# NATIONAL GUIDE TO FUNDING FOR LIBRARIES AND INFORMATION SERVICES

## Sixth Edition

**Compiled by**

The Foundation Center

**Edited by**

Jeffrey A. Falkenstein

The Foundation Center

JUL - 2 2002

# CONTRIBUTING STAFF

| | |
|---|---|
| **Senior Vice President for Information Resources and Publishing** | Rick Schoff |
| **Manager of Reference Book Publishing** | Jeffrey A. Falkenstein |
| **Contributing Editors** | David Clark |
| | Phyllis Edelson |
| | David Jacobs |
| | Francine Jones |
| | Melissa Lunn |
| | Rebecca MacLean |
| | Jose Santiago |
| **Senior Database Editor** | Margaret Feczko |
| **Coordinator of Information Control** | Yinebon Iniya |
| **Publishing Database Administrator** | Kathye Giesler |
| **Database Operations Assistant** | Emmy So |
| **Director of Design and Production** | Cheryl L. Loe |
| **Production Associate** | Christine Innamortao |
| **Manager of Bibliographic Services** | Sarah Collins |
| **Public Services Assistant** | Jimmy Tom |

The editor gratefully acknowledges the many other Foundation Center staff who contributed support, encouragement, and information that was indispensable to the preparation of this volume. Special mention should be made of the staff members of the New York, Washington, D.C., Cleveland, San Francisco, and Atlanta libraries who assisted in tracking changes in foundation information. We would like to express our appreciation as well to the many foundations that cooperated fully in updating information prior to the compilation of this volume.

# CONTENTS

# INTRODUCTION:
# FOUNDATION AND CORPORATE SUPPORT FOR
# LIBRARIES AND INFORMATION SERVICES

In 2000, over 50,000 active private and community foundations in America awarded over $23.2 billion in grants to nonprofit organizations across the country and abroad. Corporate contributions for both company-sponsored foundations (whose giving is included in the above $23.2 billion figure) and direct corporate giving programs amounted to approximately $3 billion. Although foundation and corporate donations represent but a small fraction of total philanthropic giving in the U.S., they are still a key source of support for many programs.

This volume is intended as a starting point for grantseekers looking for foundation, corporate and other charitable support for libraries and information services. It contains a total of 799 entries including 727 grantmaking foundations, 17 direct corporate giving programs and 55 public charities (including 42 community foundations) that have shown a substantial interest in libraries or information services, either as part of their stated fields of interest or through the actual grants of $10,000 or more reported to the Foundation Center in the latest year of record. Grants for libraries and information services are listed for 91 of the foundations in this volume. These 606 grants represent over $140 million in support for a variety of organizations concerned with libraries and information services, including academic libraries, public libraries, special collections, and information networks for social service and health organizations, among others.

Each entry in the *Guide* was carefully evaluated by Foundation Center staff to ensure that the grantmaker possesses a sufficient interest in libraries and information services, either stated or demonstrated. Often, a grantmaker claims interest not only programs related to libraries and information services but in dozens of widely diverse fields. To determine if inclusion in this *Guide* is warranted in such cases, consideration is given to the grantmaker's purpose statement, giving limitations, and, if they exist, subject-related grants. Grantseekers should be aware that inclusion does not imply that these grantmakers will consider all programs for libraries and information services.

Keep in mind that some grantmakers support particular programs because of their interest in a specific community or organization. Others may do so because the program relates to a highly specific subject interest of the grantmaker, such as public libraries, or various information and referral service organizations. Still others are interested in building the capacity of nonprofit institutions by providing specific types of support such as operating costs or challenge grants. Grantseekers are therefore urged to read each foundation and corporate giving program description carefully to determine the nature of the grantmaker's interests and to note any restrictions on giving that would prevent the grantmaker from considering their proposal.

## MORE PRECISE INDEXING

Since 1989 the Foundation Center has used a Grants Classification System (GCS) based on the National Taxonomy of Exempt Entities (NTEE), a comprehensive organizational coding scheme developed by the National Center for Charitable Statistics (NCCS) that was adopted by the IRS in 1995. The GCS builds on the NTEE and is used by the Center to provide subject, types of support, and other grants information both online through two DIALOG files (a product of Knight-Ridder Information Services) and in print through *The Foundation Grants Index* and related publications.

This edition of the *National Guide to Funding for Libraries and Information Services* represents, in part, the culmination of a major project to utilize the more comprehensive and precise GCS terminology across all Foundation Center publications and files. This process has resulted in the Center maintaining a more unified system of classification. The enhancements to this *Guide* resulting from the implementation of unified indexing terms include:

1. A section in grantmaker descriptive entries identifying any international giving interests of an organization. Because of the conversion to the GCS terminology, the number of index terms describing the countries, continents, and regions in which

grantmakers have giving interests has expanded from a few dozen to over 200, providing a much greater level of specificity.

2. The full scope of the terminology used to describe a grantmaker's areas of interests has also expanded following the conversion to unified GCS subject terms. The "Fields of Interest" section of each grantmaker descriptive entry will now include all indexed subject terms for the organization, rather than listing only its primary areas of giving. The "Purpose and Activities" section contains a more general statement of foundation funding priorities.

## WHAT IS A FOUNDATION?

The Foundation Center defines a foundation as a nongovernmental, nonprofit organization with its own funds (usually derived from a single source, either an individual, family, or corporation) and a program managed by its own trustees and directors, which was established to maintain or aid educational, social, charitable, or other activities serving the common welfare, primarily by making grants to other nonprofit organizations.

The Internal Revenue Service code defines the category of "private foundation" only by exclusion of other nonprofit organizations, a circumstance that has led to some confusion. David Freedman, former president of the Council on Foundations, explains the Code's definition in his book *The Handbook on Private Foundations:*

> Starting with the universe of voluntary organizations described in section 501(c)(3), the Code excludes broad groups, e.g., churches, schools, hospitals, governmental units, publicly supported charities and their affiliates. Publicly supported charities are those which derive much of their general support from the public and reach out in other ways to a public constituency. All of the above kinds of excluded organizations are commonly referred to as 'public charities.' Section 501(c)(3) organizations remaining after these exclusions are, without more precise definition, 'private foundations.' One important result: organizations are included in the remainder as private foundations that are not really grantmaking foundations at all. These may include museums, homes for the aged, and libraries, among others, if they, while serving the public, happen to have been endowed by an individual or single family, or if they were established as public charities and lose that status by failing to prove they have received ongoing financial support from the general public.

A private **independent foundation** most commonly derives its assets from an individual, family, or group of individuals. The foundation may function under the voluntary direction of family members, or may bear a family name but have independent boards of trustees and professional staffs. Typically, independent foundations have broad charters which allow a range of giving activities, but in practice most limit their giving to a few specific fields of interest and to a specific geographic area.

**Operating foundations** are also private foundations under tax laws, but their primary purpose is to operate research, social welfare, or other charitable programs determined by the donor or governing body. Some grants may be made outside the foundation, but the majority of the foundation's funds are expended on its own programs.

**Corporations** contribute through foundations, direct giving programs, or both:

**Corporate** or **company-sponsored** foundations are created and funded by business corporations for the purpose of making grants and performing other philanthropic activities. Legally, they are separate from the sponsoring corporation and are governed by the same federal rules and regulations as independent foundations. Company-sponsored foundations are generally managed by a board of directors that includes corporate officials but may also include individuals with no corporate affiliation. Giving programs often focus on communities where the company has operations, and on research and education in fields related to company activities.

**Direct corporate giving** refers to all other giving by a company, that is, money not turned over to a foundation to administer. Direct giving programs are unregulated and restricted only by the limit of taxable earnings allowed as charitable deductions. In addition to cash contributions, corporate giving may include non-cash gifts of goods and services referred to as "in-kind" giving. Donations of company products, supplies, and equipment—from computers to food—is the most common form of in-kind giving. Other types of support include technical assistance and use of office space. Direct giving programs and foundations often share the same staff, although some companies keep these functions administratively separate.

**Public charities,** in general, are organizations that are tax-exempt under code section 501(c)(3) and are classified by the IRS as a public charity and not a private foundation. Public charities typically derive their funding or support substantially from the general public in carrying out their social, educational, religious, or other charitable activities serving the common welfare. Some public charities engage in grantmaking activities, although most engage in direct service or other tax-exempt activities. Public charities are eligible for maximum income tax-deductible contributions from the public and are not subject to the same rules and restrictions as private foundations. Some are also referred to as "public foundations" or "publicly supported foundations" and may use the term "foundation" in their names.

**Community foundations** are public charities supported by and operated for a specific community or region. They receive their funds from a variety of donors; in fact, their endowments are frequently composed of a number of different trust funds, some of which bear their donors' names. Their grantmaking activities are administered by a governing body or distribution committee representative of community interests. Although community foundations may support a wide range of activities, their grants are generally restricted to charitable organizations in their city or region.

Grantseekers should be aware that an increasing number of for-profit business have also adopted "foundation" as part of their name to promote their activities. While there are no legal restrictions on the use of the word "foundation," it is important for grantseekers to understand that many of these groups do not make grants and are not governed by the same rules and regulations as private foundations or nonprofit groups.

## GRANTSEEKING FROM FOUNDATIONS

Foundations receive many thousands of worthy requests each year. Most of these requests are declined because there are not enough funds to go around or because the application clearly falls outside the foundation's fields of interest. Some of the applications denied are poorly prepared and do not reflect a careful analysis of the applicant organization's needs, its credibility, or its capacity to carry out the proposed project. Sometimes the qualifications of the organization's staff are not well established; the budget or the means of evaluating the project may not be presented convincingly; or the organization may not have asked itself whether it is especially suited to make a contribution to the solution of the problem, whether it can provide the service proposed, or whether others are not already effectively engaged in the same activity.

The first step in researching foundation funding support is to analyze your own program and organization to determine the need you plan to address, the audience you will serve, and the amount and type of support you need. Become familiar with the basic facts about foundations in general and how they operate. Consider other sources of funding, such as individual contributors, government grants, earned income possibilities, and so on. Although foundations are an important source of support for nonprofit organizations, their giving represents a relatively small percentage of the total philanthropic dollars contributed annually, and an even smaller percentage of the total when government grants and earned income are included. If you are new to grantseeking, we strongly urge you to visit one of the Foundation Center's many Cooperating Collections. They provide free access to a core collection of Foundation Center publications, as well as other materials on funding sources, program planning, and fundraising.

Once you have determined the amount and type of foundation support you need and the reasons why you are

seeking support, this *Guide* can help you develop an initial list of foundations that might be interested in funding your project. In determining whether or not it is appropriate to approach a particular foundation with a grant request, keep in mind the following questions:

1. Does the foundation's interest for libraries and information services include the specific type of service or program you are proposing?

2. Does it seem likely that the foundation will make a grant in your geographic area?

3. Does the amount of money you are requesting fit within the foundation's grant range?

4. Does the foundation have any policy prohibiting grants for the type of support you are requesting?

5. Does the foundation prefer to make grants that cover the full cost of a project or do they favor projects where other foundations or funding sources share the cost?

6. What types of organizations does the foundation tend to support?

7. Does the foundation have specific application deadlines and procedures or does it review proposals continuously?

Some of these questions can be answered from the information provided in this *Guide*, but grantseekers will almost always want to consult a few additional resources before submitting a request for funding. If the foundation issues an annual report, application guidelines, or other printed materials describing its program, it is advisable to obtain copies and study them carefully before preparing your proposal. The foundation's annual information return (Form 990-PF) includes a list of all grants paid by the foundation in addition to basic data about its finances, officers, and giving policies. Copies of these returns are available for examination at most of the Foundation Center's cooperating libraries.

The foundations listed in this *Guide* by no means represent all of the possible foundation funding sources for programs related to libraries and information services. There are a number of foundations, including some 519 community foundations across the country, that support a wide variety of programs within a specific community or region. Grantseekers should learn as much as possible about the foundations in their own area, particularly when they are seeking relatively small grants for projects with purely local impact. Be sure to check any local or state directories of which the Foundation Center is currently aware. Copies of these directories are almost always available for use at your local Foundation Center cooperating library.

The Foundation Center publishes several national directories on an annual basis. *The Foundation Directory* describes the top 10,000 foundations by total giving. *The*

*Foundation Directory Part 2* provides information on the second tier of foundations, the next 10,000 foundations by total giving. Both the *Directory* and the *Directory Part 2* entries include a list of selected grants whenever available, providing concrete examples of a foundation's giving. The *Directory* and *Directory Part 2* are arranged by state and include a geographic index to help you identify foundations located or interested in your specific community. The Foundation Center also publishes the *Guide to U.S. Foundations, Their Trustees, Officers, and Donors*, which provides basic address and financial information on over 50,000 active grantmaking foundations in the United States, as well as fully indexed listings to all foundation trustees/directors, officers, and donors. The *Guide to U.S. Foundations* is arranged alphabetically by state. Within states, foundations are listed in descending order by annual giving amount.

For those who want more detailed information on how to identify appropriate foundation funding sources, the Center also publishes *Foundation Fundamentals*. This guide takes you step-by-step through the research strategies developed and taught by the Foundation Center, describing in the process how to gather the facts you need to best approach foundations for funding. All Foundation Center publications can be examined free of charge at Foundation Center libraries.

## GRANTSEEKING FROM CORPORATIONS

The research process for corporate funding is similar to other institutional grantseeking: identifying companies that might be interested in an organization's mission and program, learning as much as possible about those companies, determining the best method of approach, and articulating program objectives so as to be in line with the company's giving rationale. It differs from researching other institutional funders, however, in that it is often more difficult to uncover the needed information. There is great diversity in method and style of giving among corporations, and companies are often looking for a quid pro quo for their giving. Because many corporations see their giving not in terms of altruism but as a responsibility or simply good business, corporate philanthropy is often considered something of an oxymoron. Soliciting support from corporations, therefore, often requires a shift in perspective, from appealing to a company's benevolence to promoting its self-interest.

Identifying corporations to approach is accomplished in several ways. Directories such as the *National Directory of Corporate Giving* describe companies with known corporate giving programs. These guides can help you identify a corporation's subject interests, geographical giving patterns, and/or the benefits it hopes to derive from its giving. General business directories aid in the search, as do the books and guides listed in the bibliography. Staff members, your organization's board, and volunteers often

know or work for companies that ultimately may be able to provide funds. The telephone book is another good resource for tracking down local businesses.

After a list of likely prospects is compiled, you should continue your efforts to locate additional information about the company, its primary and secondary business activities, its officers, giving history, and any details helpful in understanding its giving rationale. Understanding why a company gives is essential, as it may point to a match of the grantseeker's programmatic goals and the corporation's giving goals. Although determining the reasons a company makes contributions can be difficult, it can be accomplished through careful research, including studying annual reports and the materials issued by other organizations the company has supported, as well as by speaking directly with company officials whenever possible.

This kind of research usually uncovers the best method for approaching a company with a request for support. Companies with formal giving programs may have guidelines and application procedures and require a written proposal, while companies with informal giving programs may be better approached through personal contacts made by board members or volunteers. Once the approach is determined, however, a written or oral presentation that articulates how your organization's programs fit into the company's giving rationale should be prepared.

Ultimately, the more you know about a company, the better your chance of obtaining support. A company should not be approached without some knowledge of its business activities or past giving history, as that may jeopardize your chances of receiving funding. This does not mean that corporations without a record of grantmaking should be ignored. Creative fundraisers have found ways of encouraging companies of all sizes, from small businesses to large corporations, to assist in their activities. Success in acquiring such support, however, is usually the result of good research and good contacts. The job of the corporate fundraiser is to be imaginative and thorough, calling on all the knowledge, people, and ideas available. It means learning where to ask, how to ask, and what to ask.

## SOURCES OF INFORMATION

Foundation Center publications examine giving interests in two broad ways: what the grantmaker states as its purpose and what can be observed from a listing of its actual grants. In preparing the *National Guide to Funding for Libraries and Information Services* we drew on five important tools to identify grantmakers with a specific interest in programs for libraries or information services in addition to those that make contributions for related projects as part of a broader giving program:

1. *The Foundation Directory* provides descriptions of the nation's largest foundations (the top 10,000 by total giving). The statements of purpose for each foundation listed in the *Directory* are drawn from the descriptions provided by foundations in their annual reports, informational brochures or other publications, responses to our annual questionnaire mailings, and a broad analysis of the foundation's grantmaking program over the last three years. Although some of these statements provide very specific information about the foundation's giving interests, many were developed to last for substantial periods of time and, thus, left purposely broad to allow for future shifts in emphasis. To illustrate a foundation's giving pattern, lists of up to ten selected grants are included.

2. *The Foundation Directory Part 2* provides information on the second tier of U.S. grantmaking foundations, (the next 10,000 largest foundations by total giving). Like the *Directory*, the *Directory Part 2* provides lists of up to ten selected grants whenever available.

3. The *National Directory of Corporate Giving* is the source of information on corporate grantmakers. The fifth edition of the directory, published in 1999, profiles 2,568 companies making contributions to nonprofit organizations. It includes entries describing 1,023 direct corporate giving programs and 1,891 corporate foundations. The most comprehensive directory on corporate giving available, it lists only corporations that provided information to the Center or for which public documents on giving were available.

4. The Center's *Foundation Grants Index* database, which records actual grants of $10,000 or more reported to the Center by approximately 1,016 major foundations, provides a more detailed picture of foundation giving interests. Each grant record includes the name and location of the organization receiving the grant, the amount of money awarded, and a brief description of the purpose for which the grant was made. Center staff analyze and index each grant by subject focus, type of organization receiving the grant, the type of support provided, and the special population group, if any, to be served by the program.

These four sources, as well as the public charities included on *FC Search* (see Resources of the Foundation Center for more details), provide all the information on foundations, corporate giving, public charities, and grants included in this *Guide*.

# HOW TO USE THE *NATIONAL GUIDE TO FUNDING FOR LIBRARIES AND INFORMATION SERVICES*

When using the *Guide* to identify potential funding sources, grantseekers are urged to read each foundation description carefully to determine the nature of the grantmaker's interests and to note any restrictions on giving that would prevent the foundation from considering their proposal. Many foundations limit their giving to a particular subject field or geographic area; others are unable to provide certain types of support, such as funds for buildings and equipment or for general operating budgets. Even when a grantmaker has not provided an explicit limitations statement, restrictions on giving may exist. This is often the case with entries updated from public records. Further research into the giving patterns of these grantmakers is necessary before applying for funds.

## ARRANGEMENT

The *Guide* is arranged alphabetically by state and, within states, by foundation name. Each descriptive entry is assigned a sequence number; references in the indexes are to these entry numbers.

## WHAT'S IN AN ENTRY?

There are 34 basic data elements that could be included in a descriptive entry. The content of entries varies widely due to differences in the size and nature of foundation programs and the availability of information from foundations. Specific data elements that could be included are:

1. The full legal **name of the foundation.**

2. The **former name** of the foundation.

3. The **street address, city, and zip code** of the foundation's principal office.

4. The **telephone number** of the foundation.

5. The name and title of the **contact person** at the foundation.

6. Any **additional address** (such as a separate application address) supplied by the foundation. Additional telephone or FAX numbers also may be listed here.

7. **Establishment data,** including the legal form (usually a trust or corporation) and the year and state in which the foundation was established.

8. The **donor(s)** or principal contributor(s) to the foundation, including individuals, families, and corporations. If a donor is deceased, the symbol ‡ follows the name.

9. **Foundation type:** community, company-sponsored, independent, or operating.

10. The **year-end date** of the foundation's accounting period for which financial data is supplied.

11. **Assets:** the total value of the foundation's investments at the end of the accounting period. In a few instances, foundations that act as "pass-throughs" for annual corporate or individual gifts report zero assets.

12. **Asset type:** generally, assets are reported at market value (M) or ledger value (L).

13. **Gifts received:** the total amount of new capital received by the foundation in the year of record.

14. **Expenditures:** total disbursements of the foundation, including overhead expenses (salaries; investment, legal, and other professional fees; interest; rent; etc.) and federal excise taxes, as well as the total amount paid for grants, scholarships, and matching gifts.

15. The total amount of **qualifying distributions** made by the foundation in the year of record. This figure includes all grants paid, qualifying administrative expenses, loans and program-related investments, set-asides, and amounts paid to acquire assets used directly in carrying out charitable purposes.

16. The dollar value and number of **grants paid** during the year, with the largest grant paid **(high)** and smallest grant paid **(low)**. When supplied by the foundation, the average range of grant payments is also indicated. Grant figures generally do not include commitments for future payment or amounts spent for grants to individuals, employee matching gifts, loans, or foundation-administered programs.

17. The total dollar value of **set-asides** made by the foundation during the year. Although set-asides count as qualifying distributions toward the foundation's annual payout requirement, they are distinct from any amounts listed as grants paid.

18. The total amount and number of **grants made directly to or on behalf of individuals,** including scholarships, fellowships, awards, and medical payments. When supplied by the foundation, high, low, and average range are also indicated.

19. The dollar amount and number of **employee matching gifts** awarded, generally by company-sponsored foundations.

20. The total dollars expended for **programs administered by the foundation** and the number of foundation-administered programs. These programs can include museums or other institutions supported exclusively by the foundation, research programs administered by the foundation, etc.

21. The dollar amount and number of **loans** made to nonprofit organizations by the foundation. These can include program-related investments, emergency loans to help nonprofits that are waiting for grants or other income payments, etc. When supplied by the foundation, high, low, and average range are also indicated.

22. The number of **loans to individuals** and the total amount loaned. When supplied by the foundation, high, low, and average range are also indicated.

23. The monetary value and number of **in-kind gifts.**

24. The **purpose and activities,** in general terms, of the foundation. This statement reflects funding interests as expressed by the foundation or, if no foundation statement is available, an analysis of the actual grants awarded by the foundation during the most recent two-year period for which public records exist. Many foundations leave statements of purpose intentionally broad, indicating only the major program areas within which they fund. More specific areas of interest can often be found in the "Fields of Interest" section of the entry.

25. The **fields of interest** reflected in the foundation's giving program. The terminology used in this section has been revised and expanded for this edition in accordance with the Foundation Center's Grants Classification System (GCS).

26. The **international giving interests** of the foundation.

27. The **types of support** (such as endowment funds, support for buildings and equipment, fellowships, etc.) offered by the foundation. Definitions of the terms used to describe the forms of support available are provided at the beginning of the Types of Support Index at the back of this volume.

28. Any stated **limitations** on the foundation's giving program, including geographic preferences, restrictions by subject focus or type of recipient, or specific types of support the foundation cannot provide. It is noted here if a foundation does not accept unsolicited applications.

29. **Publications** or other printed materials distributed by the foundation that describe its activities and giving program. These can include annual or multi-year reports, newsletters, corporate giving reports, informational brochures, grant lists, etc. It is also noted whether a foundation will send copies of its IRS information return (Form 990-PF) on request.

30. **Application information,** including the preferred form of application, the number of copies of proposals requested, application deadlines, frequency and dates of board meetings, and the general amount of time the foundation requires to notify applicants of the board's decision. Some foundations have indicated that their funds are currently committed to ongoing projects.

31. The names and titles of **officers, principal administrators, trustees, or directors,** and members of other governing bodies. An asterisk following the individual's name indicates an officer who is also a trustee or director.

32. The number of professional and support **staff** employed by the foundation, and an indication of part-time or full-time status of these employees, as reported by the foundation.

33. **EIN:** the Employer Identification Number assigned to the foundation by the Internal Revenue Service for tax purposes. This number can be useful when ordering microfilm or paper copies of the foundation's annual information return, Form 990-PF.

34. **Recent grants for libraries and information services** awarded in 1998–2000. Entries include the name and location of the recipient, the grant amount and year awarded, and, where available, a brief description of the purpose of the grant.

## INDEXES

Six indexes to the descriptive entries are provided at the back of the book to assist grantseekers and other users of this *Guide:*

1. The **Index to Donors, Officers, Trustees** is an alphabetical list of individual and corporate donors, officers, and members of governing boards whose names appear in the descriptive entries. Many grantseekers find this index helpful in determining

whether current or prospective members of their own governing boards, alumni of their schools, or current contributors are affiliated with other foundations.

2. The **Geographic Index** references foundation entries by the state and city in which the foundation maintains its principal offices. The index includes "see-also" references at the end of each state section to indicate foundations that have made substantial grants in that state but are located elsewhere. Foundations that award grants on a national, regional, or international basis are indicated in bold type. The remaining foundations generally limit their giving to the state or city in which they are located.

3. The **Types of Support Index** provides access to foundation entries by the specific types of support the foundation awards. A glossary of the forms of support listed appears at the beginning of the index. Under each type of support term, entry numbers are listed by the state location and abbreviated name of the foundation. Foundations that award grants on a national, regional, or international basis are indicated in bold type. When using this index, grantseekers should focus on foundations located in their own state that offer the specific type of support needed, or on foundations listed in bold type if their program has national impact.

4. The **Index to Grantmakers by Subject** provides access to the giving interests of foundations based on the "Fields of Interest" sections of their entries. The terminology in the index has been revised and expanded to allow for greater precision in identifying subject areas, and now conforms to the Foundation Center's Grants Classification System (GCS). A list of subject headings for international and foreign programs is provided at the beginning of the index. Under each subject term, entry numbers are listed by the state location and abbreviated name of the foundation. As in the Types of Support Index, foundations that award grants on a national, regional, or international basis are indicated in bold type. Again, grantseekers should focus on foundations located in their own state or on foundations listed in bold type if their program is national in scope.

5. The **Index to Grants by Subject** provides access to the individual grants included in this *Guide*. For each subject term, grants are listed first by foundation entry number, then by grant number within the foundation entry.

6. The **Grantmaker Name Index** is an alphabetical list of all foundations and giving programs appearing in this *Guide*. Former names of foundations appear with "see" references to the appropriate entry numbers.

# GLOSSARY

The following list includes important terms used by grantmakers and grantseekers. A number of sources have been consulted in compiling this glossary, including *The Handbook on Private Foundations,* by David F. Freeman and the Council on Foundations (New York: The Foundation Center, 1991); *The Law of Tax-Exempt Organizations,* 7th Edition, by Bruce R. Hopkins (New York: John Wiley & Sons, 1998); and the *NSFRE Fund-Raising Dictionary,* (New York, John Wiley & Sons, 1996).

**Annual Report:** A *voluntary* report issued by a foundation or corporation that provides financial data and descriptions of grantmaking activities. Annual reports vary in format from simple typewritten documents listing the year's grants to detailed publications that provide substantial information about the grantmaking program.

**Assets:** The amount of capital or principal—money, stocks, bonds, real estate, or other resources—controlled by the foundation or corporate giving program. Generally, assets are invested and the income is used to make grants.

**Beneficiary:** In philanthropic terms, the donee or grantee receiving funds from a foundation or corporate giving program is the beneficiary, although society benefits as well. Foundations whose legal terms of establishment restrict their giving to one or more named beneficiaries are not included in this publication.

**Bricks and Mortar:** An informal term for grants for buildings or construction projects.

**Capital Support:** Funds provided for endowment purposes, buildings, construction, or equipment, and including, for example, grants for "bricks and mortar."

**Challenge Grant:** A grant awarded that will be paid only if the donee organization is able to raise additional funds from another source(s). Challenge grants are often used to stimulate giving from other donors. (*See also* **Matching Grant**)

**Community Foundation:** A 501(c)(3) organization that makes grants for charitable purposes in a specific community or region. Funds are usually derived from many donors and held in an endowment independently administered; income earned by the endowment is then used to make grants. Although a few community foundations may be classified by the IRS as private foundations, most are classified as public charities eligible for maximum income tax-deductible contributions from the general public. (*See also* **501(c)(3); Public Charity**)

**Community Fund:** An organized community program which makes annual appeals to the general public for funds that are usually not retained in an endowment but are used for the ongoing operational support of local social and health service agencies. (*See also* **Federated Giving Program**)

**Company-Sponsored Foundation** (also referred to as Corporate Foundation): A private foundation whose grant funds are derived primarily from the contributions of a profit-making business organization. The company-sponsored foundation may maintain close ties with the donor company, but it is an independent organization with its own endowment and is subject to the same rules and regulations as other private foundations. (*See also* **Private Foundation**)

**Cooperative Venture:** A joint effort between or among two or more grantmakers (including foundations, corporations, and government agencies). Partners may share in funding responsibilities or contribute information and technical resources.

**Corporate Giving Program:** A grantmaking program established and administered within a profit-making company. Corporate giving programs do not have a separate endowment and their annual grant totals are generally more directly related to current profits. They are not subject to the same reporting requirements as private foundations. Some companies make charitable contributions through both a corporate giving program and a company-sponsored foundation.

**Distribution Committee:** The board responsible for making grant decisions. For community foundations, it is intended to be broadly representative of the community served by the foundation.

**Donee:** The recipient of a grant. (Also known as the grantee or the beneficiary.)

**Donor:** The individual or organization that makes a grant or contribution. (Also known as the grantor.)

**Employee Matching Gift:** A contribution to a charitable organization by a company employee that is matched by a similar contribution from the employer. Many corporations have employee matching gift programs in higher education that stimulate their employees to give to the college or university of their choice.

**Endowment:** Funds intended to be kept permanently and invested to provide income for continued support of an organization.

**Expenditure Responsibility:** In general, when a private foundation makes a grant to an organization that is not classified by the IRS as a "public charity," the foundation is required by law to provide some assurance that the funds will be used for the intended charitable purposes. Special reports on such grants must be filed with the IRS. Most grantee organizations are public charities and many foundations do not make "expenditure responsibility" grants.

**Family Foundation:** An independent private foundation whose funds are derived from members of a single family. Family members often serve as officers or board members of the foundation and have a significant role in grantmaking decisions. (*See also* **Operating Foundation; Private Foundation; Public Charity**)

**Federated Giving Program:** A joint fundraising effort usually administered by a nonprofit "umbrella" organization which in turn distributes contributed funds to several nonprofit agencies. United Way and community chests or funds, the United Jewish Appeal and other religious appeals, the United Negro College Fund, and joint arts councils are examples of federated giving programs. (*See also* **Community Fund**)

**501(c)(3):** The section of the Internal Revenue code that defines nonprofit, charitable (as broadly defined), tax-exempt organizations; 501(c)(3) organizations are further defined as public charities, private operating foundations, and private non-operating foundations. (*See also* **Operating Foundation; Private Foundation; Public Charity**)

**Form 990-PF:** The annual information return that all private foundations must submit to the IRS each year and which is also filed with appropriate state officials. The form requires information on the foundation's assets, income, operating expenses, contributions and grants, paid staff and salaries, program funding areas, grantmaking guidelines and restrictions, and grant application procedures. Foundation Center libraries maintain files of 990-PFs for public inspection.

**General Purpose Foundation:** An independent private foundation that awards grants in many different fields of interest. (*See also* **Special Purpose Foundation**)

**General Purpose Grant:** A grant made to further the general purpose or work of an organization, rather than for a specific purpose or project. (*See also* **Operating Support Grant**)

**Grantee Financial Report:** A report detailing how grant funds were used by an organization. Many corporations require this kind of report from grantees. A financial report generally includes a listing of all expenditures from grant funds as well as an overall organizational financial report covering revenue and expenses, assets and liabilities.

**Grassroots Fundraising:** Efforts to raise money from individuals or groups from the local community on a broad basis. Usually an organization's own constituents—people who live in the neighborhood served or clients of the agency's services—are the sources of these funds. Grassroots fundraising activities include membership drives, raffles, auctions, benefits, and a range of other activities.

**Independent Foundation:** A grantmaking organization usually classified by the IRS as a private foundation. Independent foundations may also be known as family foundations, general purpose foundations, special purpose foundations, or private non-operating foundations. The Foundation Center defines independent foundations and company-sponsored foundations separately; however, federal law normally classifies both as private, non-operating foundations subject to the same rules and requirements. (*See also* **Private Foundation**)

**In-Kind Contributions:** Contributions of equipment, supplies, or other property as distinguished from monetary grants. Some organizations may also donate space or staff time as an in-kind contribution.

**Matching Grant:** A grant that is made to match funds provided by another donor. (*See also* **Challenge Grant; Employee Matching Gift**)

**Operating Foundation:** A 501(c)(3) organization classified by the IRS as a private foundation whose primary purpose is to conduct research, social welfare, or other programs determined by its governing body or establishment charter. Some grants may be made, but the sum is generally small relative to the funds used for the foundation's own programs. (*See also* **501(c)(3)**)

**Operating Support Grant:** A grant to cover the regular personnel, administrative, and other expenses of an existing program or project. (*See also* **General Purpose Grant**)

**Payout Requirement:** The minimum amount that private foundations are required to expend for charitable purposes (includes grants and, within certain limits, the administrative cost of making grants). In general, a private foundation must meet or exceed an annual payout requirement of five percent of the average market value of the foundation's assets.

**Private Foundation:** A nongovernmental, nonprofit organization with funds (usually from a single source, such as an individual, family, or corporation) and program managed by its own trustees or directors that was established to maintain or aid social, educational, religious, or other charitable activities serving the common welfare, primarily through the making of grants. "Private foundation" also means an organization that is tax-exempt under code section 501(c)(3) and is classified by the IRS as a private foundation as defined in the code. The code definition usually, but not always, identifies a foundation with the characteristics first described. (*See also* **501(c)(3); Public Charity**)

**Program Amount:** Funds that are expended to support a particular program administered internally by the foundation or corporate giving program.

**Program Officer:** A staff member of a foundation who reviews grant proposals and processes applications for the board of trustees. Only a small percentage of foundations have program officers.

**Program-Related Investment (PRI):** A loan or other investment (as distinguished from a grant) made by a foundation or corporate giving program to another organization for a project related to the grantmaker's stated charitable purpose and interests. Program-related investments are often made from a revolving fund; the foundation generally expects to receive its money back with interest or some other form of return at less than current market rates, and it then becomes available for further program-related investments.

**Proposal:** A written application, often with supporting documents, submitted to a foundation or corporate giving program in requesting a grant. Preferred procedures and formats vary. Consult published guidelines.

**Public Charity:** In general, an organization that is tax-exempt under code section 501(c)(3) and is classified by the IRS as a public charity and not a private foundation. Public charities generally derive their funding or support primarily from the general public in carrying out their social, educational, religious, or other charitable activities serving the common welfare. Some public charities engage in grantmaking activities, although most engage in direct service or other tax-exempt activities. Public charities are eligible for maximum income tax-deductible contributions from the public and are not subject to the same rules and restrictions as private foundations. Some are also referred to as "public foundations" or "publicly supported organizations" and may use the term "foundation" in their names. (*See also* **501(c)(3); Private Foundation**)

**Qualifying Distributions:** Expenditures of private foundations used to satisfy the annual payout requirement. These can include grants, reasonable administrative expenses, set-asides, loans and program-related investments, and amounts paid to acquire assets used directly in carrying out exempt purposes.

**Query Letter:** A brief letter outlining an organization's activities and its request for funding sent to a foundation or corporation to determine whether it would be appropriate for that organization to submit a full grant proposal. Many grantmakers prefer to be contacted in this way before receiving a full proposal.

**RFP:** Request For Proposal. When the government issues a new contract or grant program, it sends out RFPs to agencies that might be qualified to participate. The RFP lists project specifications and application procedures. A few foundations occasionally use RFPs in specific fields, but most prefer to consider proposals that are initiated by applicants.

**Seed Money:** A grant or contribution used to start a new project or organization. Seed grants may cover salaries and other operating expenses of a new project.

**Set-Asides:** Funds set aside by a foundation for a specific purpose or project that are counted as qualifying distributions toward the foundation's annual payout requirement. Amounts for the project must be paid within five years of the first set-aside.

**Special Purpose Foundation:** A private foundation that focuses its grantmaking activities in one or a few special areas of interest. For example, a foundation may only award grants in the area of cancer research or child development. (*See also* **General Purpose Foundation**)

**Technical Assistance:** Operational or management assistance given to nonprofit organizations. It can include fundraising assistance, budgeting and financial planning, program planning, legal advice, marketing, and other aids to management. Assistance may be offered directly by a foundation or corporate staff member, or be offered in the form of a grant to pay for the services of an outside consultant. (*See also* **In-Kind Contributions**)

**Trustee:** A member of a governing board. A foundation's board of trustees meets to review grant proposals and make decisions. Often also referred to as a "director" or "board member."

# BIBLIOGRAPHY OF FUNDING FOR LIBRARIES AND INFORMATION SERVICES

This selected bibliography is compiled from the Foundation Center's bibliographic database. Many of the items are available for free reference use in the Center's New York City, Washington, D.C., Cleveland, San Francisco, and Atlanta libraries and in many of its Cooperating Collections throughout the United States. For further references on such topics as fundraising and proposal development, see *The Literature of the Nonprofit Sector Online* at the Foundation Center's Web site: http://lnps.fdncenter.org.

*American Library Directory 2000–2001.* 53rd ed. New York, NY: R.R. Bowker Co., 2000. 2 v. ISBN 0-8352-4280-3

Lists public, academic, government, and special libraries in the United States, Puerto Rico, U.S.-administered regions, Mexico, and Canada. Arranged geographically; entries for each state, region, and province open with statistical information regarding public libraries; entries for each city begin with population figures and area code. Entries include the name and address of the library, names of key personnel, and information on the library's holdings.

Balas, Janet L. "Online Help for Library Strategic Planners." *Computers in Libraries,* vol. 19 (January 1999): p. 40–2.

Bogart, Dave (ed.) *The Bowker Annual Library and Book Trade Almanac.* 45th ed. New York, NY: R.R. Bowker Co., 2000. x, 857 p. ISBN 0-8352-4324-9

Contains statistical, tabular, and general information related to libraries and the book trade, including details on funding programs and grantmaking agencies. Contains a calendar of association meetings and promotional events.

Brazin, Lillian R. "A Grant Writers' Application of the Internet." *Bottom Line,* vol. 12 (No. 3, 1999): p. 120–2.

Advice and tips on using the Internet to full advantage in library fundraising and grant writing. Includes numerous Web addresses related to private and government funding.

Camarena, Janet. "A Wealth of Information on Foundations and the Grant Seeking Process." *Computers in Libraries,* vol. 20 (May 2000): p. 27–31.

Provides advice to grantseekers who are fundraising for libraries; provides the names of the top ten foundations that funded libraries or library science in 1998, and the top ten grants. In addition to a discussion of the services of the Foundation Center, provides proposal writing basics, suggests further reading, and lists online resources.

Corson-Finnerty, Adam; Blanchard, Laura. *Fundraising and Friend-raising on the Web.* Chicago, IL: American Library Association, 1998. viii, 122 p. ISBN 0-8389-0727-X

Intended for library administrators, but with approaches that will succeed for any nonprofit, the books offers advice on such topics as developing and measuring the impact of a Web site; creating donor recognition in cyberspace; delivering your site directly to potential donors on disk or CD-ROM; fundraising with digital cash. Throughout, examples currently on the Web are provided. A CD-ROM disk is included.

Dolnick, Sandy (ed.) *Friends of Libraries Sourcebook.* 3rd ed. Chicago, IL: American Library Association, 1996. xiii, 313 p. ISBN 0-8389-0685-0

Identifies the benefits and pitfalls of organizing friends groups for libraries. Provides specific suggestions for managing, recruiting, publicizing, and fundraising by friends groups, and offers a chapter on library foundations. Includes bibliography.

Dundjerski, Marina. "New Chapter at a Storied Foundation." *Chronicle of Philanthropy,* vol. 11 (11 March 1999): p. 1, 7–8, 10.

After an extensive review, the Carnegie Corporation of New York plans to overhaul its grantmaking programs by focusing on libraries, schoolteacher training, international development, and political and social issues.

Foundation Center. *Grants for Information Technology.* New York, NY: Foundation Center, 2000. xvi, 157 p. (Grant Guide; No. 12). ISBN 0-87954-930-0

Lists 2,708 grants of $10,000 or more made by 417 foundations, mostly in 1998 and 1999, for engineering and technology research and services; computer science; data processing; telephone, telegraph, and telecommunications services; electronic messaging, including the Internet or World Wide Web, e-mail, and interactive television and video; and computer systems and equipment, including hardware, software, CD-ROMs, local area networks, wide area networks, and other automated, digital, multimedia, or on-line systems.

Foundation Center. *Grants for Libraries and Information Services.* New York, NY: Foundation Center, 2000. xviii, 142 p. (Grant Guide; No. 13). ISBN 0-87954-931-9

Lists 2,534 grants of $10,000 or more made by 607 foundations, mostly in 1998 and 1999, to public, academic, research, school, and special libraries, as well as to archives and information centers for construction, operations, equipment, acquisitions, computerization, and library science education. Grants are indexed by recipient name, location, and subject.

"FunderSearch: Corporate Funders that Support Libraries." *Corporate Giving Watch,* vol. 17 (February 1998): p. 17.

Fundukian, Laurie (ed.) "New Directions Result from Extensive Review: Carnegie Corporation of New York Reshapes Funding Initiatives." *Foundation Giving Watch,* vol. 14 (June 1999): p. 1–2.

The Carnegie Corporation of New York has decided to prioritize their funding in the areas of education, international development, democracy, public libraries, and international peace and security issues.

Gordon, Margaret; Gordon, Andrew; Moore, Elizabeth. "New Computers Bring New Patrons." *Library Journal,* vol. 126 (15 February 2001): p. 134–8.

An analysis of the impact of the Library Program of the Bill and Melinda Gates Foundation, based on findings from 5 states: Alabama, Arkansas, Florida, Louisiana, and Mississippi.

Graubard, Stephen R. (ed.); LeClerc, Paul. *Books, Bricks & Bytes: Libraries in the Twenty-first Century.* New Brunswick, NJ: Transaction Publishers, 1998. xviii, 361 p. ISBN 1-56000-986-

Hopwood, Susan H. "Long-range Planning and Funding for Innovation." *Computers in Libraries,* vol. 19 (January 1999): p. 22–4, 26–7.

Describes the successful use of strategic planning by the staff of Marquette University Libraries, which included building a new computer classroom with the financial help of the school's Parents Association.

Kniffel, Leonard. "Backing up the Gates Millions: TRI Life in the Fast Lane." *American Libraries,* vol. 29 (March 1998): p. 56–8.

Staff at the Technology Resource Institute (TRI) are scrambling to provide technical support for the $400 million commitment made to libraries by Bill Gates. Technology Resource Institute and the Gates Library Foundation (GLF) are two independent foundations that work together: the latter focuses on policy and the implementation goals of the grants, while the former provides set-up and technical support, staff training, and software updates to the libraries as they are awarded grants by GLF. TRI was officially incorporated as a foundation in 1997, and operates with grant money provided by the Gates Library Foundation. Provides contact information for TRI.

Lapsley, Andrea. "Major Donors, Major Gifts." *Bottom Line,* vol. 9 (Summer 1996): p. 40–3.

Gives a basic overview of major gift solicitation for libraries.

Lipowicz, Alice. "Savvy, Fundraising Skills Speak Volumes at Library: New Executive-Elizabeth Rohatyn." *Crain's New York Business,* vol. 12 (1–7 January 1996): p. 13.

Profiles Elizabeth Rohatyn, the new chairwoman of the Board of Trustees at the New York Public Library.

May, Heather. "An Unusual Group of Supporters Helps the Library Grow at Brandeis U." *Chronicle of Higher Education,* vol. 53 (20 September 1996): p. A43–4.

Discusses Brandeis University National Women's Committee, which raised fifty-four million dollars for the university's three libraries.

Miskelly, Matthew (ed.) *Directory of Special Libraries and Information Centers.* 25th ed. Detroit, MI: Gale Research, 2000. 3 vols. 2 v. ISBN 0-7876-3506-5

Guide to more than 24,500 special libraries, research libraries, information centers, archives, and data centers maintained by government agencies, business, industry, newspapers, educational institutions, nonprofit organizations, and societies in the fields of science and engineering, medicine, law, art, religion, the social sciences, and humanistic studies. Subject index.

Morad, Deborah J. (ed.); Schoenenberger, Lori (ed.) "FunderSearch: Funders that Support Libraries." *Foundation Giving Watch,* vol. 17 (February 1998): p. 17.

Morad, Deborah J. (ed.); Schoenenberger, Lori (ed.) "Gates Library Foundation Issues Guidelines: Grants Fund Computers for Libraries in Low-income Areas." *Foundation Giving Watch,* vol. 17 (February 1998): p. 1–2.

Oder, Norman. "Carnegie Corporation Gives $15M to 25 Urban Libraries." *Library Journal,* vol. 124 (July 1999): p. 14–5.

Three New York City public libraries and 22 others around the country will receive substantial grants from the Carnegie Corporation of New York.

Perry, Emma Bradford. "Winning Money: a Team Approach to Grant Writing." *Computers in Libraries,* vol. 20 (May 2000): p. 33–6.

Describes how the author, dean of libraries at Southern University in Baton Rouge, assembled a team to be responsible for grant writing, and how the team functions. To date, they have achieved nearly a million dollars in support for technology and computer training.

Sommerfeld, Meg. "Founder of Dell Computer Creates Foundation." *Chronicle of Philanthropy,* vol. 12 (10 February 2000): p. 12.

Michael Dell, founder of the Dell Computer Corporation, and his wife, Susan, have contributed $114 million worth of stock to establish the Michael and Susan Dell Foundation. The Dells have focused their giving in the Austin, Texas area, supporting a children's hospital, the public library system and the United Way. In addition, they have given $1.9 million to Insure-a-Kid, a program that helps provide health insurance to children from low-income families.

Special Libraries Association. *Enhancing Competitiveness in the Information Age: Strategies and Tactics for Special Librarians and Information Professionals.* Washington, DC: Special Libraries Association, 1997. v, 64 p. ISBN 0-87111-476-3

St. Clair, Guy. *Change Management in Action: the InfoManage Interviews.* Washington, DC: Special Libraries Association, 1999. xviii, 470 p. ISBN 0-87111-500-X

St. Lifer, Evan. "Nothin' but Net: Gates Foundation Wires Alabama." *Library Journal,* vol. 123 (15 April 1998): p. 36–9.

Steele, Victoria; Elder, Stephen D. *Becoming a Fundraiser: the Principles and Practice of Library Development.* 2nd ed. Chicago, IL: American Library Association, 2000. iv, 138 p. ISBN 0-8389-0783-0

Offers a complete look at library fundraising for library administrators. Discusses fundraising principles based on leadership and participation of library directors. Ten chapters include discussion of librarians' attitudes and fears about raising money, guiding the library director in building and working with a development team or with friends groups, and soliciting major gifts. Includes bibliographical references and index.

Stehle, Vince. "Gates's Two Hundred Million Dollar Gift to Libraries Prompts Praise and Skepticism." *Chronicle of Philanthropy,* vol. 9 (10 July 1997): p. 10.

Taft Group (ed.) *The Big Book of Library Grant Money: Profiles of Private and Corporate Foundations and Direct Corporate Givers Receptive to Library Grant Proposals.* 1998–99 ed. Chicago, IL: American Library Association, 1998. xiv, 1433 p. ISBN 0-8389-0739-3

Profiles foundations and corporate grantmakers identified either by having made grants to libraries or by having listed libraries as typical recipients. Entries are arranged in alphabetical order by grantmaker name and include contact information, financial summary, contributions summary, corporate officers, giving officers, application information, grants analysis, and recent grants. Indexed by headquarters location, by operating location, by officer's and director's names, by grant recipients by state, by library recipients by state, and by grantmaker name.

Tillman, Hope N. (ed.) *Internet Tools of the Profession: A Guide for Information Professionals.* 2nd ed. Washington, DC: Special Libraries Association, 1997. v, 249 p. ISBN 0-87111-467-4 ($41)

*Washington Area Library Directory.* 2nd ed. Washington, DC: District of Columbia Library Association, 1996. 194 p. ISBN 0-9635577-2-6

Weingand, Darlene E. *Customer Service Excellence: A Concise Guide for Librarians.* Chicago, IL: American Library Association, 1997. xii, 136 p. ISBN 0-8389-0689-3

# RESOURCES OF THE FOUNDATION CENTER

The Foundation Center is a national service organization founded and supported by foundations to provide a single authoritative source of information on foundation and corporate giving. The Center's programs are designed to help grantseekers select those funders which may be most interested in their projects from the more than 58,000 active U.S. grantmakers. Among its primary activities toward this end are publishing reference books and CD-ROMs, and offering online searchable databases on foundation and corporate philanthropy; disseminating information on grantmaking, grantseeking, and related subjects through its site on the World Wide Web; offering educational courses and workshops; and a nationwide network of libraries/resource centers and cooperating collections.

Publications of the Foundation Center are the primary working tools of every serious grantseeker. They are also used by grantmakers, scholars, journalists, and legislators—in short, by anyone seeking any type of factual information on philanthropy. All private foundations and a significant number of corporate grantmakers actively engaged in grantmaking, regardless of size or geographic location, are included in one or more of the Center's publications. The publications are of three kinds: directories that describe specific funders, characterizing their program interests and providing fiscal and personnel data; grants indexes that list and classify by subject recent foundation and corporate awards; and guides, monographs, and bibliographies that introduce the reader to funding research, elements of proposal writing, and nonprofit management issues.

For those who wish to access information on grantmakers and their grants electronically, the Center issues *FC Search: The Foundation Center's Database on CD-ROM* containing the full universe of over 58,000 grantmakers and more than 246,000 associated grants. *The Foundation Directory on CD-ROM* and *The Foundation Directory Online* are searchable electronic databases that provide access to over 10,000 of the nation's largest foundations. *The Foundation Directory Online Plus* contains the top 10,000+ foundations plus a searchable database of 170,000+ grants. *The Foundation Directory Online Premium* includes 20,000+ foundations plus 170,000+ grants. *The Foundation Directory Online Platinum* includes over 58,000 grantmakers plus 170,000 grants. In addition, the Center's award-winning Web site features a wide array of free information about the philanthropic community.

The Foundation Center's publications and electronic products may be ordered from the Foundation Center, 79 Fifth Avenue, New York, NY 10003-3076, or online at our Web site. For more information about any aspect of the Center's programs or for the name of the Center's library collection nearest you, call 1-800-424-9836, or visit us on the Web at www.fdncenter.org. Please visit our Web site for the most current information available on new products and services of the Foundation Center.

## GENERAL RESEARCH DIRECTORIES

### THE FOUNDATION DIRECTORY, 2001 Edition

*The Foundation Directory* has been widely known and respected in the field for more than 40 years. It includes the latest information on the 10,000 largest U.S. foundations based on total giving. The 2001 Edition includes over 1,000 foundations that are new to this edition. *Directory* foundations hold more than $403 billion in assets and award $21 billion in grants annually.

Each *Directory* entry contains precise information on application procedures, giving limitations, types of support awarded, the publications of each foundation, and foundation staff. In addition, each entry features such vital data as the grantmaker's giving interests, financial data, grant amounts, address, and telephone number. This edition includes over 33,000 selected grants. The Foundation Center works closely with foundations to ensure the accuracy and timeliness of the information provided.

The *Directory* includes indexes by foundation name; subject areas of interest; names of donors, officers, and trustees; geographic location; international interests; types of support awarded; and grantmakers new to the volume. Also included are analyses of the foundation community by geography, asset and grant size, and the different foundation types.

*Also available on CD-ROM and Online.*
*See sections on CD-ROMs and Online Databases.*
*March 2001*
*ISBN 0-87954-944-0 / $215*
*Published annually*

## THE FOUNDATION DIRECTORY PART 2, 2001 Edition

Following in the tradition of *The Foundation Directory*, *The Foundation Directory Part 2* brings you the same thorough coverage for the next largest set of 10,000 foundations. It includes *Directory*-level information on mid-sized foundations, an important group of grantmakers responsible for millions of dollars in funding annually. Essential data on foundations is included along with more than 27,000 recently awarded foundation grants, providing an excellent overview of the foundations' giving interests. Quick access to foundation entries is facilitated by seven indexes, including foundation name; subject areas of interest; names of donors, officers, and trustees; geographic location; international interests; types of support awarded; and grantmakers new to the volume.

*March 2001 / ISBN 0-87954-945-9 / $185*
*Published annually*

## THE FOUNDATION DIRECTORY SUPPLEMENT

*The Foundation Directory Supplement* provides the latest-breaking information on *Foundation Directory* and *Foundation Directory Part 2* grantmakers six months after those volumes are published. Each year, thousands of policy and staff changes occur at these foundations. Fundraisers need to know about these crucial changes as rapidly as possible, as they may affect the way fundraisers prepare their grant proposals. The *Supplement* ensures that users of the *Directory* and *Directory Part 2* always have the latest addresses, contact names, policy statements, application guidelines, and financial data for the foundations they're approaching for funding.

*September 2001 / ISBN 0-87954-947-6/ $125*
*Published annually*

## GUIDE TO U.S. FOUNDATIONS, THEIR TRUSTEES, OFFICERS, AND DONORS

This powerful fundraising reference tool provides fundraisers with current, accurate information on 58,000 private and community foundations in the U.S. The two-volume set also includes a master list of the names of the people who establish, oversee, and manage those institutions. With access to this information, fundraisers can facilitate their funding research by discovering the philanthropic connections of current donors, board members, volunteers, and prominent families in their geographic area. Because it provides a comprehensive list of U.S. foundations and the people who govern them, the *Guide to U.S. Foundations* also helps fundraisers follow up on any giving leads they may uncover. Each entry includes asset and giving amounts as well as geographic limitations, allowing fundraisers to quickly determine whether or not to pursue a particular grant source.

The *Guide to U.S. Foundations* is the only source of published data on thousands of local foundations. (It includes more than 31,000 grantmakers not covered in other print publications.) Each entry also tells you whether you can find more extensive information on the grantmaker in another Foundation Center reference work.

*April 2001 / 0-87954-947-5 / $225*
*Published annually*

## THE FOUNDATION 1000

Nonprofit fundraisers and other researchers have access to annually published, comprehensive reports on the 1,000 largest foundations in the country. *The Foundation 1000* provides access to extensive and accurate information on this set of powerful funders. *Foundation 1000* grantmakers hold over $234 billion in assets and each year award close to 250,000 grants worth $10 billion to nonprofit organizations nationwide.

*The Foundation 1000* provides the most thorough analyses available of the 1,000 largest foundations and their extensive grant programs, including all the data fundraisers need most when applying for grants from these top-level foundations. Each multi-page foundation profile features a full foundation portrait, a detailed breakdown of the foundation's grant programs, and extensive lists of recently awarded foundation grants.

Five indexes give fundraisers the opportunity to target potential funders in a variety of ways: by subject field, type of support, geographic location, international giving, and the names of foundation officers, donors, and trustees.

*November 2000 / ISBN 0-87954-913-0 / $295*
*Published annually*

## NATIONAL DIRECTORY OF CORPORATE GIVING, 7th Edition

Each year, corporations donate billions of dollars to nonprofit organizations. To help fundraisers tap into this vital source of funding, the *National Directory of Corporate Giving* offers authoritative information on approximately 3,000 company-sponsored foundations and direct corporate giving programs.

Fundraisers who want access to current, accurate fundraising facts on corporate philanthropies will benefit from the full range of data in this volume. The *National Directory of Corporate Giving* features detailed portraits of close to 1,900 company-sponsored foundations plus 1,000+ direct corporate giving programs. Fundraisers will find essential information on these corporate grantmakers, including application information, key personnel, types of support generally awarded, giving limitations, financial data, and purpose and activities statements. Also included in the 7th Edition are over 6,500 selected grants. These grants give you the best indication of a grantmaker's funding priorities by identifying nonprofits it has already funded. The volume also provides data on the companies that sponsor foundations and direct-giving programs—essential background information for corporate grant searches. Each entry gives the company's name and address, a listing of its types of business, its financial data (complete with *Forbes* and *Fortune* ratings), a listing of its subsidiaries, divisions, plants, and offices, and a charitable-giving statement.

The *National Directory of Corporate Giving* also features an extensive bibliography to guide you to further research on corporate funding. Seven essential indexes help you target funding prospects by geographic region; international giving; types of support; subject area; officers, donors, and trustees; types of business; and the names of the corporation, its foundation, and its direct-giving program.

*October 2001 / ISBN 0-87954-965-3 / $195*
*Published biennially*

## CORPORATE FOUNDATION PROFILES, 11th Edition

This biennially updated volume includes comprehensive information on 207 of the largest corporate foundations in the U.S., grantmakers who each give at least $1.2 million annually. Each profile includes foundation giving interests, application guidelines, recently awarded grants, information on the sponsoring company, and many other essential fundraising facts. A section on financial data provides a summary of the size and grantmaking capacity of each foundation and contains a list of assets, gifts or contributions, grants paid, operating programs, expenditures, scholarships, and loans. A quick-scan appendix lists core financial data on some 1,300 additional corporate foundations, all of which give at least $50,000 in grants every year. Five indexes help grantseekers search for prospective funders by names of donors, officers, trustees, and staff; subject area; types of support; geographic region; and international giving.

*March 2000 / ISBN 0-87954-867-3 / $155*
*Published biennially*

## SOUTHEASTERN FOUNDATIONS II: A Profile of the Region's Grantmaking Community, 2nd Edition

*Southeastern Foundations II* provides a detailed examination of foundation philanthropy in the booming 12-state Southeast region. The report includes an overview of the Southeast's share of all U.S. foundations, measures the growth of Southeastern foundations since 1992, profiles Southeastern funders by type, size, and geographic focus, compares broad giving trends of Southeastern and all U.S. foundations in 1992 and 1997, and details giving by non-Southeastern grantmakers to recipients in the region. *Produced in cooperation with the Southeastern Council of Foundations*

*November 1999 / ISBN 0-87954-775-8 / $19.95*

## NEW YORK STATE FOUNDATIONS: A Comprehensive Directory, 7th Edition

*New York State Foundations* offers fundraisers complete coverage of over 7,000 independent, corporate, and community foundations that fund New York nonprofits. Close to 5,900 of these foundations are located in New York state. An additional 1,200+ are out-of-state grantmakers with a documented interest in New York. Every entry has been drawn from the most current sources of information available,

including IRS 990-PF returns and, in many cases, the foundations themselves. The volume includes descriptions of 12,600 recently awarded grants, the best indication of a grantmaker's giving interests. Six time-saving indexes offer quick access to foundations according to their fields of interest; international interests; types of support awarded; city and county; names of donors, officers, and trustees; and foundation names.

*July 2001 / ISBN 0-87954-955-6 / $180*
*Published biennially*

## DIRECTORY OF MISSOURI GRANTMAKERS, 4th Edition

The *Directory of Missouri Grantmakers* provides a comprehensive guide to grantmakers in the state—close to 1,500 foundations, corporate giving programs, and public charities—from the largest grantmakers to local family foundations. The volume will facilitate your grantseeking with information-filled entries that list giving amounts, fields of interest, purpose statements, selected grants, and much more. Indexes help you target the most appropriate funders by subject interest, types of support, and names of key personnel.

*June 2001 / ISBN 0-87954-956-4 / $75*
*Published biennially*

## FOUNDATION GRANTS TO INDIVIDUALS, 11th Edition

The only publication devoted entirely to foundation grant opportunities for qualified individual applicants, the 11th Edition of this volume features more than 3,800 entries, all of which profile foundation grants to individuals. Entries include foundation addresses and telephone numbers, financial data, giving limitations, and application guidelines. This volume will save individual grantseekers countless hours of research.

*May 2001 / ISBN 0-87954-948-3 / $65*
*Published biennially*

# SUBJECT DIRECTORIES

The Foundation Center's National Guide to Funding series is designed to facilitate grantseeking within specific fields of nonprofit activity. Each of the directories described below performs the crucial first step of fundraising research by identifying a set of grantmakers that have already stated or demonstrated an interest in a particular field. Fact-filled entries provide access to foundation addresses, financial data, giving priorities, application procedures, contact names, and key officials. Many entries also feature recently awarded grants, the best indication of a grantmaker's funding priorities. A variety of indexes help fundraisers target potential grant sources by subject area, geographic preferences, types of support, and the names of donors, officers, and trustees.

*Subject guides are published biennially.*

## GUIDE TO FUNDING FOR INTERNATIONAL AND FOREIGN PROGRAMS, 5th Edition

The *Guide to Funding for International and Foreign Programs* covers over 1,000 grantmakers interested in funding projects with an international focus, both within the U.S. and abroad. Program areas covered include international relief, disaster assistance, human rights, civil liberties, community development, education, and much more. The volume also includes descriptions of more than 8,900+ recently awarded grants.

*May 2000 / ISBN 0-87954-903-3 / $125*

## NATIONAL GUIDE TO FUNDING IN AGING, 6th Edition

This volume provides essential facts on close to 1,400 grantmakers with a specific interest in the field of aging. This funding tool includes up-to-date addresses, financial data, giving priorities statements, application procedures, contact names, and key officials. The volume also provides recent grants lists with descriptions of over 2,200 grants for nearly 500 foundation entries. Section II of this volume includes basic descriptions and contact information for approximately 85 voluntary organizations which offer valuable technical assistance or information to older Americans and the agencies that serve them.

*June 2000 / ISBN 0-87954-904-1 / $115*

## NATIONAL GUIDE TO FUNDING IN AIDS, 2nd Edition

This volume covers more than 500 foundations, corporate giving programs, and public charities that support AIDS- and HIV-related nonprofit organizations involved in direct relief, medical research, legal aid, preventative education, and other programs to empower persons with AIDS and AIDS-related diseases. Nearly 500 recently awarded grants show the types of projects funded by grantmakers.

*July 2001 / ISBN 0-87954-950-5 / $115*

## NATIONAL GUIDE TO FUNDING IN ARTS AND CULTURE, 6th Edition

This volume covers more than 7,500 grantmakers with an interest in funding art-colonies, dance companies, museums, theaters, and countless other types of arts and culture projects and institutions. The volume also includes more than 16,500 descriptions of recently awarded grants.

*May 2000 / ISBN 0-87954-906-8 / $155*

## NATIONAL GUIDE TO FUNDING FOR THE ENVIRONMENT AND ANIMAL WELFARE, 5th Edition

This guide covers over 2,900 grantmakers that fund nonprofits involved in international conservation, ecological research, waste reduction, animal welfare, and much more. The volume includes descriptions of over 7,200 recently awarded grants.

*June 2000 / ISBN 0-87954-907-6 / $115*

## NATIONAL GUIDE TO FUNDING IN HEALTH, 7th Edition

The *National Guide to Funding in Health* contains essential facts on over 10,000 grantmakers interested in funding hospitals, universities, research institutes, community-based agencies, national health associations, and a broad range of other health-related programs and services. The volume also includes descriptions of more than 15,900 recently awarded grants.

*June 2001 / ISBN 0-87954-951-3 / $155*

## NATIONAL GUIDE TO FUNDING IN HIGHER EDUCATION, 6th Edition

The *National Guide to Funding in Higher Education* includes information on over 7,200 grantmakers with an interest in funding colleges, universities, graduate programs, and research institutes, as well as descriptions of more than 18,000 recently awarded grants.

*June 2000 / ISBN 0-87954-905-X / $175*

## NATIONAL GUIDE TO FUNDING FOR LIBRARIES AND INFORMATION SERVICES, 6th Edition

This volume provides essential data on nearly 800 grantmakers that support a wide range of organizations and initiatives, from the smallest public libraries to major research institutions, academic/research libraries, art, law, and medical libraries, and other specialized information centers. The volume also includes descriptions of over 600 recently awarded grants.

*June 2001 / ISBN 0-87954-953-X / $115*

## NATIONAL GUIDE TO FUNDING IN RELIGION, 6th Edition

With this volume, fundraisers who work for nonprofits affiliated with religious organizations have access to information on over 8,400 grantmakers that have demonstrated or stated an interest in funding churches, missionary societies, religious welfare and education programs, and many other types of projects and institutions. The volume also includes descriptions of more than 10,000 recently awarded grants.

*May 2001 / ISBN 0-87954-952-1 / $155*

# GRANT DIRECTORIES

### GRANT GUIDES

Designed for fundraisers who work within defined fields of nonprofit development, this series of guides lists actual foundation grants of $10,000 or more in 25 key areas of grantmaking.

Each title in the series affords immediate access to the names, addresses, and giving limitations of the foundations listed. The grant descriptions provide fundraisers with the grant recipient's name and location; the amount of the grant;

the date the grant was authorized; and a description of the grant's intended use.

In addition, each *Grant Guide* includes three indexes, which help fundraisers target possible sources of funding by the type of organization generally funded by the grantmaker, the subject focus of the foundation's grants, and the geographic area in which the foundation has already funded projects.

Each *Grant Guide* also includes a concise overview of the foundation spending patterns within the specified field. The introduction uses a series of statistical tables to document such important findings as (1) the 25 top funders in your area of interest (by total dollar amount of grants); (2) the 15 largest grants reported; (3) the total dollar amount and number of grants awarded for specific types of support, recipient organization type, and population group; and (4) the total grant dollars received in each U.S. state and many foreign countries.

The *Grant Guide* series gives fundraisers the data they need to target foundations making grants in their field, to network with organizations that share their goals, and to tailor their grant applications to the specific concerns of grantmakers as expressed by the grants they have already made.

*Series published annually in December /
2000 / 2001 Editions / $75 each*

## THE FOUNDATION GRANTS INDEX, 2001 Edition

A foundation's recently awarded grants offer the best indication of its future funding priorities. The 2001 (29th) Edition of *The Foundation Grants Index*—the volume fundraisers have relied upon since 1970—is the most current and accurate source of information on recent grantmaker awards. The *Grants Index* has steadily expanded its coverage since the 1st Edition: it now covers the grantmaking programs of over 1,000 of the largest independent, corporate, and community foundations in the U.S. and includes more than 100,000 grant descriptions in all.

The *Grants Index* is designed for fast and easy grants-based research. Grant descriptions are divided into 28 broad subject areas such as health, higher education, and arts and culture. Within each of these broad fields, the grant descriptions are listed geographically by state and alphabetically by the name of the foundation, an arrangement that helps fund-raisers find prospective funders who share their program interests *and* fund projects within their geographic region.

*December 2000 / ISBN 0-87954-914-9 / $165*

# GUIDEBOOKS, MANUALS, AND REPORTS

## AIDS FUNDRAISING

Published in conjunction with Funders Concerned About AIDS, this guide helps nonprofit groups plan a strategy for raising money. *AIDS Fundraising* covers a vast array of money-generating initiatives, from membership drives to special events, direct mail, and grant applications.
*July 1991 / ISBN 0-87954-390-6 / $10*

## ARTS FUNDING: A Report on Foundation Trends, 3rd Edition

The report focuses on grantmaking in 1996 and analyzes over 11,000 arts grants awarded by 800+ foundations, providing a detailed picture of giving priorities in the field. This new edition of *Arts Funding* includes several enhancements, such as an analysis of arts grantmakers and recipients by region, an examination of the impact of smaller grants on the field, and brief profiles of arts grantmakers that support individual artists.
*November 1998 / ISBN 0-87954-813-4 / $19.95*

## ARTS FUNDING 2000:
### Funder Perspectives on Current and Future Trends
### by Loren Renz and Caron Atlas

*Arts Funding 2000* explores the current state of arts grantmaking and previews emerging themes and issues. Based on in-depth interviews with 35 leading foundations and corporations nationwide, conducted in 1999, the report offers an inside perspective on recent changes in arts funding priorities and strategies and on factors affecting decision-making. Important issues and opportunities facing the arts community and arts funders at the turn of the century are identified. Conducted in cooperation with Grantmakers in the Arts.
*November 1999 / ISBN 0-87954-776-6 / $14.95*

## FAMILY FOUNDATIONS:
### A Profile of Funders and Trends

*Family Foundations* is an essential resource for anyone interested in understanding the fastest growing segment of foundation philanthropy. The report provides the most comprehensive measurement to date of the size and scope of the U.S. family foundation community. Through the use of objective and subjective criteria, the report identifies the number of family foundations and their distribution by region and state, size, geographic focus, and decade of establishment; and includes analyses of staffing and public reporting by these funders. *Family Foundations* also examines trends in giving by a sample of larger family foundations between 1993 and 1998 and compares these patterns with independent foundations overall. Prepared in cooperation with the National Center for Family Philanthropy.
*August 2000 / ISBN 0-87954-917-3 / $19.95*

## HEALTH POLICY GRANTMAKING:
### A Report on Foundation Trends

*Health Policy Grantmaking* explores broad trends in grantmaker support for health policy-related activities during the 1990s, a period of dramatic growth in health policy funding. This report investigates health policy's share of all giving for health, presents areas of growth in health policy funding, spotlights emerging topics in the field, and identifies leading grantmakers by amount of funding and programmatic interests.

*September 1998 / ISBN 0-87954-814 -2 / $14.95*

### INTERNATIONAL GRANTMAKING II:
#### An Update on U.S. Foundation Trends, 2nd Edition

An update to 1997's groundbreaking *International Grantmaking* study, this report documents trends in international giving by U.S. foundations in the late 1990s. Based on a sample of over 570 foundations, *International Grantmaking II* identifies shifts in international giving priorities, types of support provided, recipients funded, and countries/regions targeted for support. The report also includes an overview of recent events and factors shaping the international funding environment; and perspectives on the changing funding climate based on a 2000 survey of more than 25 leading international grantmakers. Prepared in cooperation with the Council on Foundations.

*November 2000 / ISBN 0-87954-916-5 / $35*

### THE FOUNDATION CENTER'S GRANTS CLASSIFICATION SYSTEM INDEXING MANUAL WITH THESAURUS, Revised Edition

A complete "how-to" guide, the *Grants Classification Manual* provides an essential resource for any organization that wants to classify foundation grants or their recipients. The *Manual* includes a complete set of all classification codes to facilitate precise tracking of grants and recipients by subject, recipient type, and population categories. It also features a completely revised thesaurus to help identify the "official" terms and codes that represent thousands of subject areas and recipient types in the Center's system of grants classification.

*May 1995 / ISBN 0-87954-644-1 / $95*

### FOUNDATION FUNDAMENTALS:
#### A Guide for Grantseekers, 6th Edition

This comprehensive, easy-to-read guidebook shows you how to use print and electronic funding research directories and databases to develop your prospect list; how to use the World Wide Web to locate information on potential funders; how to target grantmakers by subject interest, types of support, and geographic area; how to shape your proposal to reflect the special concerns of corporate funders; and much more! The 6th Edition is fully revised with up-to-date charts and worksheets to help you manage your fundraising program.

*August 1999 / ISBN 0-87954-869-X / $24.95*

### THE FOUNDATION CENTER'S USER-FRIENDLY GUIDE:
#### A Grantseeker's Guide to Resources, 4th Edition

This helpful book answers the most commonly asked questions about grantseeking in an upbeat, easy-to-read style.

Specifically designed for novice grantseekers, the *User-Friendly Guide* leads the reader through the maze of unfamiliar jargon and wide range of research guides used successfully by professional fundraisers every day. Whether a grantseeker needs $100 or $100,000 for his or her project or organization, *The Foundation Center's User-Friendly Guide* offers an excellent first step in the fundraising process.

*July 1996 / ISBN 0-87954-666-2 / $14.95*

### FOUNDATIONS TODAY SERIES, 2001 Edition

The successor to the Foundation Center's popular *Foundation Giving* report, the *Foundations Today Series* provides the latest information on foundation growth and trends in foundation giving. A subscription to the 2001 Edition of the *Foundations Today Series* includes copies of all four reports and the estimates update (as they are published) for one low price.

***Foundation Giving Trends: Update on Funding Priorities***—Examines 1999 grantmaking patterns of a sample of more than 1,000 larger U.S. foundations and compares current giving priorities with trends since 1980. *January 2001*

***Foundation Growth and Giving Estimates: 2000 Preview***—Provides a first look at estimates of foundation giving for 2000 and final statistics on actual giving and assets for 1999. Presents new top 100 foundation lists. *March 2001*

***Foundation Yearbook: Facts and Figures on Private and Community Foundations***—Documents the growth in number, giving, and assets of all active U.S. foundations from 1975 through 1999. *June 2001*

***Foundation Staffing: Update on Staffing Trends of Private and Community Foundations***—Examines changes in the staffing patterns of U.S. foundations through mid-2001, based on an annual survey of nearly 3,000 staffed foundations. *September 2001*

***Foundation Reporting: Update on Public Reporting Trends of Private and Community Foundations***—Documents changes in voluntary reporting patterns of U.S. foundations through mid-2001, based on an annual survey of more than 3,000 foundations that issued publications. *November 2001*

*Annual 2001 / ISBN 0-87954-957-2 / $95*

### THE FOUNDATION CENTER'S GUIDE TO GRANTSEEKING ON THE WEB, 2001 Edition

Learn how to maximize use of the World Wide Web for your funding research! Packed with a wealth of information, the *Guide to Grantseeking on the Web* provides both novice and experienced Web users with a gateway to the numerous online resources available to grantseekers. Foundation Center staff experts have team-authored this guide, contributing their extensive knowledge of Web content as well as their tips and strategies on how to evaluate and use Web-based funding materials. Presented in a concise, "how-to" style, the *Guide* will introduce you to the World Wide Web and structure your funding research with a toolkit of resources. These resources include foundation and corporate Web sites, searchable databases for grantseeking, government funding sources, online journals, and interactive services on the Web for grantseekers.

*September 2001 / Book / ISBN 0-87954-966-1 / $19.95*
*CD-ROM / ISBN 0-87954-967-X / $19.95*
*Book and CD-ROM / $29.95*

### THE FOUNDATION CENTER'S GUIDE TO PROPOSAL WRITING, 3rd Edition

The *Guide* is a comprehensive manual on the strategic thinking and mechanics of proposal writing. It covers each step of the process, from pre-proposal planning to the writing itself to the essential post-grant follow-up. The book features many extracts from actual grant proposals and also includes candid advice from grantmakers on the "do's and don't's" of proposal writing. Written by a professional fundraiser who has been creating successful proposals for more than 25 years, *The Foundation Center's Guide to Proposal Writing* offers the kind of valuable tips and in-depth, practical instruction that no other source provides.

*February 2001 / ISBN 0-87954-958-0 / $34.95*

### THE PRI DIRECTORY:
### Charitable Loans and Other Program-Related Investments by Foundations

Certain foundations have developed an alternative financing approach—known as program-related investing—for supplying capital to the nonprofit sector. PRIs have been used to support community revitalization, low-income housing, microenterprise development, historic preservation, human services, and more. This directory lists leading PRI providers and includes tips on how to seek out and manage PRIs. Foundation listings include funder name and state; recipient name, city, and state (or country); and a description of the project funded. There are several helpful indexes to guide PRI-seekers to records by foundation/recipient location, subject/type of support, and recipient name, as well as an index to officers, donors, and trustees.

*February 2001 / ISBN 0-87954-915-7 / $75*

## OTHER PUBLICATIONS

### AMERICA'S NONPROFIT SECTOR: A Primer, 2nd Edition
### by Lester M. Salamon

In this revised edition of his classic book, Lester M. Salamon clarifies the basic structure and role of the nonprofit sector in the U.S. Moreover, he places the nonprofit sector into context in relation to the government and business sectors. He also shows how the position of the nonprofit sector has changed over time, both generally and in the major fields in which the sector is active. Illustrated with numerous charts and tables, Salamon's book is an easy-to-understand primer for government officials, journalists, and students—in short, for anyone who wants to comprehend the makeup of America's nonprofit sector.

*February 1999 / ISBN 0-87954-801-0 / $14.95*

### BEST PRACTICES OF EFFECTIVE NONPROFIT ORGANIZATIONS: A Practitioner's Guide
### by Philip Bernstein

This volume provides guidance for any nonprofit professional eager to advance your organization's goals. Philip Bernstein has drawn on his own extensive experience as a nonprofit executive, consultant, and volunteer to produce this review of "best practices" adopted by successful nonprofit organizations. The author identifies and explains the procedures which provide the foundation for social achievement in all nonprofit fields. Topics include defining purposes and goals, creating comprehensive financing plans, evaluating services, and effective communication.

*February 1997 / ISBN 0-87954-755-3 / $29.95*

### THE BOARD MEMBER'S BOOK, 2nd Edition
### by Brian O'Connell

Based on his extensive experience working with and on the boards of voluntary organizations, Brian O'Connell has developed this practical guide to the essential functions of voluntary boards. O'Connell offers practical advice on how to be a more effective board member as well as on how board members can help their organizations make a difference. He also provides an extensive reading list. *The Board Member's Book* is an invaluable instructional and inspirational tool for anyone who works on or with a voluntary board.

*October 1993 / ISBN 0-87954-502-X / $24.95*

### CAREERS FOR DREAMERS AND DOERS: A Guide to Management Careers in the Nonprofit Sector
### by Lilly Cohen and Dennis R.Young

A comprehensive guide to management positions in the nonprofit world, *Careers for Dreamers and Doers* offers practical advice for starting a job search and suggests strategies used by successful managers throughout the voluntary sector.

*November 1989 / ISBN 0-87954-294-2 / $24.95*

### ECONOMICS FOR NONPROFIT MANAGERS
### by Dennis R. Young and Richard Steinberg

*Economics for Nonprofit Managers* is a complete course in the economic issues faced by America's nonprofit decision-makers. Young and Steinberg treat micro-economic analysis as an indispensable skill for nonprofit managers. They introduce and explain concepts such as opportunity cost, analysis at the margin, market equilibrium, market failure, and cost-benefit analysis. This volume also focuses on issues of particular concern to nonprofits, such as the economics of fundraising and volunteer recruiting, the regulatory environment, the impact of competition on nonprofit performance, interactions among sources of revenue, and much more.

*July 1995 / ISBN 0-87954-610-7 / $34.95*

## HANDBOOK ON PRIVATE FOUNDATIONS
### by David F. Freeman and the Council on Foundations

This publication provides a thorough look at the issues facing the staff and boards of private foundations in the U.S. Author David F. Freeman offers sound advice on establishing, staffing, and governing foundations and provides insights into legal and tax guidelines as well. Each chapter concludes with a useful annotated bibliography. Sponsored by the Council on Foundations.

*September 1991*
*Softbound: ISBN 0-87954-404-X / $29.95*
*Hardbound: ISBN 0-87954-403-1 / $39.95*

## THE NONPROFIT ENTREPRENEUR: Creating Ventures to Earn Income
### Edited by Edward Skloot

In a well-organized topic-by-topic approach to nonprofit venturing, nonprofit consultant and entrepreneur Edward Skloot demonstrates how nonprofits can launch successful earned-income enterprises without compromising their missions. Skloot has compiled a collection of writings by the nation's top practitioners and advisors in nonprofit enterprise. Topics covered include legal issues, marketing techniques, business planning, avoiding the pitfalls of venturing for smaller nonprofits, and a special section on museums and their retail operations.

*September 1988 / ISBN 0-87954-239-X / $19.95*

## A NONPROFIT ORGANIZATION OPERATING MANUAL: Planning for Survival and Growth
### by Arnold J. Olenick and Philip R. Olenick

This straightforward, all-inclusive desk manual for nonprofit executives covers all aspects of starting and managing a nonprofit. The authors discuss legal problems, obtaining tax exemption, organizational planning and development, and board relations; operational, proposal, cash, and capital budgeting; marketing, grant proposals, fundraising, and for-profit ventures; computerization; and tax planning and compliance.

*July 1991 / ISBN 0-87954-293-4 / $29.95*

## PEOPLE POWER: SERVICE, ADVOCACY, EMPOWERMENT
### by Brian O'Connell

Throughout his career, Brian O'Connell has broadened the impact of his own nonprofit work with thoughtful essays, speeches, and op-ed articles. *People Power,* a selection of

O'Connell's most powerful writings, provides thought-provoking commentary on the nonprofit world. The 25+ essays included in this volume range from keen analyses of the role of voluntarism in American life, to sound advice for nonprofit managers, to suggestions for developing and strengthening the nonprofit sector of the future. Anyone involved in the nonprofit world will appreciate O'Connell's penetrating insights.

*October 1994 / ISBN 0-87954-563-1 / $24.95*

## PROMOTING ISSUES AND IDEAS: A Guide to Public Relations for Nonprofit Organizations, Revised edition
### by M Booth & Associates

M Booth & Associates are specialists in promoting the issues and ideas of nonprofit groups. Their book presents proven strategies that will attract the interest of the people you wish to influence and inform. Included are the "nuts-and-bolts" of advertising, publicity, speech-making, lobbying, and special events; how to write and produce informational literature that leaps off the page; public relations on a shoe-string budget; how to plan and evaluate PR efforts; the use of rapidly evolving communication technologies; and a new chapter on crisis management.

*December 1995 / ISBN 0-87954-594-1 / $29.95*

## RAISE MORE MONEY FOR YOUR NONPROFIT ORGANIZATION: A Guide to Evaluating and Improving Your Fundraising
### by Anne L. New

In *Raise More Money,* Anne New sets guidelines for a fundraising program that will benefit the incipient as well as the established nonprofit organization. The author divides her text into three sections: "The Basics," which delineates the necessary steps a nonprofit must take before launching a development campaign; "Fundraising Methods," which encourages organizational self-analysis and points the way to an effective program involving many sources of funding; and "Fundraising Resources," a 20-page bibliography that highlights the most useful research and funding directories available.

*January 1991 / ISBN 0-87954-388-4 / $14.95*

## SECURING YOUR ORGANIZATION'S FUTURE: A Complete Guide to Fundraising Strategies, Revised Edition
### by Michael Seltzer

In this completely updated edition, Michael Seltzer acts as your personal fundraising consultant. Beginners get bottom-line facts and easy-to-follow worksheets; veteran fundraisers receive a complete review of the basics plus new money-making ideas. Seltzer supplements his text with an extensive bibliography of selected readings and resource organizations. Highly recommended for use as a text in nonprofit management programs at colleges and universities.

*February 2001 / ISBN 0-87954-900-9 / $34.95*

## SUCCEEDING WITH CONSULTANTS: Self-Assessment for the Changing Nonprofit
### by Barbara Kibbe and Fred Setterberg

This inspirational book, written by Barbara Kibbe and Fred Setterberg and supported by the David and Lucile Packard Foundation, guides nonprofits through the process of selecting and utilizing consultants to strengthen their organization's operations. The book emphasizes self assessment tools and covers six different areas in which a nonprofit organization might benefit from a consultant's advice: governance, planning, fund development, financial management, public relations and marketing, and quality assurance.

*April 1992 / ISBN 0-87954-450-3 / $19.95*

## THE 21ST CENTURY NONPROFIT
### by Paul B. Firstenberg

In *The 21st Century Nonprofit,* Paul B. Firstenberg provides nonprofit managers with the know-how to make their organizations effective agents of change. *The 21st Century Nonprofit* encourages managers to adopt strategies developed by the for-profit sector in recent years. These strategies will help them to expand their revenue base by diversifying grant sources, exploit the possibilities of for-profit enterprises, develop human resources by learning how to attract and retain talented people, and explore the nature of leadership through short profiles of three nonprofit CEOs.

*July 1996 / ISBN 0-87954-672-7 / $34.95*

# MEMBERSHIP PROGRAM

## ASSOCIATES PROGRAM
### Direct Line to Fundraising Information

The Associates Program puts important facts and figures on your desk through an e-mail and toll-free telephone reference service, helping you to:

- identify potential sources of foundation funding for your organization; and
- gather important information to use in targeting and presenting your proposals effectively.

Your annual membership in the Associates Program gives you vital information on a timely basis, saving you hundreds of hours of research time.

- Membership in the Associates Program entitles you to important funding information, including information from:
  - foundation and corporate annual reports, brochures, press releases, grants lists, and other announcements
  - IRS 990-PF information returns for 50,000+ active grantmaking U.S. foundations—often the only source of information on small foundations

  - books and periodicals on the grantmaking field, including regulation and nonprofit management
- The annual fee of $595 for the Associates Program entitles you to ten free reference requests per month. Additional reference requests can be made at the rate of $30 per ten questions.
- Membership in the Associates Program allows you to request custom searches of the Foundation Center's computerized databases, which contain information on more than 53,000 U.S. foundations and corporate givers. There is an additional cost for this service.
- Associates Program members may request photocopies of key documents. Important information from 990-PFs, annual reports, application guidelines, and other resources can be copied and either mailed or faxed to your office. The fee for this service, available only to Associate Members, is $2.00 for the first page of material and $1.00 for each additional page. Fax service is available at an additional charge.
- All Associates Program members receive the Associates Program quarterly newsletter, which provides news and information about new foundations, changes in boards of directors, new programs, and publications from both the Foundation Center and other publishers in the field.
- New benefit—Members now receive two special e-mail reports each month; one listing a minimum of 75 new or emerging foundations not yet listed in our directories or on our Web site, and a second e-mail report listing updates on current grantmaker profiles.
- Coming soon—Access to all program services via Associates Program Online.

Thousands of professional fundraisers find it extremely cost-effective to rely on the Center's Associates Program. Put our staff of experts to work for your fundraising program. For more information call 1-800-424-9836, or visit our World Wide Web site at www.fdncenter.org.

# CD-ROMs

## FC SEARCH: The Foundation Center's Database on CD-ROM, Version 5.0

The Foundation Center's comprehensive database of grantmakers and their associated grants can be accessed in this fully searchable CD-ROM format. *FC Search* contains the Center's entire universe of over 58,000 grantmaker records, including all known active foundations and corporate giving programs in the United States. It also includes over 246,000 newly reported grants from the largest foundations and the names of more than 250,000 trustees, officers, and donors which can be quickly linked to their foundation affiliations. Users can also link from *FC Search* to the Web sites of close to 2,000 grantmakers and 1,000+ corporations.**

Grantseekers and other researchers may select multiple criteria and create customized prospect lists which can be printed or saved. Basic or Advanced search modes and special search options enable users to make searches as broad or as specific as required. Up to 21 different criteria may be selected:

- grantmaker name
- grantmaker type
- grantmaker city
- grantmaker state
- geographic focus
- fields of interest
- types of support
- total assets
- total giving
- trustees, officers, and donors
- establishment date
- corporate name
- corporate location
- recipient name
- recipient city
- recipient state
- recipient type
- subject
- grant amount
- year grant authorized
- text search field

*FC Search* is a sophisticated fundraising research tool, but it is also user-friendly. It has been developed with both the novice and experienced researcher in mind. Assistance is available through Online Help, a *User Manual* that accompanies *FC Search,* as well as through a free User Hotline.

FC Search, *Version 5.0, spring 2001 (prices include fall 2001 Update disk plus one* User Manual*).*
*Standalone (single user) version: $1,195*
*Local Area Network (2–8 users in one building) version: $1,895\**
*Additional copies of* User Manual: *$19.95*
*New editions of* FC Search *are released each spring.*
*\*Larger local area network versions, site licenses, and wide area network versions are also available. For more information, call* the **Electronic Product Support Line (Mon–Fri., 9 am–5 pm EST) 1-800-478-4661.**

### THE FOUNDATION DIRECTORY ON CD-ROM, Version 2.0

For the first time, users can search for funding prospects from among the same set of 10,000+ *Foundation Directory*-size foundations that appear in our print *Directory,* using the fast-speed search capabilities and high-powered features only available via CD-ROM!

*The Foundation Directory on CD-ROM:* includes over 3,800 foundation records which list approximately 10 sample grants; features a searchable index of 62,000 trustees, officers, and donors; links to over 900 foundation Web sites and the Foundation Center's Web site; includes extensive Help file and printed user guide; features Boolean operators between fields; the ability to store search schemes and mark records for use in future sessions; a wide range of printing and saving options; alphabetical or total giving sort; and the ability to affix searchable notes to personalize grantmaker

records; and allows users to create customized prospect lists by selecting from 12 search fields:

- grantmaker name
- grantmaker state
- grantmaker city
- fields of interest
- types of support
- trustees, officers, and donors
- geographic focus
- grantmaker type
- total giving
- total assets
- establishment date
- text search

The Foundation Directory on CD-ROM *(includes March 2001 release and Fall 2001 Update disk)*
*Standalone (single-user) version: $295*
*Local Area Network version (2–8 users in one building): $595*

### THE FOUNDATION DIRECTORY 1 & 2 ON CD-ROM

We've combined the authoritative data found in our two print classics, *The Foundation Directory* and *The Foundation Directory Part 2,* to bring you 20,000 of the nation's largest and mid-sized foundations in this new CD-ROM product. Search for funding prospects by choosing from 12 search fields (see *Foundation Directory on CD-ROM* fields listed above). The CD-ROM includes links to close to 1,000 foundation Web sites, a list of sample grants in 6,800+ foundation records, and a searchable index of over 100,000 trustees, officers, and donors.

The Foundation Directory 1 & 2 on CD-ROM *(includes March 2001 release and Fall 2001 Update disk)*
*Standalone (single-user) version: $495*
*Local Area Network version (2-8 users in one building): $795*

### THE FOUNDATION GRANTS INDEX ON CD-ROM

The same data found in our classic print publication, *The Foundation Grants Index,* is available for the first time in a fast-speed CD-ROM format. Search our database of close to 100,000 recently awarded grants by the largest 1,000 funders to help you target foundations by the grants they have already awarded. Choose from twelve search fields:

- Recipient Name
- Recipient State
- Recipient City
- Recipient Type
- Grantmaker Name
- Grantmaker State
- Geographic Focus
- Subject
- Types of Support
- Grant Amount
- Year Authorized
- Text Search

The Foundation Grants Index on CD-ROM
*December 2000/ Single User / ISBN 0-87954-954-8 /$195*
*Call 1-800-478-4661 for network versions.*

## FOUNDATION GRANTS TO INDIVIDUALS ON CD-ROM, Version 2.0

The Foundation Center's new funding research tool, Foundation Grants to Individuals on CD-ROM, is an essential resource that no financial aid office, funding library, or individual grantseeker should be without. It includes over 4,200 foundations and public charities that provide support to individual grantseekers for research, education, general welfare, arts and culture, and more. Grantmaker records include current information: address, contact name, financial data, application information, program descriptions, and more.

The CD-ROM includes nine search fields: geographic focus, fields of interest, types of support, company name, school name, grantmaker name, grantmaker city, grantmaker state, and text search. Special features include flexible printing and saving options; the ability to mark records and save search schemes; and a searchable notepad function for devising a tickler system. In addition, the CD-ROM connects users to a special Web page with further resources for individual grantseekers.

*June 2001/ Single-user / ISBN 0-87954-949-1 / $75*

*Call 1-800-478-4661 for network versions.*

## GUIDE TO GREATER WASHINGTON D.C. GRANTMAKERS ON CD-ROM

Compiled with the assistance of the Washington Regional Association of Grantmakers, an organization with a unique local perspective on the dynamics of D.C. grantmaking, this CD-ROM covers over 1,500 grantmakers located in the D.C. region or that have an interest in D.C.-area nonprofits. It also contains close to 1,800 selected grants and a searchable index of 8,000+ trustees, officers, and donors and their grantmaker affiliations.

Users can generate prospect lists within seconds, using twelve search fields. Grantmaker portraits feature crucial information: address, phone number, contact name, financial data, giving limitations, and names of key officials. For the large foundations—those that give at least $50,000 in grants per year—the volume provides even more data, including application procedures and giving interest statements.

The CD-ROM links to more than 150 grantmaker Web sites; connects to a special Web page with resources of value to D.C. grantseekers; and offers flexible printing and saving options and the ability to mark records.

*June 2000 / Single-user: 0-87954-912-2 / $75*
*Local Area Network:* 0-87954-899-1 / $125*

*\*A local area network is defined as 2-8 users within one building.*

## SYSTEM CONFIGURATIONS FOR CD-ROM PRODUCTS

- Windows-based PC
- Microsoft Windows™ ME, Windows™ 98, Windows™ 95, Windows™ 2000 or Windows™ NT
- Pentium microprocessor
- 16MB memory

*\*\*Internet access and Netscape's Navigator or Communicator or Microsoft's Internet Explorer browser required to access grantmaker Web sites and Foundation Center Web site.*

# ONLINE DATABASES

## THE FOUNDATION DIRECTORY ONLINE SUBSCRIPTION SERVICE

### The Foundation Directory Online

Search for prospects from among the nation's largest 10,000+ foundations. Perform searches using up to seven search fields and print results that appear in the browser window.

*Monthly subscriptions start at $19.95 per month*
*Annual subscriptions start at $195 per year*

### The Foundation Directory Online Plus

Plus service allows users to search the 10,000+ largest foundations in the U.S.—plus 170,000 grants awarded by the largest 1,100 foundations.

*Monthly subscriptions start at $29.95 per month*
*Annual subscriptions start at $295 per year*

### The Foundation Directory Online Premium

Research and identify more foundation funding sources online than ever before with *The Foundation Directory Online Premium*. In addition to featuring 20,000 of the nation's large and mid-sized foundations—twice the number of foundations included in the other subscription services—*Premium* service includes a searchable database of 170,000 grants awarded by the top 1,100 U.S. foundations.

*Monthly subscriptions start at $59.95 per month*
*Annual subscriptions start at $595 per year*

### The Foundation Directory Online Platinum

Search our entire universe of U.S. foundations, corporate giving programs, and grantmaking public charities - 58,000 funders in all - in our most comprehensive online subscription service. In addition to more funders, you'll get access to more in-depth data. Only *The Foundation Directory Online Platinum* offers extensive program details for 1,000+

leading foundations; detailed application guidelines for 6,000+ foundations; and sponsoring company information for corporate givers. This service also includes a searchable file of approximately 170,000 grants awarded by the top 1,100 funders.

*Monthly subscriptions start at $149.95*
*Annual subscriptions start at $995*

**Foundation and grants data are updated monthly for the above databases. Monthly, annual, and multi-user subscription options are available.**
**Please visit www.fconline.fdncenter.org to subscribe.**

### DIALOG

The Center's grantmaker and grants databases are also available online through The Dialog Corporation. For further information, contact The Dialog Corporation at 1-800-334-2564.

### DIALOG User Manual and Thesaurus, Revised Edition

The *User Manual and Thesaurus* is a comprehensive guide that will help you retrieve essential fundraising facts quickly and easily. It will greatly facilitate your foundation and corporate giving research through our databases, offered online through Dialog.

*November 1995 / ISBN 0-87954-595-X / $50*

# FOUNDATION CENTER'S WORLD WIDE WEB SITE (www.fdncenter.org)

*Your gateway to philanthropy on the Web*

The Foundation Center's World Wide Web site (www.fdncenter.org) is fast becoming the premier online source of fundraising information. Updated and expanded on a daily basis, the Center's site provides grantseekers, grantmakers, researchers, journalists, and the general public with easy access to a range of valuable resources, among them:

- A Grantmaker Information directory with links to more than 1,700 individual grantmaker sites—the most comprehensive and useful directory of its kind on the Internet.

- *Philanthropy News Digest,* a weekly compendium of philanthropy-related articles abstracted from major print and online media outlets. Also available as a listserv.

- *The Literature of the Nonprofit Sector Online,* a searchable bibliographical database with 18,000+ entries of works in the field of philanthropy, over 12,000 of which are abstracted.

- An Online Library, with comprehensive answers to FAQs, an online librarian to field questions about grantseeking and the Foundation Center, annotated links to useful nonprofit resources, and online orientations to the grantseeking process—one for individual grantseekers, the other for fundraisers at nonprofit organizations.

- Our popular Proposal Writing Short Course, an extensive glossary, bibliographies, a prospect worksheet, and common grant application forms.

- Information about Center-sponsored orientations, training programs, and seminars.

- The locations of our 200+ Cooperating Collections nationwide, and the activities and resources at our five main libraries.

- Foundation Finder, our free foundation look-up tool that provides a foundation's contact information and brief background data, such as type of foundation, assets, total giving, and EIN.

- A special section For Grantmakers offers funders the opportunity to help get the word out about their work, answers frequently asked questions, and informs grantmakers on recent developments in the field and how the Center assists grantees and applicants.

- Sector Search is a search tool that continuously crawls the Web sites of thousands of private, corporate, community foundations, grantmaking public charities, and nonprofit organizations, and provides relevant, accurate search results. Search by organization type, subject, or individual's name.

All this and more is available at our Web site. The Center's publications and electronic resources can be ordered via the site's printable or interactive order forms. Visit our Web site often for information on new products and services.

# FOUNDATION CENTER COOPERATING COLLECTIONS    FREE FUNDING INFORMATION CENTERS

The Foundation Center is an independent national service organization established by foundations to provide an authoritative source of information on foundation and corporate giving. The New York, Washington D.C., Atlanta, Cleveland, and San Francisco reference collections operated by the Foundation Center offer a wide variety of services and comprehensive resources on foundations and grants. Cooperating Collections are libraries, community foundations, and other nonprofit agencies that make accessible a collection of Foundation Center publications, as well as a variety of supplementary materials and education programs in areas useful to grantseekers. The collection includes:

FC SEARCH: THE FOUNDATION CENTER'S DATABASE ON CD-ROM
THE FOUNDATION DIRECTORY 1 AND 2, AND SUPPLEMENT
FOUNDATION FUNDAMENTALS
THE FOUNDATION 1000

FOUNDATIONS TODAY SERIES
FOUNDATION GRANTS TO INDIVIDUALS
THE FOUNDATION CENTER'S GUIDE TO GRANTSEEKING ON THE WEB
THE FOUNDATION CENTER'S GUIDE TO PROPOSAL WRITING

GUIDE TO U.S. FOUNDATIONS, THEIR TRUSTEES, OFFICERS, AND DONORS
NATIONAL DIRECTORY OF CORPORATE GIVING
NATIONAL GUIDE TO FUNDING IN.... (SERIES)

All five Foundation Center libraries and most Cooperating Collections have *FC: Search: The Foundation Center's Database on CD-ROM* available for public use and provide Internet access. Increasingly, those seeking information on fundraising and nonprofit management are referring to our Web site (http://www.fdncenter.org) and others for a wealth of data and advice on grantseeking, including links to foundation IRS information returns (990-PFs). Because the Cooperating Collections vary in their hours, it is recommended that you call the collection in advance of a visit. To check on new locations or current holdings, call toll-free 1-800-424-9836, or visit our site at http://fdncenter.org/collections/index.html.

## REFERENCE COLLECTIONS OPERATED BY THE FOUNDATION CENTER

| THE FOUNDATION CENTER | THE FOUNDATION CENTER | THE FOUNDATION CENTER | THE FOUNDATION CENTER | THE FOUNDATION CENTER |
|---|---|---|---|---|
| 2nd Floor | 312 Sutter St., Suite 606 | 1627 K St., NW | Kent H. Smith Library | Suite 150, Grand Lobby |
| 79 Fifth Ave. | San Francisco, CA 94108 | Washington, DC 20006 | 1422 Euclid, Suite 1356 | Hurt Bldg., 50 Hurt Plaza |
| New York, NY 10003 | (415) 397-0902 | (202) 331-1400 | Cleveland, OH 44115 | Atlanta, GA 30303 |
| (212) 620-4230 | | | (216) 861-1933 | (404) 880-0094 |

**ALABAMA**

BIRMINGHAM PUBLIC LIBRARY
Government Documents
2100 Park Place
Birmingham  35203
(205) 226-3620

HUNTSVILLE PUBLIC LIBRARY
915 Monroe St.
Huntsville  35801
(256) 532-5940

AUBURN UNIVERSITY AT MONTGOMERY LIBRARY
7300 University Dr.
Montgomery  36124-4023
(334) 244-3200

**ALASKA**

CONSORTIUM LIBRARY
3211 Providence Dr.
Anchorage  99508
(907) 786-1848

JUNEAU PUBLIC LIBRARY
292 Marine Way
Juneau  99801
(907) 586-5267

**ARIZONA**

FLAGSTAFF CITY-COCONINO COUNTY PUBLIC LIBRARY
300 W. Aspen Ave.
Flagstaff  86001
(520) 779-7670

PHOENIX PUBLIC LIBRARY
Information Services Department
1221 N. Central Ave.
Phoenix  85004
(602) 262-4636

TUCSON PIMA LIBRARY
101 N. Stone Ave.
Tucson  87501
(520) 791-4393

**ARKANSAS**

WESTARK COMMUNITY COLLEGE—BOREHAM LIBRARY
5210 Grand Ave.
Ft. Smith  72913
(501) 788-7200

CENTRAL ARKANSAS LIBRARY SYSTEM
100 Rock St.
Little Rock  72201
(501) 918-3000

**CALIFORNIA**

HUMBOLDT AREA FOUNDATION
Rooney Resource Center
373 Indianola
Bayside  95524
(707) 442-2993

VENTURA COUNTY COMMUNITY FOUNDATION
Resource Center for Nonprofit Organizations
1317 Del Norte Rd., Suite 150
Camarillo  93010-8504
(805) 988-0196

FRESNO REGIONAL FOUNDATION
Nonprofit Advancement Center
3425 N. First St., Suite 101
Fresno  93726
(559) 226-0216

CENTER FOR NONPROFIT MANAGEMENT IN SOUTHERN CALIFORNIA
Nonprofit Resource Library
606 South Olive St. #2450
Los Angeles 90014
(213) 623-7080

PHILANTHROPY RESOURCE CENTER
Flintridge Foundation
1040 Lincoln Ave, Suite 100
Pasadena 91103
(626) 449-0839

GRANT & RESOURCE CENTER OF NORTHERN CALIFORNIA
Bldg. C, Suite A
2280 Benton Dr.
Redding  96003
(530) 244-1219

LOS ANGELES PUBLIC LIBRARY
West Valley Regional Branch Library
19036 Van Owen St.
Reseda  91335
(818) 345-4393

RICHMOND PUBLIC LIBRARY
325 Civic Center Plaza
Richmond  94804
(510) 620-6555

RIVERSIDE PUBLIC LIBRARY
3581 Mission Inn Ave.
Riverside  92501
(909) 782-5201

SACRAMENTO PUBLIC LIBRARY
328 I St., 2nd Floor
Sacramento  95814
(916) 264-2772

SAN DIEGO FOUNDATION
Funding Information Center
1420 Kettner Blvd., Suite 500
San Diego  92101
(619) 235-2300

NONPROFIT DEVELOPMENT LIBRARY
1922 The Alameda, Suite 212
San Jose  95126
(408) 248-9505

PENINSULA COMMUNITY FOUNDATION
Peninsula Nonprofit Center
1700 S. El Camino Real, #R201
San Mateo  94402-3049
(650) 358-9392

LOS ANGELES PUBLIC LIBRARY
San Pedro Regional Branch
931 S. Gaffey St.
San Pedro  90731
(310) 548-7779

VOLUNTEER CENTER OF GREATER ORANGE COUNTY
Nonprofit Resource Center
1901 E. 4th St., Suite 100
Santa Ana  92705
(714) 953-5757

SANTA BARBARA PUBLIC LIBRARY
40 E. Anapamu St.
Santa Barbara  93101-1019
(805) 962-7653

SANTA MONICA PUBLIC LIBRARY
1343 6th St.
Santa Monica  90401-1603
(310) 458-8600

SONOMA COUNTY LIBRARY
3rd & E Sts.
Santa Rosa  95404
(707) 545-0831

SEASIDE BRANCH LIBRARY
550 Harcourt Ave.
Seaside  93955
(831) 899-8131

SONORA AREA FOUNDATION
20100 Cedar Rd., N.
Sonora  95370
(209) 533-2596

**COLORADO**

PENROSE LIBRARY
20 N. Cascade Ave.
Colorado Springs 80903
(719) 531-6333

DENVER PUBLIC LIBRARY
10 W. 14th Ave. Pkwy.
Denver  80204
(303) 640-6200

**CONNECTICUT**

DANBURY PUBLIC LIBRARY
170 Main St.
Danbury  06810
(203) 797-4527

GREENWICH LIBRARY
101 W. Putnam Ave.
Greenwich  06830
(203) 622-7900

HARTFORD PUBLIC LIBRARY
500 Main St.
Hartford  06103
(860) 543-8656

NEW HAVEN FREE PUBLIC LIBRARY
133 Elm St.
New Haven  06510-2057
(203) 946-7091

**DELAWARE**

UNIVERSITY OF DELAWARE
Hugh Morris Library
Newark  19717-5267
(302) 831-2432

**FLORIDA**

VOLUSIA COUNTY LIBRARY CENTER
City Island
105 E. Magnolia Ave.
Daytona Beach  32114-4484
(386) 257-6036

NOVA SOUTHEASTERN UNIVERSITY
Einstein Library
3301 College Ave.
Fort Lauderdale  33314
(954) 262-4601

INDIAN RIVER COMMUNITY COLLEGE
Learning Resources Center
3209 Virginia Ave.
Fort Pierce  34981-5596
(561) 462-4757

# FOUNDATION CENTER COOPERATING COLLECTIONS

JACKSONVILLE PUBLIC LIBRARIES
Grants Resource Center
122 N. Ocean St.
Jacksonville 32202
(904) 630-2665

MIAMI-DADE PUBLIC LIBRARY
Humanities/Social Science
101 W. Flagler St.
Miami 33130
(305) 375-5575

ORANGE COUNTY LIBRARY SYSTEM
Social Sciences Department
101 E. Central Blvd.
Orlando 32801
(407) 425-4694

SELBY PUBLIC LIBRARY
Reference
1331 1st St.
Sarasota 34236
(941) 316-1181

TAMPA-HILLSBOROUGH COUNTY
PUBLIC LIBRARY
900 N. Ashley Dr.
Tampa 33602
(813) 273-3652

COMMUNITY FOUNDATION OF PALM
BEACH & MARTIN COUNTIES
324 Datura St., Suite 340
West Palm Beach 33401
(561) 659-6800

**GEORGIA**

ATLANTA-FULTON PUBLIC LIBRARY
Foundation Collection—Ivan Allen
  Department
1 Margaret Mitchell Square
Atlanta 30303-1089
(404) 730-1909

UNITED WAY OF CENTRAL GEORGIA
Community Resource Center
277 Martin Luther King Jr. Blvd.,
  Suite 301
Macon 31201
(912) 738-3949

SAVANNAH STATE UNIVERSITY
Asa Gordon Library
Thompkins Rd.
Savannah 31404
(912) 356-2185

THOMAS COUNTY PUBLIC LIBRARY
201 N. Madison St.
Thomasville 31792
(912) 225-5252

**HAWAII**

UNIVERSITY OF HAWAII
Hamilton Library
2550 The Mall
Honolulu 96822
(808) 956-7214

HAWAII COMMUNITY FOUNDATION
FUNDING RESOURCE LIBRARY
900 Fort St., Suite 1300
Honolulu 96813
(808) 537-6333

**IDAHO**

BOISE PUBLIC LIBRARY
Funding Information Center
715 S. Capitol Blvd.
Boise 83702
(208) 384-4024

CALDWELL PUBLIC LIBRARY
1010 Dearborn St.
Caldwell 83605
(208) 459-3242

**ILLINOIS**

DONORS FORUM OF CHICAGO
208 S. LaSalle, Suite 735
Chicago 60604
(312) 578-0175

EVANSTON PUBLIC LIBRARY
1703 Orrington Ave.
Evanston 60201
(847) 866-0300

ROCK ISLAND PUBLIC LIBRARY
401 19th St.
Rock Island 61201-8143
(309) 732-7323

UNIVERSITY OF ILLINOIS
AT SPRINGFIELD, LIB 23
Brookens Library
Springfield 62794-9243
(217) 206-6633

**INDIANA**

EVANSVILLE–VANDERBURGH
PUBLIC LIBRARY
22 SE 5th St.
Evansville 47708
(812) 428-8200

ALLEN COUNTY PUBLIC LIBRARY
900 Webster St.
Ft. Wayne 46802
(219) 421-1200

INDIANAPOLIS–MARION COUNTY
PUBLIC LIBRARY
Social Sciences
40 E. St. Clair
Indianapolis 46206
(317) 269-1733

VIGO COUNTY PUBLIC LIBRARY
1 Library Square
Terre Haute 47807
(812) 232-1113

**IOWA**

CEDAR RAPIDS PUBLIC LIBRARY
500 1st St., SE
Cedar Rapids 52401
(319) 398-5123

SOUTHWESTERN COMMUNITY
COLLEGE
Learning Resource Center
1501 W. Townline Rd.
Creston 50801
(515) 782-7081

PUBLIC LIBRARY OF DES MOINES
100 Locust
Des Moines 50309-1791
(515) 283-4152

SIOUX CITY PUBLIC LIBRARY
Siouxland Funding Research Center
529 Pierce St.
Sioux City 51101-1203
(712) 255-2933

**KANSAS**

PIONEER MEMORIAL LIBRARY
375 West 4th St.
Colby 67701
(785) 462-4470

DODGE CITY PUBLIC LIBRARY
1001 2nd Ave.
Dodge City 67801
(316) 225-0248

TOPEKA AND SHAWNEE COUNTY
PUBLIC LIBRARY
1515 SW 10th Ave.
Topeka 66604
(785) 580-4400

WICHITA PUBLIC LIBRARY
223 S. Main St.
Wichita 67202
(316) 261-8500

**KENTUCKY**

WESTERN KENTUCKY UNIVERSITY
Helm-Cravens Library
Bowling Green 42101-3576
(270) 745-6163

LEXINGTON PUBLIC LIBRARY
140 E. Main St.
Lexington 40507-1376
(859) 231-5520

**LOUISIANA**

LOUISVILLE FREE PUBLIC LIBRARY
301 York St.
Louisville 40203
(502) 574-1617

EAST BATON ROUGE PARISH LIBRARY
Centroplex Branch Grants Collection
120 St. Louis
Baton Rouge 70802
(225) 389-4967

BEAUREGARD PARISH LIBRARY
205 S. Washington Ave.
De Ridder 70634
(318) 463-6217

OUACHITA PARISH PUBLIC LIBRARY
1800 Stubbs Ave.
Monroe 71201
(318) 327-1490

NEW ORLEANS PUBLIC LIBRARY
Business & Science Division
219 Loyola Ave.
New Orleans 70112
(504) 596-2580

SHREVE MEMORIAL LIBRARY
424 Texas St.
Shreveport 71120-1523
(318) 226-5894

**MAINE**

UNIVERSITY OF SOUTHERN
MAINE LIBRARY
Maine Philanthropy Center
314 Forrest Ave.
Portland 04104-9301
(207) 780-5029

**MARYLAND**

ENOCH PRATT FREE LIBRARY
Social Science & History
400 Cathedral St.
Baltimore 21201
(410) 396-5430

**MASSACHUSETTS**

ASSOCIATED GRANT MAKERS
55 Court St.
Room 520
Boston 02108
(617) 426-2606

BOSTON PUBLIC LIBRARY
Soc. Sci. Reference
700 Boylston St.
Boston 02116
(617) 536-5400

WESTERN MASSACHUSETTS FUNDING
RESOURCE CENTER
65 Elliot St.
Springfield 01101-1730
(413) 452-0697

WORCESTER PUBLIC LIBRARY
Grants Resource Center
160 Fremont St.
Worcester 01603
(508) 799-1655

**MICHIGAN**

ALPENA COUNTY LIBRARY
211 N. 1st St.
Alpena 49707
(517) 356-6188

UNIVERSITY OF
MICHIGAN–ANN ARBOR
Graduate Library
Reference & Research Services
  Department
Ann Arbor 48109-1205
(734) 763-1539

WILLARD PUBLIC LIBRARY
Nonprofit & Funding Resource
  Collections
7 W. Van Buren St.
Battle Creek 49017
(616) 968-8166

HENRY FORD CENTENNIAL LIBRARY
16301 Michigan Ave.
Dearborn 48124
(313) 943-2330

WAYNE STATE UNIVERSITY
Purdy/Kresge Library
265 Cass Ave.
Detroit 48202
(313) 577-6424

MICHIGAN STATE UNIVERSITY
LIBRARIES
Main Library
Funding Center
100 Library
East Lansing 48824-1049
(517) 353-8818

FARMINGTON COMMUNITY LIBRARY
32737 W. 12 Mile Rd.
Farmington Hills 48334
(248) 553-0300

UNIVERSITY OF MICHIGAN—FLINT
Frances Willson Thompson Library
Flint 48502-1950
(810) 762-3413

GRAND RAPIDS PUBLIC LIBRARY
60 Library Plaza NE
Grand Rapids 49503-3093
(616) 456-3600

MICHIGAN TECHNOLOGICAL
UNIVERSITY
Van Pelt Library
1400 Townsend Dr.
Houghton 49931
(906) 487-2507

NORTHWESTERN MICHIGAN COLLEGE
Mark & Helen Osterlin Library
1701 E. Front St.
Traverse City 49684
(616) 922-1060

**MINNESOTA**

DULUTH PUBLIC LIBRARY
520 W. Superior St.
Duluth 55802
(218) 723-3802

SOUTHWEST STATE UNIVERSITY
University Library
N. Hwy. 23
Marshall 56253
(507) 537-6108

MINNEAPOLIS PUBLIC LIBRARY
Sociology Department
300 Nicollet Mall
Minneapolis 55401
(612) 630-6300

ROCHESTER PUBLIC LIBRARY
101 2nd St. SE
Rochester 55904-3777
(507) 285-8002

ST. PAUL PUBLIC LIBRARY
90 W. 4th St.
St. Paul 55102
(651) 266-7000

**MISSISSIPPI**

JACKSON/HINDS LIBRARY SYSTEM
300 N. State St.
Jackson 39201
(601) 968-5803

**MISSOURI**

CLEARINGHOUSE FOR
MIDCONTINENT FOUNDATIONS
University of Missouri—Kansas City
Center for Business Innovation
4747 Troost
Kansas City 64113-0680
(816) 235-1176

KANSAS CITY PUBLIC LIBRARY
311 E. 12th St.
Kansas City 64106
(816) 701-3541

METROPOLITAN ASSOCIATION FOR PHILANTHROPY, INC.
211 N. Broadway, Suite 1200
St. Louis   63102
(314) 621-6220

SPRINGFIELD-GREENE COUNTY LIBRARY
The Library Center
4653 S. Campbell
Springfield   65810
(417) 874-8110

**MONTANA**

MONTANA STATE UNIVERSITY—BILLINGS
Library—Special Collections
1500 N. 30th St.
Billings   59101-0245
(406) 657-1687

BOZEMAN PUBLIC LIBRARY
220 E. Lamme
Bozeman   59715
(406) 582-2402

MONTANA STATE LIBRARY
Library Services
1515 E. 6th Ave.
Helena   59620-1800
(406) 444-3004

UNIVERSITY OF MONTANA
Mansfield Library
32 Campus Dr. #9936
Missoula   59812-9936
(406) 243-6800

**NEBRASKA**

UNIVERSITY OF NEBRASKA—LINCOLN
Love Library
14th & R Sts.
Lincoln   68588-2848
(402) 472-2848

OMAHA PUBLIC LIBRARY
W. Dale Clark Library
Social Sciences Dept.
215 S. 15th St.
Omaha   68102
(402) 444-4826

**NEVADA**

CLARK COUNTY LIBRARY
1401 E. Flamingo
Las Vegas   89119
(702) 733-3642

WASHOE COUNTY LIBRARY
301 S. Center St.
Reno   89501
(775) 327-8312

**NEW HAMPSHIRE**

CONCORD PUBLIC LIBRARY
45 Green St.
Concord   03301
(603) 225-8670

PLYMOUTH STATE COLLEGE
Herbert H. Lamson Library
Plymouth   03264
(603) 535-2258

**NEW JERSEY**

CUMBERLAND COUNTY LIBRARY
800 E. Commerce St.
Bridgeton   08302
(856) 453-2210

FREE PUBLIC LIBRARY OF ELIZABETH
11 S. Broad St.
Elizabeth   07202
(908) 354-6060

NEWARK ENTERPRISE COMMUNITY RESOURCE DEVELOPMENT CENTER
303-309 Washington St.
Newark   07102
(973) 624-8300

COUNTY COLLEGE OF MORRIS
Learning Resource Center
214 Center Grove Rd.
Randolph   07869
(973) 328-5296

NEW JERSEY STATE LIBRARY
185 W. State St.
Trenton   08625-0520
(609) 292-6220

**NEW MEXICO**

NEW MEXICO STATE LIBRARY
Information Services
1209 Camino Carlos Rey
Santa Fe   87505-9860
(505) 476-9702

**NEW YORK**

NEW YORK STATE LIBRARY
Humanities Reference
Cultural Education Center, 6th Fl.
Empire State Plaza
Albany   12230
(518) 474-5355

SUFFOLK COOPERATIVE LIBRARY SYSTEM
627 N. Sunrise Service Rd.
Bellport   11713
(516) 286-1600

BROOKLYN PUBLIC LIBRARY
Social Sciences/Philosophy Division
Grand Army Plaza
Brooklyn   11238
(718) 230-2122

BUFFALO & ERIE COUNTY PUBLIC LIBRARY
Business, Science & Technology Dept.
1 Lafayette Square
Buffalo   14203-1887
(716) 858-7097

HUNTINGTON PUBLIC LIBRARY
338 Main St.
Huntington   11743
(631) 427-5165

QUEENS BOROUGH PUBLIC LIBRARY
Social Sciences Division
89-11 Merrick Blvd.
Jamaica   11432
(718) 990-0700

LEVITTOWN PUBLIC LIBRARY
1 Bluegrass Ln.
Levittown   11756
(516) 731-5728

ADRIANCE MEMORIAL LIBRARY
Special Services Department
93 Market St.
Poughkeepsie   12601
(914) 485-3445

ROCHESTER PUBLIC LIBRARY
Social Sciences
115 South Ave.
Rochester   14604
(716) 428-8120

ONONDAGA COUNTY PUBLIC LIBRARY
447 S. Salina St.
Syracuse   13202-2494
(315) 435-1900

UTICA PUBLIC LIBRARY
303 Genesee St.
Utica   13501
(315) 735-2279

WHITE PLAINS PUBLIC LIBRARY
100 Martine Ave.
White Plains   10601
(914) 422-1480

YONKERS PUBLIC LIBRARY
Reference Department, Getty Square Branch
7 Main St.
Yonkers   10701
(914) 476-1255

**NORTH CAROLINA**

PACK MEMORIAL LIBRARY
Community Foundation of Western North Carolina
67 Haywood St.
Asheville   28802
(704) 254-4960

THE DUKE ENDOWMENT
100 N. Tryon St., Suite 3500
Charlotte   28202-4012
(704) 376-0291

DURHAM COUNTY PUBLIC LIBRARY
300 N. Roxboro
Durham   27702
(919) 560-0100

FORSYTH COUNTY PUBLIC LIBRARY
660 W. 5th St.
Winston-Salem   27101
(336) 727-2680

**NORTH DAKOTA**

BISMARCK PUBLIC LIBRARY
515 N. 5th St.
Bismarck   58501-4081
(701) 222-6410

FARGO PUBLIC LIBRARY
102 N. 3rd St.
Fargo   58102
(701) 241-1491

**OHIO**

STARK COUNTY DISTRICT LIBRARY
715 Market Ave. N.
Canton   44702
(330) 452-0665

PUBLIC LIBRARY OF CINCINNATI & HAMILTON COUNTY
Grants Resource Center
800 Vine St.—Library Square
Cincinnati   45202-2071
(513) 369-6000

COLUMBUS METROPOLITAN LIBRARY
Business and Technology
96 S. Grant Ave.
Columbus   43215
(614) 645-2590

DAYTON & MONTGOMERY COUNTY PUBLIC LIBRARY
Grants Information Center
215 E. Third St.
Dayton   45402
(937) 227-9500

MANSFIELD/RICHLAND COUNTY PUBLIC LIBRARY
42 W. 3rd St.
Mansfield   44902
(419) 521-3100

TOLEDO–LUCAS COUNTY PUBLIC LIBRARY
325 Michigan St.
Toledo   43612
(419) 259-5209

PUBLIC LIBRARY OF YOUNGSTOWN & MAHONING COUNTY
305 Wick Ave.
Youngstown   44503
(330) 744-8636

MUSKINGUM COUNTY LIBRARY
220 N. 5th St.
Zanesville   43701
(740) 453-0391

**OKLAHOMA**

OKLAHOMA CITY UNIVERSITY
Dulaney Browne Library
2501 N. Blackwelder
Oklahoma City   73106
(405) 521-5822

TULSA CITY–COUNTY LIBRARY
400 Civic Center
Tulsa   74103
(918) 596-7977

**OREGON**

OREGON INSTITUTE OF TECHNOLOGY
Library
3201 Campus Dr.
Klamath Falls   97601-8801
(541) 885-1770

PACIFIC NON-PROFIT NETWORK
Southern Oregon University
1600 N. Riverside #1094
Medford 97501
(541) 779-6044

MULTNOMAH COUNTY LIBRARY
801 SW 10th Ave.
Portland 97205
(503) 248-5123

OREGON STATE LIBRARY
State Library Bldg.
250 N.Winter St. NE
Salem   97301-3950
(503) 378-4277

**PENNSYLVANIA**

NORTHAMPTON COMMUNITY COLLEGE
Learning Resources Center
3835 Green Pond Rd.
Bethlehem   18017
(610) 861-5360

ERIE COUNTY LIBRARY SYSTEM
160 E. Front St.
Erie   16507
(814) 451-6927

DAUPHIN COUNTY LIBRARY SYSTEM
Central Library
101 Walnut St.
Harrisburg   17101
(717) 234-4976

LANCASTER COUNTY PUBLIC LIBRARY
125 N. Duke St.
Lancaster   17602
(717) 394-2651

FREE LIBRARY OF PHILADELPHIA
Regional Foundation Center
1901 Vine St.
Philadelphia   19103-1189
(215) 686-5423

CARNEGIE LIBRARY OF PITTSBURGH
Foundation Collection
4400 Forbes Ave.
Pittsburgh   15213-4080
(412) 622-1917

POCONO NORTHEAST DEVELOPMENT FUND
James Pettinger Memorial Library
1151 Oak St.
Pittston   18640-3795
(570) 655-5581

READING PUBLIC LIBRARY
100 S. 5th St.
Reading   19602
(610) 655-6355

MARTIN LIBRARY
159 E. Market St.
York   17401
(717) 846-5300

# FOUNDATION CENTER COOPERATING COLLECTIONS

## RHODE ISLAND

PROVIDENCE PUBLIC
LIBRARY
225 Washington St.
Providence   02906
(401) 455-8088

## SOUTH CAROLINA

ANDERSON COUNTY LIBRARY
300 N. McDuffie
Anderson   29622
(864) 260-4500

CHARLESTON COUNTY LIBRARY
68 Calhoun St.
Charleston   29401
(843) 805-6930

SOUTH CAROLINA STATE LIBRARY
1500 Senate St.
Columbia   29211-1469
(803) 734-8666

COMMUNITY FOUNDATION OF
GREATER GREENVILLE
27 Cleveland St., Suite 101
Greenville   29601
(864) 233-5925

## SOUTH DAKOTA

SINTE GLESKA UNIVERSITY LIBRARY
Rosebud Sioux Reservation
Mission   57555-0107
(605) 856-2355

SOUTH DAKOTA STATE LIBRARY
800 Governors Dr.
Pierre   57501-2294
(605) 773-3131
(800) 592-1841 (SD residents)

DAKOTA STATE LIBRARY
Nonprofit Grants Assistance
2505 Career Ave.
Sioux Falls   57108
(605) 367-5380

SIOUXLAND LIBRARIES
201 N. Main Ave.
Sioux Falls   57104
(605) 367-8720

## TENNESSEE

UNITED WAY OF GREATER
CHATTANOOGA
Center for Nonprofits
406 Frazier Ave.
Chattanooga   37405
(423) 265-0514

KNOX COUNTY PUBLIC LIBRARY
500 W. Church Ave.
Knoxville   37902
(865) 215-8751

MEMPHIS & SHELBY COUNTY
PUBLIC LIBRARY
1850 Peabody Ave.
Memphis   38104
(901) 725-8877

NASHVILLE PUBLIC LIBRARY
Business Information Division
225 Polk Ave.
Nashville   37203
(615) 862-5842

## TEXAS

NONPROFIT RESOURCE CENTER
Funding Information Library
500 S. Chestnut, Suite 1511
Abilene   79604
(915) 677-8166

AMARILLO AREA FOUNDATION
Grants Center
801 S. Filmore, Suite 700
Amarillo 79101
(806) 376-4521

HOGG FOUNDATION
Regional Foundation Library
3001 Lake Austin Blvd., Suite 400
Austin 78703
(512) 471-5041

BEAUMONT PUBLIC LIBRARY
801 Pearl St.
Beaumont   77704-3827
(409) 838-6606

CORPUS CHRISTI PUBLIC LIBRARY
Funding Information Center
805 Comanche St.
Reference Dept.
Corpus Christi   78401
(361) 880-7000

DALLAS PUBLIC LIBRARY
Urban Information
1515 Young St.
Dallas   75201
(214) 670-1487

SOUTHWEST BORDER NONPROFIT
RESOURCE CENTER
1201 W. University Dr.
Edinburgh 78539
(956) 384-5920

FUNDING INFORMATION CENTER
OF FORT WORTH
329 S. Henderson
Ft. Worth   76132
(817) 334-0228

HOUSTON PUBLIC LIBRARY
Bibliographic Information Center
500 McKinney
Houston   77002
(713) 236-1313

NONPROFIT MANAGEMENT AND
VOLUNTEER CENTER
Laredo Public Library
1120 E. Calton Rd.
Laredo   78041
(956) 795-2400

LONGVIEW PUBLIC LIBRARY
222 W. Cotton St.
Longview   75601
(903) 237-1350

LUBBOCK AREA FOUNDATION, INC.
1655 Main St., Suite 209
Lubbock   79401
(806) 762-8061

NONPROFIT RESOURCE CENTER
OF TEXAS
111 Soledad, Suite 200
San Antonio   78212-8270
(210) 227-4333

WACO-MCLENNAN COUNTY LIBRARY
1717 Austin Ave.
Waco   76701
(254) 750-5941

NORTH TEXAS CENTER FOR
NONPROFIT MANAGEMENT
1105 Holliday
Wichita Falls   76301
(940) 322-4961

## UTAH

SALT LAKE CITY PUBLIC LIBRARY
209 E. 500 S.
Salt Lake City   84111
(801) 524-8200

## VERMONT

VERMONT DEPT. OF LIBRARIES
Reference & Law Info. Services
109 State St.
Montpelier   05609
(802) 828-3261

## VIRGINIA

WASHINGTON COUNTY
PUBLIC LIBRARY
205 Oak Hill St.
Abingdon   24210
(540) 676-6222

HAMPTON PUBLIC LIBRARY
4207 Victoria Blvd.
Hampton   23669
(757) 727-1312

RICHMOND PUBLIC LIBRARY
Business, Science & Technology
101 E. Franklin St.
Richmond   23219
(804) 646-7223

ROANOKE CITY PUBLIC
LIBRARY SYSTEM
Main Library
706 S. Jefferson
Roanoke   24016
(540) 853-2471

## WASHINGTON

MID-COLUMBIA LIBRARY
1620 South Union St.
Kennewick 99338
(509) 783-7878

REDMOND REGIONAL LIBRARY
15990 NE 85th
Redmond   98052
(425) 885-1861

SEATTLE PUBLIC LIBRARY
Fundraising Resource Center
1000 4th Ave.
Seattle   98104
(206) 386-4620

SPOKANE PUBLIC LIBRARY
Funding Information Center
901 W. Main Ave.
Spokane   99201
(509) 444-5300

UNIVERSITY OF WASHINGTON
TACOMA LIBRARY
1900 Commerce St.
Tacoma   98402-3100
(253) 692-4440

GREATER WENATCHEE COMMUNITY
FOUNDATION AT THE WENATCHEE
PUBLIC LIBRARY
310 Douglas St.
Wenatchee   98807
(509) 662-5021

## WEST VIRGINIA

KANAWHA COUNTY PUBLIC LIBRARY
123 Capitol St.
Charleston   25301
(304) 343-4646

## WISCONSIN

UNIVERSITY OF WISCONSIN–MADISON
Memorial Library, Grants Information
Center
728 State St.
Madison   53706
(608) 262-3242

MARQUETTE UNIVERSITY
MEMORIAL LIBRARY
Funding Information Center
1415 W. Wisconsin Ave.
Milwaukee   53201-3141
(414) 288-1515

UNIVERSITY OF WISCONSIN—
STEVENS POINT
Library—Foundation Collection
900 Reserve St.
Stevens Point   54481-3897
(715) 346-2540

## WYOMING

CASPER COLLEGE
Goodstein Foundation Library
125 College Dr.
Casper   82601
(307) 268-2269

LARAMIE COUNTY COMMUNITY
COLLEGE
Instructional Resource Center
1400 E. College Dr.
Cheyenne   82007-3299
(307) 778-1206

CAMPBELL COUNTY PUBLIC LIBRARY
2101 4-J Rd.
Gillette   82718
(307) 687-0115

TETON COUNTY LIBRARY
125 Virginian Ln.
Jackson   83001
(307) 733-2164

ROCK SPRINGS LIBRARY
Grantwriting Collection
400 C St.
Rock Springs   82901
(307) 352-6667

## PUERTO RICO

UNIVERSIDAD DEL SAGRADO
CORAZON
M.M.T. Guevara Library
Santurce   00914
(787) 728-1515

Participants in the Foundation Center's Cooperating Collections network are libraries or nonprofit information centers that provide fundraising information and other funding-related technical assistance in their communities. Cooperating Collections agree to provide free public access to a basic collection of Foundation Center publications during a regular schedule of hours, offering free funding research guidance to all visitors. Many also provide a variety of services for local nonprofit organizations, using staff or volunteers to prepare special materials, organize workshops, or conduct orientations.

The Foundation Center welcomes inquiries from libraries or information centers in the U.S. interested in providing this type of public information service, particularly for communities with special need for this information. If you are interested in establishing a funding information library for the use of nonprofit organizations in your area or in learning more about the program, please contact a coordinator of Cooperating Collections: Erika Wittlieb, The Foundation Center, 79 Fifth Avenue, New York, NY 10003 (e-mail: eaw@fdncenter.org) or Janet Camarena, The Foundation Center, 312 Sutter Street, Suite 606, San Francisco, CA 94108 (e-mail: jfc@fdncenter.org).

# DESCRIPTIVE DIRECTORY

# DESCRIPTIVE DIRECTORY

## ALABAMA

### 1
**Crampton Trust**
c/o Regions Bank
P.O. Box 2527
Mobile, AL 36622 (334) 690-1411
*Contact:* R.B. Doyle, III

Established in 1993 in AL.
**Donor(s):** Katharine C. Cochrane.‡
**Grantmaker type:** Independent foundation
**Financial data** (yr. ended 12/31/99): Assets,
$22,529,602 (M); expenditures, $858,632;
qualifying distributions, $654,868; giving
activities include $653,441 for 21 grants (high:
$150,000; low: $4,000).
**Purpose and activities:** Giving primarily for arts
and culture, a public library, education, and
health and human services.
**Fields of interest:** Museums (art); arts/cultural
programs; libraries (public); education; health
care; health associations; food banks; human
services; children & youth, services.
**Types of support:** General/operating support;
capital campaigns; building/renovation;
equipment; endowments; program-related
investments/loans.
**Limitations:** Giving primarily in southwestern
AL, including Baldwin, Clarke, Escambia,
Mobile, Monroe and Washington counties.
**Application information:** Application form not
required.
    *Deadline(s):* None
**Trustee:** Regions Bank.
**Distribution Committee:** Gilbert F. Dukes, Jr.,
John C. Johnson, Mabel B. Ward.
**EIN:** 636181261

### 2
**First National Bank of Brewton, Alabama
    Charitable Foundation**
P.O. Drawer 469
Brewton, AL 36427 (334) 867-3231
*Contact:* Raymond Lynn

**Donor(s):** First National Bank of Brewton,
Alabama.
**Grantmaker type:** Company-sponsored
foundation
**Financial data** (yr. ended 12/31/99): Assets,
$1,034,812 (M); expenditures, $52,317;
qualifying distributions, $47,381; giving
activities include $47,381 for 55 grants (high:
$10,000; low: $50).

**Purpose and activities:** Giving primarily for
religion, education, human services and
community.
**Fields of interest:** Secondary school/education;
higher education; libraries/library science;
education; health associations; youth, services;
community development; government/public
administration; religion; general charitable
giving.
**Types of support:** General/operating support;
building/renovation.
**Limitations:** Giving limited to Escambia County,
AL.
**Application information:** Application form not
required.
    *Initial approach:* Letter
    *Deadline(s):* None
**Trustees:** Gaillard Bixler, Broox G. Garrett, Jr.,
Billy Joe Griffin, J. Stephen Nelson, Earl H.
Weaver.
**EIN:** 630935188

### 3
**Linn-Henley Charitable Trust**
c/o Compass Bank, Trust Dept.
P.O. Box 10566
Birmingham, AL 35296
*Contact:* Mitzie Hall

Trust established in 1965 in AL.
**Donor(s):** Walter E. Henley.‡
**Grantmaker type:** Independent foundation
**Financial data** (yr. ended 03/31/98): Assets,
$7,350,646 (M); expenditures, $419,111;
qualifying distributions, $333,459; giving
activities include $333,459 for 20 grants (high:
$125,000; low: $500).
**Purpose and activities:** Giving primarily for
higher education; support also for hospitals,
libraries, and cultural programs.
**Fields of interest:** Arts/cultural programs; higher
education; libraries/library science; religion.
**Types of support:** Capital campaigns; research;
matching/challenge support.
**Limitations:** Giving limited to Jefferson County,
AL.
**Application information:**
    *Initial approach:* Letter
    *Deadline(s):* None
**Trustees:** Arthur Henley, Compass Bank.
**EIN:** 636051833

### 4
**Gloria Narramore Moody Foundation, Inc.**
P.O. Box 1029
Tuscaloosa, AL 35403 (205) 333-1440
*Contact:* Pamela Penick, Admin. Asst.
*FAX:* (205) 333-1449; E-mail:
gnm87678@aol.com

Established in 1990 in AL.
**Donor(s):** Frank M. Moody, Sr.‡
**Grantmaker type:** Independent foundation
**Financial data** (yr. ended 12/31/98): Assets,
$894,183 (M); gifts received, $250,820;
expenditures, $240,569; qualifying distributions,
$236,498; giving activities include $221,175 for
37 grants (high: $34,725; low: $300).
**Purpose and activities:** Giving to higher
education, the arts and culture, and public
services.
**Fields of interest:** Performing arts; music;
orchestra (symphony); humanities; libraries
(public).
**Types of support:** General/operating support;
continuing support; capital campaigns;
building/renovation; endowments; program
development; fellowships; grants to individuals.
**Limitations:** Giving primarily in AL.
**Publications:** Financial statement, application
guidelines (including application guidelines).
**Application information:** Application form
required.
    *Initial approach:* Letter
    *Copies of proposal:* 6
    *Deadline(s):* None
    *Board meeting date(s):* Quarterly
**Officers and Directors:*** Gloria N. Moody,*
Pres.; Celeste Burnum,* V.P.; Hugh Rowe
Thomas,* V.P.; Larry W. O'Neal,* Treas.; David
Davis, Sara Moody.
**Number of staff:** 1 part-time professional.
**EIN:** 634020569

### 5
**Estelle, Abe and Majorie Sanders
    Tennessee Foundation**
c/o Regions Bank
P.O. Box 680
Huntsville, AL 35804 (256) 535-0370
*Application address:* c/o Board of Directors, P.O.
Box 54, Winchester, TN 37398-0054

Established in 1997.
**Grantmaker type:** Independent foundation
**Financial data** (yr. ended 12/31/99): Assets,
$1,279,825 (M); expenditures, $69,534;
qualifying distributions, $55,374; giving
activities include $56,000 for 9 grants (high:
$36,000; low: $5,000).
**Purpose and activities:** Giving for the benefit of
the people of Franklin County, TN.

**Fields of interest:** Museums (specialized); college (community/junior); libraries (public).
**Limitations:** Giving primarily in TN.
**Application information:**
*Initial approach:* Letter
*Deadline(s):* None
**Directors:** Brenda Cannon, Melinda Huffman, Samuel H. Paplanus, M.D., Cowman Simmons, Fricks Stewart.
**EIN:** 636190924

## 6
## M. W. Smith, Jr. Foundation
c/o AmSouth Bank of Alabama
P.O. Drawer 1628
Mobile, AL 36633-1628
*Contact:* Kenneth E. Niemeyer

Trust established in 1960 in AL.
**Donor(s):** M.W. Smith, Jr.‡
**Grantmaker type:** Independent foundation
**Financial data** (yr. ended 06/30/99): Assets, $2,821,890 (M); expenditures, $153,955; qualifying distributions, $123,130; giving activities include $99,000 for 17 grants (high: $18,500; low: $1,000).
**Purpose and activities:** Giving primarily to the arts, education, the environment, and community development.
**Fields of interest:** Arts/cultural programs; elementary/secondary education; higher education; libraries/library science; natural resource conservation & protection; community development; Protestant agencies & churches; disabled.
**Types of support:** General/operating support; continuing support; annual campaigns; building/renovation; equipment; land acquisition; endowments; debt reduction; emergency funds; program development; conferences/seminars; publication; seed money; scholarship funds; research; matching/challenge support.
**Limitations:** Giving primarily in AL. No grants to individuals; no loans.
**Application information:** Application form not required.
*Initial approach:* Letter
*Copies of proposal:* 1
*Deadline(s):* None
*Board meeting date(s):* May and Nov.
*Final notification:* 1 month
**Officers and Distribution Committee:*** Maida S. Pearson,* Chair.; Mary M. Riser,* Secy.; Joeseph Baker, Jr., Louis M. Finlay, Jr., John H. Martin.
**Trustee:** AmSouth Bank of Alabama.
**Number of staff:** None.
**EIN:** 636018078

## 7
## The Julius E. Talton, Jr. and Ruth J. Talton Charitable Trust
P.O. Box 799
Selma, AL 36701

Established in 1997 in AL.
**Donor(s):** Julius E. Talton.
**Grantmaker type:** Independent foundation
**Financial data** (yr. ended 12/31/99): Assets, $1,021,064 (M); expenditures, $68,041; qualifying distributions, $62,861; giving

activities include $63,392 for 9 grants (high: $26,000; low: $500).
**Purpose and activities:** Giving for religion, libraries and human services.
**Fields of interest:** Libraries/library science; Salvation Army; religion.
**Limitations:** Applications not accepted. No grants to individuals.
**Application information:** Contributes only to pre-selected organizations.
**Trustees:** Julius E. Talton, Jr., Ruth J. Talton, The Peoples Bank and Trust Co.
**EIN:** 726173130

## 8
## Vulcan Materials Company Foundation ▼
P.O. Box 385014
Birmingham, AL 35238-5014 (205) 298-3229
*Contact:* Mary S. Russom, Secy.-Treas.

Established in 1987 in AL.
**Donor(s):** Vulcan Materials Co.
**Grantmaker type:** Company-sponsored foundation
**Financial data** (yr. ended 11/30/99): Assets, $7,690,338 (M); gifts received, $118,245; expenditures, $2,361,854; qualifying distributions, $2,361,854; giving activities include $2,355,919 for 692 grants (high: $167,834; low: $20; average: $500–$10,000).
**Purpose and activities:** Support for health care and welfare agencies, youth and recreational organizations, educational institutions, arts organizations, and environmental organizations.
**Fields of interest:** Visual arts; performing arts; music; humanities; arts/cultural programs; education, association; early childhood education; child development, education; elementary school/education; secondary school/education; higher education; adult/continuing education; adult education—literacy & basic skills; libraries/library science; reading; education; environment; substance abuse, services; human services; children & youth, services; child development, services; family services; race/intergroup relations; community development; public policy, research; government/public administration; public affairs; minorities; disabled; economically disadvantaged.
**Types of support:** General/operating support; continuing support; annual campaigns; capital campaigns; endowments; program development; seed money; scholarship funds; research; employee-related scholarships; in-kind gifts; matching/challenge support.
**Limitations:** Giving primarily in regions where major company facilities are located: AL, FL, GA, IA, IL, IN, KS, KY, LA, MS, NC, SC, TN, TX, and WI. No support for political or religious organizations, or organizations with discriminatory practices. No grants to individuals (except for employee-related scholarships).
**Publications:** Newsletter, occasional report, informational brochure (including application guidelines).
**Application information:** Application form not required.
*Initial approach:* 1- or 2-page letter
*Copies of proposal:* 1
*Deadline(s):* None

*Board meeting date(s):* Quarterly
**Officers and Trustees:*** D.M. James,* Chair.; W.F. Denson III,* Pres.; Mary S. Russom, Secy.-Treas.; G.M. Badgett III, P.J. Clemens III, J.A. Heilala.
**Number of staff:** 1 full-time professional; 1 part-time support.
**EIN:** 630971859
**Recent grants for library/information services:**
**8-1** Ascension Parish Library Board, Donaldsonville, LA, $20,000. 1998.

# ALASKA

## 9
## Alaska Conservation Foundation
441 W. 5th Ave., Ste. 402
Anchorage, AK 99501-2340 (907) 276-1917
*Contact:* Deborah L. Williams, Exec. Dir.
*FAX:* (907) 274-4145; E-mail: acfinfo@akcf.org; URL: http://www.akcf.org

Established in 1980 in AK.
**Grantmaker type:** Community foundation
**Financial data** (yr. ended 06/30/99): Assets, $4,045,107 (M); gifts received, $1,874,552; expenditures, $3,361,476; giving activities include $1,881,203 for grants and $1,077,009 for foundation-administered programs.
**Purpose and activities:** Awards grants to protect the integrity of Alaskan ecosystems and promote sustainable livelihoods among Alaskan communities and peoples; awards to honor outstanding environmental volunteer activists and professionals, and to sustain community development.
**Fields of interest:** Environment, research; natural resource conservation & protection; environmental education; environment; wildlife preservation & protection; wildlife, sanctuaries; economic development; community development; social sciences, public policy; public affairs, information services.
**Types of support:** General/operating support; continuing support; equipment; emergency funds; program development; conferences/seminars; publication; seed money; internship funds; research; technical assistance; consulting services; program evaluation; grants to individuals; scholarships—to individuals; matching/challenge support.
**Limitations:** Giving primarily in AK. No grants for annual campaigns, deficit financing, building funds, land acquisition, renovation projects, general or special endowments, or exchange programs; no student loans.
**Publications:** Annual report (including application guidelines), program policy statement, application guidelines, financial statement, grants list, informational brochure, newsletter.
**Application information:** Request grant guidelines. Application form required.
*Initial approach:* Letter or telephone
*Copies of proposal:* 1
*Deadline(s):* Varies
*Board meeting date(s):* Feb., May, and Sept.
*Final notification:* 2 weeks after board meeting

**Officers and Trustees:*** Matt Kirchhoff,* Chair.; David Rockefeller, Jr.,* Vice-Chair.; Peg Tileston,* Secy.-Treas.; Deborah L. Williams, Exec. Dir.; Ben Barerra, Rick Caulfield, Dalee Sambo Dorough, Bert Fingerhut, Celia Hunter, Heather Kendall-Miller, Robert Glenn Ketchum, Bill Lazar, Eric Myers, Ted Smith, William Wiener, Jr., Steve Williams.
**Number of staff:** 4 full-time professional; 3 full-time support.
**EIN:** 920061466

---

**10**
**The Doyon Foundation**
201 1st Ave., Ste. 300
Fairbanks, AK 99701 (907) 459-2040
*Contact:* Miranda Wright, Exec. Dir.
*FAX:* (907) 459-2065

Established in 1988 in AK.
**Donor(s):** Doyon Ltd.
**Grantmaker type:** Company-sponsored foundation
**Financial data** (yr. ended 10/31/98): Assets, $4,049,824 (M); gifts received, $3,541,016; expenditures, $732,024; qualifying distributions, $268,318; giving activities include $268,318 for grants to individuals.
**Purpose and activities:** Giving focuses on Native Americans.
**Fields of interest:** History & archaeology; arts/cultural programs; higher education; libraries/library science; education; Native Americans.
**Types of support:** Scholarship funds.
**Limitations:** Giving primarily in AK.
**Publications:** Newsletter, occasional report, informational brochure.
**Application information:** Application form required.
*Deadline(s):* None
*Board meeting date(s):* Quarterly
**Officers:** Donald Peter, Pres.; Kathy Wilson, V.P.; Betty Jean Olin, Secy.-Treas.; Miranda Wright, Exec. Dir.
**Directors:** Rebecca Gallen, Mike Irwin.
**Number of staff:** 2 full-time professional.
**EIN:** 943089624

---

# ARIZONA

**11**
**American Foundation**
(Formerly American Support Foundation)
4518 N. 32nd St.
Phoenix, AZ 85018 (602) 955-4770
*Contact:* Dina Pelletier, Dir. of Comm.
*FAX:* (602) 955-4707; E-mail:
grantinfo@americanfdn.org; URL: http://
www.americanfoundation.org

Became a public charity in Jan. 1999.
**Grantmaker type:** Public charity
**Financial data** (yr. ended 12/31/97): Assets, $17,855,359 (M); gifts received, $19,166,463; expenditures, $1,737,799; giving activities include $337,357 for 69 grants (high: $67,585; low: $100).

**Purpose and activities:** The foundation's emphasis is on education, health, environmental issues, religion, community development, and the arts and sciences.
**Fields of interest:** Arts/cultural programs; education; environment; health care; community development; philanthropy/voluntarism, information services; science; religion.
**Limitations:** Giving on a national basis. No grants to individuals.
**Application information:** Application form required.
*Initial approach:* E-mail for grant application information
*Copies of proposal:* 1
*Deadline(s):* May 1 and Oct. 1
*Final notification:* July 1 and Dec. 1
**Board:** R.R. Badowski, John Goodson, Robert Miller, Benson S. Schaub.
**Number of staff:** 11 full-time professional; 1 part-time support.
**EIN:** 942832530

---

**12**
**Dr. Lloyd and Kay Chapman Charitable Fund**
3730 E. Menlow St.
Mesa, AZ 85215-1717

Established in 1989 in OH and AZ.
**Donor(s):** Lloyd Chapman, Katherine E. Chapman.
**Grantmaker type:** Independent foundation
**Financial data** (yr. ended 12/31/98): Assets, $2,726,779 (M); expenditures, $131,251; qualifying distributions, $92,927; giving activities include $85,451 for 36 grants (high: $6,500; low: $20).
**Purpose and activities:** Giving primarily for higher education and human services.
**Fields of interest:** Higher education; libraries/library science; health care; health associations; human services; federated giving programs; marine science.
**Limitations:** Applications not accepted. Giving primarily in FL. No grants to individuals.
**Application information:** Contributes only to pre-selected organizations.
**Officers and Trustees:*** Lloyd Chapman,* Pres.; Donald L. Chapman, V.P.; Katherine E. Chapman,* Secy.-Treas.
**EIN:** 311285588

---

**13**
**Southwestern Foundation for Education and Historical Preservation**
P.O. Box 40380
Tucson, AZ 85717-0380 (520) 327-1215
*Contact:* Timothy N. Gardner, Chair., or Dianne M. Bret Harte, Exec. Dir.
*FAX:* (520) 320-9126

Established in 1992 in AZ.
**Donor(s):** Jane Harrison Ivancovich.‡
**Grantmaker type:** Independent foundation
**Financial data** (yr. ended 12/31/99): Assets, $7,498,827 (M); expenditures, $494,939; qualifying distributions, $368,533; giving activities include $368,533 for 26 grants (high: $25,000; low: $1,000).

**Purpose and activities:** Focus is on education and historical preservation in the southwestern U.S.
**Fields of interest:** Museums; historic preservation/historical societies; elementary/secondary education; higher education; libraries/library science.
**International interests:** Mexico.
**Types of support:** Annual campaigns; capital campaigns; building/renovation; equipment; endowments; conferences/seminars; publication; fellowships; scholarship funds; research; matching/challenge support.
**Limitations:** Giving limited to northern Mexico and the southwestern U.S., with emphasis on Tucson, AZ. No grants to individuals directly.
**Application information:** Application form not required.
*Initial approach:* Letter
*Copies of proposal:* 1
*Deadline(s):* One month preceding meeting
*Board meeting date(s):* Mar. and Nov.
*Final notification:* Two weeks following meeting
**Officer and Trustees:*** Timothy N. Gardner,* Chair.; Dianne M. Bret Harte, Exec. Dir.; Hermann Bleibtreu, Michael Hard, Jessica Harrison, Ruth McCormick Tankersley.
**Number of staff:** 1 part-time professional; 1 part-time support.
**EIN:** 860701832

---

# ARKANSAS

**14**
**Elizabeth Fletcher Dishongh Charitable Trust**
c/o Regions Bank, Trust Dept.
P.O. Box 1471
Little Rock, AR 72203

Established in 1996 in AR.
**Grantmaker type:** Independent foundation
**Financial data** (yr. ended 09/30/99): Assets, $2,677,323 (M); gifts received, $10,692; expenditures, $150,129; qualifying distributions, $135,078; giving activities include $120,000 for 5 grants of $24,000 each.
**Purpose and activities:** Giving for relief service, cultural institutes, and religion.
**Fields of interest:** Arts, multipurpose centers/programs; libraries/library science; Salvation Army; federated giving programs; Christian agencies & churches.
**Limitations:** Applications not accepted. Giving limited to Little Rock, AR. No grants to individuals.
**Application information:** Contributes only to pre-selected organizations.
**Trustee:** Regions Bank.
**EIN:** 716168209

## 15
## Ottenheimer Brothers Foundation

425 Capitol Ave., Ste. 1533
Little Rock, AR 72201
*Contact:* E. Grainger Williams, Chair., Projects Comm.
*Application address:* 7509 Cantrell Rd., Ste. 223, Little Rock, AR 72211

Established in 1965 in AR.
**Donor(s):** Gus Ottenheimer,‡ Leonard J. Ottenheimer,‡ Gladys Ottenheimer Hirsch,‡ Joseph B. Hirsch.‡
**Grantmaker type:** Independent foundation
**Financial data** (yr. ended 04/30/99): Assets, $5,623,154 (M); expenditures, $279,672; qualifying distributions, $218,782; giving activities include $202,200 for 16 grants (high: $62,500; low: $125).
**Purpose and activities:** Giving for building construction projects in the health and higher education fields in Little Rock, AR, and surrounding areas.
**Fields of interest:** Higher education; libraries/library science; hospitals (general); community development.
**Types of support:** Building/renovation.
**Limitations:** Giving primarily in the Little Rock, AR, area. No grants to individuals or for scholarships.
**Application information:** Application form not required.
  *Initial approach:* Letter
  *Copies of proposal:* 1
  *Deadline(s):* None
  *Board meeting date(s):* Bimonthly
  *Final notification:* 1 week after board meeting
**Officers:** Edward M. Penick, Sr., Chair.; Steve Bauman, Secy.-Treas.
**Directors:** Larry Alman, Gus Blass III, Judy Grundfest, Fred Selz, Sam C. Sowell, Sam B. Strauss, Jr., E. Grainger Williams.
**Number of staff:** 1 part-time support.
**EIN:** 716059988

# CALIFORNIA

## 16
## The Ahmanson Foundation ▼

9215 Wilshire Blvd.
Beverly Hills, CA 90210 (310) 278-0770
*Contact:* Leonard E. Walcott, Jr., V.P. and Managing Dir.

Incorporated in 1952 in CA.
**Donor(s):** Howard F. Ahmanson,‡ Dorothy G. Sullivan,‡ William H. Ahmanson, Robert H. Ahmanson.
**Grantmaker type:** Independent foundation
**Financial data** (yr. ended 10/31/99): Assets, $940,763,817 (M); gifts received, $61,330,500; expenditures, $50,500,445; qualifying distributions, $45,605,103; giving activities include $45,618,397 for 501 grants (high: $5,000,000; low: $1,000; average: $10,000–$25,000).
**Purpose and activities:** Emphasis on higher and other education, the arts and humanities, medicine and health, and a broad range of

human service programs, including youth organizations.
**Fields of interest:** Visual arts; museums; performing arts; humanities; arts/cultural programs; elementary school/education; secondary school/education; higher education; nursing school/education; adult education—literacy & basic skills; libraries/library science; reading; education; health care; health associations; biomedicine; domestic violence prevention; human services; youth, services; homeless, human services; minorities; economically disadvantaged; homeless.
**Types of support:** Capital campaigns; building/renovation; equipment; land acquisition; endowments; emergency funds; program development; scholarship funds; matching/challenge support.
**Limitations:** Giving primarily in southern CA, with emphasis on the Los Angeles area. No grants to individuals, or for continuing support, annual campaigns, deficit financing, professorships, internships, fellowships, film production, media projects, seminars, general research and development, underwriting, or exchange programs; no loans.
**Publications:** Annual report (including application guidelines), application guidelines.
**Application information:** Application form not required.
  *Initial approach:* Letter of inquiry or proposal
  *Copies of proposal:* 1
  *Deadline(s):* None
  *Board meeting date(s):* 4 times annually
  *Final notification:* 30 to 60 days
**Officers and Trustees:*** Robert H. Ahmanson,* Pres.; Leonard E. Walcott, Jr.,* V.P. and Managing Dir.; William Hayden Ahmanson,* V.P.; Karen A. Hoffman, Secy. and Prog. Off.; Kristen K. O'Connor, Treas.; Howard F. Ahmanson, Jr., William Howard Ahmanson, Daniel N. Belin, Lloyd E. Cotsen, Robert M. DeKruif, Robert F. Erburu.
**Number of staff:** 8 full-time professional; 2 part-time professional; 2 full-time support.
**EIN:** 956089998
**Recent grants for library/information services:**
**16-1** DVeal Family and Youth Services, Pasadena, CA, $10,000. For refurbishment and furnishings for D'Veal Family Life Center library. 1999.
**16-2** EdSource, Menlo Park, CA, $10,000. For publications. 1999.
**16-3** Foundation Center, NYC, NY, $15,000. For general support. 1999.
**16-4** Hillel Hebrew Academy, Beverly Hills, CA, $15,000. Toward library equipment. 1999.
**16-5** Huntington Library, Art Collections and Botanical Gardens, San Marino, CA, $1,000,000. Toward construction of Botanical Resource and Education Center. 1999.
**16-6** Huntington Library, Art Collections and Botanical Gardens, San Marino, CA, $1,000,000. Toward acquisition of Sanford and Helen Berger William Morris Collection. 1999.
**16-7** Huntington Library, Art Collections and Botanical Gardens, San Marino, CA, $50,000. For continued support toward Garden's Initiative. 1999.
**16-8** Huntington Library, Art Collections and Botanical Gardens, San Marino, CA,

$50,000. Toward acquisition of engraved plate for Audubon's Birds of America. 1999.
**16-9** Huntington Library, Art Collections and Botanical Gardens, San Marino, CA, $10,000. For continued support toward acquisition of sculpture, Diana. 1999.
**16-10** Huntington Library, Art Collections and Botanical Gardens, San Marino, CA, $10,000. Toward acquisition of sculpture, Diana. 1999.
**16-11** Library Foundation of Los Angeles, Los Angeles, CA, $250,000. Toward Reading Club and Grandparents and Books programs. 1999.
**16-12** Saint Peters Episcopal School, San Pedro, CA, $10,000. Toward library books. 1999.
**16-13** Southern California Institute of Architecture, Los Angeles, CA, $15,000. For book acquisitions for Kappe Library. 1999.
**16-14** University of California at Los Angeles Foundation, University Research Library, Los Angeles, CA, $1,000,000. Toward Discretionary Endowment Fund for Head of Special Collections. 1999.
**16-15** University of California at Los Angeles Foundation, University Research Library, Los Angeles, CA, $300,000. Toward book acquisitions for Ahmanson-Murphy Aldine Collection. 1999.
**16-16** University of California at Los Angeles Foundation, William Andrews Clark Memorial Library, Los Angeles, CA, $281,500. For publication of exhibition catalog, The World From Here: Treasures of the Great Libraries of Los Angeles. 1999.
**16-17** University of California at Los Angeles Foundation, William Andrews Clark Memorial Library, Los Angeles, CA, $50,000. Toward book aquisitions. 1999.
**16-18** University of California at Los Angeles Foundation, William Andrews Clark Memorial Library, Los Angeles, CA, $20,000. Toward post-doctoral fellowships. 1999.
**16-19** University of California at Los Angeles Foundation, William Andrews Clark Memorial Library, Los Angeles, CA, $10,000. Toward undergraduate fellowships. 1999.
**16-20** University of Richmond, Richmond, VA, $15,000. Toward acquisition of 17th and 18th century European materials for Music Library and Art History Department. 1999.
**16-21** Woodbury University, Burbank, CA, $25,000. Toward library computer wiring and acquisition of architecture books. 1999.

## 17
## AIDS Project Los Angeles, Inc.

1313 N. Vine St.
Los Angeles, CA 90028 (323) 993-1600
*Contact:* Craig E. Thompson, Exec. Dir.
*Additional tel.:* (800) 367-AIDS (CA HIV/AIDS Hotline), (323) 993-1500 (AIDS Project Los Angeles Clientline; FAX: (323) 993-1598; URL: http://www.apla.org

Established in 1983 in CA.
**Grantmaker type:** Public charity
**Financial data** (yr. ended 06/30/99): Assets, $16,205,299 (L); gifts received, $10,360,179; expenditures, $16,382,956; giving activities include $621,504 for grants and $967,154 for in-kind gifts.

**Purpose and activities:** The project is dedicated to improving the lives of people affected by HIV disease by providing direct services; reducing the incidence of HIV infection through risk reduction education; and advocating for fair and effective public policy.

**Fields of interest:** Education; medicine/medical care, information services; medicine/medical care, public education; AIDS; human services.

**Types of support:** General/operating support; program development; publication; research; consulting services.

**Limitations:** Applications not accepted.

**Publications:** Newsletter.

**Application information:** Contributes only to pre-selected organizations; Unsolicited requests for funds not considered or acknowledged.

**Officers and Directors:** Eric G. Bing, Ph.D.,* Co-Chair.; Leslie Margolin,* Co-Chair.; John Douponce,* Co Vice-Chair.; Jeffrey Haber,* Co Vice-Chair.; Mark Juhas,* Secy.; Tim Aldrete,* Treas.; Craig E. Thompson, Exec. Dir.; Christine Baranski, Stephen Bennett, Angelia Bibbs-Sanders, Les Bider, and 19 additional directors.

**Number of staff:** 170

**EIN:** 953842506

---

**18**

## Auburn Community Foundation

P.O. Box 7306
Auburn, CA 95604 (530) 885-4920
*Contact:* Betty Palmer, Secy.

Established in 1946 in CA.

**Donor(s):** Rhea Trittenbach,‡ Auburn Faith Hospital.

**Grantmaker type:** Independent foundation

**Financial data** (yr. ended 12/31/99): Assets, $4,000,000 (M); expenditures, $210,000; qualifying distributions, $200,000; giving activities include $200,000 for grants (high: $65,000; low: $300).

**Purpose and activities:** Giving to general charitable giving.

**Fields of interest:** Performing arts; historic preservation/historical societies; elementary/secondary education; youth development, scouting agencies (general); human services; children & youth, services; community development; public affairs, information services.

**Types of support:** Capital campaigns; building/renovation; equipment; emergency funds; program development; conferences/seminars; seed money; internship funds; matching/challenge support.

**Limitations:** Giving limited to the Auburn, CA, area. No grants to individuals.

**Publications:** Informational brochure.

**Application information:** Application form not required.

> *Initial approach:* Letter
> *Copies of proposal:* 15
> *Deadline(s):* None
> *Board meeting date(s):* 3rd Thurs. in Mar., June, Sept., and Dec.

**Officers and Directors:** D.R. Robinson,* Pres.; Harry E. Sands,* V.P.; Janice Forbes, 2nd V.P.; James Carlisle,* Treas.; Susann Baldo, John Briner, Mary Ann Hamilton, Bruce Lyon, Basilio Procissi, Thomas Propp, Kelley Richardson, Victor Roumage, Keith Sparks, H. Ray Yamaski.

**Number of staff:** 1 part-time professional.

**EIN:** 946093213

---

**19**

## The Francis Bacon Foundation, Inc.

100 E. Corson St., Ste. 200
Pasadena, CA 91103-3841

Incorporated in 1938 in CA.

**Donor(s):** Walter Conrad Arensberg,‡ Louise Stevens Arensberg.‡

**Grantmaker type:** Independent foundation

**Financial data** (yr. ended 12/31/99): Assets, $4,091,365 (M); gifts received, $306,783; expenditures, $256,201; qualifying distributions, $220,394; giving activities include $203,000 for 1 grant.

**Purpose and activities:** Support for a library.

**Fields of interest:** Libraries/library science.

**Types of support:** Conferences/seminars; professorships; publication; matching/challenge support.

**Limitations:** Applications not accepted. Giving limited to CA. No grants to individuals, or for building or endowment funds, or operating budgets; no loans.

**Publications:** Informational brochure.

**Application information:** Contributes only to pre-selected organizations.

> *Board meeting date(s):* Bimonthly beginning in Jan., on third Wed. of the month

**Members:** Richard Fadem, Henry J. Gibbons, Corene L. Pindroh, Jack T. Ryburn, Karl L. Swaidan.

**Number of staff:** 2 full-time professional; 1 part-time professional; 1 full-time support.

**EIN:** 951921362

---

**20**

## The Baker Fund

1900 Ave. of the Stars, Ste. 630
Los Angeles, CA 90067 (310) 552-9822
*Contact:* Solomon R. Baker, Pres.

Established in 1996 in CA.

**Donor(s):** Solomon R. Baker.

**Grantmaker type:** Independent foundation

**Financial data** (yr. ended 04/30/99): Assets, $2,824,315 (M); expenditures, $158,348; qualifying distributions, $151,717; giving activities include $151,618 for 6 grants (high: $100,000; low: $618).

**Purpose and activities:** The fund is principally interested in medical research in autism and the care or therapy of autistic individuals.

**Fields of interest:** Libraries/library science; medical care, in-patient care; medical research, named diseases; human services; federated giving programs.

**Types of support:** Research.

**Limitations:** Giving primarily in CA. No grants to individuals.

**Application information:** Application form not required.

> *Initial approach:* Brief proposal
> *Deadline(s):* None

**Officers and Directors:** Solomon R. Baker,* Chair. and Pres.; Rebecca D. Baker,* V.P.; Robert J. Plourde,* Secy.; Eric H. Baker, Richard H. Barker, Al Marsella.

**EIN:** 954591581

---

**21**

## The Baker Street Foundation

135 Main St., Ste. 1140
San Francisco, CA 94105

Established in 1993 in CA.

**Donor(s):** Mary M. Miner.

**Grantmaker type:** Independent foundation

**Financial data** (yr. ended 12/31/98): Assets, $39,815,186 (M); expenditures, $1,977,969; qualifying distributions, $1,825,434; giving activities include $1,822,500 for 42 grants (high: $325,000; low: $1,000).

**Purpose and activities:** Funding primarily for human services, and arts and culture.

**Fields of interest:** Arts/cultural programs; elementary/secondary education; libraries/library science; health care; medical research; human services; foundations (public).

**Limitations:** Applications not accepted. Giving primarily in San Francisco, CA. No grants to individuals.

**Application information:** Contributes only to pre-selected organizations.

**Officers and Directors:** Mary M. Miner,* Pres.; Andrew Dudnick,* Secy.; Roy Bukstein,* C.F.O.; Justine Miner, Nicola Miner.

**EIN:** 943192365

---

**22**

## The Bandai Foundation

5551 Katella Ave.
Cypress, CA 90630
*Application address:* c/o The Burkett Group, Bob Burkett, 2828 Dumfries Rd., Los Angeles, CA 90064, tel.: (310) 836-7777

Established in 1995 in CA.

**Grantmaker type:** Operating foundation

**Financial data** (yr. ended 12/31/98): Assets, $9,547,735 (M); gifts received, $37,313; expenditures, $632,461; qualifying distributions, $574,937; giving activities include $484,140 for 35 grants (high: $100,000; low: $100).

**Fields of interest:** Theater; libraries/library science; animal welfare; medical care, in-patient care; arthritis; muscular dystrophy; AIDS; children & youth, services; international affairs; science.

**Application information:** Application form not required.

> *Deadline(s):* None

**Officers:** Makoto Yamashina, Chair. and Pres.; Takeshi Nojima, Secy.-Treas.

**EIN:** 330655933

---

**23**

## Banky La Rocque Foundation

5332 Harbor St.
Los Angeles, CA 90040
*Contact:* Robert P. Vossler, C.F.O.

Established in 1981 in CA.

**Donor(s):** Vilma Banky La Rocque.‡

**Grantmaker type:** Independent foundation

**Financial data** (yr. ended 12/31/98): Assets, $4,708,095 (M); expenditures, $146,921; qualifying distributions, $133,000; giving activities include $133,000 for 21 grants (high: $25,000; low: $1,000).

**Fields of interest:** Arts, information services; scholarships/financial aid; health care; boys &

girls clubs; YM/YWCAs & YM/YWHAs; children & youth, services.
**Limitations:** Giving primarily in CA. No grants to individuals.
**Application information:**
  *Initial approach:* Letter
  *Deadline(s):* None
**Officers and Directors:** Phyllis K. Wolf,* C.E.O.; Robert P. Vossler,* C.F.O.; Donna Deitch.
**EIN:** 953637348

**24**

## The Bartman Foundation
11777 San Vicente Blvd., No. 600
Los Angeles, CA 90049-5051

Established in 1969.
**Donor(s):** N. Bartman,‡ Cecile C. Bartman.
**Grantmaker type:** Independent foundation
**Financial data** (yr. ended 12/31/99): Assets, $10,309,209 (M); expenditures, $642,394; qualifying distributions, $502,231; giving activities include $505,600 for 69 grants (high: $100,000; low: $25).
**Purpose and activities:** Giving primarily for education; funding also for human services, medical research, community development, and federated giving programs.
**Fields of interest:** Arts/cultural programs; education; libraries/library science; health associations; medical research; human services; community development; federated giving programs; religion.
**Limitations:** Applications not accepted. Giving primarily in CA. No grants to individuals.
**Application information:** Contributes only to pre-selected organizations.
**Trustee:** Cecile C. Bartman.
**EIN:** 237005283

**25**

## Sam & Roslyn Berkman Family Foundation
1024 Cove Way
Beverly Hills, CA 90210
*Contact:* Sam Berkman, Pres.

Established in 1967 in CA.
**Donor(s):** Sam Berkman, Roslyn K. Berkman.
**Grantmaker type:** Independent foundation
**Financial data** (yr. ended 03/31/00): Assets, $1,314,420 (M); gifts received, $4,000; expenditures, $82,436; qualifying distributions, $77,859; giving activities include $78,135 for 19 grants (high: $15,000; low: $500).
**Purpose and activities:** Giving for public education and community projects.
**Fields of interest:** Arts/cultural programs; higher education; libraries/library science; Jewish federated giving programs; Jewish agencies & temples.
**Types of support:** General/operating support; continuing support; scholarship funds.
**Limitations:** Applications not accepted. Giving primarily in Los Angeles, CA. No grants to individuals.
**Application information:** Contributes only to pre-selected organizations.
**Officers and Directors:** Sam Berkman,* Pres. and Treas.; Roslyn K. Berkman,* V.P. and Secy.; Louis D. Berkman, Neil G. Berkman, Susan M. Berkman.
**Number of staff:** None.

**EIN:** 952505127

**26**

## Robert C. & Lois C. Braddock Charitable Foundation
1221 Broadway, 21st Fl.
Oakland, CA 94612-1837 (510) 451-3300
*Contact:* Robert C. Braddock, Jr., Tr.

Classified as a private operating foundation in 1992.
**Donor(s):** Robert C. Braddock, Lois C. Braddock.
**Grantmaker type:** Operating foundation
**Financial data** (yr. ended 06/30/99): Assets, $7,062,837 (M); gifts received, $250,000; expenditures, $451,410; qualifying distributions, $421,364; giving activities include $421,364 for 22 grants (high: $98,800; low: $2,000).
**Purpose and activities:** Giving primarily for a public library and a business college, as well as for education, conservation and preservation, health associations, food services, human services, churches, and an aeronautical organization.
**Fields of interest:** Higher education; business school/education; libraries (public); natural resource conservation & protection; health associations; food services; human services; space/aviation; Christian agencies & churches.
**Limitations:** Giving primarily in CA.
**Application information:**
  *Initial approach:* Letter
  *Deadline(s):* None
**Trustees:** Lois C. Braddock, Robert C. Braddock, Jr., Cheryl Lee Keemar.
**EIN:** 680234966

**27**

## Allan Braun Foundation
P.O. Box 557
Solvang, CA 93464

Established in 1990 in CA as partial successor to The Braun Foundation.
**Grantmaker type:** Independent foundation
**Financial data** (yr. ended 12/31/97): Assets, $853,828 (M); expenditures, $346,133; qualifying distributions, $339,398; giving activities include $341,000 for 8 grants (high: $200,000; low: $1,500).
**Fields of interest:** Museums; music; historic preservation/historical societies; vocational education, post-secondary; libraries/library science; disabled.
**Limitations:** Applications not accepted. Giving primarily in CA. No grants to individuals.
**Application information:** Contributes only to pre-selected organizations.
**Officers and Directors:** C. Allan Braun,* Pres.; Dorrie Braun,* Secy.-Treas.; C. William Braun.
**EIN:** 770251424

**28**

## Brewster West Foundation
c/o Barbara Brewster Johnson
57 Post St., Ste. 503
San Francisco, CA 94104

Established in 1994 in CA.
**Donor(s):** Eric Johnson.

**Grantmaker type:** Independent foundation
**Financial data** (yr. ended 12/31/99): Assets, $4,461,303 (M); expenditures, $275,086; qualifying distributions, $228,461; giving activities include $218,000 for 24 grants (high: $25,000; low: $1,000).
**Purpose and activities:** Giving for Christian organizations, environmental conservation organizations, cultural institutes and youth services.
**Fields of interest:** Museums; higher education; college; libraries/library science; hospices; religion.
**Limitations:** Applications not accepted. Giving primarily in CA. No grants to individuals.
**Application information:** Contributes only to pre-selected organizations.
**Trustees:** Barbara B. Johnson, Eric L. Johnson, Martine B. Larsen.
**EIN:** 680343603

**29**

## C.M.J. Private Foundation
1130 Sacramento St.
San Francisco, CA 94108

**Donor(s):** Christopher James.
**Grantmaker type:** Independent foundation
**Financial data** (yr. ended 11/30/99): Assets, $1,604,762 (M); gifts received, $739,018; expenditures, $62,805; qualifying distributions, $62,566; giving activities include $62,575 for 5 grants (high: $35,000; low: $75).
**Purpose and activities:** Giving for education and family services.
**Fields of interest:** Libraries/library science; family services.
**Limitations:** No grants to individuals.
**Officers and Directors:** Christopher M. James,* Pres.; Nathaniel A. Morrison,* Secy.; Laura Anne James, S. Laughran.
**EIN:** 133864227

**30**

## Central Africa Foundation-USA
c/o Daniel M. Herscher
10100 Santa Monica Blvd., Ste. 250
Los Angeles, CA 90067

Established in 1995 in VA.
**Grantmaker type:** Independent foundation
**Financial data** (yr. ended 03/31/97): Assets, $319,571 (M); expenditures, $3,411,843; qualifying distributions, $3,112,514; giving activities include $3,112,913 for 17 grants (high: $2,300,100; low: $2,000).
**Fields of interest:** Libraries (special); health care; mental health/crisis services, alliance; AIDS; athletics/sports, racquet sports; international relief; community development, formal/general education; trade boards.
**Limitations:** Applications not accepted. Giving on an international basis. No grants to individuals.
**Application information:** Contributes only to pre-selected organizations.
**Officer:** Daniel M. Hercher, Treas.
**Directors:** J. Daniel Phillips, Man. Dir.; Chester Crocker, William Foege, Daniel Jorgensen.
**EIN:** 541750759

## 31
### Cheeryble Foundation

c/o Manny Flekman & Co.
9171 Wilshire Blvd., Ste. 530
Beverly Hills, CA 90210 (310) 274-5847
*Contact:* Zora Charles, Pres. and Secy.

Established in 1987 in CA.
**Donor(s):** Les Charles, Zora Charles.
**Grantmaker type:** Independent foundation
**Financial data** (yr. ended 12/31/99): Assets,
$1,915,530 (M); gifts received, $300,000;
expenditures, $304,989; qualifying distributions,
$302,980; giving activities include $302,980 for
42 grants (high: $40,000; low: $100).
**Fields of interest:** Museums (art); arts/cultural
programs; libraries/library science; natural
resource conservation & protection;
environment; family planning; human services;
women.
**Types of support:** General/operating support.
**Limitations:** Giving primarily in CA. No grants
to individuals.
**Application information:** Application form not
required.
   *Initial approach:* Letter
   *Deadline(s):* None
**Officers:** Zora Charles, Pres. and Secy.; Les
Charles, C.F.O.
**EIN:** 954121906

## 32
### Clarence B. & Joan F. Coleman Charitable Foundation

2401 Merced St.
San Leandro, CA 94577-4210 (510) 357-0220
*Contact:* Clarence B. Coleman, Pres.

Established in 1986 in CA.
**Donor(s):** Clarence B. Coleman, Joan F.
Coleman.
**Grantmaker type:** Independent foundation
**Financial data** (yr. ended 12/31/98): Assets,
$3,236,754 (L); gifts received, $156,155;
expenditures, $200,557; qualifying distributions,
$167,014; giving activities include $167,015 for
grants.
**Purpose and activities:** Giving primarily for
youth organizations, higher education,
museums, and health.
**Fields of interest:** Arts, multipurpose
centers/programs; museums; higher education;
libraries (school); medical care, in-patient care;
youth, services; Jewish agencies & temples.
**Types of support:** General/operating support;
continuing support; capital campaigns;
building/renovation; endowments; debt
reduction; emergency funds; program
development; curriculum development;
scholarship funds; research.
**Limitations:** Giving primarily in CA, with
emphasis on local agencies. No grants to
individuals directly.
**Application information:** Application form not
required.
   *Board meeting date(s):* Late Aug. or 1st week
   of Sept.
**Officers and Directors:*** Clarence B. Coleman,*
Pres.; Joan F. Coleman,* Secy.; Barbara Frey,*
C.F.O.
**EIN:** 942973572

## 33
### James S. Copley Foundation

7776 Ivanhoe Ave.
P.O. Box 1530
La Jolla, CA 92038-1530 (858) 454-0411
*Contact:* Terry L. Gilbert, Foundation Admin.

Incorporated in 1953 in CA.
**Donor(s):** The Copley Press Inc.
**Grantmaker type:** Company-sponsored
foundation
**Financial data** (yr. ended 12/31/99): Assets,
$30,903,356 (M); gifts received, $21,182;
expenditures, $3,000,017; qualifying
distributions, $2,665,582; giving activities
include $2,631,902 for 154 grants (high:
$500,000; low: $10; average: $500–$10,000)
and $65,841 for 201 employee matching gifts.
**Purpose and activities:** Support for higher and
secondary education, including an employee
matching gift program, performing arts groups
and other cultural programs, community funds,
journalism, social services, hospices and
hospitals, the aged, and youth and child
development.
**Fields of interest:** Journalism & publishing;
museums; performing arts; dance; theater;
music; arts/cultural programs; child
development, education; elementary
school/education; secondary school/education;
higher education; adult education—literacy &
basic skills; libraries/library science; reading;
education; hospitals (general); health care;
substance abuse, services; health associations;
AIDS; recreation; human services; youth,
services; child development, services; hospices;
aging, centers & services; homeless, human
services; federated giving programs; aging.
**Types of support:** Capital campaigns;
building/renovation; equipment; land
acquisition; endowments; employee matching
gifts.
**Limitations:** Giving primarily in immediate
circulation areas of company newspapers: San
Diego, Torrance, and San Pedro, CA; and
Aurora, Galesburg, Elgin, Joliet, Springfield,
Lincoln, Naperville, Peoria, Plainfield, and
Waukegan, IL. No support for religious,
fraternal, or athletic organizations, government
agencies, local chapters of national
organizations, or public elementary or
secondary schools. No grants to individuals, or
for research, public broadcasting systems,
publications, conferences, unrestricted
purposes, operating budgets, or large
campaigns; no loans.
**Publications:** Informational brochure (including
application guidelines).
**Application information:** Application form not
required.
   *Initial approach:* Letter
   *Copies of proposal:* 1
   *Deadline(s):* Delivered by Jan. 2 for spring
   meeting
   *Board meeting date(s):* Spring
   *Final notification:* 2 to 3 weeks following
   meeting, otherwise within 1 week
**Officers and Directors:*** Helen K. Copley,*
Chair.; David C. Copley,* Pres.; Robert F.
Crouch, V.P.; Alex De Bakcsy,* V.P.; Karl
Zobell,* V.P.; Charles F. Patrick,* Secy.-Treas.
**Number of staff:** None.
**EIN:** 956051770

## 34
### C. M. and Edna P. Cotton Family Foundation

2237 Donnie Rd.
Newport Beach, CA 92660

Established in 1962.
**Donor(s):** Charles P. Cotton, Priscilla C. Clark.
**Grantmaker type:** Independent foundation
**Financial data** (yr. ended 08/31/99): Assets,
$1,538,854 (M); expenditures, $84,361;
qualifying distributions, $68,477; giving
activities include $70,000 for 12 grants (high:
$15,000; low: $1,000).
**Purpose and activities:** Giving to human
services.
**Fields of interest:** Libraries/library science;
natural resource conservation & protection;
hospitals (general); health associations; human
services.
**Limitations:** Applications not accepted. Giving
primarily in CA. No grants to individuals.
**Application information:** Contributes only to
pre-selected organizations.
**Officers and Trustees:*** Charles B. Cotton,*
Pres.; John P. Cotton,* V.P. and Treas.; Robert C.
Gannon, Jr.,* Secy.; Christopher C. Clark,
Charles P. Cotton, Cynthia Cotton Fowler,
Gregory D. Fuss, Christina C. Gannon.
**EIN:** 956097315

## 35
### Delzell Foundation, Inc.

c/o J. Trager
6380 Wilshire Blvd., Ste. 1111
Los Angeles, CA 90048 (310) 540-9370
*Contact:* Robert M. Delzell, Chair.

Established in 1996 in CA.
**Donor(s):** Robert M. Delzell.
**Grantmaker type:** Independent foundation
**Financial data** (yr. ended 12/31/98): Assets,
$9,128 (L); gifts received, $87,275;
expenditures, $87,275; qualifying distributions,
$87,275; giving activities include $64,000 for 4
grants (high: $50,000; low: $1,500).
**Purpose and activities:** To improve the medical
and cultural welfare in St. Petersburg, Russia.
**Fields of interest:** Theater; opera; libraries
(medical).
**International interests:** Russia.
**Limitations:** Giving primarily in St. Petersburg,
Russia.
**Application information:** Application form not
required.
   *Deadline(s):* None
**Officers:** Robert M. Delzell, Chair. and Pres.;
Tatiana Polzik, Secy.
**Director:** Eugene Polzik.
**EIN:** 330725441

## 36
### Edmund D. Edelman Foundation

c/o Jules Glazer
9531 Via Ricardo
Burbank, CA 91504-1215

Established in 1995 in CA.
**Grantmaker type:** Independent foundation
**Financial data** (yr. ended 12/31/98): Assets,
$1,141,987 (M); expenditures, $60,660;
qualifying distributions, $56,678; giving

activities include $56,000 for 19 grants (high: $10,000; low: $500).
**Purpose and activities:** Giving primarily for music programming.
**Fields of interest:** Music; arts/cultural programs; higher education; libraries/library science; religion.
**Limitations:** Applications not accepted. Giving primarily in CA. No grants to individuals.
**Application information:** Contributes only to pre-selected organizations.
**Officers and Directors:** Edmund D. Edelman,* Pres.; Mari Edelman,* Secy.; Loren Rothschild,* C.F.O.
**EIN:** 954507828

---

**37**
## The Endurance Fund
c/o Far West Capital Management
4749 Nicasio Valley Rd.
Nicasio, CA 94946
*Contact:* Robert G. Schiro, Tr.

Established in 1993 in CA.
**Grantmaker type:** Independent foundation
**Financial data** (yr. ended 12/31/99): Assets, $4,149,437 (M); expenditures, $134,390; qualifying distributions, $62,615; giving activities include $61,958 for 53 grants (high: $5,100; low: $40).
**Purpose and activities:** There are no restrictions or limitations on awards such as by geographical areas, charitable fields, kinds of institutions or other factors.
**Fields of interest:** Elementary school/education; libraries/library science.
**Limitations:** Giving primarily in CA.
**Application information:** Application form not required.
   *Initial approach:* Purpose of the grant and verification of the tax-exempt status of donees
   *Deadline(s):* None
**Trustees:** Dorene C. Schiro, Robert G. Schiro.
**EIN:** 943170349

---

**38**
## The Essick Foundation, Inc.
1379 La Solana Dr.
Altadena, CA 91001
*Contact:* Robert Essick, Pres.

Incorporated in 1947 in CA.
**Donor(s):** Jeanette Marie Essick,‡ Bryant Essick, Essick Investment Co.
**Grantmaker type:** Independent foundation
**Financial data** (yr. ended 12/31/99): Assets, $3,151,971 (M); expenditures, $180,157; qualifying distributions, $156,902; giving activities include $147,250 for 8 grants (high: $93,000; low: $500).
**Purpose and activities:** Giving mainly to local organizations in which the donors are interested, with emphasis on higher education and libraries.
**Fields of interest:** Higher education; libraries/library science.
**Types of support:** General/operating support; endowments.
**Limitations:** Giving primarily in CA. No grants to individuals.

**Application information:** Application form not required.
   *Initial approach:* Letter
   *Deadline(s):* None
   *Board meeting date(s):* Apr., Nov., and as needed
   *Final notification:* Varies
**Officers and Directors:** Robert N. Essick, Pres.; Jenijoy La Belle, V.P. and Secy.; James Stanger.
**EIN:** 956048985

---

**39**
## The Folger, Levin, & Kahn Philanthropic Fund
(Formerly Folger & Levin Philanthropic Fund)
c/o Janice B. Lawrence
275 Battery St., 23rd Fl.
San Francisco, CA 94111-3305

Established in 1992 in CA.
**Grantmaker type:** Independent foundation
**Financial data** (yr. ended 12/31/99): Assets, $12,932 (M); gifts received, $47,274; expenditures, $60,430; qualifying distributions, $60,427; giving activities include $60,430 for grants.
**Fields of interest:** Museums; libraries (public); legal services; human services; civil rights; federated giving programs.
**Limitations:** Applications not accepted. Giving primarily in San Francisco, CA. No grants to individuals.
**Application information:** Contributes only to pre-selected organizations.
**Officers:** John P. Levin, Pres.; Peter M. Folger, V.P.; Teressa K. Lippert, Secy.-Treas.
**EIN:** 943161483

---

**40**
## Foothill Independent Bancorp Foundation
510 S. Grand Ave., Ste. 204
Glendora, CA 91741-2017
*Contact:* George E. Langley, Dir.

Established in 1995 in CA.
**Donor(s):** Foothill Independent Bancorp.
**Grantmaker type:** Independent foundation
**Financial data** (yr. ended 12/31/99): Assets, $44,474 (M); gifts received, $61,000; expenditures, $69,430; qualifying distributions, $69,400; giving activities include $69,400 for 3 grants (high: $55,900; low: $5,000).
**Purpose and activities:** Giving primarily for health and human services that serve the needs of residents of southern CA.
**Fields of interest:** Education, single organization support; libraries (public); medicine/medical care, single organization support; hospitals (general); human services; YM/YWCAs & YM/YWHAs.
**Limitations:** Giving limited to southern CA.
**Application information:**
   *Initial approach:* Letter
   *Deadline(s):* None
**Directors:** Charles G. Boone, William V. Landecena, George E. Langley, Orville L. Mestad, Douglas F. Tessitor, Max E. Williams, and 3 additional directors.
**EIN:** 954554550

---

**41**
## The Frankel Foundation
c/o Katz, Fram & Co.
11620 Wilshire Blvd., Ste. 580
Los Angeles, CA 90025

Established in 1988 in NY; funded in 1989.
**Donor(s):** Raymond Frankel.
**Grantmaker type:** Independent foundation
**Financial data** (yr. ended 05/31/99): Assets, $7,197,403 (M); gifts received, $59,690; expenditures, $272,650; qualifying distributions, $261,582; giving activities include $267,485 for 28 grants (high: $60,000; low: $50).
**Purpose and activities:** Giving for education, the environment, and Jewish organizations.
**Fields of interest:** Higher education; libraries (academic/research); environment; human services; Jewish agencies & temples.
**Limitations:** Applications not accepted. Giving primarily in CA. No grants to individuals.
**Application information:** Contributes only to pre-selected organizations.
**Trustees:** Belinda Frankel, Maxine Frankel, Raymond Frankel, Marvin Sears.
**EIN:** 133187074

---

**42**
## Charles M. Geschke and Nancy A. Geschke Foundation
220 University Ave.
Los Altos, CA 94022
*Contact:* Charles M. Geschke, Pres.

Established in 1987 in CA.
**Donor(s):** Charles M. Geschke, Nancy A. Geschke.
**Grantmaker type:** Independent foundation
**Financial data** (yr. ended 09/30/99): Assets, $5,357,971 (M); expenditures, $48,704; qualifying distributions, $44,473; giving activities include $42,753 for grants.
**Purpose and activities:** Giving for the arts and education.
**Fields of interest:** Arts/cultural programs; libraries/library science; education.
**Limitations:** No grants to individuals.
**Application information:** Application form not required.
   *Initial approach:* Letter
   *Deadline(s):* None
**Officers and Directors:** Charles M. Geschke,* Pres.; Nancy A. Geschke,* Secy.-Treas.; Kathleen A. Geschke.
**EIN:** 943052556

---

**43**
## J. Paul Getty Trust ▼
1200 Getty Ctr. Dr., Ste. 800
Los Angeles, CA 90049-1685   (310) 440-7320
*Contact:* The Getty Grant Program
*FAX:* (310) 440-7703; URL: http://www.getty.edu/grant

Operating trust established in 1953 in CA as J. Paul Getty Museum; Grant Program established in 1984.
**Donor(s):** J. Paul Getty.‡
**Grantmaker type:** Operating foundation
**Financial data** (yr. ended 06/30/99): Assets, $8,729,628,798 (M); gifts received, $1,539,337; expenditures, $223,678,070; qualifying

---

distributions, $240,036,421; giving activities include $11,109,386 for 158 grants (high: $2,000,000; low: $50; average: $3,000–$250,000), $2,166,508 for 168 grants to individuals (high: $76,265; low: $500; average: $3,000–$75,000), $1,315,965 for 185 employee matching gifts and $234,729,428 for 4 foundation-administered programs.

**Purpose and activities:** The J. Paul Getty Trust is a private operating foundation dedicated to the visual arts and humanities. The Getty Grant Program, the philanthropic arm of the trust, fosters work of exceptional merit for which resources are otherwise limited. It supports a wide range of projects that promote research in the history of art and related fields, advancement of the understanding of art, and conservation of cultural heritage. Grants are awarded to institutions and individuals throughout the world. In addition to the Grant Program, the Getty Trust is comprised of the J. Paul Getty Museum, the Getty Research Institute, the Getty Conservation Institute, and the Getty Museum Management Institute.

**Fields of interest:** Arts, cultural/ethnic awareness; visual arts; architecture; art conservation; museums; art history; history & archaeology; historical activities; historic preservation/historical societies; arts/cultural programs; minorities.

**Types of support:** Program development; publication; fellowships; internship funds; research; employee matching gifts; grants to individuals; matching/challenge support.

**Limitations:** Giving on an international basis. No grants for operating or endowment purposes, construction or maintenance of buildings, or acquisition of works of art.

**Publications:** Informational brochure, grants list, application guidelines, occasional report, annual report.

**Application information:** Detailed guidelines that outline eligibility requirements, deadlines, application procedures, review process, and notification dates for most of the grant categories are available online at the foundation's Web site and from the Grant Program office. Before submitting an application, potential applicants should request the detailed guidelines for the grant category in which they intend to request funding. If applicants are uncertain about which detailed guidelines to request, they should contact the Grant Program office for assistance.

*Initial approach:* Letter
*Deadline(s):* Varies by grant category. Generally, deadlines for residential and nonresidential research grants are Nov. 1
*Board meeting date(s):* As necessary
*Final notification:* Generally 6 months

**Officers and Trustees:** Robert F. Erburu,* Chair.; Barry Munitz,* Pres. and C.E.O.; Stephen D. Rountree, Exec. V.P. and C.O.O.; Russell S. Gould, Sr. V.P., Finance and Investments; John Walsh, V.P. and Dir., Museum; Penny Cobey, Acting Genl. Counsel; Lewis W. Bernard, John H. Biggs, Louise H. Bryson, Ramon C. Cortines, Barbara Fleischman, David P. Gardner, Vartan Gregorian, Agnes Gund, Helene L. Kaplan, Luis Nogales, Blenda J. Wilson, Ira E. Yellin.
**Number of staff:** 1324
**EIN:** 951790021
**Recent grants for library/information services:**

**43-1** American Academy in Rome, NYC, NY, $129,000. For photography archive project. 1998.

**43-2** American School of Classical Studies at Athens, Athens, Greece, $230,000. For research library consortium on-line catalog. 1998.

**43-3** Auckland Institute and Museum, Auckland, New Zealand, $250,000. For architectural conservation program. 1998.

**43-4** British Architectural Library Trust, London, England, $92,472. For photography archive project. 1998.

**43-5** Espoo-Vantaa Polytechnic, Department of Conservation Studies, Vantaa, Finland, $55,000. For library acquisitions. 1998.

**43-6** Fundacion Espigas, Buenos Aires, Argentina, $112,000. For Documentation Center for the History of Argentine Art. 1998.

**43-7** Huntington Library, Art Collections and Botanical Gardens, San Marino, CA, $18,000. For electronic cataloguing initiative planning in Art Division. 1998.

**43-8** Huntington Library, Art Collections and Botanical Gardens, San Marino, CA, $10,200. For continued support for multicultural internships. 1998.

**43-9** Los Angeles County Public Library Foundation, Downey, CA, $80,000. 1998.

**43-10** Ministere de la Culture et de la Francophonie, Centre de Chaillot pour le patrimoine monumental et urbain, Paris, France, $248,100. For Mediatheque archival project. 1998.

**43-11** National Library of South Africa, Cape Town, South Africa, $20,000. For mid-career training at New York Public Library and Library of Congress. 1998.

**43-12** Social and Public Art Resource Center, Venice, CA, $10,200. For multicultural internships. 1998.

## 44
## Hattie Givens Testamentary Trust
1017 W. 18th St.
Merced, CA 95340 (209) 722-7429
*Contact:* Trustees

Established in 1976 in CA.
**Donor(s):** Hattie Givens.‡
**Grantmaker type:** Independent foundation
**Financial data** (yr. ended 12/31/99): Assets, $2,413,684 (M); expenditures, $125,931; qualifying distributions, $95,364; giving activities include $95,364 for 32 grants (high: $16,000; low: $50).

**Purpose and activities:** Support limited to Masonic charities; giving primarily for health care, including grants for medical assistance to individuals; support also for hospices, the handicapped, family services, secondary education, and other community organizations within Merced County, CA.

**Fields of interest:** Museums; music; secondary school/education; libraries/library science; health care; health associations; family services; hospices; women, centers & services; disabled; women; economically disadvantaged.

**Types of support:** Building/renovation; endowments; emergency funds; program development.

**Limitations:** Giving limited to Merced County, CA. No grants for scholarships.

**Publications:** Financial statement.
**Application information:** Completion of application form required for individuals.
*Copies of proposal:* 1
*Deadline(s):* None
*Board meeting date(s):* Monthly
**Officers:** Ira Herring, Chair.; Ralph Busby, Secy.; J. Don Brammer, Fin. Off.
**Board Members:** James Fletcher, Ricky Wallace.
**Number of staff:** None.
**EIN:** 946430302

## 45
## Glendale Community Foundation
327 Arden Ave., Ste. 201
Glendale, CA 91203 (818) 241-8040
*Contact:* Thomas R. Miller, Exec. Dir.
*Mailing address:* P.O. Box 313, Glendale, CA 91209-0313; FAX: (818) 241-8045; E-mail: gcfndn@earthlink.net; URL: http://www.cwire.com/GCF

Incorporated in 1956 in CA.
**Donor(s):** Albert Dunford,‡ Pearl Gray,‡ Maryon Greaves,‡ Don Packer,‡ Juanita Duncan,‡ Bernie Larson,‡ Dorothy Larson.‡
**Grantmaker type:** Community foundation
**Financial data** (yr. ended 08/31/99): Assets, $5,007,351 (M); gifts received, $750,738; expenditures, $415,505; giving activities include $240,431 for 147 grants (high: $40,970; low: $100; average: $100–$40,970).

**Purpose and activities:** Giving primarily for social services; support also for the performing arts, medical centers, the handicapped, and higher education. Funding for capital (hard asset) items and programming.

**Fields of interest:** Performing arts; arts/cultural programs; higher education; adult education—literacy & basic skills; libraries (public); education; hospitals (general); disasters, preparedness & services; recreation; human services; family services; hospices; aging, centers & services; disabled; economically disadvantaged.

**Types of support:** Equipment; program development; scholarship funds; technical assistance; scholarships—to individuals; matching/challenge support; student loans—to individuals.

**Limitations:** Giving limited to the Glendale, CA, area, including Montrose, La Crescenta, La Canada Flintridge, and Verdugo City.

**Publications:** Annual report, informational brochure, application guidelines, newsletter, financial statement.

**Application information:** Application form not required.
*Initial approach:* Letter or telephone
*Copies of proposal:* 1
*Deadline(s):* Mar. 1, June 1, Sept. 1 and Dec. 1
*Board meeting date(s):* 6 times a year
*Final notification:* Within 6 to 8 weeks
**Officers and Trustees:** Richard Jouroyan,* Pres.; Frank Leone,* Secy.; Stephen Bache,* C.F.O.; Eric Ashton, Jim Bishop, Jim Cashion, Glenn Cornwell, Sharon Dobbs, Raul Flamenco, Frank Gladstone, David Greenbaum, Margaret Hayhurst, Greg Jones, Roubina Khoylian, Joe Lazara, Jean Maluccio, George McCullough, Alice Petrossian, Don Russ, Sally Schnitger, John Simpson, Genevieve Sultenfuss, Gerry Tomsic, Ante Trinidad, Charles Whitesell.

**Number of staff:** 1 full-time professional; 1 part-time professional; 1 part-time support.
**EIN:** 956068137

## 46
## Robert and Susan Green Foundation
2601 Mariposa St.
San Francisco, CA 94110 (415) 865-1700
*Contact:* Robert L. Green, Pres.

Established in 1986 in CA as a public charity; reclassified by the IRS as a private foundation in 1991.
**Grantmaker type:** Independent foundation
**Financial data** (yr. ended 12/31/98): Assets, $658,705 (M); expenditures, $233,732; qualifying distributions, $223,783; giving activities include $224,723 for 42 grants (high: $39,780; low: $50).
**Fields of interest:** Museums (art); arts/cultural programs; elementary/secondary education; libraries/library science; education; human services; federated giving programs; Jewish federated giving programs.
**Limitations:** Giving primarily in CA.
**Application information:**
  *Initial approach:* Letter
  *Deadline(s):* None
**Officer:** Robert L. Green, Pres.
**EIN:** 943025003

## 47
## The Hanover Foundation
9401 Wilshire Blvd., No. 1201
Beverly Hills, CA 90212

Established in 1983.
**Donor(s):** Ralph J. Shapiro, Shirley Shapiro, Flavia J. Kavanau, Kihi Foundation, Knoll International Holdings, Inc.
**Grantmaker type:** Independent foundation
**Financial data** (yr. ended 01/31/00): Assets, $3,169,285 (M); gifts received, $205,380; expenditures, $752,351; qualifying distributions, $713,444; giving activities include $712,742 for 111 grants (high: $470,297; low: $45).
**Purpose and activities:** Giving primarily to United Way; also giving for education, health, human services, legal organizations and conservation.
**Fields of interest:** Museums; museums (history); arts/cultural programs; higher education; theological school/education; libraries/library science; education; natural resource conservation & protection; health associations; medical research; legal services; human services; YM/YWCAs & YM/YWHAs; children & youth, services; foundations (community); federated giving programs; Jewish agencies & temples; disabled.
**Types of support:** General/operating support.
**Limitations:** Giving primarily in southern CA. No grants to individuals.
**Application information:** Application form not required.
  *Deadline(s):* None
**Officers:** Ralph J. Shapiro, Chair.; Shirley Shapiro, Pres.; Alison D. Shapiro, V.P. and Secy.; Peter W. Shapiro, V.P. and Treas.
**EIN:** 953887151

## 48
## Heller Charitable and Educational Fund
P.O. Box 247
Kentfield, CA 94914
*Contact:* Ruth B. Heller, Corresponding Secy.

Established in 1951 in CA.
**Donor(s):** Members of the Heller family.
**Grantmaker type:** Independent foundation
**Financial data** (yr. ended 12/31/99): Assets, $2,014,807 (M); expenditures, $91,166; qualifying distributions, $80,843; giving activities include $80,000 for 11 grants (high: $10,000; low: $2,000).
**Purpose and activities:** The fund seeks to: 1) promote prison reform, especially programs to develop alternatives to incarceration; 2) support programs for research, litigation, or other means of arresting despoliation of the natural environment and help preserve open space lands for agriculture, wilderness, and recreation through purchase and other means; and 3) support the acquisition of books, periodicals, and other educational materials for libraries.
**Fields of interest:** Libraries (public); natural resource conservation & protection; environment; civil rights, advocacy.
**Types of support:** Land acquisition; program development; research.
**Limitations:** Giving primarily in CA. No grants to individuals, or for capital projects; no loans.
**Publications:** Application guidelines.
**Application information:** Application form not required.
  *Initial approach:* Proposal (no more than 5 pages)
  *Copies of proposal:* 4
  *Deadline(s):* Jan. 1
  *Board meeting date(s):* Spring
  *Final notification:* 2nd quarter of year
**Officers and Trustees:*** Rolf Lygren,* Pres.; Ruth Heller, V.P. and Corresponding Secy.; F. Jerome Tone IV,* Treas.; Janet Harckham, Peter Harckham, Olivia Mandell, Peter Mandell.
**Number of staff:** None.
**EIN:** 946066671

## 49
## The William and Flora Hewlett Foundation ▼
525 Middlefield Rd., Ste. 200
Menlo Park, CA 94025 (650) 329-1070
*Contact:* Paul Brest, Pres.
*FAX:* (650) 329-9342; URL: http://www.hewlett.org

Incorporated in 1966 in CA.
**Donor(s):** Flora Lamson Hewlett,‡ William R. Hewlett.
**Grantmaker type:** Independent foundation
**Financial data** (yr. ended 12/31/99): Assets, $2,738,945,087 (M); expenditures, $109,583,761; qualifying distributions, $93,521,066; giving activities include $86,449,400 for 683 grants (high: $3,500,000; low: $5,000; average: $50,000–$200,000), $1,055,010 for employee matching gifts and $460,702 for foundation-administered programs.
**Purpose and activities:** Emphasis on conflict resolution, the environment, performing arts, education at both the K-12 and the college/university level, population studies, and family and community development.

**Fields of interest:** Performing arts; dance; theater; music; arts/cultural programs; elementary/secondary education; higher education; libraries (academic/research); natural resource conservation & protection; environment; family planning; youth development, services; family services; urban/community development; community development; population studies; international studies; public policy, research; minorities.
**International interests:** Latin America.
**Types of support:** General/operating support; continuing support; land acquisition; emergency funds; program development; seed money; employee matching gifts; matching/challenge support.
**Limitations:** Giving limited to the San Francisco Bay Area, CA, for family and community development program; performing arts primarily limited to the Bay Area; environment programs limited to North American West. No support for medicine and health-related projects, law, criminal justice, and related fields, juvenile, delinquency or drug and alcohol addiction, prevention or treatment programs, problems of the elderly and the handicapped, or television or radio projects. No grants to individuals, or for building funds or capital construction funds, basic research, equipment, seminars, conferences, festivals, touring costs, fundraising drives, scholarships, or fellowships; no loans.
**Publications:** Annual report (including application guidelines), program policy statement, application guidelines, informational brochure, grants list.
**Application information:** Proposals sent via E-mail or FAX not considered. Application form not required.
  *Initial approach:* Letter of inquiry
  *Copies of proposal:* 1
  *Deadline(s):* Arts: Jan. 6, music; Apr. 1, theater; July 1, dance, film, & video orgs.; Conflict: Jan. 1, theory devel. orgs. & intl. orgs.; July 1, promotional orgs. & consensus building, public participation and policymaking orgs.; Oct. 1, practitioner orgs.
  *Board meeting date(s):* Jan., Apr., July, and Oct.
  *Final notification:* 2 to 3 months
**Officers and Directors:*** Walter B. Hewlett,* Chair.; Paul Brest, Pres.; Marianne Pallotti, V.P. and Corp. Secy.; William F. Nichols, Treas.; Robert F. Erburu, James C. Gaither, Eleanor H. Gimon, H. Irving Grousbeck, Richard A. Hackborn, Mary H. Jaffe, Herant Katchdourian, M.D., Richard Levin, Condoleeza Rice.
**Number of staff:** 20 full-time professional; 11 full-time support; 4 part-time support.
**EIN:** 941655673
**Recent grants for library/information services:**
**49-1** Allied Fellowship Service, Oakland, CA, $50,000. For Family Resource Network project. 1999.
**49-2** Bay Area School Reform Collaborative, San Francisco, CA, $500,000. For Bay Area National Digital Library project. 1999.
**49-3** Council on Library and Information Resources, DC, $300,000. For general support. 1999.
**49-4** Foundation Center, NYC, NY, $100,000. For general support of national and San Francisco offices. 1999.

**49-5** Greater Bay Area Family Resource Network, San Francisco, CA, $130,000. For Employment Journey project. 1999.

**49-6** Greatschools.net, San Francisco, CA, $350,000. For general support. 1999.

---

### 50
### Hexcel Foundation
c/o Hexcel Corp.
5794 W. Las Positas Blvd.
Pleasanton, CA 94588
*Contact:* Ron Ziemba
*Application address:* 2 Stamford Plz., Stamford, CT 06901, tel.: (203) 969-0666

Established in 1984 in CA.
**Donor(s):** Hexcel Corp.
**Grantmaker type:** Company-sponsored foundation
**Financial data** (yr. ended 06/30/99): Assets, $190,405 (M); expenditures, $111,898; qualifying distributions, $109,691; giving activities include $109,691 for 54 grants (high: $15,000; low: $20).
**Purpose and activities:** Contributions to: 1) endeavors dedicated to science, engineering, and technology-museums, science fairs, and special events in key operating cities or those which are nationally significant; 2) education-direct financial aid to higher education and scholarship funds, with special consideration given to those institutions offering degrees related to materials science, and scholarships for students studying materials science; 3) youth activities-groups promoting leadership skills and civic responsibility, job training, and sports; 4) civic and community improvement and cultural activities-local or regional civic and economic groups in support of the free enterprise system or betterment of the community, including cultural activities, planning and urban development organizations.
**Fields of interest:** Media/communications; performing arts; arts/cultural programs; higher education; libraries/library science; education; natural resource conservation & protection; environment; wildlife preservation & protection; hospitals (general); medical care, rehabilitation; health care; substance abuse, services; mental health/crisis services; health associations; employment; human services; youth, services; urban/community development; community development; economics; government/public administration; disabled; economically disadvantaged.
**Types of support:** General/operating support; capital campaigns; scholarship funds.
**Limitations:** Giving limited to Casa Grande and Chandler, AZ, San Francisco, Dublin, Pleasanton, Livermore, and Chatsworth, CA, Reno, NV, Lancaster, OH, Pottsville, PA, Graham and Seguin, TX, and Burlington, WA. No support for religious organizations, veterans' or labor groups, or groups which affect only a small segment of the community. No grants to individuals.
**Publications:** Application guidelines.
**Application information:**
   *Initial approach:* Letter
   *Deadline(s):* None
**Officers and Trustee:\*** John J. Lee, Pres.; Rodney P. Jenks, Secy.; Stephen Forsyth,\* Treas.
**EIN:** 942972860

---

### 51
### John Brockway Huntington Foundation
c/o Peter K. Maier
80 E. Sir Francis Drake Blvd., 4th Fl.
Larkspur, CA 94939

Established in 1997 in CA.
**Donor(s):** John B. Huntington Charitable Trust.
**Grantmaker type:** Independent foundation
**Financial data** (yr. ended 12/31/98): Assets, $1,886,871 (M); gifts received, $681,879; expenditures, $94,435; qualifying distributions, $80,100; giving activities include $80,100 for grants (high: $15,000).
**Purpose and activities:** Funding for higher education and education related needs.
**Fields of interest:** Arts/cultural programs; libraries/library science; education.
**Limitations:** Applications not accepted. Giving primarily in CA and OR. No grants to individuals.
**Application information:** Contributes only to pre-selected organizations.
**Officer:** Peter K. Maier, Pres.
**Directors:** Julie Huntington De Polo, Elizabeth Huntington, Marian Huntington Schinske.
**EIN:** 943252483

---

### 52
### William H. Hurt Foundation, Inc.
(Formerly William H. Hurt Charities, Inc.)
333 S. Hope St., 50th Fl.
Los Angeles, CA 90071-1406

Established in 1961 in CA.
**Donor(s):** William H. Hurt.
**Grantmaker type:** Independent foundation
**Financial data** (yr. ended 12/31/99): Assets, $5,154,200 (M); gifts received, $576,011; expenditures, $244,425; qualifying distributions, $215,548; giving activities include $212,295 for 144 grants (high: $10,000; low: $6).
**Fields of interest:** Arts, multipurpose centers/programs; museums (art); arts/cultural programs; secondary school/education; higher education; libraries (public); education; hospitals (general); Boy Scouts; foundations (community).
**Limitations:** Applications not accepted. Giving primarily in CA. No grants to individuals.
**Application information:** Contributes only to pre-selected organizations.
**Officers:** William H. Hurt, Pres.; Sarah S. Hurt, V.P.; Kelley A. Purnell, V.P.; Courtney D. Macmillan, Secy.; Kathleen C. Hurt, Treas.
**Directors:** Bernadette Glenn-Murray, Michael T. Kerr, Robert G. Kirby, Terrence A. Macmillan, Mark L. Purnell, Briant W. Smith.
**EIN:** 956118626

---

### 53
### Lawrence E. & Elaine Smith Irell Foundation
1800 Ave. of the Stars, Ste. 900
Los Angeles, CA 90067-4211

Established in 1961.
**Grantmaker type:** Independent foundation
**Financial data** (yr. ended 12/31/99): Assets, $1,320,031 (M); expenditures, $72,003; qualifying distributions, $63,370; giving

activities include $63,315 for 41 grants (high: $25,000; low: $50).
**Fields of interest:** Libraries/library science; education; health care; mental health, treatment; health associations; human services; Jewish federated giving programs; general charitable giving.
**Limitations:** Applications not accepted. Giving primarily in CA. No grants to individuals.
**Application information:** Contributes only to pre-selected organizations.
**Trustees:** Elaine Smith Irell, Eugene H. Irell, Lawrence E. Irell, Stephen C. Irell.
**EIN:** 956058214

---

### 54
### The James Irvine Foundation ▼
1 Market St.
Steuart Tower, Ste. 2500
San Francisco, CA 94105 (415) 777-2244
*Contact:* Stefani Jacobson, Asst. Grants Mgr.
*FAX:* (415) 777-0869; Southern CA office: 777 S. Figueroa St., Ste. 740, Los Angeles, CA 90017-5430; tel.: (213) 236-0552; FAX: (213) 236-0537; URL: http://www.irvine.org

Incorporated in 1937 in CA.
**Donor(s):** James Irvine.‡
**Grantmaker type:** Independent foundation
**Financial data** (yr. ended 12/31/99): Assets, $1,605,121,505 (M); gifts received, $4,000; expenditures, $65,902,617; qualifying distributions, $55,219,931; giving activities include $48,922,963 for 438 grants (high: $1,070,000; low: $600; average: $20,000–$250,000) and $1,290,660 for 4 foundation-administered programs.
**Purpose and activities:** Giving primarily for the arts, higher education, workforce development, civic culture, sustainable communities, and children, youth, and families.
**Fields of interest:** Arts, multipurpose centers/programs; arts, cultural/ethnic awareness; folk arts; arts councils; performing arts; performing arts centers; dance; ballet; theater; orchestra (symphony); opera; higher education; college; university; higher education reform; natural resource conservation & protection; employment, services; employment, job counseling; employment, training; employment, retraining; youth development, centers & clubs; Camp Fire; youth development, services; race/intergroup relations; community development, management/technical aid; community development, volunteer services; community development, neighborhood development; economic development; rural development; nonprofit management; philanthropy/voluntarism, association; philanthropy/voluntarism, administration/regulation; philanthropy/voluntarism, information services; foundations (public); foundations (community); voluntarism promotion; philanthropy/voluntarism; public policy, research.
**Types of support:** General/operating support; program development; seed money; technical assistance; program evaluation; program-related investments/loans; employee matching gifts; matching/challenge support.

**Limitations:** Giving limited to CA. No support for agencies receiving substantial government support. No grants to individuals.
**Publications:** Annual report, grants list.
**Application information:** Application form not required.
> *Initial approach:* Letter, telephone, or website for information
> *Copies of proposal:* 2
> *Deadline(s):* None
> *Final notification:* Within 8 months
**Officers and Directors:\*** James C. Gaither,\* Chair.; Donn B. Miller,\* Vice-Chair.; Dennis A. Collins,\* C.E.O. and Pres.; Larry R. Fies, C.F.O. and Treas.; James E. Canales, V.P. and Corp. Secy.; Kathryn L. Wheeler, Hon. Dir.; Samuel H. Armacost, Joan F. Lane, Cheryl White Mason, Patricia Pineda, Gary B. Pruitt, Toby Rosenblatt, Forrest N. Shumway, Peter W. Stanley, Ph.D., Edward Zapanta, M.D.
**Number of staff:** 24 full-time professional; 1 part-time professional; 16 full-time support.
**EIN:** 941236937
**Recent grants for library/information services:**
**54-1** California Health Foundation and Trust, Sacramento, CA, $80,000. For continued support of California TeleHealth/Telemedicine Center at Rural Healthcare Center of California Healthcare Association. Grants in the program area of Health will be discontinued after 1999. 1999.
**54-2** Foundation Center, NYC, NY, $150,000. Toward new facility in San Francisco. 1999.
**54-3** Greater Bay Area Family Resource Network, San Francisco, CA, $400,000. For continued support of welfare-to-work demonstration program, including three distinct models of public/private employment partnerships in San Francisco, Sacramento and South Hayward. 1999.

---

## 55
### George Frederick Jewett Foundation
The Russ Bldg.
235 Montgomery St., Ste. 612
San Francisco, CA 94104 (415) 421-1351
*Contact:* Ann D. Gralnek, Sr. Advisor
*FAX:* (415) 421-0721; E-mail:
TFBjewettf@aol.com or ADGjewettf@aol.com

Trust established in 1957 in MA.
**Donor(s):** George Frederick Jewett.‡
**Grantmaker type:** Independent foundation
**Financial data** (yr. ended 12/31/98): Assets, $37,083,414 (M); gifts received, $289,644; expenditures, $1,942,725; qualifying distributions, $1,833,325; giving activities include $1,560,000 for 95 grants (high: $100,000; low: $850; average: $5,000–$20,000).
**Purpose and activities:** To carry on the charitable interests of the donor to stimulate, encourage, and support activities of established, voluntary, nonprofit organizations which are of importance to human welfare. Interests include arts and culture, music, education, libraries, environment (with particular emphasis on land conservation, oceanographic studies and population), protection of environment, including population issues and scientific research, health and social services.
**Fields of interest:** Music; arts/cultural programs; libraries (public); education; environment, land

resources; environment, beautification programs; environmental education; environment; health care; human services; science, research; marine science.
**Types of support:** General/operating support; building/renovation; equipment; land acquisition; program development; seed money; research; technical assistance; matching/challenge support.
**Limitations:** Giving primarily in San Francisco, CA, Spokane, WA, and in geographic areas of which trustees and family members have knowledge. No support for private or operating foundations or organizations which receive support from public tax funds. No grants to individuals, or for emergency funds (except for disaster relief), purchase of tickets or support of fundraising events; no loans.
**Publications:** Annual report (including application guidelines), application guidelines, program policy statement.
**Application information:** Formal application by invitation only; unsolicited requests for funds not considered. Application form required.
> *Initial approach:* Letter of inquiry
> *Copies of proposal:* 1
> *Deadline(s):* Quarterly: Mar., June, Sept., and Dec.
> *Board meeting date(s):* Within the annual grant cycle and no later than mid-Dec.
**Trustees:** George Frederick Jewett, Jr., Chair.; Margaret Jewett Greer, William Hershey Greer, Jr., Lucille McIntyre Jewett.
**Number of staff:** 1 part-time professional; 1 full-time support.
**EIN:** 046013832

---

## 56
### Thomas and Dorothy Leavey Foundation ▼
4680 Wilshire Blvd.
Los Angeles, CA 90010 (323) 930-4252
*Contact:* Kathleen Leavey McCarthy, Acting Chair.

Trust established in 1952 in CA.
**Donor(s):** Thomas E. Leavey,‡ Dorothy E. Leavey.
**Grantmaker type:** Independent foundation
**Financial data** (yr. ended 12/31/99): Assets, $317,992,049 (M); expenditures, $9,026,357; qualifying distributions, $6,314,789; giving activities include $5,728,844 for 66 grants (high: $1,000,000; low: $1,000; average: $10,000–$250,000) and $488,981 for 125 grants to individuals (high: $124,759; low: $1,333; average: $1,750–$4,000).
**Purpose and activities:** Giving primarily for hospitals, medical research, higher and secondary education, and Catholic church groups; provides scholarships to children of employees of Farmers Group, Inc.
**Fields of interest:** Secondary school/education; higher education; hospitals (general); medical research; Roman Catholic agencies & churches.
**Types of support:** General/operating support; employee-related scholarships.
**Limitations:** Giving primarily in southern CA.
**Application information:**
> *Initial approach:* Letter
> *Copies of proposal:* 1
> *Deadline(s):* None
> *Board meeting date(s):* As required

**Trustees:** Kathleen Leavey McCarthy, Acting Chair.; L. Castruccio, Leo E. Denlea, Jr., Michael Enright, Joseph James Leavey.
**Number of staff:** None.
**EIN:** 956060162
**Recent grants for library/information services:**
**56-1** University of Southern California, Los Angeles, CA, $1,000,000. For library landscape project. 1999.

---

## 57
### The Thomas J. Long Foundation ▼
2950 Buskirk Ave., Ste. 160
Walnut Creek, CA 94596 (925) 944-3800
*Contact:* Marcia A. Sander
*FAX:* (925) 287-8879

Established in 1972.
**Donor(s):** Thomas J. Long.‡
**Grantmaker type:** Independent foundation
**Financial data** (yr. ended 12/31/99): Assets, $90,485,741 (M); expenditures, $5,201,299; qualifying distributions, $4,691,660; giving activities include $4,793,720 for 45 grants (high: $1,000,000; low: $1,120; average: $10,000–$60,000).
**Purpose and activities:** Giving primarily for higher education, the arts, and health associations.
**Fields of interest:** Higher education; libraries/library science; health care; youth development, services.
**Limitations:** Giving primarily in CA.
**Application information:** Application form required.
> *Initial approach:* Letter requesting guidelines
> *Deadline(s):* Apr. 1 or Oct. 1
> *Board meeting date(s):* Annually
**Officers and Trustees:\*** William G. Combs,\* Pres.; Robert M. Coakley, V.P.; Howard H. Bell, Secy.; Lolita L. Lowry,\* Treas.; Sidne J. Long, Jill M. Rapier, Thomas R. Sweeney.
**EIN:** 237180712

---

## 58
### Bertha Russ Lytel Foundation
P.O. Box 893
Ferndale, CA 95536
*Contact:* George Hindley, Mgr.

Established in 1974 in CA.
**Donor(s):** Bertha Russ Lytel,‡ L.D. O'Rourke,‡ Rachel H. Hauge.‡
**Grantmaker type:** Independent foundation
**Financial data** (yr. ended 09/30/99): Assets, $15,712,742 (M); gifts received, $96,622; expenditures, $883,960; qualifying distributions, $743,401; giving activities include $728,605 for 39 grants (high: $115,000; low: $300; average: $300–$115,000).
**Purpose and activities:** Giving primarily to social service agencies for the aged and handicapped, civic and cultural programs, including libraries and museums, elementary and higher education, health associations, including hospitals and hospices, and agricultural and nursing scholarship funds.
**Fields of interest:** Museums; arts/cultural programs; elementary school/education; higher education; libraries/library science; education; hospitals (general); substance abuse, services; health associations; human services; hospices;

aging, centers & services; government/public administration; disabled; aging.
**Types of support:** General/operating support; continuing support; building/renovation; equipment; seed money; scholarship funds; matching/challenge support.
**Limitations:** Giving limited to Humboldt County, CA. No grants to individuals, or for annual campaigns, emergency or endowment funds, deficit financing, land acquisition, renovations, research, demonstration projects, or publications; no loans.
**Publications:** Application guidelines.
**Application information:** Application form required.
   *Initial approach:* Letter
   *Copies of proposal:* 8
   *Deadline(s):* 1st Thur. of each month
   *Board meeting date(s):* Monthly
   *Final notification:* 30 to 60 days
**Officers and Directors:*** Charles M. Lawrence,* Pres.; James K. Morrison,* Secy.; George Hindley, Mgr.; Betty Diehl, Charles Lakin, Tom Renner, Jack Russ, Jack Smith.
**Number of staff:** 1 part-time professional.
**EIN:** 942271250

## 59
## Glen & Ellen McLaughlin Foundation
14016 Camino Barco
Saratoga, CA  95070  (408) 867-5366
*Contact:* Glen McLaughlin, Pres.
*FAX:* (408) 867-5817; E-mail:
vla@ix.netcom.com

Established in 1994 in CA.
**Donor(s):** Glen McLaughlin, Ellen McLaughlin.
**Grantmaker type:** Independent foundation
**Financial data** (yr. ended 06/30/99): Assets, $3,131,770 (M); expenditures, $171,530; qualifying distributions, $132,501; giving activities include $138,060 for 35 grants (high: $20,000; low: $200; average: $200–$20,000).
**Purpose and activities:** Giving primarily for education.
**Fields of interest:** Higher education; libraries/library science; medical care, in-patient care; Boy Scouts; youth development, services.
**Types of support:** Annual campaigns; endowments; professorships; seed money; scholarship funds; matching/challenge support.
**Limitations:** Giving on a national basis. No grants to individuals.
**Application information:**
   *Initial approach:* Letter
   *Deadline(s):* None
**Officers:** Glen McLaughlin, Pres. and V.P.; Helen E. O'Rourke, V.P. and Secy.; Ellen McLaughlin, V.P. and Treas.
**EIN:** 770388864

## 60
## The Bill Muster Foundation
4640 Admiralty Way, Ste. 402
Marina Del Rey, CA  90292
*Contact:* Vicki F. Magasinn, Pres.

Established in 1988 in CA.
**Grantmaker type:** Independent foundation
**Financial data** (yr. ended 11/30/99): Assets, $1,336,408 (M); expenditures, $79,804; qualifying distributions, $60,035; giving

activities include $60,035 for 74 grants (high: $10,000; low: $50).
**Purpose and activities:** Giving for museums, recreation, and human services.
**Fields of interest:** Education; health associations; recreation, information services; human services; religion.
**Limitations:** Applications not accepted. No grants to individuals.
**Application information:** Contributes only to pre-selected organizations.
**Officers and Director:*** Vicki F. Magasinn,* Pres.; Arnold Magasinn, Secy. and C.F.O.
**EIN:** 954215790

## 61
## The Peter & Mary Muth Foundation
c/o Kushner, Smith, Joanou & Gregson, LLP
2 Park Plz., Ste.550
Irvine, CA  92614-8515

Established in 1984 in CA.
**Donor(s):** Orco Block Co., Inc.
**Grantmaker type:** Independent foundation
**Financial data** (yr. ended 12/31/98): Assets, $1,283,760 (M); expenditures, $368,108; qualifying distributions, $357,707; giving activities include $360,000 for 13 grants (high: $12,000; low: $5,000).
**Purpose and activities:** Giving primarily to the arts and to Roman Catholic federated giving programs.
**Fields of interest:** Arts/cultural programs; libraries (special); federated giving programs; Roman Catholic federated giving programs.
**Limitations:** Applications not accepted. No grants to individuals.
**Application information:** Contributes only to pre-selected organizations.
**Officers:** Verlyn N. Jensen, Pres.; Robert Pralle, V.P.; Richard J. Muth, Secy.; Mary Muth, C.F.O.
**Number of staff:** 1 part-time professional.
**EIN:** 330016627

## 62
## Maury and Lillian Novak Charitable Trust
530 B St., No. 1810
San Diego, CA  92101  (858) 239-1151
*Contact:* Earl Feldman, Tr.

Established in 1997 in CA.
**Grantmaker type:** Independent foundation
**Financial data** (yr. ended 12/31/99): Assets, $2,247,329 (M); expenditures, $141,128; qualifying distributions, $120,460; giving activities include $96,915 for 11 grants (high: $48,000; low: $25).
**Purpose and activities:** Funding primarily for Jewish organizations.
**Fields of interest:** Museums; choreography; libraries/library science; neighborhood centers; Jewish agencies & temples.
**Limitations:** Applications not accepted. Giving primarily in CA, Washington, DC, and NY. No grants to individuals.
**Application information:** Contributes only to pre-selected organizations.
**Trustee:** Earl N. Feldman.
**EIN:** 336201249

## 63
## The Joseph R. Parker Foundation
1000 4th St., Ste. 570
San Rafael, CA  94901

Established in 1994 in CA.
**Grantmaker type:** Independent foundation
**Financial data** (yr. ended 12/31/99): Assets, $2,320,211 (M); expenditures, $158,352; qualifying distributions, $123,707; giving activities include $123,500 for 34 grants (high: $14,500; low: $1,000).
**Purpose and activities:** Giving for medical and human services, education, community services and for the arts.
**Fields of interest:** Higher education; libraries/library science; education; hospitals (general); hospices; religion.
**Limitations:** Applications not accepted. Giving primarily in CA. No grants to individuals.
**Application information:** Contributes only to pre-selected organizations.
**Trustees:** Paul Eveloff, D.K. Macdonald, Joan M. Woodson.
**EIN:** 686084391

## 64
## Paul & Nancy Pelosi Charitable Foundation
1 Bush St., No. 1100
San Francisco, CA  94104
*Contact:* Paul Pelosi, Tr.

Established in 1991 in CA.
**Donor(s):** Nancy Pelosi, Paul Pelosi.
**Grantmaker type:** Independent foundation
**Financial data** (yr. ended 12/31/99): Assets, $526,336 (M); gifts received, $207,000; expenditures, $69,180; qualifying distributions, $66,925; giving activities include $66,925 for 22 grants (high: $10,000; low: $425).
**Fields of interest:** Museums (art); opera; historic preservation/historical societies; libraries/library science; education; health associations; foundations (public).
**Limitations:** Giving primarily in CA. No grants to individuals.
**Trustee:** Paul F. Pelosi.
**EIN:** 943150212

## 65
## The Lesly & Pat Sajak Foundation
301 N. Lake Ave., Ste. 310
Pasadena, CA  91101-4108

Established in 1995 in CA.
**Donor(s):** Pat Sajak, Lesly Sajak.
**Grantmaker type:** Independent foundation
**Financial data** (yr. ended 12/31/98): Assets, $266,831 (M); gifts received, $50,000; expenditures, $78,648; qualifying distributions, $77,945; giving activities include $78,000 for 9 grants (high: $25,000; low: $5,000).
**Purpose and activities:** Giving for art and culture.
**Fields of interest:** Arts/cultural programs; education, research; libraries (public); education; foundations (public); general charitable giving.
**Limitations:** Applications not accepted. Giving primarily in CA. No grants to individuals.

**Application information:** Contributes only to pre-selected organizations.
**Officers:** Pat Sajak, Pres.; Lesly Sajak, Secy.; Gregory B. Stanislawski, Treas.
**EIN:** 954511126

## 66
## Stephen C. & Patricia A. Schott Foundation
404 Saratoga Ave., Ste. 100
Santa Clara, CA 95050

**Donor(s):** SCS Development, Patricia A. Schott, Stephen C. Schott.
**Grantmaker type:** Independent foundation
**Financial data** (yr. ended 12/31/99): Assets, $2,884,142 (M); expenditures, $109,281; qualifying distributions, $85,915; giving activities include $85,915 for 35 grants (high: $12,500; low: $50).
**Purpose and activities:** Giving for Christian churches and agencies, education, youth services, and for federated giving programs.
**Fields of interest:** Libraries (public); education; youth, services; federated giving programs; Christian agencies & churches.
**Limitations:** Applications not accepted. Giving primarily in CA. No grants to individuals.
**Application information:** Contributes only to pre-selected organizations.
**Officers:** Stephen C. Schott, Pres. and Treas.; Patricia A. Schott, V.P.; Daniel M. Ikeda, Secy.
**EIN:** 943192795

## 67
## The E. L. and Ruth B. Shannon Foundation
1000 S. Fremont Ave.
Alhambra, CA 91803-1366

Established in 1991 in CA.
**Donor(s):** E.L. Shannon, Jr., Ruth B. Shannon.
**Grantmaker type:** Independent foundation
**Financial data** (yr. ended 12/31/99): Assets, $3,305,050 (M); gifts received, $363,888; expenditures, $185,015; qualifying distributions, $131,692; giving activities include $131,692 for 98 grants (high: $18,900; low: $25).
**Fields of interest:** Arts/cultural programs; higher education; libraries/library science; hospitals (general); youth development, centers & clubs; human services; Christian agencies & churches.
**Limitations:** Applications not accepted. Giving primarily in southern CA. No grants to individuals.
**Application information:** Contributes only to pre-selected organizations.
**Officers and Directors:*** Ruth B. Shannon,* Pres.; Michael L. Shannon,* Secy.; E.L. Shannon, Jr.,* Treas.; Kathryn Shannon Johnson, Bruce L. Shannon.
**EIN:** 954348050

## 68
## The Stephen M. Silberstein Foundation
29 Eucalyptus Rd.
Belvedere, CA 94920 (415) 435-1692
*Contact:* Steven Silberstein, Pres.

Established in 1997 in CA.
**Donor(s):** Stephen M. Silberstein.

**Grantmaker type:** Independent foundation
**Financial data** (yr. ended 12/31/98): Assets, $12,696,261 (M); expenditures, $144,817; qualifying distributions, $119,418; giving activities include $125,000 for 2 grants (high: $100,000; low: $25,000).
**Purpose and activities:** Giving for the arts and education.
**Fields of interest:** Historical activities; libraries/library science.
**Types of support:** General/operating support.
**Limitations:** Giving primarily in CA. No grants to individuals.
**Application information:** Application form required.
*Deadline(s):* None
**Officers:** Stephen M. Silberstein, Pres.; Paul Silberstein, Secy. and C.F.O.
**EIN:** 911852739

## 69
## Simpson PSB Fund
P.O. Box 359
Lafayette, CA 94549-0359 (925) 284-7048
*Contact:* Barclay Simpson

Established in 1988 in CA.
**Donor(s):** Simpson Manufacturing Co., Inc.
**Grantmaker type:** Company-sponsored foundation
**Financial data** (yr. ended 12/31/98): Assets, $52,164,287 (M); expenditures, $789,710; qualifying distributions, $791,170; giving activities include $787,600 for 45 grants (high: $500,000; low: $500).
**Purpose and activities:** Giving primarily for education.
**Fields of interest:** Museums; arts/cultural programs; higher education; business school/education; libraries/library science; human services.
**Limitations:** Giving primarily in CA. No grants to individuals.
**Application information:**
*Initial approach:* Letter
*Deadline(s):* None
**Officer and Directors:*** Charles A. Lee,* Treas.; Jules F. Bonjour.
**EIN:** 680168017

## 70
## The Smittcamp Family Foundation
8100 N. Minnewana
Clovis, CA 93611

Established in 1996 in CA.
**Grantmaker type:** Independent foundation
**Financial data** (yr. ended 12/31/99): Assets, $1,564,189 (M); gifts received, $608,931; expenditures, $1,114,519; qualifying distributions, $1,090,240; giving activities include $1,090,750 for 17 grants (high: $1,000,000; low: $250).
**Purpose and activities:** Giving primarily for libraries and hospitals.
**Fields of interest:** Higher education; libraries (public); education; hospitals (specialty); health care; human services; children & youth, services.
**Limitations:** Giving limited to CA. No grants to individuals, no loans.
**Officers:** Earl S. Smittcamp, Pres.; Muriel Smittcamp, Secy.-Treas.

**Directors:** Carol Copeland, Elizabeth Kimball, Robert Smittcamp, William Smittcamp.
**EIN:** 770343026

## 71
## Sonora Area Foundation
20100 Cedar Rd., No. E
P.O. Box 577
Sonora, CA 95370-0577 (209) 533-2596
*Contact:* Mick Grimes, Exec. Dir.
*FAX:* (209) 533-2412; E-mail: acorn@sonora-area.org; URL: http://www.sonora-area.org

Established in 1989 in CA.
**Grantmaker type:** Community foundation
**Financial data** (yr. ended 12/31/99): Assets, $8,500,000 (L); gifts received, $372,000; expenditures, $467,000; giving activities include $166,101 for 26 grants (high: $50,000; low: $500; average: $500–$50,000), $21,472 for 32 grants to individuals (high: $3,600; low: $200; average: $200–$3,600) and $50,000 for 1 foundation-administered program.
**Fields of interest:** Visual arts; performing arts; music; arts/cultural programs; early childhood education; child development, education; elementary school/education; libraries/library science; education; environment; animal welfare; hospitals (general); health care; substance abuse, services; mental health/crisis services; health associations; alcoholism; food services; recreation; human services; children & youth, services; child development, services; family services; hospices; aging, centers & services; women, centers & services; community development; voluntarism promotion; disabled; aging; women; economically disadvantaged.
**Types of support:** General/operating support; continuing support; building/renovation; equipment; emergency funds; program development; conferences/seminars; seed money; curriculum development; scholarship funds; technical assistance; consulting services; program evaluation; scholarships—to individuals; matching/challenge support.
**Limitations:** Giving limited to Tuolumne County, CA. No support for sectarian purposes, private foundations, or political purposes. No grants for annual or capital campaigns, endowment funds, or debt retirement.
**Publications:** Annual report, financial statement, grants list, application guidelines, occasional report, informational brochure, newsletter (including application guidelines).
**Application information:** Application form required.
*Initial approach:* Telephone, letter, or FAX
*Copies of proposal:* 1
*Deadline(s):* Last day of every month
*Board meeting date(s):* Monthly
**Officers and Trustees:*** Bill Coffill,* Pres.; Jim Gianelli,* V.P.; Marilyn Knudson,* Secy.; Joan Bergsund, Treas.; Mick Grimes, Exec. Dir.; Mike Albrecht, Pat Jones, Todd Simonson.
**Number of staff:** 1 full-time professional; 1 full-time support; 2 part-time support.
**EIN:** 931023051

## 72
### Steiner Family Foundation, Inc.
18 Manzanita Pl.
Mill Valley, CA 94941

Established in 1987 in CA.
**Grantmaker type:** Independent foundation
**Financial data** (yr. ended 06/30/98): Assets,
$1,149,245 (M); expenditures, $72,624;
qualifying distributions, $58,625; giving
activities include $58,625 for grants.
**Fields of interest:** Libraries/library science;
natural resource conservation & protection;
environment.
**Limitations:** Applications not accepted. Giving
primarily in the San Francisco Bay Area, CA. No
grants to individuals.
**Application information:** Contributes only to
pre-selected organizations.
**Officers:** Lynn S. Wasser, Pres.; Sharon A. Davis,
Secy.; Heather Wasser, C.F.O.
**EIN:** 954133581

## 73
### Laura May Stewart Trust
P.O. Box BD
Beaumont, CA 92223 (909) 922-0024
*Contact:* Judith Hawkins, Secy., Distrib. Comm.
*FAX:* (909) 922-0998

Established in 1975 in CA.
**Donor(s):** Laura May Stewart.‡
**Grantmaker type:** Independent foundation
**Financial data** (yr. ended 05/31/99): Assets,
$2,457,044 (M); expenditures, $107,490;
qualifying distributions, $77,284; giving
activities include $59,151 for 20 grants (high:
$10,000; low: $250).
**Purpose and activities:** Giving primarily to
educational organizations.
**Fields of interest:** Museums; performing arts;
theater; language & linguistics; literature;
arts/cultural programs; early childhood
education; elementary school/education;
secondary school/education; libraries/library
science; education; hospitals (general); health
associations; crime/law enforcement; nutrition;
recreation; human services; children & youth,
services; family services; homeless, human
services; community development; voluntarism
promotion; government/public administration;
economically disadvantaged; homeless.
**Types of support:** General/operating support;
equipment; emergency funds; program
development; in-kind gifts; matching/challenge
support.
**Limitations:** Giving limited to the
Banning-Beaumont, CA, area. No grants to
individuals.
**Publications:** Application guidelines.
**Application information:** Application form
required.
*Initial approach:* Letter
*Copies of proposal:* 4
*Deadline(s):* 2 weeks before board meeting
*Board meeting date(s):* 4 times a year
**Trustee:** Wells Fargo Private Banking Group.
**Number of staff:** 1 part-time professional.
**EIN:** 956527634

## 74
### Irving & Jean Stone Foundation
1360 Summitridge Place
Beverly Hills, CA 90210

**Donor(s):** Jean Stone.
**Grantmaker type:** Independent foundation
**Financial data** (yr. ended 12/31/98): Assets,
$226,828 (M); gifts received, $15,000;
expenditures, $72,806; qualifying distributions,
$71,250; giving activities include $71,385 for
15 grants (high: $50,000; low: $25).
**Fields of interest:** Museums (history); university;
libraries (public); animals/wildlife; Jewish
federated giving programs.
**Types of support:** Scholarship funds.
**Limitations:** Applications not accepted. Giving
primarily in Los Angeles, CA. No grants to
individuals.
**Application information:** Contributes only to
pre-selected organizations.
**Officers:** Jean Stone, Pres.; George Sidney, Secy.
**EIN:** 956050151

## 75
### Robert K. and Barbara J. Straus Family Foundation, Inc.
(Formerly Penelope Straus More Family
Foundation)
200 E. Carrillo St., Ste. 202
Santa Barbara, CA 93101

Established in 1987 in NY.
**Donor(s):** Robert K. Straus.‡
**Grantmaker type:** Independent foundation
**Financial data** (yr. ended 12/31/99): Assets,
$3,273,197 (M); expenditures, $142,470;
qualifying distributions, $129,076; giving
activities include $124,100 for 31 grants (high:
$62,100; low: $250).
**Fields of interest:** Historic
preservation/historical societies; arts/cultural
programs; higher education; libraries/library
science; education; human services; children &
youth, services; federated giving programs;
Christian agencies & churches.
**Limitations:** Applications not accepted. Giving
primarily in CA. No grants to individuals.
**Application information:** Contributes only to
pre-selected organizations.
**Officers and Directors:*** Penelope Straus
More,* Pres.; Christopher Straus, V.P. and Treas.;
Marshall H. Turner, Jr.,* Secy.; Thomas H.
Clynes, Jr., Braden More.
**EIN:** 133377987

## 76
### Barry Taper Foundation
9460 Wilshire Blvd., Ste. 800
Beverly Hills, CA 90212-2644 (310) 550-8688
*Contact:* Craig Cooper, C.F.O.

Established in 1960.
**Donor(s):** Barry H. Taper.
**Grantmaker type:** Independent foundation
**Financial data** (yr. ended 03/31/99): Assets,
$191,329 (M); gifts received, $146,677;
expenditures, $120,935; qualifying distributions,
$119,647; giving activities include $113,148 for
39 grants (high: $52,000; low: $15).
**Purpose and activities:** Giving for arts and
culture, education and health and medicine.

**Fields of interest:** Arts/cultural programs;
elementary/secondary education;
libraries/library science; federated giving
programs; general charitable giving.
**Limitations:** Giving primarily in CA. No grants
to individuals.
**Application information:** Application form not
required.
*Initial approach:* Letter
*Deadline(s):* None
**Officers:** Barry H. Taper, Pres.; Rose Marie
Barnhart, Secy.; Craig Cooper, C.F.O.
**EIN:** 956027375

## 77
### Weingart Foundation ▼
1055 W. 7th St., Ste. 3050
Los Angeles, CA 90017-2305 (213) 688-7799
*Contact:* Fred Ali, Pres. and C.A.O.
*FAX:* (213) 688-1515; E-mail:
info@weingartfund; URL: http://
www.weingartfnd.org

Incorporated in 1951 in CA.
**Donor(s):** Ben Weingart,‡ Stella Weingart.‡
**Grantmaker type:** Independent foundation
**Financial data** (yr. ended 06/30/00): Assets,
$873,857,709 (M); expenditures, $41,857,568;
qualifying distributions, $37,106,418; giving
activities include $35,393,413 for 444 grants
(high: $2,500,000; low: $1,000; average:
$1,000–$250,000) and $323,103 for 169
employee matching gifts.
**Purpose and activities:** Support for community
services, health and medicine, including a
student loan program, and public policy, with
strong emphasis on programs for children and
youth, education, and social services.
**Fields of interest:** Museums; performing arts;
music; language & linguistics; literature;
arts/cultural programs; early childhood
education; child development, education;
elementary school/education; secondary
school/education; higher education; adult
education—literacy & basic skills; reading;
education; hospitals (general); medical care,
rehabilitation; nursing care; health care;
substance abuse, services; health associations;
AIDS; delinquency prevention/services; legal
services; crime/law enforcement; recreation;
youth development, services; human services;
children & youth, services; child development,
services; family services; hospices;
minorities/immigrants, centers & services;
homeless, human services; community
development; leadership development;
minorities; disabled; economically
disadvantaged; homeless.
**Types of support:** Capital campaigns;
building/renovation; equipment; program
development; seed money; scholarship funds;
employee matching gifts; matching/challenge
support.
**Limitations:** Giving limited to 7 southern CA
counties; Los Angeles, Kern, Orange, Santa
Barbara, Riverside, San Bernadino, and Ventura.
No support for environmental or religious
programs, political refugee or international
concerns, federated fundraising groups, or
national organizations. No grants to individuals,
or for endowment funds, normal operating
expenses, annual campaigns, emergency funds,
deficit financing, land acquisition, scholarships,

fellowships, seminars, conferences, publications, workshops, travel, surveys, films, medical research, or publishing activities.
**Publications:** Annual report (including application guidelines), application guidelines, newsletter.
**Application information:** The foundation does not accept "test letters" by Fax or E-mail. Student loan program limited to 14 private colleges and universities in southern CA. Application form required.
*Initial approach:* Brief "test letter"
*Copies of proposal:* 3
*Deadline(s):* None
*Board meeting date(s):* Bimonthly, except July and Aug.
*Final notification:* 3 to 4 months
**Officers and Directors:\*** Steven D. Broidy,\* Chair. and C.E.O.; Fred Ali, Pres. and C.A.O.; Ann L. Van Dormolen, V.P. and Treas.; Laurence A. Wolfe, V.P. and Secy.; Andrew E. Bogen, Murray L. Galinson, John T. Gurash, William D. Schulte, Dennis Stanfill.
**Number of staff:** 7 full-time professional; 5 full-time support; 3 part-time support.
**EIN:** 956054814
**Recent grants for library/information services:**
**77-1** Foundation Center, NYC, NY, $25,000. Toward program serving foundations and other grantmakers. 1999.
**77-2** Huntington Library, Art Collections and Botanical Gardens, San Marino, CA, $1,750,000. For construction of Weingart Botanical Teaching Center. 1999.
**77-3** Huntington Library, Art Collections and Botanical Gardens, San Marino, CA, $10,000. For lecture series. 1999.
**77-4** Library Foundation of Los Angeles, Los Angeles, CA, $100,000. For renovation and expansion of library's TeenScape project. 1999.
**77-5** Los Angeles County Public Library Foundation, Downey, CA, $100,000. Toward support of library-based homework center project. 1999.
**77-6** School of Theology of Claremont, Claremont, CA, $75,000. To renovate library. 1999.
**77-7** South Pasadena Educational Foundation, South Pasadena, CA, $20,000. For Libraries Without Walls collaborative partnership. 1999.
**77-8** University of Southern California, Los Angeles, CA, $10,000. For Friends of USC Library Scripter Award. 1999.

## 78
### Harvey P. & Frances H. White Foundation
2520 San Elijo Ave.
Cardiff, CA 92007

Established in 1993 in CA.
**Donor(s):** Frances H. White, Harvey P. White.
**Grantmaker type:** Independent foundation
**Financial data** (yr. ended 12/31/99): Assets, $8,990,013 (M); gifts received, $8,064,693; expenditures, $1,585,665; qualifying distributions, $1,581,634; giving activities include $1,581,634 for 75 grants (high: $316,255; low: $200).
**Fields of interest:** Performing arts; higher education; libraries (public); education; human services; Protestant agencies & churches.

**Limitations:** Applications not accepted. Giving primarily in CA. No grants to individuals.
**Application information:** Contributes only to pre-selected organizations.
**Officers and Directors:\*** Harvey P. White,\* C.E.O.; Frances H. White,\* C.F.O.; Katherine D. White.
**EIN:** 330572273

## 79
### The Gary and Karen Winnick Foundation
360 N. Crescent Dr.
Beverly Hills, CA 90210
*Contact:* Rosalie Zalis, Secy.

Established in 1983 in MD.
**Donor(s):** Gary Winnick, Karen Winnick, L.P. Pah.
**Grantmaker type:** Independent foundation
**Financial data** (yr. ended 12/31/99): Assets, $26,030,170 (M); gifts received, $14,283,410; expenditures, $4,654,542; qualifying distributions, $4,647,669; giving activities include $4,646,803 for 167 grants (high: $400,000; low: $75).
**Purpose and activities:** Giving primarily to Jewish organizations and for education, medical research, and health care.
**Fields of interest:** Arts/cultural programs; higher education; libraries/library science; education; health associations; AIDS; Jewish federated giving programs; Jewish agencies & temples.
**International interests:** Israel.
**Limitations:** Giving in the U.S., with strong emphasis on CA and NY. No grants to individuals.
**Application information:**
*Initial approach:* 3-page proposal
*Deadline(s):* None
**Officers and Directors:\*** Gary Winnick,\* Chair.; Karen Winnick,\* Pres.; Rosalie Zalis, Secy.; Gregg Ritchie, C.F.O. and Treas.; Lod Cook, Edward Sanders.
**EIN:** 953855792

# COLORADO

## 80
### El Pomar Foundation ▼
10 Lake Cir.
Colorado Springs, CO 80906 (719) 633-7733
*Contact:* William J. Hybl, Chair.
*Additional tel.:* (800) 554-7711; FAX: (719) 577-5702; URL: http://www.elpomar.org

Incorporated in 1937 in CO.
**Donor(s):** Spencer Penrose,‡ Mrs. Spencer Penrose.‡
**Grantmaker type:** Independent foundation
**Financial data** (yr. ended 12/31/99): Assets, $492,653,986 (M); gifts received, $32,180; expenditures, $22,485,120; qualifying distributions, $19,916,499; giving activities include $15,485,711 for 406 grants (high: $2,000,000; low: $1,000; average: $5,000–$100,000), $2,599,559 for 4 foundation-administered programs and $86,181 for in-kind gifts.

**Purpose and activities:** Grants only to nonprofit organizations for public, educational, arts and humanities, health, and welfare purposes, including child welfare, the disadvantaged, and housing; municipalities may request funds for specific projects.
**Fields of interest:** Media/communications; visual arts; museums; performing arts; theater; music; humanities; historic preservation/historical societies; arts/cultural programs; child development, education; elementary school/education; secondary school/education; vocational education; higher education; adult/continuing education; adult education—literacy & basic skills; libraries/library science; reading; education; natural resource conservation & protection; environment; hospitals (general); pharmacology; health care; substance abuse, services; health associations; employment; food services; nutrition; housing/shelter, development; recreation; human services; children & youth, services; child development, services; family services; hospices; aging, centers & services; homeless, human services; community development; voluntarism promotion; transportation; minorities; disabled; aging; economically disadvantaged; homeless.
**Types of support:** General/operating support; continuing support; capital campaigns; building/renovation; equipment; land acquisition; emergency funds; program development; scholarship funds; program-related investments/loans; employee matching gifts.
**Limitations:** Giving limited to CO. No support for organizations that distribute funds to other grantees, religious or political organizations, primary or secondary education, or for camps or seasonal facilities. No grants to individuals, or for annual campaigns, travel, film or other media projects, conferences, deficit financing, endowment funds, research, matching gifts, seed money, or publications.
**Publications:** Annual report (including application guidelines), application guidelines, grants list, informational brochure.
**Application information:** Application form not required.
*Initial approach:* Proposal
*Copies of proposal:* 1
*Deadline(s):* None
*Board meeting date(s):* 6 to 8 times a year
*Final notification:* 90 days
**Officers and Trustees:\*** William J. Hybl,\* Chair. and C.E.O.; R. Thayer Tutt, Jr.,\* Pres. and C.I.O.; Robert J. Hilbert,\* V.P., Admin. and Secy.-Treas.; David J. Palenchar, V.P., Progs.; Judith M. Bell, Cortlandt S. Dietler, Kent O. Olin, Brenda J. Smith, William R. Ward.
**Number of staff:** 29 full-time professional; 17 full-time support; 3 part-time support.
**EIN:** 846002373
**Recent grants for library/information services:**
**80-1** Old Colorado City Historical Society, Colorado Springs, CO, $10,000. To preserve computer documents. 1998.
**80-2** Penrose-Saint Francis Health Care System, Webb Library, Colorado Springs, CO, $122,000. For Cancer Center. 1998.

## 81
## Martin & Deborah Flug Foundation
(Formerly Margulf Foundation, Inc.)
616 E. Hyman Ave., No. 2-D
Aspen, CO 81611

Established in 1977 in NY and DE.
**Donor(s):** Martin Flug, James Flug, Robert Flug, Barbara Colin, Gulftech International, Inc.
**Grantmaker type:** Independent foundation
**Financial data** (yr. ended 11/30/98): Assets, $4,957,215 (M); gifts received, $600,000; expenditures, $452,341; qualifying distributions, $428,105; giving activities include $440,294 for 25 grants (high: $275,000; low: $50).
**Purpose and activities:** Support given to organizations that provide scholarships, support the arts, or provide community services.
**Fields of interest:** Arts/cultural programs; elementary/secondary education; higher education; libraries/library science; human services; Jewish federated giving programs.
**Types of support:** General/operating support; capital campaigns; scholarship funds.
**Limitations:** Applications not accepted. Giving primarily in Aspen, CO. No grants to individuals.
**Application information:** Contributes only to pre-selected organizations.
**Officers and Directors:** Martin Flug,* Pres.; Jeremy Flug,* V.P.; Steve Hall, Secy.-Treas.
**EIN:** 132927245

## 82
## Gates Family Foundation ▼
(Formerly Gates Foundation)
3200 Cherry Creek S. Dr., Ste. 630
Denver, CO 80209-3247 (303) 722-1881
*Contact:* C. Thomas Kaesemeyer, Exec. Dir.
*FAX:* (303) 698-9031; E-mail:
info@GatesFamilyFdn.org; URL: http://
www.gatesFamilyFdn.org

Incorporated in 1946 in CO.
**Donor(s):** Charles C. Gates, Sr.,‡ Hazel Gates,‡ John Gates.‡
**Grantmaker type:** Independent foundation
**Financial data** (yr. ended 12/31/99): Assets, $240,180,985 (M); gifts received, $2,000,000; expenditures, $10,651,047; qualifying distributions, $9,329,557; giving activities include $8,840,895 for 90 grants (high: $800,000; low: $1,000; average: $5,000–$100,000).
**Purpose and activities:** To promote the health, welfare, and broad education of mankind, whether by means of research, grants, publications, and the foundation's own agencies and activities, or through cooperation with agencies and institutions already in existence. Grants primarily for education and youth services, including leadership development; public policy; historic preservation, humanities, and cultural affairs; health care, including cost reduction; and human services.
**Fields of interest:** Visual arts; museums; performing arts; dance; theater; music; humanities; historic preservation/historical societies; arts/cultural programs; adult/continuing education; adult education—literacy & basic skills; libraries/library science; reading; education; natural resource conservation & protection; recreation; youth development, services; youth

development; human services; youth, services; aging, centers & services; economics; government/public administration; leadership development; aging.
**Types of support:** Capital campaigns; building/renovation; equipment; land acquisition; endowments; fellowships; matching/challenge support.
**Limitations:** Giving limited to CO, with emphasis on the Denver area, except for foundation-initiated grants. No support for private foundations, medical facilities, or individual public schools of public school districts. No grants to individuals, or for operating budgets, medical research, annual campaigns, emergency funds, deficit financing, purchase of tickets for fundraising dinners, parties, balls, or other social fundraising events, purchase of vehicles or office equipment, conferences, meetings, research, or scholarships; no loans.
**Publications:** Annual report (including application guidelines), grants list.
**Application information:** If the summary proposal seems to dovetail with the current interests of the foundation additional information will be required. A Common Grant Application form will be provided for this purpose. Application form not required.
  *Initial approach:* Telephone call or short summary proposal
  *Copies of proposal:* 1
  *Deadline(s):* Jan. 15, Apr. 1, July 15, and Oct. 1
  *Board meeting date(s):* Approx. Apr. 1, June 15, Oct. 1, and Dec. 15
  *Final notification:* 2 weeks following meetings
**Officers and Trustees:** Diane Gates Wallach,* Pres.; Charles G. Cannon,* V.P.; C. Thomas Kaesemeyer, Secy. and Exec. Dir.; Thomas C. Stokes,* Treas.; Christina H. Turissini, Compt.; George B. Beardsley, Charles C. Gates, Valerie Gates, William W. Grant III, Mike Wilfley.
**Number of staff:** 4 full-time professional; 1 full-time support.
**EIN:** 840474837
**Recent grants for library/information services:**
**82-1** Carnegie Public Library of Monte Vista, Monte Vista, CO, $50,000. Toward restoration and expansion. 1999.
**82-2** Park County Public Library System, Bailey, CO, $31,750. Toward completion of Phase I renovations to Bailey Public Library. 1999.
**82-3** Western Museum of Mining and Industry, Colorado Springs, CO, $21,133. Toward cataloging and archival storage of Winfield Scott Stratton Collection. 1999.

## 83
## Joslin-Needham Family Foundation
c/o Farmers State Bank, Brush
200 Clayton St.
Brush, CO 80723 (970) 842-5101
*Contact:* Judy Gunnon
*Application address:* P.O. Box 324, Brush, CO 80723

Established in 1964.
**Donor(s):** Gladys Joslin.‡
**Grantmaker type:** Independent foundation
**Financial data** (yr. ended 12/31/98): Assets, $5,739,770 (M); expenditures, $294,561; qualifying distributions, $270,858; giving

activities include $257,704 for 14 grants (high: $67,893; low: $300).
**Purpose and activities:** Giving primarily to a public library district, a municipality, and social services.
**Fields of interest:** Libraries/library science; health associations; human services; government/public administration.
**Types of support:** General/operating support; equipment; scholarship funds.
**Limitations:** Giving primarily in the Brush, CO, area.
**Application information:** Application form not required.
  *Initial approach:* Letter
  *Deadline(s):* None
**Directors:** Robert U. Hansen, Robert Pettys.
**Trustee:** Farmers State Bank, Brush.
**EIN:** 846038670

## 84
## Kinder Morgan Foundation
(Formerly KN Energy Foundation)
370 Van Gordon St.
P.O. Box 281304
Lakewood, CO 80228-8304 (303) 763-3471
*Contact:* Maureen Bulkley, Comm. Rels. Coord.
*FAX:* (303) 914-4757; E-mail:
maureen_bulkley@kindermorgan.com; URL:
http://www.kindermorgan.com/
community_support

Established in 1990 in CO.
**Donor(s):** K N Energy, Inc., Kinder Morgan, Inc.
**Grantmaker type:** Company-sponsored foundation
**Financial data** (yr. ended 12/31/98): Assets, $5,338,800 (M); expenditures, $309,234; qualifying distributions, $297,356; giving activities include $304,010 for 187 grants (high: $15,000; low: $25; average: $1,000–$5,000).
**Purpose and activities:** The foundation is dedicated to supporting nonprofit programs that enhance the quality of life for everyone in Kinder Morgan communities through charitable contributions to youth and education. The foundation makes grants for capital purchase and program support that range from $1,000 to $5,000. It also provides a limited matching gift program for employees of Kinder Morgan.
**Fields of interest:** Elementary/secondary education; higher education; libraries/library science; children & youth, services.
**Types of support:** Capital campaigns; program development; employee matching gifts.
**Limitations:** Giving primarily in areas of company operations. No support for political causes, programs outside the U.S., or projects of religious denominations. No grants to individuals, or for scholarships, advertising, travel, athletic team sponsorship, or for operating expenses.
**Publications:** Informational brochure (including application guidelines).
**Application information:** Contact foundation to receive application form and guidelines. Application form required.
  *Initial approach:* Proposal (not to exceed 3 pages), including cover letter and application form
  *Copies of proposal:* 1
  *Deadline(s):* Jan. 15, Mar. 15, May 15, July 15, Sep. 15, Nov. 15

*Board meeting date(s):* Funding decisions made bimonthly
**Directors:** Michael Morgan, Larry S. Pierce, James E. Street, Daniel E. Watson.
**EIN:** 841148161

---

**85**
**Kitzmiller-Bales Trust**
P.O. Box 96
Wray, CO 80758 (970) 332-3484
*Contact:* Robert U. Hansen, Tr.
*Additional tel.:* (970) 332-4824

Established in 1984 in CO.
**Donor(s):** Edna B. Kitzmiller.‡
**Grantmaker type:** Independent foundation
**Financial data** (yr. ended 12/31/99): Assets, $11,469,540 (M); expenditures, $554,339; qualifying distributions, $538,829; giving activities include $537,597 for 13 grants (high: $155,285; low: $1,550).
**Fields of interest:** Historic preservation/historical societies; arts/cultural programs; libraries/library science; education; hospitals (general); medical care, rehabilitation; health care; health associations; recreation; aging, centers & services; community development; federated giving programs; government/public administration; aging.
**Types of support:** Continuing support; capital campaigns; building/renovation; equipment; program development; matching/challenge support.
**Limitations:** Giving limited to projects benefiting the area of East Yuma County School District, RJ-2, CO.
**Application information:** Application form not required.
  *Initial approach:* Letter
  *Copies of proposal:* 1
  *Deadline(s):* None
  *Final notification:* Following board meetings
**Trustees:** Duard Fix, Robert U. Hansen, Farmers State Bank, Brush.
**Number of staff:** None.
**EIN:** 846178085

---

**86**
**The Pioneer Fund**
1801 California St., Ste. 4500
Denver, CO 80202

Established in 1960 in IL.
**Donor(s):** Helen M. McLoraine.
**Grantmaker type:** Independent foundation
**Financial data** (yr. ended 12/31/99): Assets, $22,306,296 (M); gifts received, $1,590,000; expenditures, $597,572; qualifying distributions, $575,500; giving activities include $575,500 for 2 grants (high: $575,000; low: $500).
**Purpose and activities:** Giving for a public library, and the Salk Institute for Biological Studies.
**Fields of interest:** Libraries/library science; biological sciences.
**Types of support:** Endowments.
**Limitations:** Applications not accepted. Giving primarily in La Jolla, CA and Denver, CO. No grants to individuals.
**Application information:** Contributes only to pre-selected organizations.

**Officers and Directors:\*** Helen M. McLoraine,* Pres. and Treas.; Robert T. Birdsong,* V.P.; Robert Anderson,* Secy.
**EIN:** 366108943

---

**87**
**Eleanore Mullen Weckbaugh Foundation**
P.O. Box 3486
Englewood, CO 80155-3486 (303) 471-1301
*Contact:* Therese A. Polakovic, Pres.

Established in 1975.
**Donor(s):** Eleanore Mullen Weckbaugh.‡
**Grantmaker type:** Independent foundation
**Financial data** (yr. ended 03/31/00): Assets, $11,198,414 (M); expenditures, $579,100; qualifying distributions, $510,260; giving activities include $436,435 for 43 grants (high: $40,000; low: $75).
**Purpose and activities:** Emphasis on Roman Catholic church support, grants also for higher and secondary education, libraries, museums and the performing arts, hospitals, health agencies, employment, child welfare and development, and women.
**Fields of interest:** Museums; performing arts; language & linguistics; literature; arts/cultural programs; elementary/secondary education; child development, education; secondary school/education; higher education; adult/continuing education; libraries (public); education; hospitals (general); health associations; employment; human services; children & youth, services; child development, services; women, centers & services; Christian agencies & churches; religion; women; general charitable giving.
**Types of support:** General/operating support; scholarship funds.
**Limitations:** Giving primarily in CO. No grants to individuals.
**Application information:** The foundation accepts the Common Grant Application form. Application form required.
  *Initial approach:* Letter
  *Copies of proposal:* 1
  *Deadline(s):* Feb. 1, May 1, Aug. 1, and Nov. 1
  *Board meeting date(s):* Mar., June, Sept., and Dec.
**Officers and Trustees:\*** Therese A. Polakovic,* Pres.; Michael J. Polakovic,* V.P. and Secy.; Edward J. Limes,* Treas.; Jean P. Guyton, Michael J. Lascor.
**Number of staff:** 3 part-time professional.
**EIN:** 237437761

---

# CONNECTICUT

**88**
**Alden-Wright Foundation, Inc.**
18 Beach Dr.
Darien, CT 06820

Established in 1997 in CT.
**Donor(s):** Philip T. Wright, Virginia A. Wright.
**Grantmaker type:** Independent foundation
**Financial data** (yr. ended 12/31/99): Assets, $3,683,323 (M); expenditures, $158,314;

qualifying distributions, $137,449; giving activities include $137,000 for 18 grants (high: $21,000; low: $2,000).
**Purpose and activities:** Giving for education, health, and human services.
**Fields of interest:** Libraries (public); health care; human services; federated giving programs.
**Types of support:** Scholarship funds.
**Limitations:** Applications not accepted. Giving primarily in CT. No grants to individuals.
**Application information:** Contributes only to pre-selected organizations.
**Officers and Directors:\*** Philip T. Wright,* Pres. and Treas.; Virginia A. Wright,* V.P. and Secy.; Ann W. Franke, Wendy W. Marrinan, Sandra C. Wright, Steven A. Wright.
**EIN:** 061482991

---

**89**
**The Auerbach Schiro Foundation**
15 Porter Rd.
West Hartford, CT 06117
*Contact:* Elizabeth A. Schiro, Tr.

Established in 1993 in CT.
**Donor(s):** Schiro Fund, Inc.
**Grantmaker type:** Independent foundation
**Financial data** (yr. ended 12/31/99): Assets, $2,273,726 (M); expenditures, $83,174; qualifying distributions, $78,895; giving activities include $80,000 for 57 grants (high: $38,374; low: $30).
**Purpose and activities:** Giving to Jewish agencies, community services, the arts and for children and youth services.
**Fields of interest:** Museums (art); college; libraries (public); children & youth, services; Jewish federated giving programs.
**Types of support:** General/operating support; continuing support; annual campaigns; equipment; land acquisition; program development; seed money; scholarship funds; program-related investments/loans; scholarships—to individuals.
**Limitations:** Applications not accepted. Giving primarily in CT.
**Application information:** Contributes only to pre-selected organizations.
**Trustees:** Stephen L. Bayer, Elizabeth A. Schiro.
**EIN:** 133692236

---

**90**
**Bodenwein Public Benevolent Foundation**
777 Main St. CTEH402228
Hartford, CT 06115 (860) 986-7696
*Contact:* Marjorie Alexandre Davis

Established in 1938 in CT.
**Donor(s):** The Day Trust, Theodore Bodenwein.‡
**Grantmaker type:** Independent foundation
**Financial data** (yr. ended 12/31/99): Assets, $527,718 (M); expenditures, $316,776; qualifying distributions, $311,126; giving activities include $311,126 for 51 grants (high: $25,000; low: $511).
**Purpose and activities:** Giving to social service and health agencies, including AIDS support, the fine and performing arts and other cultural programs, youth and child welfare agencies, civic affairs and community development groups, education, and minority programs.

**Fields of interest:** Visual arts; museums; performing arts; theater; language & linguistics; literature; arts/cultural programs; early childhood education; child development, education; adult/continuing education; adult education—literacy & basic skills; libraries/library science; reading; education; environment; animal welfare; hospitals (general); family planning; medical care, rehabilitation; health care; substance abuse, services; mental health/crisis services; health associations; alcoholism; cancer research; AIDS research; legal services; youth development, services; human services; children & youth, services; child development, services; family services; aging, centers & services; women, centers & services; minorities/immigrants, centers & services; community development; voluntarism promotion; Jewish federated giving programs; engineering & technology; science; government/public administration; transportation; leadership development; religion; minorities; aging; women.
**Types of support:** Capital campaigns; equipment; program development; publication; seed money; scholarship funds; matching/challenge support.
**Limitations:** Giving limited to Lyme, Old Lyme, East Lyme, Waterford, New London, Montville, Groton, Ledyard, Stonington, and North Stonington, CT.
**Publications:** Informational brochure (including application guidelines).
**Application information:** Each applicant may submit only 1 grant application per calendar year. Application form required.
*Copies of proposal:* 5
*Deadline(s):* May 15 and Nov. 15
*Board meeting date(s):* Jan. and July
*Final notification:* Feb. 1 and Aug. 1
**Trustee:** Fleet Bank.
**Number of staff:** None.
**EIN:** 066030548

## 91
## Robert G. Burton Charitable Foundation
170 Clapboard Ridge Rd.
Greenwich, CT 06831
*Contact:* Robert Burton, Tr.

Established in 1992.
**Donor(s):** Robert G. Burton.
**Grantmaker type:** Independent foundation
**Financial data** (yr. ended 06/30/99): Assets, $1,439,473 (M); gifts received, $462,500; expenditures, $97,893; qualifying distributions, $87,600; giving activities include $87,600 for 8 grants (high: $25,000; low: $1,000).
**Purpose and activities:** Giving for higher education and for education scholarships.
**Fields of interest:** Libraries/library science; higher education; education.
**Limitations:** Giving primarily in the Greenwich, CT, area. No grants to individuals.
**Trustees:** Paula M. Burton, Robert G. Burton, Leonard C. Green.
**EIN:** 061354439

## 92
## Champion International Corporation Contributions Program
1 Champion Plz.
Stamford, CT 06921 (203) 358-7000
*Contact:* Eileen McSweeney, Dir., Contribs.
*FAX:* (203) 358-6622

**Grantmaker type:** Corporate giving program
**Financial data** (yr. ended 12/31/99): Total giving, $8,000,000; giving activities include $7,870,000 for 350 grants (high: $125,000; low: $1,000; average: $2,500–$5,000) and $130,000 for 30 grants to individuals (high: $2,500; low: $500; average: $500–$2,500).
**Purpose and activities:** Champion makes charitable contributions to nonprofit organizations involved with arts and culture, education, the environment, health and human services, disease, community development, science, public affairs, and minorities. Support is limited to areas of company operations.
**Fields of interest:** Visual arts; museums; performing arts; arts/cultural programs; education, association; higher education; business school/education; engineering school/education; adult education—literacy & basic skills; libraries/library science; reading; education; natural resource conservation & protection; environment; hospitals (general); health care; health organizations; youth, services; human services; community development; engineering & technology; science; public affairs; minorities.
**Types of support:** General/operating support; continuing support; capital campaigns; endowments; program development; employee volunteer services; employee matching gifts; employee-related scholarships; matching/challenge support.
**Limitations:** Giving limited to areas of company operations. No support for political candidates or organizations, religious, veterans', or fraternal organizations not of benefit to the entire community, or United Way-supported organizations. No grants to individuals (except for employee-related scholarships), or for dinners, benefits, conferences, one-time activities, advertisements, or sports events.
**Publications:** Informational brochure (including application guidelines), corporate giving report.
**Application information:** The Public Affairs Department handles giving. The company has a staff that only handles contributions. Application form not required.
*Initial approach:* Contact headquarters for guidelines
*Copies of proposal:* 1
*Deadline(s):* None
*Final notification:* 3 weeks if approved
**Number of staff:** 1 full-time professional; 1 part-time professional; 1 full-time support.

## 93
## The Community Foundation of Southeastern Connecticut
(Formerly The Pequot Community Foundation, Inc.)
1 Union Plz.
P.O. Box 769
New London, CT 06320 (860) 442-3572
*Contact:* Alice F. Fitzpatrick, Exec. Dir.
*FAX:* (860) 442-0584; E-mail: jenno@cfsect.org;
URL: http://www.cfsect.org

Established in 1982 in CT.
**Donor(s):** J. Martin Leatherman,‡ Beatrice G. McEwen,‡ Dorothy Morgan,‡ Jim Smith, members of the White Family.
**Grantmaker type:** Community foundation
**Financial data** (yr. ended 12/31/99): Assets, $22,865,750 (L); gifts received, $1,143,196; expenditures, $1,214,710; giving activities include $912,155 for 150 grants (high: $55,000; low: $500; average: $2,000–$10,000).
**Purpose and activities:** The Community Foundation of Southeastern Connecticut permanently strengthens our shared community through the promotion of local philanthropy and the responsible stewardship of endowed funds.
**Fields of interest:** Arts/cultural programs; libraries/library science; scholarships/financial aid; education; natural resource conservation & protection; environment; health care; substance abuse, services; mental health/crisis services; human services; children & youth, services; family services; aging, centers & services; women, centers & services; community development; voluntarism promotion; disabled; aging; women; economically disadvantaged.
**Types of support:** General/operating support; building/renovation; equipment; emergency funds; program development; seed money; scholarship funds; consulting services; scholarships—to individuals.
**Limitations:** Giving limited to southeastern CT, including East Lyme, Groton, Ledyard, Lyme, Montville, New London, North Stonington, Old Lyme, Salem, Stonington, and Waterford. No support for sectarian or religious programs. No grants to individuals (except for scholarships awarded by nomination only), or for endowment, memorial, or building funds, deficit financing, or annual campaigns; no loans.
**Publications:** Annual report (including application guidelines), application guidelines, financial statement, grants list, newsletter.
**Application information:** Application form available on foundation website. Application form required.
*Initial approach:* Telephone or letter
*Copies of proposal:* 2
*Deadline(s):* Nov. 15; Apr. 1 for scholarship applications
*Board meeting date(s):* Jan., Mar., June, Sept., and Nov.
*Final notification:* Grants are distributed in Mar.; scholarships are awarded in June
**Officers and Trustees:\*** Jane Bredeson,\* Pres.; George Willauer,\* V.P.; Roger Gross,\* Secy.; Walter Baker,\* Treas.; Alice F. Fitzpatrick, Exec. Dir.; and 22 additional trustees.
**Number of staff:** 3 full-time professional; 1 full-time support; 1 part-time support.
**EIN:** 061080097

## 94
**The Dibner Fund, Inc.** ▼
44 Old Ridgefield Rd.
P.O. Box 7575
Wilton, CT  06897  (203) 761-9904
*Contact:* Marci B. Sternheim, Ph.D., Exec. Dir.
*FAX:* (203) 761-9989; E-mail:
dibnerfund@worldnet.att.net

Incorporated in 1957 in CT.
**Donor(s):** Barbara Dibner,‡ Bern Dibner,‡ David Dibner.
**Grantmaker type:** Independent foundation
**Financial data** (yr. ended 12/31/99): Assets, $104,592,354 (M); expenditures, $6,803,394; qualifying distributions, $6,650,274; giving activities include $6,270,239 for 71 grants (high: $2,095,700; low: $1,000; average: $2,000–$50,000).
**Purpose and activities:** Support in seven particular areas: environment (emphasis on clean water and rivers); history of science and technology; humanitarian causes; Jewish heritage and culture; peaceful coexistence; science education (emphasis on support for science/math literacy and careers for minorities, including Native Americans, and girls/women); also giving for selected community organizations.
**Fields of interest:** Higher education; education; environment; disasters, preparedness & services; peace; engineering & technology; science; minorities; Native Americans.
**International interests:** Europe; Israel.
**Types of support:** Program development; conferences/seminars; scholarship funds.
**Limitations:** Giving primarily in CT, MA, and NY. No support for religious sects or institutions, or political parties or programs. No grants to individuals, or generally for building or endowment funds, scholarships, fellowships (except through universities, educational agencies and/or specific academic programs) capital expenditures, or matching gifts; no loans.
**Publications:** Program policy statement, application guidelines.
**Application information:** Application form not required.
  *Initial approach:* Letter
  *Copies of proposal:* 1
  *Deadline(s):* None
  *Board meeting date(s):* Quarterly
**Officers and Trustees:*** David Dibner,* Pres.; Brent Dibner, V.P.; Frances K. Dibner,* V.P.; George M. Szabad,* Secy.-Treas.; Marci B. Sternheim, Ph.D., Exec. Dir.; Michael Cohen, Stewart Greenfield, Stephen D. Shapiro, Warren Shine.
**Number of staff:** 1 full-time professional; 1 full-time support.
**EIN:** 066038482
**Recent grants for library/information services:**
**94-1** Massachusetts Institute of Technology, Burndy Library, Cambridge, MA, $409,200. 1998.
**94-2** Smithsonian Institution, DC, $19,300. For libraries. 1998.

## 95
**Richard Davoud Donchian Charitable Foundation, Inc.**
(Formerly Richard Davoud Donchian Foundation)
c/o Fogerty, Cohen, Selby, & Hemiroff, LLC
P.O. Box 2508
Greenwich, CT  06836-2250
*Contact:* Geoffrey M. Parkinson, Dir.
*Application address:* 35 Mason St., Greenwich, CT 06830

Established in 1991 in CT; reincorporated in 1998.
**Donor(s):** Richard D. Donchian.
**Grantmaker type:** Independent foundation
**Financial data** (yr. ended 12/31/99): Assets, $11,971,686 (M); gifts received, $28,490; expenditures, $517,988; qualifying distributions, $393,511; giving activities include $307,000 for 14 grants (high: $100,000; low: $1,000).
**Purpose and activities:** Giving primarily for the arts, education, and human services.
**Fields of interest:** Arts/cultural programs; libraries/library science; education; health care, support services; human services; urban/community development.
**Limitations:** Giving primarily in CT and NY.
**Application information:**
  *Deadline(s):* None
**Directors:** Geoffrey M. Parkinson, Leland C. Selby, Clark M. Whittemore, Jr.
**EIN:** 061514402

## 96
**Howard A. Fromson Foundation, Inc.**
(Formerly Fromson Foundation, Inc.)
c/o Anocoil Corp.
60 E. Main St., P.O. Box 1318
Rockville, CT  06066

Established in 1982 in CT.
**Donor(s):** Howard A. Fromson, Anocoil Corp.
**Grantmaker type:** Company-sponsored foundation
**Financial data** (yr. ended 11/30/99): Assets, $614,657 (M); gifts received, $75,900; expenditures, $82,307; qualifying distributions, $65,550; giving activities include $65,550 for 26 grants (high: $16,000; low: $250).
**Purpose and activities:** Giving primarily in the areas of education and health.
**Fields of interest:** Ballet; libraries (public); education; Christian agencies & churches.
**Limitations:** Giving primarily in the northeastern U.S., with emphasis on CT.
**Application information:** Application form not required.
  *Initial approach:* Letter
  *Deadline(s):* None
**Officer:** Howard A. Fromson, Pres.
**EIN:** 061074374

## 97
**Kenneth K. Mills Trust for First Congregational Church of Washington**
c/o BankBoston, N.A.
P.O. Box 2210
Waterbury, CT  06720
*Application address:* c/o Principal, Shepaug Valley Regional High School, Roxbury, CT 06783, tel.: (860) 868-7326

**Grantmaker type:** Independent foundation
**Financial data** (yr. ended 12/31/98): Assets, $3,251,404 (M); expenditures, $162,952; qualifying distributions, $139,522; giving activities include $140,867 for 3 grants (high: $104,900; low: $1,000).
**Purpose and activities:** Support primarily for Protestant organizations and libraries, also awards scholarships to residents of Washington, CT, who are graduates of Shepaug Valley High School and plan to attend Rutgers University.
**Fields of interest:** Libraries/library science; Protestant agencies & churches.
**Types of support:** General/operating support; scholarships—to individuals.
**Limitations:** Giving limited to Washington, CT.
**Application information:** Applicants for scholarships must be nominated by high school principal. Unsolicited requests for funds not accepted.
**Trustee:** BankBoston, N.A.
**EIN:** 066119402

## 98
**New Britain Foundation for Public Giving**
29 Russell St.
New Britain, CT  06052  (860) 229-6018
*Contact:* Mary-Ellen Powell, Exec. Dir.
*FAX:* (860) 229-2641; E-mail: nbf@nbfoundation.org; URL: http://www.nbfoundation.org

Established in 1941 in CT.
**Grantmaker type:** Community foundation
**Financial data** (yr. ended 12/31/99): Assets, $30,892,754 (M); gifts received, $607,002; expenditures, $1,249,094; giving activities include $795,786 for 116 grants (high: $25,000; low: $100).
**Purpose and activities:** To meet the needs of the greater New Britain, CT, community through support of programs dedicated to health and human services, children, youth, education, rehabilitation services, arts, culture, and civic affairs.
**Fields of interest:** Arts/cultural programs; child development, education; secondary school/education; libraries/library science; education; hospitals (general); family planning; health care; substance abuse, services; mental health/crisis services; health associations; domestic violence prevention; youth development, services; human services; children & youth, services; child development, services; family services; aging, centers & services; homeless, human services; community development; leadership development; African Americans; Latinos; disabled; aging; people with AIDS (PWAs); economically disadvantaged; homeless; general charitable giving.
**Types of support:** General/operating support; continuing support; capital campaigns; building/renovation; equipment; emergency

funds; program development; conferences/seminars; seed money; curriculum development; scholarship funds; technical assistance; consulting services; scholarships—to individuals; matching/challenge support.
**Limitations:** Giving limited to central CT, with emphasis on New Britain. No support for religious activities. No grants to individuals (except through scholarships), or for annual endowment campaigns or budget deficits.
**Publications:** Annual report (including application guidelines), newsletter, financial statement, application guidelines.
**Application information:** Proposals should be no longer than 5 pages in length and contain a cover sheet. Application form not required.
  *Initial approach:* Letter or telephone
  *Copies of proposal:* 15
  *Deadline(s):* None
  *Board meeting date(s):* Mar., June, Sept., and Dec.
**Officers and Directors:*** Connie Collins,* Chair.; Kenneth Julian,* Treas.; Mary-Ellen Powell, Exec. Dir.; Diane Alverio, Charles Bauer, Donald Davidson, Carol Gordon, Edward Januszewski, Charles Jones, Nancy Judd, Peter Rosa, Robert A. Scalise, Jr., Talcott Stanley, Lindsley Wellman.
**Number of staff:** 2 full-time professional; 4 part-time professional; 1 full-time support.
**EIN:** 066036461

## 99
### The 1919 Foundation, Inc.
c/o Gilbridge, Tusa, Last & Spellans, LLC
31 Brookside Dr.
Greenwich, CT 06830

Established in 1997.
**Grantmaker type:** Independent foundation
**Financial data** (yr. ended 12/31/99): Assets, $1,070,929 (M); expenditures, $73,503; qualifying distributions, $69,190; giving activities include $65,000 for 6 grants (high: $25,000; low: $5,000).
**Fields of interest:** Libraries/library science; environment, land resources; hospices; religion.
**Limitations:** Applications not accepted. Giving primarily in CT, NY, and PA. No grants to individuals.
**Application information:** Contributes only to pre-selected organizations.
**Officers:** Justine F. Theurkauf, Pres.; O. Robert Theurkauf, V.P.; Thomas P. Spellane, Secy.
**EIN:** 061502375

## 100
### The Frank Loomis Palmer Fund
c/o Shipman & Goodwin, LLP
1 American Row
Hartford, CT 06115 (860) 986-4071
*Contact:* Sheilah Rostow, V.P., Fleet Bank

Trust established in 1936 in CT.
**Donor(s):** Virginia Palmer.‡
**Grantmaker type:** Independent foundation
**Financial data** (yr. ended 07/31/98): Assets, $35,109,091 (M); expenditures, $1,430,071; qualifying distributions, $1,317,465; giving activities include $1,185,488 for 55 grants (high: $82,500; low: $1,000).

**Purpose and activities:** Grants to encourage new projects and to provide seed money, with emphasis on child welfare and family services and youth agencies; support also for civic groups, cultural programs, social services, and educational programs.
**Fields of interest:** Performing arts; arts/cultural programs; elementary school/education; secondary school/education; higher education; adult/continuing education; libraries/library science; education; natural resource conservation & protection; environment; hospitals (general); family planning; health care; health associations; AIDS; alcoholism; AIDS research; legal services; safety/disasters; children & youth, services; family services; hospices; aging, centers & services; minorities/immigrants, centers & services; community development; engineering & technology; science; government/public administration; transportation; religion; minorities; aging.
**Types of support:** Equipment; program development; conferences/seminars; publication; seed money; scholarship funds; research; consulting services; matching/challenge support.
**Limitations:** Giving limited to New London, CT. No grants to individuals, or for endowment funds.
**Publications:** Informational brochure (including application guidelines).
**Application information:** Application form required.
  *Initial approach:* Telephone
  *Copies of proposal:* 1
  *Deadline(s):* May 15 and Nov. 15
  *Board meeting date(s):* Jan. and July
  *Final notification:* Feb. 1 and Aug. 1
**Trustee:** Fleet Bank.
**Number of staff:** None.
**EIN:** 066026043

## 101
### The Rayonier Foundation
(Formerly The ITT Rayonier Foundation)
1177 Summer St.
Stamford, CT 06905-5529 (203) 348-7000
*Contact:* Jay A. Fredericksen, V.P.
*Scholarship application address:* College Scholarship Svc., P.O. Box 6730, Princeton, NJ 08541, tel.: (609) 951-1248

Incorporated in 1952 in NY.
**Donor(s):** Rayonier Inc.
**Grantmaker type:** Company-sponsored foundation
**Financial data** (yr. ended 12/31/98): Assets, $5,210,255 (M); gifts received, $239,000; expenditures, $716,977; qualifying distributions, $694,184; giving activities include $598,111 for 367 grants and $102,905 for grants to individuals.
**Purpose and activities:** Created as a medium to meet civic responsibilities in the areas of company operations and educational institutions related to Rayonier recruitment or to forest industry specializations. Grants to educational associations for scholarships, hospitals for buildings and equipment, health agencies and community funds, the arts, and environmental organizations; scholarships to individuals residing in areas of company operations in Nassau County, FL, Wayne

County, GA, and Clallam, Mason, and Grays Harbor counties, WA.
**Fields of interest:** Performing arts; libraries/library science; education; natural resource conservation & protection; hospitals (general); medical care, rehabilitation; substance abuse, services; mental health/crisis services; health associations; alcoholism; recreation; human services; children & youth, services; family services; women, centers & services; minorities/immigrants, centers & services; community development; voluntarism promotion; federated giving programs; engineering & technology; science; economics; minorities; disabled; women; economically disadvantaged.
**Types of support:** General/operating support; continuing support; annual campaigns; capital campaigns; building/renovation; equipment; land acquisition; endowments; debt reduction; emergency funds; program development; seed money; scholarship funds; research; employee matching gifts; employee-related scholarships; in-kind gifts; matching/challenge support.
**Limitations:** Giving primarily in areas of company operations in FL, GA, and WA. No loans.
**Application information:** Application form required for scholarships.
  *Initial approach:* Letter or proposal
  *Copies of proposal:* 1
  *Deadline(s):* Nov. 15 for scholarships
  *Board meeting date(s):* Feb.
  *Final notification:* Scholarship awards announced in Apr.
**Officers and Directors:*** Ronald M. Gross,* Chair. and Pres.; Jay A. Fredericksen,* V.P.; John B. Canning, Secy.; Macdonald Auguste, Treas.; Kenneth P. Janette, Cont.; William S. Berry, W. Lee Nutter.
**EIN:** 136064462

## 102
### Clinton S. Roberts Foundation, Inc.
P.O. Box 1399
201 West St.
Bristol, CT 06011-1399
*Contact:* Christopher Ziogas, Exec. Dir.

Established in 1987.
**Grantmaker type:** Independent foundation
**Financial data** (yr. ended 12/31/98): Assets, $8,125,049 (M); gifts received, $642,882; expenditures, $677,434; qualifying distributions, $550,891; giving activities include $555,015 for 35 grants (high: $150,000; low: $1,000).
**Fields of interest:** University; libraries (public); athletics/sports, baseball; boys clubs; boys & girls clubs; YM/YWCAs & YM/YWHAs; Protestant agencies & churches.
**Limitations:** Giving limited to the greater Bristol, CT, area.
**Application information:**
  *Initial approach:* Letter
**Officer:** Christopher Ziogas, Exec. Dir.
**Directors:** Linda Arbesman, Ellen Ferrier.
**EIN:** 222867088

## 103

**Roosa Family Foundation**
c/o Fleet Bank
777 Main St., CTMOH18A
Hartford, CT 06115 (860) 986-4071
*Application address:* c/o Florence E. Roosa, 275
Steele Rd., Apt. 418A, West Hartford, CT 06117

Established in 1994 in CT.
**Grantmaker type:** Independent foundation
**Financial data** (yr. ended 12/31/98): Assets,
$1,542,554 (M); expenditures, $383,788;
qualifying distributions, $371,417; giving
activities include $358,000 for 5 grants (high:
$340,000; low: $1,000).
**Purpose and activities:** Giving primarily for
health.
**Fields of interest:** Libraries (public); health care.
**Limitations:** Giving primarily in CT.
**Application information:**
    *Initial approach:* Proposal
    *Deadline(s):* None
**Trustee:** Fleet Bank.
**EIN:** 223295175

## 104

**Sayles & Maddocks Family Foundation**
c/o Cummings & Lockwood
P.O. Box 120
Stamford, CT 06904
*Contact:* John M. Baldwin, Pres.
*Application address:* P.O. Box 287, Goshen, CT
06756

Established in 1993 in CT.
**Donor(s):** Dolores M. Sayles,‡ Madison Sayles.‡
**Grantmaker type:** Independent foundation
**Financial data** (yr. ended 12/31/97): Assets,
$3,244,707 (M); expenditures, $176,219;
qualifying distributions, $143,342; giving
activities include $142,400 for 21 grants (high:
$20,000; low: $2,000).
**Fields of interest:** Orchestra (symphony); higher
education; libraries/library science; hospitals
(general); human services; American Red Cross;
Christian agencies & churches.
**Limitations:** Applications not accepted. Giving
primarily in CT and MA. No grants to
individuals.
**Application information:** Contributes only to
pre-selected organizations.
**Officers and Trustees:*** John M. Baldwin,* Pres.;
Marilyn M. Kerney,* V.P.; John R. Musicaro, Jr.,*
Secy.; David M. Harris,* Treas.
**EIN:** 066395098

## 105

**Tenneco Automotive Inc. Corporate
    Giving Program**
(Formerly Tenneco Inc. Corporate Giving
Program)
1275 King St.
Greenwich, CT 06831-2946
*Contact:* John J. Castellani, Exec. V.P.

**Grantmaker type:** Corporate giving program
**Purpose and activities:** Emphasis on elementary
and secondary education, including a Tenneco
Presidential Scholarship Program for students at
Jefferson Davis High School in the inner city of
Houston, TX. The scholarship carries a
maximum award of $4,000 for those ninth

graders who are able to maintain a 2.5 grade
point average and meet other academic
requirements. To be eligible, students must also
attend two summer enrichment sessions, which
Tenneco helped develop under the sponsorship
of a local philanthropic foundation and a local
university.
**Fields of interest:** Museums; theater; humanities;
historic preservation/historical societies;
arts/cultural programs; education, association;
education, research; early childhood education;
elementary school/education; secondary
school/education; higher education; engineering
school/education; adult education—literacy &
basic skills; libraries/library science; reading;
education; natural resource conservation &
protection; environment; hospitals (general);
health care; alcoholism; health organizations;
medical research; crime/law enforcement; food
services; housing/shelter, development; youth
development, services; human services; youth,
services; hospices; aging, centers & services;
women, centers & services; homeless, human
services; urban/community development;
community development; engineering; public
policy, research; government/public
administration; leadership development;
minorities; aging; women; economically
disadvantaged; homeless.
**International interests:** United Kingdom.
**Types of support:** Capital campaigns;
building/renovation; professorships; fellowships;
internship funds; scholarship funds; research;
employee volunteer services; loaned talent; use
of facilities; sponsorships; employee matching
gifts; donated equipment; donated products;
in-kind gifts; matching/challenge support.
**Limitations:** Giving on an international basis in
areas of company operations in CT, GA, IL, MI,
NY, TN, TX, VA, WI, Canada, and the United
Kingdom. No support for political, religious,
fraternal, or veterans' organizations. No grants to
individuals.
**Publications:** Corporate report, informational
brochure (including application guidelines).
**Application information:** The corporate offices
in Greenwich, CT, and Lake Forest, IL, handle
giving. Application form not required.
    *Initial approach:* Letter of inquiry on
        organization letterhead to headquarters or
        nearest company facility
    *Copies of proposal:* 1
    *Deadline(s):* Before Aug. 15 for the following
        year
    *Board meeting date(s):* 2nd Tuesday in Jan.
    *Final notification:* 12 weeks following
        submission of proposal
**Administrator:** Christine Sweetser Gable,
Contribs. Coord.
**Number of staff:** 1 part-time professional; 2
part-time support.

## 106

**Thomaston Savings Bank Foundation, Inc.**
P.O. Box 907
Thomaston, CT 06787
*Contact:* James Nicol, Secy.
*Application address:* 203 Main St., Thomaston,
CT 06787, tel: (860) 283-4373

Established in 1997.
**Grantmaker type:** Independent foundation

**Financial data** (yr. ended 12/31/98): Assets,
$3,258,148 (M); expenditures, $100,142;
qualifying distributions, $81,126; giving
activities include $80,500 for 19 grants (high:
$18,000; low: $1,000).
**Purpose and activities:** Giving primarily for
education, youth programs, and community
services.
**Fields of interest:** Elementary/secondary
education; libraries/library science; children &
youth, services; human services, emergency aid;
religion.
**Limitations:** Giving limited to Bethlehem,
Harwinton, Litchfield, Morris, Plymouth,
Thomaston, Watertown, and Woodbury, CT.
**Application information:**
    *Initial approach:* Proposal
**Officers and Trustees:*** Francis Kaminski,*
Chair.; Peter Dahlin,* Pres.; James Nicol, Secy.;
David Carlson, Treas.; Walter Barber, Paul
Broomhead, George Cocco, George Green,
James Kaniewski, Roger Perreault, George
Seabourne.
**EIN:** 061483909

## 107

**The Weller Foundation, Inc.**
P.O. Box 1145
Woodbury, CT 06798 (203) 263-0229
*Contact:* JoAnn E. Davies, Mgr.

Established in 1959 in CT.
**Grantmaker type:** Independent foundation
**Financial data** (yr. ended 12/31/99): Assets,
$2,904,413 (M); expenditures, $104,071;
qualifying distributions, $100,571; giving
activities include $10,700 for 34 grants (high:
$6,000; low: $100) and $50,663 for 56 grants to
individuals (high: $2,500; low: $100).
**Purpose and activities:** Provides scholarships
and awards to high school students in five CT
communities for higher and vocational
education; grants also for health associations,
youth organizations, higher education, and
community development.
**Fields of interest:** Higher education;
libraries/library science; education; children &
youth, services.
**Types of support:** General/operating support;
scholarships—to individuals.
**Limitations:** Giving limited to Easton-Redding,
Monroe, Newtown, Shelton, and Trumbull, CT.
**Application information:** Contact foundation for
application procedures for the various awards
and scholarship programs. Application form
required.
**Officers and Trustees:*** Michael J. Smith,*
Chair.; Louis J. LaCroce,* Vice-Chair.; Alexander
Fraser,* Secy.; Brian E. Skinner,* Treas.; JoAnn E.
Davies,* Mgr.; Michael Zabinski.
**EIN:** 066068987

## 108

**The David, Helen, and Marian Woodward
    Fund-Watertown**
(also known as Marian W. Ottley
Trust-Watertown)
Box 817
Watertown, CT 06795-0817
*Contact:* M. Heminway Merriman, 2nd Member,
Selection Comm.

Trust established in 1975 in GA.
**Donor(s):** Marian W. Ottley.‡
**Grantmaker type:** Independent foundation
**Financial data** (yr. ended 05/31/98): Assets, $19,677,592 (M); expenditures, $720,814; qualifying distributions, $629,164; giving activities include $624,870 for 32 grants (high: $100,000; low: $700).
**Purpose and activities:** Giving primarily for secondary, elementary, and early childhood education, social services, health services, and libraries. Support for building funds for education and hospitals.
**Fields of interest:** Museums; education, fund raising; early childhood education; elementary school/education; secondary school/education; libraries/library science; education; environment; hospitals (general); medical care, rehabilitation; health care; health associations; human services; youth, services; hospices; Christian agencies & churches; Native Americans.
**Types of support:** Capital campaigns; building/renovation; equipment; endowments; scholarship funds.
**Limitations:** Giving limited to local organizations in New England and NY. No support for institutions of higher education, or organizations lacking 501(c)(3) tax-exempt status. No grants to individuals, or for general operating funds; generally no multi-year grants.
**Publications:** Application guidelines.
**Application information:** Education awards limited to the pre-collegiate level. Application form not required.
  *Initial approach:* 2-page letter
  *Copies of proposal:* 3
  *Deadline(s):* May 15
  *Board meeting date(s):* May 7
**Selection Committee:** Anne Fitzgerald, M. Heminway Merriman, William J. Zito, M.D.
**Trustee:** First National Bank of Atlanta.
**Number of staff:** None.
**EIN:** 586222005

---

# DELAWARE

---

### 109
### Crystal Trust ▼
1088 DuPont Bldg.
Wilmington, DE  19898  (302) 774-8421
*Contact:* Stephen C. Doberstein, Dir.

Trust established in 1947 in DE.
**Donor(s):** Irenee duPont.‡
**Grantmaker type:** Independent foundation
**Financial data** (yr. ended 12/31/99): Assets, $200,657,492 (M); expenditures, $9,622,378; qualifying distributions, $8,691,093; giving activities include $9,003,350 for 100 grants (high: $2,000,000; low: $5,000; average: $10,000–$100,000).
**Purpose and activities:** Giving mainly for higher and secondary education and social and family services, including youth and child welfare agencies, family planning, and programs for the aged, the disadvantaged, and the homeless; support also for the arts and cultural programs, health and hospitals, conservation programs,

and historical preservation. Needs of the State of Delaware have priority.
**Fields of interest:** Museums; music; arts/cultural programs; secondary school/education; higher education; libraries/library science; education; natural resource conservation & protection; hospitals (general); family planning; health care; health associations; food services; housing/shelter, development; human services; children & youth, services; family services; hospices; aging, centers & services; homeless, human services; aging; economically disadvantaged; homeless.
**Types of support:** Capital campaigns; building/renovation; equipment; land acquisition.
**Limitations:** Giving primarily in DE, with emphasis on Wilmington. No grants to individuals, or for endowment funds, research, scholarships, fellowships, or matching gifts.
**Publications:** Informational brochure (including application guidelines).
**Application information:** Application form not required.
  *Initial approach:* Proposal
  *Copies of proposal:* 1
  *Deadline(s):* Sept. 30
  *Board meeting date(s):* Nov.
  *Final notification:* Dec. 15
**Director:** Stephen C. Doberstein.
**Trustees:** Irenee duPont, Jr., David Greenewalt, Eleanor S. Maroney.
**Number of staff:** 1 part-time professional; 1 part-time support.
**EIN:** 516015063
**Recent grants for library/information services:**
**109-1** Folger Shakespeare Library, DC, $75,000. For renovations. 1998.
**109-2** Lewes Public Library, Lewes, DE, $75,000. For capital campaign. 1998.
**109-3** Rehoboth Beach Public Library, Rehoboth Beach, DE, $35,000. For capital campaign. 1998.

### 110
### Delaware Medical Education Foundation
1925 Lovering Ave.
Wilmington, DE  19806-2147  (302) 658-7596
*Contact:* Mark A. Meister, Sr., Exec. Dir.
*FAX:* (302) 658-9669; E-mail: cmh@medsocdel.org; URL: http://www.medsocdel.org/DMEF.htm

Established in 1992 in DE.
**Grantmaker type:** Public charity
**Financial data** (yr. ended 12/31/98): Assets, $227,612; gifts received, $194,596; expenditures, $42,127; giving activities include $37,518 for grants.
**Purpose and activities:** The foundation provides Delaware physicians with up-to-the-minute clinical information in the field of medical sciences; sponsors programs to educate the public on medical issues; and helps fund the Physicians' Health Programs in coordination with the State Board of Medical Practice.
**Fields of interest:** Medicine/medical care, information services; medicine/medical care, public education.
**Types of support:** Program development.
**Limitations:** Giving limited to DE.
**Application information:**
  *Initial approach:* Letter

**Officers:** Janice Tildon-Burton, M.D., Chair.; Mansour Saberi, M.D., Vice-Chair.; Richard Sherman, M.D., Secy.-Treas.; Mark A. Meister, Sr., Exec. Dir.
**Directors:** Raafat Abdel-Misih, Alfonso P. Carlo, Katherine Esterly, James Grill, John Kramer, Carol A. Tavani, Samuel M. Wilson, M.D.
**EIN:** 510343625

### 111
### The Marmot Foundation
100 W. 10th St., Ste. 1109
Wilmington, DE  19801-1694  (302) 654-2477
*Contact:* Charles F. Gummey, Jr., Secy. (for DE organizations), or Willis H. duPont, Chair. (for FL organizations)
*Application address for FL organizations:* P.O. Box 2468, Palm Beach, FL 33480

Established in 1968 in DE.
**Donor(s):** Margaret F. duPont Trust.
**Grantmaker type:** Independent foundation
**Financial data** (yr. ended 12/31/99): Assets, $41,069,727 (M); expenditures, $1,959,395; qualifying distributions, $1,799,359; giving activities include $1,800,100 for 102 grants (high: $70,000; low: $100; average: $500–$50,000).
**Purpose and activities:** Support for hospitals, health, higher and secondary education, (including libraries), community funds, cultural programs, (including museums), youth agencies, social services, literacy programs, and environmental and ecological organizations.
**Fields of interest:** Museums; arts/cultural programs; secondary school/education; higher education; adult education—literacy & basic skills; libraries/library science; reading; natural resource conservation & protection; environment; hospitals (general); family planning; health care; health associations; housing/shelter, development; human services; children & youth, services; hospices; homeless, human services; homeless.
**Types of support:** Capital campaigns; building/renovation; equipment; research; matching/challenge support.
**Limitations:** Giving primarily in DE and FL. No support for religious organizations. No grants to individuals, or for operating budgets, endowments or scholarships; no loans.
**Application information:** Application form not required.
  *Initial approach:* Letter
  *Copies of proposal:* 1
  *Deadline(s):* Apr. 30 and Oct. 31
  *Board meeting date(s):* May and Nov.
  *Final notification:* 2 weeks after board meeting
**Officers and Trustees:*** Willis H. duPont,* Chair.; Charles F. Gummey,* Secy.; Lammot Joseph duPont, Miren deA. duPont, George S. Harrington, Miren duPont Sanchez.
**Number of staff:** None.
**EIN:** 516022487

**112**
**The Nick and Alma Robson Foundation**
c/o J.P. Morgan Svcs., Inc.
P.O. Box 6089
Newark, DE 19714-6089
*Contact:* Sybil Ann Robson, Dir.
*Application address:* 2021 S. Lewis, Ste. 740,
Tulsa, OK 74104

Established in 1992 in TX.
**Grantmaker type:** Independent foundation
**Financial data** (yr. ended 06/30/98): Assets,
$5,862,469 (M); expenditures, $237,947;
qualifying distributions, $214,953; giving
activities include $219,493 for 5 grants (high:
$93,875; low: $10,000).
**Purpose and activities:** Giving primarily for
education and to Methodist organizations.
**Fields of interest:** Libraries (public); education;
human services, special populations; Protestant
agencies & churches.
**Limitations:** Giving primarily in OK.
**Application information:**
*Initial approach:* Letter
*Deadline(s):* None
**Officers and Directors:*** John N. Robson,* Pres.;
John Joseph Robson,* V.P.; Sybil Ann Robson,*
V.P.; Bruce Allen Robson,* Secy.-Treas.; Alma
Lavon Robson, Edward Dodge Robson.
**EIN:** 752438350

**113**
**Ross Foundation, Inc.**
P.O. Box 4300
Wilmington, DE 19807

Established in 1960.
**Grantmaker type:** Independent foundation
**Financial data** (yr. ended 09/30/99): Assets,
$871,460 (M); expenditures, $63,515;
qualifying distributions, $62,649; giving
activities include $62,500 for 62 grants (high:
$11,100; low: $25).
**Purpose and activities:** Giving for education,
federated giving programs, and the environment.
**Fields of interest:** Museums; libraries/library
science; education; natural resource
conservation & protection; federated giving
programs.
**Limitations:** Applications not accepted. Giving
on a national basis. No grants to individuals.
**Application information:** Contributes only to
pre-selected organizations.
**Officers:** Donald P. Ross, Jr., Pres.; Robert H.
Bolling, Jr., V.P.; Wilhelmina duPont Ross, V.P.;
Sheila Ross, Secy.; Carl E. Golt, Treas.
**Director:** Joan R. Bolling.
**EIN:** 516015081

**114**
**Zock Endowment Trust**
c/o J.P. Morgan Svcs., Inc.
P.O. Box 6089
Newark, DE 19714-6089
*Contact:* Sara M. Zock, Tr.
*Application address:* 506 Crescent Pkwy., Sea
Girt, NJ 08750

Established in 1970.
**Grantmaker type:** Independent foundation
**Financial data** (yr. ended 09/30/99): Assets,
$3,976,670 (M); expenditures, $173,577;

qualifying distributions, $165,140; giving
activities include $136,000 for 21 grants (high:
$15,000; low: $1,000).
**Purpose and activities:** Giving primarily for
libraries, social services and Lutheran
organizations; support also for education and
health.
**Fields of interest:** Libraries (public); education;
environment; health associations; human
services; Protestant agencies & churches.
**Limitations:** Giving primarily in NJ and PA. No
grants to individuals.
**Application information:** Application form not
required.
*Deadline(s):* None
**Trustees:** Robert A. Zock, Sara M. Zock.
**EIN:** 226098288

# DISTRICT OF COLUMBIA

**115**
**The Baruch Fund**
2700 Chesapeake St., N.W.
Washington, DC 20008
*Contact:* Jordan J. Baruch, Tr.

Established about 1964 as the Jordan J. Baruch
Foundation.
**Donor(s):** Jordan J. Baruch, Rhoda W. Baruch.
**Grantmaker type:** Independent foundation
**Financial data** (yr. ended 12/31/97): Assets,
$5,006,621 (M); gifts received, $350,000;
expenditures, $744,240; qualifying distributions,
$572,783; giving activities include $582,430 for
206 grants (high: $23,000; low: $13).
**Purpose and activities:** Giving primarily for
education, environmental causes, community
programs, and Jewish organizations.
**Fields of interest:** Arts/cultural programs; higher
education; libraries/library science;
botanical/landscape services; environment,
beautification programs; environment; hospitals
(general); medical research, association;
children & youth, services; civil rights, equal
rights; federated giving programs; Jewish
agencies & temples.
**Limitations:** Giving primarily in Washington DC,
New York, NY and PA. No grants to individuals.
**Application information:**
*Initial approach:* Letter
*Deadline(s):* None
**Trustees:** Jordan J. Baruch, Lawrence K. Baruch,
Rhoda W. Baruch.
**Number of staff:** None.
**EIN:** 046112483

**116**
**Benton Foundation**
1800 K St., N.W., 2nd Fl.
Washington, DC 20006 (202) 638-5770
*Contact:* Larry Kirkman, Pres.
*E-mail:* Sandy@benton.org; *URL:* http://
www.benton.org

Incorporated in 1948 in NY.
**Donor(s):** William Benton.‡
**Grantmaker type:** Independent foundation

**Financial data** (yr. ended 12/31/98): Assets,
$17,620,317 (M); gifts received, $2,799,354;
expenditures, $5,243,749; qualifying
distributions, $5,085,841; giving activities
include $468,572 for 27 grants (high: $75,000;
low: $1,000; average: $100–$5,000) and
$3,699,332 for 4 foundation-administered
programs.
**Purpose and activities:** The Benton Foundation's
mission is to realize the social benefits made
possible by the public interest use of
communications, because the foundation
believes that communications in the public
interest is essential to a strong democracy. The
foundation bridges the worlds of philanthropy,
community practice, and public policy. It
develops and provides effective information and
communication tools and strategies to equip
and engage individuals and organizations in the
emerging digital and communications
environment.
**Fields of interest:** Media/communications;
arts/cultural programs; libraries/library science;
health care; children & youth, services; public
policy, research; telecommunications.
**Types of support:** Conferences/seminars;
internship funds; research; technical assistance.
**Limitations:** Applications not accepted.
**Publications:** Program policy statement,
occasional report, informational brochure,
financial statement, newsletter.
**Application information:** Disbursements
primarily through operating projects initiated by
the board of directors; few direct grants awarded.
*Board meeting date(s):* Mar. and Nov.
**Officers and Directors:*** Charles Benton,*
Chair.; Larry Kirkman,* Pres.; Karen Menichelli,
Exec. V.P.; Henry Rivera,* Treas.; Susan N. Bales,
Dir. of Children's Prog.; Anne Green, Dir.,
Grantmaking; Doug Moss, Dir., Finance and
Admin.; David Weiner, Dir., Newstadt Ctr.;
Michael Litz, C.T.O.; Mark Lloyd,* Genl.
Counsel; Worth Bruntjen, Robert Furniss, Harold
Richman, Terry Tinson Saario, Jorge Reina
Schement, Paul Simon.
**Number of staff:** 19 full-time professional; 1
part-time professional; 4 full-time support.
**EIN:** 136075750

**117**
**The Robert and Mary Haft Foundation,
Inc.**
3000 K St., N.W., Ste. 105
Washington, DC 20007
*Contact:* Robert M. Haft, Pres.

Established in 1997 in MD.
**Donor(s):** Mary Z. Haft, Robert M. Haft.
**Grantmaker type:** Independent foundation
**Financial data** (yr. ended 12/31/97): Assets,
$1,291,213 (M); gifts received, $1,453,820;
expenditures, $50,680; qualifying distributions,
$50,530; giving activities include $44,050 for
14 grants (high: $6,300; low: $100).
**Purpose and activities:** Giving primarily to
education, health care, children and youth
services, philanthropy and voluntarism groups,
and religious organizations.
**Fields of interest:** Libraries (public); reading;
hospitals (specialty); speech & hearing centers;
health associations; children & youth, services;
international relief; foundations (private

operating); philanthropy/voluntarism; Roman Catholic agencies & churches.
**Application information:**
*Initial approach:* Proposal
*Deadline(s):* None
**Officers:** Robert M. Haft, Pres.; Mary Z. Haft, V.P.
**EIN:** 522034198

## 118
## National Home Library Foundation
1920 N St., N.W., Ste. 300
Washington, DC 20036 (202) 293-3860
*Contact:* Lynda J. Robb, Pres.

Incorporated in 1932 in DC.
**Donor(s):** Sherman F. Mittell.‡
**Grantmaker type:** Independent foundation
**Financial data** (yr. ended 12/31/98): Assets, $913,459 (M); expenditures, $122,821; qualifying distributions, $106,216; giving activities include $88,829 for 22 grants (high: $15,000; low: $899).
**Purpose and activities:** To assist in the distribution of books and other forms of reading materials to libraries and to community groups with limited resources or abilities to otherwise procure these materials; to assist in the support, promotion and development of programs with the goal of combating illiteracy and/or to encourage an interest in reading and the literary arts among all ages; and to encourage the development of programs relating primarily to literary or cultural topics that utilize various means of communications.
**Fields of interest:** Media/communications; language & linguistics; literature; adult education—literacy & basic skills; libraries/library science; reading.
**Types of support:** Matching/challenge support.
**Limitations:** No grants to individuals, or for building or endowment funds, operating budgets, conferences, scholarships, fellowships, or matching gifts; no loans.
**Publications:** Multi-year report (including application guidelines).
**Application information:** Application form not required.
*Initial approach:* Proposal
*Copies of proposal:* 1
*Deadline(s):* Submit application 4 weeks prior to board meetings
*Board meeting date(s):* Mar., June, and Oct.
*Final notification:* 3 months
**Officers and Directors:*** Lynda J. Robb,* Pres.; Alice B. Popkin,* V.P.; Ervin S. Duggan,* Secy.-Treas.; Heidi I. Halleck, Exec. Dir.; Michael R. Gardner, Bernard M.W. Knox, Leonard H. Marks, Ann Bradford Mathias.
**Number of staff:** 1 part-time professional; 1 part-time support.
**EIN:** 526051013

## 119
## The Leonard & Elaine Silverstein Family Foundation
(Formerly Silverstein Family Foundation)
1776 K St., N.W., Ste. 800
Washington, DC 20006-2301

Established in 1965 in DC.
**Donor(s):** Leonard L. Silverstein.
**Grantmaker type:** Independent foundation

**Financial data** (yr. ended 11/30/99): Assets, $825,430 (M); gifts received, $62,062; expenditures, $83,800; qualifying distributions, $75,269; giving activities include $71,500 for 10 grants (high: $20,000; low: $500).
**Purpose and activities:** Giving primarily for the arts and education.
**Fields of interest:** Museums; performing arts; historic preservation/historical societies; elementary/secondary education; libraries (special).
**Limitations:** Applications not accepted. Giving primarily in Washington, DC. No grants to individuals.
**Application information:** Contributes only to pre-selected organizations.
**Officers:** Elaine W. Silverstein, Pres.; Leonard L. Silverstein, V.P.; Susan Silverstein Scott, Secy.-Treas.
**EIN:** 520845731

## 120
## Special Libraries Association
(also known as SLA)
1700 18th St., N.W.
Washington, DC 20009 (202) 234-4700
*Contact:* David Bender, Exec. Dir.; or Lynn Woodbury
*FAX:* (202) 265-9317; E-mail: RESEARCH@SLA.org; URL: http://www.SLA.org

Established in 1909 in NY.
**Grantmaker type:** Public charity
**Financial data** (yr. ended 12/31/97): Assets, $9,593,252 (L); gifts received, $501,094; expenditures, $6,467,689; giving activities include $32,490 for grants to individuals.
**Purpose and activities:** The association advances the leadership role of the special librarian/information professional by putting knowledge to work in society. Funded research must focus on one of the areas specified in the association's Research Agenda: future technology in the special library; current user issues; measures of productivity and value; client-user satisfaction measures; and staffing.
**Fields of interest:** Libraries (special); education, information services.
**Types of support:** Research.
**Publications:** Annual report, informational brochure, newsletter, financial statement, application guidelines.
**Application information:** Grant applicant must be member of library or information science profession. The majority of grant awards are made from restricted funds. Application form required.
*Initial approach:* Letter
*Deadline(s):* Feb. 28
*Board meeting date(s):* Jan., June, and Oct.
*Final notification:* Shortly after June board meeting
**Officers and Directors:*** Susan D. Mattia,* Pres.; David Bender, Exec. Dir.
**Number of staff:** 22 full-time professional; 1 part-time professional; 14 full-time support; 2 part-time support.
**EIN:** 135404745

## 121
## The Telecommunications Infrastructure Assistance Fund for the City of Washington, D.C., Inc.
1401 New York Ave., N.W., Ste. 600
Washington, DC 20005-6200

Established in 1997 in DC as a company-sponsored operating foundation.
**Donor(s):** Bell Atlantic - Washington, DC, Inc.
**Grantmaker type:** Operating foundation
**Financial data** (yr. ended 12/31/98): Assets, $1,208,280 (M); gifts received, $2,000,000; expenditures, $2,781,044; qualifying distributions, $2,781,044; giving activities include $2,781,044 for foundation-administered programs.
**Purpose and activities:** Giving to provide public schools and libraries with high speed connections to the internet and local computer networks.
**Fields of interest:** Elementary/secondary education; libraries/library science; telecommunications.
**Limitations:** Applications not accepted. Giving limited to Washington, DC. No grants to individuals.
**Application information:** Contributes only to pre-selected organizations.
**Officers and Directors:*** Marlene L. Johnson,* Pres.; Joyce Clements-Smith,* V.P.; Ulysses Keyes,* Secy.; Alan Bobowski, Treas.; Marie C. Johns, Deborah M. Royster.
**EIN:** 522026610

## 122
## Wilkes, Artis, Hedrick & Lane Foundation
1666 K St., N.W., Ste. 300
Washington, DC 20006-2866 (202) 457-7800
*Contact:* Robert L. Gorham, Pres.

Established in 1982 in DC.
**Donor(s):** Wilkes, Artis, Hedrick & Lane, Norman M. Glasgow, Sr., Albert L. Ledgard, Jr., Stanley J. Fineman, Whayne S. Quin, Allen Jones, Jr., Robert L. Gorham, Charles A. Camalier III, C. Francis Murphy, Maureen E. Dwyer, Joseph B. Whitebread, Jr.
**Grantmaker type:** Company-sponsored foundation
**Financial data** (yr. ended 09/30/99): Assets, $70,920 (M); gifts received, $79,502; expenditures, $75,852; qualifying distributions, $75,337; giving activities include $75,305 for 51 grants (high: $12,600; low: $25).
**Purpose and activities:** Giving primarily for higher education.
**Fields of interest:** Arts/cultural programs; higher education; libraries/library science; hospitals (general); community development; general charitable giving.
**Limitations:** Giving primarily in Washington, DC. No grants to individuals.
**Application information:** Application form not required.
*Initial approach:* Letter
*Deadline(s):* None
**Officers and Directors:*** Robert L. Gorham,* Pres.; Stanley J. Fineman,* V.P.; Norman M. Glasgow, Jr.,* V.P.; Whayne S. Quin,* Secy.; Joseph B. Whitebread, Jr.,* Treas.
**EIN:** 521272246

# FLORIDA

## 123
## BCR Foundation, Inc.
P.O. Box 13307
Pensacola, FL 32591-3307 (850) 438-2509
*Contact:* Betty G. Rainwater, Pres.

Established in 1986.
**Grantmaker type:** Independent foundation
**Financial data** (yr. ended 08/31/99): Assets,
$6,843,413 (M); expenditures, $110,645;
qualifying distributions, $51,600; giving
activities include $51,600 for 14 grants (high:
$10,200; low: $1,000).
**Purpose and activities:** Giving primarily for
social services, including programs for children;
support also for arts and culture, and
conservation.
**Fields of interest:** Orchestra (symphony);
libraries (public); natural resource conservation
& protection; wildlife, sanctuaries; human
services; children & youth, services; aging,
centers & services.
**Types of support:** Capital campaigns;
emergency funds; matching/challenge support.
**Limitations:** Giving primarily in FL. No grants to
individuals.
**Application information:** Application form not
required.
　*Deadline(s):* None
**Officers and Trustees:*** Betty Gregg Rainwater,*
Pres. and Treas.; Betty Nickenson,* Secy.
**Number of staff:** 1
**EIN:** 592728836

## 124
## Community Services of Bay County, Inc.
P.O. Box 15483
Panama City, FL 32406

Established in 1980.
**Grantmaker type:** Independent foundation
**Financial data** (yr. ended 12/31/98): Assets,
$2,920,276 (M); expenditures, $141,946;
qualifying distributions, $128,460; giving
activities include $103,000 for 25 grants (high:
$20,000; low: $500).
**Purpose and activities:** Giving primarily to
health and human services.
**Fields of interest:** Museums (children's);
orchestra (symphony); college
(community/junior); libraries/library science;
animal welfare; hospitals (general); cerebral
palsy; muscular dystrophy; boys & girls clubs;
youth development, scouting agencies (general);
youth development, business; American Red
Cross; Salvation Army; children & youth,
services; family services; federated giving
programs.
**Limitations:** Applications not accepted. Giving
limited to FL. No grants to individuals.
**Application information:** Contributes only to
pre-selected organizations.
**Officers:** Lola Bowditch, Pres.; John Holloman,
V.P.; Shirley Philips, 2nd V.P.; Rick Fulton, 3rd
V.P. and Admin.; Kathy Stanley, Secy.; Richard
Youd, Treas.

**Directors:** Milton Acton, Richard Cueroni,
Charley Gramling, K.C. Holyfield, Rayford
Lloyd, Louella Washington, Clark Whitehorn.
**EIN:** 591681213

## 125
## The Doyle Foundation, Inc.
14 Ambleside Dr.
Clearwater, FL 33756
*Contact:* Frederick E. Fisher, Secy.
*Application address:* 1166 Lindenwood Dr.,
Tarpon Springs, FL 34689, tel.: (727) 942-7003

Established in 1995 in FL.
**Grantmaker type:** Independent foundation
**Financial data** (yr. ended 12/31/99): Assets,
$4,236,941 (M); expenditures, $154,541;
qualifying distributions, $147,402; giving
activities include $148,250 for 13 grants (high:
$50,000; low: $2,250).
**Purpose and activities:** Giving primarily for
youth services.
**Fields of interest:** Libraries (public); recreation,
community facilities; youth development;
religion.
**Limitations:** Giving limited to FL.
**Application information:** Application form
required.
　*Copies of proposal:* 4
　*Deadline(s):* Nov. 30
**Officers:** Daniel M. Doyle, Pres.; Rosaleen J.
Doyle, V.P.; Frederick E. Fisher, Secy.
**Directors:** Margaret Doyle Carter, Daniel M.
Doyle, Jr.
**EIN:** 593311469

## 126
## Eagles Memorial Foundation, Inc.
4710 14th St. W.
Bradenton, FL 34207 (941) 758-5456
*Contact:* Thomas J. McGriff, Exec. Secy.
*Application address:* c/o Richard J. Steinberg,
Golden Eagle Fund, P.O. Box 25916,
Milwaukee, WI 53225-0916

Established in 1944.
**Grantmaker type:** Public charity
**Financial data** (yr. ended 05/31/98): Assets,
$16,699,438; gifts received, $556,302;
expenditures, $1,445,891.
**Purpose and activities:** Grants to organizations
are made through the Golden Eagle Fund,
which supports the aged, nutrition, public
libraries, and Eagle Village, Inc. The foundation
supports scientific research to discover the
cause, treatment, and possible cure for
Alzheimer's disease. The foundation also gives
for educational and medical purposes to
children of deceased Eagle servicemen and
women, law officers, firefighters, and EMS
workers.
**Fields of interest:** Libraries/library science;
nutrition; aging, centers & services; aging;
economically disadvantaged.
**Types of support:** Program development;
research; grants to individuals; scholarships—to
individuals.
**Limitations:** Giving on a national basis. No
grants to individuals (except for scholarships
and medical expense assistance to Eagle
members and families), hospices, private
nursing homes, or Aerie clubs.

**Publications:** Financial statement, informational
brochure.
**Application information:** Alzheimer grant
requests must include research project
description sheet written on the letterhead of the
applying medical institution. Application form
required.
　*Copies of proposal:* 1
　*Deadline(s):* None
**Officers and Directors:*** E.L. "Bud" Collett,*
Chair.; Dale E. Webster,* Vice-Chair.; Thomas J.
McGriff,* Exec. Secy.; Vincent Cherry,* Secy.;
Richard Downer, James Valentine.
**EIN:** 396126176

## 127
## Elizabeth Eaton Charitable Trust
(Formerly Charles & Elizabeth Eaton Charitable
Trust)
c/o First Union National Bank
5327 Gulf Dr.
Holmes Beach, FL 34217
*Contact:* R. Chris Jones, Trust Off., First Union
National Bank

Established in 1969 in FL.
**Grantmaker type:** Independent foundation
**Financial data** (yr. ended 12/31/99): Assets,
$1,192,128 (M); gifts received, $52,223;
expenditures, $76,351; qualifying distributions,
$53,462; giving activities include $52,223 for
11 grants (high: $11,121; low: $500).
**Purpose and activities:** Giving to cultural and
educational institutions.
**Fields of interest:** Museums; history &
archaeology; higher education; libraries/library
science.
**Types of support:** General/operating support.
**Limitations:** Giving limited to Manatee County,
FL. No grants to individuals.
**Application information:** Application form not
required.
　*Copies of proposal:* 3
　*Deadline(s):* None
　*Board meeting date(s):* Varies
　*Final notification:* Dec.
**Trustee:** First Union National Bank.
**Number of staff:** None.
**EIN:** 596234709

## 128
## The Flaherty Family Foundation
c/o William Flaherty
315 Chapel Hill Rd.
Palm Beach, FL 33480-4124

Established in 1990 in NY.
**Donor(s):** Clementina S. Flaherty, William E.
Flaherty.
**Grantmaker type:** Independent foundation
**Financial data** (yr. ended 12/31/99): Assets, $0
(M); gifts received, $809,785; expenditures,
$758,583; qualifying distributions, $758,583;
giving activities include $743,680 for 85 grants
(high: $75,000; low: $20).
**Purpose and activities:** Giving primarily for
human services.
**Fields of interest:** Arts/cultural programs; higher
education; libraries (school); education; natural
resource conservation & protection; hospitals
(general); human services; children & youth,
services.

**Limitations:** Applications not accepted. Giving primarily in FL and NY. No grants to individuals.
**Application information:** Contributes only to pre-selected organizations.
**Trustees:** Clementina S. Flaherty, William E. Flaherty.
**EIN:** 133599123

## 129
## Fred O. Funkhouser Charitable Foundation
2122 Devonshire Way
Palm Beach Gardens, FL  33418

**Grantmaker type:** Independent foundation
**Financial data** (yr. ended 08/31/99): Assets, $2,471,122 (M); expenditures, $359,509; qualifying distributions, $250,000; giving activities include $250,000 for 7 grants (high: $100,000; low: $5,000).
**Purpose and activities:** Giving for education and public libraries.
**Fields of interest:** Higher education; libraries (public).
**Limitations:** Applications not accepted. Giving primarily in VA. No grants to individuals.
**Application information:** Contributes only to pre-selected organizations.
**Trustee:** Janice Scaglione.
**EIN:** 656243936

## 130
## Green Family Foundation, Inc.
2601 S. Bayshore Dr., Ste. 1775
Coconut Grove, FL  33133

Established in 1991 in FL.
**Donor(s):** Steven J. Green.
**Grantmaker type:** Independent foundation
**Financial data** (yr. ended 12/31/99): Assets, $9,216,898 (M); gifts received, $541,702; expenditures, $1,804,891; qualifying distributions, $1,802,311; giving activities include $1,527,528 for 37 grants (high: $411,594; low: $250).
**Purpose and activities:** Giving primarily for arts and culture, education and human services.
**Fields of interest:** Museums (art); arts/cultural programs; higher education; libraries/library science; education; hospitals (general); human services; American Red Cross; federated giving programs.
**Limitations:** Applications not accepted. Giving primarily in FL. No grants to individuals.
**Application information:** Contributes only to pre-selected organizations.
**Officer:** Jeffrey A. Sapchik, Pres.
**Director:** Kimberly Green.
**EIN:** 650284913

## 131
## The Thomas M. and Irene B. Kirbo Charitable Trust ▼
112 W. Adams St., Ste. 1111
Jacksonville, FL  32202  (904) 354-7212
*Contact:* R. Murray Jenks, Pres.

Established in 1959 in GA.
**Donor(s):** Thomas M. Kirbo,‡ Irene B. Kirbo.
**Grantmaker type:** Independent foundation

**Financial data** (yr. ended 09/30/98): Assets, $50,098,882 (M); expenditures, $3,923,921; qualifying distributions, $3,729,095; giving activities include $3,189,600 for 105 grants (high: $225,000; low: $1,150; average: $5,000–$50,000).
**Purpose and activities:** Giving primarily for religion, hospitals, universities, and youth.
**Fields of interest:** Higher education; libraries/library science; hospitals (general); youth, services; Christian agencies & churches.
**Limitations:** Giving primarily in FL and GA. No grants to individuals.
**Application information:** Application form required.
    *Deadline(s):* None
**Officers and Trustees:\*** Bruce W. Kirbo,\* Chair.; R. Murray Jenks,\* Pres.; John T. Jenks, Margaret L. Kirbo.
**EIN:** 592151720
**Recent grants for library/information services:**
131-1 Decatur County Board of Education, Bainbridge, GA, $109,000. For public school libraries. 1998.

## 132
## Kenneth A. Lattman Foundation, Inc.
721 Biltmore Way, Ste. 302
Coral Gables, FL  33134
*Contact:* Elliott Abramson, Dir.

Established in 1997 in FL.
**Grantmaker type:** Independent foundation
**Financial data** (yr. ended 12/31/99): Assets, $1,926,424 (M); gifts received, $192; expenditures, $117,814; qualifying distributions, $112,624; giving activities include $113,980 for 26 grants (high: $35,000; low: $50).
**Purpose and activities:** Giving for health and human services, and for Jewish organizations.
**Fields of interest:** Orchestra (symphony); higher education; medical school/education; libraries (academic/research).
**Limitations:** Giving primarily in FL.
**Application information:** Application form not required.
    *Initial approach:* Letter
    *Deadline(s):* None
**Directors:** Elliott Abramson, Jerome Abramson, Shelley Abramson, Alex Lattman, Norma Lattman, Daniel Lyons, Monica Lyons.
**EIN:** 311466884

## 133
## Carmen Rebozo Foundation, Inc.
c/o Charles Rebozo
1570 Madruga Ave., Ste. 305
Coral Gables, FL  33146  (305) 704-0022
*Contact:* Olga Guilarte, Secy.

Established in 1985 in FL.
**Donor(s):** Charles G. Rebozo,‡ Mary Bouterse.
**Grantmaker type:** Independent foundation
**Financial data** (yr. ended 06/30/99): Assets, $12,339,437 (M); gifts received, $4,317,032; expenditures, $1,113,182; qualifying distributions, $1,043,343; giving activities include $1,071,500 for 2 grants (high: $541,500; low: $530,000).
**Purpose and activities:** Giving primarily to benefit a private library, and for a Boys and Girls club.

**Fields of interest:** Libraries/library science; boys & girls clubs.
**Limitations:** Applications not accepted. Giving primarily in FL. No grants to individuals.
**Application information:** Contributes only to pre-selected organizations.
**Officers and Directors:\*** Robert H. Abplanalp,\* Chair. and Pres.; Tricia Nixon Cox,\* V.P.; Julie Nixon Eisenhower,\* V.P.; Charles F. Rebozo,\* V.P.; Thomas H. Wakefield,\* V.P.; Olga Guilarte,\* Secy.; Mary Bouterse, Christina Gilbert.
**EIN:** 592667397

## 134
## Schultz Foundation, Inc.
Schultz Bldg.
P.O. Box 1200
Jacksonville, FL  32201  (904) 354-3603
*Contact:* John R. Schultz, V.P.
*Application address:* 118 W. Adams St., Ste. 600, Jacksonville, FL 32202

Established in 1964 in FL.
**Donor(s):** Mae W. Schultz,‡ Genevieve S. Ayers,‡ Frederick H. Schultz, Nancy R. Schultz.
**Grantmaker type:** Independent foundation
**Financial data** (yr. ended 12/31/99): Assets, $5,375,244 (M); expenditures, $158,322; qualifying distributions, $100,750; giving activities include $100,750 for grants.
**Fields of interest:** Media/communications; film/video; visual arts; museums; performing arts; dance; music; history & archaeology; historic preservation/historical societies; arts/cultural programs; early childhood education; adult/continuing education; libraries/library science; education; natural resource conservation & protection; environment; wildlife preservation & protection; hospitals (general); family planning; health care; substance abuse, services; AIDS; AIDS research; youth development, services; human services; children & youth, services; civil rights; urban/community development; federated giving programs; government/public administration; leadership development; Christian agencies & churches; minorities; general charitable giving.
**Types of support:** General/operating support.
**Limitations:** Giving primarily in Jacksonville, FL, and GA. No grants to individuals.
**Publications:** Annual report.
**Application information:** Telephone calls not considered. Application form not required.
    *Initial approach:* Letter
    *Deadline(s):* None
    *Board meeting date(s):* Dec.
**Officers and Trustees:\*** Clifford G. Schultz II,\* Pres.; John R. Schultz, V.P.; Catherine Kelly, Frederick H. Schultz, Jr., Nancy R. Schultz.
**Number of staff:** 1 part-time professional.
**EIN:** 591055869

## 135
## Louis C. Skinner Foundation, Inc.
c/o Ronald Herzog, CPA
300 Sevilla Ave., Ste. 215
Coral Gables, FL  33134

Established in 1984 in FL.
**Donor(s):** Louis C. Skinner, Jr.

**Grantmaker type:** Independent foundation
**Financial data** (yr. ended 09/30/99): Assets, $120,649 (M); gifts received, $257,772; expenditures, $250,086; qualifying distributions, $250,058; giving activities include $250,000 for 1 grant.
**Purpose and activities:** Giving to education and libraries.
**Fields of interest:** Libraries (school).
**Limitations:** Applications not accepted. Giving primarily in Asheville, NC. No grants to individuals.
**Application information:** Contributes only to pre-selected organizations.
**Officers and Directors:*** Louis C. Skinner,* Pres.; Ronald E. Herzog,* V.P.
**EIN:** 133247530

## 136
## The Spurlino Foundation
4809 A Ehrlich Rd.
Tampa, FL 33624
*Contact:* Cyrus W. Spurlino, Tr.
*Application address:* 7224 N. Mobley Rd., Odessa, FL 33556

Established in 1986 in FL.
**Donor(s):** Cyrus W. Spurlino.
**Grantmaker type:** Independent foundation
**Financial data** (yr. ended 11/30/99): Assets, $4,795,016 (L); gifts received, $1,756,165; expenditures, $120,000; qualifying distributions, $120,000; giving activities include $120,000 for 20 grants (high: $10,000; low: $3,000).
**Purpose and activities:** Giving for children's services, higher education, and federated giving programs.
**Fields of interest:** University; libraries/library science; health associations; children & youth, services; federated giving programs.
**Limitations:** Giving primarily in Tampa, FL. No grants to individuals.
**Application information:** Application form not required.
*Deadline(s):* None
**Trustee:** Cyrus W. Spurlino.
**EIN:** 596875441

## 137
## The Toffey Family Charitable Trust
12784 Mariner Ct.
Palm City, FL 34990

Established in 1990.
**Donor(s):** H. James Toffey, Mrs. H. James Toffey.
**Grantmaker type:** Independent foundation
**Financial data** (yr. ended 06/30/98): Assets, $1,217,238 (M); gifts received, $661,500; expenditures, $74,045; qualifying distributions, $73,913; giving activities include $73,913 for 42 grants (high: $50,000; low: $25).
**Fields of interest:** Arts/cultural programs; higher education; libraries/library science; health associations; federated giving programs; religion.
**Limitations:** Applications not accepted. Giving primarily in Hanover, NH. No grants to individuals.
**Application information:** Contributes only to pre-selected organizations.
**Trustees:** Debora Toffey Puckette, H. James Toffey, James W. Toffey, Sally N. Toffey.
**EIN:** 136955166

## 138
## Dr. Richard D. Williams Foundation
(Formerly Richard D. Williams, Slatington Scholarship Fund and Trust)
1314 N. Lakeside Dr.
Lake Worth, FL 33460-1918
*Contact:* Richard Williams, Tr.

Established in 1992 in PA.
**Donor(s):** Richard D. Williams.
**Grantmaker type:** Independent foundation
**Financial data** (yr. ended 12/31/99): Assets, $1,742,611 (M); gifts received, $70,000; expenditures, $86,147; qualifying distributions, $85,422; giving activities include $85,205 for 12 grants (high: $32,275; low: $655).
**Purpose and activities:** Giving to higher education.
**Fields of interest:** Higher education; libraries/library science.
**Types of support:** Scholarship funds; scholarships—to individuals.
**Limitations:** Giving primarily in FL and PA.
**Application information:** Applicants chosen by guidance counselor of high school; approved by trustees. Application form not required.
**Trustees:** Howard Cyr, Gerald Geiger, Richard D. Williams.
**EIN:** 526490235

# GEORGIA

## 139
## Arnold Fund
c/o Alston & Bird, 1 Atlantic Ctr.
1201 W. Peachtree St., Ste. 4200
Atlanta, GA 30309-3400 (404) 881-7886
*Contact:* John C. Sawyer, Exec. Dir.

Established in 1952 in GA.
**Donor(s):** Florence Arnold,‡ Robert O. Arnold.‡
**Grantmaker type:** Independent foundation
**Financial data** (yr. ended 12/31/99): Assets, $27,081,521 (M); expenditures, $1,368,150; qualifying distributions, $1,149,123; giving activities include $1,171,991 for 47 grants (high: $200,000; low: $500).
**Fields of interest:** Performing arts; music; higher education; libraries/library science; education; biomedicine; medical research.
**Limitations:** Giving primarily in Newton County, GA. No grants to individuals.
**Application information:**
*Initial approach:* Letter
*Deadline(s):* None
*Board meeting date(s):* Spring and fall
**Officer:** John C. Sawyer, Exec. Dir.
**Trustees:** Robert Fowler III, David Newman, Frank Turner.
**Number of staff:** None.
**EIN:** 586032079

## 140
## The Azalea Foundation
(Formerly JVM & JKM Foundation)
P.O. Box 20567
St. Simons Island, GA 31522
*Contact:* Jeanne Manning, Pres.

Established in 1993.
**Grantmaker type:** Independent foundation
**Financial data** (yr. ended 11/30/99): Assets, $10,000,000 (M); expenditures, $553,217; qualifying distributions, $470,870; giving activities include $470,870 for 63 grants (average: $140–$45,000).
**Purpose and activities:** Giving primarily for education, youth services, health, and the arts.
**Fields of interest:** Media/communications; museums; arts/cultural programs; libraries/library science; education; children & youth, services.
**Limitations:** Giving on a national basis, with some emphasis on Slynn County, GA, and Santa Fe County, NM. No grants to individuals.
**Application information:** Contributes mostly to pre-selected organizations. Applications accepted only from Slynn County, GA and Santa Fe County, NM areas, and from projects serving children and families at risk.
*Initial approach:* Letter
*Board meeting date(s):* Varies
**Officers and Trustees:*** Jeanne K. Manning,* Pres.; James V. Manning,* V.P.
**EIN:** 226617071

## 141
## Callaway Foundation, Inc. ▼
209 Broome St.
P.O. Box 790
La Grange, GA 30241 (706) 884-7348
*Contact:* J.T. Gresham, Pres.
*FAX:* (706) 884-0201

Incorporated in 1943 in GA.
**Donor(s):** Textile Benefit Assn., Callaway Mills, Callaway Institute, Inc.
**Grantmaker type:** Independent foundation
**Financial data** (yr. ended 09/30/99): Assets, $216,456,504 (M); expenditures, $10,521,782; qualifying distributions, $9,474,057; giving activities include $9,310,092 for 77 grants (high: $1,158,319; low: $500; average: $1,000–$100,000) and $965,800 for 5 in-kind gifts.
**Purpose and activities:** Giving for elementary, higher, and secondary education, including libraries and buildings, and equipment; health and hospitals; community funds; care for the aged; community development; historic preservation; and church support.
**Fields of interest:** Historic preservation/historical societies; elementary school/education; secondary school/education; higher education; libraries/library science; education; hospitals (general); health care; health associations; aging, centers & services; community development; Christian agencies & churches; aging; general charitable giving.
**Types of support:** General/operating support; continuing support; annual campaigns; capital campaigns; building/renovation; equipment; land acquisition; in-kind gifts; matching/challenge support.

**Limitations:** Giving primarily in GA, with emphasis on the City of La Grange and Troup County. No grants to individuals, or for endowment funds, deficit financing, scholarships, or fellowships; no loans.
**Publications:** Annual report (including application guidelines).
**Application information:** Application form not required.
*Initial approach:* Letter
*Copies of proposal:* 1
*Deadline(s):* End of month preceding board meetings
*Board meeting date(s):* Jan., Apr., July, and Oct.
*Final notification:* 2 months
**Officers:** J.T. Gresham, Pres., Treas., and Genl. Mgr.; D. Ray McKenzie, Jr., V.P.; C.L. Pitts, Secy.
**Trustees:** Mark Clayton Callaway, Jane Alice Craig, Ellen H. Harris, Charles D. Hudson, Jr., Ida H. Hughes.
**Number of staff:** None.
**EIN:** 580566147
**Recent grants for library/information services:**
141-1 Troup-Harris-Coweta Regional Library, La Grange, GA, $175,768. For Integrated Library Computer System. 1999.

**142**
**Paul & Mary Cancellarini Charitable Trust**
864 Ashfield Dr.
Decatur, GA 30030

Established in 1995 in CT and GA.
**Grantmaker type:** Independent foundation
**Financial data** (yr. ended 12/31/98): Assets, $1,550,301 (M); expenditures, $92,736; qualifying distributions, $75,337; giving activities include $75,431 for 8 grants (high: $16,776; low: $6,710).
**Purpose and activities:** Giving primarily for education, health, and religious organizations.
**Fields of interest:** Libraries/library science; education; hospitals (general); nursing care; cancer; eye diseases; Roman Catholic agencies & churches.
**Limitations:** Applications not accepted. Giving limited to CT. No grants to individuals.
**Application information:** Contributes only to pre-selected organizations.
**Trustees:** Keith Mattioli, Wallace Mattioli.
**EIN:** 066414334

**143**
**Georgia Humanities Council**
(Formerly Georgia Endowment for the Humanities)
50 Hurt Plz., S.E., Ste. 1565
Atlanta, GA 30303-2915 (404) 523-6220
*Contact:* Laura Thomson, Prog. Off.
*FAX:* (404) 523-5702; E-mail: info@georgiahumanities.org; URL: http://www.georgiahumanities.org

Established in 1971 in GA.
**Grantmaker type:** Public charity
**Financial data** (yr. ended 10/31/99): Assets, $915,806 (L); gifts received, $616,523; expenditures, $777,050; giving activities include $121,284 for grants.
**Purpose and activities:** The council supports humanities-based projects in Georgia and works to promote public awareness about humanities

topics through special events, book discussions, and an awards banquet honoring humanities leaders.
**Fields of interest:** Museums; humanities; libraries (public); education.
**Types of support:** Program development; conferences/seminars.
**Limitations:** Giving limited to GA. No grants to individuals, or for overhead, construction, entertainment, travel, research, or creative/performing arts programs.
**Publications:** Newsletter, multi-year report, application guidelines.
**Application information:** See Web site for further information and application forms. Application form required.
*Initial approach:* Letter or telephone
*Deadline(s):* Feb. 1, Apr. 1, June 1, Aug. 1, Oct. 1, and Dec. 1 for Planning Consultant Grants and Special Program Grants; Apr. 1 and Oct. 1 for Public Program Grants; Apr. 1 for Conference Grants; Oct. 1 for Teacher Enrichment Grants
**Officers and Directors:*** Thomas Dasher, Ph.D.,* Chair.; O. Ben Harris,* Vice-Chair.; Jamil S. Zainaldin,* Pres.; Edward Cashin,* Secy.; Donna Buchanan,* Treas.; and 16 additional directors.
**Number of staff:** 6
**EIN:** 510180861

**144**
**Joe E. Johnston Foundation**
c/o SunTrust Bank, Atlanta
P.O. Box 4655
Atlanta, GA 30302-4655
*Application address:* c/o A. Smith Johnston, 8632 Main St., Woodstock, GA 30188

Established in 1980 in GA.
**Grantmaker type:** Independent foundation
**Financial data** (yr. ended 03/31/99): Assets, $2,386,510 (M); expenditures, $123,443; qualifying distributions, $108,774; giving activities include $100,000 for 19 grants (high: $25,000; low: $1,000).
**Purpose and activities:** Giving primarily for youth programs, community development, and religious organizations.
**Fields of interest:** Libraries (school); children & youth, services; community development; Protestant agencies & churches; general charitable giving.
**Types of support:** General/operating support.
**Limitations:** Giving primarily in Woodstock, GA.
**Application information:**
*Initial approach:* Letter
*Deadline(s):* None
**Officer:** Debbie Couch, Secy.
**Advisors:** Alice Booth, Lynn H. Johnston, Smith L. Johnston.
**Trustee:** SunTrust Bank, Atlanta.
**EIN:** 581364875

**145**
**Margaret Lee Martin Charitable Trust**
P.O. Box 9626
Savannah, GA 31412
*Application address:* The Martin Scholarship Committee, c/o James M. Floyd, Sr., The Hinesville Bank, P.O. Box 1009, Hinesville, GA 31313

Established in 1995 in GA.
**Grantmaker type:** Independent foundation
**Financial data** (yr. ended 12/31/99): Assets, $12,060,057 (M); expenditures, $458,114; qualifying distributions, $400,914; giving activities include $362,468 for 12 grants (high: $158,283; low: $2,083).
**Purpose and activities:** Applicant must be a legal resident of Liberty County, GA, or the child of a legal resident of Liberty County, GA; be in the top 10 percent of their high school class, score a minimum of 1000 on the SAT or the equivalent on the ACT, and must be accepted by and/or attending a regionally accredited college, university, or nursing school.
**Fields of interest:** Museums; arts/cultural programs; libraries/library science; Girl Scouts; federated giving programs; religion.
**Types of support:** Scholarship funds; scholarships—to individuals.
**Limitations:** Giving limited to Liberty County, GA.
**Application information:**
*Deadline(s):* May 1
*Final notification:* varies
**Trustees:** James M. Floyd, Sr., Bank of America.
**Number of staff:** 1 part-time professional.
**EIN:** 586305150

**146**
**Mary Lane Morrison Foundation, Inc.**
5745 Ogeechee Rd.
Savannah, GA 31405-9505
*Contact:* Howard J. Morrison, Jr., Pres.
*E-mail:* howardmorrison@mindspring.com

Established in 1995 in GA.
**Grantmaker type:** Independent foundation
**Financial data** (yr. ended 12/31/98): Assets, $2,403,472 (M); expenditures, $102,267; qualifying distributions, $96,665; giving activities include $94,250 for 42 grants (high: $15,000; low: $250).
**Purpose and activities:** Giving for higher education, libraries, and family planning.
**Fields of interest:** Higher education; libraries/library science; education; family planning.
**Limitations:** Giving primarily in GA. No grants to individuals.
**Application information:**
*Initial approach:* Letter
*Copies of proposal:* 1
*Deadline(s):* None
*Board meeting date(s):* Dec. 1
*Final notification:* Dec. 1
**Officers:** Howard J. Morrison, Jr., Pres.; Mary Reynolds Morrison, V.P.; Mary Thiesen Morrison, Secy.; Howard J. Morrison III, Treas.
**EIN:** 582173256

## 147
### The Newland Family Foundation, Inc.
(Formerly The DSN Foundation)
230 Hampton Ct.
Athens, GA  30605-1404  (706) 543-3938
*Contact:* Dorothy Sams Newland, Pres.
*FAX:* (706) 354-6694; E-mail:
dorothy-jim-newland@juno.com

Established in 1994 in GA.
**Donor(s):** Dorothy Sams Newland.
**Grantmaker type:** Independent foundation
**Financial data** (yr. ended 12/31/99): Assets,
$1,923,277 (M); expenditures, $97,040;
qualifying distributions, $94,369; giving
activities include $91,000 for 17 grants (high:
$10,000; low: $2,000).
**Purpose and activities:** To support programs
primarily in the areas of human social services
with emphasis on those benefiting the elderly
and children; education, including libraries;
health; and the environment; with an emphasis
on those programs within the Athens-Clarke
County, GA, area.
**Fields of interest:** Libraries/library science;
education; environment; housing/shelter,
homeless; aging, centers & services; boys & girls
clubs; youth development; Protestant agencies
& churches.
**Types of support:** General/operating support;
capital campaigns; building/renovation;
equipment; emergency funds; program
development; seed money; curriculum
development; matching/challenge support.
**Limitations:** Giving primarily in GA.
**Publications:** Annual report, informational
brochure (including application guidelines).
**Application information:** Application form not
required.
*Initial approach:* Letter
*Copies of proposal:* 1
*Deadline(s):* None
*Board meeting date(s):* Quarterly
**Officers and Board Members:*** Dorothy Sams
Newland,* Pres.; Harriet Newland Hulsey,* V.P.;
James L. Newland, Jr.,* V.P.; James L. Newland,*
Secy.-Treas.; R. Drew Hulsey, Jr., Tina Lowe
Newland.
**Number of staff:** None.
**EIN:** 582142455

## 148
### The Price-Campbell Foundation
900 Pineridge Dr.
Valdosta, GA  31602  (912) 242-1348
*Contact:* Barbara K. Passmore, Tr.

**Donor(s):** Mildred M. Price.‡
**Grantmaker type:** Independent foundation
**Financial data** (yr. ended 04/30/99): Assets,
$3,125,186 (M); expenditures, $175,092;
qualifying distributions, $163,582; giving
activities include $142,000 for 12 grants (high:
$25,000; low: $1,000) and $11,250 for 3 grants
to individuals of $3,750 each.
**Purpose and activities:** Awards postgraduate
scholarships in the fields of medicine and law to
students at three universities in GA; support also
for conservation, social services, youth services
and arts.
**Fields of interest:** Higher education; medical
school/education; libraries (public);
scholarships/financial aid; natural resource

conservation & protection; environment; Boy
Scouts; human services.
**Types of support:** Scholarships—to individuals.
**Limitations:** Giving primarily in Lowndes
County, GA.
**Application information:** Application form not
required.
*Initial approach:* Letter or telephone for
guidelines
*Deadline(s):* None
**Trustees:** Lucy Acree, John R. Bennett, Barbara
K. Passmore.
**EIN:** 581530873

## 149
### Lewis Hall & Mildred Sasser Singletary
###   Foundation, Inc.
P.O. Box 1095
Thomasville, GA  31799  (912) 226-1011
*Contact:* Tonya McCorkle
*FAX:* (912) 226-5744

Established in 1990.
**Grantmaker type:** Independent foundation
**Financial data** (yr. ended 12/31/99): Assets,
$36,765,522 (M); gifts received, $11,945;
expenditures, $1,702,318; qualifying
distributions, $1,463,845; giving activities
include $1,463,845 for grants (average:
$1,000–$1,000,000).
**Fields of interest:** Elementary/secondary
education; secondary school/education; libraries
(public); libraries (special); environmental
education; animal welfare; animal population
control; Boy Scouts; YM/YWCAs & YM/YWHAs;
adoption; international affairs; foundations
(community); Christian agencies & churches;
Protestant agencies & churches.
**Types of support:** Seed money;
matching/challenge support.
**Limitations:** Giving limited to the southeastern
U.S. No grants to individuals.
**Application information:** Application guidelines
available. Application form not required.
*Initial approach:* Letter
*Copies of proposal:* 1
*Deadline(s):* Sept. 30
*Board meeting date(s):* Dec.
*Final notification:* Dec.
**Officers and Directors:*** Karen S. Leabo,* Pres.;
Richard L. Singletary,* V.P.; Thomas H. Vann,
Jr.,* Secy.; Richard L. Singletary, Jr.,* Treas.;
Milton Gardner, Greg Hamil, Jeanne S. Hamil, J.
Philip Leabo, J. Philip Leabo, Jr., JoAnn Leabo,
Julia Singletary, Karen L. Singletary, Lewis Hall
Singletary II, Rebecca Singletary, Tim Singletary.
**Number of staff:** 1 part-time professional.
**EIN:** 581906094

## 150
### Williams Family Foundation of Georgia,
###   Inc.
P.O. Box 378
Thomasville, GA  31799
*Contact:* Elizabeth C. Prance, Exec. Secy.
*FAX:* (912) 228-7780

Established in 1980 in GA.
**Donor(s):** Diane W. Parker, Marguerite N.
Williams,‡ Thomas L. Williams III, Bennie G.
Williams.‡

**Grantmaker type:** Independent foundation
**Financial data** (yr. ended 11/30/99): Assets,
$48,078,002 (M); gifts received, $27,922,156;
expenditures, $1,129,171; qualifying
distributions, $937,635; giving activities include
$912,500 for 20 grants (high: $350,000; low:
$1,000).
**Fields of interest:** Visual arts; museums;
performing arts; historic preservation/historical
societies; arts/cultural programs; secondary
school/education; higher education;
libraries/library science; education; natural
resource conservation & protection;
environment; wildlife preservation & protection;
family services; community development;
government/public administration.
**Types of support:** General/operating support;
building/renovation; program development;
matching/challenge support.
**Limitations:** Giving primarily in GA, with
emphasis on Thomasville and Thomas County.
No grants to individuals.
**Publications:** Corporate giving report,
application guidelines, informational brochure
(including application guidelines).
**Application information:** New contributions
limited due to numerous commitments.
Application form required.
*Initial approach:* Letter
*Copies of proposal:* 1
*Deadline(s):* Mar. 15 and Aug. 15
*Board meeting date(s):* May and Oct.
**Officers and Directors:*** Thomas L. Williams
III,* Pres.; Diane W. Parker,* V.P.; Bernard
Lanigan, Jr.,* Treas.; Joseph E. Beverly, Frederick
E. Cooper, Lawrence A. Harmon, Stephen T.
Parker, Thomas W. Parker, Thomas H. Vann, Jr.,
Alston P. Watt.
**Number of staff:** 1 part-time support.
**EIN:** 581414850

# HAWAII

## 151
### The Richard T. Mamiya Charitable
###   Foundation
1001 Bishop St., Pacific Twr., Ste. 1760
Honolulu, HI  96813
*Contact:* Richelle M. Fujioka, Secy.
*Application address:* 1014 Waa Kava Pl.,
Honolulu, HI 96822, tel.: (808) 538-7322

Established in 1983 in HI.
**Grantmaker type:** Independent foundation
**Financial data** (yr. ended 09/30/99): Assets,
$3,505,990 (M); expenditures, $151,385;
qualifying distributions, $129,694; giving
activities include $65,000 for 1 grant.
**Purpose and activities:** Funding to preserve and
organize historical medical records.
**Fields of interest:** Libraries (medical).
**Types of support:** Capital campaigns.
**Limitations:** Giving primarily in HI. No grants to
individuals.
**Application information:** Application form not
required.
*Deadline(s):* None

**Officers:** Richard T. Mamiya, Pres.; Lauree Ann Weaver, V.P.; Richelle M. Fujioka, Secy.; Christin Mamiya, Treas.
**Directors:** Deidre Mamiya, Jonathan Mamiya, Matthew Mamiya, Richard G. Mamiya, Monica McLaren.
**EIN:** 990226498

# IDAHO

## 152
## The ALSAM Foundation ▼
P.O. Box 1760
Eagle, ID  83616   (208) 854-0414
*Contact:* George L. Moosman, Pres.

Established in 1984.
**Donor(s):** L. S. Skaggs.
**Grantmaker type:** Independent foundation
**Financial data** (yr. ended 06/30/99): Assets, $130,626,960 (M); expenditures, $7,418,159; qualifying distributions, $6,600,368; giving activities include $6,271,376 for 15 grants (high: $4,631,501; low: $1,000).
**Purpose and activities:** Giving primarily for education, religion, animal welfare, medical research, and human services.
**Fields of interest:** Arts education; theological school/education; scholarships/financial aid; education; wildlife preservation & protection; medical research; food services; housing/shelter; human services, homeless, human services; Roman Catholic federated giving programs; science, research; religion; economically disadvantaged; homeless; general charitable giving.
**Types of support:** Scholarship funds.
**Limitations:** Applications not accepted. No grants to individuals.
**Application information:** Contributes only to pre-selected organizations. Unsolicited requests for funds not accepted.
**Officer:** George L. Moosman, Pres.
**Trustee:** The Northern Trust Co.
**Number of staff:** 1 full-time professional; 1 part-time professional; 1 part-time support.
**EIN:** 742364289
**Recent grants for library/information services:**
**152-1** Brigham Young University, Provo, UT, $3,000,000. For capital campaign for library addition. 1998.

## 153
## The Campion Foundation
P.O. Box 538
Ketchum, ID  83340
*Contact:* Thomas B. Campion, Pres. or Lynn H. Campion, V.P.

Established in 1993.
**Donor(s):** Thomas B. Campion, Lynn H. Campion, Helen K. and Arthur E. Johnson Foundation.
**Grantmaker type:** Independent foundation
**Financial data** (yr. ended 11/30/98): Assets, $1,774 (M); gifts received, $10,000; expenditures, $80,445; qualifying distributions,

$80,445; giving activities include $80,000 for grants.
**Fields of interest:** Arts/cultural programs; libraries/library science; education; human services; foundations (community).
**Limitations:** Giving primarily in Boise, Hailey, Ketchum, and Sun Valley, ID.
**Application information:**
*Initial approach:* Letter
*Deadline(s):* None
**Officers and Directors:\*** Thomas B. Campion,\* Pres.; Lynn H. Campion,\* V.P.; Ashley Campion, Berit Campion.
**EIN:** 841250400

## 154
## The James & Barbara Cimino Foundation, Inc.
P.O. Box 448
Sun Valley, ID  83353-0448   (208) 622-4556
*Contact:* Christine Bender, Secy.-Treas.

Established in 1995 in ID.
**Donor(s):** James N. Cimino, Barbara Cimino, Robert Cimino.
**Grantmaker type:** Independent foundation
**Financial data** (yr. ended 06/30/99): Assets, $1,254,054 (M); expenditures, $96,898; qualifying distributions, $86,221; giving activities include $87,049 for 16 grants (high: $25,000; low: $1,000).
**Purpose and activities:** Giving primarily for the arts, education, and human services.
**Fields of interest:** Media/communications; humanities; higher education; libraries/library science; natural resource conservation & protection; boys & girls clubs; YM/YWCAs & YM/YWHAs; hospices.
**Limitations:** No grants to individuals.
**Application information:**
*Initial approach:* Letter
*Deadline(s):* None
**Officers and Directors:\*** James N. Cimino,\* Pres.; Barbara Cimino,\* V.P.; Christine Bender,\* Secy.-Treas.; David Cimino, James A. Cimino, Robert Cimino.
**EIN:** 820474867

## 155
## J. R. Simplot Foundation, Inc.
c/o Adelia Simplot, Comm. Rels. Coord.
P.O. Box 27
Boise, ID  83707-0027
*FAX:* (208) 389-7515

Established in 1953.
**Grantmaker type:** Independent foundation
**Financial data** (yr. ended 09/30/99): Assets, $40,841,575 (M); gifts received, $38,593,750; expenditures, $3,450,708; qualifying distributions, $2,551,021; giving activities include $2,507,347 for grants (high: $2,160,965).
**Fields of interest:** Arts/cultural programs; libraries/library science; education; human services; community development, neighborhood development; public affairs, government agencies.
**Types of support:** General/operating support; continuing support; capital campaigns; building/renovation; endowments; scholarship funds; in-kind gifts; matching/challenge support.

**Limitations:** Applications not accepted. Giving limited to ID headquarters and company locations of the J.R. Simplot Co. No grants to individuals.
**Application information:** Contributes only to pre-selected organizations.
**Officers:** J.R. Simplot, Pres.; Don J. Simplot, V.P.; Ronald N. Graves, Secy.; James D. Crawford, Treas.
**EIN:** 826003437

## 156
## The Whittenberger Foundation
(Formerly Claude R. and Ethel B. Whittenberger Foundation)
P.O. Box 1073
Caldwell, ID  83606   (208) 459-3402
*Contact:* William J. Rankin, Chair., or Margaret Gigray, Vice-Chair.
*FAX:* (208) 459-0096

Established in 1970 in ID; commenced grantmaking activities in 1973.
**Donor(s):** Ethel B. Whittenberger.‡
**Grantmaker type:** Independent foundation
**Financial data** (yr. ended 12/31/99): Assets, $6,413,814 (M); expenditures, $391,019; qualifying distributions, $214,128; giving activities include $208,815 for 48 grants (high: $41,763; low: $500; average: $1,000–$5,000).
**Purpose and activities:** Giving for youth and children, and education; some support for cultural programs and public libraries in southwestern ID.
**Fields of interest:** Arts/cultural programs; libraries/library science; education; children & youth, services.
**Limitations:** Giving limited to southwestern ID, with emphasis on Treasure Valley. No grants to individuals, or for endowment funds.
**Publications:** Program policy statement, application guidelines, informational brochure, multi-year report.
**Application information:** Application form required.
*Initial approach:* Letter or telephone requesting application form
*Copies of proposal:* 5
*Deadline(s):* Aug. 31
*Board meeting date(s):* Apr., July, Sept., and Nov.
*Final notification:* Dec.
**Officers:** William J. Rankin, Chair.; Margaret Gigray, Vice-Chair.; Joe Miller, Secy.
**Directors:** D. Whitman Jones, Donald D. Price, M.D.
**Number of staff:** None.
**EIN:** 237092604

# ILLINOIS

## 157
## Allen-Heath Memorial Foundation
222 N. LaSalle St., Ste. 300
Chicago, IL  60601-1081

Incorporated in 1947 in CA.
**Donor(s):** Harriet A. Heath,‡ John E.S. Heath.‡

**Grantmaker type:** Independent foundation
**Financial data** (yr. ended 12/31/99): Assets,
$3,606,064 (M); expenditures, $381,514;
qualifying distributions, $310,000; giving
activities include $310,000 for 24 grants (high:
$28,000; low: $5,000).
**Purpose and activities:** Grants to a limited
number of educational institutions, hospitals,
museums, air safety organizations, and other
charitable institutions.
**Fields of interest:** Museums; arts/cultural
programs; higher education; libraries/library
science; hospitals (general); safety/disasters;
children & youth, services; hospices; aging,
centers & services; women, centers & services;
community development; federated giving
programs; aging; women.
**Types of support:** General/operating support;
program development.
**Limitations:** Applications not accepted. Giving
on a national basis. No support for religious or
foreign organizations, private foundations, or
conduit organizations. No grants to individuals;
no loans.
**Publications:** Annual report.
**Application information:** Contributes only to
pre-selected organizations. Unsolicited requests
for funds not considered.
 *Board meeting date(s):* Nov.
**Officers and Directors:\*** Charles K. Heath,\*
Pres.; Ruth R. Hooper,\* V.P.; James Harbert,
Secy.-Treas.; Nolan H. Baird, Jr.
**Number of staff:** None.
**EIN:** 363056910

## 158
## American Library Association
50 E. Huron St.
Chicago, IL 60611-2795 (800) 545-2433
*Contact:* Peggy Barber, Assoc. Exec. Dir., Comm.
*TDD:* (888) 814-7692; FAX: (312) 440-9374;
E-mail: ala@ala.org; URL: http://www.ala.org

**Grantmaker type:** Public charity
**Financial data** (yr. ended 08/31/99): Assets,
$32,765,815; gifts received, $2,801,532;
expenditures, $35,051,400; giving activities
include $451,788 for grants (high: $225,916;
low: $2,000; average: $2,000–$225,916) and
$304,500 for 116 grants to individuals (high:
$6,000; low: $2,500).
**Purpose and activities:** The association provides
leadership for the development, promotion, and
improvement of library and information services
and the profession of librarianship in order to
enhance learning and ensure access to
information for all.
**Fields of interest:** Media/communications;
libraries/library science; libraries (public);
libraries (school); libraries (academic/research);
reading; children & youth, services; youth,
services; civil liberties, first amendment;
computer science; minorities; Asians/Pacific
Islanders; African Americans; Latinos; Native
Americans.
**Types of support:** General/operating support;
program development; seed money; fellowships;
research; grants to individuals; scholarships—to
individuals; in-kind gifts.
**Application information:** Application form
required.
 *Deadline(s):* Dec. 1

**Officers and Directors:\*** Nancy C. Kranich,\*
Pres.; Liz Bishoff,\* Treas.; William R. Gordon,
Exec. Dir.; Camilla Alire, Alice M. Calabrese,
Julie Cummins, Martin J. Gomez, Robert R.
Newlen, Mary E. Raphael, Sally Gardner Reed.
**EIN:** 362166947

## 159
## Bank One Foundation
(Formerly First National Bank of Chicago
Foundation)
1 Bank One Plz., Ste. 0308
Chicago, IL 60670 (312) 407-8052
*Contact:* James E. Donovan

Incorporated in 1961 in IL.
**Donor(s):** The First National Bank of Chicago.
**Grantmaker type:** Company-sponsored
foundation
**Financial data** (yr. ended 12/31/99): Assets,
$6,637,456 (M); gifts received, $2,000,000;
expenditures, $9,721,714; qualifying
distributions, $10,246,184; giving activities
include $9,708,684 for 288 grants (high:
$1,990,000; low: $500; average:
$1,000–$200,000) and $537,500 for 8 loans.
**Purpose and activities:** Giving primarily for
human services, including housing programs
and race relations; community development,
civic affairs, and crime and law enforcement;
education, especially business and other higher
education, libraries, and education building
funds; and the arts and culture, including
museums, music, dance, and the theater.
**Fields of interest:** Visual arts; museums;
performing arts; dance; theater; music;
arts/cultural programs; education, fund raising;
higher education; business school/education;
libraries/library science; education; natural
resource conservation & protection;
environment; crime/law enforcement;
housing/shelter, development; human services;
youth, services; minorities/immigrants, centers &
services; race/intergroup relations; civil rights;
urban/community development; business &
industry; community development; federated
giving programs; government/public
administration; minorities.
**Types of support:** General/operating support;
continuing support; annual campaigns; capital
campaigns; building/renovation; endowments;
fellowships; employee matching gifts; in-kind
gifts; matching/challenge support.
**Limitations:** Giving limited to the metropolitan
Chicago, IL, area. No support for fraternal or
religious organizations, preschool, elementary,
or secondary education, public agencies, or
United Way/Crusade of Mercy-supported
agencies. No grants to individuals, or for
emergency funds, deficit financing, land
acquisition, research, publications, conferences,
or multi-year operating pledges; no loans
(except for program-related investments).
**Publications:** Informational brochure (including
application guidelines).
**Application information:** Application form not
required.
 *Initial approach:* Letter
 *Copies of proposal:* 1
 *Deadline(s):* None
 *Board meeting date(s):* Mar., June, Sept., and
  Dec.
 *Final notification:* 3 months

**Officers and Directors:\*** Diane M. Smith,\* Pres.;
William P. Boardman,\* V.P.; Gerald E. Buldak,\*
V.P.; Stanley J. Calderon,\* V.P.; Mary L. Decker,\*
V.P.; William M. Farrow,\* V.P.; Jacqueline A.
Hurlbutt,\* V.P.; Patricia Hurston,\* V.P.; Norma J.
Lauder,\* V.P.; John Q. McKinnon,\* V.P.; Timothy
P. Moen,\* V.P.; Ilona M. Berry, Secy.; James E.
Donovan, Treas.
**Number of staff:** 2 full-time professional; 1
full-time support.
**EIN:** 366033828

## 160
## Bellebyron Foundation
c/o D.B. Smith
3600 W. Lake Ave.
Glenview, IL 60025
*Contact:* Stephen Byron Smith, Pres.

Established in 1983 in IL.
**Donor(s):** Harold Byron Smith.
**Grantmaker type:** Independent foundation
**Financial data** (yr. ended 12/31/98): Assets,
$8,959,991 (M); expenditures, $1,888,833;
qualifying distributions, $1,878,013; giving
activities include $1,879,580 for 13 grants (high:
$500,088; low: $500).
**Purpose and activities:** Giving primarily for the
arts, education and health care.
**Fields of interest:** Libraries/library science;
education; horticulture & garden clubs;
hospitals (general); youth development.
**Limitations:** Giving primarily in IL.
**Application information:**
 *Initial approach:* Letter
 *Deadline(s):* None
**Officers:** Stephen B. Smith, Pres.; Christopher
Byron Smith, V.P.; Harold Byron Smith, Jr., Secy.;
David B. Smith, Treas.
**EIN:** 366058056

## 161
## Bound to Stay Bound Books Foundation
73 Central Park Plz. E.
Jacksonville, IL 62650-2070

Established in 1984.
**Donor(s):** Bound To Stay Bound Books, Inc.
**Grantmaker type:** Company-sponsored
foundation
**Financial data** (yr. ended 12/31/99): Assets,
$3,584,974 (M); gifts received, $100,000;
expenditures, $185,372; qualifying distributions,
$167,650; giving activities include $167,400 for
grants.
**Fields of interest:** Elementary/secondary
education; higher education; libraries/library
science; human services.
**Limitations:** Applications not accepted. Giving
primarily in Jacksonville, IL.
**Application information:** Unsolicited requests
for funds not considered.
**Trustee:** Elliott State Bank.
**EIN:** 376227827

## 162
## T. Kimball Brooker Foundation
1500 N. Lake Shore Dr.
Chicago, IL 60610

Incorporated in 1986 in IL.
**Donor(s):** T. Kimball Brooker.
**Grantmaker type:** Independent foundation
**Financial data** (yr. ended 10/31/99): Assets, $1,307,434 (M); expenditures, $91,717; qualifying distributions, $87,081; giving activities include $80,800 for 15 grants (high: $25,250; low: $100).
**Purpose and activities:** Support for private and university libraries and opera.
**Fields of interest:** Music; opera; libraries (school); education.
**Limitations:** Applications not accepted. Giving on a national basis. No grants to individuals.
**Application information:** Contributes only to pre-selected organizations.
**Officers and Directors:*** T. Kimball Brooker,* Pres. and Treas.; James M. Trapp,* V.P.; Robert D. Loprete,* Secy.
**EIN:** 363481541

## 163
## The Charles and Marie Caestecker Foundation
20 S. Clark St., Ste. 2310
Chicago, IL 60603
*Scholarship application address:* c/o Guidance Counselor, Green Lake Public High School, Green Lake, WI 54941

Established about 1967.
**Donor(s):** Charles E. Caestecker.‡
**Grantmaker type:** Independent foundation
**Financial data** (yr. ended 04/30/99): Assets, $2,144,453 (M); expenditures, $1,145,518; qualifying distributions, $1,127,621; giving activities include $1,131,435 for 15 grants (high: $1,000,000; low: $1,000) and $1,281 for 3 grants to individuals (high: $1,007; low: $67).
**Purpose and activities:** Giving primarily for a symphony. Giving also for a public library and higher education, including scholarships to graduates of Green Lake Public High School, WI.
**Fields of interest:** Orchestra (symphony); higher education; libraries (public); scholarships/financial aid; hospitals (general).
**Types of support:** General/operating support; building/renovation; scholarship funds; scholarships—to individuals.
**Limitations:** Giving primarily in WI.
**Application information:** Application form required for scholarships.
*Deadline(s):* Feb. 1 of graduation year for scholarships
**Trustee:** Thomas E. Caestecker.
**EIN:** 363154453

## 164
## Centralia Foundation
115 E. 2nd St.
Centralia, IL 62801
*Contact:* Bill Sprehe, Tr.

Established in 1943.
**Donor(s):** Rollen Robinson, Lecta Rae Robinson.
**Grantmaker type:** Operating foundation
**Financial data** (yr. ended 09/30/99): Assets, $23,661,841 (M); gifts received, $1,270,112; qualifying distributions, $1,300,255; giving activities include $50,991 for 19 grants (high: $13,473; low: $1,084), $41,900 for 46 grants to individuals

(high: $4,500; low: $250) and $1,001,087 for 3 foundation-administered programs.
**Purpose and activities:** Giving for civic affairs, churches, and a hospital; also awards interest-free loans for graduate and undergraduate education to local students. The foundation operates and maintains a park system and a Carillon Bell Tower.
**Fields of interest:** Libraries (public); scholarships/financial aid; hospitals (general); government/public administration; Protestant agencies & churches.
**Types of support:** General/operating support; scholarships—to individuals; student loans—to individuals.
**Limitations:** Giving primarily in Centralia, Odin and Sandoval, IL.
**Application information:** Scholarship applicants must have attended a Centralia, IL area high school.
**Officers and Trustees:*** Wendell Lamblin,* Chair.; Verle Besant,* Vice-Chair.; Lloyd Allen, Bruce Geary, John Lackey, David Perrine, William Sprehe.
**EIN:** 376029269

## 165
## CharitaBulls
Chicago Bulls, Inc.
1901 W. Madison St.
Chicago, IL 60612 (312) 455-4000
*Contact:* Stuart Bookman, Community Svcs. Dept.

**Grantmaker type:** Public charity
**Financial data** (yr. ended 06/30/98): Assets, $8,686,953; gifts received, $269,307; expenditures, $526,500.
**Purpose and activities:** The foundation raises and contributes funds to projects benefiting worthy causes in the Chicago, Illinois, area, such as basketball court renovation programs, midnight basketball, Special Olympics, and an upgrading equipment project of the Chicago Public Library.
**Fields of interest:** Libraries (public); parks/playgrounds; athletics/sports, basketball; athletics/sports, Special Olympics.
**Types of support:** Building/renovation; equipment; program development.
**Limitations:** Giving primarily in Chicago, IL.
**EIN:** 363544506

## 166
## Chicago Board of Trade Foundation
141 W. Jackson Blvd., Ste. 1740-A
Chicago, IL 60604
*Contact:* Judith Singband

Established in 1984 in IL.
**Donor(s):** Chicago Board of Trade.
**Grantmaker type:** Company-sponsored foundation
**Financial data** (yr. ended 06/30/99): Assets, $4,188,683 (M); expenditures, $184,584; qualifying distributions, $170,000; giving activities include $170,000 for 29 grants (high: $20,000; low: $2,000).
**Purpose and activities:** Support for rehabilitation and the handicapped; arts and culture, including libraries and museums; education, including higher education and science and

technology; youth and child development; wildlife; and media and communications.
**Fields of interest:** Media/communications; museums; theater; arts/cultural programs; child development, education; higher education; adult/continuing education; adult education—literacy & basic skills; libraries/library science; reading; education; wildlife preservation & protection; medical care, rehabilitation; mental health/crisis services; cancer; cancer research; human services; children & youth, services; child development, services; community development; engineering & technology; science; minorities; disabled; economically disadvantaged.
**Types of support:** General/operating support; continuing support; annual campaigns; capital campaigns; endowments.
**Limitations:** Giving limited to Chicago, IL. No grants to individuals.
**Application information:** Application form not required.
*Initial approach:* Letter
*Copies of proposal:* 1
*Deadline(s):* Feb. 15
*Board meeting date(s):* 1st quarter annually
*Final notification:* Within 30 days
**Officer:** Dena Cooperman, Admin.
**EIN:** 363348469

## 167
## The Chicago Community Trust and Affiliates ▼
222 N. LaSalle St., Ste. 1400
Chicago, IL 60601-1009 (312) 372-3356
*Contact:* Ms. Sandy Chears, Grants Mgr. (grants to organizations)
*TDD:* (312) 853-0394; FAX: (312) 580-7411; E-mail: sandy@cct.org; URL: http://www.cct.org

Established in 1915 in IL by bank resolution and declaration of trust.
**Donor(s):** Albert W. Harris, and members of the Harris family.
**Grantmaker type:** Community foundation
**Financial data** (yr. ended 09/30/99): Assets, $1,059,750,098 (M); gifts received, $30,481,515; expenditures, $38,470,213; giving activities include $29,000,000 for grants.
**Purpose and activities:** Established for such charitable purposes as will best make for the mental, moral, intellectual and physical improvement, assistance and relief of the inhabitants of the County of Cook, State of Illinois. Grants for both general operating support and specific programs and projects in the areas of health, social services, education, arts and humanities, and civic affairs; awards fellowships to individuals in leadership positions in local community service organizations.
**Fields of interest:** Visual arts; performing arts; arts/cultural programs; child development, education; elementary school/education; secondary school/education; higher education; libraries/library science; environment; health care; health associations; AIDS; housing/shelter, development; youth development, services; human services; children & youth, services; child development, services; aging, centers & services; women, centers & services; minorities/immigrants, centers & services; homeless, human services; economic development; community development; public

policy, research; government/public administration; leadership development; minorities; disabled; aging; women; homeless.
**Types of support:** General/operating support; continuing support; capital campaigns; building/renovation; equipment; land acquisition; emergency funds; program development; seed money; research; technical assistance; program evaluation; program-related investments/loans; employee matching gifts; matching/challenge support.
**Limitations:** Giving primarily in Cook County, IL. No support for religious purposes. No grants to individuals (except for limited fellowship programs), or for annual campaigns, deficit financing, endowment funds, publications, conferences, or scholarships; no support for the purchase of computer hardware; no general operating support for agencies or institutions whose program activities substantially duplicate those already undertaken by others.
**Publications:** Annual report, informational brochure, financial statement, application guidelines, newsletter.
**Application information:** Application form required for various special programs.
   *Initial approach:* Proposal
   *Copies of proposal:* 2
   *Deadline(s):* Proposals scheduled for next available board meeting; no set deadline
   *Board meeting date(s):* Jan., May, and Sept.
   *Final notification:* 4 to 6 months after submission
**Officers:** Donald M. Stewart, Pres. and C.E.O.; Carol Y. Crenshaw, C.F.O.
**Executive Committee:** James J. Glasser, Chair.; Milton Davis, Vice-Chair.; Prudence R. Beidler, Heather M. Bilandic, Martin R. Castro, Marshall Field V, Sue Ling Gin, Martin J. Koldyke, Mercedes A. Laing, Homer J. Livingston, John D. Nichols, Virginia F. Ojeda.
**Trustees:** American National Bank and Trust Co. of Chicago, Bank of America, Bank One, Corp., The Chicago Trust Co., Harris Trust & Savings Bank, LaSalle National Bank, The Northern Trust Co., Pullman Bank and Trust Co., U.S. Bank, N.A.
**Number of staff:** 24 full-time professional; 1 part-time professional; 9 full-time support; 3 part-time support.
**EIN:** 362167000
**Recent grants for library/information services:**
**167-1** Chicago Historical Society, Chicago, IL, $72,478. For Studs Terkel audio archives project. 1999.
**167-2** Chicago Public Library Foundation, Chicago, IL, $300,000. For continued support of NatureConnections. 1999.
**167-3** Chicago Public Library Foundation, Chicago, IL, $85,000. For Chicago Matters series in conjunction with The Chicago Reporter, WBEZ-FM and WTTW Channel 11. 1999.
**167-4** Connection Resource Services, Libertyville, IL, $24,000. For salary of van driver and family worker. Grant made through Chicago Community Foundation. 1999.
**167-5** Connection Resource Services, Libertyville, IL, $10,000. 1999.
**167-6** Donors Forum of Chicago, Chicago, IL, $100,000. For leadership fund. 1999.
**167-7** Donors Forum of Chicago, Chicago, IL, $25,000. For Fund for Immigrants and

Refugees. Grant made through Chicago Community Foundation. 1999.
**167-8** Donors Forum of Chicago, Chicago, IL, $20,000. For Giving Voice to Your Heart education and publicity project. Grant made through Chicago Community Foundation. 1999.
**167-9** Donors Forum of Chicago, Chicago, IL, $18,480. 1999.
**167-10** Foundation Center, NYC, NY, $10,000. 1999.

### 168
### The Comer Foundation
c/o Neal Gerber & Eisenberg
2 N. LaSalle St.
Chicago, IL 60602
*Contact:* Stephanie Comer, Fdn. Mgr.

Established in 1986 in IL.
**Donor(s):** Gary C. Comer, Frances Comer.
**Grantmaker type:** Independent foundation
**Financial data** (yr. ended 12/31/99): Assets, $14,511,420 (M); expenditures, $2,762,231; qualifying distributions, $2,605,186; giving activities include $2,578,493 for 73 grants (high: $416,236; low: $500; average: $1,000–$30,000).
**Purpose and activities:** Giving primarily for environmental protection, medicine, arts and cultural organizations, human services, and education.
**Fields of interest:** Museums; arts/cultural programs; libraries/library science; education; natural resource conservation & protection; zoos/zoological societies; hospitals (general); public health; AIDS; human services; children & youth, services.
**Types of support:** General/operating support; continuing support; program development; internship funds; scholarship funds.
**Limitations:** Applications not accepted. Giving primarily in Chicago, IL. No grants to individuals.
**Application information:** Contributes only to pre-selected organizations.
**Officers:** Stephanie Comer, Pres.; Frances Comer, V.P. and Secy.; Gary C. Comer, Treas.
**Number of staff:** 1 full-time professional.
**EIN:** 363522486

### 169
### Deering Foundation
410 N. Michigan Ave., Rm. 590
Chicago, IL 60622

Incorporated in 1956 in IL.
**Donor(s):** Barbara D. Danielson, Richard E. Danielson, Jr., Marion D. Campbell, Miami Corp.
**Grantmaker type:** Independent foundation
**Financial data** (yr. ended 11/30/99): Assets, $17,979,393 (M); expenditures, $720,617; qualifying distributions, $713,376; giving activities include $711,000 for 15 grants (high: $250,000; low: $1,000).
**Purpose and activities:** Giving primarily to affiliated foundations; some support also for education, health, and the arts.
**Fields of interest:** Museums; libraries (special); education; hospitals (general); health associations; Alzheimer's disease; federated giving programs.

**Types of support:** General/operating support.
**Limitations:** Applications not accepted. Giving primarily in ID, IL and MA. No grants to individuals.
**Application information:** Contributes only to pre-selected organizations.
**Officers and Directors:** Barbara S.D. Danielson, Pres.; Candida D. Burnap,* V.P.; Charles E. Schroeder,* Secy.-Treas.; Charles E. Seitz, Richard Strachan, Stephen M. Strachan, Jocelyn D. Tennille.
**EIN:** 366051876

### 170
### Dillon Foundation ▼
P.O. Box 537
Sterling, IL 61081 (815) 626-9000
*Contact:* Peter W. Dillon, Pres.
*FAX:* (815) 626-4000

Incorporated in 1953 in IL.
**Donor(s):** Members of the Dillon family.
**Grantmaker type:** Independent foundation
**Financial data** (yr. ended 10/31/99): Assets, $79,164,463 (M); expenditures, $4,514,709; qualifying distributions, $3,878,316; giving activities include $3,634,109 for 122 grants (high: $752,422; low: $323; average: $1,000–$25,000) and $223,889 for in-kind gifts.
**Purpose and activities:** Support for local community economic development and civic and urban affairs; technology and other education; social services and youth; historic preservation and museums; recreation; and libraries in and around Sterling, IL.
**Fields of interest:** Museums; historic preservation/historical societies; vocational education, post-secondary; libraries/library science; education; employment; recreation; human services; children & youth, services; community development; government/public administration; general charitable giving.
**Types of support:** General/operating support; continuing support; annual campaigns; capital campaigns; building/renovation; equipment; land acquisition; endowments; emergency funds; program development; seed money; scholarship funds; in-kind gifts; matching/challenge support.
**Limitations:** Giving primarily in the Sterling, IL, area. No grants to individuals; no loans.
**Application information:** Application form not required.
   *Initial approach:* Letter
   *Copies of proposal:* 1
   *Deadline(s):* None
   *Board meeting date(s):* Feb. and Aug.
   *Final notification:* As soon as possible
**Officers and Directors:** Peter W. Dillon,* Pres.; John P. Conway,* V.P. and Secy.; James M. Boesen,* Treas.; Margo Dillon, Michael W. Dillon, Gale D. Inglee, Mark C. Inglee, Tom Lexvold.
**Number of staff:** 1 part-time support.
**EIN:** 366059349

## 171

### The Donnelley Foundation

(Formerly Elliott and Ann Donnelley Foundation)
360 N. Michigan Ave., Ste. 1009
Chicago, IL 60601-3803
*Contact:* Thomas E. Donnelley, II, Pres.

Incorporated in 1954 in IL.
**Donor(s):** Elliott Donnelley,‡ Ann S. Hardy,
Thomas E. Donnelley II, James R. Donnelley,
Barbara C. Donnelley, Nina H. Donnelley,
Robert G. Donnelley, Miranda S. Donnelley.
**Grantmaker type:** Independent foundation
**Financial data** (yr. ended 12/31/99): Assets,
$8,756,242 (M); gifts received, $234,779;
expenditures, $227,665; qualifying distributions,
$212,269; giving activities include $197,752 for
182 grants (high: $10,000; low: $100; average:
$50–$20,000).
**Purpose and activities:** Giving primarily to
wildlife conservation, youth welfare, libraries,
historic preservation, and educational and
medical institutions with whom the foundation
directors have long-term relationships and/or
serve on the boards.
**Fields of interest:** Museums; historic
preservation/historical societies; libraries/library
science; education; wildlife preservation &
protection; hospitals (general); children & youth,
services.
**Types of support:** General/operating support;
continuing support; annual campaigns; capital
campaigns; building/renovation; endowments;
seed money; matching/challenge support.
**Limitations:** Applications not accepted. Giving
primarily in CA, CT, IL, MT, OR, and VT. No
grants to individuals.
**Application information:** Contributes only to
pre-selected organizations.
*Board meeting date(s):* As required
**Officers:** Thomas E. Donnelley II, Pres.; James
R. Donnelley, 1st V.P.; David E. Donnelley, V.P.
and Secy.; Robert G. Donnelley, V.P. and Treas.
**Number of staff:** None.
**EIN:** 366066894

## 172

### Gaylord and Dorothy Donnelley Foundation ▼

35 E. Wacker Dr., Ste. 2600
Chicago, IL 60601-2102 (312) 977-2700
*Contact:* Judith M. Stockdale
*FAX:* (312) 977-1686; URL: http://www.gddf.org

Incorporated in 1952 in IL.
**Donor(s):** Gaylord Donnelley,‡ Dorothy Ranney
Donnelley.
**Grantmaker type:** Independent foundation
**Financial data** (yr. ended 12/31/98): Assets,
$82,317,160 (M); gifts received, $2,716,247;
expenditures, $4,315,982; qualifying
distributions, $3,573,877; giving activities
include $3,040,673 for 198 grants (high:
$167,000; low: $500; average:
$3,000–$25,000) and $10,000 for 1
foundation-administered program.
**Purpose and activities:** Primary areas of interest
include conservation and environment,
education, arts and culture, and short term food
and shelter programs.
**Fields of interest:** Arts/cultural programs;
education; natural resource conservation &
protection; environment; agriculture;

housing/shelter, development; youth
development.
**Types of support:** General/operating support;
program development.
**Limitations:** Giving primarily in the Chicago, IL,
area and in the Lowcountry area of SC. No
support for religious purposes. No grants to
individuals, or for pledges, endowments, capital
campaigns, benefits, conferences, meetings,
eradication of deficits, publications, films,
videos, fundraising events, or matching gifts; no
loans.
**Publications:** Annual report, application
guidelines.
**Application information:** Telephone or FAX
requests not considered. Application form
required.
*Initial approach:* Letter requesting guidelines
*Copies of proposal:* 1
*Deadline(s):* None
*Board meeting date(s):* Spring, summer, and
fall
**Officers and Directors:*** Strachan Donnelley,
Ph.D.,* Chair.; Dorothy Ranney Donnelley,*
Vice-Chair.; Elliott R. Donnelley,* Vice-Chair.;
Laura Donnelley-Morton,* Vice-Chair.; Robert T.
Carter,* Secy.; Robert W. Carton, M.D., Treas.;
Judith M. Stockdale, Exec. Dir.; Deborah
Gillespie, Dir., Admin.; Jane Rishel, Life Dir.;
Gerald W. Adelmann, James B. Edwards,
D.M.D., Joel L. Fleishman, Coy Johnston,
Challis M. Lowe.
**Number of staff:** 1 full-time professional.
**EIN:** 366108460
**Recent grants for library/information services:**
**172-1** American Friends of Cambridge
University, NYC, NY, $167,000. To endow
full-time fellow librarian for Parker Library.
1998.
**172-2** American Friends of Cambridge
University, NYC, NY, $167,000. To endow
full-time fellow librarian for Parker Library.
1998.
**172-3** Chicago Public Library Foundation,
Chicago, IL, $25,000. For Project MIND:
Meeting Information Needs Democratically.
1998.
**172-4** Native American Educational Services
(NAES), Chicago, IL, $15,000. For position of
Librarian/Archivist and for endowment. 1998.
**172-5** Newberry Library, Center for Public
Programs, Chicago, IL, $50,000. 1998.
**172-6** Newberry Library, Center for Public
Programs, Chicago, IL, $25,000. 1998.

## 173

### Arnold & Mildred Erickson Charitable Foundation, Inc.

c/o National Bank & Trust Co. of Sycamore
230 W. State St.
Sycamore, IL 60178 (815) 895-2125
*Contact:* Diane Florschuetz, Asst. V.P. and Trust
Off., National Bank & Trust Co. of Sycamore

**Grantmaker type:** Independent foundation
**Financial data** (yr. ended 12/31/98): Assets,
$2,016,441 (M); expenditures, $100,806;
qualifying distributions, $88,565; giving
activities include $30,000 for 3 grants of
$10,000 each and $55,500 for 22 grants to
individuals (high: $3,500; low: $2,500).

**Purpose and activities:** Scholarships only to
graduates of Kaneland School District and
Central Community School District No. 301, IL.
**Fields of interest:** Libraries/library science;
Protestant agencies & churches.
**Types of support:** Scholarships—to individuals.
**Limitations:** Giving limited to residents of IL.
**Application information:** Application form
required.
*Initial approach:* Request application form
*Deadline(s):* Mar. 1
**Officers:** Wayne E. Byerhof, Pres.; Howard A.
Heidlauf, Secy.-Treas.
**Directors:** Stephen Cooper, John Johnsen, James
Robison.
**EIN:** 366998667

## 174

### The First National Bank of Chicago Corporate Giving Program

c/o Community Affairs
1 First National Plz., Mail Ste. 0356
Chicago, IL 60670-0356 (312) 732-6948
*Contact:* Diane M. Smith, V.P.
*FAX:* (312) 732-2437

**Grantmaker type:** Corporate giving program
**Purpose and activities:** In making contributions,
the company seeks to improve the quality of life
in metropolitan Chicago, IL, by assisting in the
social, economic, and cultural development of
the community.
**Fields of interest:** Museums; performing arts;
dance; theater; music; arts/cultural programs;
higher education; business school/education;
libraries/library science; education; natural
resource conservation & protection;
environment; crime/law enforcement;
housing/shelter, development; human services;
minorities/immigrants, centers & services;
race/intergroup relations; urban/community
development; community development;
federated giving programs; government/public
administration; minorities.
**Types of support:** Annual campaigns; capital
campaigns; building/renovation; endowments;
fellowships; matching/challenge support.
**Limitations:** Giving primarily in the Chicago, IL,
metropolitan area. No support for religious or
fraternal organizations, preschool, elementary or
secondary schools, or public agencies; no
additional support of individual agencies
receiving support from the United Way/Crusade
of Mercy unless a community/neighborhood
organization involved in housing, commercial,
or industrial development. No grants to
individuals, or for multi-year operating pledges
or consecutive multi-year pledges.
**Application information:** Application form not
required.
*Initial approach:* Letter
*Copies of proposal:* 1
*Deadline(s):* None
*Board meeting date(s):* Mar., June, Sept., and
Dec.
*Final notification:* 3 months
**Number of staff:** 2 full-time professional; 1
full-time support.

## 175
### The Joseph B. Glossberg Foundation
455 Cityfront Plz., Ste. 3000
Chicago, IL 60611

Established in 1997 in IL.
**Donor(s):** Joseph B. Glossberg.
**Grantmaker type:** Independent foundation
**Financial data** (yr. ended 12/31/99): Assets, $119,695 (M); gifts received, $71,557; expenditures, $133,403; qualifying distributions, $132,483; giving activities include $132,965 for 39 grants (high: $33,000; low: $10).
**Purpose and activities:** Giving for higher education, the humanities, athletic programs, libraries, youth music education, music programs and human services.
**Fields of interest:** Music; humanities; arts, services; libraries (school); education, services; medical care, rehabilitation; athletics/sports, school programs; human services.
**Limitations:** Applications not accepted. No grants to individuals.
**Application information:** Contributes only to pre-selected organizations.
**Officers and Directors:*** Joseph B. Glossberg,* Pres. and Treas.; Madeleine K. B. Glossberg,* V.P. and Secy.; John C. Stiefel,* V.P.
**EIN:** 364119754

## 176
### The H.B.B. Foundation
400 N. Michigan Ave., Ste. 1120
Chicago, IL 60611

Established in 1964 in IL.
**Grantmaker type:** Independent foundation
**Financial data** (yr. ended 12/31/99): Assets, $8,862,942 (M); expenditures, $470,949; qualifying distributions, $436,824; giving activities include $382,000 for 58 grants (high: $25,000; low: $500).
**Purpose and activities:** Giving primarily for health services and the arts.
**Fields of interest:** Museums; arts/cultural programs; libraries (public); education; environment; hospitals (general); family services, counseling; disabled; general charitable giving.
**Limitations:** Applications not accepted. Giving in the U.S., with emphasis on CO, CT, IL, MA, NH, and VA. No grants to individuals.
**Application information:** Contributes only to pre-selected organizations.
**Officers and Directors:*** Elizabeth B. Tieken,* Pres.; Theodore D. Tieken, Jr.,* V.P. and Secy.; Mark Stephenitch,* Treas.; Elizabeth Kirkpatrick, Nancy B. Tieken.
**EIN:** 366104969

## 177
### Helen M. Harrison Foundation
70 W. Madison, Ste. 620
Chicago, IL 60602
*Contact:* Timothy G. Carroll, Tr.

Established in 1986 in IL.
**Donor(s):** Helen M. Harrison Trust.
**Grantmaker type:** Independent foundation
**Financial data** (yr. ended 12/31/99): Assets, $17,621,265 (M); expenditures, $825,924; qualifying distributions, $726,845; giving

activities include $656,750 for 67 grants (high: $500,000; low: $750).
**Purpose and activities:** Giving primarily to a university and its affiliates; support also for community development, including youth services and community organizations.
**Fields of interest:** Arts/cultural programs; secondary school/education; higher education; libraries/library science; children & youth, services; community development; foundations (community); Protestant agencies & churches.
**Limitations:** Applications not accepted. Giving primarily in Chicago and Oak Park, IL. No grants to individuals.
**Application information:** Contributes only to pre-selected organizations.
**Trustees:** George E. Barnes, Philip M. Burno, Timothy G. Carroll, Raymond Kratzer.
**EIN:** 363475137

## 178
### Mary Heath Foundation
c/o Old National Trust
P.O. Box 10
Oblong, IL 62449 (618) 592-5029
*Contact:* Jimmy J. Rogers, V.P.
*FAX:* (618) 592-3135; *E-mail:* jimmy_rogers@oldnational.com

Established in 1994 in IL.
**Grantmaker type:** Independent foundation
**Financial data** (yr. ended 12/31/99): Assets, $5,521,000 (M); expenditures, $221,954; qualifying distributions, $167,545; giving activities include $167,545 for 35 grants (high: $30,000; low: $1,000).
**Purpose and activities:** Support primarily for organizations sponsoring projects in the areas of public health, safety, recreation, and education in IL.
**Fields of interest:** Arts, multipurpose centers/programs; adult/continuing education; libraries/library science; education, PTA groups; food banks; housing/shelter, development; disasters, fire prevention/control; parks/playgrounds; youth development, centers & clubs; residential/custodial care; aging, centers & services; community development, neighborhood development.
**Types of support:** Building/renovation; equipment; program development.
**Limitations:** Giving limited to IL. No grants to individuals, or for endowments, deficit reduction, fundraising, or political campaigns.
**Application information:** Contact foundation for application guidelines. Application form required.
 *Initial approach:* Proposal
 *Copies of proposal:* 6
 *Deadline(s):* May 1 and Nov.1
**Advisory Committee:** Radford Burkett, Thomas Eden, Steve Holliday, Myrl Littlejohn, Thomas Pearce.
**Officer:** Jimmy J. Rogers, V.P.
**EIN:** 371330907

## 179
### Hoellen Family Foundation
1940 W. Irving Park Rd.
Chicago, IL 60613
*Contact:* John J. Hoellen, Pres.

Established in 1983.
**Donor(s):** John J. Hoellen.
**Grantmaker type:** Independent foundation
**Financial data** (yr. ended 12/31/98): Assets, $1,830,556 (M); expenditures, $108,275; qualifying distributions, $104,000; giving activities include $104,000 for 11 grants (high: $50,000; low: $1,000).
**Purpose and activities:** Giving primarily for education.
**Fields of interest:** Arts/cultural programs; higher education; libraries/library science; health care; Christian agencies & churches.
**Limitations:** Giving limited to Chicago, IL metropolitan area.
**Application information:** Application form not required.
 *Deadline(s):* None
**Officers and Directors:*** John J. Hoellen,* Pres.; Rev. George A. Rice, Secy.-Treas.; Mary Jane Hoellen.
**EIN:** 363209348

## 180
### Hume Foundation
P.O. Box 677
Mendota, IL 61342 (815) 539-6355
*Contact:* Marsha Jones, Treas.

Established in 1993 in IL.
**Donor(s):** Horace D. Hume.
**Grantmaker type:** Independent foundation
**Financial data** (yr. ended 12/31/99): Assets, $1,138,720 (L); expenditures, $69,986; qualifying distributions, $66,991; giving activities include $67,500 for 18 grants (high: $6,000; low: $1,000).
**Purpose and activities:** Giving for historical preservation, Christian organizations, and education.
**Fields of interest:** Historic preservation/historical societies; libraries/library science; Christian agencies & churches.
**Types of support:** General/operating support; building/renovation.
**Limitations:** Giving primarily in Mendota, IL.
**Application information:**
 *Initial approach:* Letter
 *Deadline(s):* None
**Officers and Directors:*** Horace D. Hume,* Pres.; Michelle H. Babin,* Secy.; Marsha H. Jones,* Treas.
**EIN:** 363890112

## 181
### The Lawlor Foundation
c/o William J. Lawlor, III
3 1st National Plz., Ste. 5100
Chicago, IL 60602

Established in 1988 in IL.
**Donor(s):** William J. Lawlor,‡ William J. Lawlor III.
**Grantmaker type:** Independent foundation
**Financial data** (yr. ended 12/31/98): Assets, $1,100,784 (M); gifts received, $16,506; expenditures, $61,675; qualifying distributions, $54,043; giving activities include $47,000 for 24 grants (high: $4,000; low: $500).
**Purpose and activities:** Giving to education, the arts, community services and religion.

**Fields of interest:** Arts/cultural programs; libraries/library science; education; environment; human services; religion.
**Limitations:** Applications not accepted. Giving primarily in Chicago, IL. No grants to individuals.
**Application information:** Contributes only to pre-selected organizations.
**Officers and Directors:*** William J. Lawlor III,* Pres. and Secy.-Treas.; Blair Lawlor,* V.P.; Michael J. Lawlor, Exec. Dir.; John F. Lawlor.
**EIN:** 363620712

## 182
### The Lumpkin Foundation
7200 Sears Twr.
233 S. Wacker Dr.
Chicago, IL 60606
*Contact:* Lisa Barr, Exec. Dir.
*Application address:* 121 S. 17th St., Mattoon, IL 61938, tel.: (217) 235-3361; URL: http://www.lumpkinfoundation.org

Incorporated in 1953 in IL.
**Donor(s):** Besse Adamson Lumpkin,‡ Mary G. Lumpkin,‡ Richard Adamson Lumpkin,‡ Illinois Consolidated Telephone Co., Richard Anthony Lumpkin.
**Grantmaker type:** Independent foundation
**Financial data** (yr. ended 12/31/99): Assets, $29,319,279 (M); expenditures, $1,399,372; qualifying distributions, $1,141,314; giving activities include $1,116,500 for 161 grants (high: $168,000; low: $250).
**Purpose and activities:** Giving primarily for conservation and human services.
**Fields of interest:** Libraries (public); education; natural resource conservation & protection; human services; children, services.
**Types of support:** Program development; seed money; internship funds; matching/challenge support.
**Limitations:** Giving primarily in central IL. No grants to individuals.
**Publications:** Application guidelines.
**Application information:** Application form required.
  *Initial approach:* Letter
  *Copies of proposal:* 1
  *Deadline(s):* None
  *Board meeting date(s):* Feb., Apr., June, Sept. and Nov.
**Officers and Directors:*** Margaret Lumpkin Keon,* Pres.; Pamela Ryan Keon,* V.P.; S.L. Grissom, Secy.; Richard Anthony Lumpkin,* Treas.; Elizabeth Lumpkin Celio, John W. Sparks, Mary Lee Lumpkin Sparks.
**Number of staff:** 1 full-time professional; 1 part-time support.
**EIN:** 237423640

## 183
### Marion Memorial Health Foundation
P.O. Box 1815
Marion, IL 62959 (618) 997-5341
*Contact:* Harlean Miller, V.P.

Established in 1996 in IL.
**Grantmaker type:** Independent foundation
**Financial data** (yr. ended 12/31/98): Assets, $1,041,827 (M); expenditures, $59,612; qualifying distributions, $56,588; giving

activities include $40,072 for 9 grants (high: $25,000; low: $161) and $7,750 for 14 grants to individuals (high: $1,000; low: $250).
**Purpose and activities:** Giving for health and medical services, and youth and family services.
**Fields of interest:** Nursing school/education; libraries (medical); health care clinics & centers; youth development; family services.
**Limitations:** Giving primarily in IL.
**Application information:** Applications for scholarships available in high school guidance departments or the administration office at Marion Memorial Hospital. Application form required.
  *Initial approach:* Letter stating educational goals, needs, interests, and future plans
  *Deadline(s):* None
**Officers:** Ben Bruce, Pres.; Harlean Miller, V.P.; Kerry Hudgens, Secy.-Treas.
**Board Members:** Mike Bradley, Judy Broemmel, Stephanie Elkins, Todd Goodman, Larry Hughes, Nita Joyner, Tom Keim, Nancy Kirschner, Earl Parks, John Power, Lu Queen, Larry Sanders, J. David Thompson, Erin Ward.
**EIN:** 371316969

## 184
### Moen Foundation
(Formerly Stanadyne Foundation)
c/o First National Bank of Chicago
1 S. Northwest Hwy.
Park Ridge, IL 60068 (847) 518-7392

Trust established in 1958 in IL.
**Donor(s):** Stanadyne, Inc.
**Grantmaker type:** Company-sponsored foundation
**Financial data** (yr. ended 12/31/98): Assets, $20,658 (M); expenditures, $78,337; qualifying distributions, $75,075; giving activities include $73,239 for 167 grants (high: $18,750; low: $20).
**Purpose and activities:** Giving to federated giving programs, education, human services, and public service organizations.
**Fields of interest:** Television; radio; ballet; orchestra (symphony); music, choral; education, information services; higher education; college; university; libraries/library science; education; zoos/zoological societies; hospitals (general); mental health, association; cystic fibrosis; cancer; heart & circulatory diseases; muscular dystrophy; multiple sclerosis; Alzheimer's disease; diabetes; athletics/sports, Special Olympics; youth development, centers & clubs; boys & girls clubs; Big Brothers/Big Sisters; Boy Scouts; Salvation Army; hospices; civil rights, minorities; federated giving programs.
**Limitations:** Applications not accepted. Giving on a national basis. No grants to individuals.
**Application information:** Contributes only to pre-selected organizations.
**Trustee:** First National Bank of Chicago.
**EIN:** 237421900

## 185
### Myers Charitable Trust
c/o Norwest Bank Illinois, N.A.
121 W. 1st St.
Geneseo, IL 61254 (309) 944-5361
*Contact:* Judy Konecki, Tr.

Established in 1997 in IL.
**Grantmaker type:** Independent foundation
**Financial data** (yr. ended 12/31/99): Assets, $1,324,841 (M); expenditures, $80,979; qualifying distributions, $67,231; giving activities include $47,109 for 2 grants (high: $23,555; low: $23,554) and $17,215 for 6 grants to individuals (high: $5,000; low: $637).
**Purpose and activities:** Giving primarily for libraries and hospitals. Scholarships awarded to students seeking a degree in medicine, dentistry, law or nursing.
**Fields of interest:** Dental school/education; law school/education; medical school/education; libraries (public); scholarships/financial aid; hospitals (general).
**Limitations:** Giving primarily in Geneseo, IL.
**Application information:**
  *Initial approach:* Call for scholarship application form
  *Deadline(s):* None
  *Board meeting date(s):* Within 3 months
**Trustees:** Judy Konecki, Norwest Bank Illinois, N.A.
**EIN:** 367233377

## 186
### OMRON Foundation, Inc.
c/o OMRON Systems, Inc.
1 E. Commerce Dr.
Schaumburg, IL 60173 (847) 843-7900
*Contact:* Nicholas Hahn, Dir.
*FAX:* (847) 240-5362

Established in 1989 in IL.
**Donor(s):** OMRON Systems, Inc., OMRON Management Center of America, OMRON Systems of America, Inc., OMRON Healthcare, Inc., OMRON Advanced Systems, Inc., OMRON Office Automation Products, Inc.
**Grantmaker type:** Company-sponsored foundation
**Financial data** (yr. ended 03/31/98): Assets, $1,306,657 (M); gifts received, $300,017; expenditures, $325,936; qualifying distributions, $323,199; giving activities include $323,482 for 135 grants (high: $50,000; low: $15).
**Purpose and activities:** Primary areas of interest include higher and other education, the handicapped, cultural programs, the environment, and the elderly.
**Fields of interest:** Museums; performing arts; music; humanities; language & linguistics; literature; arts/cultural programs; education; fund raising; early childhood education; child development, education; secondary school/education; higher education; adult/continuing education; libraries/library science; education; natural resource conservation & protection; energy; environment; wildlife preservation & protection; medical care, rehabilitation; health care; substance abuse, services; mental health/crisis services; health associations; cancer; alcoholism; biomedicine; medical research; cancer research; employment; safety/disasters; youth development, citizenship; human services; children & youth, services; child development, services; hospices; aging, centers & services; women, centers & services; minorities/immigrants, centers & services; homeless, human services; international economic development; peace; foreign policy; human rights (international); international

affairs; race/intergroup relations; civil rights; community development; voluntarism promotion; federated giving programs; engineering & technology; science; population studies; public policy, research; public affairs, citizen participation; public affairs; minorities; disabled; aging; women; immigrants/refugees; homeless; general charitable giving.
**International interests:** Asia; Japan.
**Types of support:** General/operating support; continuing support; building/renovation; scholarship funds; employee matching gifts; employee-related scholarships; in-kind gifts.
**Limitations:** Giving primarily in Chicago, IL; minor support for organizations outside IL. No grants to individuals (except for employee-related scholarships).
**Publications:** Grants list, informational brochure, program policy statement, application guidelines.
**Application information:** Application form not required.
   *Initial approach:* Letter
   *Deadline(s):* None
   *Board meeting date(s):* Quarterly
**Officers and Directors:*** Yoshio Tateisi,* Pres.; Hideki Masuda,* V.P.; Masatoshi Yajima, Secy.; Fumitaka Hosomi, Treas.; Shingo Areghi, Nicholas Hahn, Frank Zorn.
**EIN:** 363644055

## 187
## Pritzker Foundation ▼
200 W. Madison St., 38th Fl.
Chicago, IL  60606  (312) 750-8400
*Contact:* Glen Miller, V.P. and Treas.

Incorporated in 1944 in IL.
**Donor(s):** Members of the Pritzker family.
**Grantmaker type:** Independent foundation
**Financial data** (yr. ended 12/31/98): Assets, $607,070,781 (M); gifts received, $37,008,124; expenditures, $24,022,867; qualifying distributions, $22,718,601; giving activities include $22,687,557 for 225 grants (high: $12,000,000; low: $50; average: $100–$10,000).
**Purpose and activities:** Grants largely for higher education, including medical education, and religious welfare funds; giving also for hospitals, temple support, and cultural programs.
**Fields of interest:** Arts/cultural programs; higher education; medical school/education; hospitals (general); human services; religious federated giving programs; Jewish agencies & temples.
**Limitations:** Applications not accepted. Giving on a national basis, with some emphasis on Chicago, IL. No grants to individuals.
**Application information:** Contributes only to pre-selected organizations.
   *Board meeting date(s):* Dec. and as required
**Officers and Directors:*** Robert A. Pritzker,* Pres.; Simon Zunamon, V.P. and Secy.; Glen Miller, V.P. and Treas.; Nicholas J. Pritzker,* V.P.; Penny S. Pritzker,* V.P.; Thomas J. Pritzker,* V.P.
**Number of staff:** None.
**EIN:** 366058062
**Recent grants for library/information services:**
187-1 Chicago Public Library Foundation, Chicago, IL, $200,000. For continued general operating support. 1998.

187-2 Chicago Public Library Foundation, Chicago, IL, $75,000. For continued general operating support. 1998.
187-3 Chicago Public Library Foundation, Chicago, IL, $20,000. For continued general operating support. 1998.
187-4 Northwestern University, Evanston, IL, $2,000,000. For continued general support of Pritzker Library in Chicago. 1998.

## 188
## Puckett Foundation
c/o Fairfield National Bank
P.O. Box 429
Fairfield, IL  62837-0429  (618) 842-2107

**Donor(s):** B. Earl Puckett.
**Grantmaker type:** Independent foundation
**Financial data** (yr. ended 12/31/99): Assets, $1,742,841 (M); expenditures, $65,675; qualifying distributions, $61,301; giving activities include $42,000 for 3 grants (high: $20,000; low: $2,000) and $16,000 for 9 grants to individuals (high: $2,000; low: $1,000).
**Purpose and activities:** Awards scholarships to graduates of Fairfield Community High School.
**Fields of interest:** Libraries (public); scholarships/financial aid; hospitals (general).
**Types of support:** Equipment; program development; scholarships—to individuals.
**Limitations:** Giving primarily in Fairfield, IL.
**Publications:** Application guidelines.
**Application information:** Application form required.
   *Deadline(s):* Mar. 1 for scholarships; none for grants
   *Final notification:* Apr. 15 for scholarships
**Trustee:** Fairfield National Bank.
**EIN:** 136115138

## 189
## Rauch Family Foundation II, Inc.
1705 2nd Ave., Ste. 424
Rock Island, IL  61201  (309) 788-2300
*Contact:* Samuel Gilman, Dir.

Established in 1987 in IL.
**Grantmaker type:** Independent foundation
**Financial data** (yr. ended 12/31/99): Assets, $1,535,181 (M); expenditures, $74,847; qualifying distributions, $63,330; giving activities include $63,330 for 12 grants (high: $13,000; low: $583).
**Purpose and activities:** Giving to programs and projects for the enhancement of Judaism and its traditions and people.
**Fields of interest:** Libraries (public); Jewish agencies & temples.
**Types of support:** Curriculum development; scholarships—to individuals.
**Limitations:** Giving primarily in Rock Island, IL.
**Publications:** Annual report (including application guidelines).
**Application information:** Application form required.
   *Deadline(s):* May 1
   *Final notification:* Sept. 1
**Directors:** Samuel Gilman, Dorothy Versman.
**EIN:** 363570748

## 190
## Franklin I. and Irene List Saemann Foundation
(Formerly Franklin I. Saemann Foundation)
P.O. Box 105
Morrison, IL  61270  (815) 772-2121
*Contact:* Walter C. Kilgus, Fdn. Mgr.
*FAX:* (815) 772-2026; E-mail: saemann@soltec.net

Established in 1983 in IN.
**Donor(s):** Franklin I. Saemann,‡ Irene L. Saemann.‡
**Grantmaker type:** Independent foundation
**Financial data** (yr. ended 06/30/99): Assets, $13,105,169 (M); gifts received, $1,494,527; expenditures, $1,481,862; qualifying distributions, $528,000; giving activities include $527,000 for 30 grants (high: $250,000; low: $100).
**Purpose and activities:** Giving primarily for education and human services, with an emphasis on funding for libraries and literacy programs.
**Fields of interest:** Higher education; libraries/library science; hospitals (general); human services; children & youth, services; community development; philanthropy/voluntarism.
**Publications:** Informational brochure (including application guidelines).
**Application information:** Application form required.
   *Initial approach:* Letter
   *Deadline(s):* Apr. 1
   *Board meeting date(s):* Quarterly; June for considering grant applications
**Trustees:** Amy Kilgus Chamley, Joann A. Kilgus, Thomas E. List, June Waller, Katherine A. Waller.
**Number of staff:** 1 full-time professional; 3 full-time support.
**EIN:** 626171002

## 191
## Dr. Scholl Foundation ▼
11 S. LaSalle St., Ste. 2100
Chicago, IL  60603-1302  (312) 782-5210
*Contact:* Pamela Scholl, Pres.

Incorporated in 1947 in IL.
**Donor(s):** William M. Scholl, M.D.‡
**Grantmaker type:** Independent foundation
**Financial data** (yr. ended 12/31/98): Assets, $205,598,216 (M); expenditures, $13,981,831; qualifying distributions, $11,806,325; giving activities include $11,190,728 for 431 grants (high: $500,000; low: $2,000; average: $10,000–$100,000).
**Purpose and activities:** Support for private education at all levels, including elementary, secondary, and postsecondary schools, colleges and universities, and medical and nursing institutions; general charitable programs, including grants to hospitals, and programs for children, the developmentally disabled, and senior citizens; and civic, cultural, social welfare, economic, and religious activities.
**Fields of interest:** Film/video; visual arts; museums; performing arts; dance; theater; history & archaeology; arts/cultural programs; elementary/secondary education; early childhood education; child development, education; elementary school/education;

secondary school/education; higher education; business school/education; law school/education; medical school/education; adult education—literacy & basic skills; libraries/library science; reading; education; natural resource conservation & protection; animal welfare; hospitals (general); nursing care; health care; mental health/crisis services; health associations; cancer; heart & circulatory diseases; AIDS; alcoholism; medical research; cancer research; heart & circulatory research; AIDS research; delinquency prevention/services; legal services; housing/shelter, development; human services; children & youth, services; child development, services; family services; hospices; aging, centers & services; minorities/immigrants, centers & services; homeless, human services; civil rights; community development; Jewish federated giving programs; engineering & technology; computer science; science; economics; government/public administration; Roman Catholic agencies & churches; religion; minorities; disabled; aging; economically disadvantaged; homeless.
**Types of support:** Building/renovation; equipment; endowments; program development; conferences/seminars; fellowships; research.
**Limitations:** Giving in the U.S., with emphasis on IL. No support for public education. No grants to individuals, or for general support, continuing support, operating budgets, deficit financing, or unrestricted purposes.
**Publications:** Informational brochure (including application guidelines), application guidelines.
**Application information:** The scholarship program for the children of company employees has been discontinued. Applications sent by FAX not accepted. Application form required.
   *Copies of proposal:* 1
   *Deadline(s):* May 15
   *Board meeting date(s):* Feb., May, Aug., and Oct.
   *Final notification:* Nov.
**Officers and Trustees:*** William H. Scholl, Chair.; Pamela Scholl,* Pres.; Jack E. Scholl,* Secy.; David L. Royalty, Treas.; Neil Flanagin, Jeanne M. Scholl, Michael W. Scholl, Susan Scholl, Douglas C. Witherspoon.
**Number of staff:** 4 full-time professional; 1 part-time professional; 3 full-time support.
**EIN:** 366068724
**Recent grants for library/information services:**
**191-1** Cambridge Foundation, Cambridge, England, $162,800. For development of University Library. 1998.
**191-2** Chicago Public Library Foundation, Chicago, IL, $25,000. For computer literacy training. 1998.
**191-3** Newberry Library, Chicago, IL, $50,000. For Scholl Center endowment. 1998.
**191-4** Saint Augustine College, Chicago, IL, $10,000. Toward library materials. 1998.

---

**192**
### Elizabeth A. Smysor Charitable Trust
P.O. Box 1389
Murphysboro, IL  62966

Established in 1994 in IL.
**Grantmaker type:** Independent foundation

**Financial data** (yr. ended 07/31/99): Assets, $4,071,921 (M); expenditures, $273,850; qualifying distributions, $215,942; giving activities include $217,403 for 14 grants (high: $45,000; low: $2,025).
**Purpose and activities:** Contributes only for projects within the cities of Murphysboro & Ava, IL.
**Fields of interest:** Arts/cultural programs; secondary school/education; libraries/library science; community development, neighborhood development.
**Limitations:** Giving limited to Murphysboro and Ava, IL. No grants to individuals.
**Application information:** Application form required.
   *Initial approach:* Request application
   *Deadline(s):* Mar. 1
**Officers:** Thomas H. Jones, Chair.; Frank Cheatnam, Vice-Chair.; James A. Lawder, Jr., Secy.-Treas.
**Governors:** L.D. Allen, Scott Draves, Bert Ozburn, William Wilson.
**EIN:** 376243123

---

**193**
### The Swearingen Foundation
c/o Amoco Bldg.
200 E. Randolph St., Ste. 7906
Chicago, IL  60601

Established in 1996.
**Donor(s):** John E. Swearingen.
**Grantmaker type:** Independent foundation
**Financial data** (yr. ended 12/31/98): Assets, $3,422,130 (M); gifts received, $1,008,976; expenditures, $312,227; qualifying distributions, $253,446; giving activities include $256,677 for 47 grants (high: $100,000; low: $27).
**Purpose and activities:** Giving for higher education, medical centers, and to Federated giving programs.
**Fields of interest:** Museums; arts/cultural programs; higher education; libraries/library science; education; hospitals (general); boys & girls clubs; human services; Salvation Army; federated giving programs; Protestant agencies & churches; religion.
**Limitations:** Applications not accepted. Giving primarily in IL. No grants to individuals.
**Application information:** Contributes only to pre-selected organizations.
**Directors:** John F. Swearingen, Linda Swearingen-Arnold, Sally Swearingen-Origer, Marcia Swearingen-Pfleeger.
**EIN:** 367164493

---

**194**
### Sycamore Charities, Inc.
c/o National Bank & Trust Co.
230 W. State St.
Sycamore, IL  60178-1419

Established in 1958.
**Grantmaker type:** Independent foundation
**Financial data** (yr. ended 11/30/99): Assets, $1,534,407 (M); expenditures, $80,207; qualifying distributions, $67,145; giving activities include $68,944 for 16 grants (high: $29,787; low: $500).
**Purpose and activities:** Giving for education, health, and recreation.

**Fields of interest:** Libraries (public); health care; recreation.
**Limitations:** Applications not accepted. Giving primarily in IL. No grants to individuals.
**Application information:** Contributes only to pre-selected organizations.
**Officers:** Robert C. Johnson, Pres.; Howard A. Heidlauf, Secy.-Treas.
**Director:** John W. Ovitz, Jr.
**Agent:** National Bank & Trust Co.
**EIN:** 237425092

---

**195**
### The Tesuque Foundation, Inc.
c/o Sandra L. Soltis
300 S. Riverside Plz., Ste. 660
Chicago, IL  60606-6613
*Contact:* David Wilson

Established in 1990 in NY.
**Donor(s):** Andrea Wilson,‡ Fred W. Wilson.‡
**Grantmaker type:** Independent foundation
**Financial data** (yr. ended 12/31/98): Assets, $12,352,918 (M); expenditures, $531,057; qualifying distributions, $423,067; giving activities include $323,067 for 5 grants (high: $250,000; low: $5,000) and $100,000 for 5 grants to individuals of $20,000 each.
**Fields of interest:** Arts/cultural programs; libraries/library science; medical research; general charitable giving.
**Types of support:** General/operating support.
**Limitations:** Applications not accepted. Giving primarily in IL. No grants to individuals.
**Application information:** Contributes only to pre-selected organizations. Unsolicited requests for funds not considered.
**Officers and Directors:*** Pamela Wilson,* Pres.; David Wilson,* V.P.; Tom Ryckman, Secy.-Treas.
**Number of staff:** None.
**EIN:** 133579598

---

**196**
### John E. Timm Charitable Trust
c/o State Bank of Arthur
411 S. Vine St.
Arthur, IL  61911   (217) 543-2111
*Contact:* Board of Directors

Established in 1977.
**Grantmaker type:** Independent foundation
**Financial data** (yr. ended 12/31/98): Assets, $1,311,004 (M); expenditures, $48,889; qualifying distributions, $42,960; giving activities include $26,960 for 3 grants (high: $10,960; low: $6,000) and $16,000 for 30 grants to individuals (high: $1,600; low: $83).
**Purpose and activities:** Awards scholarships for higher education to Arthur and Lexington high school graduates.
**Fields of interest:** Secondary school/education; libraries/library science; federated giving programs.
**Types of support:** General/operating support; equipment; scholarship funds.
**Limitations:** Giving limited to Arthur, IL.
**Application information:**
   *Initial approach:* Letter
   *Deadline(s):* None
**Trustee:** State Bank of Arthur.
**EIN:** 371023095

## 197
## Vermilion Healthcare Foundation
702 N. Logan
Danville, IL  61832  (217) 431-7021
*Contact:* Valeria Saikley

Established in 1994.
**Grantmaker type:** Independent foundation
**Financial data** (yr. ended 09/30/99): Assets, $13,100,146 (M); expenditures, $1,290,918; qualifying distributions, $1,183,819; giving activities include $1,189,744 for 21 grants (high: $732,984; low: $2,930).
**Purpose and activities:** Support primarily for a medical center; giving also for research, education, and social and youth services.
**Fields of interest:** Libraries/library science; education; hospitals (general); human services; children & youth, services.
**Limitations:** Giving limited to Danville, IL. No grants to individuals.
**Publications:** Program policy statement, application guidelines.
**Application information:**
*Initial approach:* Telephone
*Copies of proposal:* 8
*Deadline(s):* Mar. 15, June 15, Sept. 15, and Dec. 15
*Board meeting date(s):* Last Wed. in Jan., Apr., July, and Oct.
**Officers:** W. John Shane, Chair.; Mary Michael Bateman, Vice-Chair.; Michael Mulcahey, Secy.-Treas.
**Directors:** Thomas Bott, H. Michael Finkle, Robert Hoecker, Robert Kesler, Mark Layden, Bruce Meachum, Robert Muirhead, Judd Peck, Rebecca Schlect, Frank Young.
**EIN:** 371225688

## 198
## Bernard and Rochelle Zell Charitable Trust
980 N. Michigan Ave., Ste. 1380
Chicago, IL  60611-4501

Established in 1986 in IL.
**Donor(s):** Rochelle Zell.
**Grantmaker type:** Independent foundation
**Financial data** (yr. ended 04/30/99): Assets, $1,851,368 (M); gifts received, $378,237; expenditures, $1,111,804; qualifying distributions, $1,110,181; giving activities include $1,111,210 for 73 grants (high: $884,700; low: $100).
**Purpose and activities:** Giving primarily to libraries, arts and cultural programs, Jewish organizations, and for education and medical research.
**Fields of interest:** Arts/cultural programs; libraries/library science; education; medical research; Jewish agencies & temples.
**Limitations:** Applications not accepted. Giving primarily in Chicago, IL. No grants to individuals.
**Application information:** Contributes only to pre-selected organizations.
**Trustee:** Roger S. Baskes.
**EIN:** 363440025

# INDIANA

## 199
## Auburn Foundry Foundation
c/o National City Bank
P.O. Box 110
Fort Wayne, IN  46801
*Contact:* David Fink, Tr.
*Application address:* c/o Auburn Foundry, Inc., 635 W. 11th St., Auburn, IN 46706; FAX: (219) 925-7944; E-mail: dfink@fwl.com

Established in 1955.
**Donor(s):** Auburn Foundry, Inc.
**Grantmaker type:** Company-sponsored foundation
**Financial data** (yr. ended 02/28/00): Assets, $1,434,540 (M); expenditures, $74,909; qualifying distributions, $72,205; giving activities include $68,500 for grants.
**Purpose and activities:** Funding primarily for arts and cultural programs, higher education, libraries, scholarships/financial aid, safety/disasters, human services, and youth services.
**Fields of interest:** Arts/cultural programs; higher education; libraries/library science; scholarships/financial aid; safety/disasters; human services; YM/YWCAs & YM/YWHAs; youth, services.
**Types of support:** General/operating support; continuing support; annual campaigns; capital campaigns; scholarship funds.
**Limitations:** Giving primarily in IN.
**Application information:** Application form not required.
*Initial approach:* Letter
*Copies of proposal:* 1
*Deadline(s):* None
*Board meeting date(s):* Jan., Apr., July, and Oct.
**Trustees:** David Fink, John Fink, William E. Fink, National City Bank.
**EIN:** 356019220

## 200
## Booe-Inlow-d'Arlier Memorial Charitable Foundation
P.O. Box 98
Covington, IN  47932
*Contact:* Kip White, Tr.
*Application address:* 3 Fountain Sq., Covington, IN 47932

Established in 1980 in IN.
**Donor(s):** George d'Arlier.‡
**Grantmaker type:** Independent foundation
**Financial data** (yr. ended 09/30/99): Assets, $4,087,936 (M); expenditures, $224,125; qualifying distributions, $204,610; giving activities include $177,242 for grants.
**Purpose and activities:** Support for local public libraries and summer study-abroad programs in France for local area high school students.
**Fields of interest:** Secondary school/education; libraries/library science.
**International interests:** France.
**Types of support:** Building/renovation.
**Limitations:** Applications not accepted. Giving primarily in Veedersburg, IN, and to

organizations that benefit residents or former residents.
**Application information:** Unsolicited requests for funds not accepted.
**Trustees:** Kip White, The Fountain Trust Co.
**EIN:** 311001831

## 201
## The Community Foundation of Muncie and Delaware County, Inc.
P.O. Box 807
Muncie, IN  47308-0807  (765) 747-7181
*Contact:* Roni Johnson, Exec. Dir.
*FAX:* (765) 289-7770; E-mail: cfmd@ecicnet.org

Incorporated in 1985 in IN.
**Grantmaker type:** Community foundation
**Financial data** (yr. ended 12/31/99): Assets, $28,734,707 (M); gifts received, $2,320,964; expenditures, $1,520,336; giving activities include $1,214,094 for grants.
**Purpose and activities:** Support for the improvement of the quality of life; primary areas of interest include economic development, cultural programs, educational programs, charitable organizations, and community betterment.
**Fields of interest:** Theater; arts/cultural programs; education, association; libraries/library science; education; environment; health care; health associations; crime/law enforcement; human services; youth, services; minorities/immigrants, centers & services; community development; economics; minorities.
**Types of support:** General/operating support; capital campaigns; building/renovation; equipment; program development; conferences/seminars; seed money; scholarship funds; technical assistance; grants to individuals; scholarships—to individuals; in-kind gifts; matching/challenge support.
**Limitations:** Giving limited to Muncie and Delaware County, IN. No support for religious purposes or public agency projects. No grants for endowment support or budget deficits.
**Publications:** Annual report, application guidelines, newsletter, informational brochure (including application guidelines), occasional report, financial statement, informational brochure.
**Application information:** Application form required.
*Initial approach:* Letter
*Copies of proposal:* 12
*Deadline(s):* 4th Fri. of Jan., Apr., July, and Oct.
*Board meeting date(s):* 3rd Mon. of each month
*Final notification:* 3rd Mon. of Feb., May, Aug., and Nov.
**Officers and Trustees:*** Steve Anderson,* Pres.; Wilbur Davis, V.P.; Mary Sissel,* Secy.; R. David Hoover, Treas.; Roni Johnson, Exec. Dir.
**Number of staff:** 1 full-time professional; 1 part-time professional; 1 full-time support.
**EIN:** 351640051

## 202

## Decatur County Community Foundation, Inc.

P.O. Box 72
101 E. Main St., Ste. 1
Greensburg, IN 47240 (812) 662-6364
*Contact:* Michelle Anderson, Exec. Dir.
*FAX:* (812) 662-8704

Established in 1992 in IN.
**Grantmaker type:** Community foundation
**Financial data** (yr. ended 12/31/99): Assets, $6,259,865 (M); gifts received, $1,720,835; expenditures, $435,761; giving activities include $358,371 for 46 grants (high: $28,000; low: $416; average: $416–$28,000).
**Purpose and activities:** Giving for community development, human services, and recreation programs.
**Fields of interest:** Arts/cultural programs; libraries (public); education; health care; recreation; aging, centers & services; homeless, human services; community development.
**Types of support:** Equipment; emergency funds; seed money; scholarship funds; technical assistance; scholarships—to individuals; matching/challenge support.
**Limitations:** Giving primarily in Decatur County, IN.
**Publications:** Annual report (including application guidelines), financial statement, occasional report, application guidelines.
**Application information:** Application form required.
*Initial approach:* Letter of inquiry
*Copies of proposal:* 10
*Deadline(s):* Feb. 1, May 1, Aug. 1, and Nov. 1
*Final notification:* Normally within 1-month
**Officers and Directors:*** William O. Smith,* Pres.; Toni Collins,* V.P.; Bob Blankman,* Secy.-Treas.; Michelle Anderson, Exec. Dir.; Edna Domingo, Phyllis Hamilton, Albert Knecht, Jr., David Miers, Jerry Westhafer.
**Number of staff:** 1 full-time professional.
**EIN:** 351870979

## 203

## Dekko Foundation, Inc. ▼

P.O. Box 548
Kendallville, IN 46755-0548 (219) 347-1278
*Contact:* Richard Mappin, Pres.
*FAX:* (219) 347-7103; E-mail: dekko@noble.cioe; URL: http://www.dekkofoundation.org

Established in 1981 in IN.
**Donor(s):** Chester E. Dekko.‡
**Grantmaker type:** Independent foundation
**Financial data** (yr. ended 08/31/99): Assets, $195,481,101 (M); gifts received, $2,725,000; expenditures, $4,169,216; qualifying distributions, $3,534,339; giving activities include $2,897,619 for 94 grants (high: $488,500; average: $1,000–$25,000).
**Purpose and activities:** Support primarily for philanthropy, human service organizations, K-12 educational programs, and early childhood development.
**Fields of interest:** Museums; early childhood education; elementary school/education; secondary school/education; adult/continuing education; libraries/library science; education.

**Types of support:** General/operating support; annual campaigns; capital campaigns; building/renovation; equipment; endowments; program development; conferences/seminars; seed money; curriculum development; technical assistance; matching/challenge support.
**Limitations:** Giving primarily in Limestone County, AL; Clarke, Decatur, Lucas, Ringgold, and Union counties, IA; Noble, DeKalb, Whitley, Steuben, LaGrange, and Kosciousko counties, IN; and Lincoln and Giles counties, TN. No grants to individuals.
**Publications:** Biennial report, newsletter, application guidelines.
**Application information:** Application form not required.
*Initial approach:* Letter
*Copies of proposal:* 1
*Board meeting date(s):* Six times per year
**Officers and Directors:*** Lorene Salsbery,* C.E.O.; Richard Mappin, Pres.; Erica D. Dekko,* V.P.; Chester E. Dekko, Jr.
**Number of staff:** 4 full-time professional; 3 full-time support.
**EIN:** 351528135

## 204

## The W. C. Griffith Foundation

c/o National City Bank, Indiana
101 W. Washington St., Ste. 600E, Box 5031
Indianapolis, IN 46255

Trust established in 1959 in IN.
**Donor(s):** William C. Griffith,‡ Ruth Perry Griffith.‡
**Grantmaker type:** Independent foundation
**Financial data** (yr. ended 11/30/98): Assets, $17,721,651 (M); expenditures, $718,564; qualifying distributions, $658,281; giving activities include $636,100 for 104 grants (high: $50,000; low: $1,000; average: $1,000–$15,000).
**Purpose and activities:** Support primarily for hospitals, health associations, medical and cancer research, the arts, including music and museums, community funds and development, higher, secondary, and other education, family planning services, child welfare, the homeless, the environment, libraries, and Christian religious organizations.
**Fields of interest:** Museums; music; arts/cultural programs; secondary school/education; higher education; libraries/library science; education; environment; hospitals (general); family planning; health associations; cancer; medical research; cancer research; children & youth, services; homeless, human services; community development; federated giving programs; Christian agencies & churches; minorities; homeless.
**Types of support:** Continuing support; capital campaigns; building/renovation.
**Limitations:** Giving primarily in Indianapolis, IN. No grants to individuals, or for scholarships or fellowships.
**Application information:** Application form not required.
*Initial approach:* Letter
*Copies of proposal:* 1
*Deadline(s):* None
*Board meeting date(s):* June and Nov.
**Trustee:** National City Bank, Indiana.

**Advisors:** Ruthelen Griffith Burns, Charles P. Griffith, Jr., Walter S. Griffith, William C. Griffith III, Wendy Griffith Kortepeter.
**Number of staff:** 1 part-time support.
**EIN:** 356007742

## 205

## The Floyd A. and Frieda S. Guynn Foundation

c/o Norwest Bank Indiana, N.A.
P.O. Box 960
Fort Wayne, IN 46801-2363 (219) 461-6444

Established in 1987 in IN.
**Grantmaker type:** Independent foundation
**Financial data** (yr. ended 06/30/00): Assets, $1,277,916 (M); expenditures, $77,530; qualifying distributions, $73,589; giving activities include $66,169 for 2 grants (high: $48,324; low: $17,845).
**Purpose and activities:** Giving primarily for children in Wabash County, IN. Support also for education, health, welfare and rehabilitation of the ailing and handicapped throughout IN.
**Fields of interest:** Libraries/library science; children & youth, services.
**Limitations:** Giving primarily in Wabash County, IN.
**Application information:** Application form not required.
*Initial approach:* Letter
*Deadline(s):* None
**Trustee:** Norwest Bank Indiana, N.A.
**EIN:** 356465390

## 206

## The Indianapolis Foundation ▼

615 N. Alabama St., Rm. 119
Indianapolis, IN 46204 (317) 634-7497
*Contact:* J.A. Rosenfeld, Interim Exec. Dir.
*FAX:* (317) 684-0943; E-mail: program@cicf.org;
URL: http://www.cicf.org/About/fsetif.htm

Established in 1916 in IN by resolution of trust.
**Grantmaker type:** Community foundation
**Financial data** (yr. ended 12/31/99): Assets, $196,347,000 (M); gifts received, $7,944,856; expenditures, $15,484,483; giving activities include $13,732,801 for 149 grants (high: $500,000; low: $443; average: $1,000–$200,000).
**Purpose and activities:** Support from the unrestricted fund in the areas of arts, culture, and humanities; civic and community development; education and libraries; health and human services; and information and technology. The Indianapolis Foundation is an affiliate of the Central Indiana Community Foundation.
**Fields of interest:** Arts/cultural programs; education; medical care, rehabilitation; health care; mental health/crisis services; health associations; housing/shelter, development; human services; children & youth, services; family services; aging, centers & services; community development; government/public administration; disabled.
**Types of support:** General/operating support; annual campaigns; capital campaigns; building/renovation; equipment; land acquisition; emergency funds; program development; conferences/seminars;

publication; seed money; curriculum development; technical assistance; consulting services; program evaluation; program-related investments/loans; matching/challenge support.
**Limitations:** Giving limited to Indianapolis and Marion County, IN. No support for religious or sectarian purposes, political campaigns, or for public schools or state funded universities and colleges. No grants to individuals, or for endowment funds, long-term funding, travel, annual appeals, fundraising events, post-event funding, operating budgets, medical, scientific, or academic research, publications, films, audio/visual, or media publication; generally no loans.
**Publications:** Annual report (including application guidelines), newsletter, informational brochure.
**Application information:** Applicants must meet with a member of the program staff before submitting a formal proposal. Application form required.

> *Initial approach:* Brief letter of inquiry or telephone
> *Copies of proposal:* 8
> *Deadline(s):* Consult with program staff
> *Board meeting date(s):* Feb., May, June, Sept., and Nov.
> *Final notification:* Immediately following meetings

**Officers and Trustees:*** Robert T. Grand,* Chair.; Charles A. Pechette,* Vice-Chair.; Milton O. Thompson,* Secy.; J.A. Rosenfeld, Interim Exec. Dir.; Rexford C. Early, Martha D. Lamkin.
**Trustee Banks:** Bank One, Bank One, Indianapolis, N.A., Fifth Third Bank, First of America Bank, N.A., The Huntington National Bank, Key Trust Co. of Indiana, N.A., National City Bank of Indiana, Union Bank & Trust Co.
**Number of staff:** None.
**EIN:** 350868115
**Recent grants for library/information services:**
**206-1** Arlington High School, Indianapolis, IN, $18,000. For school library's collection development. 1999.
**206-2** Arsenal Technical High School, Indianapolis, IN, $18,000. For school library's collection development. 1999.
**206-3** Beech Grove High School, Beech Grove, IN, $18,000. For school library's collection development. 1999.
**206-4** Ben Davis Senior High School, Indianapolis, IN, $16,000. For school library's collection development. 1999.
**206-5** Bishop Chatard High School, Indianapolis, IN, $18,000. For school library's collection development. 1999.
**206-6** Brebeuf Preparatory School, Indianapolis, IN, $18,000. For school library's collection development. 1999.
**206-7** Broad Ripple High School, Indianapolis, IN, $16,000. For school library's collection development. 1999.
**206-8** Cardinal Ritter Junior-Senior High School, Indianapolis, IN, $16,462. For school library's collection development. 1999.
**206-9** Cathedral High School, Indianapolis, IN, $18,000. For school library's collection development. 1999.
**206-10** Childrens Museum of Indianapolis, Indianapolis, IN, $200,000. For Children's Museum Library. 1999.

**206-11** Covenant Christian High School, Indianapolis, IN, $18,000. For school library's collection development. 1999.
**206-12** Decatur Central High School, Indianapolis, IN, $18,000. For school library's collection development. 1999.
**206-13** Eliza Hendricks High School, Indianapolis, IN, $16,000. For school library's collection development. 1999.
**206-14** Emmerich Manual High School, Indianapolis, IN, $18,000. For school library's collection development. 1999.
**206-15** Franklin Central High School, Indianapolis, IN, $18,000. For school library's collection development. 1999.
**206-16** Heritage Christian Schools, Indianapolis, IN, $18,000. For school library's collection development. 1999.
**206-17** Indiana School for the Blind, Indianapolis, IN, $16,000. For school library's collection development. 1999.
**206-18** Indiana School for the Deaf, Indianapolis, IN, $18,000. For school library's collection development. 1999.
**206-19** Indiana University-Purdue University, Indianapolis, IN, $250,000. For Joseph and Matthew Payton Philanthropic Studies Library Endowment. 1999.
**206-20** Indianapolis Museum of Art, Stout Library, Indianapolis, IN, $10,000. For technical conversion fund. 1999.
**206-21** Indianapolis Public Schools, Indianapolis, IN, $200,000. For Africa, Spirit of the Continent Project, collection development initiative to increase resources and teacher knowledge about Africa. 1999.
**206-22** Indianapolis Public Schools, Indianapolis, IN, $18,000. For Alternative School library's collection development. 1999.
**206-23** Indianapolis-Marion County Public Library Foundation, Indianapolis, IN, $2,500,000. For matching grant for endowment. 1999.
**206-24** Indianapolis-Marion County Public Library, Indianapolis, IN, $136,884. For IMA library catalog conversion/merge project. 1999.
**206-25** Indianapolis-Marion County Public Library, Indianapolis, IN, $117,305. For Children's Museum Library. 1999.
**206-26** Indianapolis-Marion County Public Library, Indianapolis, IN, $43,000. For Social Assets and Vulnerabilities Indicators (SAVI) project. 1999.
**206-27** International Center of Indianapolis, Indianapolis, IN, $10,000. For computer equipment. 1999.
**206-28** Lawrence Central High School, Indianapolis, IN, $18,000. For school library's collection development. 1999.
**206-29** Lawrence North High School, Indianapolis, IN, $16,500. For school library's collection development. 1999.
**206-30** Lutheran High School, Indianapolis, IN, $16,000. For school library's collection development. 1999.
**206-31** North Central High School, Indianapolis, IN, $18,000. For school library's collection development. 1999.
**206-32** Northwest High School, Indianapolis, IN, $18,000. For school library's collection development. 1999.

**206-33** Park Tudor School, Indianapolis, IN, $18,000. For school library's collection development. 1999.
**206-34** Perry Meridian High School, Indianapolis, IN, $18,000. For school library's collection development. 1999.
**206-35** Pike High School, Indianapolis, IN, $18,000. For school library's collection development. 1999.
**206-36** Roncalli High School, Indianapolis, IN, $18,000. For school library's collection development. 1999.
**206-37** Scecina Memorial High School, Indianapolis, IN, $18,000. For school library's collection development. 1999.
**206-38** Southport High School, Southport, IN, $18,000. For school library's collection development. 1999.
**206-39** Speedway High School, Indianapolis, IN, $18,000. For school library's collection development. 1999.
**206-40** Warren Central High School, Indianapolis, IN, $18,000. For school library's collection development. 1999.

### 207
### International Palace of Sports, Inc.
P.O. Box 332
North Webster, IN  46555  (219) 834-4422
*Contact:* Joan Rhodes, Secy.-Treas.

**Grantmaker type:** Independent foundation
**Financial data** (yr. ended 03/31/98): Assets, $4,392,529 (M); expenditures, $240,635; qualifying distributions, $154,761; giving activities include $142,557 for 34 grants (high: $2,000; low: $250) and $65,907 for 38 grants to individuals (high: $45,000; low: $250).
**Purpose and activities:** Scholarships only to graduates of school districts within Wawasee, Warsaw or Whitko, IN. Also some support for community projects and programs.
**Fields of interest:** Libraries/library science; education; recreation, community facilities; youth, services.
**Types of support:** Scholarship funds; scholarships—to individuals.
**Limitations:** Giving limited to the Wawasee, Warsaw, and Whitko, IN school districts.
**Application information:** Application form required.

> *Deadline(s):* Mar. 31

**Officers:** Richard Long, Pres.; Joan Rhodes, Secy.-Treas.
**EIN:** 351331032

### 208
### Journal-Gazette Foundation, Inc.
701 S. Clinton St.
Fort Wayne, IN  46802  (219) 424-5257
*Contact:* Richard G. Inskeep, Pres.

Established in 1985 in IN.
**Donor(s):** Journal-Gazette Co., Richard G. Inskeep, Harriett J. Inskeep.
**Grantmaker type:** Company-sponsored foundation
**Financial data** (yr. ended 12/31/99): Assets, $8,034,554 (M); gifts received, $87,563; expenditures, $684,195; qualifying distributions, $675,168; giving activities include $675,168 for 95 grants (high: $103,350; low: $40).

**Purpose and activities:** Giving primarily for education and human services.
**Fields of interest:** Arts/cultural programs; higher education; libraries/library science; education; health care; medical research; human services; YM/YWCAs & YM/YWHAs; children & youth, services; federated giving programs; Christian agencies & churches.
**Types of support:** General/operating support; capital campaigns.
**Limitations:** Giving limited to northeastern IN. No grants to individuals.
**Application information:**
  *Initial approach:* Letter
  *Deadline(s):* None
  *Board meeting date(s):* Quarterly
**Officers and Directors:\*** Richard G. Inskeep,\* Pres.; Jerry D. Fox, Secy.-Treas.; Harriett J. Inskeep, Julie Inskeep Walda.
**EIN:** 311134237

---

**209**
**Marshall County Community Foundation, Inc.**
P.O. Box 716
Plymouth, IN  46563  (219) 935-5159
*Contact:* R. Jeffrey Honzik, Exec. Dir.

Established in 1991 in IN.
**Grantmaker type:** Community foundation
**Financial data** (yr. ended 06/30/99): Assets, $11,715,032 (M); gifts received, $3,397,564; expenditures, $531,790; giving activities include $294,453 for 71 grants (high: $53,378; low: $91) and $51,555 for 18 grants to individuals (high: $37,424; low: $100; average: $1,000–$2,000).
**Fields of interest:** Arts/cultural programs; secondary school/education; higher education; libraries (public); scholarships/financial aid; wildlife preservation & protection; hospitals (general); parks/playgrounds; recreation; community development; government/public administration; Protestant agencies & churches.
**Types of support:** General/operating support; endowments; publication; scholarship funds; consulting services; scholarships—to individuals.
**Limitations:** Giving limited to Marshall County, IN.
**Publications:** Annual report (including application guidelines), financial statement, grants list, newsletter, informational brochure (including application guidelines), program policy statement, application guidelines.
**Officers and Directors:\*** William Erwin, Pres.; Elwood Hillis, V.P.; Lynn Overmyer,\* Secy.; Glenn Borden,\* Treas.; R. Jeffrey Honzik, Exec. Dir.; Janet Anglemyer, Mark Batman, Ginny Gibson, Ron Gifford, Chuck Lewallen, Fred Lintner, Capt. William W. Pippenger, Sarah Smith.
**Number of staff:** 2 full-time professional.
**EIN:** 351826870

---

**210**
**The Martin Foundation, Inc.** ▼
500 Simpson Ave.
Elkhart, IN  46515  (219) 295-3343
*Contact:* Elizabeth L. Martin, Co-Pres.

Incorporated in 1953 in IN.

**Donor(s):** Ross Martin,‡ Esther Martin,‡ Lee Martin, Geraldine F. Martin.
**Grantmaker type:** Independent foundation
**Financial data** (yr. ended 06/30/99): Assets, $62,062,417 (M); expenditures, $2,945,060; qualifying distributions, $2,279,208; giving activities include $2,208,375 for 72 grants (high: $950,000; low: $500; average: $1,000–$25,000).
**Purpose and activities:** Emphasis on education and social services, including programs for women and youth, environmental and conservation organizations; support also for cultural programs, public interest programs, and international development.
**Fields of interest:** Media/communications; museums; arts/cultural programs; early childhood education; higher education; adult/continuing education; libraries/library science; education; natural resource conservation & protection; environment; animal welfare; wildlife preservation & protection; family planning; medical care, rehabilitation; mental health/crisis services; housing/shelter, development; human services; youth, services; family services; women, centers & services; minorities/immigrants, centers & services; international economic development; peace; community development; federated giving programs; population studies; public affairs; minorities; women; economically disadvantaged.
**Limitations:** Giving primarily in IN; limited national and international support. No grants to individuals.
**Publications:** Annual report (including application guidelines).
**Application information:** Application form not required.
  *Initial approach:* Letter
  *Copies of proposal:* 1
  *Deadline(s):* None
  *Board meeting date(s):* As required
  *Final notification:* 4 to 8 weeks
**Officers and Directors:\*** Geraldine F. Martin,\* Chair.; Elizabeth L. Martin,\* Co-Pres.; Jennifer L. Martin,\* Co-Pres.; Casper Martin,\* Treas.; Lee Martin, Rex Martin.
**Number of staff:** None.
**EIN:** 351070929

---

**211**
**Rieke Corporation Foundation**
c/o Norwest Bank Indiana, N.A.
P.O. Box 960
Fort Wayne, IN  46801-6632
*Contact:* Donald E. Kelly, Tr.
*Application address:* c/o Rieke Corp., 500 W. 7th St., Auburn, IN 46706-2289, tel.: (219) 925-3700

**Donor(s):** Rieke Corp.
**Grantmaker type:** Company-sponsored foundation
**Financial data** (yr. ended 12/31/99): Assets, $1,420,411 (M); gifts received, $20,000; expenditures, $58,052; qualifying distributions, $52,635; giving activities include $47,200 for 12 grants (high: $15,000; low: $500).
**Purpose and activities:** Giving for community, youth and human services.
**Fields of interest:** Museums; libraries/library science; animal welfare; human services; youth,

services; aging, centers & services; disabled; aging.
**Limitations:** Giving limited to Auburn, IN.
**Application information:**
  *Initial approach:* Letter or telephone
  *Deadline(s):* Aug. 31
**Trustee:** Norwest Bank Indiana, N.A.
**EIN:** 510158651

---

**212**
**Jennie Thompson Foundation, Inc.**
P.O. Box 176
Ligonier, IN  46767-0176  (219) 894-3931
*Contact:* Samuel W. Patton, Jr., Pres.

Established in 1976.
**Grantmaker type:** Independent foundation
**Financial data** (yr. ended 12/31/98): Assets, $2,523,323 (M); expenditures, $65,934; qualifying distributions, $49,990; giving activities include $46,550 for 5 grants (high: $35,600; low: $950).
**Purpose and activities:** Giving to youth programs and civic projects.
**Fields of interest:** Elementary/secondary education; libraries (public); youth development, services; public affairs, government agencies.
**Types of support:** General/operating support; equipment.
**Limitations:** Giving limited to the West Noble, IN, area.
**Application information:** Application form required.
  *Deadline(s):* None
**Officers:** Samuel W. Patton, Jr., Pres.; Richard D. Brown, V.P.; Howard K. Heckner, Secy.; Maltha M. Burke, Treas.
**EIN:** 237450325

---

**213**
**The Vahn Family Foundation, Inc.**
2336 Turnberry Ln.
Fort Wayne, IN  46804
*Contact:* Sherry S. Connelly, Secy.-Treas.
*Application address:* 11008 Carnoustie Ln., Fort Wayne, IN 46814

Established in 1997 in IN.
**Donor(s):** James M. Vahn, Mrs. James M. Vahn.
**Grantmaker type:** Independent foundation
**Financial data** (yr. ended 12/31/99): Assets, $2,726,540 (M); gifts received, $973,086; expenditures, $62,682; qualifying distributions, $61,242; giving activities include $56,883 for 29 grants (high: $9,400; low: $100).
**Purpose and activities:** Giving for museums, education, and human services.
**Fields of interest:** Museums; libraries/library science; YM/YWCAs & YM/YWHAs.
**Application information:**
  *Initial approach:* Letter
  *Deadline(s):* None
**Officers and Directors:\*** James M. Vahn,\* Chair; Majorie Lee Vahn,\* Pres.; Sherry S. Connelly,\* Secy.-Treas.; Deborah Vahn Gilreath, Stephanie S. Moen, James M. Vahn III.
**EIN:** 352008538

## 214
**Helen P. Van Arnam Foundation, Inc.**
111 E. Wayne St., Ste. 800
Fort Wayne, IN 46802-2603 (219) 424-8000
*Contact:* Jeanne E. Longsworth, Secy.-Treas.

Established in 1996 in IN.
**Donor(s):** Helen P. Van Arnam.‡
**Grantmaker type:** Independent foundation
**Financial data** (yr. ended 12/31/99): Assets,
$1,755,912 (M); expenditures, $95,888;
qualifying distributions, $79,911; giving
activities include $67,513 for 11 grants (high:
$14,300; low: $2,500).
**Purpose and activities:** Giving primarily to arts
and culture, orchestra, and boy scouts.
**Fields of interest:** Orchestra (symphony);
libraries (public); Boy Scouts.
**Limitations:** Giving limited to Fort Wayne, IN.
**Application information:**
  *Initial approach:* Letter
  *Deadline(s):* None
**Officers and Directors:*** John F. Bonsib,* Pres.;
Maurice C. Keltsch,* V.P.; Jeanne E.
Longsworth,* Secy.-Treas.; Patricia E. Bonsib.
**EIN:** 351927467

# IOWA

## 215
**AmerUs Group Charitable Foundation**
(Formerly American Mutual Life/Amerus
Charitable Foundation)
699 Walnut St.
Des Moines, IA 50309 (515) 283-2371
*Contact:* Ted Wheat, V.P., Comm. Rels.

Established in 1994 in IA.
**Donor(s):** American Mutual Life Insurance Co.,
AmerUs Group Co.
**Grantmaker type:** Company-sponsored
foundation
**Financial data** (yr. ended 12/31/98): Assets,
$9,538,566 (M); gifts received, $406,433;
expenditures, $582,008; qualifying distributions,
$545,426; giving activities include $564,695 for
123 grants (high: $150,000; low: $25).
**Fields of interest:** Visual arts;
elementary/secondary education; higher
education; medical school/education;
theological school/education; libraries (public);
natural resource conservation & protection;
botanical gardens; Boy Scouts; YM/YWCAs &
YM/YWHAs; youth, services; hospices; civil
rights, minorities; community development,
public policy.
**Limitations:** Giving primarily in IA.
**Application information:**
  *Deadline(s):* None
**Officers:** Sam C. Kalainov, Pres.; Roger Fors,
V.P., Investments; Ted W. Wheat, V.P., Comm.
Rels.; James A. Smallenberger, Secy.; Michael G.
Fraizer, Treas.
**Directors:** Roger K. Brooks, Thomas C.
Godlasky.
**EIN:** 421431745

## 216
**Edith Curtis Armstrong & Florence E.
  Curtis Foundation**
246 Woodlawn Ct.
Clinton, IA 52732
*Contact:* David Shaff, Pres.

Established in 1954.
**Grantmaker type:** Independent foundation
**Financial data** (yr. ended 12/31/99): Assets,
$2,178,222 (M); expenditures, $454,349;
qualifying distributions, $421,037; giving
activities include $422,505 for 21 grants (high:
$355,000; low: $100).
**Fields of interest:** Higher education;
libraries/library science; education; human
services; federated giving programs.
**Types of support:** General/operating support;
building/renovation; equipment.
**Limitations:** Giving primarily in the Clinton, IA,
area. No grants to individuals.
**Application information:** Application form not
required.
  *Initial approach:* Proposal
  *Deadline(s):* None
**Officers:** David O. Shaff, Pres.; Dee Willoughby,
V.P. and Secy.-Treas.
**Directors:** Everett Eslinger.
**EIN:** 426054969

## 217
**Homer G. Barr Trust**
P.O. Box 370
Webster City, IA 50595
*Application address:* c/o First American Bank,
1207 Central Ave., Fort Dodge, IA 50501, tel.:
(515) 832-1133

Established in 1997 in IA.
**Grantmaker type:** Independent foundation
**Financial data** (yr. ended 12/31/99): Assets,
$973,440 (M); expenditures, $92,153;
qualifying distributions, $61,861; giving
activities include $56,149 for 13 grants (high:
$7,500; low: $1,000) and $8,000 for 2 grants to
individuals of $4,000 each.
**Purpose and activities:** Scholarships are for
individuals attending accredited divinity schools.
**Fields of interest:** Theological school/education;
libraries/library science; scholarships/financial
aid; education; Alzheimer's disease; human
services; children & youth, services; family
services; Christian agencies & churches.
**Types of support:** General/operating support;
scholarships—to individuals.
**Limitations:** Giving limited to IA.
**Application information:** Application form
required.
  *Deadline(s):* None
**Trustee:** First American Bank.
**EIN:** 426299595

## 218
**Lavern T. Busse & Audrey Busse
  Foundation**
2129 North Towne Ln., N.E., Ste. B
Cedar Rapids, IA 52402

Established in 1990 in TX.
**Donor(s):** Lavern T. Busse, Audrey Busse.
**Grantmaker type:** Independent foundation

**Financial data** (yr. ended 12/31/98): Assets,
$2,168,453 (M); gifts received, $49,438;
expenditures, $58,671; qualifying distributions,
$56,090; giving activities include $56,000 for
14 grants (high: $20,000; low: $1,000).
**Purpose and activities:** Giving for higher
education, religion, cultural organizations, and
federated giving programs.
**Fields of interest:** Historic preservation/historical
societies; higher education; libraries/library
science; health associations; cancer research;
camps; federated giving programs; Protestant
agencies & churches.
**Limitations:** Applications not accepted. No
grants to individuals.
**Application information:** Contributes only to
pre-selected organizations.
**Trustees:** Audrey Busse, Jeffrey Busse, Lavern T.
Busse, Lori A. Busse, Lisa Busse Carpentier.
**EIN:** 752342746

## 219
**Roy J. Carver Charitable Trust ▼**
202 Iowa Ave.
Muscatine, IA 52761-3733 (319) 263-4010
*Contact:* Troy K. Ross, Ph.D., Exec. Admin.
*FAX:* (319) 263-1547; E-mail:
info@carvertrust.org; URL: http://
www.carvertrust.org

Established in 1982 in IA.
**Donor(s):** Roy J. Carver, Sr.‡
**Grantmaker type:** Independent foundation
**Financial data** (yr. ended 04/30/00): Assets,
$299,286,217 (M); expenditures, $15,386,319;
qualifying distributions, $14,464,591; giving
activities include $14,032,071 for 145 grants
(high: $2,000,000; low: $1,050; average:
$10,000–$150,000).
**Purpose and activities:** Support primarily for
biomedical and scientific research and programs
addressing the educational needs of youth.
**Fields of interest:** Elementary/secondary
education; higher education; libraries/library
science; biomedicine; medical research; youth
development; science, research.
**Types of support:** Capital campaigns;
building/renovation; equipment; program
development; conferences/seminars;
professorships; seed money; curriculum
development; scholarship funds; research.
**Limitations:** Giving primarily in IA. No support
for religious activities or political organizations.
No grants to individuals, or for endowments,
fundraising benefits, program advertising,
annual operating support.
**Publications:** Biennial report, informational
brochure (including application guidelines).
**Application information:** Proposals must be
accompanied by a standardized cover sheet
available from the trust. Application form not
required.
  *Initial approach:* Letter
  *Copies of proposal:* 1
  *Deadline(s):* Feb. 15, May 15, Aug. 15, and
    Nov. 15
  *Board meeting date(s):* 3rd fri. of Apr., July.,
    Oct., and Jan.
**Officers and Trustees:*** Arthur E. Dahl,* Chair.;
Roy J. Carver, Jr.,* Vice-Chair.; Lucille A.
Carver,* Secy.; Troy K. Ross, Ph.D., Exec.
Admin.; Willard L. Boyd, William F. Cory, J.
Larry Griffith, Clay LeGrand.

**Number of staff:** 4 full-time professional; 1 full-time support; 1 part-time support.
**EIN:** 421186589
**Recent grants for library/information services:**
**219-1** Albert City Public Library, Albert City, IA, $10,000. For construction of new library. 1999.
**219-2** Alden Public Library, Alden, IA, $20,000. To construct new building addition. 1999.
**219-3** Anita Public Library, Anita, IA, $19,964. For furnishings for library. 1999.
**219-4** Bremwood Lutheran Childrens Home, Waterloo, IA, $250,000. To construct alternative education center and recreation complex. 1999.
**219-5** Central College, Pella, IA, $40,000. For campus library automation project. 1999.
**219-6** Davenport Public Library, Davenport, IA, $100,000. To renovate Special Collections Center. 1999.
**219-7** Eldora Public Library, Eldora, IA, $40,000. To construct new library building. 1999.
**219-8** Family Resources, Bettendorf, IA, $25,025. For technological improvements to information management system. 1999.
**219-9** Fayette Community Library, Fayette, IA, $20,000. To construct addition to existing library. 1999.
**219-10** Fort Dodge Public Library Foundation, Fort Dodge, IA, $60,000. To construct new library. 1999.
**219-11** Glidden, City of, Glidden Public Library, Glidden, IA, $20,000. To construct new public library building. 1999.
**219-12** Harlan Community Library, Harlan, IA, $10,000. For furnishings for newly renovated children's section. 1999.
**219-13** Iowa College Foundation, Des Moines, IA, $300,000. For continued support for Library Challenge Grant program. 1999.
**219-14** Iowa Falls, City of, Carnegie Ellsworth Public Library, Iowa Falls, IA, $40,000. For technology for new library. 1999.
**219-15** Kingsley Public Library, Kingsley, IA, $20,000. For furnishings and technology for new library. 1999.
**219-16** Monmouth College, Monmouth, IL, $1,000,000. For renovation of Library and to upgrade Dorothy Peterson Dahl Computer Center. 1999.
**219-17** Mount Saint Clare College, Clinton, IA, $120,000. To expand Library's electronic research databases. 1999.
**219-18** Preston Public Library, Preston, IA, $20,000. To construct new library. 1999.
**219-19** Solon Public Library, Solon, IA, $20,000. To construct new library building. 1999.
**219-20** Tama Public Library, Tama, IA, $40,000. To construct new library building. 1999.
**219-21** University of Iowa Foundation, Iowa City, IA, $269,512. For new Science Library Information Literacy Initiative. 1999.
**219-22** Washta Public Library, Washta, IA, $20,000. For furnishings, shelving and technology for new library space. 1999.
**219-23** Waterloo Public Library, Waterloo, IA, $60,000. For library automation. 1999.
**219-24** Woodbine Carnegie Public Library, Woodbine, IA, $20,000. To construct new library addition. 1999.

**220**
**Community Foundation of Waterloo/Cedar Falls & Northeast Iowa**
(Formerly Waterloo Civic Foundation)
P.O. Box 1176
Waterloo, IA 50704 (319) 287-9106
*Contact:* Mary Ann Burk, Pres. and C.E.O.
*FAX:* (319) 287-9105; E-mail: mburk927@aol.com

Incorporated in 1956 in IA.
**Grantmaker type:** Community foundation
**Financial data** (yr. ended 04/30/99): Assets, $15,648,626 (M); gifts received, $6,516,783; expenditures, $1,218,824; giving activities include $1,058,889 for grants.
**Purpose and activities:** To promote, encourage, and aid recreational, benevolent, charitable, medical, scientific, literary, educational, and research organizations' projects of work in Waterloo and northeast IA.
**Fields of interest:** Arts/cultural programs; child development, education; libraries/library science; education; recreation; human services; children & youth, services; child development, services; family services; minorities/immigrants, centers & services; minorities; general charitable giving.
**Types of support:** Continuing support; equipment; emergency funds; professorships; publication; seed money; research; exchange programs; matching/challenge support.
**Limitations:** Giving limited to the Waterloo/Cedar Falls, IA, area. No grants to individuals, or for annual campaigns, operating budgets, renovation projects, or conferences and seminars.
**Publications:** Application guidelines, financial statement, grants list, informational brochure (including application guidelines).
**Application information:** Application form required.
*Copies of proposal:* 1
*Deadline(s):* Apr. 1 and Oct. 1
*Board meeting date(s):* 1st Monday in June and Dec.
**Officer:** Mary Ann Burk, Pres. and C.E.O.
**Number of staff:** 1 full-time professional; 1 part-time support.
**EIN:** 426060414

**221**
**The Cathrine Vincent Deardorf Charitable Foundation**
c/o First American Bank
P.O. Drawer 798
Fort Dodge, IA 50501-0798 (515) 955-0679
*Contact:* Susie Kieler

Established in 1994 in IA.
**Grantmaker type:** Independent foundation
**Financial data** (yr. ended 12/31/99): Assets, $9,452,719 (M); gifts received, $2,006; expenditures, $494,121; qualifying distributions, $412,970; giving activities include $419,969 for 24 grants (high: $200,000; low: $500).
**Purpose and activities:** Giving primarily for the community, including arts and culture, education, and health and human services.
**Fields of interest:** Arts, multipurpose centers/programs; performing arts; elementary/secondary education; libraries/library science; health care,

reproductive health; human services; children & youth, services.
**Limitations:** Giving limited to Webster County, IA. No support for religious activities and groups. No grants to individuals.
**Application information:** Application form not required.
*Initial approach:* Letter
*Deadline(s):* None
**Officers:** Hans Nielsen, Pres.; Jane Gibb, V.P.; Judy Perkins, Secy.-Treas.
**Trustees:** Delores Garst, James A. Kerkhove.
**EIN:** 426496438

**222**
**Farrer Endowment Foundation**
10 1st St., N.W.
P.O. Box 1567
Mason City, IA 50402-1567
*Contact:* Gerald M. Stambaugh, Secy.

Established in 1986 in IA.
**Grantmaker type:** Independent foundation
**Financial data** (yr. ended 12/31/98): Assets, $2,734,968 (M); expenditures, $164,040; qualifying distributions, $135,004; giving activities include $135,004 for 40 grants (high: $10,000; low: $1,000).
**Purpose and activities:** Giving primarily for youth services and public libraries.
**Fields of interest:** Libraries/library science; animal welfare; human services; children & youth, services.
**Limitations:** Giving primarily in Mason, IA.
**Application information:** Application form not required.
*Initial approach:* Letter
*Deadline(s):* Apr. 30
**Officers:** Keith P. Sanborn, Pres. and Treas.; James R. Heiny, V.P.; Gerald M. Stambaugh, Secy.
**EIN:** 421214699

**223**
**The Ralph & Sylvia G. Green Charitable Foundation**
1801 2nd Ave.
Des Moines, IA 50314
*Contact:* Ann G. Anderson, Pres.

Established in 1983 in IA.
**Donor(s):** Ralph Green.‡
**Grantmaker type:** Independent foundation
**Financial data** (yr. ended 12/31/99): Assets, $1,341,402 (M); expenditures, $62,464; qualifying distributions, $61,140; giving activities include $61,810 for 26 grants (high: $10,000; low: $45; average: $45–$10,000).
**Purpose and activities:** Giving for the arts, education, the environment, and human services.
**Fields of interest:** Arts/cultural programs; higher education; libraries/library science; natural resource conservation & protection; human services; general charitable giving.
**Types of support:** General/operating support; annual campaigns; capital campaigns; endowments; seed money.
**Limitations:** Giving primarily in Des Moines, IA. No grants to individuals.
**Application information:** Application form not required.

*Initial approach:* Letter
*Copies of proposal:* 1
*Deadline(s):* None
*Board meeting date(s):* Quarterly
*Final notification:* Upon action of the board
**Officers and Directors:*** Ann G. Anderson,*
Pres. and Secy.; Sigurd Anderson,* V.P. and Treas.
**Number of staff:** None.
**EIN:** 421208959

## 224
## Heath Foundation, Inc.

c/o Keele Law Offices
P.O. Box 156
West Liberty, IA 52776-0156
*Contact:* Dennis Batty, Secy.-Treas.
*Application address:* P.O. Box 78, West Liberty,
IA 52776, tel.: (319) 627-2191

**Grantmaker type:** Operating foundation
**Financial data** (yr. ended 12/31/98): Assets,
$193,790 (M); expenditures, $214,891;
qualifying distributions, $214,891; giving
activities include $213,960 for 10 grants (high:
$100,000; low: $500).
**Purpose and activities:** Giving primarily for the
construction of a library and a community
center in West Liberty, IA, as well as for
education and human services.
**Fields of interest:** Libraries (public); education;
human services; community development.
**Limitations:** Giving primarily in West Liberty, IA.
No grants to individuals.
**Application information:**
*Initial approach:* Proposal
*Deadline(s):* None
**Officers:** James R. Keele, Pres.; Thomas C.
Brooke, V.P.; Dennis Batty, Secy.-Treas.
**EIN:** 421367113

## 225
## Herbert Hoover Foundation, Inc.

c/o Tom Walsh
P.O. Box 400
West Branch, IA 52358

Established in 1986 in NY.
**Grantmaker type:** Independent foundation
**Financial data** (yr. ended 12/31/98): Assets,
$4,651,782 (M); expenditures, $239,564;
qualifying distributions, $197,777; giving
activities include $198,000 for 3 grants (high:
$95,000; low: $35,000).
**Fields of interest:** Libraries/library science;
parks/playgrounds; boys clubs; public policy,
research.
**Limitations:** Applications not accepted. Giving
primarily in IA. No grants to individuals.
**Application information:** Contributes only to
pre-selected organizations.
**Officers and Trustees:*** Paul L. Davies, Jr.,*
Pres.; Herbert Hoover III,* V.P. and Secy.-Treas.;
Tom Walsh, Exec. Dir; Peter B. Bedford, Andrew
Hoover, Robert H. Malott, Jeremiah Milbank,
Robert J. Swain, Dean A. Watkins.
**EIN:** 136101789

## 226
## Kent-Stein Foundation

c/o Grain Processing Corp.
1600 Oregon St.
Muscatine, IA 52761
*Contact:* Nellie L. Ziegenhorn, Mgr., Admin.
Svcs.

Established in 1945 in IA.
**Donor(s):** Grain Processing Corp.
**Grantmaker type:** Independent foundation
**Financial data** (yr. ended 12/31/99): Assets,
$3,178,157 (M); expenditures, $671,645;
qualifying distributions, $542,778; giving
activities include $544,800 for 15 grants (high:
$200,000; low: $3,000).
**Fields of interest:** Higher education;
libraries/library science; human services.
**Limitations:** Applications not accepted. Giving
primarily in IA. No grants to individuals.
**Application information:** Contributes only to
pre-selected college funds.
**Trustees:** J.H. Kent, J.L. Lamb, S.G. Stein IV.
**Number of staff:** None.
**EIN:** 426058939

## 227
## R. J. McElroy Trust ▼

KWWL Bldg., Ste. 318
500 E. 4th St.
Waterloo, IA 50703 (319) 287-9102
*Contact:* Linda L. Klinger, Exec. Dir.
*FAX:* (319) 287-9105; E-mail:
mcelroy@cedarnet.org; URL: http://
www.cedarnet.org/mcelroy/index.html

Established in 1965 in IA; private foundation
status attained in 1984.
**Donor(s):** R.J. McElroy.
**Grantmaker type:** Independent foundation
**Financial data** (yr. ended 12/31/99): Assets,
$50,633,387 (M); expenditures, $3,139,114;
qualifying distributions, $2,803,336; giving
activities include $2,638,919 for 139 grants
(high: $253,892; low: $50; average:
$1,000–$50,000) and $80,464 for 36 grants to
individuals (high: $14,200; low: $1,000).
**Purpose and activities:** Primary emphasis on
higher education, especially scholarship and
loan programs; public secondary education,
particularly for the disadvantaged; early
childhood and elementary education and
programs for minorities; and youth, including
internships. Giving also for the arts, recreation,
and the environment; some support through
matching funds and fellowships for graduate
study.
**Fields of interest:** Visual arts; performing arts;
arts/cultural programs; early childhood
education; child development, education;
elementary school/education; secondary
school/education; higher education; education;
environment; recreation; youth development,
services; human services; children & youth,
services; child development, services;
leadership development; minorities;
economically disadvantaged.
**Types of support:** Capital campaigns;
building/renovation; equipment; emergency
funds; program development; professorships;
seed money; fellowships; internship funds;
scholarship funds; research; matching/challenge
support.

**Limitations:** Giving primarily in the KWWL
viewing area, 22 counties in northeast IA. No
grants to individuals (except for fellowship
program).
**Publications:** Informational brochure (including
application guidelines), program policy
statement, grants list, application guidelines.
**Application information:** Application form not
required.
*Copies of proposal:* 1
*Deadline(s):* Mar. 1, June 1, Sept. 1, and Dec.
1
*Board meeting date(s):* Monthly
*Final notification:* May 1, Aug. 1, Nov. 1, and
Feb. 1
**Officers and Trustees:*** James B. Waterblury,*
Chair.; Linda L. Klinger, Exec. Dir.; Raleigh D.
Buckmaster, Ross D. Christensen.
**Number of staff:** 1 full-time professional; 1
part-time support.
**EIN:** 426173496
**Recent grants for library/information services:**
**227-1** Aplington Legion Memorial Library,
Aplington, IA, $15,000. For library and
community center expansion project. 1999.
**227-2** Charles City Public Library, Charles City,
IA, $15,000. For library building project.
1999.
**227-3** City Library, Harpers Ferry, IA, $15,000.
For renovation project. 1999.
**227-4** Farmersburg Library, Farmersburg, IA,
$10,000. For new library building. 1999.
**227-5** Fayette Community Library, Fayette, IA,
$10,000. For renovations. 1999.
**227-6** Northeast Iowa Regional Library System,
Waterloo, IA, $25,000. For computers. 1999.
**227-7** Solon Public Library, Solon, IA, $10,000.
For children's wing construction. 1999.
**227-8** Sumner, City of, Sumner, IA, $40,000. For
Project REACH: Summer Public Library and
Family Aquatic Center. 1999.
**227-9** Tama Public Library, Tama, IA, $15,000.
For Tama Library 2000. 1999.
**227-10** Wartburg College, Waverly, IA,
$100,000. For Wartburg Learner's Library.
1999.
**227-11** Waterloo Public Library, Waterloo, IA,
$12,000. For Reach Out and Read at Peoples
Community Health Clinic. 1999.

## 228
## The H. Filmore and Marjory M. Melick Foundation

413 N. Calhoun
West Liberty, IA 52776-1344

**Donor(s):** H. Filmore Melick, Marjory M. Melick.
**Grantmaker type:** Independent foundation
**Financial data** (yr. ended 12/31/99): Assets,
$1,389,010 (M); gifts received, $257,190;
expenditures, $55,293; qualifying distributions,
$50,000; giving activities include $50,000 for 1
grant.
**Purpose and activities:** Giving for library
construction.
**Fields of interest:** Libraries (public); education;
neighborhood centers.
**Limitations:** Applications not accepted. Giving
primarily in West Liberty, IA. No grants to
individuals.
**Application information:** Contributes only to
pre-selected organizations.

Advisory Committee and Trustees:* Craig A. Bieber, H. Filmore Melick,* Marjory M. Melick,* Gene H. Snapp, Jr.
EIN: 421406715

## 229
## The Melsa Foundation
c/o James Melsa
2001 Indian Grass Ct.
Ames, IA 50014-7838

Established in 1996 in IA.
**Donor(s):** James L. Melsa, Katherine S. Melsa.
**Grantmaker type:** Independent foundation
**Financial data** (yr. ended 12/31/98): Assets, $1,512,511 (M); expenditures, $53,168; qualifying distributions, $47,051; giving activities include $51,040 for 12 grants (high: $14,290; low: $250).
**Purpose and activities:** Giving for Jewish agencies, art and cultural organizations, health and medical services and human services.
**Fields of interest:** Libraries/library science; education; boys & girls clubs; human services; children & youth, services; Christian agencies & churches.
**Limitations:** Applications not accepted. No grants to individuals.
**Application information:** Contributes only to pre-selected organizations.
**Officers:** James L. Melsa, Pres. and Treas.; Katherine Melsa, V.P. and Secy.
EIN: 421464665

## 230
## MidAmerican Energy Holdings Company Contributions Program
P.O. Box 9244
Des Moines, IA 50306-9244 (515) 242-4099
*Contact:* Paul J. Leighton, Secy.

**Grantmaker type:** Corporate giving program
**Purpose and activities:** As a corporate citizen, the company will engage actively in the promotion of the welfare of its communities. To that end, MidAmerican will support charities, take part in civic activities, and participate in special projects. The company urges its employees to exercise their responsibilities as citizens in a similar manner.
**Fields of interest:** Visual arts; performing arts; humanities; arts/cultural programs; education, association; education, research; education, fund raising; early childhood education; higher education; business school/education; adult/continuing education; libraries/library science; education; medical care, rehabilitation; health care; substance abuse, services; health associations; health organizations; housing/shelter, development; recreation; youth development, services; human services; children & youth, services; youth, services; family services; hospices; homeless, human services; civil rights; urban/community development; community development; federated giving programs; engineering & technology; science; government/public administration; leadership development; minorities; disabled; homeless; general charitable giving.
**Types of support:** General/operating support; continuing support; annual campaigns; capital campaigns; building/renovation; endowments;

emergency funds; program development; scholarship funds; employee matching gifts; employee-related scholarships; in-kind gifts.
**Limitations:** Giving primarily in headquarters and company locations. No support for religious, veterans, or political organizations unless funds are used for general public.
**Publications:** Annual report (including application guidelines).
**Application information:** Application form not required.
*Initial approach:* Letter to headquarters or nearest company facility
*Copies of proposal:* 1
*Deadline(s):* None
*Final notification:* Monthly

## 231
## Grace Bott Millar Charitable Trust
c/o Keokuk Savings Bank
501 Main St.
Keokuk, IA 52632-5449

**Grantmaker type:** Independent foundation
**Financial data** (yr. ended 12/31/98): Assets, $1,371,381 (M); expenditures, $58,778; qualifying distributions, $48,742; giving activities include $48,742 for 17 grants (high: $10,000; low: $300).
**Purpose and activities:** Giving for youth and community services, and for religion.
**Fields of interest:** Arts/cultural programs; libraries/library science; education; recreation; Big Brothers/Big Sisters; youth development; human services; Christian agencies & churches.
**Limitations:** Applications not accepted. Giving primarily in Keokuk, IA. No grants to individuals.
**Application information:** Contributes only to pre-selected organizations.
**Trustees:** J.A. Concannon, E.K. Johnstone, Keokuk Savings Bank.
EIN: 426374807

## 232
## Helen J. Urban and Thomas Nelson Urban, Sr. Charitable Foundation II
317 6th Ave., Ste. 1200
Des Moines, IA 50309-4195
*Contact:* Daniel J. Martineau, Tr.
*Application address:* 201 S. 7th St., Aspen, CO 81611; E-mail:djmartineau@aol.com

Established in 1995 in IA.
**Grantmaker type:** Independent foundation
**Financial data** (yr. ended 06/30/99): Assets, $2,180,004 (M); expenditures, $125,342; qualifying distributions, $120,700; giving activities include $120,500 for 5 grants (high: $15,000; low: $10,000).
**Purpose and activities:** Giving primarily for education, fuel cell technology, and alternative energy.
**Fields of interest:** Higher education; libraries/library science; engineering & technology.
**Types of support:** Continuing support; annual campaigns; seed money; internship funds; research; matching/challenge support.
**Limitations:** No grants to individuals.
**Application information:**
*Copies of proposal:* 3
*Deadline(s):* Mar. 15

*Board meeting date(s):* Fall (annually)
*Final notification:* May 1
**Trustee:** Daniel James Martineau.
EIN: 421441830

## 233
## Helen J. Urban and Thomas Nelson Urban, Sr. Charitable Foundation IV
317 6th Ave., Ste. 1200
Des Moines, IA 50309-4195

Established in 1995 in IA.
**Donor(s):** Helen J. Urban.‡
**Grantmaker type:** Independent foundation
**Financial data** (yr. ended 06/30/99): Assets, $2,139,016 (M); expenditures, $108,152; qualifying distributions, $91,500; giving activities include $91,500 for 14 grants (high: $15,000; low: $500).
**Purpose and activities:** Giving for education, environmental conservation and human services.
**Fields of interest:** Design; museums; libraries/library science; education; environment; housing/shelter.
**Limitations:** Giving on a national basis. No grants to individuals.
**Trustees:** Aundra E. Urban, Ian Nelson Urban, Tao Bernardus Urban, Theodore Steven Urban.
EIN: 421441832

## 234
## The Wellmark Foundation
(Formerly The IASD Health Care Foundation)
636 Grand Ave., Sta. 150
Des Moines, IA 50309 (515) 245-4572
*Contact:* Dr. Sheila Riggs, Exec. Dir.
*FAX:* (515) 248-7325; E-mail: WMFoundation@wellmark.com; URL: http://www.wellmark.com/community/wellmark_foundation/wellmark_foundation_funding.htm

Established in 1991 in IA.
**Donor(s):** Blue Cross and Blue Shield of Iowa, Blue Cross and Blue Shield of South Dakota, Wellmark, Inc.
**Grantmaker type:** Company-sponsored foundation
**Financial data** (yr. ended 12/31/99): Assets, $16,794,501 (M); gifts received, $175,351; expenditures, $1,834,206; qualifying distributions, $1,652,668; giving activities include $1,660,700 for 52 grants (high: $192,500; low: $4,500; average: $9,000–$30,000).
**Purpose and activities:** Health improvement agenda focuses on encouraging preventive services and health promotions in the communities of IA and SD.
**Fields of interest:** Health care, infants; public health, communicable diseases; mental health/crisis services, information services; substance abuse, services; smoking; cancer; alcoholism.
**Types of support:** Program development; conferences/seminars; seed money; curriculum development.
**Limitations:** Giving limited to IA and SD. No grants to individuals.
**Publications:** Annual report, newsletter, informational brochure (including application guidelines).

**Application information:** Application form not
required.
*Copies of proposal:* 10
*Deadline(s):* 3 times annually
*Board meeting date(s):* Quarterly
*Final notification:* 1 week after board action
**Officers:** John Forsyth, Chair.; Janet Griffin,
Secy.; Richard C. Anderson, Treas.
**Number of staff:** 1 part-time professional.
**EIN:** 421368650

# KANSAS

**235**
## Bramlage Family Foundation
820 S. Adams
Junction City, KS  66441
*Contact:* Dorothy O. Bramlage, Pres.

Established in 1997 in KS.
**Donor(s):** Dorothy O. Bramlage, Fred C.
Bramlage.
**Grantmaker type:** Independent foundation
**Financial data** (yr. ended 12/31/99): Assets,
$884,582 (M); gifts received, $4,000;
expenditures, $57,776; qualifying distributions,
$56,153; giving activities include $56,500 for
11 grants (high: $10,000; low: $500).
**Purpose and activities:** Giving for higher
education, scouting organizations, and for
public institutes, including libraries.
**Fields of interest:** Libraries (public);
scholarships/financial aid; education; Boy
Scouts; Girl Scouts.
**Limitations:** Giving primarily in KS.
**Application information:** Application form not
required.
*Initial approach:* Letter
*Deadline(s):* None
**Officers:** Dorothy O. Bramlage, Pres.; Dorothy
B. Willcoxon, Secy.; F. Robert Bramlage, Treas.
**EIN:** 742822314

**236**
## Garvey Kansas Foundation
301 N. Main, Ste. 1300
Wichita, KS  67202

Incorporated in 1964 in KS.
**Donor(s):** Jean K. Garvey, Willard W. Garvey,
Garvey International, Inc., Petroleum, Inc.
**Grantmaker type:** Independent foundation
**Financial data** (yr. ended 12/31/97): Assets,
$1,473,736 (M); gifts received, $325,551;
expenditures, $78,003; qualifying distributions,
$74,574; giving activities include $73,700 for
48 grants (high: $25,000; low: $50).
**Purpose and activities:** Giving primarily for
secondary and higher education, and Protestant
church support; support also for community
funds and legal interest foundations.
**Fields of interest:** Elementary/secondary
education; libraries/library science; education;
children & youth, services.
**Types of support:** General/operating support;
building/renovation; scholarship funds.

**Limitations:** Applications not accepted. Giving
primarily in Wichita, KS. No grants to
individuals, or for endowment funds; no loans.
**Application information:** Contributes only to
pre-selected organizations.
*Board meeting date(s):* Jan., Apr., July, and Oct.
**Officer:** John K. Garvey, Pres.
**EIN:** 486115213

**237**
## Victor Murdock Foundation
c/o Bank of America
P.O. Box 1122
Wichita, KS  67201-9974  (316) 261-4218
*Contact:* Pamela J. Beim, V.P., Bank of America

Established in 1974 in KS.
**Grantmaker type:** Independent foundation
**Financial data** (yr. ended 12/31/98): Assets,
$1,103,855 (M); expenditures, $86,557;
qualifying distributions, $74,411; giving
activities include $72,296 for 17 grants (high:
$8,500; low: $300).
**Purpose and activities:** Giving for the arts,
education, health, and human services.
**Fields of interest:** Media/communications;
journalism & publishing; museums; performing
arts; music; humanities; history & archaeology;
language & linguistics; literature; historic
preservation/historical societies; arts/cultural
programs; early childhood education; child
development, education; elementary
school/education; secondary school/education;
higher education; adult education—literacy &
basic skills; libraries/library science; reading;
education; speech & hearing centers; health
care; mental health/crisis services; health
associations; human services; children & youth,
services; child development, services; hospices;
aging, centers & services; disabled; aging;
economically disadvantaged; general charitable
giving.
**Types of support:** Building/renovation;
equipment; scholarship funds.
**Limitations:** Giving limited to the Wichita, KS,
area. Generally, no grants to individuals.
**Application information:** Application form not
required.
*Initial approach:* Letter
*Copies of proposal:* 6
*Deadline(s):* Sept. 30
*Board meeting date(s):* Nov.
**Trustee:** Bank of America.
**Number of staff:** None.
**EIN:** 486190755

**238**
## Rose Spurrier Scholarship Fund
P.O. Box 473
Kingman, KS  67068-0473  (316) 532-3113
*Contact:* Robert S. Wunsch, Tr.

Established in 1984 in KS.
**Grantmaker type:** Independent foundation
**Financial data** (yr. ended 12/31/99): Assets,
$1,993,510 (M); expenditures, $145,500;
qualifying distributions, $124,158; giving
activities include $17,974 for 2 grants (high:
$12,974; low: $5,000) and $92,250 for 29
grants to individuals (high: $22,150; low: $400).

**Purpose and activities:** Awards scholarships for
higher education to qualified graduates of
Kingman City High School, Kingman, KS.
**Fields of interest:** Secondary school/education;
higher education; libraries/library science.
**Types of support:** Scholarship funds;
scholarships—to individuals.
**Limitations:** Giving primarily in Kingman, KS.
**Application information:**
*Initial approach:* Letter or telephone
*Final notification:* Decisions announced at the
commencement exercises of Kingman City
High School
**Trustees:** Charles Crouch, D.L. Meisenheimer,
Robert S. Wunsch.
**EIN:** 480978238

# KENTUCKY

**239**
## The Community Foundation of Louisville, Inc. ▼
(Formerly Louisville Community Foundation,
Inc.)
Waterfront Plz. Bldg., Ste. 1110
325 W. Main St.
Louisville, KY  40202  (502) 585-4649
*Contact:* C. Dennis Riggs, Pres. and C.E.O.
*FAX:* (502) 587-7484; E-mail:
commfdn@cflouisville.org; URL: http://
www.cflouisville.org

Established in 1916 in KY; reorganized in 1984.
**Grantmaker type:** Community foundation
**Financial data** (yr. ended 06/30/99): Assets,
$116,641,946 (M); gifts received, $13,175,791;
expenditures, $8,352,491; giving activities
include $6,415,229 for 395 grants (high:
$1,006,110; low: $100; average:
$5,000–$25,000).
**Purpose and activities:** The mission of the
foundation is to enrich the quality of life for all
citizens in the Louisville area by being a leader
in attracting, mobilizing, and focusing
philanthropic resources to meet community
needs for generations to come. Giving for health
and human services, arts and humanities,
education, and the environment; support also
for scholarships. The current focus of
grantmaking from unrestricted funds is to help
children and families in poverty achieve
self-sufficiency.
**Fields of interest:** Humanities; arts/cultural
programs; education; environment; human
services.
**Types of support:** General/operating support;
continuing support; annual campaigns; capital
campaigns; building/renovation; equipment;
endowments; emergency funds; program
development; publication; seed money;
scholarship funds; research; technical
assistance; scholarships—to individuals;
matching/challenge support.
**Limitations:** Giving limited to Louisville and
Jefferson County, KY. No support for sectarian
purposes. No grants to individuals (except for
scholarships).

**Publications:** Annual report, program policy statement, application guidelines, newsletter, informational brochure.
**Application information:** Grantmaking in areas of community need as decided by board; unsolicited requests for funds not considered. Application form required.
> *Board meeting date(s):* Mar., June, Sept., and Dec.
**Officers and Directors:*** W. Barrett Nichols,* Chair.; Michael B. Mountjoy, CPA,* Vice-Chair.; C. Dennis Riggs, Pres. and C.E.O.; Susan V. Nicholson, V.P. and C.F.O.; Kathy B. Steward, V.P., Fund Devel.; Marie E. Porter, Jr.,* Secy.; and additional directors.
**Number of staff:** 8 full-time professional; 1 part-time professional; 4 full-time support.
**EIN:** 310997017
**Recent grants for library/information services:**
**239-1** Louisville Free Public Library, Louisville, KY, $550,941. 1998.

### 240
### Gordon Foundation, Inc.
715 Alta Vista Rd.
Louisville, KY 40206-3865
*Contact:* Stanley J. Gordon, Jr.

Established in 1992 in KY.
**Donor(s):** Stanley J. Gordon, Jr., Denise J. Gordon.
**Grantmaker type:** Independent foundation
**Financial data** (yr. ended 12/31/98): Assets, $673,812 (M); expenditures, $289,049; qualifying distributions, $289,045; giving activities include $289,045 for 28 grants (high: $80,000; low: $45).
**Purpose and activities:** Giving for education, health, human services, and community development.
**Fields of interest:** Higher education; libraries/library science; health associations; human services; Salvation Army; community development; voluntarism promotion; Christian agencies & churches.
**Application information:** Application form not required.
> *Deadline(s):* None
**Directors:** Denise J. Gordon, Randall B. Hockensmith, J. Clifton Mahaffey.
**EIN:** 611230889

### 241
### LG&E Energy Foundation, Inc.
220 W. Main St.
Louisville, KY 40202 (502) 627-3337
*Contact:* Shauna Cole, Grants Admin.
*FAX:* (502) 627-3629

Established in 1994 in KY.
**Grantmaker type:** Independent foundation
**Financial data** (yr. ended 12/31/99): Assets, $19,902,471 (M); expenditures, $2,530,231; qualifying distributions, $2,294,559; giving activities include $2,311,744 for 91 grants (high: $402,868; low: $1,000).
**Fields of interest:** Museums (art); ballet; orchestra (symphony); arts/cultural programs; secondary school/education; higher education; university; libraries/library science; libraries (public); education; Boy Scouts; Salvation Army; science.

**Types of support:** General/operating support; annual campaigns; capital campaigns; building/renovation; program development; seed money; scholarship funds; employee matching gifts; matching/challenge support.
**Limitations:** Giving primarily in areas of company service in KY. No support for religious, political, labor, or veterans' organizations, or for fraternal societies. No grants to individuals, or for dinners, raffles, or prize-oriented activities.
**Application information:** Corporate Contributions Request form may be obtained from the foundation. Application form required.
> *Initial approach:* Contact the foundation for application guidelines
> *Copies of proposal:* 1
> *Deadline(s):* Varies
> *Board meeting date(s):* Quarterly
**Officers and Directors:*** Roger W. Hale,* Pres.; Charles A. Markel III,* V.P.; John McCall, V.P.; Grant Ringel, V.P.; Victor A. Stafferi,* V.P.; Stephen R. Wood, V.P.
**Number of staff:** 1 full-time professional.
**EIN:** 611257368

### 242
### Herman H. Nettelroth Fund
c/o PNC Bank, N.A.
Citizens Plz.
Louisville, KY 40296 (502) 581-4669
*Contact:* Mark P. Snyder, Trust Admin., PNC Bank, N.A.

Established in 1955 in KY.
**Grantmaker type:** Independent foundation
**Financial data** (yr. ended 07/31/99): Assets, $2,780,026 (M); expenditures, $74,505; qualifying distributions, $65,024; giving activities include $64,955 for 6 grants (high: $35,000; low: $4,000).
**Purpose and activities:** Giving primarily for scholarship and community funds; support also for bird sanctuaries, children's playgrounds, day nurseries, and children's books for public libraries.
**Fields of interest:** Higher education; libraries (public); wildlife, bird preserves; parks/playgrounds; children, day care; federated giving programs.
**Types of support:** General/operating support; building/renovation; equipment; scholarship funds.
**Limitations:** Giving limited to Jefferson County, KY.
**Application information:** Application form not required.
> *Initial approach:* Letter or proposal
> *Copies of proposal:* 4
> *Deadline(s):* Sept. 30
> *Board meeting date(s):* Nov.
**Trustee:** PNC Bank, N.A.
**EIN:** 616020294

### 243
### Paradis Foundation, Inc.
1801 Watterson Tr.
P.O. Box 32230
Louisville, KY 40232-2230 (502) 491-4000
*Contact:* Pat Riddle, Secy.

Established in 1978.
**Donor(s):** Bramco, Inc.

**Grantmaker type:** Independent foundation
**Financial data** (yr. ended 03/31/99): Assets, $1,437,186 (M); expenditures, $85,431; qualifying distributions, $80,507; giving activities include $81,500 for 16 grants (high: $10,000; low: $1,000).
**Purpose and activities:** Giving for education, family and youth services, and religion.
**Fields of interest:** Arts/cultural programs; secondary school/education; higher education; libraries/library science; education; human services.
**Limitations:** Giving primarily in Louisville, KY. No grants to individuals.
**Application information:** Application form not required.
> *Initial approach:* Letter
> *Deadline(s):* None
**Officers and Directors:*** Joseph A. Paradis,* Pres.; Joseph A. Paradis III,* V.P.; Pat Riddle, Secy.; Charles H. Leis,* Treas.; Steven J. Paradis.
**EIN:** 310908284

### 244
### C. F. Pollard Foundation, Inc.
P.O. Box 40
10500 U.S. Hwy. 42
Goshen, KY 40026
*Contact:* Lisa A. Kaster, Secy.

Established in 1993 in KY.
**Donor(s):** Carl F. Pollard.
**Grantmaker type:** Independent foundation
**Financial data** (yr. ended 12/31/99): Assets, $2,563,948 (M); expenditures, $169,462; qualifying distributions, $157,192; giving activities include $158,110 for 20 grants (high: $75,000; low: $110; average: $110–$75,000).
**Fields of interest:** Museums; libraries/library science; education; general charitable giving.
**Limitations:** Giving primarily in KY. No grants to individuals.
**Application information:** Application form not required.
> *Initial approach:* Letter
> *Deadline(s):* None
**Officers:** Carl F. Pollard, Pres.; Elizabeth B. Pollard, V.P.; Stuart B. Pollard, V.P.; Lisa A. Kaster, Secy.
**EIN:** 611246295

### 245
### Charlotte M. Richardt Charitable Trust
c/o Ronald G. Keeping, Tr.
P.O. Box 5
Henderson, KY 42419-0005

Established in 1996 in KY.
**Donor(s):** Charlotte M. Richardt.‡
**Grantmaker type:** Independent foundation
**Financial data** (yr. ended 12/31/99): Assets, $3,210,549 (M); expenditures, $1,001,392; qualifying distributions, $975,161; giving activities include $959,000 for 8 grants (high: $274,000; low: $68,500) and $13,850 for 5 grants to individuals (high: $3,600; low: $1,250).
**Purpose and activities:** Giving primarily to an association for blind people and a humane society; funding also for health associations and libraries.

**Fields of interest:** Museums (art); libraries (public); animal welfare; cancer; eye diseases; heart & circulatory diseases; boys & girls clubs.
**Limitations:** Applications not accepted. Giving primarily in IN. No grants to individuals.
**Application information:** Contributes only to pre-selected organizations.
**Trustee:** Ronald G. Keeping.
**EIN:** 616233945

# LOUISIANA

**246**
**The Booth-Bricker Fund**
826 Union St., Ste. 300
New Orleans, LA  70112  (504) 581-2430
*Contact:* Gray S. Parker, Chair.

Established in 1966 in LA.
**Donor(s):** John F. Bricker, Nina B. Bricker.‡
**Grantmaker type:** Independent foundation
**Financial data** (yr. ended 12/31/99): Assets, $38,358,342 (M); expenditures, $2,127,288; qualifying distributions, $1,690,078; giving activities include $1,663,164 for 99 grants (high: $105,284; low: $50; average: $2,000–$80,000).
**Purpose and activities:** Giving primarily for the purpose of promoting, developing, and fostering religious, charitable, scientific, literary, and educational programs.
**Fields of interest:** Visual arts; museums; performing arts; theater; historic preservation/historical societies; arts/cultural programs; education, fund raising; elementary/secondary education; early childhood education; child development, education; secondary school/education; higher education; theological school/education; adult education—literacy & basic skills; libraries/library science; reading; education; environment; hospitals (general); speech & hearing centers; health care; mental health/crisis services; health associations; cancer; biomedicine; medical research; cancer research; crime/law enforcement; food services; human services; youth, services; child development, services; family services; aging, centers & services; homeless, human services; Roman Catholic agencies & churches; religion; aging; economically disadvantaged; homeless; general charitable giving.
**Types of support:** Capital campaigns; building/renovation; equipment; endowments; debt reduction; professorships; publication; scholarship funds; research; employee matching gifts; matching/challenge support.
**Limitations:** Giving primarily in LA, with emphasis on New Orleans. No grants to individuals, or for operating or maintenance costs.
**Application information:** Videotapes not accepted. Application form not required.
*Initial approach:* Letter or proposal
*Deadline(s):* None
*Board meeting date(s):* Quarterly
**Officers and Trustees:*** Gray S. Parker,* Chair.; Donald J. Nalty,* Secy.; Ingrid C. Laffont, Treas.; Dorothy R. Boyle, Robert F. Goodwin, Henry N.

Kuechler III, Charles B. Mayer, Nathaniel P. Phillips, Jr., H. Hunter White, Jr.
**EIN:** 720818077

**247**
**Huie-Dellmon Trust**
P.O. Box 330
Alexandria, LA  71309
*Contact:* Richard L. Crowell, Jr., Tr.

Established around 1976.
**Grantmaker type:** Independent foundation
**Financial data** (yr. ended 12/31/99): Assets, $10,404,931 (M); expenditures, $510,042; qualifying distributions, $505,212; giving activities include $493,195 for 42 grants (high: $50,000; low: $195).
**Purpose and activities:** Support for hospitals, Protestant giving, higher and secondary education, and a library.
**Fields of interest:** Secondary school/education; higher education; libraries/library science; hospitals (general); Protestant agencies & churches.
**Types of support:** General/operating support; continuing support; annual campaigns; capital campaigns; building/renovation; equipment; endowments; program development; professorships; scholarship funds; research; matching/challenge support.
**Limitations:** Giving limited to central LA. No grants to individuals.
**Application information:** Application form not required.
*Initial approach:* Letter
**Trustees:** Richard L. Crowell, Jr., Nancy C. Owens.
**Number of staff:** None.
**EIN:** 720809684

# MAINE

**248**
**The Aldermere Foundation**
(also known as Albert H. Chatfield, Jr. & Marion W. Chatfield Trust f/b/o The Aldermere Foundation)
c/o Trust Co. of Maine
P.O. Box 2639
Bangor, ME  04402-2639
*Contact:* Susan L. Kenney
*FAX:* (207) 941-2498

Established in 1977 in ME.
**Grantmaker type:** Independent foundation
**Financial data** (yr. ended 12/31/98): Assets, $1,375,083 (M); expenditures, $70,838; qualifying distributions, $66,538; giving activities include $67,000 for 20 grants (high: $42,000; low: $1,000).
**Purpose and activities:** Giving primarily for the arts, education, and religious organizations.
**Fields of interest:** Arts education; museums (art); arts/cultural programs; libraries (public); wildlife preservation & protection; YM/YWCAs & YM/YWHAs; Christian agencies & churches.
**Types of support:** General/operating support.

**Limitations:** Giving primarily in ME. No grants to individuals.
**Application information:** Application form not required.
*Copies of proposal:* 1
*Deadline(s):* None
**Trustee:** Trust Co. of Maine.
**EIN:** 016059906

**249**
**The Brook Family Foundation**
9 Korhonen Rd.
Norway, ME  04268

Established in 1995 in ME.
**Grantmaker type:** Independent foundation
**Financial data** (yr. ended 03/31/99): Assets, $3,450,265 (M); expenditures, $201,186; qualifying distributions, $160,435; giving activities include $155,996 for 19 grants (high: $30,000; low: $500).
**Purpose and activities:** Giving primarily for education and disaster relief.
**Fields of interest:** Television; elementary/secondary education; libraries (public); natural resource conservation & protection; hospitals (general); youth development, services; American Red Cross; international relief; Roman Catholic agencies & churches.
**Limitations:** Giving primarily in MA and ME. No grants to individuals.
**Officer:** Paul F. Brook, Secy.-Treas.
**Directors:** Jacqueline C. Brook, Robert L. Brook, Shirley W. Brook.
**EIN:** 010499178

**250**
**Robert H. & Eleanor S. Heald Trust**
c/o Rendle A. Jones
P.O. Box 190
Camden, ME  04843

Established in 1995 in ME.
**Grantmaker type:** Independent foundation
**Financial data** (yr. ended 12/31/98): Assets, $1,994,140 (M); expenditures, $71,801; qualifying distributions, $57,548; giving activities include $49,453 for 5 grants (high: $13,737; low: $5,495).
**Purpose and activities:** Giving primarily for education and religious organizations.
**Fields of interest:** Historic preservation/historical societies; secondary school/education; libraries (public); recreation; Protestant agencies & churches.
**Limitations:** Applications not accepted. Giving primarily in Union, ME. No grants to individuals.
**Application information:** Contributes only to pre-selected organizations.
**Trustee:** Rendle A. Jones.
**EIN:** 016131271

**251**
**Irving Tanning Co. Charitable Trust**
Main St.
P.O. Box 239
Hartland, ME  04943-0239

Established in 1994.

**Donor(s):** Irving Tanning Co.
**Grantmaker type:** Independent foundation
**Financial data** (yr. ended 12/31/99): Assets, $334,692 (M); expenditures, $211,246; qualifying distributions, $207,181; giving activities include $207,559 for 28 grants (high: $100,000; low: $25).
**Purpose and activities:** Giving for community centers, fire departments, and for health and human services.
**Fields of interest:** Higher education; libraries/library science.
**Limitations:** Applications not accepted. Giving primarily in ME. No grants to individuals.
**Application information:** Contributes only to pre-selected organizations.
**Trustees:** Stephen Graebert, C. Perry Harrison, Richard C. Larochelle.
**EIN:** 016126344

---

**252**
**Max Kagan Family Foundation**
P.O. Box 2182, Redington N.
Kingfield, ME   04947
*Contact:* Irving Kagan, Tr.

Established in 1955 in ME.
**Grantmaker type:** Independent foundation
**Financial data** (yr. ended 12/31/99): Assets, $2,442,491 (M); expenditures, $147,874; qualifying distributions, $127,166; giving activities include $129,434 for 77 grants (high: $15,000; low: $100).
**Fields of interest:** Higher education; libraries/library science; education; health associations; human services; Jewish federated giving programs; Jewish agencies & temples.
**Limitations:** Giving primarily in FL, MA, and ME.
**Application information:** Application form not required.
*Deadline(s):* None
**Trustees:** Jerome Grossman, Irving Kagan, Ronald Striar.
**EIN:** 016019033

---

**253**
**The Clarence E. Mulford Trust**
P.O. Box 290
Fryeburg, ME   04037   (207) 935-2061
*Contact:* David R. Hastings II, Tr.

Trust established in 1950 in ME.
**Donor(s):** Clarence E. Mulford.‡
**Grantmaker type:** Independent foundation
**Financial data** (yr. ended 12/31/97): Assets, $8,827,842 (M); expenditures, $383,849; qualifying distributions, $336,069; giving activities include $306,422 for 24 grants (high: $186,572; low: $150).
**Purpose and activities:** Giving primarily to religious, charitable, scientific, literary or educational organizations, and for the prevention of cruelty to children or animals.
**Fields of interest:** Secondary school/education; libraries/library science; education; animal welfare; human services; community development; Christian agencies & churches.
**Limitations:** Giving primarily in Fryeburg, ME, and neighboring towns. No grants to individuals, or for building or endowment funds, scholarships, fellowships, or matching gifts; no loans.

**Application information:** Application form not required.
*Initial approach:* Letter
*Copies of proposal:* 3
*Deadline(s):* Preferably in June or Dec., no later than July 10 or Jan. 10
*Board meeting date(s):* Jan. and July
*Final notification:* Positive replies only
**Trustees:** David R. Hastings II, Peter G. Hastings.
**EIN:** 010247548

---

**254**
**The Margaret Chase Smith Foundation**
c/o Merton G. Henry
10 Free St., P.O. Box 4510
Portland, ME   04112

Established in 1983 in ME.
**Donor(s):** Margaret Chase Smith,‡ Alden B. Dow Charitable Trust, Dexter Shoe Co.
**Grantmaker type:** Independent foundation
**Financial data** (yr. ended 12/31/99): Assets, $13,192,072 (M); gifts received, $102,543; expenditures, $690,855; qualifying distributions, $575,532; giving activities include $542,532 for 3 grants (high: $510,884).
**Purpose and activities:** Support primarily for an affiliated library to conduct programs and provide research fellowships; funding also for education and human services.
**Fields of interest:** History & archaeology; libraries/library science; education; military/veterans' organizations.
**Types of support:** Conferences/seminars; curriculum development; fellowships.
**Limitations:** Applications not accepted. Giving primarily in ME. No grants to individuals.
**Application information:** Contributes only to pre-selected organizations.
*Board meeting date(s):* June and Dec.
**Officers:** Merton G. Henry, Pres. and Treas.; Michael J. Quinlan, Secy.
**Directors:** John Bernier, Charles L. Cragin, David E. Fry, E. Ray Hearn, Georgia McKearly.
**Number of staff:** 1 part-time professional.
**EIN:** 010388680

---

**255**
**Virginia Hodgkins Somers Foundation**
(Formerly Somers Foundation)
c/o Peoples Heritage Bank
217 Main St.
Lewiston, ME   04240
*Contact:* Gordon C. Ayer, Tr.
*Application address:* 18 Summer St., Kennebunk, ME 04043; E-mail: tropical@cybertours.com

Established in 1991 in ME.
**Donor(s):** Virginia Hodgkins Somers.‡
**Grantmaker type:** Independent foundation
**Financial data** (yr. ended 09/30/99): Assets, $7,795,959 (M); expenditures, $521,956; qualifying distributions, $438,241; giving activities include $435,000 for 13 grants (high: $100,000; low: $5,000).
**Purpose and activities:** Giving primarily to education, charitable matters pertaining to children, and human services.
**Fields of interest:** Arts/cultural programs; elementary/secondary education; higher education; libraries/library science; youth

development, centers & clubs; children & youth, services.
**Limitations:** Giving primarily in ME and NY.
**Application information:** Application form required.
*Copies of proposal:* 1
*Deadline(s):* None
*Board meeting date(s):* Quarterly
**Trustees:** Gordon C. Ayer, Susan W. Ayer, Peoples Heritage Bank.
**Number of staff:** 1 part-time professional.
**EIN:** 016109747

---

# MARYLAND

---

**256**
**Darby Foundation**
P.O. Box 1660
Easton, MD   21601
*Contact:* Katherine D. Brady, Tr.

Established in 1966 in NJ.
**Donor(s):** Nicholas F. Brady.
**Grantmaker type:** Independent foundation
**Financial data** (yr. ended 12/31/99): Assets, $2,033,269 (M); expenditures, $175,676; qualifying distributions, $171,372; giving activities include $172,533 for 23 grants (high: $50,000; low: $33).
**Fields of interest:** Museums; historic preservation/historical societies; libraries/library science; human services; children & youth, services; Roman Catholic agencies & churches.
**Limitations:** Giving primarily in Washington, DC, NJ, and NY.
**Application information:**
*Initial approach:* Letter
*Deadline(s):* None
**Trustees:** Katherine D. Brady, Nicholas F. Brady.
**EIN:** 136212178

---

**257**
**Gorlitz Foundation, Ltd.**
(Formerly Samuel J. Gorlitz Foundation)
6916 Carmichael Dr.
Bethesda, MD   20817
*Contact:* Samuel J. Gorlitz, Pres.

Established in 1986 in MD.
**Grantmaker type:** Independent foundation
**Financial data** (yr. ended 12/31/99): Assets, $3,349,841 (M); expenditures, $247,812; qualifying distributions, $174,393; giving activities include $151,646 for 112 grants (high: $27,500; low: $15).
**Purpose and activities:** Giving primarily for the arts and Jewish organizations.
**Fields of interest:** Arts/cultural programs; libraries (public); education; human services; Jewish federated giving programs; Jewish agencies & temples.
**Limitations:** Giving primarily in Washington, DC, MD, and NY.
**Application information:**
*Initial approach:* Letter
*Deadline(s):* None
**Officers:** Samuel J. Gorlitz, Pres. and Treas.; Grace K. Gorlitz, V.P. and Treas.

EIN: 521439097

**Number of staff:** 1 part-time professional.
EIN: 136001167

**Number of staff:** 1 part-time professional.
EIN: 521358159

## 258
## Guerrieri Family Foundation
P.O. Box 680
Ocean City, MD   21843

Established in 1997 in MD.
**Donor(s):** Alan Guerrieri, Guerrieri Venture
Partnership.
**Grantmaker type:** Independent foundation
**Financial data** (yr. ended 12/31/99): Assets,
$2,716,397 (M); gifts received, $1,266,125;
expenditures, $430,377; qualifying distributions,
$423,167; giving activities include $423,167 for
17 grants (high: $133,500; low: $50).
**Purpose and activities:** Giving primarily for
education and libraries.
**Fields of interest:** Libraries/library science;
education.
**Limitations:** Applications not accepted. Giving
primarily in MD. No grants to individuals.
**Application information:** Contributes only to
pre-selected organizations.
**Officers:** Alan Guerrieri, Pres.; Michael S.
Guerrieri, Secy.; Cathi G. Chandler, Treas.
EIN: 522038684

## 259
## The Knapp Foundation, Inc.
P.O. Box O
St. Michaels, MD   21663   (410) 745-5660
*Contact:* Ruth M. Capranica, V.P. and Secy.

Incorporated in 1929 in NC.
**Donor(s):** Joseph Palmer Knapp.‡
**Grantmaker type:** Independent foundation
**Financial data** (yr. ended 12/31/99): Assets,
$27,856,300 (M); expenditures, $1,080,857;
qualifying distributions, $977,989; giving
activities include $928,313 for 32 grants (high:
$250,000; low: $3,000) and $18,016 for 1
program-related investment.
**Purpose and activities:** Grants primarily for
conservation and preservation of wildlife and
wildfowl, and for assistance to college and
university libraries in the purchasing of reading
materials and equipment to improve education.
**Fields of interest:** Higher education;
libraries/library science; wildlife preservation &
protection.
**Types of support:** Equipment;
matching/challenge support.
**Limitations:** Giving limited to the U.S., primarily
in the eastern region, including CT, FL, GA, MA,
MD, ME, NC, NH, NJ, NY, PA, RI, SC, VA, and
VT. No support for foreign projects. No grants to
individuals, or for endowment or building funds,
operating budgets, or research.
**Publications:** Application guidelines.
**Application information:** Application form not
required.
  *Initial approach:* Letter
  *Copies of proposal:* 1
  *Deadline(s):* None
  *Board meeting date(s):* Dec.; executive board
    meets quarterly
  *Final notification:* 90 days
**Officers and Trustees:\*** Antoinette P. Vojvoda,*
Pres.; Ruth M. Capranica,* V.P. and Secy.; Steven
F. Capranica,* Treas.; Krista L. Hodgkin,
Margaret P. Newcombe, Sylvia V. Penny.

## 260
## Marpat Foundation, Inc.
P.O. Box 1769
Silver Spring, MD   20915-1769
*Contact:* Mrs. Joan F. Koven, Secy.-Treas.
*E-mail:* jkoven@aol.com; URL: http://
fdncenter.org/grantmaker/marpat

Incorporated in 1985 in MD.
**Donor(s):** Marvin Breckinridge Patterson.
**Grantmaker type:** Independent foundation
**Financial data** (yr. ended 12/31/99): Assets,
$14,580,064 (M); expenditures, $1,525,099;
qualifying distributions, $1,398,471; giving
activities include $1,357,300 for 134 grants
(high: $23,000; low: $3,000; average:
$5,000–$30,000).
**Purpose and activities:** Grants will be made
primarily to established charitable organizations
whose activities are personally known to the
directors and based in or benefiting the greater
Washington, DC, metropolitan area. Grants will
be made to the following: organizations that
advance international understanding,
universities, museums, and libraries for the
advancement and diffusion of knowledge;
organizations and schools that sponsor
programs that advocate and encourage family
planning, or promote or provide health care;
organizations promoting or conducting scientific
programs and research projects; organizations
providing services and/or education designed to
preserve natural and historical resources, or
advance the knowledge of mankind's history
and cultural past; and organizations that
promote volunteer participation in, and citizen
involvement with such organizations.
**Fields of interest:** Visual arts; museums;
performing arts; historic preservation/historical
societies; arts/cultural programs; higher
education; libraries/library science; education;
natural resource conservation & protection;
environment; family planning; health care;
human services; voluntarism promotion; science.
**Types of support:** General/operating support;
building/renovation; equipment; program
development; publication.
**Limitations:** Giving primarily in the metropolitan
Washington, DC, area. No support for projects
or organizations for any weapons development.
No grants to individuals, or for endowment
funds or medical research.
**Publications:** Informational brochure (including
application guidelines), application guidelines,
grants list.
**Application information:** Request summary
sheet from foundation. Application form
required.
  *Initial approach:* Letter or proposal (no more
    than 2 pages)
  *Copies of proposal:* 3
  *Deadline(s):* Sept. 15
  *Board meeting date(s):* Dec.
  *Final notification:* After Dec. 15
**Officers and Directors:\*** Marvin Breckinridge
Patterson,* Pres.; Ellen Bozman, V.P.; Isabella G.
Breckinridge,* V.P.; Sherrill M. Houghton, V.P.;
Polly Krakora, V.P.; Christine Minter-Dowd,*
V.P.; Thomas W. Richards,* V.P.; Samuel N.
Stokes,* V.P.; Joan F. Koven,* Secy.-Treas.

## 261
## The Harvey M. Meyerhoff Fund, Inc.
25 S. Charles St.
Baltimore, MD   21201

Established in 1994 in MD.
**Grantmaker type:** Independent foundation
**Financial data** (yr. ended 12/31/99): Assets,
$10,724,976 (M); expenditures, $606,324;
qualifying distributions, $540,266; giving
activities include $548,500 for 43 grants (high:
$100,000; low: $600).
**Purpose and activities:** Giving primarily for the
arts, education, and health services; support also
for Jewish organizations and agencies.
**Fields of interest:** Orchestra (symphony);
libraries/library science; scholarships/financial
aid; health associations; Jewish agencies &
temples.
**Limitations:** Applications not accepted. Giving
primarily in MD. No grants to individuals.
**Application information:** Contributes only to
pre-selected organizations.
**Officers:** Harvey M. Meyerhoff, Pres.; Lee M.
Hendler, V.P. and Secy.; Terry M. Rubenstein,
V.P. and Treas.
**Trustees:** Jill M. Hieronimus, Joseph Meyerhoff II.
EIN: 521904818

## 262
## Leon & Marianne Minkoff Family
## Foundation, Inc.
9108 Gaither Rd.
Gaithersburg, MD   20877

Established in 1986 in MD.
**Donor(s):** Leon P. Minkoff, Marianne Minkoff.
**Grantmaker type:** Independent foundation
**Financial data** (yr. ended 12/31/98): Assets,
$185,065 (M); expenditures, $127,092;
qualifying distributions, $124,107; giving
activities include $123,681 for 33 grants (high:
$30,000; low: $25).
**Purpose and activities:** Giving for religion and
community service organizations.
**Fields of interest:** Libraries (special); education;
medical research; human services; Jewish
federated giving programs; Jewish agencies &
temples.
**Limitations:** Applications not accepted. Giving
primarily in FL and Washington, DC. No grants
to individuals.
**Application information:** Contributes only to
pre-selected organizations.
**Officers:** Marianne Minkoff, Pres.; Paul N.
Chod, Treas.
EIN: 521499816

## 263
## G. Frank Thomas Foundation, Inc.
c/o Mercantile-Safe Deposit & Trust Co.
766 Old Hammonds Ferry Rd.
Linthicum, MD   21090-1323   (301) 237-5933
*Contact:* Charles F. Trunk III, Secy.
*Application address:* 506 Fairview Ave.,
Frederick, MD 21701, tel.: (301) 663-6592

Established in 1954 in MD.
**Grantmaker type:** Independent foundation
**Financial data** (yr. ended 12/31/98): Assets, $4,924,325 (M); expenditures, $255,485; qualifying distributions, $226,204; giving activities include $230,000 for 21 grants (high: $25,000; low: $3,000).
**Purpose and activities:** Giving primarily for higher education and hospitals.
**Fields of interest:** Museums (history); higher education; libraries (public); hospitals (general); human services.
**Limitations:** Giving primarily in Frederick County, MD. No grants to individuals.
**Application information:** Application form not required.
  *Initial approach:* Letter
  *Deadline(s):* Nov. 1
**Officers and Directors:*** Pamela I. Martin,* Pres.; Charles F. Trunk III,* Secy.; Helen B. Young,* Treas.; Adrian L. Winpigler.
**EIN:** 526039803

## 264
## The Westport Fund
2901 Boston St., Ste. 607
Baltimore, MD 21224-4891

Established in 1943.
**Donor(s):** Milton McGreevy,‡ Jean McGreevy Green.
**Grantmaker type:** Independent foundation
**Financial data** (yr. ended 12/31/97): Assets, $6,203,376 (M); expenditures, $426,449; qualifying distributions, $351,351; giving activities include $353,000 for 143 grants (high: $50,000; low: $250).
**Purpose and activities:** Funding primarily for education and community and human services.
**Fields of interest:** Television; museums; museums (children's); ballet; theater; orchestra (symphony); opera; music, choral; music, ensembles & groups; historic preservation/historical societies; arts/cultural programs; elementary/secondary education; higher education; college; libraries (public); vocational education; hospitals (general); family planning; cancer; crime/violence prevention; food banks; boys & girls clubs; human services; Salvation Army; hospices; community development; federated giving programs; Christian agencies & churches; women.
**Types of support:** General/operating support; continuing support; annual campaigns; capital campaigns; building/renovation; equipment; endowments; publication; curriculum development; scholarship funds; research.
**Limitations:** Applications not accepted. No grants to individuals, or for consulting services, deficit financing, exchange programs, internships, matching funds, land acquisition, seed money, or technical assistance; no loans.
**Application information:** Contributes only to pre-selected organizations.
**Officers:** Gail McGreevy Harmon, Pres.; Jean McGreevy Green, Secy.; Annie James McGreevy, Treas.
**Number of staff:** None.
**EIN:** 446007971

## 265
## Mary H. Agostine Trust
c/o BankBoston, N.A.
P.O. Box 1861
Boston, MA 02105-1861

Established in 1983.
**Grantmaker type:** Independent foundation
**Financial data** (yr. ended 12/31/99): Assets, $1,512,951 (M); expenditures, $279,287; qualifying distributions, $270,990; giving activities include $272,340 for 1 grant.
**Fields of interest:** Libraries/library science; general charitable giving.
**Limitations:** Applications not accepted. Giving primarily in MA. No grants to individuals.
**Application information:** Contributes only to pre-selected organizations.
**Trustee:** BankBoston, N.A.
**EIN:** 046489996

## 266
## American Optical Foundation
P.O. Box 1, Tax Dept.
Southbridge, MA 01550 (508) 765-9711
*Contact:* Gary Bridgeman, Tr.
*Application address:* c/o American Optical Corp., 14 Mechanic St., Southbridge, MA 01550

Established in 1968.
**Donor(s):** American Optical Corp.
**Grantmaker type:** Company-sponsored foundation
**Financial data** (yr. ended 12/31/99): Assets, $1,909,900 (M); expenditures, $94,193; qualifying distributions, $89,858; giving activities include $40,450 for 14 grants (high: $33,000; low: $50) and $35,075 for 33 grants to individuals (high: $4,000; low: $25).
**Purpose and activities:** Scholarships only for children of American Optical Corp. employees.
**Fields of interest:** Libraries/library science; education; youth, services.
**Types of support:** General/operating support; employee-related scholarships.
**Limitations:** Giving primarily in MA.
**Application information:** Application form required.
  *Deadline(s):* Apr. 25
**Trustees:** Gary Bridgeman, Allen Skott, John Van Dyke, American Optical Corp.
**EIN:** 046028058

## 267
## Austin Foundation, Inc.
c/o Carl E. York, Jr.
175 Federal St.
Boston, MA 02110

Established in 1972.
**Donor(s):** John F. Austin, Jr., Carl E. York, Jr.
**Grantmaker type:** Independent foundation
**Financial data** (yr. ended 12/31/99): Assets, $2,765,623 (M); gifts received, $93,500; expenditures, $133,748; qualifying distributions,

$102,613; giving activities include $93,225 for 8 grants (high: $30,000; low: $1,000).
**Purpose and activities:** Giving primarily for public libraries.
**Fields of interest:** Museums; libraries (public); hospitals (general).
**Limitations:** Applications not accepted. Giving primarily in MA. No grants to individuals.
**Application information:** Contributes only to pre-selected organizations.
**Officers and Directors:*** John F. Austin, Jr.,* Pres.; Carl E. York, Jr.,* V.P.; Duan K. Tuttle.
**EIN:** 237259956

## 268
## Adelaide Breed Bayrd Foundation
28 Pilgrim Rd.
Melrose, MA 02176 (781) 662-7342
*Contact:* Russell E. Watts, M.D., Pres.

Incorporated in 1927 in MA.
**Donor(s):** Frank A. Bayrd,‡ Blanche S. Bayrd.‡
**Grantmaker type:** Independent foundation
**Financial data** (yr. ended 12/31/99): Assets, $4,808,437 (M); gifts received, $444,993; expenditures, $495,835; qualifying distributions, $452,348; giving activities include $437,865 for 57 grants (high: $59,790; low: $1,000).
**Purpose and activities:** To support primarily those activities in which the donors' mother took an active interest. This includes local hospitals, social welfare concerns, libraries, youth-oriented programs, and cultural activities. The foundation does not grant individual scholarships but does fund ten scholarships annually through the Malden High School in MA. All grants must in some manner benefit the citizens of Malden.
**Fields of interest:** Arts/cultural programs; adult/continuing education; libraries/library science; education; hospitals (general); health care; health associations; human services; children & youth, services; family services; hospices; aging, centers & services; community development; aging; general charitable giving.
**Types of support:** Annual campaigns; capital campaigns; building/renovation; equipment; emergency funds; program development; scholarship funds.
**Limitations:** Giving limited to the metropolitan Boston, MA, area, with emphasis on Malden. No support for national or out-of-state organizations or the performing arts. No grants to individuals (except for scholarships supplementary to the will of Blanche Bayrd), or for matching or challenge grants, demonstration projects, conferences, publications, or research; no loans.
**Publications:** Annual report (including application guidelines).
**Application information:** Application form not required.
  *Initial approach:* Proposal
  *Copies of proposal:* 1
  *Deadline(s):* Submit proposal preferably in Dec. or Jan.; deadline Apr. 1
  *Board meeting date(s):* 2nd Tues. in Feb.; special meetings usually held in Apr. or May to consider grant requests
  *Final notification:* Generally in Apr. or May
**Officers and Trustees:*** Russell E. Watts, M.D.,* Pres.; Susan C. Mansur,* Treas.; Florence C.

Burns, C. Henry Kezer, Fred I. Lamson, William H. Marshall, Jean H. Stearns, H. Allen Stevens.
**Number of staff:** 1 part-time professional; 1 part-time support.
**EIN:** 046051258

**269**
**Brigham Hill Foundation**
128 Brigham Hill Rd.
North Grafton, MA 01536 (508) 829-1121
*Contact:* Donald F. Dillman, Mgr.

Established in 1989 in MA.
**Donor(s):** Peter H. Williams, Washington Mills Co., Washington Mills Electro-Minerals.
**Grantmaker type:** Independent foundation
**Financial data** (yr. ended 12/31/99): Assets, $422,035 (M); gifts received, $60,000; expenditures, $181,704; qualifying distributions, $180,775; giving activities include $180,775 for 18 grants (high: $101,000; low: $75).
**Purpose and activities:** Giving for the arts, education, and human services.
**Fields of interest:** Arts/cultural programs; higher education; libraries/library science; human services; federated giving programs.
**Limitations:** Giving primarily in MA. No grants to individuals.
**Application information:**
 *Initial approach:* Proposal
 *Deadline(s):* None
**Officers:** Peter H. Williams, Chair.; Henry C. Horner, Secy.; Shirley J. Williams, Treas.; Donald F. Dillman, Mgr.
**EIN:** 043066922

**270**
**Burnham Foundation, Inc.**
P.O. Box 1400
Boston, MA 02205
*Contact:* Charles A. Rosebrock, Treas.
*Application address:* c/o Nutter, McClennen & Fish, 1 International Pl., Boston, MA 02710, tel.: (617) 439-2000

Established in 1989 in MA.
**Donor(s):** George R. Burnham.‡
**Grantmaker type:** Operating foundation
**Financial data** (yr. ended 12/31/99): Assets, $1,716,732 (M); expenditures, $91,588; qualifying distributions, $75,895; giving activities include $68,100 for 24 grants (high: $10,000; low: $400).
**Purpose and activities:** Giving for the environment, Christian organizations, and libraries.
**Fields of interest:** Libraries/library science; education; natural resource conservation & protection; environment; hospitals (general); human services; Christian agencies & churches; general charitable giving.
**Types of support:** General/operating support; scholarships—to individuals.
**Limitations:** Giving limited to MA.
**Application information:** Application form required for scholarships.
 *Initial approach:* Letter for grants
 *Deadline(s):* None
**Officers and Directors:*** Charles P. Burnham, Pres.; Charles A. Rosebrock, Treas. and Clerk; Lynn Lamar.
**EIN:** 222979498

**271**
**Community Foundation of Western Massachusetts**
1500 Main St., Ste. 622
P.O. Box 15769
Springfield, MA 01115 (413) 732-2858
*Contact:* Kent W. Faerber, Pres.
*FAX:* (413) 733-8565; E-mail: wmass@communityfoundation.org

Established in 1991 in MA.
**Grantmaker type:** Community foundation
**Financial data** (yr. ended 03/31/00): Assets, $67,117,988 (M); gifts received, $9,724,587; expenditures, $10,516,219; giving activities include $9,431,576 for grants.
**Fields of interest:** Performing arts; historic preservation/historical societies; arts/cultural programs; education, fund raising; adult/continuing education; adult education—literacy & basic skills; libraries/library science; reading; education; natural resource conservation & protection; environment; wildlife preservation & protection; hospitals (general); family planning; medical care, rehabilitation; health care; substance abuse, services; health associations; cancer; heart & circulatory diseases; AIDS; cancer research; heart & circulatory research; AIDS research; delinquency prevention/services; crime/law enforcement; housing/shelter, development; safety/disasters; recreation; human services; children & youth, services; aging, centers & services; women, centers & services; minorities/immigrants, centers & services; human rights (international); civil rights; community development; voluntarism promotion; public policy, research; public affairs; minorities; Native Americans; disabled; aging; women; gays/lesbians; economically disadvantaged.
**Types of support:** Capital campaigns; building/renovation; equipment; program development; conferences/seminars; publication; seed money; fellowships; scholarship funds; technical assistance; matching/challenge support.
**Limitations:** Giving limited to western MA, with emphasis on Hampden County and Springfield. No support for political or religious organizations, private secondary or higher education. No grants to individuals directly, or for operating budgets, endowments, fundraising events, tickets for benefits, courtesy advertising, academic or medical research or multi-year funding.
**Publications:** Annual report (including application guidelines), grants list, informational brochure, application guidelines, newsletter.
**Application information:** Application form required.
 *Initial approach:* Telephone
 *Copies of proposal:* 3
 *Deadline(s):* 1st of Feb., May, Aug., and Nov.
 *Board meeting date(s):* Quarterly
 *Final notification:* Within 2 months
**Officers and Trustees:*** Thomas Wheeler,* Chair.; Alfred L. Griggs, Vice-Chair.; Kent W. Faerber,* Pres.; Lester L. Halpern, Treas.; Robert B. Atkinson, Charles P. Barker, Helen D. Blake, Kenneth C. Boutin, Randolph W. Bromery, Ph.D., Bruce Brown, Marcia Burrick, Robert S. Cohn, Robert Carroll, Stephen A. Davis, Sandra Eagleton, Helen S. Fuller, John G. Gallup,

Harold Grinspoon, Kurt M. Hertzfeld, William A. Sandri, Orlando Isaza, David Starr, Carol Leary, Judith Plotkin-Goldberg, Jean Salter Roetter, William Sadowsky, Albert E. Steiger, Jr., Marcellette G. Williams, R. Lyman Wood, Angela Wright, Richard Zilewicz.
**Number of staff:** 6 full-time professional; 1 part-time professional; 6 full-time support.
**EIN:** 223089640

**272**
**Concord's Home for the Aged**
110 Walden St.
Concord, MA 01742

Established around 1957; Classified as a private operating foundation in 1989.
**Grantmaker type:** Operating foundation
**Financial data** (yr. ended 11/30/99): Assets, $8,870,132 (M); expenditures, $468,049; qualifying distributions, $467,249; giving activities include $196,900 for 20 grants (high: $75,000; low: $100) and $5,000 for 9 grants to individuals (high: $1,250; low: $150).
**Purpose and activities:** Operates and maintains a home for the elderly.
**Fields of interest:** Libraries/library science; hospitals (general).
**Types of support:** General/operating support.
**Limitations:** Applications not accepted. Giving limited to Concord, MA. No grants to individuals.
**Application information:** Contributes only to pre-selected organizations.
**Officers:** Patricia Carey, Chair.; Tryntje Hawks, Pres.; Thomas M. Ruggles, V.P.; Laura Ells, Secy.; Jane M. Brooks, Treas.; Patricia McAlpine, Mgr.
**EIN:** 042103762

**273**
**The William F. Connell Charitable Trust**
c/o Lynch, Brewer, Hoffman & Sands, LLP
101 Federal St., 22nd Fl.
Boston, MA 02110-1800

Established in 1986 in MA.
**Donor(s):** William F. Connell.
**Grantmaker type:** Independent foundation
**Financial data** (yr. ended 12/31/99): Assets, $939,306 (M); expenditures, $50,243; qualifying distributions, $47,000; giving activities include $47,000 for 8 grants (high: $10,000; low: $1,000).
**Purpose and activities:** Giving for youth services and Catholic organizations.
**Fields of interest:** Secondary school/education; libraries (public); Roman Catholic agencies & churches; general charitable giving.
**Limitations:** Applications not accepted. Giving primarily in MA. No grants to individuals.
**Application information:** Contributes only to pre-selected organizations.
**Trustees:** Terence A. Connell, Timothy P. Connell, William C. Connell, Courtenay E. Connell-Toner, Monica C. Healey, Lisa T. McNamara.
**EIN:** 222778156

## 274
### Eleanor Cray Cottle Charitable Trust
53 Woodchuck Hill Rd.
Harvard, MA 01451
*Contact:* Trustees

Established in 1969 in MA.
**Donor(s):** Eleanor Cray Cottle.
**Grantmaker type:** Independent foundation
**Financial data** (yr. ended 12/31/98): Assets, $1,506,024 (M); expenditures, $109,660; qualifying distributions, $76,335; giving activities include $76,300 for 18 grants (high: $19,000; low: $100).
**Purpose and activities:** Giving to education and Christian agencies.
**Fields of interest:** Museums; historic preservation/historical societies; higher education; libraries (public); health care; Roman Catholic agencies & churches.
**Limitations:** Giving primarily in Boston, MA. No grants to individuals.
**Application information:**
*Initial approach:* Letter
*Deadline(s):* None
**Trustees:** Evelyn Adams Hammershaimb, Francis S. Holt.
**EIN:** 237052778

## 275
### The Crozier Family Charitable Foundation
41 Ridge Hill Farm Rd.
Wellesley, MA 02482

Established in 1997 in MA.
**Donor(s):** William M. Crozier, Jr.
**Grantmaker type:** Independent foundation
**Financial data** (yr. ended 12/31/99): Assets, $1,298,993 (M); gifts received, $253,679; expenditures, $60,651; qualifying distributions, $55,844; giving activities include $58,746 for 83 grants (high: $13,047; low: $1,000).
**Purpose and activities:** Giving for the arts, education, hospitals, and religious organizations.
**Fields of interest:** Orchestra (symphony); arts/cultural programs; higher education; libraries/library science; hospitals (general); federated giving programs; religion.
**Limitations:** Applications not accepted. Giving limited to MA. No grants to individuals.
**Application information:** Contributes only to pre-selected organizations.
**Trustees:** Abigail P. Crozier, Matthew E. Crozier, Patience W. Crozier, Prudence S. Crozier, William M. Crozier, Jr.
**EIN:** 043368611

## 276
### CYRK International Foundation
3 Pond Rd.
Gloucester, MA 01930

Established in 1994 in MA.
**Donor(s):** Patrick D. Brady, Gregory P. Shlopak.
**Grantmaker type:** Independent foundation
**Financial data** (yr. ended 12/31/99): Assets, $2,137,206 (M); expenditures, $110,565; qualifying distributions, $98,332; giving activities include $94,912 for 8 grants (high: $85,000; low: $50).

**Purpose and activities:** Giving for community affairs, Christian churches, and medical and health research.
**Fields of interest:** Libraries/library science; education; medicine/medical care, research; health associations; recreation; human services; Christian agencies & churches.
**Limitations:** Applications not accepted. Giving primarily in MA. No grants to individuals.
**Application information:** Contributes only to pre-selected organizations.
**Trustees:** Edna Brady, James T. Brady, Patrick D. Brady.
**EIN:** 043240308

## 277
### The Fred Harris Daniels Foundation, Inc.
c/o BankBoston, N.A.
100 Front St.
Worcester, MA 01608 (617) 434-1670
*Contact:* Bruce G. Daniels, Pres., or Georgia Beit, Asst. Secy.

Incorporated in 1949 in MA.
**Donor(s):** Fred H. Daniels,‡ Eleanor G. Daniels.‡
**Grantmaker type:** Independent foundation
**Financial data** (yr. ended 10/31/99): Assets, $18,384,197 (M); expenditures, $685,202; qualifying distributions, $632,716; giving activities include $623,252 for 85 grants (high: $40,000; low: $1,000; average: $1,000–$50,000).
**Purpose and activities:** Grants for the advancement of the sciences, including marine and medical sciences; support also for secondary and higher education, health services and hospitals, including programs for the mentally ill, community funds, social and family services, including museums, music organizations, historical preservation, libraries, and Protestant giving.
**Fields of interest:** Museums; performing arts; music; historic preservation/historical societies; arts/cultural programs; secondary school/education; higher education; adult education—literacy & basic skills; libraries/library science; reading; education; hospitals (general); family planning; health care; mental health/crisis services; health associations; biomedicine; medical research; youth development, services; human services; children & youth, services; family services; federated giving programs; marine science; engineering & technology; science; leadership development; Protestant agencies & churches; general charitable giving.
**Types of support:** General/operating support; continuing support; annual campaigns; capital campaigns; building/renovation; equipment; land acquisition; endowments; emergency funds; program development; scholarship funds; matching/challenge support.
**Limitations:** Giving primarily in the Worcester, MA, area. No grants to individuals, or for seed money or deficit financing; no loans.
**Application information:** Application form not required.
*Initial approach:* Letter
*Copies of proposal:* 1
*Deadline(s):* Mar. 1, June 1, Sept. 1, and Dec. 1
*Board meeting date(s):* Mar., June, Sept., and Dec.

*Final notification:* 1 to 3 months after meeting
**Officers and Directors:** Bruce G. Daniels,* Pres.; Eleanor D. Hodge,* V.P.; William S. Nicholson,* Secy.; William O. Pettit, Jr.,* Treas.; Jonathan D. Blake, Fred H. Daniels II, Janet B. Daniels, Amy B. Key, Sarah D. Morse, David A. Nicholson, Meridith D. Wesby.
**Number of staff:** None.
**EIN:** 046014333

## 278
### Eaton Foundation
255 State St.
Boston, MA 02109-2617 (617) 482-8260
*Contact:* Janet E. Sanders, Tr.

Established in 1953 in MA.
**Grantmaker type:** Independent foundation
**Financial data** (yr. ended 12/31/99): Assets, $1,721,898 (M); gifts received, $40,341; expenditures, $91,789; qualifying distributions, $85,063; giving activities include $79,500 for 46 grants (high: $10,000; low: $500).
**Purpose and activities:** Giving for hospitals, education, medical research, youth services, art and cultural programs, and for community and public services.
**Fields of interest:** Museums; arts/cultural programs; higher education; libraries/library science; education; environment; hospitals (general); health care; boys & girls clubs; youth development; human services; Salvation Army.
**Types of support:** General/operating support.
**Limitations:** Giving primarily in MA. No grants to individuals.
**Application information:** Grants awarded annually in Nov. and Dec.
*Initial approach:* Letter
**Trustees:** Frank O. Adams, Janet E. Sanders.
**EIN:** 046017700

## 279
### Kendall C. and Anna Ham Charitable Foundation, Inc.
c/o Paul L. Brigham
10 Park St.
Northborough, MA 01532
*Contact:* Frank J. Connolly, Jr., Secy.
*Application address:* P.O. Box 263, Jackson, NH 03846; E-mail: THCF@lamdmarknet.net

Established in 1994.
**Grantmaker type:** Independent foundation
**Financial data** (yr. ended 12/31/98): Assets, $12,447,139 (M); gifts received, $958,678; expenditures, $698,910; qualifying distributions, $768,606; giving activities include $551,822 for 57 grants (high: $150,000; low: $100).
**Fields of interest:** Historic preservation/historical societies; libraries/library science; health care; housing/shelter; human services, special populations.
**Types of support:** Annual campaigns; capital campaigns; building/renovation; equipment; land acquisition; endowments; debt reduction; program development; seed money; matching/challenge support.
**Limitations:** Giving limited to the Lakes Region, ME, and the Washington Valley area, NH.
**Publications:** Annual report, application guidelines, program policy statement.

**Application information:** Application form required.

*Deadline(s):* 90 days prior to board meeting
*Board meeting date(s):* Jan., Apr., July, and Oct.
*Final notification:* Following meeting
**Officers:** Paul L. Brigham, Jr., Pres.; Frank J. Connolly, Jr., Secy.
**Directors:** Bruce A. Chalmers, Robert J. Murphy, Alan Ordway.
**Number of staff:** 1 full-time professional; 1 part-time support.
**EIN:** 223080012

### 280
### Hathaway Memorial Charitable Trust
c/o BankBoston, N.A.
P.O. Box 1861
Boston, MA 02105 (617) 434-4644
*Contact:* Augusta Haydock, Chair.

Established in 1988 in MA.
**Grantmaker type:** Independent foundation
**Financial data** (yr. ended 07/31/99): Assets, $2,027,164 (M); expenditures, $74,441; qualifying distributions, $56,577; giving activities include $55,300 for 17 grants (high: $10,000; low: $500).
**Purpose and activities:** Giving for children, family and human services, and for religion.
**Fields of interest:** Historic preservation/historical societies; libraries/library science; education; human services; family services; hospices; government/public administration; Protestant agencies & churches.
**Types of support:** General/operating support; building/renovation; equipment; emergency funds; program development; conferences/seminars; publication; seed money; curriculum development; scholarship funds; matching/challenge support.
**Limitations:** Giving limited to the Somerset, MA area.
**Application information:** Application form not required.

*Initial approach:* Letter
*Copies of proposal:* 1
*Board meeting date(s):* Late May and June
*Final notification:* Mid to late July
**Trustee:** BankBoston, N.A.
**Number of staff:** None.
**EIN:** 046599655

### 281
### High Meadow Foundation, Inc.
c/o Country Curtains, Inc.
Main St.
Stockbridge, MA 01262 (413) 298-5565
*Contact:* Jane P. Fitzpatrick, Chair. or John H. Fitzpatrick, Pres.

Established in 1984 in MA.
**Donor(s):** John H. Fitzpatrick, Jane P. Fitzpatrick, Country Curtains, Inc., Housatonic Curtain Co., Red Lion Inn, Country Curtains Retail.
**Grantmaker type:** Independent foundation
**Financial data** (yr. ended 09/30/99): Assets, $2,027,799 (M); gifts received, $1,216,411; expenditures, $1,366,003; qualifying distributions, $1,365,321; giving activities include $1,353,877 for 411 grants (high: $153,000; low: $25) and $10,000 for 20 grants to individuals.

**Purpose and activities:** Support primarily for the performing arts, especially theater and music, and other cultural organizations; giving also for health, social services, and education.
**Fields of interest:** Visual arts; museums; performing arts; theater; music; humanities; arts/cultural programs; education, fund raising; elementary school/education; higher education; libraries/library science; family planning; health care; mental health/crisis services; health associations; cancer; medical research; cancer research; human services; children & youth, services; family services; women, centers & services; homeless, human services; international relief; community development; religion; Native Americans; women; homeless.
**Types of support:** Continuing support; annual campaigns; capital campaigns; building/renovation; equipment; debt reduction; emergency funds; program development; program-related investments/loans; employee-related scholarships; matching/challenge support.
**Limitations:** Giving primarily in Berkshire County, MA.
**Application information:** Application form not required.

*Initial approach:* Letter
*Deadline(s):* None
**Officers and Directors:*** Jane P. Fitzpatrick,* Chair. and Treas.; John H. Fitzpatrick,* Pres.; Robert B. Trask, Clerk; JoAnn Fitzpatrick Brown, Nancy J. Fitzpatrick, Tamara T. Stevens.
**Number of staff:** 1
**EIN:** 222527419

### 282
### Institution for Savings in Newburyport & Its Vicinity Charitable Foundation, Inc.
93 State St.
P.O. Box 510
Newburyport, MA 01950 (978) 462-3106

Established in 1997 in MA.
**Donor(s):** 1820 Security Corp.
**Grantmaker type:** Independent foundation
**Financial data** (yr. ended 06/30/99): Assets, $2,483,070 (M); expenditures, $165,250; qualifying distributions, $135,851; giving activities include $150,000 for 9 grants (high: $100,000; low: $2,500).
**Purpose and activities:** Giving to women's centers, maritime associations and youth services.
**Fields of interest:** Libraries/library science; environment; parks/playgrounds; aging, centers & services; women, centers & services; community development.
**Limitations:** Giving primarily in MA.
**Officers and Trustees:*** Donald D. Mitchell,* Pres.; Patricia D. Connelly, Clerk; Mark F. Welch,* Treas.; Harvey Beit, John F. Bradshaw, Eugene E. Bucco, Hugh J. Doyle, Curtis L. Gerrish, Jr., Peter G. Kelly, Mary E. Larnard, Marjorie A. Lynn, Arthur S. Page, Jr., John H. Pramberg, Jr., S. Merrell Stearns, Michael E. Strem, Richard E. Sullivan, David M. Tierney, Jonathan J. Woodman.
**EIN:** 043353621

### 283
### Kathleen & Ronald J. Jackson Foundation
11 Lenox Cir.
Andover, MA 01810-5428

Established in 1994.
**Donor(s):** Kathleen Jackson, Ronald J. Jackson.
**Grantmaker type:** Independent foundation
**Financial data** (yr. ended 12/31/99): Assets, $3,535,611 (M); expenditures, $164,556; qualifying distributions, $156,050; giving activities include $160,000 for 15 grants (high: $60,000; low: $1,000).
**Fields of interest:** Arts/cultural programs; libraries/library science; hospitals (general).
**Limitations:** Applications not accepted. Giving primarily in Boston, MA. No grants to individuals.
**Application information:** Contributes only to pre-selected organizations.
**Trustees:** Kathleen Jackson, Ronald J. Jackson, Susan L. Jackson, Nancy A. Rushton.
**EIN:** 046762777

### 284
### Edward Bangs Kelley and Elza Kelley Foundation, Inc.
243 South St.
P.O. Drawer M
Hyannis, MA 02601 (508) 775-3117
*Contact:* Henry L. Murphy, Jr., Pres., or Rebecca J. Jason

Incorporated in 1954 in MA.
**Donor(s):** Edward Bangs Kelley,‡ Elza deHorvath Kelley.‡
**Grantmaker type:** Independent foundation
**Financial data** (yr. ended 12/31/99): Assets, $5,490,227 (M); gifts received, $1,650; expenditures, $262,525; qualifying distributions, $236,044; giving activities include $159,385 for grants and $54,400 for 73 grants to individuals (high: $2,750; low: $150; average: $157–$2,750).
**Purpose and activities:** To promote the health and welfare of inhabitants of Barnstable County, MA; grants for higher education, including scholarships, and particularly for medical and paramedical education; support also for health and hospitals, hospices, prevention of drug and alcohol abuse, child development and youth agencies, the elderly, libraries, the environment, marine sciences, and cultural programs, including museums, fine arts, theater, and the performing arts.
**Fields of interest:** Visual arts; museums; performing arts; theater; arts/cultural programs; child development, education; higher education; medical school/education; libraries/library science; education; environment; hospitals (general); health care; substance abuse, services; health associations; alcoholism; children & youth, services; child development, services; hospices; aging, centers & services; marine science; aging.
**Types of support:** General/operating support; capital campaigns; building/renovation; equipment; emergency funds; program development; seed money; scholarship funds; research; technical assistance; scholarships—to individuals; matching/challenge support.
**Limitations:** Giving limited to Barnstable County, MA. No grants to individuals (except for

scholarships), or for annual campaigns, deficit financing, land acquisition, endowment funds, exchange programs, fellowships, publications, or conferences; no loans.
**Publications:** Annual report (including application guidelines).
**Application information:** Application form required.
　*Initial approach:* Letter, followed by proposal
　*Copies of proposal:* 6
　*Deadline(s):* Apr. 30 for scholarships; no deadline for grants; grants considered Apr., July, and Oct. if greater than $2,500
　*Board meeting date(s):* Jan., Apr., July, and Oct.
　*Final notification:* 3 weeks
**Officers and Directors:*** Henry L. Murphy, Jr.,* Pres. and Admin.; Mary Louise Montgomery,* V.P.; Thomas S. Olsen,* Treas.; R. Bruce Hammatt, Jr., Clerk; Doreen Bilezikion, Jocelyn Bowman, Robert B. Hirschman, Townsend Hornor, John M. Kayajan, Kenneth S. MacAffer, Jr., Stephen W. Malaquias, M.D., Joshua A. Nickerson, Jr., Charles N. Robinson, Barbara H. Sheaffer, Hamilton N. Shepley.
**Number of staff:** 1 part-time professional; 1 part-time support.
**EIN:** 046039660

---

**285**
### John F. Kennedy Library Foundation, Inc.
Columbia Point
Boston, MA　02125-3313　(617) 929-4500
*Contact:* Megan Desnoyers, Acting Chief Archivist
*FAX:* (617) 929-4538; *E-mail:* foundation@kennedy.nara.gov; *URL:* http://www.cs.umb.edu/jfklibrary

Established in 1984.
**Grantmaker type:** Public charity
**Financial data** (yr. ended 12/31/99): Giving activities include $27,055 for 24 grants to individuals (high: $3,600; low: $200).
**Purpose and activities:** The foundation offers grants to scholars doing significant research using the holdings of the library.
**Fields of interest:** Archives.
**Types of support:** Fellowships; grants to individuals.
**Publications:** Application guidelines, informational brochure, newsletter, grants list.
**Application information:** See Web site for further information. Application form required.
　*Initial approach:* Telephone, e-mail, or typed letter
　*Deadline(s):* Mar. 15 and Aug. 15; Feb. 25 for internships
　*Final notification:* Apr. 20 and Oct. 20
**Officers and Directors:*** Paul G. Kirk, Jr.,* Chair.; Richard K. Donahue,* Vice-Chair.; Caroline B. Kennedy,* Pres.; Carolyn M. Osteen,* Secy.; John T. Fallon,* Treas.; Charles U. Daly, Exec. Dir.; James J. Blanchard, David W. Burke, William F. Connell, Jill Ker Conway, T. Jefferson Coolidge, Jr., Diddy Culliname, John J. Cullinane, John F. Dever, Jr., Gerard F. Doherty, Donald J. Dowd, John F. Farrell, Jr., Robert P. Fitzgerald, J. John Fox, Milton A. Gilbert, Carol R. Goldberg, John L. Harrington, Catherine E.C. Henn, Thomas J. Hynes, Jr., Ellen S. Jackson, Michael Kennedy, Joanna T. Lau, Patricia Kennedy Lawford, Peter S. Lynch, Edward T. Martin, Thomas J. May, Angela Menino, Sherry

H. Penny, Dennis J. Picard, Hon. David F. Powers, Patrick J. Purcell, Sumner M. Redstone, Mary L. Reed, Robert E. Riley, Edwin A. Schlossberg, Timothy P. Shriver, Stephen E. Smith, Jr.
**EIN:** 046113130

---

**286**
### Kessler Family Foundation
c/o Tanager Financial Svcs.
800 South St., Ste. 195
Waltham, MA　02453

Established in 1993 in MA.
**Donor(s):** Howard J. Kessler, Patricia M. Kessler.
**Grantmaker type:** Independent foundation
**Financial data** (yr. ended 12/31/99): Assets, $8,428,733 (M); expenditures, $642,344; qualifying distributions, $574,330; giving activities include $579,475 for 70 grants (high: $100,000; low: $100).
**Purpose and activities:** Giving primarily for education and medical research, with emphasis on cancer research.
**Fields of interest:** Arts/cultural programs; higher education; libraries (special); education; hospitals (general); health associations; medical research; cancer research; human services; federated giving programs.
**Limitations:** Applications not accepted. Giving primarily in MA. No grants to individuals.
**Application information:** Contributes only to pre-selected organizations.
**Trustees:** Howard J. Kessler, Patricia M. Kessler.
**EIN:** 043213614

---

**287**
### Knowlton Foundation for the Elderly, Inc.
c/o Elden E. Bjurling
7 Abbott St.
Gardner, MA　01440
*Contact:* Stephen A. Brooks, Pres.
*Application address:* 147 Elm St., Gardner, MA 01440, tel.: (978) 632-3198

Established in 1980 in MA.
**Grantmaker type:** Independent foundation
**Financial data** (yr. ended 03/31/99): Assets, $1,085,608 (M); expenditures, $61,624; qualifying distributions, $52,841; giving activities include $49,240 for 6 grants (high: $15,040; low: $920).
**Purpose and activities:** Aid and assistance is restricted to the elderly in the greater Gardner, MA, area.
**Fields of interest:** Libraries/library science; hospitals (general); nursing care; aging, centers & services; aging.
**Types of support:** General/operating support; grants to individuals.
**Limitations:** Giving limited to the greater Gardner, MA, area.
**Application information:**
　*Initial approach:* Letter
　*Deadline(s):* None
**Officers and Directors:*** Stephen A. Brooks,* Pres.; Nancy Anderson,* V.P.; Robert D. Hawke,* V.P.; Nancy Hawke,* Secy.; Elden E. Bjurling,* Treas.; Joseph Forte, Janet Guzzetta, Glenn Hunt, Ethel L. Kendall, Margaret Miller, Leo Reponen, Mary Ruth, Donald Stuart, John R. Tinker, Richard Tourigny.

**EIN:** 046060834

---

**288**
### David T. Langrock Foundation
c/o BankBoston, N.A.
P.O. Box 1861
Boston, MA　02105

Established in 1981.
**Donor(s):** David T. Langrock.‡
**Grantmaker type:** Independent foundation
**Financial data** (yr. ended 11/30/99): Assets, $298,107 (M); expenditures, $71,794; qualifying distributions, $67,056; giving activities include $67,000 for 6 grants (high: $20,000; low: $5,000).
**Purpose and activities:** Grants limited to exhibitions and education relating to classical art.
**Fields of interest:** Museums (specialized); arts/cultural programs; higher education; libraries (academic/research); youth development, centers & clubs.
**Limitations:** Applications not accepted. Giving limited to CT. No grants to individuals.
**Application information:** Contributes only to pre-selected organizations.
**Trustees:** BankBoston, N.A.
**EIN:** 056039393

---

**289**
### Memorial Foundation for the Blind, Inc.
(Formerly Memorial Homes for the Blind)
51 Harvard St.
Worcester, MA　01609
*Contact:* Mrs. T. Ashley Edwards, Pres.

Established in 1951.
**Grantmaker type:** Independent foundation
**Financial data** (yr. ended 03/31/00): Assets, $5,192,725 (M); expenditures, $220,891; qualifying distributions, $179,443; giving activities include $168,403 for 9 grants (high: $73,420; low: $67) and $9,219 for 6 grants to individuals (high: $3,045; low: $975).
**Purpose and activities:** Support primarily for the care of the visually handicapped.
**Fields of interest:** Radio; libraries (public); eye diseases; human services, special populations.
**International interests:** Greece.
**Types of support:** General/operating support.
**Limitations:** Giving primarily in the Worcester, MA, area.
**Application information:**
　*Initial approach:* Letter or proposal
　*Copies of proposal:* 1
　*Deadline(s):* None
**Officers and Directors:*** Mrs. T. Ashley Edwards,* Pres.; Roger W. Greene,* V.P.; Kleber A. Campbell III,* Treas.; Barbara A. Ahalt, Stephanie S. Burnett, Helen D. Fifield, Barbara Higgins, Nancy S. Hudson, Nancy Jeppson, and 9 additional directors.
**EIN:** 041611615

---

**290**
### Newburyport Howard Benevolent Society
P.O. Box 9
Newburyport, MA　01950

Established in 1971.
**Grantmaker type:** Independent foundation
**Financial data** (yr. ended 09/30/99): Assets, $3,203,049 (M); expenditures, $103,428; qualifying distributions, $90,089; giving activities include $59,011 for 11 grants (high: $20,000; low: $2,040) and $21,099 for grants to individuals.
**Purpose and activities:** Giving for welfare and social service organizations; also provides welfare assistance to low-income families and individuals.
**Fields of interest:** Libraries/library science; health care, home services; housing/shelter; human services; community development; economically disadvantaged.
**Types of support:** General/operating support; grants to individuals.
**Limitations:** Applications not accepted. Giving limited to Newburyport, MA.
**Officers:** Robert S. Walters, Pres.; John S. Grove, Secy.; Peter DeMaranville, Treas.
**EIN:** 046041304

## 291
## Neil & Anna Rasmussen Foundation
393 Estabrook Rd.
Concord, MA  01742-5604

Established in 1994 in MA.
**Donor(s):** Neil Rasmussen, Anna Rasmussen.
**Grantmaker type:** Independent foundation
**Financial data** (yr. ended 12/31/99): Assets, $7,698,921 (M); gifts received, $10,035; expenditures, $354,614; qualifying distributions, $345,270; giving activities include $346,318 for 29 grants (high: $60,000; low: $200).
**Fields of interest:** Higher education; libraries/library science; natural resource conservation & protection; hospitals (general).
**Limitations:** Applications not accepted. Giving primarily in MA. No grants to individuals.
**Application information:** Contributes only to pre-selected organizations.
**Trustees:** Anna Rasmussen, Neil Rasmussen.
**EIN:** 046771880

## 292
## Rowe Foundation
c/o Testa, Hurwitz & Thibeault
125 High St.
Boston, MA  02110  (617) 248-7426
*Contact:* Peter A. Wilson, Exec. Dir.
*FAX:* (617) 248-7100

Established in 1989 in MA.
**Donor(s):** Dorothy Rowe.‡
**Grantmaker type:** Independent foundation
**Financial data** (yr. ended 12/31/98): Assets, $1,830,376 (M); expenditures, $130,487; qualifying distributions, $114,732; giving activities include $109,500 for 12 grants (high: $28,000; low: $2,000).
**Purpose and activities:** Giving primarily for education and youth programs.
**Fields of interest:** Arts/cultural programs; higher education; libraries/library science; housing/shelter; children & youth, services.
**Limitations:** Giving primarily in MA and NM. No grants to individuals.
**Application information:** Application form required.

*Initial approach:* Telephone
*Deadline(s):* None
**Officers and Directors:*** Richard J. Testa,* Pres. and Treas.; Henry W. Comstock, Clerk; Peter A. Wilson, Exec. Dir.; Barbara DuBois.
**Number of staff:** None.
**EIN:** 043071209

## 293
## Richard Saltonstall Charitable Foundation
c/o Saltonstall & Co., Inc.
50 Congress St., Rm. 800
Boston, MA  02109  (617) 227-8660
*Contact:* Dudley H. Willis, Tr.
*Application address:* P.O. Box 730, Sherborn, MA 01770

Established in 1964 in MA.
**Donor(s):** Richard Saltonsall.‡
**Grantmaker type:** Independent foundation
**Financial data** (yr. ended 12/31/98): Assets, $22,699,622 (M); expenditures, $1,063,352; qualifying distributions, $900,000; giving activities include $900,000 for 33 grants (high: $101,666; low: $2,000).
**Fields of interest:** Arts/cultural programs; libraries/library science; natural resource conservation & protection; hospitals (general); federated giving programs.
**Limitations:** Giving primarily in MA.
**Application information:** Application form not required.
*Initial approach:* Letter
*Deadline(s):* Oct. 15
*Board meeting date(s):* Nov. and Dec.
*Final notification:* Dec.
**Trustees:** Robert A. Lawrence, Emily S. Lewis, Dudley H. Willis, Sally S. Willis.
**Number of staff:** 1 full-time professional; 1 full-time support.
**EIN:** 046078934

## 294
## Harold B. and Elizabeth L. Shattuck Memorial Fund
c/o Randolph E. Goodwin
217 Essex St.
Salem, MA  01970

Established in 1997.
**Donor(s):** Elizabeth L. Shattuck Estate.
**Grantmaker type:** Independent foundation
**Financial data** (yr. ended 04/30/99): Assets, $4,220,687 (M); expenditures, $182,203; qualifying distributions, $161,140; giving activities include $150,000 for 5 grants of $30,000 each.
**Purpose and activities:** Support for scholarships, recreation, a council on aging, historical commission, and public library in Marblehead, MA.
**Fields of interest:** Arts/cultural programs; libraries/library science; human services.
**Limitations:** Applications not accepted. Giving primarily in Marblehead, MA. No grants to individuals.
**Application information:** Contributes only to pre-selected organizations.
**Trustee:** National Grand Bank of Marblehead.
**EIN:** 043393807

## 295
## The Smith-Denison Foundation
42 Clowes Dr.
Falmouth, MA  02540  (617) 742-1818
*Contact:* Clifford A. Clark, Tr.

Established in 1986.
**Donor(s):** Mary Smith Denison.
**Grantmaker type:** Independent foundation
**Financial data** (yr. ended 05/31/99): Assets, $963,412 (M); expenditures, $65,408; qualifying distributions, $59,156; giving activities include $60,000 for 9 grants (high: $10,000; low: $5,000).
**Purpose and activities:** Giving primarily for library services and aging centers.
**Fields of interest:** Libraries/library science; aging, centers & services.
**Application information:** Application form not required.
*Deadline(s):* None
**Trustees:** Clifford A. Clark, Mary Smith Denison.
**EIN:** 112848979

## 296
## Stearns Charitable Trust
66 Commonwealth Ave.
Concord, MA  01742
*Contact:* Russell S. Beede, Tr.

Trust established in 1947 in MA.
**Donor(s):** Russell B. Stearns.‡
**Grantmaker type:** Independent foundation
**Financial data** (yr. ended 12/31/99): Assets, $9,883,551 (M); expenditures, $492,323; qualifying distributions, $434,455; giving activities include $424,500 for grants.
**Purpose and activities:** Emphasis on cultural programs, including a science museum; support also for libraries, community funds, the environment, an aquarium, and social services.
**Fields of interest:** Museums; arts/cultural programs; libraries/library science; environment; alcoholism; human services; federated giving programs.
**Types of support:** General/operating support; continuing support; annual campaigns; building/renovation; land acquisition; program development.
**Limitations:** Applications not accepted. Giving primarily in MA. No grants to individuals.
**Application information:** Contributes primarily to pre-selected organizations.
*Board meeting date(s):* As required
**Trustees:** Russell S. Beede, Virginia Stearns Gassel, Anne B. Jencks.
**Number of staff:** None.
**EIN:** 046036697

## 297
## Silva Casa Stiftung Trust
c/o Ropes & Gray
1 International Plz.
Boston, MA  02110-2624

Established in 1992.
**Grantmaker type:** Independent foundation
**Financial data** (yr. ended 06/30/99): Assets, $4,821,288 (M); expenditures, $5,744,188; qualifying distributions, $5,549,582; giving activities include $5,549,582 for 15 grants (high: $3,222,000; low: $38,664).

**Purpose and activities:** Support for medical research and human services in Switzerland.
**Fields of interest:** Higher education; health care; diabetes.
**International interests:** Switzerland.
**Limitations:** Applications not accepted. Giving on an international basis, with emphasis on Switzerland. No grants to individuals.
**Application information:** Contributes only to pre-selected organizations.
**Trustees:** Janet Briner, Max Beat Ludwig, Ewald R. Weibel.
**EIN:** 980126934
**Recent grants for library/information services:**
297-1 Schweizerisches Literaturachiv, Zurich, Switzerland, $296,685. For general support. 1998.

---

**298**
**Thomas Thompson Trust**
1 Financial Ctr.
Boston, MA   02111   (617) 951-1145
*Contact:* William B. Tyler, Tr.

Trust established in 1869 in MA.
**Donor(s):** Thomas Thompson.‡
**Grantmaker type:** Independent foundation
**Financial data** (yr. ended 05/31/98): Assets, $16,760,204 (M); expenditures, $829,904; qualifying distributions, $761,360; giving activities include $705,517 for 45 grants (high: $100,000; low: $440; average: $1,000–$18,000).
**Purpose and activities:** Giving primarily for health, education, and human services.
**Fields of interest:** Arts/cultural programs; elementary/secondary education; higher education; libraries/library science; hospitals (general); human services; children & youth, services; family services.
**Types of support:** Capital campaigns; building/renovation; equipment; emergency funds; program development; matching/challenge support.
**Limitations:** Giving limited to Rhinebeck, NY and surrounding areas, and Brattleboro, VT. No grants to individuals, or for operating budgets, continuing support, seed money, deficit financing, endowment funds, scholarships, or fellowships; no loans.
**Publications:** Application guidelines.
**Application information:** Grants awarded only to organizations that have been in operation for 3 consecutive years. Application form not required.
*Initial approach:* Telephone
*Copies of proposal:* 1
*Deadline(s):* None
*Board meeting date(s):* Monthly except Aug., and as required
*Final notification:* 6 weeks
**Trustees:** Daniel W. Fawcett, Albert Fortier, Jr., William B. Tyler.
**Number of staff:** 1 part-time professional.
**EIN:** 030179429

---

**299**
**Tillotson North Country Foundation, Inc.**
c/o Choate, Hall & Stewart
Exchange Pl., 53 State St.
Boston, MA   02109-2891

Established in 1996 in NH.
**Grantmaker type:** Independent foundation
**Financial data** (yr. ended 11/30/99): Assets, $1,051,797 (M); expenditures, $76,225; qualifying distributions, $73,436; giving activities include $74,000 for 3 grants (high: $41,000; low: $8,000).
**Purpose and activities:** Giving for hospitals and libraries.
**Fields of interest:** Libraries (public); hospitals (general).
**Limitations:** Applications not accepted. Giving primarily in NH. No grants to individuals.
**Application information:** Contributes only to pre-selected organizations.
**Officers and Directors:*** Neil Tillotson,* Pres. and Treas.; Frederick E. Tillotson, Clerk; Sam Owen, Louise Tillotson.
**EIN:** 020494246

---

**300**
**David P. Wheatland Charitable Trust**
c/o Arcadia Mgmt. Co., Inc.
31 Milk St., Rm. 1104
Boston, MA   02109   (617) 426-5755
*Contact:* Richard Wheatland, Tr.

Established in 1993 in MA.
**Donor(s):** David P. Wheatland Trust.
**Grantmaker type:** Independent foundation
**Financial data** (yr. ended 12/31/99): Assets, $7,229,411 (M); expenditures, $312,351; qualifying distributions, $309,068; giving activities include $292,000 for 4 grants (high: $165,000; low: $12,000).
**Purpose and activities:** Support for a history museum and a university historical science center.
**Fields of interest:** Museums; higher education; libraries/library science.
**Types of support:** General/operating support.
**Limitations:** Giving primarily in MA. No grants to individuals.
**Application information:** Preference given to organizations historically supported by the donor and members of his family.
*Deadline(s):* None
**Trustees:** Eileen M. Balthazard, Peter R. Seamans, Richard Wheatland.
**EIN:** 046744379

---

**301**
**White Fund, Inc.**
P.O. Box 1887
Lawrence, MA   01842   (978) 686-6151
*Contact:* Thomas F. Caffrey, Pres.
*Additional application addresses:* c/o Elizabeth A. Beland, Clerk, P.O. Box 111, North Andover, MA 01845, and c/o Robert J. Frishman, V.P., 53 Poor St., Andover, MA 01810; FAX: (978) 683-3399

Established in 1852.
**Donor(s):** Hon. Daniel A. White.‡
**Grantmaker type:** Independent foundation
**Financial data** (yr. ended 03/31/00): Assets, $1,865,273 (M); expenditures, $110,716; qualifying distributions, $99,883; giving activities include $70,305 for 19 grants (high: $20,000; low: $800; average: $1,000–$5,000).
**Purpose and activities:** Giving primarily to sponsor a lecture series and to support the

Lawrence Public Library. Support also for youth programs.
**Fields of interest:** Arts education; arts/cultural programs; libraries/library science; youth development.
**Types of support:** General/operating support; emergency funds; program development; seed money; curriculum development; technical assistance.
**Limitations:** Giving limited to the greater Lawrence, MA, area. No grants to individuals.
**Publications:** Application guidelines.
**Application information:** Associated Grantmakers Common Proposal form accepted. Application form not required.
*Initial approach:* Copies of proposal must be sent to foundation's main address as well as to two additional addresses listed
*Copies of proposal:* 3
*Deadline(s):* None
*Board meeting date(s):* Monthly
*Final notification:* After meetings
**Officers and Trustees:*** Thomas F. Caffrey,* Pres.; Robert J. Frishman,* V.P.; Elizabeth A. Beland,* Clerk and Treas.
**Number of staff:** 1 part-time support.
**EIN:** 042761754

---

# MICHIGAN

**302**
**Talbert & Leota Abrams Foundation**
1000 Michigan National Tower
Lansing, MI   48933-1736   (517) 377-0843
*Contact:* Joe C. Foster, Jr., Secy.

Established in 1960 in MI.
**Donor(s):** Leota Abrams,‡ Talbert Abrams.‡
**Grantmaker type:** Independent foundation
**Financial data** (yr. ended 12/31/99): Assets, $10,871,351 (M); expenditures, $634,077; qualifying distributions, $534,739; giving activities include $475,500 for 14 grants (high: $170,000; low: $3,000).
**Purpose and activities:** Support primarily for a library and an educational science program; giving also for universities and colleges and community funds.
**Fields of interest:** Higher education; adult education—literacy & basic skills; libraries/library science; reading; federated giving programs.
**Types of support:** Program development; scholarship funds; research.
**Limitations:** Giving primarily in central MI. No support for churches for sectarian use, or for athletic activities. No grants to individuals, or for operating or traveling expenses; no loans.
**Publications:** Annual report.
**Application information:** Application form not required.
*Initial approach:* 2-page letter
*Copies of proposal:* 1
*Deadline(s):* May 31 for next calendar year
*Board meeting date(s):* June
**Officers and Directors:*** Barbara J. Brown,* Pres.; Kyle C. Abbott,* Exec. V.P.; Fred A. Featherly, V.P.; Joe C. Foster, Jr.,* Secy.; Craig C. Brown,* Treas.; Shane A. Patzer, Tiffany L. Patzer.

**Number of staff:** 5 part-time professional.
**EIN:** 386082194

### 303
### Berrien Community Foundation, Inc.

2900 S. State St., Ste. 2E.
St. Joseph, MI 49085 (616) 983-3304
*Contact:* Margaret Poole, Exec. Dir.
*FAX:* (616) 983-4939; E-mail: mpoole@qtm.net;
URL: http://www.qtm.net/bcf

Incorporated in 1952 in MI.
**Grantmaker type:** Community foundation
**Financial data** (yr. ended 12/31/99): Assets,
$9,763,114 (M); gifts received, $831,084;
expenditures, $573,223; giving activities include
$353,419 for 89 grants (high: $24,629; low:
$62; average: $100–$17,000), $35,581 for 4
foundation-administered programs and $3,650
for 7 in-kind gifts.
**Purpose and activities:** Primary areas of interest
include youth, education, family issues, and
general charitable giving.
**Fields of interest:** Museums; music; humanities;
historic preservation/historical societies;
arts/cultural programs; elementary
school/education; secondary school/education;
adult education—literacy & basic skills;
libraries/library science; reading; education;
environment; health care; substance abuse,
services; health associations; nutrition;
safety/disasters; recreation; youth development;
human services; children & youth, services;
family services; aging, centers & services;
homeless, human services; community
development; voluntarism promotion;
engineering & technology; science; public
affairs; disabled; aging; homeless; general
charitable giving.
**Types of support:** General/operating support;
building/renovation; endowments; emergency
funds; program development; seed money;
scholarship funds; scholarships—to individuals;
in-kind gifts; matching/challenge support.
**Limitations:** Giving limited to Berrien County,
MI. No support for sectarian religious purposes.
No grants to individuals (except for
scholarships), or for consulting services,
technical assistance, operating funds, deficit
financing, or annual fund drives; no loans or
program-related investments.
**Publications:** Annual report, financial statement,
newsletter, informational brochure (including
application guidelines).
**Application information:** Application guidelines
available on request. 20 copies of application
required for youth-oriented projects only.
Application form required.
  *Initial approach:* Telephone
  *Copies of proposal:* 1
  *Deadline(s):* Sept. 1 for winter meeting; Mar. 1
    for spring meeting
  *Board meeting date(s):* Every 2 months
  *Final notification:* 10 to 14 weeks
**Officers and Trustees:*** Mark A. Miller,* Pres.;
Jim Cousins,* V.P.; Stephen Sizer,* Secy.; Sharon
Vargo,* Treas.; B. David Allen, Larry Bubb,
Elaine Chaudoir, Robert D. Gottlieb, Nadra
Kissman, Gladys Peeples-Burks, Ph.D, Marion
Preston, Joanne Sims, Gregory Vaughn.
**Number of staff:** 3 full-time professional; 1
part-time support.
**EIN:** 386057160

### 304
### Samuel Higby Camp Foundation

145 S. Jackson
P.O. Box 787
Jackson, MI 49201
*Contact:* Walter R. Boris, Chair.

Established in 1951 in MI.
**Donor(s):** Donna Ruth Camp.‡
**Grantmaker type:** Independent foundation
**Financial data** (yr. ended 12/31/98): Assets,
$2,365,908 (M); expenditures, $137,671;
qualifying distributions, $112,704; giving
activities include $113,985 for 33 grants (high:
$10,000; low: $1,000; average: $250–$5,000).
**Purpose and activities:** Giving primarily for
education, including higher and business
education, community development, and
cultural programs.
**Fields of interest:** Arts/cultural programs; higher
education; business school/education; medical
school/education; libraries/library science;
education; animal welfare; recreation; children
& youth, services; hospices; community
development; biological sciences;
government/public administration.
**Types of support:** General/operating support;
annual campaigns; capital campaigns; debt
reduction; curriculum development.
**Limitations:** Giving primarily in south central
MI, with emphasis on Jackson.
**Application information:** Application form not
required.
  *Initial approach:* Letter or proposal
  *Copies of proposal:* 1
  *Deadline(s):* Aug. 15
  *Board meeting date(s):* As needed
  *Final notification:* Oct. or Nov.
**Officers:** Walter R. Boris, Chair. and Pres.; L.S.
Sekerke, Secy.; J.W. Zuleski, Treas.
**Trustee:** H.E. Spieler.
**Number of staff:** None.
**EIN:** 381643281

### 305
### Community Foundation for Northeast Michigan

(Formerly Northeast Michigan Community
Foundation)
111 Water St.
P.O. Box 282
Alpena, MI 49707 (517) 354-6881
*Contact:* Barbara A. Willyard, Exec. Dir.
*FAX:* (517) 356-3319; E-mail:
cfnem@alpena.cc.mi.us

Incorporated in 1974 in MI.
**Grantmaker type:** Community foundation
**Financial data** (yr. ended 09/30/99): Assets,
$17,160,873 (M); gifts received, $4,425,994;
expenditures, $868,117; giving activities include
$584,634 for 433 grants (high: $106,000; low:
$8) and $86 for set-asides.
**Purpose and activities:** Primary mission of the
foundation is to provide leadership and
resources to focus both private and public
attention on the needs of the area; to enhance
the quality of life in the area through support of
a broad range of services in such fields as
human services, health, education, the arts, the
environment, disease, and civic responsibilities;
and to stimulate the establishment of

endowments and invest them wisely to serve the
residents of northeast Michigan.
**Fields of interest:** Humanities; arts/cultural
programs; environment; libraries/library science;
education; health care; health associations;
human services; children & youth, services;
government/public administration.
**Types of support:** Continuing support;
building/renovation; equipment; land
acquisition; conferences/seminars; publication;
seed money; scholarship funds; program-related
investments/loans; matching/challenge support.
**Limitations:** Giving limited to Alcona, Alpena,
Cheboygan, Crawford, Iosco, Montmorency,
Ogemaw, Oscods, Presque Isle, and
Roscommon counties, and Mackinow City, MI.
No grants to individuals, or for operating needs
or budget deficits.
**Publications:** Annual report, application
guidelines, informational brochure, newsletter,
program policy statement, financial statement.
**Application information:** Application form
required.
  *Initial approach:* Letter or telephone
  *Copies of proposal:* 10
  *Deadline(s):* Feb. 1, May 1, Aug. 1, and Nov. 1
  *Board meeting date(s):* Quarterly
  *Final notification:* Within days of board
    meeting
**Officers and Trustees:*** Charles Ingle,* Pres.;
Steven Wilson,* V.P.; Donna Garber,* Secy.;
Beach Hall,* Treas.; David Darnell, William
DesChamps, Avis Hinks, James Johnston, Robert
Kowalski, Marianne Liddell-Ray, David
Nadolsky, Vernie Nethercut, George Stevens,
John Wade, Charles Wiesen, Gary Williams.
**Number of staff:** 3 full-time professional; 2
part-time professional.
**EIN:** 237384822

### 306
### The Mignon Sherwood Delano Foundation

c/o National City Bank of MI/IL
108 E. Michigan Ave., K-B01-2A
Kalamazoo, MI 49007-3931
*Contact:* Yolanda Searles

Incorporated in 1985 in MI.
**Donor(s):** Mignon Sherwood Delano.‡
**Grantmaker type:** Independent foundation
**Financial data** (yr. ended 12/31/99): Assets,
$5,448,822 (M); expenditures, $221,372;
qualifying distributions, $221,372; giving
activities include $193,494 for grants.
**Fields of interest:** Arts/cultural programs;
libraries (public); family planning; health care;
health associations; human services; youth,
services; child development, services;
community development.
**Types of support:** General/operating support;
continuing support; building/renovation;
equipment; program development; curriculum
development.
**Limitations:** Giving limited to southwestern MI,
with emphasis on Allegan County. No grants to
individuals.
**Application information:** Application form
required.
  *Deadline(s):* Sept. 15
**Officers:** G. Philip Dietrich, Pres.; Rebecca
Burnett, V.P.
**Directors:** Ellen Altamore, Bernard Riker, Julie
Sosnowski.

Trustee: National City Bank of MI/IL.
EIN: 382557743

## 307
## Daniel and Pamella DeVos Foundation
126 Ottawa Ave., N.W., Ste. 500
Grand Rapids, MI 49503 (616) 454-4114
*Contact:* Ginny Vander Hart

Established in 1992 in MI.
**Donor(s):** The Richard and Helen DeVos Foundation.
**Grantmaker type:** Independent foundation
**Financial data** (yr. ended 12/31/98): Assets, $139,840 (M); expenditures, $240,634; qualifying distributions, $237,139; giving activities include $226,100 for 47 grants (high: $35,000; low: $100).
**Purpose and activities:** Giving for museums, performing art centers, arts and culture, education, human services and Christian agencies.
**Fields of interest:** Museums; performing arts centers; arts/cultural programs; libraries/library science; education; human services; children & youth, services; Christian agencies & churches.
**Types of support:** General/operating support; continuing support; annual campaigns; capital campaigns; building/renovation; program development; seed money; matching/challenge support.
**Limitations:** Giving primarily in Grand Rapids, MI. No grants to individuals.
**Application information:** Application form not required.
*Initial approach:* Letter
*Copies of proposal:* 1
*Deadline(s):* None
*Final notification:* 3 to 5 months
**Officers:** Daniel G. DeVos, Pres.; Pamella DeVos, V.P.; Jerry L. Tubergen, Secy.-Treas.
**Number of staff:** None.
EIN: 383035976

## 308
## The Herbert H. and Grace A. Dow Foundation ▼
1018 W. Main St.
Midland, MI 48640-4292 (517) 631-3699
*Contact:* Herbert D. Doan, Pres.
*FAX:* (517) 631-0675; E-mail: info@hhdowfdn.org

Trust established in 1936 in MI.
**Donor(s):** Grace A. Dow.‡
**Grantmaker type:** Independent foundation
**Financial data** (yr. ended 12/31/99): Assets, $570,649,673 (M); expenditures, $21,497,742; qualifying distributions, $18,572,261; giving activities include $16,437,288 for 109 grants (high: $1,487,813; low: $500; average: $10,000–$500,000).
**Purpose and activities:** Support for religious, charitable, scientific, literacy, or educational purposes for the public benefaction of the inhabitants of the city of Midland and of the people of the state of Michigan. Grants largely for education, particularly higher education, community and social services, civic improvement, conservation, scientific research, church support (only in Midland County), and

cultural programs; maintains a public horticultural garden.
**Fields of interest:** Arts/cultural programs; higher education; libraries/library science; education; natural resource conservation & protection; human services; community development; engineering & technology; science.
**Types of support:** General/operating support; building/renovation; equipment; endowments; program development; seed money; research; matching/challenge support.
**Limitations:** Giving limited to MI, with emphasis on Midland County. No support for political organizations or sectarian religious organizations or programs, other than churches in Midland County. No grants to individuals, or for travel or conferences; no loans.
**Publications:** Annual report (including application guidelines).
**Application information:** Application form not required.
*Initial approach:* Proposal
*Copies of proposal:* 1
*Deadline(s):* None
*Board meeting date(s):* Bimonthly
*Final notification:* 2 months
**Officers and Trustees:*** Herbert D. Doan,* Pres.; Margaret Ann Riecker,* V.P. and Secy.; Michael Lloyd Dow,* Treas.; Julie Carol Arbury, Bonnie B. Matheson, Frank Popoff, Margaret E. Thompson, Ruth B. Wheeler, Macauley Whiting, Jr.
**Number of staff:** None.
EIN: 381437485
**Recent grants for library/information services:**
**308-1** Michigan Information Technology Network, East Lansing, MI, $100,000. For project in collaboration with Kellogg Foundation. 1998.

## 309
## Frazier Fund, Inc.
c/o National City Bank of MI/IL
P.O. Box 580, Trust Dept.
Marquette, MI 49855 (906) 228-9500
*Contact:* Mary C. Nurmi

Established in 1980.
**Grantmaker type:** Independent foundation
**Financial data** (yr. ended 09/30/99): Assets, $1,673,554 (M); expenditures, $90,508; qualifying distributions, $81,851; giving activities include $81,851 for 13 grants (high: $20,000; low: $351).
**Purpose and activities:** Giving for libraries and community foundations.
**Fields of interest:** Libraries (public); foundations (community).
**Limitations:** Giving limited to Marquette, MI. No grants to individuals.
**Application information:**
*Initial approach:* Proposal
*Deadline(s):* Apr. 30
**Officers:** Peter W. Frazier, Pres.; Julia Q. Frazier, V.P.; William I. McDonald, Secy.; Robert J. Toutant, Treas.
**Director:** Lincoln B. Frazier, Jr.
**Custodian:** National City Bank of MI/IL.
EIN: 382287345

## 310
## The Fremont Area Community Foundation
(Formerly The Fremont Area Foundation)
4424 W. 48th St.
P.O. Box B
Fremont, MI 49412 (231) 924-5350
*Contact:* Elizabeth Cherin, Pres. and C.E.O.
*FAX:* (231) 924-5391; E-mail: gzerlaut@tfaf.org; URL: http://www.tfaf.org

Incorporated in 1951 in MI.
**Grantmaker type:** Community foundation
**Financial data** (yr. ended 12/31/99): Assets, $197,007,302 (M); gifts received, $2,723,831; expenditures, $14,705,768; giving activities include $12,671,072 for grants (high: $728,500; low: $250; average: $250–$728,500).
**Purpose and activities:** The foundation has established six broad funding categories: 1) Newaygo County Community Services: to sustain operations of this autonomous agency established for the delivery of general social welfare services and educational programs; 2) Community Development: to strengthen the municipal activities of villages, cities, governmental units, and other related organizations; 3) Education: to augment and promote the special projects of schools, libraries, and other organizations for instruction and training, and for scholarships to promote higher education and learning in specialized programs; 4) Arts and Culture: to support activities that promote appreciation of and participation in artistic expression such as music, theater, dance, sculpture, and painting; 5) Human Services: to foster the delivery of services and the operation of programs to help meet basic human needs and to support the provision of rehabilitative services; and 6) Health Care: made to health care providers and other related organizations for activities designed to promote optimal well-being and to provide health-related education. The foundation is also interested in supporting programs that address the particular needs of youth and older (aged) adults.
**Fields of interest:** Visual arts; performing arts; arts/cultural programs; libraries/library science; education; medical care, rehabilitation; health care; substance abuse, services; health associations; human services; children & youth, services; family services; aging, centers & services; community development; government/public administration; aging; economically disadvantaged.
**Types of support:** General/operating support; capital campaigns; building/renovation; equipment; endowments; emergency funds; program development; conferences/seminars; seed money; scholarship funds; technical assistance; consulting services; program evaluation; program-related investments/loans; scholarships—to individuals; matching/challenge support.
**Limitations:** Giving primarily in Newaygo County, MI. No grants to individuals (except for scholarships from specified funds of the foundation), or for contingencies, reserves, or deficit financing.
**Publications:** Annual report, application guidelines, informational brochure, financial statement, grants list, newsletter.
**Application information:** Application form required.

*Initial approach:* Letter or telephone to arrange interview
*Copies of proposal:* 10
*Deadline(s):* Feb. 15, May 15, and Sept. 15, except for emergencies
*Board meeting date(s):* Monthly
*Final notification:* 3 months
**Officers and Trustees:*** Donald J. Bont,* Chair.; Lon Vredeveld, Vice-Chair.; Gregory M. Zerlaut, C.F.O. and C.O.O.; Elizabeth Cherin, Pres. and C.E.O.; Forrest Bowman, Treas.; Carl Dekuiper, Lana A. Ford, Jack Hendon, Duane Jones, Danielle Merrill, Mary Schafer, Norma A. Schuiteman, Terry Sharp, Linda Shively, Jeffrey Thome, Josephine Toliver, Donald VanSingel.
**Number of staff:** 6 full-time professional; 6 full-time support.
**EIN:** 381443367
**Recent grants for library/information services:**
**310-1** Fremont Area District Library, Fremont, MI, $736,241. Toward district library property transfer. 1998.
**310-2** Fremont Area District Library, Fremont, MI, $500,000. For matching grant for renovation and expansion. 1998.
**310-3** Fremont Area District Library, Fremont, MI, $396,003. For matching grant for renovation and expansion. 1998.
**310-4** Fremont Area District Library, Fremont, MI, $60,000. Toward enhancement of library operations. 1998.
**310-5** Fremont Area District Library, Fremont, MI, $25,000. For endowment. 1998.
**310-6** Fremont Area District Library, Fremont, MI, $20,265. Toward Dynix Integrated Library System. 1998.
**310-7** Fremont Area District Library, Fremont, MI, $20,000. Toward improvements to temporary library building. 1998.
**310-8** Fremont Area District Library, Fremont, MI, $15,000. Toward Writers Live at the Library. 1998.
**310-9** Fremont Area District Library, Fremont, MI, $11,999. For non-fiction circulating materials. 1998.
**310-10** Fremont Area District Library, Fremont, MI, $10,000. Toward Dynix Integrated Library System. 1998.
**310-11** Grant Public Library, Grant, MI, $35,000. Toward enhancement of library operations. 1998.
**310-12** Grant Public Library, Grant, MI, $25,000. For endowment. 1998.
**310-13** Grant, City of, Grant, MI, $15,279. Toward operating support for Grant Public Library. 1998.
**310-14** Hesperia Public Library, Hesperia, MI, $40,000. Toward enhancement of library operations. 1998.
**310-15** Hesperia Public Library, Hesperia, MI, $25,000. For endowment. 1998.
**310-16** Newaygo Carnegie Library, Newaygo, MI, $40,000. Toward enhancement of library operations. 1998.
**310-17** Newaygo Carnegie Library, Newaygo, MI, $25,000. For endowment. 1998.
**310-18** Newaygo Carnegie Library, Newaygo, MI, $14,101. Toward Dynix Integrated Library System. 1998.
**310-19** Newaygo Public Schools, Newaygo, MI, $34,054. Toward Child Care Resource and Referral Program. 1998.

**310-20** White Cloud Public Library, White Cloud, MI, $50,085. Toward operating and program support. 1998.
**310-21** White Cloud Public Library, White Cloud, MI, $35,000. Toward enhancement of library operations. 1998.
**310-22** White Cloud Public Library, White Cloud, MI, $25,000. For endowment. 1998.
**310-23** White Cloud Public Library, White Cloud, MI, $14,500. Toward Community Awareness Campaign and management support. 1998.
**310-24** White Cloud Public Library, White Cloud, MI, $13,694. Toward Dynix Integrated Library System. 1998.
**310-25** White Cloud Public Library, White Cloud, MI, $11,000. Toward landscaping for new library. 1998.
**310-26** Womens Information Service, Fremont, MI, $55,500. Toward operating support for Newaygo County Outreach programs. 1998.
**310-27** Womens Information Service, Fremont, MI, $25,000. For endowment. 1998.

---

### 311
### Hillsdale County Community Foundation
52 E. Bacon St.
P.O. Box 276
Hillsdale, MI 49242-0276 (517) 439-5101
*Contact:* Jim McCall, Exec. Dir.
*FAX:* (517) 439-5109

Established in 1991 in MI.
**Grantmaker type:** Community foundation
**Financial data** (yr. ended 09/30/99): Assets, $6,270,944 (M); gifts received, $928,779; expenditures, $262,675; giving activities include $949,384 for 28 grants (high: $15,000; average: $50–$16,667), $73,518 for 90 grants to individuals (high: $5,000; low: $200; average: $200–$5,000) and $3,600 for 1 in-kind gift.
**Purpose and activities:** The foundation gives to support community organizations and services in Hillsdale County, Michigan. The foundation also administers a scholarship program for area students.
**Fields of interest:** Visual arts; performing arts; theater; arts/cultural programs; education, association; early childhood education; child development, education; elementary school/education; higher education; libraries/library science; education; natural resource conservation & protection; environment; animal welfare; hospitals (general); health care; health associations; delinquency prevention/services; crime/law enforcement; employment; food services; recreation; youth development, services; human services; children & youth, services; child development, services; family services; hospices; aging, centers & services; community development; voluntarism promotion; biological sciences; economics; leadership development; public affairs; aging; economically disadvantaged.
**Types of support:** Annual campaigns; conferences/seminars; publication; seed money; scholarship funds; employee-related scholarships; scholarships—to individuals; in-kind gifts; matching/challenge support.
**Limitations:** Giving limited to Hillsdale County, MI. No support for political, religious, or sectarian purposes. No grants to individuals

(except for scholarships), or for new building campaigns, routine maintenance, remodeling, or capital campaigns; no loans.
**Publications:** Annual report, financial statement, newsletter, informational brochure (including application guidelines), application guidelines.
**Application information:** Application form required.
*Initial approach:* Telephone or in person
*Copies of proposal:* 1
*Deadline(s):* Oct. 15 and Apr. 15
*Board meeting date(s):* 1st Tues. of the month
*Final notification:* Within 2 months
**Officer:** Jim McCall, Exec. Dir.
**Number of staff:** 3 part-time professional; 1 part-time support.
**EIN:** 383001297

---

### 312
### Clarence and Jack Himmel Foundation
3000 Town Ctr., Ste. 2150
Southfield, MI 48075-1313 (248) 353-0150
*Contact:* Robert Karbel, Pres.
*FAX:* (248) 353-7843

Established in 1975 in MI.
**Donor(s):** Clarence Himmel.‡
**Grantmaker type:** Independent foundation
**Financial data** (yr. ended 10/31/99): Assets, $2,072,643 (M); expenditures, $168,419; qualifying distributions, $111,813; giving activities include $114,200 for 60 grants (high: $10,500; low: $150).
**Purpose and activities:** Charitable contributions are made without geographical restrictions, for purposes of social services, arts, education, and health care.
**Fields of interest:** Arts/cultural programs; libraries/library science; health associations; food banks; youth development; human services; civil rights; community development; Jewish agencies & temples; disabled.
**Limitations:** Giving primarily in MI. No grants to individuals.
**Application information:**
*Deadline(s):* None
**Officers:** Robert A. Karbel, Pres. and Secy.; David Wallace, V.P.; Robert A. Rothstein, Treas.
**EIN:** 510140773

---

### 313
### Library of Michigan Foundation
717 W. Allegan St.
P.O. Box 30159
Lansing, MI 48909 (517) 373-1297
*Contact:* Sarah D. Watkins, Exec. Dir.
*FAX:* (517) 373-5815; E-mail: materman@libofmich.lib.mi.us; URL: http://www.libofmich.lib.mi.us/foundation/foundation.html

Established in 1985 in MI.
**Grantmaker type:** Public charity
**Financial data** (yr. ended 09/30/98): Assets, $1,958,778 (M); gifts received, $731,606; expenditures, $428,771.
**Purpose and activities:** The foundation's interests include libraries and literacy projects. External grantmaking is made through the program Read Indeed, and occasionally through donor-designated funds. Currently, the foundation is raising funds for literacy, rare book

preservation, and collections and technology enhancements.
**Fields of interest:** Adult education—literacy & basic skills; libraries (public).
**Types of support:** General/operating support; annual campaigns; equipment; program development; curriculum development; technical assistance; matching/challenge support.
**Limitations:** Giving limited to MI.
**Publications:** Annual report, informational brochure, newsletter, financial statement, application guidelines, grants list.
**Application information:** Application form required.
   *Initial approach:* Letter or telephone
   *Copies of proposal:* 5
   *Deadline(s):* None
   *Board meeting date(s):* Quarterly
**Officers and Directors:*** Albert F. Zehnder,* Pres.; Michelle Engler,* V.P. and Chair., Read Indeed; Pamella G. DeVos,* Secy.; Frank D. Stella,* Treas.; Sarah D. Watkins, Exec. Dir.; and 11 additional directors.
**Number of staff:** 2 full-time professional; 2 part-time support.
**EIN:** 382611742

### 314
### Meritor Automotive, Inc. Trust
c/o Tax Dept.
2135 W. Maple Rd.
Troy, MI 48084-7186
*Contact:* Jerry Rush

Established in 1997 in MI.
**Donor(s):** Meritor Automotive, Inc.
**Grantmaker type:** Company-sponsored foundation
**Financial data** (yr. ended 09/30/98): Assets, $207 (M); gifts received, $810,201; expenditures, $810,201; qualifying distributions, $0; giving activities include $806,699 for grants.
**Purpose and activities:** Giving primarily for education.
**Fields of interest:** Arts/cultural programs; elementary/secondary education; higher education; libraries (public).
**Types of support:** Employee matching gifts.
**Limitations:** Giving on a national basis.
**Application information:**
   *Initial approach:* Proposal
   *Deadline(s):* Aug.
**Officers:** Larry Yost, Pres. and C.E.O.; Gary Collins, V.P.; Dave Greenfield, Secy.; Thomas Madden, C.F.O.
**EIN:** 522089611

### 315
### Neal Sisters Foundation
c/o Bank One
111 E. Court St., Ste. 100
Flint, MI 48502-1944
*Contact:* Carl Holmes, Treas.
*Application address:* 1080 W. Northwood Dr., Caro, MI 48723

Established in 1991 in MI.
**Donor(s):** Eleanor Neal.
**Grantmaker type:** Independent foundation
**Financial data** (yr. ended 12/31/99): Assets, $1,775,017 (M); expenditures, $115,902;

qualifying distributions, $108,157; giving activities include $105,773 for 14 grants (high: $25,000; low: $1,000).
**Purpose and activities:** Preference given to qualified charities in the education field with priority in the Caro, Michigan, area.
**Fields of interest:** Higher education; libraries/library science; hospitals (general); Salvation Army; community development.
**Limitations:** Giving primarily in the Caro, MI, area. No grants to individuals.
**Application information:**
   *Initial approach:* Letter
   *Copies of proposal:* 2
   *Deadline(s):* None
**Officers and Trustees:*** Steve Fillion,* Pres.; Martha Thurston,* Secy.; Carl Holmes,* Treas.; Dolores Rock Hutchinson, Bank One.
**EIN:** 382942765

### 316
### Stuart and Barbara Padnos Foundation
1095 S. Shore Dr.
Holland, MI 49423

Established in 1995 in MI.
**Donor(s):** Stuart Padnos, Barbara Padnos.
**Grantmaker type:** Independent foundation
**Financial data** (yr. ended 12/31/98): Assets, $430,846 (M); gifts received, $238,610; expenditures, $58,760; qualifying distributions, $58,760; giving activities include $58,760 for 22 grants (high: $50,000; low: $25).
**Purpose and activities:** Giving primarily for Jewish organizations, with some giving for the arts.
**Fields of interest:** Arts/cultural programs; libraries/library science; education; human services; religion, single organization support.
**Limitations:** Applications not accepted. No grants to individuals.
**Application information:** Contributes only to pre-selected organizations.
**Director:** Stuart Padnos.
**EIN:** 383237340

### 317
### Robert W. and Maxine C. Parker Foundation, Inc.
4777 W. Liberty Rd.
Ann Arbor, MI 48103-9707

Established in 1988 in MI.
**Donor(s):** Robert W. Parker.
**Grantmaker type:** Independent foundation
**Financial data** (yr. ended 12/31/98): Assets, $1,331,198 (M); gifts received, $54,550; expenditures, $46,722; qualifying distributions, $44,510; giving activities include $43,675 for 5 grants (high: $20,000; low: $3,675; average: $3,675–$20,000).
**Purpose and activities:** Giving to religion, education, humanitarian organizations and medical services.
**Fields of interest:** Libraries/library science; Christian agencies & churches.
**Limitations:** Applications not accepted. Giving primarily in MI. No grants to individuals.
**Application information:** Contributes only to pre-selected organizations.

**Officers and Trustees:*** Robert W. Parker,* Pres.; T. Gilbert Parker,* V.P.; Johanna C. Johnson,* Secy.-Treas.; Andrew D. Parker.
**EIN:** 382795440

### 318
### The Willard G. & Jessie M. Pierce Foundation
P.O. Box 204
Hastings, MI 49058-2045

Established in 1989 in MI; funded in 1991.
**Donor(s):** Willard G. Pierce, Jessie M. Pierce.
**Grantmaker type:** Independent foundation
**Financial data** (yr. ended 12/31/99): Assets, $31,510,267 (L); gifts received, $11,127,105; expenditures, $763,988; qualifying distributions, $1,951,816; giving activities include $81,125 for 5 grants (high: $28,050; low: $1,000) and $1,700,511 for foundation-administered programs.
**Purpose and activities:** Giving primarily to Christian organizations and human services.
**Fields of interest:** Libraries (school); child abuse prevention; human services; federated giving programs; Protestant agencies & churches.
**Types of support:** Scholarship funds.
**Limitations:** Applications not accepted. Giving primarily in MI. No grants to individuals.
**Application information:** Contributes only to pre-selected organizations.
**Officers:** Arlon Elser, Pres.; Gary J. Pierce, Secy.; Willard G. Pierce, Treas.
**Directors:** G. Kent Keller, Carl Schoessel, Hilary F. Snell.
**EIN:** 382820095

### 319
### Pinney Foundation
6363 Main St.
Cass City, MI 48726

Established in 1984 in MI.
**Donor(s):** Lottie W. Pinney Irrevocable Trust.
**Grantmaker type:** Independent foundation
**Financial data** (yr. ended 12/31/98): Assets, $1,428,490 (M); expenditures, $95,328; qualifying distributions, $87,079; giving activities include $87,060 for 6 grants (high: $75,000; low: $360).
**Purpose and activities:** Giving primarily to the arts and education.
**Fields of interest:** Performing arts; libraries/library science; education.
**Limitations:** Applications not accepted. Giving limited to the Cass City, MI, area. No grants to individuals.
**Publications:** Informational brochure.
**Application information:** Contributes only to pre-selected organizations.
**Officers and Directors:*** Richard T. Donahue,* Pres.; Annette L. Pinney,* V.P.; Jude T. Patnaude,* Secy.; Glenn W. Pietenpol,* Treas.; Beverly Perry, Delbert E. Rawson, D.D.S., Barbara Tuckey, William Wallace, Michael Weaver.
**EIN:** 382517070

## 320
### Warren L. & Catherine P. Reuther Family Foundation
1655 W. 7th St.
Monroe, MI 48161

Established in 1997 in MI.
**Donor(s):** Catherine P. Reuther, Warren L. Reuther.
**Grantmaker type:** Independent foundation
**Financial data** (yr. ended 12/31/99): Assets, $1,664 (M); gifts received, $71,923; expenditures, $212,285; qualifying distributions, $210,966; giving activities include $211,000 for 6 grants (high: $100,000; low: $3,000).
**Purpose and activities:** Giving primarily for Christian organizations.
**Fields of interest:** Libraries/library science; Christian agencies & churches.
**Limitations:** Applications not accepted. Giving primarily in Toledo, OH. No grants to individuals.
**Application information:** Contributes only to pre-selected organizations.
**Officer:** Warren L. Reuther, Secy.
**EIN:** 383326929

## 321
### John & Margaret Sagan Foundation
22149 Long Blvd.
Dearborn, MI 48124

Established in 1985 in MI.
**Donor(s):** John Sagan, Margaret Sagan.
**Grantmaker type:** Independent foundation
**Financial data** (yr. ended 12/31/98): Assets, $1,925,865 (M); gifts received, $556,600; expenditures, $54,003; qualifying distributions, $49,313; giving activities include $49,250 for 22 grants (high: $6,500; low: $250).
**Purpose and activities:** Giving for higher education, religion, youth services and federated giving programs.
**Fields of interest:** Arts/cultural programs; higher education; libraries (public); hospitals (general); health care; children & youth, services; federated giving programs; Christian agencies & churches; Protestant agencies & churches.
**Limitations:** Applications not accepted. Giving primarily in the Midwest. No grants to individuals.
**Application information:** Generally contributes only to pre-selected organizations.
**Officers:** John Sagan, Pres. and Treas.; Margaret Sagan, V.P.; W. Robert Chandler, Secy.
**EIN:** 382638868

## 322
### William H. and Patricia M. Smith Foundation
7375 Woodward Ave.
Detroit, MI 48202-3121

Established in 1994 in MI.
**Donor(s):** William H. Smith.
**Grantmaker type:** Independent foundation
**Financial data** (yr. ended 06/30/99): Assets, $1,971,857 (M); expenditures, $3,812,084; qualifying distributions, $3,786,000; giving activities include $3,786,000 for 7 grants (high: $3,750,000; low: $1,000).

**Fields of interest:** Higher education; libraries/library science.
**Limitations:** Applications not accepted. Giving primarily in MI. No grants to individuals.
**Application information:** Contributes only to pre-selected organizations.
**Officers and Trustees:*** William H. Smith,* Pres.; Patricia M. Smith,* V.P.; Wendy A. Kubitskey,* Secy.-Treas.; Kendall A. Smith, Scott D. Smith.
**EIN:** 383213042

## 323
### St. Clair Foundation
P.O. Box 3636
Grand Rapids, MI 49501
*Contact:* Franklin H. Moore, Jr., Tr.
*Application address:* c/o Old Kent Bank, 200 S. Riverside, St. Clair, MI 48079

Established in 1956.
**Donor(s):** Alice W. Moore.
**Grantmaker type:** Independent foundation
**Financial data** (yr. ended 12/31/99): Assets, $1,946,675 (M); expenditures, $215,495; qualifying distributions, $206,342; giving activities include $205,900 for 13 grants (high: $143,500; low: $500).
**Purpose and activities:** Giving primarily for community services, including a community foundation and municipal agencies of St. Clair.
**Fields of interest:** Secondary school/education; libraries (public); foundations (community); community development; government/public administration.
**Limitations:** Giving limited to the city of St. Clair, MI, and its immediate vicinity. No grants to individuals.
**Application information:**
*Initial approach:* Letter
**Trustees:** Gerald M. Emig, James Fredericks, Richard Groff, Bernard Kuhn, Franklin H. Moore, Jr.
**EIN:** 386064622

## 324
### Maurice & Dorothy Stubnitz Foundation
153 E. Maumee St.
Adrian, MI 49221 (517) 263-5788
*Contact:* Charles E. Gross, Pres. and Treas.
*FAX:* (517) 265-5293

Established in 1981 in MI.
**Grantmaker type:** Independent foundation
**Financial data** (yr. ended 09/30/99): Assets, $7,457,766 (M); expenditures, $445,026; qualifying distributions, $384,682; giving activities include $392,669 for 14 grants (high: $90,000; low: $4,494).
**Fields of interest:** Arts/cultural programs; libraries/library science; education; hospitals (general).
**Types of support:** Building/renovation; equipment; land acquisition; emergency funds; program development; seed money; scholarship funds.
**Limitations:** Giving limited to the Lenawee County, MI, area. No grants to individuals.
**Publications:** Application guidelines.
**Application information:** Application form not required.
*Copies of proposal:* 5

*Deadline(s):* Apr. 30
*Board meeting date(s):* Semiannually
*Final notification:* Aug. 31
**Officers and Directors:*** Charles E. Gross,* Pres. and Treas.; Betty Gross,* V.P.; Gaylord Baker,* Secy.; James Feeney, Hildreth Spencer.
**Number of staff:** None.
**EIN:** 382392373

## 325
### Donald G. Thayer Charitable Trust
c/o Old Kent Bank
P.O. Box 3636
Grand Rapids, MI 49501-3636

Established in 1994 in MI.
**Grantmaker type:** Independent foundation
**Financial data** (yr. ended 12/31/99): Assets, $169,051 (M); expenditures, $62,275; qualifying distributions, $59,583; giving activities include $59,379 for 14 grants (high: $19,794; low: $761).
**Purpose and activities:** Giving for public schools and institutes, and for religion.
**Fields of interest:** Secondary school/education; libraries (public); education; community development, service clubs; Christian agencies & churches.
**Limitations:** Applications not accepted. Giving primarily in MI. No grants to individuals.
**Application information:** Contributes only to pre-selected organizations.
**Trustees:** George Bishop, Old Kent Bank.
**EIN:** 383206872

## 326
### Vicksburg Foundation
c/o First of America Bank-Michigan, N.A., Trust Dept.
108 E. Michigan Ave., K-B01-2A
Kalamazoo, MI 49007 (616) 376-8021
*Contact:* William Oswalt, Pres.
*FAX:* (616) 376-8040

Incorporated in 1943 in MI.
**Grantmaker type:** Independent foundation
**Financial data** (yr. ended 12/31/98): Assets, $5,405,862 (M); gifts received, $46,671; expenditures, $280,295; qualifying distributions, $255,618; giving activities include $248,001 for 16 grants (high: $95,500; low: $100).
**Purpose and activities:** To coordinate and unify the charitable and benevolent activities of the incorporators; emphasis on community programs, education, and libraries.
**Fields of interest:** Education, association; education, fund raising; libraries/library science; education; human services; community development; federated giving programs; economically disadvantaged.
**Types of support:** General/operating support; continuing support; annual campaigns; capital campaigns; building/renovation; equipment; program development; conferences/seminars; seed money; curriculum development; scholarship funds; matching/challenge support.
**Limitations:** Applications not accepted. Giving limited to MI, with emphasis on Vicksburg, Kalamazoo, and Schoolcraft.
**Publications:** Informational brochure (including application guidelines).

**Application information:** Contributes only to pre-selected organizations.

*Board meeting date(s):* Mar., June, Sept., and Dec.

**Officers and Directors:** William Oswalt,* Pres.; Jeff Kruse, Secy.-Treas.; Lloyd Appell, Dennis Boyle, Dana Downing, Warren Lawrence.
**EIN:** 386065237

---

### 327
### James & Jane Welch Foundation
c/o Old Kent Bank
P.O. Box 3636
Grand Rapids, MI 49501-3636

Established in 1990 in MI.
**Donor(s):** James C. Welch.
**Grantmaker type:** Independent foundation
**Financial data** (yr. ended 09/30/99): Assets, $4,778,551 (M); gifts received, $22,344; expenditures, $299,528; qualifying distributions, $286,202; giving activities include $289,000 for 7 grants (high: $150,000; low: $5,000).
**Fields of interest:** Libraries/library science; federated giving programs; philanthropy, named trusts.
**Limitations:** Applications not accepted. Giving primarily in the Fort Worth, TX, area. No grants to individuals.
**Application information:** Contributes only to pre-selected organizations.
**Officer:** James C. Welch, Mgr.
**Trustee:** Old Kent Bank.
**EIN:** 382927749

---

### 328
### Harvey Randall Wickes Foundation ▼
Plaza N., Ste. 472
4800 Fashion Sq. Blvd.
Saginaw, MI 48604 (517) 799-1850
*Contact:* James V. Finkbeiner, Chair.
*FAX:* (517) 799-3327

Incorporated in 1945 in MI.
**Donor(s):** Harvey Randall Wickes,‡ members of the Wickes family.
**Grantmaker type:** Independent foundation
**Financial data** (yr. ended 12/31/99): Assets, $38,043,914 (M); expenditures, $1,898,144; qualifying distributions, $1,798,748; giving activities include $1,789,330 for 40 grants (high: $312,500; low: $500; average: $5,000–$100,000).
**Purpose and activities:** Giving primarily for civic affairs groups, parks and recreation agencies; support also for a library, youth and social services, hospitals, and cultural programs.
**Fields of interest:** Arts/cultural programs; libraries/library science; education; hospitals (general); recreation; human services; children & youth, services.
**Types of support:** Annual campaigns; building/renovation; equipment; seed money.
**Limitations:** Giving limited to the Saginaw, MI, area. No support for government where support is forth coming from tax dollars. No grants to individuals, or for endowments, travel, conferences, or film or video projects; no loans.
**Publications:** Financial statement, application guidelines.
**Application information:** Application form not required.

*Initial approach:* Letter followed by proposal
*Copies of proposal:* 1
*Deadline(s):* Submit proposal 3 weeks prior to meeting
*Board meeting date(s):* Jan., Apr., June, and Oct.
**Officers and Trustees:** James V. Finkbeiner,* Chair. and Pres.; Hugo E. Braun, Jr.,* V.P. and Secy.; Lloyd J. Yeo,* Treas.; Mary Lou Case, Peter Ewend, William A. Hendrick, Richard Heuschele, Craig W. Horn, Donald E. Juenemann, Richard Katz, David F. Wallace, Richard Winters.
**Number of staff:** 2 part-time support.
**EIN:** 386061470

---

### 329
### Wickson-Link Memorial Foundation
3023 Davenport St.
P.O. Box 3275
Saginaw, MI 48605 (517) 793-9830
*Contact:* Lloyd J. Yeo, Pres.

Established in 1973 in MI.
**Donor(s):** James Wickson,‡ Meta Wickson.‡
**Grantmaker type:** Independent foundation
**Financial data** (yr. ended 12/31/99): Assets, $6,179,988 (M); expenditures, $370,699; qualifying distributions, $329,539; giving activities include $329,539 for 53 grants (high: $75,000; low: $500; average: $300–$15,000).
**Purpose and activities:** Support for community funds, social services and programs for the disadvantaged, youth and child welfare, cultural organizations, health, and education, including business and higher education, programs for minorities and early childhood education, and libraries.
**Fields of interest:** Arts/cultural programs; early childhood education; higher education; business school/education; libraries/library science; health care; health associations; human services; children & youth, services; federated giving programs; minorities; economically disadvantaged.
**Types of support:** General/operating support; annual campaigns; building/renovation; equipment.
**Limitations:** Giving primarily in Saginaw County, MI. No grants to individuals.
**Application information:** Application form not required.

*Initial approach:* Letter
*Copies of proposal:* 7
*Deadline(s):* None
*Board meeting date(s):* Quarterly
**Officers:** Lloyd J. Yeo, Pres. and Treas.; B.J. Humphreys, V.P. and Secy.
**Directors:** Louis Hanisho, Susan Piesko.
**Number of staff:** 1 part-time professional.
**EIN:** 386083931

---

### 330
### Wilkinson Foundation
c/o Comerica Bank-Detroit
P.O. Box 75000, MC 3302
Detroit, MI 48275
*Contact:* Warren S. Wilkinson, Treas.
*Application address:* 2 Woodland Pl., Grosse Pointe, MI 48230; FAX: (248) 645-6741

Established in 1986 in MI.

**Donor(s):** Warren S. Wilkinson.
**Grantmaker type:** Independent foundation
**Financial data** (yr. ended 01/31/99): Assets, $3,549,427 (M); expenditures, $186,431; qualifying distributions, $147,749; giving activities include $148,016 for 60 grants (high: $25,000; low: $100; average: $50–$15,000).
**Purpose and activities:** Giving primarily for the arts, education, health, human services, and the environment.
**Fields of interest:** Museums; museums (history); history & archaeology; arts/cultural programs; secondary school/education; higher education; libraries/library science; natural resource conservation & protection; environment; wildlife preservation & protection; hospitals (general); parks/playgrounds; human services; civil liberties, advocacy.
**Types of support:** Continuing support; annual campaigns; capital campaigns; endowments; program development; seed money.
**Limitations:** Giving primarily in southeastern MI.
**Application information:** Application form not required.

*Deadline(s):* None
*Board meeting date(s):* Feb., May, Aug., and Nov.
*Final notification:* After board meetings
**Officers and Trustees:** Todd S. Wilkinson,* Pres.; Guerin S. Wilkinson,* Secy.; Warren S. Wilkinson,* Treas.
**Number of staff:** None.
**EIN:** 386497639

---

# MINNESOTA

---

### 331
### Elmer L. & Eleanor J. Andersen Foundation
2424 Territorial Rd.
St. Paul, MN 55114 (651) 642-0127
*Contact:* Mari Oyanagi Eggum, Fdn. Admin.
*FAX:* (651) 645-4684; E-mail: eandefdn@mtn.org

Established in 1957 in MN.
**Donor(s):** Elmer L. Andersen, Eleanor J. Andersen, Anthony L. Andersen.
**Grantmaker type:** Independent foundation
**Financial data** (yr. ended 11/30/99): Assets, $8,930,168 (M); expenditures, $569,827; qualifying distributions, $537,987; giving activities include $514,977 for 164 grants (high: $70,000; low: $750; average: $750–$50,000).
**Purpose and activities:** The purpose of the foundation is to enhance the quality of the civic, cultural, educational, environmental, and social aspects of life primarily in the St. Paul, MN area.
**Fields of interest:** Media/communications; music; arts/cultural programs; higher education; libraries/library science; education; environment; human services.
**Types of support:** General/operating support; continuing support; annual campaigns; capital campaigns; building/renovation; land acquisition; endowments; debt reduction; program development; publication; seed money; curriculum development; research; technical assistance; matching/challenge support.

**Limitations:** Giving primarily in MN, with emphasis on the metropolitan St. Paul-Minneapolis area. No support for health-related projects. No grants to individuals.
**Publications:** Annual report.
**Application information:** Telephone inquiries accepted during work hours, Mon. through Fri. Application form not required.
*Initial approach:* Proposal
*Copies of proposal:* 1
*Deadline(s):* Submit proposal by Feb. 1, May 1, Aug. 1, or Nov. 1
*Board meeting date(s):* Middle of month in Mar., June, Sept., and Dec.
*Final notification:* 21 days following board meeting
**Officers and Directors:*** Tony Andersen,* Pres.; Eleanor J. Andersen,* V.P.; Terry Stye, Secy.; Julian Andersen,* Treas.; Amy Andersen, Elmer L. Andersen, Emily Andersen, Charles Dayton, Barbara B. Miller.
**Number of staff:** 1 part-time professional.
**EIN:** 416032984

## 332
## Ankeny Foundation
c/o Sargent Mgmt. Co.
4800 First Bank Pl.
Minneapolis, MN 55402
*Contact:* Jeanne Thompson, Secy.

Established in 1963.
**Donor(s):** DeWalt H. Ankeny, Jr., Sally A. Anson, Kendall A. Mix, Michael H. Ankeny.
**Grantmaker type:** Independent foundation
**Financial data** (yr. ended 03/31/00): Assets, $3,718,273 (M); expenditures, $220,246; qualifying distributions, $197,520; giving activities include $197,520 for 120 grants (high: $50,000; low: $25).
**Purpose and activities:** Giving primarily for the arts, education, and human services.
**Fields of interest:** Museums; performing arts; arts/cultural programs; higher education; libraries/library science; scholarships/financial aid; human services; YM/YWCAs & YM/YWHAs; children & youth, services; women, centers & services; federated giving programs; Christian agencies & churches.
**Types of support:** General/operating support; annual campaigns; capital campaigns; endowments; program development.
**Limitations:** Applications not accepted. Giving primarily in MN, with emphasis on Minneapolis. No grants to individuals.
**Application information:** Unsolicited general requests for funding not considered; grants to new organizations seldom considered.
**Officers and Trustees:*** DeWalt H. Ankeny, Jr.,* Pres.; Sally A. Anson,* V.P.; Jeanne Thompson, Secy.; Michael H. Ankeny,* Treas.
**Number of staff:** 1 part-time support.
**EIN:** 416024188

## 333
## William Boss Foundation
5858 Centerville Rd.
St. Paul, MN 55127-6804 (651) 653-0599
*Contact:* Dan McKeown, Treas.

Established around 1957.
**Donor(s):** The Specialty Manufacturing Co.

**Grantmaker type:** Company-sponsored foundation
**Financial data** (yr. ended 06/30/99): Assets, $3,588,806 (M); gifts received, $25,000; expenditures, $185,592; qualifying distributions, $169,701; giving activities include $171,500 for 45 grants (high: $9,500; low: $1,000).
**Purpose and activities:** Giving primarily for the arts.
**Fields of interest:** Museums; performing arts; arts/cultural programs; higher education; libraries/library science; human services; youth, services.
**Types of support:** General/operating support; program-related investments/loans.
**Limitations:** Giving primarily in MN. No grants to individuals.
**Publications:** Application guidelines.
**Application information:**
*Initial approach:* Letter
*Copies of proposal:* 3
*Deadline(s):* June 15
*Board meeting date(s):* June
*Final notification:* 30 days after board meetings
**Officers and Trustees:*** Nancy B. Sandberg,* Chair.; W. Andrew Boss,* Pres.; Heidi Sandberg McKeown,* V.P. and Secy.; Dan McKeown,* Treas.
**EIN:** 416038452

## 334
## Otto Bremer Foundation ▼
445 Minnesota St., Ste. 2000
St. Paul, MN 55101-2107 (651) 227-8036
*Contact:* John Kostishack, Exec. Dir.
*Additional tel.:* (888) 291-1123; FAX: (651) 312-3550; E-mail: obf@bremer.com; URL: http://fdncenter.org/grantmaker/bremer

Trust established in 1944 in MN.
**Donor(s):** Otto Bremer.‡
**Grantmaker type:** Independent foundation
**Financial data** (yr. ended 12/31/99): Assets, $308,530,245 (M); expenditures, $17,128,521; qualifying distributions, $15,739,721; giving activities include $12,201,221 for 586 grants (average: $900–$150,000) and $3,358,500 for 13 loans.
**Purpose and activities:** Emphasis on human rights and equality. Support also for post-secondary education, human services, health, religion, community affairs, and flood relief and recovery.
**Fields of interest:** Early childhood education; child development, education; higher education; libraries (public); education; family planning; health care; mental health/crisis services; health associations; delinquency prevention/services; domestic violence prevention; legal services; nutrition; housing/shelter, development; youth development, citizenship; human services; children & youth, services; child development, services; hospices; women, centers & services; minorities/immigrants, centers & services; homeless, human services; peace; human rights (international); civil rights, immigrants; civil rights, minorities; civil rights, disabled; civil rights, women; civil rights, aging; civil rights, gays/lesbians; race/intergroup relations; civil rights; rural development; community development; voluntarism promotion; public

affairs, citizen participation; minorities; Asians/Pacific Islanders; African Americans; Latinos; Native Americans; disabled; aging; women; people with AIDS (PWAs); gays/lesbians; immigrants/refugees; economically disadvantaged; homeless.
**Types of support:** General/operating support; continuing support; building/renovation; equipment; emergency funds; program development; conferences/seminars; seed money; internship funds; technical assistance; program evaluation; program-related investments/loans; matching/challenge support.
**Limitations:** Giving limited to cities in MN, ND, and WI where there are Bremer Bank affiliates, and to organizations addressing poverty in the city of St. Paul, MN. No support for national health organizations, sporting activities, or K-12 education. No grants to individuals, or for endowment funds, medical research, professorships, annual fund drives, benefit events, camps, or artistic or media projects.
**Publications:** Annual report (including application guidelines).
**Application information:** Application form not required.
*Initial approach:* Letter or telephone
*Copies of proposal:* 1
*Deadline(s):* Submit proposal at least 3 months before funding decision is desired
*Board meeting date(s):* Monthly
*Final notification:* 3 months
**Officer:** John Kostishack, Exec. Dir.
**Trustees:** Charlotte S. Johnson, William H. Lipschultz, Daniel C. Reardon.
**Number of staff:** 4 full-time professional; 1 part-time professional.
**EIN:** 416019050
**Recent grants for library/information services:**
**334-1** Carnegie Regional Library, Grafton, ND, $15,000. For equipment and supplies. 1999.
**334-2** Center for Cross Cultural Health, Minneapolis, MN, $20,000. For continued support for training of health care providers in meeting health care needs of ethnically, culturally, linguistically and spiritually diverse patients. 1999.
**334-3** Community Referral Agency, Milltown, WI, $75,000. For new shelter for families affected by domestic violence. 1999.
**334-4** Early Childhood Resource Center, Minneapolis, MN, $25,000. For operating support and expansion of Network for the Development of Children of Africa Descent, organization devoted to improving cultural, spiritual and educational development of African-American children. 1999.
**334-5** First Call Minnesota, Fergus Falls, MN, $10,000. To establish First Call for Help Southwest in Marshall, MN, regional clearinghouse for services and information. 1999.
**334-6** Friends of the Kandiyohi County-Willmar Public Library, Willmar, MN, $12,120. For equipment and microfiche to allow public access to past issues of local paper. 1999.
**334-7** Lake Country Community Resources, Fergus Falls, MN, $10,000. To develop regional information and referral system. 1999.
**334-8** Leach Public Library, Wahpeton, ND, $18,926. For equipment. 1999.
**334-9** Minot Public Library, Minot, ND, $50,000. To expand library building. 1999.

**334-10** Northern Waters Library Service, Ashland, WI, $48,515. To improve information access at public libraries in northwestern Wisconsin communities. 1999.
**334-11** Webster, Village of, Webster, WI, $18,032. For improvements to library. 1999.

### 335
### Federated Insurance Foundation, Inc.
121 E. Park Sq.
Owatonna, MN  55060  (507) 455-8906
*Contact:* Brian Brose, Admin.

Established in 1972.
**Grantmaker type:** Independent foundation
**Financial data** (yr. ended 12/31/99): Assets, $37,123 (M); gifts received, $46,878; expenditures, $365,521; qualifying distributions, $360,521; giving activities include $360,521 for grants.
**Purpose and activities:** Giving primarily to education and human services.
**Fields of interest:** Higher education; libraries/library science; education; wildlife preservation & protection; children & youth, services; federated giving programs; general charitable giving.
**Types of support:** General/operating support; grants to individuals; matching/challenge support.
**Limitations:** Giving primarily in MN.
**Application information:** Application form not required.
*Initial approach:* Letter
*Copies of proposal:* 1
*Deadline(s):* None
*Board meeting date(s):* As needed
**Officers:** C.I. Buxton II, Pres.; Al Annexstad, V.P.; Rick Kraus, V.P.; Kirk Nelson, V.P.; Ray Stawarz, V.P.; Greg Stroik, V.P.; J.E. Meilahn, Secy.-Treas.
**EIN:** 237173646

### 336
### Garmar Foundation
19 Airport Dr., N.
Dodge Center, MN  55927

Established in 1998 in MN.
**Donor(s):** Brandon McNeilus, Denzil McNeilus, Garwin McNeilus, Marilee McNeilus.
**Grantmaker type:** Independent foundation
**Financial data** (yr. ended 06/30/00): Assets, $22,607,432 (M); gifts received, $11,500; expenditures, $11,936,160; qualifying distributions, $11,884,501; giving activities include $11,894,351 for 30 grants (high: $10,696,063; low: $100; average: $1,000–$176,421).
**Purpose and activities:** Giving primarily to the Minnesota Conference of Seventh Day Adventists, as well as for education and human services.
**Fields of interest:** Museums (science & technology); libraries (public); education; human services; Protestant agencies & churches.
**Limitations:** Applications not accepted. Giving primarily in MN. No grants to individuals.
**Application information:** Contributes only to pre-selected organizations.
**Officers:** Garwin McNeilus, Pres.; Denzil McNeilus, V.P.; Marilee McNeilus, Secy.-Treas.
**EIN:** 411914753

### 337
### General Mills Foundation ▼
P.O. Box 1113
Minneapolis, MN  55440  (612) 540-7891
*Contact:* Reatha Clark King, Pres. and Exec. Dir.
*FAX:* (612) 540-4114; E-mail: mills999@mail.genmills.com; URL: http://www.generalmills.com/explore/community/foundation

Incorporated in 1954 in MN.
**Donor(s):** General Mills, Inc.
**Grantmaker type:** Company-sponsored foundation
**Financial data** (yr. ended 05/31/99): Assets, $39,516,993 (M); gifts received, $7,000,000; expenditures, $16,111,952; qualifying distributions, $16,010,968; giving activities include $14,294,870 for 665 grants (high: $727,943; low: $265; average: $5,000–$50,000) and $1,708,510 for employee matching gifts).
**Purpose and activities:** Grants for higher and secondary education, social services, United Ways, community funds, health, and civic and cultural activities.
**Fields of interest:** Media/communications; museums; performing arts; dance; theater; music; humanities; arts/cultural programs; early childhood education; child development, education; elementary school/education; secondary school/education; higher education; adult/continuing education; adult education—literacy & basic skills; libraries/library science; reading; education; hospitals (general); health care; substance abuse, services; health associations; cancer; AIDS; alcoholism; cancer research; AIDS research; legal services; crime/law enforcement; employment; food services; nutrition; housing/shelter, development; youth development, services; human services; children & youth, services; child development, services; family services; hospices; aging, centers & services; women, centers & services; minorities/immigrants, centers & services; homeless, human services; race/intergroup relations; urban/community development; community development; voluntarism promotion; federated giving programs; leadership development; minorities; Native Americans; disabled; aging; women; economically disadvantaged; homeless.
**Types of support:** General/operating support; capital campaigns; program development; scholarship funds; employee matching gifts.
**Limitations:** Giving primarily in areas of major parent company operations. No support for religious purposes, political, social, labor, veterans', alumni or fraternal organizations, recreation, or national or local campaigns to eliminate or control specific diseases, or athletic associations. No grants to individuals, or, generally, for endowments, research, publications, films, advertising, athletic events, testimonial dinners, workshops, symposia, travel, fundraising events, or deficit financing; no loans.
**Publications:** Corporate giving report (including application guidelines), annual report, informational brochure, application guidelines.
**Application information:** Application form is available from the foundation office but is not required. Preliminary telephone calls or

personal visits discouraged. Minnesota Common Grant Application Form accepted.
*Initial approach:* Proposal and application
*Copies of proposal:* 1
*Deadline(s):* None
*Board meeting date(s):* 4 times per year and as required
*Final notification:* 8 weeks
**Officers and Trustees:*** S.W. Sanger,* Chair. and C.E.O.; Reatha Clark King, Pres. and Exec. Dir.; David A. Nasby, V.P.; A.P. Sullivan, Jr.,* Secy.; David B. Van Benschoten, Treas.; Charles W. Gaillard, S.S. Marshall, Michael A. Peel, R.G. Viault.
**Number of staff:** 2 full-time professional; 3 full-time support.
**EIN:** 416018495
**Recent grants for library/information services:**
**337-1** Library Legacy Foundation, Toledo, OH, $35,000. For Children's Exploration Center. 1999.
**337-2** Metropolitan State University Foundation, Saint Paul, MN, $25,000. For Writing Center DECLINE Community Library and Information Access Center. 1999.
**337-3** Newton County Library System, Covington, GA, $25,000. For library materials. 1999.

### 338
### Otter Tail Power Company Contributions Program
215 S. Cascade St.
Fergus Falls, MN  56537
*Contact:* John C. MacFarlane, Chair., Pres., and C.E.O.

**Grantmaker type:** Corporate giving program
**Purpose and activities:** Otter Tail makes charitable contributions to nonprofit organizations involved with arts and culture, education, the environment, health and human services, mental health, disease, medical research, crime, recreation, youth development, community development, public affairs, minorities, disabled people, senior citizens, and economically disadvantaged people. Support is given primarily in areas of company operations.
**Fields of interest:** Visual arts; museums; performing arts; music; historic preservation/historical societies; arts/cultural programs; education, fund raising; child development, education; secondary school/education; business school/education; libraries/library science; education; environment; hospitals (general); health care; mental health/crisis services; cancer; heart & circulatory diseases; health organizations; cancer research; heart & circulatory research; medical research; crime/law enforcement; recreation; youth development; children & youth, services; child development, services; hospices; human services; community development; leadership development; public affairs; minorities; disabled; aging; economically disadvantaged.
**Types of support:** Continuing support; annual campaigns; building/renovation; equipment; endowments; conferences/seminars; employee volunteer services; use of facilities; sponsorships; employee matching gifts; donated equipment; in-kind gifts; matching/challenge support.

**Limitations:** Giving primarily in areas of company operations, particularly the Fergus Falls, MN, area.
**Application information:** The Office of the C.E.O. handles giving. Application form not required.
   *Initial approach:* Proposal to headquarters
   *Copies of proposal:* 1
   *Deadline(s):* None
   *Final notification:* 1 to 4 weeks

## 339
## WEM Foundation ▼
P.O. Box 9300, Dept. 28
Minneapolis, MN   55440-9300
(612) 742-7544
*Contact:* Robert J. Theiler, Secy.-Treas.

Established in 1988 in MN.
**Donor(s):** Whitney MacMillan, Jr.
**Grantmaker type:** Independent foundation
**Financial data** (yr. ended 12/31/99): Assets, $59,670,707 (M); gifts received, $2,144,789; expenditures, $3,241,546; qualifying distributions, $3,136,821; giving activities include $3,166,500 for 87 grants (high: $1,500,000; low: $200; average: $1,000–$25,000).
**Purpose and activities:** Giving primarily to arts and cultural programs, education, general hospitals, health associations, international affairs, and philanthropy.
**Fields of interest:** Arts/cultural programs; education; hospitals (general); health associations; international affairs, public policy; international relief; foundations (community).
**Limitations:** Applications not accepted. Giving primarily in MN. No grants to individuals.
**Application information:** Contributes only to pre-selected organizations. Unsolicited requests for funds not considered.
**Officers and Directors:*** Elizabeth S. MacMillan,* Chair.; Whitney MacMillan,* Vice-Chair.; Robert J. Theiler,* Secy.-Treas.; James Hield, Whitney MacMillan, Jr., Harriet S. Norgren.
**EIN:** 411604640
**Recent grants for library/information services:**
339-1 Anglo-American School of Moscow, Friends of the, NYC, NY, $750,000. For new school library. 1998.

# MISSOURI

## 340
## Helen S. Boylan Foundation
P.O. Box 731
320 Grant St.
Carthage, MO   64836-0731
*Contact:* James R. Spradling, Pres.

Established in 1982.
**Donor(s):** Helen S. Boylan Trust, Elbert Elwyn Boylan, Jr.
**Grantmaker type:** Independent foundation
**Financial data** (yr. ended 09/30/99): Assets, $6,377,375 (M); expenditures, $277,945; qualifying distributions, $188,924; giving

activities include $171,482 for 23 grants (high: $34,638; low: $333).
**Purpose and activities:** Giving primarily for community development, and children's services.
**Fields of interest:** Libraries (public); recreation; human services; children & youth, services; community development.
**Types of support:** Building/renovation; land acquisition.
**Limitations:** Giving primarily in MO, with emphasis on Carthage. No grants to individuals.
**Application information:** Application form not required.
   *Deadline(s):* None
**Officers and Directors:*** James R. Spradling,* Pres.; Ida S. Locarni,* V.P.; James A. Deberry,* Treas.; Charles M. Cook, Helen B. Duff, Eugene C. Hall, Jennifer A. Hering, A.W. McKinney.
**EIN:** 431254043

## 341
## E. Kemper Carter and Anna Curry Carter Community Memorial Trust
(Formerly Carter Community Memorial Trust)
c/o UMB, N.A.
P.O. Box 419692
Kansas City, MO   64141-6692   (816) 860-7711
*Contact:* Stephen J. Campbell, Trust Off., UMB, N.A.

Established in 1993 in MO.
**Grantmaker type:** Independent foundation
**Financial data** (yr. ended 12/31/99): Assets, $13,872,119 (M); expenditures, $1,438,617; qualifying distributions, $1,363,811; giving activities include $1,320,199 for 91 grants (high: $83,333; low: $1,000).
**Purpose and activities:** Giving for civic and cultural endeavors, including children and youth services and programs, education, museums and the performing arts, and community improvement.
**Fields of interest:** Museums; performing arts; higher education; libraries/library science; education; parks/playgrounds; youth development; children & youth, services; community development.
**Limitations:** Giving limited to KS and MO, with emphasis on the bi-state Kansas City area.
**Application information:**
   *Initial approach:* Letter
   *Deadline(s):* None
**Trustees:** George Hayden, UMB, N.A.
**EIN:** 436483356

## 342
## Caleb C. and Julia W. Dula Educational and Charitable Foundation
112 S. Hanley Rd.
St. Louis, MO   63105-3418   (314) 726-2800
*Contact:* James F. Mauze
*FAX:* (314) 863-3821

Established in 1995 in MO.
**Grantmaker type:** Independent foundation
**Financial data** (yr. ended 12/31/98): Assets, $45,672,064 (M); expenditures, $2,520,004; qualifying distributions, $2,260,935; giving activities include $2,100,200 for 76 grants (high: $150,000; low: $5,000).

**Purpose and activities:** Grants to charities which the Dulas supported during their lifetime, with emphasis on education, hospitals, libraries, social service agencies, child welfare, church support, cultural programs, and historic preservation.
**Fields of interest:** Historic preservation/historical societies; arts/cultural programs; libraries/library science; education; environment; health associations; human services.
**Types of support:** General/operating support.
**Limitations:** No grants to individuals.
**Application information:**
   *Initial approach:* Letter
   *Deadline(s):* Apr. 1 and Oct. 1
**Trustees:** Margaret C. Gunter, Margaret W. Kobusch, Orrin S. Wightman III.
**EIN:** 431716767

## 343
## Allen P. & Josephine B. Green Foundation
222 S. Jefferson, Rm. 108
P.O. Box 523
Mexico, MO   65265   (573) 581-5568
*Contact:* Walter G. Staley, Jr., Secy.-Treas.
*FAX:* (573) 581-1714; E-mail: green@mail itwebs.com; additional E-mail: nrcox@mailtwebs.com

Trust established in 1941 in MO.
**Donor(s):** Allen P. Green,‡ Josephine B. Green.‡
**Grantmaker type:** Independent foundation
**Financial data** (yr. ended 12/31/99): Assets, $15,960,747 (M); expenditures, $882,866; qualifying distributions, $713,914; giving activities include $722,441 for 76 grants (high: $30,000; low: $1,500).
**Purpose and activities:** Giving for human services, with emphasis on child development and the family, women, and the elderly; health services, including rehabilitation programs for drug and alcohol abuse, cancer care, and nursing; arts and humanities, especially fine and performing arts groups and historic preservation; education, including early childhood, elementary and secondary, adult and vocational, theological and medical, and other higher educational institutions, and libraries; community development and civic affairs; and environmental conservation and animal welfare.
**Fields of interest:** Performing arts; history & archaeology; historic preservation/historical societies; arts/cultural programs; early childhood education; child development, education; elementary school/education; secondary school/education; vocational education; higher education; theological school/education; adult/continuing education; adult education—literacy & basic skills; libraries/library science; reading; natural resource conservation & protection; environment; animal welfare; medical care, rehabilitation; nursing care; health care; mental health/crisis services; health associations; eye diseases; delinquency prevention/services; nutrition; human services; children & youth, services; child development, services; hospices; aging, centers & services; women, centers & services; aging; women; economically disadvantaged.
**Types of support:** Capital campaigns; building/renovation; equipment; endowments; emergency funds; program development;

conferences/seminars; seed money; curriculum development; scholarship funds; matching/challenge support.
**Limitations:** Giving primarily in MO, with special emphasis on the Mexico area; no giving outside the continental U.S. No grants to individuals, or for operating budgets; no loans.
**Publications:** Annual report (including application guidelines), grants list.
**Application information:** Application form not required.
*Initial approach:* Letter
*Copies of proposal:* 1
*Deadline(s):* Mar. 15 or Sept. 15
*Board meeting date(s):* May and Nov.
*Final notification:* 1 month
**Officers and Directors:*** Robert E. McIntosh,* Pres.; Nancy White,* V.P.; Walter G. Staley, Jr.,* Secy.-Treas.; A.D. Bond III, Christopher S. Bond, Robert R. Collins, Nancy A. Ekern, Carl D. Fuemmeler, James F. McHenry, Andrea Bond Wilson, Robert A. Wood.
**Number of staff:** 1 part-time support.
**EIN:** 436030135

## 344
## Hall Family Foundation ▼
c/o Charitable & Crown Investment-323
P.O. Box 419580
Kansas City, MO  64141-6580  (816) 274-8516
*Contact:* Jeanne Bates, V.P., John Laney, V.P., or Sally Groves, Prog. Off.

Hallmark Educational Foundation incorporated in 1943 in MO; Hallmark Education Foundation of KS incorporated in 1954 in KS; combined funds formerly known as Hallmark Educational Foundations; current name adopted due to absorption of Hall Family Foundation of Kansas in 1993.
**Donor(s):** Hallmark Cards, Inc., Joyce C. Hall,‡ E.A. Hall,‡ R.B. Hall.‡
**Grantmaker type:** Independent foundation
**Financial data** (yr. ended 12/31/99): Assets, $973,278,893 (M); expenditures, $80,651,767; qualifying distributions, $21,399,893; giving activities include $19,493,948 for 92 grants (high: $5,000,000; low: $1,000) and $274,945 for 167 grants to individuals (high: $2,250; low: $750).
**Purpose and activities:** Giving within four main areas of interest: 1) the performing and visual arts; 2) education - all levels; 3) children, youth and families; and 4) community development.
**Fields of interest:** Performing arts; arts/cultural programs; early childhood education; child development, education; elementary school/education; secondary school/education; higher education; education; housing/shelter, development; human services; youth, services; child development, services; family services; minorities/immigrants, centers & services; homeless, human services; urban/community development; community development; minorities; homeless.
**Types of support:** General/operating support; capital campaigns; building/renovation; emergency funds; program development; seed money; technical assistance; program-related investments/loans.
**Limitations:** Giving limited to Kansas City, MO. No support for international or religious organizations or for political purposes. No

grants to individuals (except for emergency aid to Hallmark Cards employees, and employee-related scholarships) or for endowment funds, travel, operating deficits, conferences, scholarly or medical research, or fundraising campaigns such as telethons.
**Publications:** Annual report, informational brochure (including application guidelines).
**Application information:** Scholarships are for the children and close relatives of Hallmark Cards employees only. Only eligible applicants should apply. Application form not required.
*Initial approach:* Letter
*Copies of proposal:* 1
*Deadline(s):* 6 weeks before board meetings
*Board meeting date(s):* Mar., June, Sept., and Dec.
*Final notification:* 6 to 8 weeks
**Officers:** William A. Hall, Pres.; John A. MacDonald, V.P. and Treas.; Jeanne Bates, V.P.; John Laney, V.P.; Danita M.H. Robinson, Secy.
**Directors:** Donald J. Hall, Chair.; Irvine O. Hockaday, Jr., David H. Hughes, Robert A. Kipp, Sandra Lawrence, John P. Mascotte, Margaret Hall Pence, Morton I. Sosland.
**Number of staff:** 2 full-time professional; 2 part-time professional; 1 full-time support.
**EIN:** 446006291
**Recent grants for library/information services:**
**344-1** Catholic Education Foundation of Northeast Kansas, Kansas City, KS, $100,000. For Monsignor Gardner Resource Center. 1999.
**344-2** Harry S. Truman Library Institute for National and International Affairs, Independence, MO, $2,000,000. For Creating a Classroom for Democracy Program. 1999.
**344-3** Tri-County Community Mental Health Services, North Kansas City, MO, $50,000. For integrated information management system. 1999.

## 345
## Fred V. & Dorothy H. Heinkel Charitable Foundation
P.O. Box 938
Columbia, MO  65205
*Contact:* Stephen B. Smith, V.P.

Established in 1982.
**Grantmaker type:** Independent foundation
**Financial data** (yr. ended 12/31/99): Assets, $4,505,669 (M); expenditures, $210,151; qualifying distributions, $177,800; giving activities include $177,800 for 11 grants (high: $59,000; low: $3,800).
**Fields of interest:** Libraries/library science; education; health associations; youth development, centers & clubs; human services.
**Limitations:** Giving primarily in Columbia, MO.
**Application information:** Application form not required.
*Initial approach:* Letter
*Deadline(s):* None
*Board meeting date(s):* Varies
**Officers:** Robert W. Maupin, Pres.; Stephen B. Smith, V.P. and Treas.; Cathy Anderson, Secy.
**EIN:** 431242045

## 346
## Mathews Foundation
1 Metropolitan Sq., Ste. 3600
211 N. Broadway
St. Louis, MO  63102  (314) 259-2315
*Contact:* John D. Schaperkotter, Tr.

Established in 1988 in MO.
**Grantmaker type:** Independent foundation
**Financial data** (yr. ended 12/31/98): Assets, $2,419,500 (M); expenditures, $117,667; qualifying distributions, $113,868; giving activities include $90,090 for 10 grants (high: $50,000; low: $1,000).
**Fields of interest:** Arts/cultural programs; libraries/library science; education; recreation.
**Limitations:** Applications not accepted. Giving primarily in MO. No grants to individuals.
**Application information:** Contributes only to pre-selected organizations.
**Trustees:** Harry B. Mathews III, John D. Schaperkotter, William M. Van Cleve.
**EIN:** 436351190

## 347
## The May Department Stores Company Foundation, Inc. ▼
(Formerly The May Stores Foundation, Inc.)
611 Olive St., Ste. 1350
St. Louis, MO  63101-1799  (314) 342-6299
*Contact:* Joni Sullivan Baker, Mgr., Corp. Comm.
*Additional tel.:* (314) 342-6403; FAX: (314) 342-4461

Incorporated in 1945 in NY.
**Donor(s):** The May Department Stores Co.
**Grantmaker type:** Company-sponsored foundation
**Financial data** (yr. ended 12/31/99): Assets, $7,042,871 (M); gifts received, $12,309,845; expenditures, $9,177,954; qualifying distributions, $8,840,222; giving activities include $8,842,313 for grants.
**Purpose and activities:** Grants to charitable and educational institutions throughout the country, with emphasis on community funds in areas of company operations; support also for cultural programs, hospitals and health care, and civic affairs.
**Fields of interest:** Arts/cultural programs; education; health care; human services; federated giving programs.
**Limitations:** Giving primarily in areas of company operations.
**Application information:** Application form not required.
*Initial approach:* Letter
**Officers and Directors:*** Jerome T. Loeb,* Pres.; Jan R. Kniffen,* V.P. and Secy.-Treas.; John L. Dunham,* V.P.; David C. Farrell,* V.P.; Robert F. Cerulli.
**Number of staff:** None.
**EIN:** 436028949
**Recent grants for library/information services:**
**347-1** Older Adult Service and Information System (OASIS), Saint Louis, MO, $900,500. For continued support. 1998.
**347-2** Older Adult Service and Information System (OASIS), Saint Louis, MO, $318,000. For continued support for Intergenerational Tutoring Program. 1998.

## 348
## Oppenstein Brothers Foundation
P.O. Box 13095
Kansas City, MO 64199-3095 (816) 234-8671
*Contact:* Sheila K. Rice, Prog. Off.

Trust established in 1975 in MO.
**Donor(s):** Michael Oppenstein.‡
**Grantmaker type:** Independent foundation
**Financial data** (yr. ended 03/31/00): Assets,
$33,760,956 (M); expenditures, $2,208,419;
qualifying distributions, $1,974,396; giving
activities include $1,974,396 for 91 grants
(average: $1,000–$200,000).
**Purpose and activities:** Grants primarily for
education (excluding scholarship assistance),
arts (primarily educational programming for
children), health services (programs that
promote wellness), and social services.
**Fields of interest:** Museums; performing arts;
theater; arts/cultural programs; early childhood
education; child development, education;
elementary school/education; secondary
school/education; higher education;
adult/continuing education; adult
education—literacy & basic skills;
libraries/library science; reading; education;
medical care, rehabilitation; health care;
substance abuse, services; mental health/crisis
services; health associations; AIDS; alcoholism;
AIDS research; delinquency prevention/services;
employment; nutrition; housing/shelter,
development; youth development, services;
human services; children & youth, services;
child development, services; family services;
aging, centers & services; minorities/immigrants,
centers & services; homeless, human services;
urban/community development; community
development; voluntarism promotion; Jewish
federated giving programs; leadership
development; Jewish agencies & temples;
minorities; disabled; aging; economically
disadvantaged; homeless.
**Types of support:** General/operating support;
capital campaigns; building/renovation;
equipment; emergency funds; program
development; seed money; curriculum
development; consulting services;
matching/challenge support.
**Limitations:** Giving limited to the metropolitan
Kansas City, MO, area. No grants to individuals,
or for annual campaigns, building funds or
expansion.
**Publications:** Multi-year report, informational
brochure (including application guidelines).
**Application information:** Application guidelines
available on request. Application form not
required.
  *Initial approach:* Telephone or letter
  *Copies of proposal:* 1
  *Deadline(s):* 3 weeks prior to board meetings
  *Board meeting date(s):* Usually bimonthly
  *Final notification:* 2 to 4 months
**Disbursement Committee:** Warren W. Weaver,
Chair.; Mary Bloch, Laura Kemper Fields, Roger
T. Hurwitz, Estelle Sosland.
**Trustee:** Commerce Bank, N.A.
**Number of staff:** None.
**EIN:** 436203035

## 349
## Margaret C. Palmer Trust
c/o Jim Owens
500 Washington Ave., Ste. 1204
St. Louis, MO 63101

Established around 1995.
**Grantmaker type:** Independent foundation
**Financial data** (yr. ended 12/31/99): Assets,
$1,565,096 (M); expenditures, $101,181;
qualifying distributions, $76,090; giving
activities include $60,000 for 2 grants of
$30,000 each.
**Purpose and activities:** Giving for libraries and
higher education scholarships.
**Fields of interest:** Higher education;
libraries/library science.
**Limitations:** Applications not accepted. Giving
primarily in MO. No grants to individuals.
**Application information:** Contributes only to
pre-selected organizations.
**Trustee:** Hon. Ronald B. Safren.
**EIN:** 396596804

## 350
## Elmer F. Pierson Foundation
1030 W. 56th St.
Kansas City, MO 64113-1113 (816) 333-3297
*Contact:* Marilyn Pierson Patterson, Pres.

Established in 1943.
**Donor(s):** E.F. Pierson.‡
**Grantmaker type:** Independent foundation
**Financial data** (yr. ended 12/31/99): Assets,
$1,838,040 (M); expenditures, $83,607;
qualifying distributions, $78,428; giving
activities include $60,550 for 64 grants (high:
$6,000; low: $50).
**Fields of interest:** Arts/cultural programs; higher
education; libraries/library science; education;
hospitals (general); human services.
**Types of support:** General/operating support.
**Limitations:** Giving limited to the Kansas City,
MO, area. No support for health organizations.
**Application information:**
  *Initial approach:* Letter
  *Deadline(s):* Oct. 15
**Officers:** Marilyn Pierson Patterson, Pres.;
Martha Ann Pierson Marquis, V.P.; Doyle
Patterson, Secy.-Treas.
**Number of staff:** None.
**EIN:** 446006295

## 351
## Pitzman Fund
c/o Bank of America
100 N. Broadway, P.O. Box 14737
St. Louis, MO 63178 (314) 466-3452
*Contact:* Ellen Crabtree, V.P., Bank of America

Established in 1944.
**Donor(s):** Frederick Pitzman.‡
**Grantmaker type:** Independent foundation
**Financial data** (yr. ended 09/30/99): Assets,
$5,080,102 (M); expenditures, $164,799;
qualifying distributions, $154,823; giving
activities include $154,300 for 62 grants (high:
$10,000; low: $500).
**Purpose and activities:** Giving primarily for
education, health, and human services.
**Fields of interest:** Arts/cultural programs;
libraries/library science; education; family

planning; medical care, rehabilitation; health
care; substance abuse, services; human services;
children & youth, services; Protestant agencies
& churches.
**Types of support:** General/operating support;
continuing support; annual campaigns.
**Limitations:** Giving primarily in St. Louis, MO.
**Application information:** Application form not
required.
  *Deadline(s):* None
**Trustees:** Caroline P. Early, Gilbert Gordon Early,
Bank of America.
**Number of staff:** None.
**EIN:** 436023901

## 352
## L. F. Richardson Foundation
P.O. Box 419692
Kansas City, MO 64141-6692
*Contact:* David A. Junge, Trust Invest. Off.

Established in 1947.
**Grantmaker type:** Independent foundation
**Financial data** (yr. ended 12/31/98): Assets,
$1,611,180 (M); expenditures, $72,466;
qualifying distributions, $57,312; giving
activities include $55,000 for 4 grants (high:
$25,000; low: $5,000).
**Purpose and activities:** Giving to Baptist
churches and community foundations.
**Fields of interest:** Libraries/library science;
federated giving programs; Protestant agencies
& churches; religion; general charitable giving.
**Types of support:** General/operating support;
capital campaigns.
**Limitations:** Applications not accepted. Giving
limited to the city of Nevada, MO. No grants to
individuals.
**Application information:** Contributes only to
pre-selected organizations.
**Trustees:** Ronald F. Fisk, Don W. Kennedy.
**Director:** Cynthia Wynn.
**Number of staff:** 1 part-time professional; 1
part-time support.
**EIN:** 436031530

## 353
## Russell Stover Candies, Inc. Corporate Giving Program
c/o Corp. Contribs.
1000 Walnut St.
Kansas City, MO 64106 (816) 842-9240

**Grantmaker type:** Corporate giving program
**Purpose and activities:** Russell Stover makes
charitable contributions to nonprofit
organizations on a case by case basis and to
libraries and parks. Support is given primarily in
areas of company operations.
**Fields of interest:** Libraries/library science;
parks/playgrounds; general charitable giving.
**Types of support:** General/operating support;
employee volunteer services; in-kind gifts.
**Limitations:** Giving primarily in areas of
company operations.
**Application information:** Application form not
required.
  *Initial approach:* Proposal to headquarters or
    nearest company facility
  *Copies of proposal:* 1
  *Deadline(s):* Oct. 31
  *Final notification:* Following review

## 354
## Arch W. Shaw Foundation
Thomasville Rte., Box 60B
Birch Tree, MO 65438 (417) 764-3701
*Contact:* William W. Shaw, Tr.
*FAX:* (417) 764-3706

Trust established in 1949 in IL.
**Donor(s):** Arch W. Shaw.‡
**Grantmaker type:** Independent foundation
**Financial data** (yr. ended 12/31/99): Assets,
$12,065,236 (M); expenditures, $659,250;
qualifying distributions, $450,171; giving
activities include $650,000 for 88 grants (high:
$25,000; low: $1,000; average:
$1,000–$25,000).
**Fields of interest:** Museums; arts/cultural
programs; education, fund raising; higher
education; business school/education;
libraries/library science; hospitals (general);
health care; medical research; hospices.
**Types of support:** General/operating support;
continuing support; annual campaigns; capital
campaigns; building/renovation; equipment;
endowments; emergency funds; program
development; seed money; scholarship funds;
research.
**Limitations:** Giving primarily in IL, MA, MO,
NY, and WI. No support for private foundations.
No grants to individuals.
**Publications:** Financial statement.
**Application information:** Application form
required.
  *Initial approach:* Letter
  *Copies of proposal:* 1
  *Deadline(s):* None
  *Board meeting date(s):* Dec.
**Trustees:** Arch W. Shaw II, Bruce P. Shaw, Roger
D. Shaw, Jr., William W. Shaw.
**Number of staff:** None.
**EIN:** 366055262

---

# MONTANA

## 355
## Boe Brothers Foundation
(Formerly The Lief Boe Charitable Trust)
c/o Al Faechner
P.O. Box 1396
Great Falls, MT 59403 (406) 727-4200

Established in 1994 in MT.
**Grantmaker type:** Independent foundation
**Financial data** (yr. ended 12/31/98): Assets,
$5,177,002 (M); expenditures, $368,907;
qualifying distributions, $340,827; giving
activities include $333,000 for 35 grants (high:
$62,600; low: $100).
**Purpose and activities:** Giving primarily for
education and human services.
**Fields of interest:** Elementary/secondary
education; higher education; libraries (public);
children & youth, services.
**Types of support:** Scholarship funds.
**Limitations:** Giving primarily in northern and
central MT. No grants to individuals.
**Application information:**
  *Initial approach:* Letter
  *Deadline(s):* None

**Trustee:** Al Faechner.
**EIN:** 841378691

## 356
## The Montana Power Foundation, Inc.
(Formerly MPCo/Entech Foundation, Inc.)
40 E. Broadway
Butte, MT 59701-9394 (406) 497-2602
*FAX:* (406) 497-2451; E-mail:
bcain@mtpower.com; URL: http://
www.mtpower.com/Community/
cm_foundation.htm

Established in 1985 in MT.
**Donor(s):** The Montana Power Co.,
Independent Power Group.
**Grantmaker type:** Company-sponsored
foundation
**Financial data** (yr. ended 12/31/98): Assets,
$173,441 (M); gifts received, $647,868;
expenditures, $724,866; qualifying distributions,
$643,091; giving activities include $603,296 for
147 grants (high: $50,000; low: $25) and
$39,855 for 43 employee matching gifts.
**Purpose and activities:** Support for colleges and
universities through grants and an employee
matching gift program; primary areas of interest
also include hospital building funds, civic
affairs, and cultural programs.
**Fields of interest:** Performing arts; arts/cultural
programs; elementary/secondary education;
higher education; libraries/library science;
education; natural resource conservation &
protection; health care; children & youth,
services; human services; community
development.
**Types of support:** General/operating support;
annual campaigns; capital campaigns;
building/renovation; equipment; endowments;
conferences/seminars; scholarship funds;
employee matching gifts; in-kind gifts.
**Limitations:** Giving primarily in areas of
company operations in MT. No support for
individual United Way agencies (except for
capital funds), fraternal, service, veterans', or
social groups, political activities or
organizations established primarily to influence
legislation, religious activities, economic or
commercial development projects, or national
health organizations. No grants to individuals
(except for scholarships), or for operating funds
(except for organizations such as the United
Way), sporting events, medical equipment,
research, or multi-year requests.
**Publications:** Annual report (including
application guidelines), financial statement.
**Application information:** Application form
required.
  *Initial approach:* Letter or telephone
  *Copies of proposal:* 1
  *Deadline(s):* None
  *Board meeting date(s):* Apr., Aug., and Dec.
  *Final notification:* 6 weeks
**Directors:** Daniel T. Berube, Alan F. Cain,
Richard F. Cromer, Robert P. Gannon, Carl
Lehrkind III, Arthur K. Neill, Jerrold P. Pederson.
**Number of staff:** 1 full-time professional.
**EIN:** 810432484

---

# NEBRASKA

## 357
## Dr. C. C. and Mabel L. Criss Memorial
  Foundation ▼
c/o U.S. Bank, N.A.
17th and Farnam Sts.
Omaha, NE 68102
*Contact:* The Trustees

Trust established in 1978 in NE.
**Donor(s):** C.C. Criss, M.D.,‡ Mabel L. Criss.‡
**Grantmaker type:** Independent foundation
**Financial data** (yr. ended 02/28/99): Assets,
$47,393,008 (M); expenditures, $3,007,754;
qualifying distributions, $2,555,900; giving
activities include $2,617,290 for 30 grants
(high: $797,314; low: $5,000).
**Purpose and activities:** Support primarily for
educational and scientific purposes, including
Creighton University's medical center; support
also for education, including higher education,
cultural agencies, youth and social service
agencies, and a hospital.
**Fields of interest:** Arts/cultural programs; higher
education; education; human services; children
& youth, services.
**Limitations:** Applications not accepted. Giving
limited to Omaha, NE. No grants to individuals.
**Application information:** Contributes only to
pre-selected organizations.
  *Board meeting date(s):* Monthly
**Trustees:** M. Philip Crummer, Stanley Davis,
Donna Turner, John J. Vinardi, U.S. Bank, N.A.
**EIN:** 470601105
**Recent grants for library/information services:**
**357-1** Ralston Public Library Foundation,
  Ralston, NE, $10,000. For general support.
  1999.
**357-2** University of Nebraska Foundation, Criss
  Library, Omaha, NE, $400,000. For general
  support. 1999.

## 358
## Karl H. & Wealtha H. Nelson Family
  Foundation
c/o George T. Blazek
8805 Indian Hills Dr., Ste. 280
Omaha, NE 68114-4077
*Contact:* William J. Roker, V.P.
*Application address:* 502 S. 14th St., Nebraska
City, NE 68410, tel.: (402) 873-5706

Established in 1993 in NE.
**Grantmaker type:** Independent foundation
**Financial data** (yr. ended 12/31/99): Assets,
$2,301,792 (M); gifts received, $1,500,000;
expenditures, $60,354; qualifying distributions,
$42,100; giving activities include $42,100 for
12 grants (high: $25,000; low: $100).
**Fields of interest:** Higher education; libraries
(public); health care, support services; disasters,
fire prevention/control.
**Application information:**
  *Initial approach:* Letter
  *Deadline(s):* None
**Officers:** William J. Roker, Pres.; Karen Nelson,
V.P.; George T. Blazer, Secy.; Andrew Grier, Treas.
**Trustee:** Wealtha H. Nelson.

EIN: 363879767

## 359
**Kitty M. Perkins Foundation**
c/o J. Richard Shoemaker
304 Nelson St.
Cambridge, NE 69022

Incorporated in 1966 in IL.
**Donor(s):** Kitty M. Perkins.‡
**Grantmaker type:** Independent foundation
**Financial data** (yr. ended 12/31/99): Assets, $14,056,060 (M); expenditures, $561,327; qualifying distributions, $549,000; giving activities include $549,000 for 37 grants (high: $235,000; low: $500).
**Purpose and activities:** Grants largely for a hospital and a law school; support also for higher education, rural libraries, medical research, and rural community hospitals.
**Fields of interest:** Higher education; libraries/library science; hospitals (general); medical research.
**Types of support:** General/operating support; continuing support; annual campaigns; capital campaigns; building/renovation; equipment; program development; professorships; research.
**Limitations:** Applications not accepted. Giving primarily in NE. No grants to individuals, or for matching gifts; no loans.
**Application information:** Contributes only to pre-selected organizations.
*Board meeting date(s):* As required
**Officers and Directors:*** J. Richard Shoemaker,* Pres.; Don C. Shoemaker,* Secy.; William Shoemaker,* Treas.; Kathryn Heitmann, George Franklin Shoemaker, Honor J. Shoemaker.
**Number of staff:** None.
EIN: 366154399

## 360
**Union Pacific Foundation ▼**
1416 Dodge St., Rm. 802
Omaha, NE 68179 (402) 271-5600
*Contact:* Ms. Darlynn Herweg, Dir.
*FAX:* (402) 271-5477; E-mail: union_pacific_foundation@notes.up.com; URL: http://www.up.com/found

Incorporated in 1959 in UT.
**Donor(s):** Union Pacific Corp.
**Grantmaker type:** Company-sponsored foundation
**Financial data** (yr. ended 12/31/98): Assets, $2,918,418 (M); gifts received, $6,571,941; expenditures, $7,598,632; qualifying distributions, $7,404,580; giving activities include $7,404,580 for 867 grants (high: $250,000; low: $500; average: $1,000–$10,000).
**Purpose and activities:** Grants primarily to non-tax-supported institutions of higher education, health (including hospitals and hospices), social services, fine and performing arts groups and other cultural programs, and environmental programs.
**Fields of interest:** Museums; performing arts; dance; theater; historic preservation/historical societies; arts/cultural programs; higher education; libraries/library science; natural resource conservation & protection; environment; hospitals (general); medical care,

rehabilitation; substance abuse, services; youth development; human services; family services; community development, single organization support; minorities; disabled; economically disadvantaged.
**Types of support:** General/operating support; continuing support; capital campaigns; building/renovation; equipment; program development; professorships; curriculum development; scholarship funds; matching/challenge support.
**Limitations:** Giving primarily in areas of company operations, with emphasis on the midwestern and western U.S.: AR, AZ, CA, CO, IA, ID, IL, KS, LA, MN, MO, MT, NE, NM, NV, OK, OR, TX, UT, WA, WI, and WY. No support for specialized national health and welfare organizations, religious or labor groups, social clubs, or fraternal or veterans' organizations; support for United Way-affiliated organizations restricted to capital projects. No grants to individuals, or for sponsorship of dinners, benefits, seminars, or other special events.
**Publications:** Application guidelines.
**Application information:** The foundation does not sponsor an employee matching gift program. Application form required.
*Initial approach:* Letter containing mission statement and use of funds requested
*Copies of proposal:* 1
*Deadline(s):* Aug. 15 for consideration in the following calendar year
*Board meeting date(s):* Late Jan. for consideration for year
*Final notification:* Feb. through Apr.
**Officers and Trustees:*** Richard K. Davidson,* Chair.; R.F. Starzel,* Pres.; J.J. Koraleski,* V.P., Finance; Carl W. von Bernuth,* Genl. Counsel; I.J. Evans.
**Number of staff:** 1 full-time professional; 1 part-time professional; 1 full-time support.
EIN: 136406825
**Recent grants for library/information services:**
**360-1** Council Bluffs Library Foundation, Council Bluffs, IA, $10,000. Toward construction of new facility. 1998.
**360-2** Fort Worth Public Library Foundation, Fort Worth, TX, $10,000. Toward expansion of facility. 1998.
**360-3** Marylhurst University, Lake Oswego, OR, $10,000. To broaden collections at Shoen Library. 1998.
**360-4** Pennsylvania State University, University Park, PA, $20,000. For library services and programs. 1998.
**360-5** Westminster College, Salt Lake City, UT, $20,000. Toward construction of new library and for scholarship aid. 1998.

---

# NEVADA

---

## 361
**Bing Fund Corporation ▼**
990 N. Sierra St.
Reno, NV 89503
*Contact:* Peter S. Bing, Pres.
*Additional address:* 9700 W. Pico Blvd., Los Angeles, CA 90035

Incorporated in 1977 in NV as partial successor to Bing Fund, Inc., incorporated in NY.
**Donor(s):** Leo S. Bing,‡ Anna Bing Arnold, Peter S. Bing.
**Grantmaker type:** Independent foundation
**Financial data** (yr. ended 05/31/99): Assets, $59,632,077 (M); gifts received, $1,011,488; expenditures, $2,258,577; qualifying distributions, $2,225,732; giving activities include $2,218,120 for 22 grants (high: $500,000; low: $12,120).
**Purpose and activities:** Giving primarily for higher education, museums, the arts, secondary education, hospitals, and family planning.
**Fields of interest:** Museums; arts/cultural programs; secondary school/education; higher education; hospitals (general); family planning.
**Limitations:** Applications not accepted. No grants for individual.
**Application information:** Contributes only to pre-selected organizations.
**Officers and Trustees:*** Peter S. Bing,* Pres. and Treas.; Robert D. Burch,* V.P. and Secy.
EIN: 942476169
**Recent grants for library/information services:**
**361-1** Huntington Library, Art Collections and Botanical Gardens, San Marino, CA, $150,000. For general support. 1999.
**361-2** Huntington Library, Art Collections and Botanical Gardens, San Marino, CA, $60,000. For The Children's Garden. 1999.
**361-3** Huntington Library, Art Collections and Botanical Gardens, San Marino, CA, $12,120. For exhibit, Votes for Women. 1999.

## 362
**The Geomar Foundation, Inc.**
c/o Wayne, Mortimer, et al.
4950 Kietzke Ln., Ste. 302
Reno, NV 89509

Established in 1989 in NV as successor to the Geomar Foundation, established in NY.
**Donor(s):** George T. Scharffenberger.
**Grantmaker type:** Independent foundation
**Financial data** (yr. ended 12/31/99): Assets, $3,415,607 (M); expenditures, $223,492; qualifying distributions, $221,971; giving activities include $220,615 for 98 grants (high: $100,000; low: $25).
**Purpose and activities:** Giving primarily for education; support also for hospitals and health services.
**Fields of interest:** Higher education; libraries/library science; hospitals (general).
**Limitations:** Applications not accepted. No grants to individuals.
**Application information:** Contributes only to pre-selected organizations.
**Officers:** George T. Scharffenberger, Pres.; Marion A. Scharffenberger, Secy.
EIN: 350677888

## 363
**Bill and Moya Lear Charitable Foundation**
P.O. Box 61000
Reno, NV 89570
*Contact:* Moya Olsen Lear, Tr.

Established in 1996 in NV.
**Donor(s):** Moya Olsen Lear.
**Grantmaker type:** Independent foundation

**Financial data** (yr. ended 12/31/97): Assets, $769,934 (M); gifts received, $498,538; expenditures, $425,146; qualifying distributions, $422,871; giving activities include $411,055 for 35 grants (high: $60,000; low: $1,500).
**Purpose and activities:** Giving primarily for arts and education.
**Fields of interest:** Museums; performing arts; elementary/secondary education; higher education; libraries/library science; health care.
**Limitations:** Giving primarily in NV.
**Application information:**
*Deadline(s):* None
**Trustees:** Harold J. Hertzberg, Moya Olsen Lear, Moya Tsatsos.
**EIN:** 880368716

## 364
### E. L. Wiegand Foundation ▼
Wiegand Ctr.
165 W. Liberty St., Ste. 200
Reno, NV  89501   (775) 333-0310
*Contact:* Kristen A. Avansino, Pres. and Exec. Dir.

Established in 1982 in NV.
**Donor(s):** Ann K. Wiegand,‡ Edwin L. Wiegand.‡
**Grantmaker type:** Independent foundation
**Financial data** (yr. ended 10/31/99): Assets, $117,212,348 (M); expenditures, $5,656,581; qualifying distributions, $5,196,867; giving activities include $4,660,907 for 76 grants (high: $350,000; low: $200; average: $10,000–$100,000).
**Purpose and activities:** The foundation makes grants primarily to develop and strengthen programs and projects: at educational institutions in the academic areas of science, business, fine arts, law, and medicine; and at health institutions in the areas of heart, eye, and cancer surgery, treatment and research, with priority given to programs and projects that benefit children. Emphasis on Roman Catholic institutions.
**Fields of interest:** Visual arts; museums; performing arts; theater; music; arts/cultural programs; elementary school/education; secondary school/education; higher education; business school/education; law school/education; medical school/education; education; hospitals (general); health care; health associations; cancer; eye diseases; heart & circulatory diseases; medical research; cancer research; eye research; heart & circulatory research; chemistry; physics; biological sciences; public affairs; Roman Catholic agencies & churches.
**Types of support:** Equipment; program development.
**Limitations:** Giving primarily in NV and adjoining western states, including AZ, CA (north of Ventura County), ID, OR, UT and WA; public affairs grants given primarily in CA, Washington, DC, and New York, NY. No support for organizations receiving significant support from the United Way or public tax funds; organizations with beneficiaries of their own choosing; or federal, state, or local government agencies or institutions. No grants to individuals, or for endowment funds, fundraising campaigns, debt reductions, emergency funding, film or media presentations, or operating funds; no loans.

**Publications:** Informational brochure (including application guidelines).
**Application information:** An informational booklet outlining the foundation's grant criteria is available on request. Application form required.
*Initial approach:* Letter
*Copies of proposal:* 1
*Deadline(s):* None
*Board meeting date(s):* Feb., June, and Oct.
*Final notification:* Within 15 days of meeting at which application is reviewed
**Officers and Trustees:\*** Raymond C. Avansino, Jr.,\* Chair.; Kristen A. Avansino, Pres. and Exec. Dir.; Michael J. Melarkey, V.P. and Secy.; James T. Carrico, Treas.; Frank J. Fahrenkopf, Jr., Harvey C. Fruehauf, Jr., Mario J. Gabelli.
**Number of staff:** None.
**EIN:** 942839372
**Recent grants for library/information services:**
**364-1** Pontifical North American College, Princeton, NJ, $103,000. For library computerization. 1998.
**364-2** Saint Patrick Seminary, Menlo Park, CA, $138,000. For library conversion. 1998.
**364-3** University of San Francisco, School of Law, San Francisco, CA, $250,000. For library project. 1998.

# NEW HAMPSHIRE

## 365
### Lane & Elizabeth C. Dwinnell Foundation
c/o Fleet Investment Svcs.
1155 Elm St., MS NHNA-E03E
Manchester, NH  03101

Established in 1997.
**Grantmaker type:** Independent foundation
**Financial data** (yr. ended 12/31/98): Assets, $3,719,922 (M); gifts received, $69,764; expenditures, $265,091; qualifying distributions, $245,872; giving activities include $225,000 for 11 grants (high: $50,000; low: $5,000).
**Purpose and activities:** Giving primarily for education and social services.
**Fields of interest:** Higher education; libraries/library science; substance abuse, treatment; mental health, residential care; human services, special populations; community development.
**Limitations:** Applications not accepted.
**Application information:** Contributes only to pre-selected organizations.
**Trustee:** Fleet Bank, N.A.
**EIN:** 161543787

## 366
### Saul O. Sidore Memorial Foundation
24 Gage Rd.
Bedford, NH  03110-5615
*Contact:* Ralph P. Sidore, Treas.

Established in 1968 in NH.
**Grantmaker type:** Independent foundation
**Financial data** (yr. ended 12/31/98): Assets, $1,481,494 (M); gifts received, $635; expenditures, $76,651; qualifying distributions,

$75,731; giving activities include $75,904 for 39 grants (high: $12,500; low: $50).
**Purpose and activities:** Giving to community and human service organizations and for education.
**Fields of interest:** Libraries/library science; education; youth development, adult and child programs; children & youth, services; foundations (community).
**Types of support:** Seed money; curriculum development.
**Limitations:** Giving primarily in NH. No grants to individuals.
**Application information:** Application form not required.
*Initial approach:* Letter
*Copies of proposal:* 1
*Deadline(s):* Mar. 31 or Sept. 30
*Board meeting date(s):* May-June and Nov.-Dec.
**Officers and Trustees:\*** Sara Mae Berman,\* Pres.; Jack B. Middleton,\* Secy.; Ralph P. Sidore,\* Treas.; Alexander Berman II, Doria Berman, Micala Sidore, Gabriel Spitz, and 5 additional trustees.
**EIN:** 237124593

# NEW JERSEY

## 367
### The Armour Family Foundation
c/o R.D. Hunter & Co., LLP
1 Mack Centre Dr.
Paramus, NJ  07652-3900

Established in 1981 in DE.
**Donor(s):** George and Frances Armour Foundation, Inc.
**Grantmaker type:** Independent foundation
**Financial data** (yr. ended 03/31/99): Assets, $2,043,792 (M); expenditures, $92,926; qualifying distributions, $72,468; giving activities include $53,425 for 21 grants (high: $10,100; low: $500).
**Purpose and activities:** Giving primarily for arts education, museums, health care and Jewish organizations.
**Fields of interest:** Museums (art); higher education; libraries (public); YM/YWCAs & YM/YWHAs; Jewish federated giving programs.
**Limitations:** Applications not accepted. Giving primarily in FL and NY. No grants to individuals.
**Application information:** Contributes only to pre-selected organizations.
**Officer:** Joan Armour Mendeall, Pres. and Secy.
**Directors:** David Armour, Frederick Sudekum.
**Number of staff:** 1 part-time professional.
**EIN:** 510257055

## 368
### Bildner Family Foundation
(Formerly KSM Foundation)
293 Eisenhower Pkwy., Ste. 150
Livingston, NJ  07039
*Contact:* Allen Bildner, Pres.

Established in 1983 in NJ.
**Donor(s):** Allen Bildner, Joan Bildner.

**Grantmaker type:** Independent foundation
**Financial data** (yr. ended 06/30/99): Assets, $9,179,935 (M); expenditures, $1,367,954; qualifying distributions, $1,235,272; giving activities include $1,235,272 for 73 grants (high: $100,000; low: $250).
**Purpose and activities:** Giving primarily for the arts and Jewish organizations.
**Fields of interest:** Theater; music; arts/cultural programs; higher education; libraries/library science; cancer; medical research; cancer research; food services; human services; Jewish federated giving programs; Jewish agencies & temples.
**Types of support:** Continuing support.
**Limitations:** Giving primarily in NJ and NY. No support for private foundations. No grants to individuals.
**Application information:**
  *Initial approach:* Letter
  *Deadline(s):* None
**Officers:** Allen Bildner, Pres.; Joan Bildner, V.P.
**Number of staff:** None.
**EIN:** 222541254

### 369
### Alonzo F. & Jennie W. Bonsal Foundation, Inc.
2 Hudson Pl.
Hoboken, NJ 07030
*Contact:* Richard I. Bonsal, Pres.

Established in 1943 in NJ.
**Grantmaker type:** Independent foundation
**Financial data** (yr. ended 12/31/99): Assets, $903,560 (M); gifts received, $9,640; expenditures, $89,214; qualifying distributions, $74,565; giving activities include $69,500 for 17 grants (high: $17,000; low: $1,000).
**Purpose and activities:** Giving for education, religion and the arts.
**Fields of interest:** Museums; performing arts; higher education; libraries/library science; hospitals (general); Protestant agencies & churches.
**Types of support:** Continuing support; annual campaigns; scholarship funds.
**Limitations:** Giving primarily in NJ. No grants to individuals directly.
**Application information:**
  *Initial approach:* Letter
**Officers and Directors:*** Richard I. Bonsal,* Pres. and Treas.; Carol Johnson Bald,* V.P.; Julia L. Bonsal,* V.P.; Margaret B. Soleau,* V.P.; John A. Ragucci, Secy.
**EIN:** 136089295

### 370
### Nancy and Herbert Burns Foundation
c/o Dorothy Eccleston
2 Golf Ave.
Maywood, NJ 07607
*Contact:* Nancy Burns, Pres.
*Application address:* 3 Bridle Way, Saddle River, NJ 07458, tel.: (201) 327-0396

Established in 1998 in NJ.
**Donor(s):** Nancy Burns.
**Grantmaker type:** Operating foundation
**Financial data** (yr. ended 12/31/99): Assets, $2,464,159 (M); gifts received, $2,282,069; expenditures, $146,313; qualifying distributions,

$144,000; giving activities include $144,000 for 12 grants (high: $25,000; low: $1,000).
**Purpose and activities:** Giving primarily to libraries, human services and children's services, particularly for food.
**Fields of interest:** Libraries (public); animal welfare; food services; human services; American Red Cross; children, services.
**Types of support:** General/operating support.
**Limitations:** Giving on a national basis. No grants to individuals.
**Application information:**
  *Initial approach:* Proposal
  *Deadline(s):* None
**Officers:** Nancy Burns, Pres.; Dorothy Eccleston, Secy.
**EIN:** 223583333

### 371
### The Cowles Charitable Trust
P.O. Box 219
Rumson, NJ 07760 (732) 936-9826
*Contact:* Gardner Cowles, III, Pres.

Trust established in 1948 in NY.
**Donor(s):** Gardner Cowles.‡
**Grantmaker type:** Independent foundation
**Financial data** (yr. ended 12/31/99): Assets, $20,509,696 (M); expenditures, $1,110,978; qualifying distributions, $794,500; giving activities include $794,500 for 137 grants (high: $45,000; low: $1,000).
**Purpose and activities:** Grants largely for arts and culture, including museums and the performing arts, education, including early childhood, higher, and secondary, hospitals and AIDS programs, social services, including family planning, and community funds.
**Fields of interest:** Visual arts; museums; performing arts; dance; theater; music; historic preservation/historical societies; arts/cultural programs; education, research; education, fund raising; early childhood education; child development, education; secondary school/education; higher education; medical school/education; adult/continuing education; adult education—literacy & basic skills; libraries/library science; reading; education; natural resource conservation & protection; environment; animal welfare; hospitals (general); family planning; health care; substance abuse, services; mental health/crisis services; health associations; cancer; AIDS; medical research; cancer research; AIDS research; food services; youth development, services; human services; children & youth, services; child development, services; family services; hospices; aging, centers & services; women, centers & services; minorities/immigrants, centers & services; homeless, human services; race/intergroup relations; civil rights; federated giving programs; population studies; leadership development; minorities; disabled; aging; women; homeless; general charitable giving.
**Types of support:** General/operating support; continuing support; annual campaigns; capital campaigns; building/renovation; equipment; endowments; emergency funds; program development; professorships; seed money; matching/challenge support.

**Limitations:** Giving primarily along the Eastern Seaboard, with emphasis on FL and NY. No grants to individuals; no loans.
**Publications:** Annual report, application guidelines.
**Application information:** Applications from any organizations submitted more than once every 12 months not considered. Telephone inquiries are not considered. Application form required.
  *Initial approach:* Letter requesting proposal cover sheet and guidelines
  *Copies of proposal:* 8
  *Deadline(s):* Dec. 1, Mar. 1, June 1, and Sept. 1
  *Board meeting date(s):* Jan., Apr., July, and Oct.
  *Final notification:* Within 2 weeks of board meeting
**Officers and Trustees:*** Gardner Cowles III,* Pres.; Mary Croft, Secy.-Treas.; Charles Cowles, Jan Cowles, Lois Cowles Harrison, Lois Eleanor Harrison, Kate Cowles Nichols, Virginia Cowles Schroth.
**Number of staff:** 1 full-time professional.
**EIN:** 136090295

### 372
### Ambrose and Ida Fredrickson Foundation
c/o First Union National Bank
190 River Rd.
Summit, NJ 07901 (908) 598-3576
*Contact:* Andrew Davis, V.P., First Union National Bank
*FAX:* (908) 598-3582

Established in 1988 in NJ.
**Donor(s):** Ambrose Fredrickson,‡ Ida Fredrickson.‡
**Grantmaker type:** Independent foundation
**Financial data** (yr. ended 12/31/99): Assets, $3,127,103 (M); expenditures, $224,292; qualifying distributions, $199,326; giving activities include $204,911 for grants.
**Fields of interest:** Elementary/secondary education; higher education; libraries/library science; hospitals (general).
**Types of support:** General/operating support; capital campaigns; building/renovation; equipment; program development; scholarship funds.
**Limitations:** Giving primarily in NJ.
**Publications:** Application guidelines.
**Application information:** Application form not required.
  *Initial approach:* Proposal
  *Copies of proposal:* 1
  *Deadline(s):* Mar. 1, June 1, Sept. 1, and Dec. 1
  *Board meeting date(s):* Jan., Apr., July, and Oct.
  *Final notification:* 1 month after board meeting
**Trustees:** Frederick A. Coombs, Rosemary M. Karl, Hugo M. Pfaltz, Richard G. Ranck, First Union National Bank.
**EIN:** 226422114

### 373
### The Raymond V. & Gladys H. Gilmartin Foundation, Inc.
c/o Raymond V. Gilmartin
308 Chelsea Manor
Park Ridge, NJ 07656

Established in 1997 in NJ.

**Donor(s):** Richard V. Gilmartin.
**Grantmaker type:** Independent foundation
**Financial data** (yr. ended 12/31/99): Assets, $494,448 (M); expenditures, $59,318; qualifying distributions, $59,133; giving activities include $59,133 for 7 grants (high: $25,633; low: $1,000).
**Purpose and activities:** Giving for museums, historical societies, libraries, hospitals, and youth programs.
**Fields of interest:** Museums; historical activities; libraries/library science; hospitals (general); children & youth, services.
**Limitations:** Applications not accepted. Giving primarily in NJ. No grants to individuals.
**Application information:** Contributes only to pre-selected organizations.
**Trustees:** Beth Gilmartin, Gladys H. Gilmartin, John Gilmartin, Raymond V. Gilmartin, Sara Gilmartin.
**EIN:** 223513913

## 374
## Heidtke Foundation, Inc.
c/o Brian J. Heidtke
585 Sparrowbush Rd.
Wyckoff, NJ   07481

Established in 1997.
**Donor(s):** Brian J. Heidtke.
**Grantmaker type:** Independent foundation
**Financial data** (yr. ended 12/31/99): Assets, $3,238,151 (M); gifts received, $659,703; expenditures, $349,147; qualifying distributions, $340,700; giving activities include $340,700 for grants (high: $148,000).
**Purpose and activities:** Giving for education and art and cultural programs.
**Fields of interest:** Theater; elementary/secondary education; higher education; libraries (special); boys & girls clubs.
**Limitations:** Applications not accepted. Giving primarily in Washington, DC, NJ, and NY. No grants to individuals.
**Application information:** Contributes only to pre-selected organizations.
**Officers:** Brian J. Heidtke, Pres.; Elizabeth Heidtke, V.P.; Darlene A. Heidtke, Secy.-Treas.
**EIN:** 223512499

## 375
## The International Foundation
170 Changebridge Rd., No. C5-4
Montville, NJ   07045   (973) 227-6107
*Contact:* Dr. Edward A. Holmes, Grants Chair.
*Additional tel.:* (971) 227-6618; FAX: (973) 227-6821

Incorporated in 1948 in DE.
**Grantmaker type:** Independent foundation
**Financial data** (yr. ended 12/31/99): Assets, $40,112,593 (M); expenditures, $1,799,988; qualifying distributions, $1,464,709; giving activities include $1,223,715 for 86 grants (high: $30,000; low: $1,615).
**Purpose and activities:** Giving to help people of developing nations in their endeavors to solve some of their problems, to attain a better standard of living, and to obtain a reasonable degree of self-sufficiency. Grants are made in general areas: 1) Agriculture: research and production, 2) Health: medical, nutrition, and

water, 3) Education: formal at all levels research, 4) Social Development: cultural, economic, community, and entrepreneurial activity, and some aid to refugees, and grants for population planning are given, and 5) Environment.
**Fields of interest:** Arts/cultural programs; libraries/library science; education; natural resource conservation & protection; environment; hospitals (general); medical care, rehabilitation; health care; health associations; AIDS; biomedicine; medical research; AIDS research; agriculture; food services; human services; international economic development; urban/community development; rural development; voluntarism promotion; marine science; engineering & technology; science; Roman Catholic agencies & churches.
**International interests:** Caribbean; Southern Africa; Latin America; Oceania; Middle East; Philippines.
**Types of support:** Building/renovation; equipment; emergency funds; program development; publication; seed money.
**Limitations:** Giving primarily in Asia, the Caribbean, Latin America, the Middle East, the Philippines, the South Pacific, and Southern Africa through U.S.-based philanthropies. No grants to individuals, or for endowment funds, operating budgets, scholarships, fellowships, matching gifts, video productions, or conferences; no loans.
**Publications:** Informational brochure (including application guidelines).
**Application information:** Application should include a SASE for reply. Application form required.
*Initial approach:* Letter requesting descriptive brochure
*Copies of proposal:* 2
*Deadline(s):* None
*Board meeting date(s):* Jan., Apr., July, and Oct.
*Final notification:* 6 months; grants paid in Dec.
**Officers and Trustees:** Edward A. Holmes,* Grants Chair.; Gary Dicovitsky, Finance Chair; Frank Madden,* Pres.; David S. Bate,* V.P.; John D. Carrico,* Secy.-Treas.; Duncan W. Clark, M.D., William McCormack, M.D.
**Number of staff:** 1 part-time professional; 1 part-time support.
**EIN:** 131962255

## 376
## Barbara Piasecka Johnson Foundation
c/o Danser Balaam & Frank
5 Independence Way
Princeton, NJ   08540
*Contact:* Beata Piasecka, Secy.

Established in 1976 in DE.
**Donor(s):** Barbara Piasecka Johnson, J. Seward Johnson, Sr.‡
**Grantmaker type:** Independent foundation
**Financial data** (yr. ended 12/31/98): Assets, $451,240 (M); gifts received, $1,500; expenditures, $74,010; qualifying distributions, $73,063; giving activities include $60,700 for 12 grants (high: $20,000; low: $70).
**Purpose and activities:** To support institutions which promote human rights in Poland, promote institutions of Polish character in the U.S. and abroad, and support artists and scientists, primarily those who are Polish or of

Polish extraction, and institutions which support such individuals.
**Fields of interest:** Journalism & publishing; visual arts; museums; performing arts; language & linguistics; literature; arts/cultural programs; higher education; medical school/education; adult/continuing education; libraries/library science; education; natural resource conservation & protection; environment; heart & circulatory diseases; medical research; heart & circulatory research; human rights (international); international affairs; civil rights; engineering & technology; biological sciences; science; international studies; religion; economically disadvantaged; general charitable giving.
**International interests:** Monaco; Poland.
**Limitations:** Giving to organizations for the benefit of Poland.
**Publications:** Application guidelines.
**Application information:** Contributes only to pre-selected organizations; unsolicited requests not considered. Scholarships and fellowships are for graduate, doctoral and postgraduate education only; no undergraduate programs considered. Application form required.
*Initial approach:* Letter or telephone
*Copies of proposal:* 1
*Deadline(s):* Mar. 30 and Sept. 1; all considered within 3-month basis
*Board meeting date(s):* July
**Officers and Trustees:** Barbara Piasecka Johnson,* Chair.; Beata P. Piasecka,* Secy.; Christopher Piasecki,* Treas.; Wojciech Piasecki.
**Number of staff:** 1 part-time professional; 1 part-time support.
**EIN:** 510201795

## 377
## The Lebensfeld Foundation
c/o VIS, Inc.
15 Exchange Pl.
Jersey City, NJ   07302-3912
*Contact:* Joseph F. Arrigo, Secy.-Treas.

Incorporated in 1959 in NY.
**Donor(s):** Harry Lebensfeld Revocable Trust.
**Grantmaker type:** Independent foundation
**Financial data** (yr. ended 08/31/99): Assets, $40,703,388 (M); gifts received, $10,771,579; expenditures, $2,483,994; qualifying distributions, $2,413,609; giving activities include $2,432,500 for 83 grants (high: $500,000; low: $250; average: $1,000–$100,000).
**Purpose and activities:** Giving primarily for health care and to health associations.
**Fields of interest:** Arts/cultural programs; elementary/secondary education; higher education; libraries/library science; education; hospitals (general); health associations; federated giving programs; Roman Catholic agencies & churches.
**Limitations:** Giving primarily in NY and PA. No grants to individuals.
**Application information:** Application form not required.
*Deadline(s):* None
**Officers and Directors:** Andrew G. Pietrini,* Pres.; Edward Brodsky,* V.P.; Joseph F. Arrigo,* Secy.-Treas.; Brian McDonnell.
**EIN:** 136086169

## 378
## Nicholas Martini Foundation
777 Passaic Ave.
Clifton, NJ 07012
*FAX:* (973) 890-1477

Established in 1986 in NJ.
**Donor(s):** Nicholas Martini.‡
**Grantmaker type:** Independent foundation
**Financial data** (yr. ended 12/31/99): Assets, $15,322,979 (M); expenditures, $635,273; qualifying distributions, $540,805; giving activities include $437,600 for grants (average: $250–$5,000).
**Purpose and activities:** The foundation supports programs in the fields of youth and education, public health and welfare, community development, and arts and humanities programs.
**Fields of interest:** Arts/cultural programs; secondary school/education; higher education; libraries/library science; hospitals (general); youth development, services; human services; children & youth, services.
**Types of support:** General/operating support; matching/challenge support.
**Limitations:** Giving primarily in Bergen, Essex, and Passaic counties, NJ. No grants to individuals.
**Publications:** Annual report, application guidelines.
**Application information:** Application form required.
  *Initial approach:* Letter requesting application form on organization letterhead; phone requests not accepted
  *Copies of proposal:* 1
  *Deadline(s):* Varies
  *Board meeting date(s):* Varies; 2 to 3 meetings per year
  *Final notification:* Varies
**Officer:** William J. Martini, Pres.
**Trustees:** Fannie Rosta, Marie Salanitri.
**EIN:** 222756049

## 379
## PaineWebber Foundation
1000 Harbor Blvd., 9th Fl., Tax Dept.
Weehawken, NJ 07087
*Contact:* Elaine Conte
*Application address:* 1285 Ave. of the Americas, New York, NY 10019

Established in 1973 in NY.
**Donor(s):** PaineWebber Inc.
**Grantmaker type:** Company-sponsored foundation
**Financial data** (yr. ended 12/31/98): Assets, $34,293,825 (M); gifts received, $2,053,828; expenditures, $1,540,805; qualifying distributions, $1,105,000; giving activities include $1,105,000 for 9 grants (high: $300,000; low: $10,000).
**Purpose and activities:** Giving primarily for health care.
**Fields of interest:** Higher education; libraries/library science; health care; cancer; human services.
**Limitations:** Giving primarily in NY. No grants to individuals.
**Application information:**
  *Initial approach:* Typewritten letter
  *Deadline(s):* Dec. 1

**Trustees:** Regina A. Dolan, Donald Marron, Mark Vassallo.
**EIN:** 046032804

## 380
## Rene S. & Rubin Rabinowitz Family Foundation
c/o Rubin Rabinowitz
2 Laurel Ave.
Clifton, NJ 07012-1217

Established in 1990 in NJ.
**Donor(s):** Rubin Rabinowitz, Rene S. Rabinowitz.
**Grantmaker type:** Independent foundation
**Financial data** (yr. ended 12/31/99): Assets, $843,811 (M); expenditures, $88,461; qualifying distributions, $86,862; giving activities include $86,862 for 19 grants (high: $40,000; low: $100).
**Purpose and activities:** Giving for Jewish federated giving programs, education, women's services and civil rights.
**Fields of interest:** Elementary/secondary education; higher education; libraries/library science; human services; Jewish federated giving programs; Jewish agencies & temples.
**Types of support:** Annual campaigns; capital campaigns.
**Limitations:** Applications not accepted. Giving primarily in NJ and New York, NY. No grants to individuals.
**Application information:** Contributes only to pre-selected organizations.
**Trustees:** Rene S. Rabinowitz, Rubin Rabinowitz.
**EIN:** 223111538

## 381
## D. M. Robb Private Foundation
(Formerly The D. M. Robb Charitable Trust)
c/o Merrill Lynch Trust Co.
P.O. Box 30531, Tax 2W
New Brunswick, NJ 08989-0531

Established in 1998 in TX.
**Donor(s):** D.M. Robb.
**Grantmaker type:** Independent foundation
**Financial data** (yr. ended 12/31/98): Assets, $3,111,461 (M); expenditures, $259,828; qualifying distributions, $203,396; giving activities include $199,121 for 4 grants (high: $85,470; low: $18,440).
**Purpose and activities:** Giving primarily to a Methodist church, as well as for scholarships and a library fund in Electra, TX.
**Fields of interest:** Libraries/library science; scholarships/financial aid; community development; Protestant agencies & churches.
**Limitations:** Applications not accepted. Giving primarily in Electra, TX. No grants to individuals.
**Application information:** Contributes only to pre-selected organizations.
**Trustee:** Merrill Lynch Trust Co. of Texas.
**EIN:** 223571387

## 382
## The Arnold A. Schwartz Foundation
c/o Bivona, Cohen, Kunzman, et al.
15 Mountain Blvd.
Warren, NJ 07059-6327
*Contact:* Edwin D. Kunzman, Pres.

Incorporated in 1953 in NJ.
**Donor(s):** Arnold A. Schwartz.‡
**Grantmaker type:** Independent foundation
**Financial data** (yr. ended 11/30/98): Assets, $7,995,784 (M); expenditures, $332,449; qualifying distributions, $300,074; giving activities include $287,370 for 54 grants (high: $20,000; low: $500; average: $1,000–$5,000).
**Purpose and activities:** Giving primarily for health and human services.
**Fields of interest:** Visual arts; performing arts; libraries/library science; hospitals (general); heart & circulatory diseases; AIDS; heart & circulatory research; AIDS research; housing/shelter, development; children & youth, services; children, services; child development, services; family services; aging, centers & services; homeless, human services; urban/community development; community development; voluntarism promotion; minorities; disabled; aging; homeless; general charitable giving.
**Types of support:** General/operating support; continuing support; annual campaigns; capital campaigns; building/renovation; equipment; program development; scholarship funds; research; matching/challenge support.
**Limitations:** Giving primarily in Middlesex, Somerset, and Union counties, NJ. No support for religious purposes. No grants to individuals, or for endowment funds; no loans.
**Publications:** Application guidelines.
**Application information:** Application form required.
  *Initial approach:* Letter
  *Copies of proposal:* 2
  *Deadline(s):* Applications accepted between Apr. 1 and Aug. 1
  *Board meeting date(s):* Feb., June, Sept., and Nov.
  *Final notification:* Nov. 30
**Officers and Trustees:*** Edwin D. Kunzman,* Pres.; Louis Harding,* V.P.; Steven Kunzman,* Secy.-Treas.; Victor DiLeo, David Lackland, Robert Shapiro, Kenneth Turnbull.
**EIN:** 226034152

## 383
## The Stern Family Foundation
(Formerly Leonard N. Stern Foundation)
c/o F. Roscitt
400 Plaza Dr.
Secaucus, NJ 07094-3688

Established in 1963 in NY.
**Donor(s):** Leonard N. Stern, Hartz Mountain Industries, Inc.
**Grantmaker type:** Independent foundation
**Financial data** (yr. ended 12/31/98): Assets, $22,861 (M); gifts received, $525,000; expenditures, $507,222; qualifying distributions, $507,222; giving activities include $505,072 for 23 grants (high: $125,000; low: $1,000).
**Purpose and activities:** Giving primarily for wildlife conservation; also giving for health and human services.

**Fields of interest:** Elementary/secondary education; libraries (public); zoos/zoological societies; health associations; human services; Jewish federated giving programs; Jewish agencies & temples.
**Types of support:** General/operating support; continuing support; building/renovation; equipment; program development; seed money; matching/challenge support.
**Limitations:** Applications not accepted. Giving primarily in the metropolitan New York, NY, area. No grants to individuals.
**Application information:** Contributes only to pre-selected organizations.
**Officers and Directors:*** Leonard N. Stern,* Pres.; Edward Stern,* V.P.; Emanuel Stern,* V.P.; Curtis Schwartz, Secy.-Treas.
**Number of staff:** 1 full-time professional; 1 full-time support.
**EIN:** 136149990

### 384
### Otto H. York Foundation, Inc.
130 Hempstead Ct.
Madison, NJ 07940 (973) 765-9352
*Contact:* Otto H. York, Pres.

Established in 1985.
**Grantmaker type:** Independent foundation
**Financial data** (yr. ended 02/28/99): Assets, $2,948,176 (M); expenditures, $95,790; qualifying distributions, $95,000; giving activities include $95,000 for 20 grants (high: $67,000; low: $1,000).
**Purpose and activities:** Giving for education, hospitals, human services and the disabled.
**Fields of interest:** University; libraries/library science; hospitals (general); human services; disabled.
**Limitations:** Giving primarily in NJ and RI. No grants to individuals.
**Application information:** Application form not required.
*Initial approach:* Letter
*Deadline(s):* None
**Officers:** Otto H. York, Pres.; Myrth York, V.P.
**EIN:** 225154083

# NEW MEXICO

### 385
### McCune Charitable Foundation ▼
(Formerly Marshall L. & Perrine D. McCune Charitable Foundation)
345 E. Alameda St.
Santa Fe, NM 87501-2229 (505) 983-8300
*Contact:* Frances R. Sowers, Assoc. Dir.
*FAX:* (505) 983-7887; E-mail: fsowers@trail.com; URL: http://www.nmmccune.org

Established in 1992 in NM.
**Donor(s):** Perrine Dixon McCune,‡ Marshall L. McCune.‡
**Grantmaker type:** Independent foundation
**Financial data** (yr. ended 12/31/98): Assets, $133,250,360 (M); expenditures, $6,869,334; qualifying distributions, $6,414,584; giving

activities include $5,090,941 for 368 grants (high: $100,000; low: $500; average: $5,000–$50,000).
**Purpose and activities:** Primary areas of interest include the arts, education, youth, health, social services and environment.
**Fields of interest:** Visual arts; museums; performing arts; dance; theater; music; history & archaeology; historic preservation/historical societies; arts/cultural programs; early childhood education; child development, education; elementary school/education; secondary school/education; vocational education; higher education; adult/continuing education; adult education—literacy & basic skills; libraries/library science; reading; education; natural resource conservation & protection; environment; animal welfare; wildlife preservation & protection; hospitals (general); family planning; medical care, rehabilitation; health care; substance abuse, services; mental health/crisis services; health associations; cancer; heart & circulatory diseases; AIDS; alcoholism; delinquency prevention/services; crime/law enforcement; employment; agriculture; food services; nutrition; housing/shelter, development; youth development, services; youth development, citizenship; human services; children & youth, services; child development, services; family services; hospices; aging, centers & services; women, centers & services; minorities/immigrants, centers & services; homeless, human services; rural development; community development; federated giving programs; public affairs, citizen participation; leadership development; public affairs; minorities; Native Americans; disabled; aging; women; gays/lesbians; economically disadvantaged; homeless.
**Types of support:** General/operating support; continuing support; annual campaigns; building/renovation; equipment; emergency funds; program development; conferences/seminars; seed money; scholarship funds; technical assistance; matching/challenge support.
**Limitations:** Giving limited to NM. No grants to individuals, or for endowments, research or voter registration drives.
**Publications:** Biennial report, application guidelines.
**Application information:** Contact foundation for current cycle dates for initial approach and deadlines; submissions received by FAX not accepted. Application form required.
*Initial approach:* Letter of inquiry ( no more than 2 pages)
*Copies of proposal:* 1
*Deadline(s):* Changes annually
*Board meeting date(s):* Changes annually
*Final notification:* Changes annually
**Officers and Directors:*** Sarah McCune Losinger,* Chair.; Owen M. Lopez, Exec. Dir.; Frances Sowers, Assoc. Dir.; James M. Edwards, John R. McCune VI.
**Number of staff:** 1 full-time professional; 1 full-time support.
**EIN:** 850429439
**Recent grants for library/information services:**
385-1 Columbus, Village of, Columbus, NM, $12,000. For operating support for community library. 1998.

385-2 Las Clinicas del Norte, El Rito, NM, $15,000. For operating support for El Rito Library. 1998.
385-3 North American Institute, Santa Fe, NM, $10,000. To establish library on North American public policy issues. 1998.
385-4 Saint Michaels High School, Santa Fe, NM, $12,000. To automate card catalogue, network with library's media center and expand collection. 1998.

# NEW YORK

### 386
### Louis and Anne Abrons Foundation, Inc. ▼
c/o First Manhattan Co.
437 Madison Ave.
New York, NY 10017 (212) 756-3376
*Contact:* Richard Abrons, Pres.

Incorporated in 1950 in NY.
**Donor(s):** Anne S. Abrons,‡ Louis Abrons.‡
**Grantmaker type:** Independent foundation
**Financial data** (yr. ended 12/31/99): Assets, $42,552,755 (M); expenditures, $3,336,399; qualifying distributions, $3,227,200; giving activities include $3,217,550 for 176 grants (high: $200,000; low: $750; average: $5,000–$60,000).
**Purpose and activities:** Giving primarily to social welfare agencies, Jewish charities, major New York, NY, institutions, civic improvement programs, education, and environmental and cultural projects.
**Fields of interest:** Museums; arts/cultural programs; dental school/education; libraries/library science; education; environment; hospitals (general); family planning; legal services; employment; human services; children & youth, services; family services; aging, centers & services; minorities/immigrants, centers & services; community development; Jewish agencies & temples; African Americans; aging; economically disadvantaged; homeless.
**Types of support:** Continuing support; annual campaigns; building/renovation; program development; scholarship funds; research; technical assistance; consulting services; program-related investments/loans.
**Limitations:** Applications not accepted. Giving primarily in the metropolitan New York, NY, area. No grants to individuals.
**Application information:** Contributes only to pre-selected organizations. Telephone calls not accepted. Unsolicited applications not considered or acknowledged.
*Board meeting date(s):* Feb., June, and Oct.
**Officers and Directors:*** Richard Abrons,* Pres.; Herbert L. Abrons,* V.P.; Rita Aranow,* V.P.; Anne Abrons,* Secy.-Treas.; Alix Abrons, Henry Abrons, John Abrons, Leslie Abrons, Peter Abrons, Judith Aranow, Vicki Feiner.
**Number of staff:** None.
**EIN:** 136061329
**Recent grants for library/information services:**
386-1 New York Public Library, NYC, NY, $30,000. 1998.

**387**

**Acorn Foundation, Inc.**
c/o The Bank of New York
1 Wall St., 28th Fl., Tax Dept.
New York, NY 10286
*Contact:* Grace K. Culbertson, Pres.
*Application address:* P.O. Box 47, Green Village,
NJ 07935, tel.: (973) 267-1742

Established in 1992 in NJ.
**Donor(s):** Grace K. Culbertson, John H.
Culbertson, Jr., Marian C. Hvolbeck, Katherine
C. Prentice.
**Grantmaker type:** Independent foundation
**Financial data** (yr. ended 12/31/98): Assets,
$2,201,315 (M); gifts received, $62,674;
expenditures, $87,538; qualifying distributions,
$64,318; giving activities include $68,135 for
33 grants (high: $6,000; low: $25).
**Fields of interest:** Arts/cultural programs;
libraries/library science; education; hospitals
(general); family planning; cancer; hospices.
**Limitations:** Giving primarily in New York, NY.
**Application information:** Application form not
required.
  *Initial approach:* Letter
  *Deadline(s):* None
**Officers:** Grace K. Culbertson, Pres.; Marian C.
Hvolbeck, V.P.; Katherine C. Prentice, Secy.;
John H. Culbertson, Jr., Treas.
**EIN:** 223079659

**388**

**Louis and Bessie Adler Foundation, Inc.**
654 Madison Ave., 14th Fl.
New York, NY 10021
*Contact:* Robert Liberman, Chair.

Incorporated in 1946 in NY.
**Donor(s):** Louis Adler,‡ Louis Adler Realty Co.,
Inc.
**Grantmaker type:** Independent foundation
**Financial data** (yr. ended 12/31/99): Assets,
$2,289,918 (M); expenditures, $179,361;
qualifying distributions, $170,925; giving
activities include $160,000 for 5 grants (high:
$70,000; low: $10,000).
**Purpose and activities:** Giving for education, the
arts, and foundations.
**Fields of interest:** Performing arts;
elementary/secondary education;
libraries/library science; libraries (public);
hospitals (general); cancer research.
**Limitations:** Applications not accepted. Giving
primarily in New York, NY. No grants to
individuals.
**Officers:** Robert Liberman, Chair. and Secy.;
Louise Grunwald, Pres. and Treas.; Barbara
Liberman, V.P.; Robert Savitt, V.P.
**EIN:** 131880122

**389**

**Agrilink Foods/Pro-Fac Foundation**
(Formerly Curtice-Burns/Pro-Fac Foundation)
P.O. Box 20670
90 Linden Oaks
Rochester, NY 14602-0670 (716) 383-1850
*Contact:* Susan C. Riker, Secy. and Tr.
*URL:* http://www.agrilinkfoods.com/corp/about/
community/index.html

Trust established in 1966 in NY.

**Donor(s):** Agrilink Foods, Inc.
**Grantmaker type:** Company-sponsored
foundation
**Financial data** (yr. ended 06/26/99): Assets,
$60,698 (M); gifts received, $150,000;
expenditures, $239,145; qualifying distributions,
$238,863; giving activities include $238,209 for
177 grants (high: $26,000; low: $100; average:
$500–$5,000).
**Purpose and activities:** Primary areas of interest
include community funds, agriculture, and
youth and child development and welfare.
Emphasis on education, including higher
education, building and scholarship funds,
literacy and programs for minorities, and
libraries; health agencies, hospital building
funds, hospices, medical research, drug abuse
and alcoholism, and rehabilitation; human
services, including women, the elderly,
minorities, the handicapped and the
disadvantaged, and housing; community
development; and cultural programs including
the fine and performing arts.
**Fields of interest:** Visual arts; museums;
performing arts; theater; arts/cultural programs;
education, fund raising; early childhood
education; child development, education;
higher education; adult education—literacy &
basic skills; libraries/library science; reading;
education; environment; hospitals (general);
family planning; medical care, rehabilitation;
health care; substance abuse, services; mental
health/crisis services; health associations;
alcoholism; medical research; agriculture;
housing/shelter, development; human services;
children & youth, services; child development,
services; hospices; minorities/immigrants,
centers & services; homeless, human services;
community development; voluntarism
promotion; federated giving programs;
minorities; disabled; economically
disadvantaged; homeless; general charitable
giving.
**Types of support:** General/operating support;
continuing support; annual campaigns; capital
campaigns; building/renovation; equipment;
endowments; program development;
conferences/seminars; professorships;
fellowships; scholarship funds; research.
**Limitations:** Giving primarily in areas of
company operations. No support for religious or
political organizations. No grants to individuals,
or for seed money, emergency funds, deficit
financing, land acquisition, matching gifts, or
publications; no loans.
**Application information:** Application form not
required.
  *Initial approach:* Proposal
  *Copies of proposal:* 1
  *Deadline(s):* None
  *Board meeting date(s):* Usually in Jan., Mar.,
  June, Aug., and Nov.
**Officers and Trustees:*** Paul Roe,* Chair.; Susan
C. Riker,* Secy.; Virginia Ford, William Rice.
**Number of staff:** 1 part-time support.
**EIN:** 166071142

**390**

**Joseph Alexander Foundation**
400 Madison Ave., Ste. 906
New York, NY 10017 (212) 355-3688

Established in 1960 in NY.

**Donor(s):** Joseph Alexander.‡
**Grantmaker type:** Independent foundation
**Financial data** (yr. ended 10/31/98): Assets,
$17,948,849 (M); expenditures, $905,783;
qualifying distributions, $880,962; giving
activities include $727,500 for 65 grants (high:
$50,000; low: $1,000).
**Purpose and activities:** Giving primarily for
education, including libraries, law and medical
schools, and other higher education; health,
especially the medical sciences and research,
AIDS programs, the elderly and hospices,
cancer care, scientific organizations, and
hospitals; museums and other arts groups; and
Israel, and Jewish welfare and religious
organizations.
**Fields of interest:** Museums; arts/cultural
programs; higher education; law
school/education; medical school/education;
libraries/library science; education; hospitals
(general); health care; health associations;
cancer; AIDS; biomedicine; medical research;
cancer research; AIDS research; human services;
hospices; aging, centers & services; Jewish
federated giving programs; chemistry;
engineering & technology; biological sciences;
science; Jewish agencies & temples; religion;
aging.
**International interests:** Israel.
**Types of support:** General/operating support;
annual campaigns; capital campaigns;
building/renovation; equipment; endowments;
program development; conferences/seminars;
curriculum development; scholarship funds;
research; exchange programs.
**Limitations:** Giving primarily in the continental
U.S., with emphasis on New York, NY; some
giving also in Israel. No grants to individuals.
**Publications:** Financial statement.
**Application information:** Application form not
required.
  *Initial approach:* Proposal
  *Copies of proposal:* 1
  *Deadline(s):* Submit proposal preferably in
  Feb. through Aug.
  *Board meeting date(s):* Jan., Apr., July, and Oct.
**Officers and Directors:*** Robert M. Weintraub,*
Pres.; Arthur S. Alfert,* V.P.; Helen Mackler,*
Secy.; Harvey A. Mackler.
**EIN:** 510175951

**391**

**Sol and Lillian Ash Foundation, Inc.**
c/o Ed Yelon
420 Lexington Ave., Ste. 2150
New York, NY 10170 (212) 687-6776
*Contact:* Robert Siegel, Pres.

Established in 1959.
**Grantmaker type:** Independent foundation
**Financial data** (yr. ended 12/31/99): Assets,
$2,090,245 (M); expenditures, $97,110;
qualifying distributions, $74,000; giving
activities include $74,000 for 16 grants (high:
$20,000; low: $1,000).
**Purpose and activities:** Giving for Jewish
organizations, museums, and cultural centers.
**Fields of interest:** Libraries/library science; boys
clubs; Jewish federated giving programs; Jewish
agencies & temples.
**Limitations:** Giving primarily in the greater New
York, NY, area.
**Application information:**

*Initial approach:* Letter
*Deadline(s):* None
**Officers:** Robert Siegel, Pres.; Edward Yelon, Treas.
**EIN:** 136159050

## 392
### AT&T Foundation ▼
32 Ave. of the Americas, 6th Fl.
New York, NY 10013 (212) 387-4801
*Contact:* Timothy J. McClimon, Exec. Dir.
*FAX:* (212) 387-4882; E-mail:
Mcclimon@att.com; URL: http://www.att.com/
foundation

Established in 1984 in NY.
**Donor(s):** American Telephone and Telegraph
Co., Western Electric Fund, AT&T Corp.
**Grantmaker type:** Company-sponsored
foundation
**Financial data** (yr. ended 12/31/98): Assets,
$81,274,194 (M); gifts received, $36,621,716;
expenditures, $48,508,420; qualifying
distributions, $45,327,214; giving activities
include $42,810,641 for 1,723 grants (high:
$1,000,000; low: $10; average:
$20,000–$100,000) and $3,059,804 for 13,661
employee matching gifts.
**Purpose and activities:** The foundation invests
globally in projects that are at the intersection of
community needs and AT&T's business interests.
Emphasis is placed on programs that serve the
needs of people in communities where AT&T
has a significant business presence; initiatives
that use technology in innovative ways; and
programs that AT&T employees are actively
involved with as contributors and/or volunteers.
**Fields of interest:** Arts, alliance; arts,
multipurpose centers/programs; arts,
cultural/ethnic awareness; arts councils;
media/communications; visual arts; museums;
performing arts; performing arts centers; dance;
music; arts, services; elementary/secondary
education; higher education; teacher
school/education; engineering
school/education; continuing education/lifelong
learning; libraries/library science; education,
community/cooperative; natural resource
conservation & protection; public health; AIDS;
safety/disasters, volunteer services; disasters,
preparedness & services; youth development;
human services; women, centers & services;
international exchange; international affairs;
civil rights; economic development; community
development; philanthropy/voluntarism;
science; public affairs.
**International interests:** Canada; France;
Netherlands; United Kingdom; Germany;
Mexico; Argentina; Brazil; Colombia; Chile;
Peru; India; China; Taiwan; Japan.
**Types of support:** General/operating support;
annual campaigns; emergency funds; program
development; conferences/seminars; curriculum
development; technical assistance; employee
matching gifts; matching/challenge support.
**Limitations:** Applications not accepted. Giving
on a national and international basis, primarily
to Los Angeles and San Francisco, CA; Denver,
CO; Washington, DC; Miami, FL; Chicago, IL;
NJ; NY; Pittsburgh and Philadelphia PA; and
Seattle, WA. No support for religious
organizations for sectarian purposes, political
campaign, or disease-related health associations

other than AIDS-related programs, child care
and elder care centers, sports teams, or
sports-related activities, planetariums, zoos, or
historic buildings or villages. No grants to
individuals, or for capital development,
scholarships endowments, deficit financing,
medical research projects, operating expenses
or capital campaigns of local health or human
service agencies other than hospitals, the
purchase or installation of computers, modems,
printers, telephones, facsimile machines, wiring
or other equipment, construction or renovation,
competitions, or land acquisition; no advertising
or sponsorship purchases or equipment
donations.
**Publications:** Biennial report.
**Application information:** Unsolicited
applications not considered.
*Board meeting date(s):* Monthly
**Officers and Trustees:\*** Richard J. Martin,\*
Chair.; Esther Silver-Parker,\* Pres.; Marilyn
Reznick, V.P., Education Prog.; Suzanne Sato,
V.P., Arts and Culture Prog.; Mitzi Vaimberg,
V.P., Civic and Community Svc. Prog.; Vivian
Nero, Secy.; Robert E. Angelica, Treas.; Timothy
J. McClimon, Exec. Dir.; Harold W. Burlingame,
David Condit, John C. Guerra, Jr., William H.
Oliver, Barbara Peda, Ray Robinson.
**Number of staff:** 9 full-time professional; 3
full-time support.
**EIN:** 133166495
**Recent grants for library/information services:**
**392-1** Americans for the Arts, DC, $35,000.
1999.
**392-2** Brooklyn Public Library, Brooklyn, NY,
$50,000. 1999.
**392-3** Broward Public Library Foundation, Fort
Lauderdale, FL, $10,000. 1999.
**392-4** Charities Aid Foundation, West Malling,
England, $35,000. 1999.
**392-5** Chicago Public Library Foundation,
Chicago, IL, $200,000. 1999.
**392-6** Council for Basic Education, DC,
$130,500. 1999.
**392-7** Filipino American Heritage Institute, Los
Angeles, CA, $10,000. 1999.
**392-8** Indianapolis-Marion County Public
Library Foundation, Indianapolis, IN,
$30,000. 1999.
**392-9** Library of Congress, DC, $300,000. 1999.
**392-10** National Archives, Foundation for the,
DC, $250,000. 1999.
**392-11** Public Library of Charlotte and
Mecklenburg County, Charlotte, NC,
$10,000. 1999.
**392-12** San Jose Public Library Foundation, San
Jose, CA, $22,000. 1999.
**392-13** United States Educational Foundation in
India, New Delhi, India, $20,000. 1999.
**392-14** Westchester Library System, Elmsford,
NY, $21,000. 1999.

## 393
### The B & L Foundation
c/o Bernard Palitz
221 E. 70th St., Box 2520
New York, NY 10021

Established about 1963.
**Donor(s):** Bernard Palitz.
**Grantmaker type:** Independent foundation
**Financial data** (yr. ended 12/31/99): Assets,
$3,888,156 (M); expenditures, $297,060;

qualifying distributions, $199,213; giving
activities include $202,197 for 45 grants (high:
$76,750; low: $25).
**Purpose and activities:** Giving primarily for the
arts and education.
**Fields of interest:** Museums; arts/cultural
programs; higher education; libraries/library
science; Jewish agencies & temples.
**Limitations:** Giving primarily in MA and NY. No
grants to individuals.
**Trustee:** Bernard Palitz.
**EIN:** 136064168

## 394
### The George F. Baker Trust
767 5th Ave., Ste. 2850
New York, NY 10153 (212) 755-1890
*Contact:* Miss Rocio Suarez, Exec. Dir.

Trust established in 1937 in NY.
**Donor(s):** George F. Baker.‡
**Grantmaker type:** Independent foundation
**Financial data** (yr. ended 12/31/98): Assets,
$27,200,479 (M); expenditures, $5,752,887;
qualifying distributions, $5,520,129; giving
activities include $5,095,640 for 84 grants
(high: $2,000,000; low: $1,000; average:
$10,000–$100,000).
**Purpose and activities:** Giving primarily for
higher and secondary education, hospitals,
social services, civic affairs, and religious and
international affairs.
**Fields of interest:** Secondary school/education;
higher education; natural resource conservation
& protection; hospitals (general); human
services; international affairs; government/public
administration; religion.
**Types of support:** General/operating support;
matching/challenge support.
**Limitations:** Giving primarily in the eastern U.S.,
with some emphasis on the New York, NY, area.
No grants to individuals, or for scholarships; no
loans.
**Publications:** Annual report.
**Application information:** Application form not
required.
*Initial approach:* Letter with brief outline of
proposal
*Copies of proposal:* 1
*Deadline(s):* None
*Board meeting date(s):* June and Nov.
*Final notification:* Up to 6 months
**Officer:** Rocio Suarez, Exec. Dir.
**Trustees:** Anthony K. Baker, George F. Baker III,
Kane K. Baker, Citibank, N.A.
**Number of staff:** 1 full-time professional.
**EIN:** 136056818
**Recent grants for library/information services:**
**394-1** Dartmouth College, Hanover, NH,
$2,000,000. Toward renovation of Baker
Library and new Berry Library. 1998.

## 395
### The George Balanchine Foundation, Inc.
161 W. 61st St.
New York, NY 10023-7900 (212) 262-0700
*Contact:* Leslie Hansen Kopp, Genl. Admin.
*FAX:* (212) 262-2892; E-mail:
GeorgeBalanchineFoundation@Balanchine.org

Established in 1983; status changed to a public
charity in 1992.

**Grantmaker type:** Public charity
**Financial data** (yr. ended 12/31/99): Assets, $1,092,575 (M); gifts received, $60,107; expenditures, $274,364; giving activities include $158,344 for grants.
**Fields of interest:** Dance; ballet; archives.
**Publications:** Newsletter, informational brochure.
**Application information:**
   *Initial approach:* Letter
   *Deadline(s):* None
**Officers and Directors:*** Barbara Horgan,* Chair.; Paul H. Epstein,* Pres.; Karin Anny Hannelore Gewirtz,* V.P.; Nancy Reynolds,* Secy.; Lorie Barber,* Treas.
**Number of staff:** 1 full-time professional; 1 part-time professional.
**EIN:** 133180628

### 396
### The Barker Welfare Foundation ▼
P.O. Box 2
Glen Head, NY  11545  (516) 759-5592
*Contact:* Mrs. Sarane H. Ross, Pres.
*FAX:* (516) 759-5497

Incorporated in 1934 in IL.
**Donor(s):** Mrs. Charles V. Hickox.‡
**Grantmaker type:** Independent foundation
**Financial data** (yr. ended 09/30/99): Assets, $66,538,388 (M); expenditures, $3,963,190; qualifying distributions, $3,341,605; giving activities include $3,046,245 for 164 grants (high: $100,000; low: $3,500; average: $7,500–$15,000) and $58,755 for employee matching gifts.
**Purpose and activities:** Grants to established organizations and charitable institutions, with emphasis on youth and families, museums and the fine and performing arts, child welfare and youth agencies, health services and rehabilitation, welfare, aid to the handicapped, family planning, libraries, the environment, recreation, and elderly programs.
**Fields of interest:** Visual arts; museums; arts/cultural programs; libraries/library science; environment; health care; mental health/crisis services; recreation; human services; children & youth, services; disabled.
**Types of support:** General/operating support; continuing support; annual campaigns; building/renovation; equipment.
**Limitations:** Giving primarily in Chicago, IL, Michigan City, IN, and New York, NY. No support for political activities, national health, welfare, or education agencies, institutions or funds. No grants to individuals, or for endowment funds, seed money, emergency funds, deficit financing, scholarships, fellowships, medical or scientific research, films or videos, or conferences; no loans.
**Publications:** Annual report, application guidelines.
**Application information:** Proposals must be completed according to the foundation's guidelines and grants process in order to be considered for funding. Grants to Chicago agencies are by invitation only. Proposals sent by FAX not considered. Application form required.
   *Initial approach:* 2- to 3-page letter of inquiry
   *Copies of proposal:* 2
   *Deadline(s):* Feb. 1 and Aug. 1
   *Board meeting date(s):* May and Nov.

*Final notification:* After board meeting for positive response; any time for negative response
**Officers and Directors:*** Mrs. Sarane H. Ross,* Pres.; Katrina H. Becker,* V.P. and Secy.; Thomas P. McCormick,* Treas.; Diane Curtis, Charles C. Hickox, Danielle A. Hickox, John B. Hickox, Linda J. Hickox, Mary Lou Linnen, Alline Matheson, Sarane R. O'Connor, Alexander B. Ross.
**Number of staff:** 2 full-time professional; 1 part-time support.
**EIN:** 366018526
**Recent grants for library/information services:**
**396-1** Brooklyn Public Library, Brooklyn, NY, $20,000. For Kids Connection Program. 1999.
**396-2** Chicago Public Library Foundation, Chicago, IL, $100,000. For Project MIND: Meeting Information Needs Democratically. 1999.
**396-3** New York Public Library, NYC, NY, $20,000. For page program. 1999.

### 397
### The Birkelund Fund
c/o Barry Strauss Assoc., Ltd.
245 5th Ave., Ste. 1102
New York, NY  10016-8775

Established in 1989 in NY.
**Donor(s):** John P. Birkelund.
**Grantmaker type:** Independent foundation
**Financial data** (yr. ended 04/30/00): Assets, $11,805,727 (M); gifts received, $930,659; expenditures, $761,123; qualifying distributions, $713,885; giving activities include $711,125 for 21 grants (high: $535,000; low: $500).
**Purpose and activities:** Giving primarily for education, including public libraries.
**Fields of interest:** Humanities; higher education; libraries (public); international affairs.
**Limitations:** Applications not accepted. Giving primarily in NJ and NY. No grants to individuals.
**Application information:** Contributes only to pre-selected organizations.
**Officer and Directors:*** John P. Birkelund,* Pres.; Immanuel Kohn.
**EIN:** 133539224

### 398
### Blue Hill Road Foundation, Inc.
c/o Leshkowitz & Co.
270 Madison Ave.
New York, NY  10016
*Contact:* Fred Lee Barber, Pres.
*Application address:* 8 E. 96th St., New York, NY 10028, tel.: (212) 532-5550

Established in 1994 in NY.
**Donor(s):** Fred Lee Barber Co., Inc.
**Grantmaker type:** Independent foundation
**Financial data** (yr. ended 12/31/99): Assets, $1,340,888 (M); gifts received, $186,186; expenditures, $44,017; qualifying distributions, $42,808; giving activities include $42,808 for 9 grants (high: $13,000; low: $1,000).
**Purpose and activities:** Giving primarily for education and hospitals.
**Fields of interest:** University; libraries (public); hospitals (general).
**Limitations:** Giving primarily in NY. No grants to individuals.

**Application information:**
   *Initial approach:* Letter
   *Deadline(s):* None
**Officers:** Fred Lee Barber, Pres.; David Barber, Secy.; Daniel Barber, Treas.
**EIN:** 133799422

### 399
### Madeline and Kevin Brine Charitable Trust
c/o Sanford C. Bernstein & Co., Inc.
767 5th Ave.
New York, NY  10153-0185
*Contact:* Kevin R. Brine, Tr.

Established in 1989 in NY.
**Donor(s):** Madeline Brine, Kevin R. Brine.
**Grantmaker type:** Independent foundation
**Financial data** (yr. ended 12/31/99): Assets, $17,967 (M); gifts received, $1,874,566; expenditures, $1,862,926; qualifying distributions, $1,862,097; giving activities include $1,862,831 for 14 grants (high: $1,025,000; low: $250).
**Purpose and activities:** Giving primarily for the arts, including museums; for leadership programs; and for education.
**Fields of interest:** Museums; elementary/secondary education; higher education; libraries/library science; leadership development.
**Limitations:** Applications not accepted. Giving primarily in New York, NY. No grants to individuals.
**Application information:** Contributes only to pre-selected organizations.
**Trustees:** Kevin R. Brine, Madeline Brine.
**Number of staff:** None.
**EIN:** 133549098

### 400
### Gladys Brooks Foundation
1055 Franklin Ave., Ste. 102
Garden City, NY  11530-5723  (516) 746-6103
*Contact:* Jessica L. Rutledge
*URL:* http://www.gladysbrooksfoundation.org

Established in 1981 in NY.
**Donor(s):** Gladys Brooks Thayer.‡
**Grantmaker type:** Independent foundation
**Financial data** (yr. ended 12/31/98): Assets, $36,709,197 (M); expenditures, $1,661,595; qualifying distributions, $1,482,018; giving activities include $1,247,000 for 23 grants (high: $107,500; low: $5,000; average: $50,000–$100,000).
**Purpose and activities:** The foundation's primary purpose is to provide for the intellectual, moral, and physical welfare of the people of this country by establishing and supporting nonprofit libraries, educational institutions, hospitals, and clinics.
**Fields of interest:** Higher education; libraries/library science; hospitals (general); health care.
**Types of support:** Building/renovation; equipment; endowments; scholarship funds.
**Limitations:** Giving limited to CT, Washington, DC, DE, IN, MA, MD, ME, NC, NH, NJ, NY, OH, PA, RI, SC, VA, VT, and WV. No grants to individuals, or for research.

**Publications:** Annual report (including application guidelines), program policy statement.
**Application information:** Application form required.
>   *Initial approach:* Letter
>   *Copies of proposal:* 2
>   *Deadline(s):* June 19
>   *Board meeting date(s):* Bimonthly
>   *Final notification:* Dec.

**Board of Governors:** Harman Hawkins, Chair.; James J. Daly, Secy.; Thomas Q. Morris, M.D., U.S. Trust Co. of New York.
**Number of staff:** 1 full-time professional.
**EIN:** 132955337

## 401
## Burke Family Foundation

c/o Daniel Burke
20 Island Dr.
Rye, NY   10580-4306

Established in 1997 in NY.
**Donor(s):** Daniel Burke.
**Grantmaker type:** Independent foundation
**Financial data** (yr. ended 12/31/98): Assets, $2,014,595 (M); expenditures, $962,983; qualifying distributions, $962,983; giving activities include $962,983 for 25 grants (high: $200,000; low: $1,500).
**Purpose and activities:** Giving primarily for education and health care.
**Fields of interest:** Elementary school/education; higher education; libraries (public); hospitals (general).
**Limitations:** Applications not accepted. Giving primarily in, but not limited to, Portland, ME, New York, NY, and VT. No grants to individuals.
**Application information:** Contributes only to pre-selected organizations.
**Trustees:** Daniel Burke, Harriet Burke.
**EIN:** 137119979

## 402
## Calf Island Foundation

c/o Bear Stearns Co.
245 Park Ave.
New York, NY   10167
*Contact:* William Jennings, Jr., Pres.

Established in 1987.
**Donor(s):** William M. Jennings, Jr.
**Grantmaker type:** Independent foundation
**Financial data** (yr. ended 01/31/00): Assets, $403,989 (M); gifts received, $46,469; expenditures, $61,570; qualifying distributions, $60,847; giving activities include $61,500 for grants.
**Purpose and activities:** Giving for education and to medical centers.
**Fields of interest:** Libraries (school); museums (history); hospitals (general); girls clubs.
**Types of support:** General/operating support.
**Limitations:** Applications not accepted. Giving limited to NY. No grants to individuals.
**Application information:** Contributes only to pre-selected organizations.
**Officer and Directors:** William Mitchell Jennings, Jr.,* Pres.; Elizabeth B. Dater.
**EIN:** 066304990

## 403
## The Carbetz Foundation, Inc.

c/o U.S. Trust Co. of New York
114 W. 47th St.
New York, NY   10036
*Contact:* Carl H. Pforzheimer III, Pres.
*Application address:* 650 Madison Ave., 23rd Fl., New York, NY 10022

Established in 1987.
**Donor(s):** Elizabeth S. Pforzheimer, Carl H. Pforzheimer III.
**Grantmaker type:** Independent foundation
**Financial data** (yr. ended 12/31/99): Assets, $23,310 (M); gifts received, $195,758; expenditures, $172,354; qualifying distributions, $167,377; giving activities include $167,750 for 24 grants (high: $100,000; low: $500).
**Purpose and activities:** Giving for education, libraries, and health and human services.
**Fields of interest:** Orchestra (symphony); higher education; libraries/library science; health care; human services.
**Limitations:** Giving primarily in New York, NY. No grants to individuals; no loans.
**Application information:**
>   *Initial approach:* Letter
>   *Deadline(s):* None

**Officers:** Carl H. Pforzheimer III, Pres.; Elizabeth S. Pforzheimer, V.P.; Martin F. Richman, Secy.
**EIN:** 133431027

## 404
## Carnegie Corporation of New York ▼

437 Madison Ave.
New York, NY   10022   (212) 371-3200
*Contact:* Edward Sermier, V.P.
*FAX:* (212) 754-4073; *URL:* http://www.carnegie.org

Incorporated in 1911 in NY.
**Donor(s):** Andrew Carnegie.‡
**Grantmaker type:** Independent foundation
**Financial data** (yr. ended 09/30/99): Assets, $1,705,527,531 (M); gifts received, $50,015; expenditures, $70,317,034; qualifying distributions, $61,268,493; giving activities include $49,649,695 for 304 grants (high: $2,051,517; low: $975) and $1,789,771 for 5 foundation-administered programs.
**Purpose and activities:** The advancement and diffusion of knowledge and understanding among the peoples of the U.S. and of certain countries that are or have been members of the British Overseas Commonwealth. The foundation's current program goals are as follows: 1) Education, including teacher education and liberal arts education; 2) International Peace and Security; 3) International Development; and 4) Democracy.
**Fields of interest:** Education, research; early childhood education; child development, education; elementary school/education; secondary school/education; education; health care; health associations; gun control; human services; children & youth, services; child development, services; women, centers & services; minorities/immigrants, centers & services; international economic development; peace; arms control; foreign policy; international affairs; civil rights, minorities; civil rights, women; race/intergroup relations; civil rights; science; public policy, research;

telecommunications, electronic messaging services; minorities; Asians/Pacific Islanders; African Americans; Latinos; Native Americans; women; immigrants/refugees; economically disadvantaged.
**International interests:** Caribbean; Sub-Saharan Africa; South Africa.
**Types of support:** Program development; continuing support; conferences/seminars; publication; seed money; curriculum development; research.
**Limitations:** Giving primarily in the U.S. Some grants in commonwealth Sub-Saharan Africa, South Africa, and the Caribbean. No support for facilities of educational or human services institutions. No grants for scholarships, fellowships (except for internal fellowhip program), travel, basic operating expenses or endowments; no program-related investments.
**Publications:** Annual report (including application guidelines), informational brochure, grants list, occasional report, newsletter.
**Application information:** Application form not required.
>   *Initial approach:* Letter
>   *Copies of proposal:* 9
>   *Deadline(s):* None
>   *Board meeting date(s):* Feb., Apr., June, and Oct.
>   *Final notification:* Within 4 months

**Officers and Trustees:** Hon. Thomas H. Kean,* Chair.; Helene L. Kaplan,* Vice-Chair.; Vartan Gregorian,* Pres.; Neil Grabois, V.P. and Dir. Strategic Planning and Prog. Coord.; Susan King, V.P., Public Affairs; Edward Sermier, V.P. and C.A.O.; D. Ellen Shuman, V.P. and C.I.O.; Dorothy Wills Knapp, Secy. and Prog. Off.; Jeanmarie C. Grisi, Treas.; Caryl P. Haskins, Hon. Tr.; Teresa F. Heinz, James A. Johnson, Martin L. Leibowitz, Vincent A. Mai, Shirley M. Malcom, Henry Muller, Sam Nunn, Olara A. Otunnu, James J. Renier, Raymond W. Smith, Marta Tienda, Judy Woodruff.
**Number of staff:** 45 full-time professional; 3 part-time professional; 32 full-time support; 4 part-time support.
**EIN:** 131628151
**Recent grants for library/information services:**
**404-1** Africa Fund, NYC, NY, $300,000. For final grant toward promoting involvement of state and municipal officials in U.S. policy toward Africa. 1999.
**404-2** Atlanta-Fulton County Public Library Foundation, Atlanta, GA, $500,000. Toward multicultural literacy project. 1999.
**404-3** Biblioteca Carnegie, San Juan, PR, $500,000. Toward development of young adult collection and outreach programs for young adults. 1999.
**404-4** Boston Public Library Foundation, Boston, MA, $500,000. Toward expansion of literacy services at all branch libraries and creation of neighborhood history centers in seven branch libraries. 1999.
**404-5** Brooklyn Public Library, Brooklyn, NY, $1,000,000. Toward reading program for children and core collections for English for speakers of other languages at every branch library. 1999.
**404-6** Carnegie Library of Pittsburgh, Pittsburgh, PA, $500,000. Toward system-wide preservation and access project. 1999.

**404-7** Chicago Public Library Foundation, Chicago, IL, $500,000. Toward Teen Reading Project. 1999.

**404-8** Cleveland Public Library, Cleveland, OH, $500,000. Toward literacy project for young children. 1999.

**404-9** Denver Public Library, Denver, CO, $500,000. Toward special acquisitions for foreign language collections, enhancement of services to children and augmentation of core collections. 1999.

**404-10** Detroit Public Library, Detroit, MI, $500,000. Toward project for young adolescents. 1999.

**404-11** District of Columbia Public Library Foundation, DC, $500,000. Toward expansion of library services on literacy, services to adolescents and special exhibition on Harlem Renaissance. 1999.

**404-12** Enoch Pratt Free Library, Baltimore, MD, $500,000. Toward expansion of youth services and foreign language collections. 1999.

**404-13** Free Library of Philadelphia Foundation, Philadelphia, PA, $500,000. Toward enhancement and expansion of after-school program. 1999.

**404-14** Houston Public Library, Houston, TX, $500,000. Toward library programs for Hispanic users. 1999.

**404-15** Human Serve Campaign, NYC, NY, $10,000. Toward final report and archive of materials. 1999.

**404-16** Indianapolis-Marion County Public Library Foundation, Indianapolis, IN, $500,000. Toward enhancement and expansion of foreign language collections. 1999.

**404-17** International Council of Scientific Unions, Paris, France, $38,000. For review and synthesis of literature on public libraries in Africa by International Network for the Availability of Scientific Publications. 1999.

**404-18** Kansas City Public Library, Kansas City, MO, $500,000. Toward expansion of Books to Better Our Lives collection. 1999.

**404-19** Los Angeles Public Library, Los Angeles, CA, $500,000. Toward expansion of after-school reading club for children. 1999.

**404-20** Miami-Dade Public Library System, Miami, FL, $500,000. For acquisition of foreign language materials for immigrant populations. 1999.

**404-21** Minneapolis Public Library and Information Center, Minneapolis, MN, $500,000. Toward services for immigrant families and students. 1999.

**404-22** New Orleans Public Library Foundation, New Orleans, LA, $500,000. Toward enhanced collections for young children, adolescents and teenage parents. 1999.

**404-23** New York Public Library, NYC, NY, $2,000,000. Toward adult literacy projects, special acquisitions to strengthen core collections and preservation of materials at Schomburg Center for Research in Black Culture. 1999.

**404-24** Newark Public Library, Newark, NJ, $500,000. Toward citywide branch revitalization. 1999.

**404-25** Queens Library Foundation, Jamaica, NY, $1,000,000. Toward enhanced special collections in social sciences, math and science on diversity. 1999.

**404-26** San Antonio Public Library Foundation, San Antonio, TX, $500,000. Toward enhanced library services to children. 1999.

**404-27** San Francisco Public Library, San Francisco, CA, $500,000. Toward initiative to improve academic and job information available to adolescents. 1999.

**404-28** Seattle Public Library Foundation, Seattle, WA, $500,000. Toward enhancement and expansion of special collections of music and film for branch libraries. 1999.

## 405
## Howard and Bess Chapman Charitable Corporation

c/o Oneida Valley National Bank, Trust Dept.
160 Main St.
Oneida, NY 13421
*Contact:* Peter M. Dunn, Secy.

Established in 1989 in NY.
**Grantmaker type:** Independent foundation
**Financial data** (yr. ended 10/31/99): Assets, $3,765,854 (M); expenditures, $215,026; qualifying distributions, $193,613; giving activities include $183,075 for 20 grants (high: $46,000; low: $1,000).
**Purpose and activities:** Giving primarily for education and for human services.
**Fields of interest:** Libraries/library science; education; human services; YM/YWCAs & YM/YWHAs; children & youth, services.
**Types of support:** General/operating support; building/renovation.
**Limitations:** Giving primarily in Oneida, NY.
**Application information:** Application form not required.
*Initial approach:* Letter
*Deadline(s):* None
*Board meeting date(s):* Quarterly
**Officers and Directors:\*** John G. Haskell,\* Pres.; Robert H. Fearon, Jr.,\* V.P.; Peter M. Dunn,\* Secy. and Genl. Counsel; Steven Schneeweiss,\* Treas.; Rowland Stevens.
**Number of staff:** 1 part-time professional.
**EIN:** 161373396

## 406
## Chase Texas Foundation, Inc.

(Formerly Texas Commerce Bank Foundation, Inc.)
c/o The Chase Tax Group
52 Broadway, 8th Fl.
New York, NY 10004
*Contact:* Jana Gunter, Tr.
*Application address:* c/o The Chase Manhattan Bank, P.O. Box 2558, Houston, TX 77252, tel.: (713) 216-4004

Incorporated in 1952 in TX.
**Donor(s):** Texas Commerce Bank-Houston, N.A.
**Grantmaker type:** Company-sponsored foundation
**Financial data** (yr. ended 12/31/99): Assets, $5,828,763 (M); gifts received, $5,326,052; expenditures, $2,730,587; qualifying distributions, $2,032,004; giving activities include $2,032,004 for 206 grants (high: $550,000; low: $100).
**Purpose and activities:** Primary areas of interest include the arts, community development, housing, and civic affairs. Giving for a

community fund, higher education, and health and medical research organizations; support also for social service agencies, including programs for minorities, child welfare, the homeless, and drug abuse.
**Fields of interest:** Museums; performing arts; arts/cultural programs; early childhood education; elementary school/education; secondary school/education; higher education; adult education—literacy & basic skills; libraries/library science; reading; education; hospitals (general); health care; substance abuse, services; mental health/crisis services; health associations; cancer; alcoholism; biomedicine; medical research; cancer research; food services; housing/shelter, development; recreation; human services; family services; hospices; aging, centers & services; minorities/immigrants, centers & services; homeless, human services; race/intergroup relations; community development; voluntarism promotion; federated giving programs; government/public administration; public affairs; minorities; disabled; aging; homeless.
**Types of support:** General/operating support; continuing support; annual campaigns; capital campaigns; building/renovation; equipment; endowments; program development; conferences/seminars; research; employee matching gifts; in-kind gifts.
**Limitations:** Giving limited to Houston, TX. No grants to individuals.
**Publications:** Application guidelines.
**Application information:** Application form not required.
*Initial approach:* Formal letter of request
*Copies of proposal:* 1
*Deadline(s):* None
*Board meeting date(s):* 3 times annually
**Officers and Trustees:\*** Beverly McCaskill,\* Chair. and Pres.; Jane Gunter,\* Treas.; Debbie Siegfried.
**Number of staff:** None.
**EIN:** 746036696

## 407
## Chautauqua Region Community Foundation, Inc.

418 Spring St.
Jamestown, NY 14701 (716) 661-3390
*Contact:* Randall J. Sweeney, Exec. Dir.
*FAX:* (716) 488-0387; E-mail: crcf@crcfoline.org; URL: http://www.crcfonline.org

Incorporated in 1978 in NY.
**Grantmaker type:** Community foundation
**Financial data** (yr. ended 12/31/99): Assets, $40,282,322 (M); gifts received, $1,298,967; expenditures, $2,096,539; giving activities include $1,549,851 for 323 grants (high: $56,825; low: $15; average: $2,500–$12,000) and $5,516 for 30 grants to individuals (high: $1,000; low: $100).
**Fields of interest:** Arts/cultural programs; libraries/library science; education; housing/shelter, development; human services; children & youth, services; government/public administration; general charitable giving.
**Types of support:** General/operating support; continuing support; building/renovation; equipment; emergency funds; conferences/seminars; publication; seed money; scholarships—to individuals.

**Limitations:** Giving limited to the southern Chautauqua County, NY, area. No support for political, religious or sectarian purposes. No grants to individuals (except for scholarship grants), or for debt retirement.

**Publications:** Annual report (including application guidelines), informational brochure, newsletter, application guidelines.

**Application information:** Scholarships applications available in Nov., (1 copy required). Application form required.

*Copies of proposal:* 15

*Deadline(s):* June 1 and July 15 for scholarships; grant applications accepted from Aug. 1 to Nov. 1

*Board meeting date(s):* Monthly

*Final notification:* Late Feb. for grants; Oct. for scholarships

**Officers and Directors:*** Max R. Pickard,* Pres.; Randy M. Ordines,* V.P.; Mary Lou Scully,* Secy.; Jeanette J. Carlson,* Treas.; Daniel A. Black, Katherine K. Burch, Hon. Stephen W. Cass, Cristie L. Herbst, Bridget B. Johnson, Samuel P. Price, Jr.

**Number of staff:** 4 full-time professional; 1 part-time professional.

**EIN:** 161116837

---

**408**

## Children's Aid Association of Amsterdam, NY

P.O. Box 327

Amsterdam, NY 12010-0327 (518) 842-4259

*Contact:* Jacque Bresonis, V.P.

*Application address:* 321 Guy Park Ave., Amsterdam, NY 12010

Established around 1914 in NY.

**Grantmaker type:** Operating foundation

**Financial data** (yr. ended 05/31/99): Assets, $1,414,503 (M); gifts received, $314; expenditures, $62,775; qualifying distributions, $61,559; giving activities include $41,125 for 21 grants (high: $9,615; low: $200) and $16,200 for grants to individuals.

**Purpose and activities:** Support for needy residents of Montgomery County, NY, including scholarships and camperships.

**Fields of interest:** Music; libraries/library science; housing/shelter; recreation; youth development; human services; children & youth, services; federated giving programs; Christian agencies & churches.

**Types of support:** Program development; grants to individuals; scholarships—to individuals.

**Limitations:** Giving limited to residents of Montgomery County, NY.

**Application information:** Application form required.

*Deadline(s):* May 30

**Officers:** Karen Wright, Pres.; Jacque Bresonis, 1st V.P.; Carol Constantino, 2nd V.P.; Margo Hotaling, Corresponding Secy.; Robin Sise, Recording Secy.; Shirley Iodice, Treas.

**EIN:** 141340035

---

**409**

## China Medical Board of New York, Inc. ▼

750 3rd Ave., 23rd Fl.

New York, NY 10017-2701 (212) 682-8000

*Contact:* M. Roy Schwarz, M.D., Pres.

Incorporated in 1928 in NY.

**Donor(s):** The Rockefeller Foundation.

**Grantmaker type:** Independent foundation

**Financial data** (yr. ended 06/30/99): Assets, $216,483,947 (M); expenditures, $11,844,995; qualifying distributions, $10,730,935; giving activities include $9,725,467 for 32 grants (high: $873,873; low: $20,000; average: $100,000–$200,000) and $232,300 for 3 foundation-administered programs.

**Purpose and activities:** To extend financial aid to the Peking Union Medical College and/or like institutions in the Far East or the United States of America. The board's activities are: 1) to assist institutions in improving the health levels and services in Asian societies; and 2) to assist institutions in improving the quality and increasing the numbers of appropriate health practitioners in these societies. Supports programs in medical research, staff development, cooperative planning, and library endowment only at designated national medical schools, nursing schools, and schools of public health in Hong Kong, Indonesia, Korea, Malaysia, the Philippines, Singapore, Taiwan, Thailand, Laos, Myanmar, Tibet, and the People's Republic of China.

**Fields of interest:** Medical school/education; libraries/library science; nursing care; health care; health associations; medical research.

**International interests:** Asia; Southeast Asia; Indonesia; Malaysia; Philippines; Singapore; Thailand; China & Mongolia; Taiwan; Korea; Hong Kong.

**Types of support:** Endowments; program development; conferences/seminars; publication; fellowships; scholarship funds; research; technical assistance.

**Limitations:** Applications not accepted. Giving limited to East and Southeast Asia, including the People's Republic of China, Hong Kong, Indonesia, Korea, Malaysia, the Philippines, Singapore, Taiwan, and Thailand. No support for governments, professional societies, or research institutes not directly under medical school control. No grants to individuals, or for capital funds, operating budgets for medical care, special projects, or the basic equipping of medical schools, nursing schools, or schools of public health that are the responsibility of various governments or universities; no loans.

**Publications:** Annual report.

**Application information:** Submit request through dean's office of Asian institution in which foundation has a program of support.

*Board meeting date(s):* June and Dec.

**Officers and Trustees:*** J. Robert Buchanan, M.D.,* Chair.; M. Roy Schwarz, M.D.,* Pres.; Jean Hogan, V.P., Admin.; Robert H.M. Ferguson, Secy.; Walter G. Ehlers,* Treas.; Mary Brown Bullock, Ph.D., Loring Catlin, Jordan J. Cohen, Don Eugene Detmer, M.D., Tom G. Kessinger, Dwight H. Perkins, Ph.D., Gloria H. Spivak.

**Number of staff:** 2 full-time professional; 3 full-time support.

**EIN:** 131659619

---

**410**

## Columbian Foundation, Inc.

P.O. Box 1284

Auburn, NY 13021 (315) 255-1151

*Contact:* Peter Flint Metcalf, Pres.

*FAX:* (315) 255-3292

Established in 1957 in NY.

**Grantmaker type:** Independent foundation

**Financial data** (yr. ended 12/31/99): Assets, $2,112,377 (M); expenditures, $109,192; qualifying distributions, $98,413; giving activities include $95,180 for 26 grants (high: $13,600; low: $260).

**Purpose and activities:** Giving for education and nursing scholarships, children and youth services and clubs, federated giving programs and for art organizations.

**Fields of interest:** Museums; music; higher education; libraries/library science; health care; health associations; medical research; recreation; federated giving programs.

**Types of support:** General/operating support; capital campaigns; building/renovation; equipment; scholarship funds; research.

**Limitations:** Giving limited to Cayuga and Onondaga counties, NY. No grants to individuals, or for annual operating budgets or endowments.

**Application information:** Application form required.

*Deadline(s):* None

*Board meeting date(s):* Quarterly

**Officers and Directors:*** Peter Flint Metcalf,* Pres.; Charles R. Adams,* V.P.; Charles W. Loomis,* V.P.; Karen E. Spinelli,* Secy.; John P. McLane,* Treas.

**Number of staff:** 1 part-time support.

**EIN:** 156017838

---

**411**

## The Community Foundation of Herkimer & Oneida Counties, Inc.

(Formerly Utica Foundation, Inc.)

270 Genesee St.

Utica, NY 13502 (315) 735-8212

*Contact:* Susan D. Smith, Sr. Prog. Off.

*FAX:* (315) 735-9363; E-mail: commfdn@borg.com

Incorporated in 1952 in NY.

**Grantmaker type:** Community foundation

**Financial data** (yr. ended 12/31/99): Assets, $51,692,385 (L); expenditures, $2,073,537; giving activities include $1,421,036 for grants.

**Fields of interest:** Arts/cultural programs; higher education; libraries/library science; education; environment; hospitals (general); health care; human services; children & youth, services; family services; aging, centers & services; disabled; aging.

**Types of support:** General/operating support; capital campaigns; building/renovation; equipment; endowments; emergency funds; program development; seed money; fellowships; scholarship funds; technical assistance; consulting services; program-related investments/loans; matching/challenge support.

**Limitations:** Giving limited to Oneida and Herkimer counties, NY. No support for religious purposes or government agencies and organizations. No grants to individuals, or for ongoing operating support.

**Publications:** Annual report, application guidelines, newsletter.
**Application information:** 8 copies of proposal required for organizations within Oneida County, NY; 7 required for Herkimer County, when requested by foundation. Application form not required.

    *Initial approach:* Letter of intent
    *Deadline(s):* None
    *Board meeting date(s):* Grants committees for each county meet 5 to 6 times per year
    *Final notification:* 4 to 6 weeks
**Officers and Directors:*** Harold T. Clark, Jr.,* Pres.; Lauren E. Bull,* V.P.; Jane A. Halbritter,* V.P.; Richard Hanna,* V.P.; David L. Mathis, V.P.; Joseph H. Hobika, Sr., Secy.; Gordon M. Hayes, Exec. Dir.; Susan M. Blatt, M.D., Milton Bloch, Don Carbone, Vincent R. Corrou, Jr., Judith B. Gorman, Mary K. Griffith, Christian G. Heilmann, Camille T. Kahler, Grace McLaughlin, Earle C. Reed, William L. Schrauth, Robert N. Sheldon, Dwight E. Vicks, Jr.
**Trustee Banks:** Fleet Bank, N.A., HSBC Bank USA.
**Number of staff:** 3 full-time professional; 2 full-time support.
**EIN:** 156016932

---

### 412
### Constans Culver Foundation

c/o The Chase Manhattan Bank, N.A.
1211 Ave. of the Americas
New York, NY 10036
*Contact:* Robert Rosenthal, V.P., The Chase Manhattan Bank, N.A.

Trust established in 1965 in NY.
**Donor(s):** Erne Constans Culver.‡
**Grantmaker type:** Independent foundation
**Financial data** (yr. ended 12/31/99): Assets, $7,578,506 (M); expenditures, $428,023; qualifying distributions, $416,192; giving activities include $343,700 for 95 grants (high: $30,000; low: $500; average: $1,500–$2,500).
**Purpose and activities:** Emphasis on civic and cultural organizations, including libraries, museums, and music organizations; higher and insurance education; the disadvantaged; housing issues; military personnel; and health associations.
**Fields of interest:** Museums; music; arts/cultural programs; higher education; business school/education; libraries/library science; education; health associations; housing/shelter, development; human services; government/public administration; military/veterans' organizations; economically disadvantaged.
**Types of support:** General/operating support; continuing support; annual campaigns.
**Limitations:** Giving primarily in NY. No grants to individuals, or for endowment funds.
**Application information:** Application form not required.

    *Initial approach:* Letter or modest proposal
    *Copies of proposal:* 1
    *Deadline(s):* Submit proposal preferably in Sept.
    *Board meeting date(s):* Oct. and as required
**Trustees:** Pauline Hoffmann Herd, Pauline May Herd, Victoria Prescott Herd, The Chase Manhattan Bank, N.A.
**Number of staff:** 5 shared staff

**EIN:** 136048059

---

### 413
### Lois Lenski Covey Foundation, Inc.

c/o Moses & Singer
1301 Ave. of the Americas
New York, NY 10019-6076 (212) 554-7826
*Contact:* Arthur F. Abelman, Tr.

Established in NY.
**Donor(s):** Lois Lenski Cove.‡
**Grantmaker type:** Independent foundation
**Financial data** (yr. ended 12/31/99): Assets, $1,150,552 (M); expenditures, $66,426; qualifying distributions, $55,450; giving activities include $52,753 for 22 grants (high: $13,653; low: $500).
**Purpose and activities:** Grants to organizations that provide schoolbooks for indigent children.
**Fields of interest:** Elementary school/education; libraries/library science; libraries (school).
**Limitations:** No grants to individuals.
**Application information:** Application form required.

    *Initial approach:* Letter
    *Copies of proposal:* 1
    *Deadline(s):* None
    *Final notification:* Dec.
**Trustees:** Arthur F. Abelman, Michael C. Covey, Paul A. Covey, Stephen Covey, Gloria Koltmeyer, Paula Quint.
**Number of staff:** 1 part-time professional.
**EIN:** 136223036

---

### 414
### CTW Fund, Inc.

42 Division St.
Amsterdam, NY 12010
*Contact:* William Moore

Established in 1997 in NY.
**Grantmaker type:** Independent foundation
**Financial data** (yr. ended 12/31/99): Assets, $1,924,340 (M); gifts received, $91,500; expenditures, $122,596; qualifying distributions, $123,967; giving activities include $90,798 for 3 grants (high: $50,000; low: $8,798).
**Purpose and activities:** Giving primarily for libraries, education and the prevention of cruelty to animals.
**Fields of interest:** College; libraries (public); youth development, centers & clubs.
**Officer and Directors:*** Alan Woodmancy,* Pres.; Barbara Miller,* V.P.; William E. Moore,* Secy.; Justin C. Brusgul.
**EIN:** 141787317

---

### 415
### Lewis B. & Dorothy Cullman Foundation, Inc.

c/o Lewis B. Cullman
767 3rd Ave., 36th Fl.
New York, NY 10017 (212) 751-6655

Established in 1958 in NY.
**Donor(s):** Dorothy F. Cullman, Lewis B. Cullman.
**Grantmaker type:** Independent foundation
**Financial data** (yr. ended 11/30/99): Assets, $29,092,617 (M); gifts received, $110,431;

expenditures, $9,768,263; qualifying distributions, $9,367,163; giving activities include $9,333,673 for 49 grants (high: $2,000,000; low: $100; average: $50,000–$400,000).
**Purpose and activities:** Giving primarily for the arts.
**Fields of interest:** Museums; performing arts; arts/cultural programs.
**Limitations:** Applications not accepted. Giving primarily in NY. No grants to individuals.
**Application information:** Contributes only to pre-selected organizations.
**Officers and Directors:*** Lewis B. Cullman,* Pres.; Dorothy F. Cullman,* V.P.; John C. Emmert, Treas.; Joseph P. Kremer.
**EIN:** 510243747
**Recent grants for library/information services:**
415-1 New York Public Library, Center for Scholars and Writers, NYC, NY, $1,000,000. 1999.
415-2 New York Public Library, Division of Performing Arts, NYC, NY, $400,000. 1999.

---

### 416
### Jessie Smith Darrah Charitable Trust

c/o Citibank, N.A., C.D.S. Tax Dept.
1 Court Sq., 22nd Fl.
Long Island City, NY 11120

**Donor(s):** Jessie S. Darrah.‡
**Grantmaker type:** Independent foundation
**Financial data** (yr. ended 12/31/99): Assets, $5,134,845 (M); expenditures, $262,155; qualifying distributions, $210,238; giving activities include $206,196 for 20 grants (high: $42,300; low: $1,050).
**Purpose and activities:** Giving primarily for human services.
**Fields of interest:** Higher education; libraries/library science; human services; federated giving programs.
**Limitations:** Applications not accepted. Giving primarily in Chautauqua County, NY. No grants to individuals.
**Application information:** Contributes only to pre-selected organizations.
**Trustees:** George A. Campbell, Charles H. Price, Wilson C. Price III, James M. Smith, Charles B. Ulrich, Citibank, N.A.
**EIN:** 136129875

---

### 417
### Sarah K. deCoizart Perpetual Charitable Trust

c/o The Chase Manhattan Bank, N.A.
1 Chase Manhattan Plz., 5th Fl
New York, NY 10081 (212) 270-6305
*Contact:* Philip DiMaulo
*Application address:* c/o The Chase Manhattan Bank, N.A., 1211 Ave. of the Americas, New York, NY 10036, tel: (212) 789-5264

Established in 1995 in NY.
**Grantmaker type:** Independent foundation
**Financial data** (yr. ended 01/31/98): Assets, $30,527,761 (M); gifts received, $111,151; expenditures, $1,592,499; qualifying distributions, $1,431,086; giving activities include $1,305,000 for 66 grants (high: $35,000; low: $2,500).

**Purpose and activities:** Giving primarily for the arts, education and health and human services.
**Fields of interest:** Museums; historic preservation/historical societies; higher education; libraries/library science; education; animals/wildlife; hospitals (general); eye diseases; arthritis; youth development, scouting agencies (general).
**Limitations:** Giving primarily in New York, NY.
**Application information:** Application form not required.
*Deadline(s):* None
**Trustees:** Carl S. Forsythe III, The Chase Manhattan Bank, N.A.
**EIN:** 137046581

## 418
### Margarita Victoria Delacorte Foundation
c/o U.S. Trust Co. of New York
114 W. 47th St.
New York, NY 10036-1532
*Contact:* Margarita V. Delacorte

Established in 1966 in NY.
**Donor(s):** Margarita V. Delacorte.
**Grantmaker type:** Independent foundation
**Financial data** (yr. ended 12/31/99): Assets, $533,345 (M); expenditures, $103,394; qualifying distributions, $101,403; giving activities include $97,250 for 40 grants (high: $7,500; low: $750).
**Purpose and activities:** Support for private higher and secondary educational institutions.
**Fields of interest:** Music; higher education; libraries/library science; education; natural resource conservation & protection; human services; aging, centers & services; Christian agencies & churches.
**Limitations:** Giving primarily in New York, NY. No grants to individuals.
**Application information:**
*Initial approach:* Letter
*Deadline(s):* None
**Trustee:** U.S. Trust Co. of New York.
**EIN:** 136197777

## 419
### The Gladys Krieble Delmas Foundation ▼
521 5th Ave., Ste. 1612
New York, NY 10175-1699 (212) 687-0011
*Contact:* Kate Rushing, Admin. Asst.
*FAX:* (212) 687-8877; E-mail: Delmasfdtn@aol.com; URL: http://www.delmas.org

Established in 1976 in NY.
**Donor(s):** Gladys Krieble Delmas,‡ Jean Paul Delmas.‡
**Grantmaker type:** Independent foundation
**Financial data** (yr. ended 12/31/98): Assets, $71,271,167 (M); expenditures, $3,564,244; qualifying distributions, $3,020,594; giving activities include $2,684,800 for 119 grants (high: $130,000; low: $500; average: $5,000–$100,000) and $128,381 for 28 grants to individuals (high: $12,000; low: $1,233; average: $2,500–$12,500).
**Purpose and activities:** The foundation supports the humanities, research libraries, and New York City performing arts organizations, and has a particular interest in encouraging Venetian scholarship.

**Fields of interest:** Performing arts; humanities; libraries/library science.
**International interests:** Italy.
**Types of support:** General/operating support; endowments; research; grants to individuals.
**Limitations:** Giving on a national basis to organizations, but only in New York, NY, for performing arts grants; giving for individual research projects conducted in Venice or the Veneto, Italy. No grants to individuals (except for advanced research in Venice and the Veneto), or for building campaigns; no loans.
**Publications:** Informational brochure (including application guidelines), multi-year report.
**Application information:** Application form required for grants for independent research on Venetian history and culture.
*Initial approach:* Letter
*Deadline(s):* Dec. 15 for grants for independent research on Venetian history and culture
*Board meeting date(s):* Varies
*Final notification:* Apr. 1 for grants for independent research on Venetian history and culture
**Trustees:** Patricia H. Labalme, Joseph C. Mitchell, David H. Stam.
**Number of staff:** 1 full-time professional; 1 full-time support.
**EIN:** 510193884
**Recent grants for library/information services:**
**419-1** American Academy in Rome, Photographic Archive, NYC, NY, $40,000. 1998.
**419-2** American Antiquarian Society, Worcester, MA, $25,000. For History of the Book in America Project. 1998.
**419-3** American Friends of Cambridge University, Cambridge University Library, NYC, NY, $130,000. For illuminated medieval manuscript catalogue. 1998.
**419-4** Centro di Studi Americani, Rome, Italy, $30,000. For library fund. 1998.
**419-5** Connecticut Historical Society, Hartford, CT, $25,000. For finding aids for manuscript collections. 1998.
**419-6** Cornell University, Ithaca, NY, $40,000. For continued support of preservation and record conversion for Italian literature collections. 1998.
**419-7** Cornell University, Ithaca, NY, $10,000. For Eleusis inscriptions. 1998.
**419-8** Council on Library and Information Resources, DC, $30,000. For ACLS/CLIR digital technology task forces. 1998.
**419-9** Foundation Center, NYC, NY, $12,000. For new library and training center and general operating support. 1998.
**419-10** Harvard University, Fine Arts Library, Cambridge, MA, $10,000. For Before and After the End of Time: Architecture and the Year 1000 exhibition. 1998.
**419-11** Indiana University, School of Liberal Arts, Indianapolis, IN, $45,000. For Philanthropy Archival Collections. 1998.
**419-12** New School University, Raymond Fogelman Library, NYC, NY, $15,000. For continued support to catalog and preserve chamber music scores at Mannes College of Music. 1998.
**419-13** New York Academy of Medicine, NYC, NY, $47,000. For continued support of Humanities in Medicine Program. 1998.

**419-14** New York Public Library, Astor, Lenox and Tilden Foundations, NYC, NY, $70,000. For The Manuscripts and Archives Access Project. 1998.
**419-15** Newberry Library, Chicago, IL, $14,000. For Summer Institute in the Archival Sciences program. 1998.
**419-16** Ohio State University, Department of History, Columbus, OH, $15,000. For digital images of Attic decrees. 1998.
**419-17** Oxford University Development North America, NYC, NY, $25,000. For Finding Aids Conversion Project. 1998.
**419-18** Oxford University Development North America, Bodleian Library, NYC, NY, $25,000. For Bodleian Incunabula Project. 1998.
**419-19** Philadelphia Area Consortium of Special Collections Libraries, Philadelphia, PA, $15,050. For Encoded Archival Description training workshops at Van Pelt-Dietrich Library Center. 1998.
**419-20** Research Foundation of the City University of New York, Center for the Study of Women and Society, NYC, NY, $10,000. For Database of Classical Bibliography. 1998.
**419-21** Research Libraries Group, Mountain View, CA, $40,000. For endowment for English Short Title Catalogue (ESTC). 1998.
**419-22** Research Libraries Group, Mountain View, CA, $40,000. For archival finding aids conversion pilot program. 1998.
**419-23** Save Venice, NYC, NY, $15,000. For microfilm reader and printer. 1998.
**419-24** Society of American Archivists, Chicago, IL, $14,000. For Encoded Archival Description (EAD) program. 1998.
**419-25** Syracuse University, E. S. Bird Library, Syracuse, NY, $90,000. For continued support for historical sound recordings. 1998.
**419-26** University of London, Institute of Classical Studies, London, England, $20,000. To endow librarian traineeship. 1998.
**419-27** University of Pittsburgh, School of Information Sciences, Pittsburgh, PA, $25,000. For Working Meeting for Graduate Archival Educators. 1998.

## 420
### Deutsche Bank Americas Foundation ▼
(Formerly BT Foundation)
130 Liberty St., 10th Fl., M.S. 2107
New York, NY 10006 (212) 250-7065
*Contact:* Gary S. Hattem, Pres.
*URL:* http://www.deutschebank.com

Established as the BT Foundation in 1986 in NY; changed to Deutsche Bank Americas Foundation in 1999.
**Donor(s):** Bankers Trust Co., BT Capital Corp., Deutsche Bank Americas.
**Grantmaker type:** Company-sponsored foundation
**Financial data** (yr. ended 11/30/98): Assets, $824,853 (M); gifts received, $5,500,000; expenditures, $9,047,268; qualifying distributions, $9,054,386; giving activities include $4,264,621 for 193 grants (high: $1,118,310; low: $500; average: $5,000–$30,000) and $4,782,647 for 8 employee matching gifts.
**Purpose and activities:** The foundation administers the philanthropic activities of

Deutsche Bank within the United States, Latin America and Canada. Together with its Community Development Group, the foundation carries out the firm's corporate citizenship commitments through a program of loans, investments and grants. Based in New York City, where the majority of grants are awarded, the foundation supports nonprofit organizations that concentrate on community development, education, the arts and the environment. Deutsche Bank works in partnership with local nonprofit organizations to provide distressed communities and disadvantaged individuals with opportunities for economic advancement. The foundation seeks to enrich these communities by providing access to the arts, and encourage the exchange of creative expression between diverse communities. In addition, the bank relies on the talents of its personnel and leadership of its management to leverage its financial commitments in addressing local needs.

**Fields of interest:** Arts/cultural programs; education; environment; housing/shelter, development; urban/community development; community development.

**Types of support:** General/operating support; continuing support; capital campaigns; program development; internship funds; technical assistance; employee matching gifts.

**Limitations:** Giving primarily in areas of company operations in the U.S., Canada and Latin America. No support for religious purposes, veterans' and fraternal organizations, United Way agencies unless they provide a fundraising waiver, political parties or their candidates, or legal advocacy. No grants to individuals, or for endowment campaigns.

**Publications:** Application guidelines, annual report, newsletter.

**Application information:** Application form not required.

  *Initial approach:* Letter, not to exceed three pages
  *Deadline(s):* None

**Officers and Directors:*** Rose Tobin, C.O.O.; Gary S. Hattem,* Pres.; Robyn Brady Ince, V.P.; Robert Blank, Secy.; Sandra West, Secy.; Theresa A. Vitolo, Treas.

**Number of staff:** 3 full-time professional; 3 full-time support.

**EIN:** 133321736

**Recent grants for library/information services:**

**420-1** Charities Aid Foundation America, Alexandria, VA, $60,000. For Bankers Trust Company Donor Advised Fund. 1998.

**420-2** Charities Aid Foundation America, Alexandria, VA, $15,000. For Computer Services Center in Brazil. 1998.

**420-3** Charities Aid Foundation America, International Marketing Division, Alexandria, VA, $60,400. For Bankers Trust Company Donor Advised Fund. 1998.

**420-4** Charities Aid Foundation America, International Marketing Division, Alexandria, VA, $50,000. For Bankers Trust Company Donor Advised Fund. 1998.

**420-5** Charities Aid Foundation America, International Marketing Division, Alexandria, VA, $36,500. For Bankers Trust Company Donor Advised Fund. 1998.

**420-6** Charities Aid Foundation America, International Marketing Division, Alexandria,

VA, $25,000. For Bankers Trust Company Donor Advised Fund. 1998.

**420-7** Charities Aid Foundation America, International Marketing Division, Alexandria, VA, $20,000. For Bankers Trust Company Donor Advised Fund. 1998.

**420-8** Charities Aid Foundation America, International Marketing Division, Alexandria, VA, $18,000. For Bankers Trust Company Donor Advised Fund. 1998.

**420-9** Charities Aid Foundation America, International Marketing Division, Alexandria, VA, $13,100. For Bankers Trust Company Donor Advised Fund. 1998.

**420-10** Charities Aid Foundation America, International Marketing Division, Alexandria, VA, $10,000. For Bankers Trust Company Donor Advised Fund. 1998.

**420-11** Charities Aid Foundation America, Investors in Society, Alexandria, VA, $15,723. For Bankers Trust Company Foundation Donor Advised Fund. 1998.

**420-12** Library of Congress, DC, $60,000. For National Digital Library. 1998.

**420-13** New York Public Library, NYC, NY, $100,000. For Computer Page Program. 1998.

**420-14** University of Pennsylvania, Wharton Financial Institutions Center, Philadelphia, PA, $10,000. For Brookings-Wharton Papers on Financial Services. 1998.

---

**421**

**The James & Judith K. Dimon Foundation**
c/o Popper, Seger & Popper, LLP
192 Lexington Ave., 11th Fl.
New York, NY 10016

Established in 1996 in NY.
**Donor(s):** James Dimon, Judith K. Dimon.
**Grantmaker type:** Independent foundation
**Financial data** (yr. ended 11/30/97): Assets, $3,806,462 (M); gifts received, $3,872,604; expenditures, $440,406; qualifying distributions, $440,393; giving activities include $440,365 for grants (high: $66,000).
**Purpose and activities:** Funding primarily for arts and culture and youth services.
**Fields of interest:** Arts/cultural programs; libraries/library science; higher education; boys clubs; Big Brothers/Big Sisters; Boy Scouts; youth development, services; Jewish agencies & temples.
**Limitations:** Applications not accepted. No grants to individuals.
**Application information:** Contributes only to pre-selected organizations.
**Officers:** James Dimon, Pres.; Theodore Dimon, Secy.; Judith K. Dimon, Treas.
**EIN:** 133922199

---

**422**

**Dorys McConnell Duberg Charitable Trust**
c/o Bank of New York
1 Wall St., 28th Fl.
New York, NY 10286
*Contact:* Vincent Griffin, Jr.
*Application address:* c/o Putnam Trust Co., Pequot Ave., Southport, CT 06490

Trust established in 1969 in CT.
**Donor(s):** Dorys McConnell Faile Duberg.‡

**Grantmaker type:** Independent foundation
**Financial data** (yr. ended 01/31/98): Assets, $2,253,151 (M); expenditures, $86,735; qualifying distributions, $73,750; giving activities include $66,403 for 13 grants (high: $22,000; low: $250).
**Purpose and activities:** Giving for medical education and hospitals; support also for social service agencies, religious and denominational giving, and libraries.
**Fields of interest:** Medical school/education; libraries/library science; hospitals (general); human services.
**Types of support:** General/operating support; continuing support; program development; scholarship funds.
**Limitations:** Giving primarily in Fairfield County, CT.
**Application information:** Application form not required.
  *Deadline(s):* None
**Trustees:** David Hall Faile, Jr., John B. Faile, Robert B. Hutchinson.
**Agent:** Putnam Trust Co.
**Number of staff:** None.
**EIN:** 237016974

---

**423**

**Dyson Foundation**
25 Halcyon Rd.
Millbrook, NY 12545-9611 (845) 677-0644
*Contact:* Dean K. Stein, Deputy Exec. Dir.
*FAX:* (845) 677-0650; E-mail: info@dyson.org;
URL: http://www.dysonfoundation.org

Trust established in 1949 in NY; incorporated in 1957 in DE.
**Donor(s):** Charles H. Dyson,‡ Margaret M. Dyson.‡
**Grantmaker type:** Independent foundation
**Financial data** (yr. ended 12/31/99): Assets, $332,176,732 (M); gifts received, $5,523,289; expenditures, $16,275,585; qualifying distributions, $11,688,688; giving activities include $11,688,688 for grants (average: $25,000–$200,000) and $300,000 for 2 program-related investments.
**Purpose and activities:** While the foundation has historically made a wide variety of grants to support social, educational and cultural activities in New York City and on a national level as well, the foundation's current priorities are to support organizations active in Dutchess County and the Mid-Hudson Valley. The foundation is interested in improving the quality of life for citizens of Dutchess County, helping to provide critical services to at-risk populations in that community, strengthening the not-for-profit sector and helping to contribute to the economic revitalization and diversification of Dutchess County. The foundation is currently developing new guidelines for national grantmaking in pediatrics and child health. National grants are made through invitation of selected grantees.
**Fields of interest:** Arts/cultural programs; medical school/education; education; health care; medical research; human services; children & youth, services; economically disadvantaged.
**Types of support:** General/operating support; continuing support; capital campaigns; building/renovation; equipment; emergency

funds; program development; professorships; seed money; fellowships; scholarship funds; research; technical assistance; consulting services; program evaluation; program-related investments/loans; matching/challenge support.
**Limitations:** Giving primarily in Dutchess County, NY, and organizations providing services in Dutchess County, NY. National and other grants on a solicited basis. No support for international organizations. No grants to individuals, debt reduction, direct mail campaign or fundraising events.
**Publications:** Annual report (including application guidelines).
**Application information:** Unsolicited proposals are not accepted, but letter inquiries are welcomed. Application form not required.
*Initial approach:* 2- to 3-page letter of inquiry
*Copies of proposal:* 1
*Deadline(s):* None
*Board meeting date(s):* Quarterly
*Final notification:* At least six months
**Officers and Directors:*** Robert R. Dyson,* V.P.; John H. FitzSimmons, Secy.; Diana M. Gurieva, Exec. Dir.; Joseph V. Mariner, Jr., David Nathan, M.D.
**Number of staff:** 5 full-time professional; 1 full-time support; 2 part-time support.
**EIN:** 136084888
**Recent grants for library/information services:**
**423-1** Eastern Dutchess Rural Health Network, Poughkeepsie, NY, $20,000. For Primary Healthcare Network program, linking uninsured residents with healthcare providers. 1998.
**423-2** Marist College, Poughkeepsie, NY, $650,000. For Capital Campaign for a New Library. 1998.
**423-3** Mid-Hudson Library, Poughkeepsie, NY, $20,000. Toward development of website to link nonprofit agencies with fundraising information and resources. 1998.
**423-4** New York Academy of Medicine, NYC, NY, $15,000. For David E. Rogers Fellowship Program. 1998.

## 424
## Eckert Family Foundation
c/o Greenwich Street Capital Partners
388 Greenwich St.
New York, NY   10013

Established in 1985 in NY.
**Donor(s):** Alfred C. Eckert III.
**Grantmaker type:** Independent foundation
**Financial data** (yr. ended 07/31/97): Assets, $2,422,467 (M); gifts received, $896,003; expenditures, $125,432; qualifying distributions, $119,431; giving activities include $119,431 for 67 grants (high: $20,000; low: $10).
**Fields of interest:** Music; higher education; libraries/library science; family planning; human services; Christian agencies & churches.
**Limitations:** Applications not accepted. Giving primarily in New York, NY. No grants to individuals; no loans.
**Application information:** Contributes only to pre-selected organizations.
**Trustees:** Alfred C. Eckert, Jr., Alfred C. Eckert III, Kevin W. Kennedy.
**EIN:** 133318138

## 425
## Elster Foundation
c/o Sydney E. Goldstein
925 Delaware Ave., Apt. 6B
Buffalo, NY   14209-1843

Established in 1964 in NY.
**Donor(s):** Robert S. Elster.‡
**Grantmaker type:** Independent foundation
**Financial data** (yr. ended 12/31/99): Assets, $4,467,061 (M); expenditures, $255,333; qualifying distributions, $200,700; giving activities include $200,700 for 45 grants (high: $36,000; low: $250).
**Purpose and activities:** Giving for the arts, education, the environment, health, and Jewish organizations.
**Fields of interest:** Arts/cultural programs; higher education; libraries/library science; education; natural resource conservation & protection; hospitals (general); health care, patient services; housing/shelter, development; federated giving programs; Jewish agencies & temples.
**Types of support:** Continuing support; annual campaigns; building/renovation; emergency funds.
**Limitations:** Applications not accepted. Giving primarily in FL, Atlanta, GA, and Buffalo, NY. No grants to individuals.
**Application information:** Contributes only to pre-selected organizations.
**Trustees:** Amy Gerome-Acuff, Douglas R. Goldstein, Elizabeth Geer Goldstein, Jerome E. Goldstein, Sydney E. Goldstein.
**Number of staff:** None.
**EIN:** 166054742

## 426
## Fred L. Emerson Foundation, Inc. ▼
P.O. Box 276
Auburn, NY   13021   (315) 253-9621
*Contact:* Ronald D. West, Exec. Dir.

Incorporated in 1943 in DE.
**Donor(s):** Fred L. Emerson.‡
**Grantmaker type:** Independent foundation
**Financial data** (yr. ended 12/31/99): Assets, $92,158,304 (M); expenditures, $4,393,661; qualifying distributions, $3,900,390; giving activities include $3,840,758 for 81 grants (high: $300,000; low: $250; average: $1,000–$100,000).
**Purpose and activities:** Giving to private colleges and universities, community funds, and a library; grants also for youth and social service agencies and cultural programs.
**Fields of interest:** Arts/cultural programs; higher education; libraries/library science; human services; children & youth, services; federated giving programs.
**Types of support:** Annual campaigns; capital campaigns; building/renovation; equipment; endowments; emergency funds; program development; internship funds; scholarship funds; research; matching/challenge support.
**Limitations:** Giving primarily in Auburn, Cayuga County, and upstate NY. No grants to individuals, or for deficit financing; no loans. Support for operating budgets is discouraged.
**Publications:** Application guidelines.
**Application information:** Application form not required.
*Initial approach:* Letter, telephone, or proposal

*Copies of proposal:* 1
*Deadline(s):* May 1 and Nov. 1
*Board meeting date(s):* June and Dec.
*Final notification:* 2 to 3 weeks after board meetings (positive replies only)
**Officers and Directors:*** W. Gary Emerson,* Pres.; Anthony D. Franceschelli,* V.P.; Ronald D. West,* Secy. and Exec. Dir.; J. David Hammond,* Treas.; William F. Allyn, Christopher S. Emerson, David L. Emerson, Heather A. Emerson, Peter J. Emerson, Lori E. Robinson, Kristen E. Rubacka, Sally E. Wagner.
**Number of staff:** 1 full-time professional; 1 full-time support.
**EIN:** 156017650
**Recent grants for library/information services:**
**426-1** Seymour Library Foundation, Auburn, NY, $50,000. For endowment. 1998.

## 427
## The Charles Engelhard Foundation ▼
645 5th Ave., Ste. 712
New York, NY   10022   (212) 935-2433
*Contact:* Mary F. Ogorzaly, Secy.

Incorporated in 1940 in NJ.
**Donor(s):** Charles Engelhard,‡ Engelhard Hanovia, Inc., and others.
**Grantmaker type:** Independent foundation
**Financial data** (yr. ended 12/31/99): Assets, $145,000,000 (M); expenditures, $11,300,000; qualifying distributions, $10,500,000; giving activities include $10,616,054 for 271 grants (high: $633,000; low: $500; average: $1,000–$50,000).
**Purpose and activities:** Emphasis on higher and secondary education, and cultural, medical, religious, wildlife, and conservation organizations.
**Fields of interest:** Arts/cultural programs; secondary school/education; higher education; natural resource conservation & protection; wildlife preservation & protection; biomedicine; medical research; religion.
**Types of support:** General/operating support; continuing support; annual campaigns; capital campaigns; building/renovation; endowments; program development; conferences/seminars; publication; research; matching/challenge support.
**Limitations:** Applications not accepted. Giving on a national basis. No support for international organizations. No grants to individuals.
**Application information:** Giving only to organizations known to the trustees. Unsolicited requests for funds not considered.
*Board meeting date(s):* Quarterly
**Officers and Trustees:*** Sally E. Pingree,* Pres.; Mary F. Ogorzaly, Secy.; Edward G. Beimfohr,* Treas.; Sophie Engelhard Craighead, Anne E. de la Renta, Charlene B. Engelhard, Jane B. Engelhard, Anthony J. Gostkowski, Susan O'Connor.
**Number of staff:** 1 full-time professional; 2 part-time professional.
**EIN:** 226063032
**Recent grants for library/information services:**
**427-1** New York Public Library, NYC, NY, $100,000. 1998.
**427-2** Pierpont Morgan Library, NYC, NY, $1,045,000. For general support. 1998.

## 428
### Engineering Information Foundation
(also known as EI Foundation)
180 W. 80th St., Ste. 207
New York, NY 10024 (212) 579-7596
*Contact:* Thomas R. Buckman, Chair. and Pres.
*FAX:* (212) 579-7517; E-mail: info@eifgrants.org;
URL: http://www.eifgrants.org

Established in 1934 as a publisher of
engineering information with the legal status of
a public charity. Restructured in 1994 in NY as a
private foundation; approved July 25, 1996,
with first round of grants made in Aug. 1997.
**Grantmaker type:** Independent foundation
**Financial data** (yr. ended 12/31/99): Assets,
$9,468,548 (M); expenditures, $487,912;
qualifying distributions, $303,803; giving
activities include $291,870 for 10 grants (high:
$110,050; low: $1,000; average:
$5,000–$75,000).
**Purpose and activities:** Support for educational
research programs that advance the availability
and use of information related to engineering
and applied technologies; programs conducted
by engineering educators that encourage
women to undertake careers in engineering; and
projects to improve access to engineering
information for students and faculty of
educational institutions in developing countries.
**Fields of interest:** Women, centers & services;
science, research; science, information services;
engineering & technology.
**International interests:** Developing countries.
**Types of support:** Program development;
research; matching/challenge support.
**Limitations:** Giving on a national and
international basis. No grants for operating
expenses, campaigns, or conferences; no loans.
**Publications:** Annual report (including
application guidelines).
**Application information:** Application form not
required.
  *Initial approach:* Letter or E-mail requesting
    application guidelines
  *Copies of proposal:* 5
  *Deadline(s):* Feb. 28, June 30, and Sept. 30
  *Board meeting date(s):* Apr., Aug., and Nov.
  *Final notification:* Within 30 days of Board
    meeting
**Officers and Directors:\*** Thomas R. Buckman,\*
Chair. and Pres.; Anne M. Buck,\* Vice-Chair.
and V.P.; Hans Rutimann,\* Secy.; John J.
Regazzi, Julie A. Shimer.
**Number of staff:** 1 part-time professional.
**EIN:** 131679606

## 429
### Eugene V. Fife Family Foundation
c/o BCRS Assoc., LLC
67 Wall St., 8th Fl.
New York, NY 10005

Established in 1982 in CA.
**Donor(s):** Eugene V. Fife.
**Grantmaker type:** Independent foundation
**Financial data** (yr. ended 01/31/00): Assets,
$9,634,886 (M); gifts received, $1,393,918;
expenditures, $158,975; qualifying distributions,
$158,725; giving activities include $158,500 for
19 grants (high: $35,000; low: $2,500).
**Purpose and activities:** Giving primarily for
higher education.

**Fields of interest:** Higher education;
libraries/library science; education.
**Types of support:** General/operating support;
endowments.
**Limitations:** Applications not accepted. Giving
primarily in VA and WV. No grants to
individuals; no loans.
**Application information:** Contributes only to
pre-selected organizations.
**Trustees:** Jonathan L. Cohen, Amy S. Fife, David
Fife, Eugene V. Fife.
**EIN:** 133153715

## 430
### Leo and Julia Forchheimer Foundation ▼
(Formerly The Forchheimer Foundation)
c/o Golenbock, Eiseman, Assor & Bell
437 Madison Ave, 35th Fl.
New York, NY 10022 (212) 661-3140

Established about 1957 in NY.
**Donor(s):** Leo Forchheimer.‡
**Grantmaker type:** Independent foundation
**Financial data** (yr. ended 12/31/98): Assets,
$24,541,983 (M); expenditures, $3,382,753;
qualifying distributions, $3,119,847; giving
activities include $3,119,032 for 50 grants (high:
$500,000; low: $500; average:
$10,000–$100,000).
**Purpose and activities:** Giving primarily for
hospitals, health agencies, higher education,
including medical and technical education,
Jewish welfare funds, museums, and social
services.
**Fields of interest:** Museums; higher education;
medical school/education; hospitals (general);
health care; health associations; human
services; Jewish federated giving programs.
**International interests:** Israel.
**Limitations:** Applications not accepted. Giving
primarily in New York, NY; giving also in Israel.
**Application information:** Contributes only to
pre-selected charitable organizations.
**Officers and Directors:\*** Rudolph Forchheimer,\*
Pres.; Barbara Kamen,\* V.P.; Michael Jesselson,\*
Secy.-Treas.
**EIN:** 136075112
**Recent grants for library/information services:**
430-1 Survivors of the Shoah Visual History
  Foundation, Los Angeles, CA, $500,000.
  1998.

## 431
### Gebbie Foundation, Inc. ▼
Hotel Jamestown Bldg., Rm. 308
110 W. 3rd St.
Jamestown, NY 14701 (716) 487-1062
*Contact:* Dr. Thomas M. Cardman, Exec. Dir.
*FAX:* (716) 484-6401; E-mail:
gebfnd@netsync.net

Incorporated in 1963 in NY.
**Donor(s):** Marion B. Gebbie,‡ Geraldine G.
Bellinger.‡
**Grantmaker type:** Independent foundation
**Financial data** (yr. ended 09/30/99): Assets,
$83,313,142 (M); expenditures, $4,410,601;
qualifying distributions, $3,770,081; giving
activities include $3,666,891 for 58 grants (high:
$473,204; low: $1,000; average:
$1,000–$120,000).

**Purpose and activities:** Grants primarily for local
organizations such as hospitals, libraries, youth
agencies, cultural programs, social service
agencies, and the United Way.
**Fields of interest:** Theater; arts/cultural
programs; early childhood education;
libraries/library science; education;
environment; hospitals (general); human
services; children & youth, services; community
development; federated giving programs.
**Types of support:** General/operating support;
continuing support; annual campaigns; capital
campaigns; building/renovation; equipment;
seed money; scholarship funds;
matching/challenge support.
**Limitations:** Giving primarily in Chautauqua
County and, secondarily, in neighboring areas of
western NY. No support for sectarian or religious
organizations. No grants to individuals.
**Publications:** Annual report (including
application guidelines).
**Application information:** A signed grant
agreement is required before approval of the
grant. Application form not required.
  *Initial approach:* Letter of inquiry
  *Copies of proposal:* 12
  *Deadline(s):* Apr. 1, Aug. 1, and Dec. 1
  *Board meeting date(s):* Mar., July, and Nov.
  *Final notification:* 1 to 4 months
**Officers and Directors:\*** Charles T. Hall,\* Pres.;
Paul W. Sandberg,\* V.P.; Linda Swanson,\* Secy.;
Rhoe B. Henderson III,\* Treas.; Thomas M.
Cardman, Exec. Dir.; George A. Campbell,
Daniel Kathman, Lillian V. Ney, Bertram Parker,
Geraldine Parker.
**Number of staff:** 1 full-time professional; 2
full-time support.
**EIN:** 166050287
**Recent grants for library/information services:**
431-1 Chautauqua-Cattaraugus Library System,
  Jamestown, NY, $28,810. For renewal of
  book plan. 1998.
431-2 James Prendergast Library, Jamestown,
  NY, $37,000. For books. 1998.

## 432
### Leopold R. Gellert Family Trust
122 E. 42nd St., 34th Fl.
New York, NY 10168-0070

Established in 1962.
**Donor(s):** Robert J. Gellert, Max E. Gellert,
Donald N. Gellert.
**Grantmaker type:** Independent foundation
**Financial data** (yr. ended 05/31/99): Assets,
$1,087,341 (M); expenditures, $140,207;
qualifying distributions, $129,364; giving
activities include $129,600 for 15 grants (high:
$60,000; low: $300).
**Purpose and activities:** Giving primarily for
performing arts, education, and human services.
**Fields of interest:** Opera; performing arts,
education; music; higher education; libraries
(public); education; hospitals (general); human
services; federated giving programs.
**Limitations:** Applications not accepted. Giving
primarily in NY. No grants to individuals.
**Application information:** Contributes only to
pre-selected organizations.
**Trustees:** Donald N. Gellert, Max E. Gellert,
Robert J. Gellert, William R. Peters.
**EIN:** 136085289

**433**
**The GGM Trust**
70 E. 10 St., Ste. 6U
New York, NY 10003

Established in 1997.
**Donor(s):** Gertrude G. Michelson.
**Grantmaker type:** Independent foundation
**Financial data** (yr. ended 12/31/98): Assets,
$434,839 (M); expenditures, $104,100;
qualifying distributions, $103,178; giving
activities include $104,100 for 39 grants (high:
$36,500; low: $100).
**Purpose and activities:** Giving for legal
education and services, higher education,
religion, and for health and human services.
**Fields of interest:** Museums (children's); ballet;
theater; music; orchestra (symphony); higher
education; law school/education; libraries
(public); hospitals (general); health care, blood
supply; cerebral palsy; cancer; legal services;
food distribution, meals on wheels; YM/YWCAs
& YM/YWHAs; children, services; homeless,
human services; civil rights, minorities; civil
liberties, advocacy; gerontology; Protestant
agencies & churches; Jewish agencies & temples.
**Limitations:** Applications not accepted. Giving
primarily in NY. No grants to individuals.
**Application information:** Contributes only to
pre-selected organizations.
**Trustees:** Gertrude G. Michelson, Horace
Michelson.
**EIN:** 137097804

**434**
**Gilder Foundation, Inc.** ▼
c/o Anchin, Block & Anchin, LLP
1375 Broadway
New York, NY 10018 (212) 765-2500
*Contact:* Devon Cross, Exec. Dir.

Established in 1965 in NY.
**Donor(s):** Richard Gilder.
**Grantmaker type:** Independent foundation
**Financial data** (yr. ended 12/31/98): Assets,
$58,580,648 (M); gifts received, $7,998,319;
expenditures, $8,062,782; qualifying
distributions, $7,937,253; giving activities
include $7,716,983 for 216 grants (high:
$1,768,216; average: $5,000–$75,000).
**Purpose and activities:** Support for libraries,
scholarship funds, and secondary education;
support also for recreational programs, public
affairs organizations, and cultural groups.
**Fields of interest:** Arts/cultural programs;
education; recreation; economic development;
public affairs, association.
**Limitations:** Applications not accepted. Giving
primarily in NY. No grants to individuals.
**Application information:** Contributes only to
pre-selected organizations.
**Officers:** Richard Gilder, Jr., Pres.; Thomas L.
Rhodes, V.P.; Richard Schneidman, Secy.; David
Howe, Treas.; Devon Cross, Exec. Dir.
**EIN:** 136176041
**Recent grants for library/information services:**
**434-1** Gilder Lehrman Institute of American
History, NYC, NY, $1,768,216. For continued
support. 1998.
**434-2** New York Public Library, NYC, NY,
$10,000. 1998.
**434-3** Pierpont Morgan Library, NYC, NY,
$91,338. For continued support. 1998.

**435**
**Sol and Lillian Goldman Foundation**
c/o Solil Mgmt.
640 5th Ave., 3rd Fl.
New York, NY 10019
*Contact:* Amy Goldman

Established in 1981.
**Grantmaker type:** Independent foundation
**Financial data** (yr. ended 11/30/97): Assets,
$12,086 (M); expenditures, $138,185;
qualifying distributions, $138,127; giving
activities include $138,053 for grants.
**Fields of interest:** Libraries (public); hospitals
(general); philanthropy/voluntarism.
**Limitations:** Giving primarily in NY. No grants to
individuals.
**Application information:**
*Initial approach:* Letter
*Deadline(s):* None
**Officer:** Jane H. Goldman, Pres.
**Trustee:** Allan H. Goldman.
**EIN:** 133102400

**436**
**Barbara Lubin Goldsmith Foundation**
(Formerly Goldsmith-Perry Philanthropies, Inc.)
c/o Hecht and Co., PC
111 W. 40th St.
New York, NY 10018

Established in 1969 in NY.
**Donor(s):** Barbara Lubin Goldsmith Charitable
Trust, Joseph I. Lubin.‡
**Grantmaker type:** Independent foundation
**Financial data** (yr. ended 12/31/99): Assets,
$13,789,532 (M); expenditures, $1,512,566;
qualifying distributions, $1,278,631; giving
activities include $1,158,259 for grants.
**Purpose and activities:** Support primarily for
Jewish giving, a public library, higher education,
and cultural programs.
**Fields of interest:** Museums; arts/cultural
programs; higher education; libraries/library
science; children & youth, services; Jewish
agencies & temples.
**Limitations:** Applications not accepted. Giving
primarily in New York, NY. No grants to
individuals.
**Application information:** Contributes only to
pre-selected organizations.
**Officers and Directors:*** Barbara L. Goldsmith,*
Pres.; Alice Elgart,* Secy.
**Number of staff:** 1
**EIN:** 237031986

**437**
**Horace W. Goldsmith Foundation** ▼
375 Park Ave., Ste. 1602
New York, NY 10152 (212) 319-8700
*Contact:* James C. Slaughter, C.E.O.

Incorporated in 1955 in NY.
**Donor(s):** Horace W. Goldsmith.‡
**Grantmaker type:** Independent foundation
**Financial data** (yr. ended 12/31/99): Assets,
$860,484,602 (M); expenditures, $36,459,897;
qualifying distributions, $34,250,472; giving
activities include $33,630,300 for 502 grants
(high: $600,000; low: $5,000; average:
$5,000–$500,000).

**Purpose and activities:** Support for cultural
programs, including the performing arts and
museums; Jewish welfare funds and temple
support; hospitals and a geriatric center; and
education, especially higher education.
**Fields of interest:** Visual arts; museums;
performing arts; dance; theater; music;
arts/cultural programs; education, research;
higher education; business school/education;
libraries/library science; education; natural
resource conservation & protection; hospitals
(general); family planning; medical care,
rehabilitation; cancer; AIDS; medical research;
cancer research; AIDS research; crime/law
enforcement; human services; aging, centers &
services; homeless, human services;
international relief; Jewish federated giving
programs; Jewish agencies & temples; disabled;
aging; homeless; general charitable giving.
**International interests:** Israel.
**Types of support:** General/operating support;
continuing support; capital campaigns;
building/renovation; endowments; scholarship
funds; research; matching/challenge support.
**Limitations:** Applications not accepted. Giving
primarily in AZ, MA, and New York, NY. No
grants to individuals.
**Application information:** Foundation depends
almost exclusively on internally initiated grants.
*Board meeting date(s):* 6 times a year
**Managing Directors:** James C. Slaughter, C.E.O.;
Richard L. Menschel, Robert B. Menschel,
Thomas Slaughter, William A. Slaughter.
**Number of staff:** 1 full-time support.
**EIN:** 136107758
**Recent grants for library/information services:**
**437-1** Amagansett Free Library, Amagansett, NY,
$50,000. 1998.
**437-2** Free Library of Philadelphia Foundation,
Philadelphia, PA, $150,000. 1998.
**437-3** Gilder Lehrman Institute of American
History, NYC, NY, $50,000. 1998.
**437-4** Leo Baeck Institute, NYC, NY, $25,000.
1998.
**437-5** Rutgers, The State University of New
Jersey Foundation, New Brunswick, NJ,
$10,000. For Oral History Archives. 1998.
**437-6** YIVO Institute for Jewish Research, NYC,
NY, $25,000. 1998.

**438**
**D. S. and R. H. Gottesman Foundation**
3 Manhattanville Rd.
Purchase, NY 10577

Incorporated in 1941 in NY.
**Grantmaker type:** Independent foundation
**Financial data** (yr. ended 10/31/99): Assets,
$1,581,269 (M); expenditures, $79,600;
qualifying distributions, $77,590; giving
activities include $76,000 for 1 grant.
**Purpose and activities:** Giving primarily for a
school for the deaf.
**Fields of interest:** Education, special;
libraries/library science; disabled.
**International interests:** Israel.
**Limitations:** Applications not accepted. Giving
primarily in New York, NY; giving also in Israel.
No grants to individuals.
**Application information:** Contributes only to
pre-selected organizations.
**Officers and Directors:*** Ira D. Wallach,* Pres.;
Armand P. Bartos,* V.P.; Edgar Wachenheim III,

V.P.; Peter C. Siegfried, Secy.-Treas.; Celeste G. Bartos, Philip Mayerson, Miriam G. Wallach.
**EIN:** 136101701

### 439
### The Gramercy Park Foundation, Inc.
c/o Zemlock, Levy, Bick & Karnbad
225 Broadway
New York, NY 10007
*Contact:* Lawrence S. Karnbad

Incorporated in 1952 in NY.
**Donor(s):** Benjamin Sonnenberg, Helen Sonnenberg Tucker.
**Grantmaker type:** Independent foundation
**Financial data** (yr. ended 12/31/99): Assets, $3,905,542 (M); expenditures, $230,992; qualifying distributions, $199,734; giving activities include $199,946 for 104 grants (high: $25,100; low: $50).
**Purpose and activities:** Grants for arts and cultural programs, with emphasis on libraries and the performing arts; support also for higher education, including music education.
**Fields of interest:** Performing arts; music; arts/cultural programs; higher education; libraries/library science.
**Limitations:** Giving primarily in the metropolitan New York, NY, area. No grants to individuals.
**Application information:** Application form not required.
  *Initial approach:* Letter
  *Deadline(s):* None
**Officers:** Helen Sonnenberg Tucker, Pres.; Steven Tucker, Secy.; William Spears, Treas.
**Number of staff:** 1 part-time support.
**EIN:** 132507282

### 440
### Greenhill Family Foundation
c/o Greenhill & Co., LLC
31 W. 52nd St., 16th Fl.
New York, NY 10019 (212) 408-0666
*Contact:* Robert F. Greenhill, Tr.

Established in 1997.
**Donor(s):** Robert F. Greenhill.
**Grantmaker type:** Independent foundation
**Financial data** (yr. ended 12/31/98): Assets, $2,516,966 (M); expenditures, $154,579; qualifying distributions, $149,057; giving activities include $150,000 for 20 grants (high: $80,000; low: $300).
**Purpose and activities:** Support primarily for a library and a photography center. Funding also for education and federated giving programs.
**Fields of interest:** Photography; libraries (public); education; federated giving programs.
**Limitations:** Giving primarily in CT, MA, and NY.
**Application information:**
  *Initial approach:* Letter
  *Deadline(s):* None
**Trustees:** Gayle G. Greenhill, Robert F. Greenhill.
**EIN:** 061488779

### 441
### Alexis Gregory Foundation
c/o Vendome Press
1370 Ave. of the Americas, No. 2003
New York, NY 10019-4602
*Contact:* Alexis Gregory, Pres.

Established in 1986 in NY.
**Donor(s):** Alexis Gregory.
**Grantmaker type:** Independent foundation
**Financial data** (yr. ended 12/31/98): Assets, $2,699,978 (M); gifts received, $253,759; expenditures, $169,738; qualifying distributions, $159,226; giving activities include $153,500 for 20 grants (high: $106,000; low: $100).
**Purpose and activities:** Giving primarily for education purposes.
**Fields of interest:** Museums; arts/cultural programs; libraries/library science; health associations; AIDS; AIDS research; human services; Jewish agencies & temples.
**Limitations:** Giving primarily in NY.
**Application information:** Application form not required.
  *Initial approach:* Letter or proposal
  *Deadline(s):* None
**Officers:** Alexis Gregory, Pres.; Peter Gregory, V.P.; Larry Levett, Secy.
**EIN:** 133201280

### 442
### Hebrew Technical Institute
c/o O'Connor, Davies & Co.
60 E. 42nd St.
New York, NY 10165-3698
*Contact:* Anita Goldberg
*Application address:* c/o Lawrence Properties, 855 Ave. of the Americas, New York, NY 10020

Established in 1884.
**Grantmaker type:** Independent foundation
**Financial data** (yr. ended 12/31/97): Assets, $3,652,337 (M); gifts received, $21,471; expenditures, $377,813; qualifying distributions, $363,105; giving activities include $359,500 for 14 grants (high: $60,000; low: $9,000).
**Purpose and activities:** Support for technical and vocational education.
**Fields of interest:** Museums (science & technology); vocational education; higher education; engineering school/education; libraries (public); employment, services.
**Types of support:** General/operating support.
**Limitations:** Giving primarily in NY. No grants to individuals.
**Application information:** Application form not required.
  *Deadline(s):* None
  *Board meeting date(s):* Quarterly
**Directors:** Catherine H. Behrend, Lawrence A. Benenson, Andrew Berkman, Seth H. Dubin, John R. Menke, Herbert A. Raisler, Hyman B. Ritchin, Sandra Priest Rose, Robert Rosenthal, Bruce D. Schlechter, Charles S. Weilman.
**EIN:** 135562240

### 443
### The Heckscher Foundation for Children ▼
17 E. 47th St.
New York, NY 10017 (212) 371-7775
*Contact:* Virginia Sloane, Pres.
*FAX:* (212) 371-7787

Incorporated in 1921 in NY.
**Donor(s):** August Heckscher.‡
**Grantmaker type:** Independent foundation
**Financial data** (yr. ended 12/31/99): Assets, $121,323,392 (M); expenditures, $3,574,813; qualifying distributions, $3,396,661; giving activities include $3,015,911 for 194 grants (high: $140,000; low: $139; average: $100–$25,000).
**Purpose and activities:** To promote the welfare of children; grants particularly for child welfare and family service agencies, education, recreation, music and the performing arts, health and hospitals, summer youth programs and camps, and aid to the handicapped.
**Fields of interest:** Museums; performing arts; arts/cultural programs; early childhood education; child development, education; libraries/library science; education; environment; hospitals (general); health care; substance abuse, services; health associations; recreation; human services; youth, services; child development, services; family services; homeless, human services; minorities; disabled; economically disadvantaged.
**Types of support:** Capital campaigns; building/renovation; equipment; program development; seed money; curriculum development; scholarship funds; matching/challenge support.
**Limitations:** Giving primarily in the greater New York, NY, area. No grants to individuals, or for operating budgets, annual campaigns, deficit financing, fellowships, or endowment funds; no loans.
**Publications:** Application guidelines, informational brochure.
**Application information:** Application form not required.
  *Initial approach:* Letter or proposal
  *Copies of proposal:* 1
  *Deadline(s):* None
  *Board meeting date(s):* Jan., Mar., May, July, Sept., and Nov.
  *Final notification:* 2 months
**Officers and Trustees:\*** Howard G. Sloane,\* Chair.; Virginia Sloane,\* Pres.; William D. Hart, Jr.,\* Secy.; Phyllis Fannan, Carole S. Landman, Gail Meyers, George Noumair, Fred Obser, Howard Rosenbaum, Marlene Shyer, Arthur J. Smadbeck, Louis Smadbeck, Jr., Mina Smadbeck, Paul Smadbeck.
**Number of staff:** 1 full-time professional; 2 part-time professional.
**EIN:** 131820170
**Recent grants for library/information services:**
**443-1** Citizens Advice Bureau, Bronx, NY, $10,000. 1998.

### 444
### Heilbrunn Foundation
c/o Herbert Paul
370 Lexington Ave., Rm. 1001
New York, NY 10017-2416

Established in 1960.

**Donor(s):** Robert Heilbrunn, Berkshire Hathaway, Inc.
**Grantmaker type:** Independent foundation
**Financial data** (yr. ended 12/31/99): Assets, $1,991,428 (M); gifts received, $171,929; expenditures, $4,309,750; qualifying distributions, $4,309,750; giving activities include $4,302,669 for 54 grants (high: $1,948,750; low: $40).
**Fields of interest:** Arts, multipurpose centers/programs; museums; higher education; libraries (public); health associations; human services; Jewish federated giving programs; Jewish agencies & temples; general charitable giving.
**Limitations:** Applications not accepted. Giving primarily in New York, NY. No grants to individuals.
**Application information:** Contributes only to pre-selected organizations.
**Officers:** Robert Heilbrunn, Pres.; Harriet Heilbrunn, Secy.-Treas.
**EIN:** 136138257

---

**445**

**Heineman Foundation for Research, Educational, Charitable and Scientific Purposes, Inc.**
c/o Brown Brothers Harriman Trust Co.
63 Wall St.
New York, NY 10005

Incorporated in 1947 in DE.
**Donor(s):** Dannie N. Heineman.‡
**Grantmaker type:** Independent foundation
**Financial data** (yr. ended 12/31/99): Assets, $18,197,414 (M); expenditures, $748,686; qualifying distributions, $663,910; giving activities include $638,000 for 11 grants (high: $128,000; low: $25,000).
**Purpose and activities:** Primary areas of interest include the medical sciences and physics. Support for research programs in mathematical sciences and medicine; grants for higher education, specialized libraries (including the Heineman Library of Rare Books and Manuscripts given to the Pierpont Morgan Library, New York), music schools, and two annual physics awards.
**Fields of interest:** Visual arts; performing arts; dance; theater; music; language & linguistics; literature; arts/cultural programs; education, research; early childhood education; child development, education; elementary school/education; higher education; adult/continuing education; adult education—literacy & basic skills; libraries/library science; reading; education; natural resource conservation & protection; energy; environment; wildlife preservation & protection; health care; health associations; heart & circulatory diseases; biomedicine; medical research; heart & circulatory research; food services; human services; children & youth, services; child development, services; women, centers & services; race/intergroup relations; civil rights; physical/earth sciences; chemistry; mathematics; physics; engineering & technology; biological sciences; science; minorities; women; economically disadvantaged.
**Types of support:** General/operating support; endowments; program development;

publication; seed money; fellowships; research; technical assistance.
**Limitations:** Giving on a national basis. No grants to individuals.
**Application information:** Application form not required.
*Copies of proposal:* 1
*Board meeting date(s):* Apr. and Nov.
**Officers:** Ann R. Podlipny, Pres.; Maria Heineman Bergendahl, V.P.; Andrew Podlipny, Secy.; Agnes Gautier, Treas.
**Directors:** Anders Bergendahl, Edith Fehr, Marilyn Heineman, June Heineman-Morris, Joan Heineman-Schur, Glen Morris, David Heineman Rose, James A. Rose, Marian Heineman Rose, Simon Rose.
**Number of staff:** None.
**EIN:** 136082899

---

**446**

**Hazen B. Hinman, Sr. Foundation, Inc.**
530 Henry St.
Rome, NY 13440 (315) 336-5500
*Contact:* Mark F. Hinman, Treas.

Established in 1988 in NY.
**Grantmaker type:** Operating foundation
**Financial data** (yr. ended 12/31/98): Assets, $17,995 (M); gifts received, $60,000; expenditures, $66,673; qualifying distributions, $66,531; giving activities include $66,535 for 50 grants (high: $10,000; low: $35).
**Fields of interest:** Higher education; libraries/library science; health associations; Girl Scouts; human services; federated giving programs; Christian agencies & churches; general charitable giving.
**Types of support:** General/operating support.
**Limitations:** Giving primarily in central NY.
**Application information:**
*Initial approach:* Proposal
*Deadline(s):* None
**Officers:** A. Buol Hinman, Pres.; Mark F. Hinman, Treas.
**Directors:** David N. Hinman, Kirk B. Hinman.
**EIN:** 166093005

---

**447**

**The Howard and Bush Foundation, Inc.**
2 Belle Ave.
Troy, NY 12180 (518) 271-1134
*Contact:* Deborah Byers

Incorporated in 1961 in CT.
**Donor(s):** Edith Mason Howard,‡ Julia Howard Bush.‡
**Grantmaker type:** Independent foundation
**Financial data** (yr. ended 12/31/98): Assets, $4,573,518 (M); expenditures, $534,250; qualifying distributions, $503,432; giving activities include $467,570 for grants (average: $5,000–$30,000).
**Purpose and activities:** Emphasis on arts and culture, education, civic and urban affairs, and social service and health programs that benefit residents of Rensselaer County, NY.
**Fields of interest:** Arts/cultural programs; adult education—literacy & basic skills; libraries/library science; education; health care; home services; community development.

**Types of support:** Building/renovation; equipment; program development; seed money; matching/challenge support.
**Limitations:** Giving limited to programs that benefit residents of Rensselaer County, NY. Generally no support for government or largely tax-supported agencies, or churches not connected with the founders. No grants to individuals, or for endowment funds, operating budgets, reserve or revolving funds, or deficit financing.
**Publications:** Application guidelines, grants list.
**Application information:** Application form required.
*Initial approach:* Brief letter or telephone
*Copies of proposal:* 6
*Deadline(s):* Feb. 14, and Sept. 1 for concept papers
*Board meeting date(s):* Apr. and Oct.
*Final notification:* Within 14 days after board meeting
**Officers, Directors and Trustees:*** David S. Haviland,* Pres.; Margaret Mochan,* V.P.; Donald C. Bowes,* Secy.; David W. Parmelee,* Treas.; Judith A. Barnes.
**Number of staff:** None.
**EIN:** 066059063

---

**448**

**Hudson River Bancorp, Inc. Foundation**
1 Hudson City Centre
P.O. Box 76
Hudson, NY 12534 (518) 828-4760
*Contact:* Holly Rappleyea

Established in 1998 in NY.
**Donor(s):** Hudson River Bank & Trust Co.
**Grantmaker type:** Company-sponsored foundation
**Financial data** (yr. ended 03/31/99): Assets, $5,611,561 (M); gifts received, $5,200,120; expenditures, $147,323; qualifying distributions, $135,996; giving activities include $95,006 for 100 grants (high: $25,000; low: $25).
**Purpose and activities:** Giving primarily to public libraries.
**Fields of interest:** Education; libraries/library science; hospitals (general); youth, services.
**Limitations:** Giving primarily in upstate NY.
**Application information:** Application form not required.
*Initial approach:* Telephone
*Deadline(s):* None
**Officers and Directors:*** Marilyn A. Herrington,* Pres.; William H. Jones,* V.P.; Stanley Bardwell, M.D.,* Treas.; Earl Schram.
**EIN:** 223595668

---

**449**

**The Huguenot Society of America**
122 E. 58th St.
New York, NY 10022

Established in 1883 in NY.
**Grantmaker type:** Independent foundation
**Financial data** (yr. ended 02/28/98): Assets, $3,996,899 (M); gifts received, $1,615; expenditures, $166,227; qualifying distributions, $140,259; giving activities include $89,159 for 23 grants (high: $37,750; low: $700).

**Purpose and activities:** Giving limited to scholarships for higher education at listed colleges to descendants of Huguenots.
**Fields of interest:** History & archaeology; historic preservation/historical societies; libraries/library science.
**Limitations:** Applications not accepted. No grants to individuals.
**Application information:** Contributes only to pre-selected organizations.
**Officers:** William W. Reese, Pres.; Mieke Armstrong, Secy.; Courtney A. Haff, Treas.
**Number of staff:** 1 part-time support.
**EIN:** 136117102

### 450
### Nila B. Hulbert Foundation
6 Ford Ave.
Oneonta, NY 13820-1898 (607) 432-6720
*Contact:* Henry L. Hulbert, Tr.

Established about 1971.
**Donor(s):** Nila B. Hulbert.
**Grantmaker type:** Independent foundation
**Financial data** (yr. ended 12/31/99): Assets, $8,239,790 (M); expenditures, $383,780; qualifying distributions, $374,041; giving activities include $319,934 for 23 grants (high: $140,000; low: $500).
**Purpose and activities:** Giving primarily for the arts, education, and human services.
**Fields of interest:** Higher education; libraries/library science; hospitals (general); recreation; human services; community development.
**Limitations:** Giving primarily in Oneonta, NY.
**Application information:**
  *Initial approach:* Letter
  *Deadline(s):* Sept. 30
**Trustees:** Henry L. Hulbert, J. Burton Hulbert, William H. Hulbert.
**EIN:** 237039996

### 451
### The Hultquist Foundation
c/o Morgan Stanley & Co.
1221 Ave. of the Americas
New York, NY 10020
*Contact:* Timothy Hultquist, Pres.

Established in 1991 in DE.
**Donor(s):** Timothy Hultquist.
**Grantmaker type:** Independent foundation
**Financial data** (yr. ended 12/31/98): Assets, $2,618,574 (M); expenditures, $116,797; qualifying distributions, $114,500; giving activities include $114,500 for 17 grants (high: $27,500; low: $1,000).
**Purpose and activities:** Giving to Christian organizations, secondary education, substance abuse treatment centers and human service organizations.
**Fields of interest:** Elementary/secondary education; university; libraries/library science; medical research; human services; youth, services.
**Types of support:** General/operating support; capital campaigns; building/renovation; emergency funds; scholarship funds; research.
**Limitations:** Applications not accepted. Giving primarily in Fairfield County, CT, and the

metropolitan New York, NY, area. No grants to individuals.
**Application information:**
  *Board meeting date(s):* Varies
**Officers:** Timothy Hultquist, Pres.; Cynthia M. Hultquist, V.P.
**Director:** Wayne B. Hultquist.
**Number of staff:** None.
**EIN:** 980120582

### 452
### Graham Hunter Foundation, Inc.
c/o Saint Andrew's Society
20 Corporate Woods Blvd., Ste. 600
Albany, NY 12211-2396
*Contact:* Thomas G. Burke, V.P.

Established in 1946 in NY.
**Donor(s):** Graham Hunter.‡
**Grantmaker type:** Independent foundation
**Financial data** (yr. ended 12/31/97): Assets, $2,177,407 (M); expenditures, $126,364; qualifying distributions, $101,501; giving activities include $92,546 for 24 grants (high: $39,346; low: $300).
**Purpose and activities:** Grants primarily for a library; some support for higher education, including medical education.
**Fields of interest:** Arts/cultural programs; higher education; libraries/library science; health care.
**Limitations:** Applications not accepted. No grants to individuals.
**Application information:** Contributes only to pre-selected organizations.
**Officers:** Carol Hunter Kelley, Pres.; William R. MacClarence, V.P. and Secy.; Thomas G. Burke, V.P. and Treas.
**Trustee:** Thomas W. Burke.
**EIN:** 136161726

### 453
### International Paper Company Foundation ▼
2 Manhattanville Rd.
Purchase, NY 10577 (914) 397-1500
*Contact:* Phyllis Epp, Exec. Dir.
*FAX:* (914) 397-1505; URL: http://www.internationalpaper.com/our_world/outreach_frame.html

Incorporated in 1952 in NY.
**Donor(s):** International Paper Co.
**Grantmaker type:** Company-sponsored foundation
**Financial data** (yr. ended 12/31/98): Assets, $59,891,397 (M); gifts received, $317,388; expenditures, $5,227,210; qualifying distributions, $4,842,286; giving activities include $4,640,905 for grants (high: $250,000; low: $20).
**Purpose and activities:** Grants are primarily for model projects in company communities with focus on pre-college levels of education, programs for minorities and women in the sciences, health and welfare services for children, and community and cultural affairs. Operates EDCORE (Education and Community Resources Program) in selected International Paper communities for public schools by invitation only.
**Fields of interest:** Arts/cultural programs; early childhood education; elementary

school/education; secondary school/education; vocational education; engineering school/education; adult/continuing education; adult education—literacy & basic skills; libraries/library science; reading; education; environment; health care; substance abuse, services; human services; children & youth, services; rural development; engineering; minorities; economically disadvantaged.
**Types of support:** General/operating support; continuing support; program development; seed money; curriculum development; fellowships; employee matching gifts; matching/challenge support.
**Limitations:** Giving primarily in communities where there are company plants and mills, and in Memphis, TN. No support for athletic organizations or religious groups. No grants to individuals, or for endowment funds or capital expenses; no loans.
**Publications:** Annual report, occasional report, informational brochure (including application guidelines), grants list, application guidelines.
**Application information:** Address requests from organizations in company communities to the local company contact person; no applications accepted for EDCORE (Education and Community Resources) Program or for fellowships. Application form required.
  *Initial approach:* Letter, telephone, or proposal with application to local facility
  *Copies of proposal:* 1
  *Deadline(s):* Mar. 1 for current year funding
  *Board meeting date(s):* June
  *Final notification:* July
**Officers and Directors:*** James E. Lee,* Pres.; Carol Samalin, Secy.; Robert Hunkeler, Treas.; Phyllis Epp, Exec. Dir.; John T. Dillon, James P. Melican, Jr.
**Trustee:** State Street Corp.
**Number of staff:** 2 full-time professional; 2 part-time support.
**EIN:** 136155080

### 454
### John Alfred & Oscar Johnson Memorial Trust
c/o The Chase Manhattan Bank, N.A.
P.O. Box 1412
Rochester, NY 14603-1412
*Contact:* Carole W. Sellstrom, Coord.
*Application address:* 9-11 E. 4th St., P.O. Box 50, Jamestown, NY 14702, tel.: (716) 484-7190

Established in 1996 in NY.
**Donor(s):** John Alfred Johnson.‡
**Grantmaker type:** Independent foundation
**Financial data** (yr. ended 01/31/99): Assets, $9,142,454 (M); expenditures, $583,575; qualifying distributions, $522,008; giving activities include $446,915 for 27 grants (high: $200,000; low: $300).
**Purpose and activities:** Support for charitable, religious, and educational organizations that benefit the citizens of Jamestown, NY. Consideration will also be given to organizations that carry out the enrichment of Swedish heritage.
**Fields of interest:** Higher education; libraries (public); education; health care; Salvation Army; YM/YWCAs & YM/YWHAs; family services; civic centers; Protestant agencies & churches.

**Limitations:** Giving primarily in Jamestown, NY, and the surrounding areas. No grants to individuals, or for scholarships.
**Application information:**
  *Initial approach:* Written application
  *Deadline(s):* June 1 and Dec. 1
**Trustees:** John L. Sellstrom, The Chase Manhattan Bank, N.A.
**EIN:** 166438291

## 455
## Rita J. and Stanley H. Kaplan Foundation, Inc.
866 United Nations Plz., Ste. 306
New York, NY  10017  (212) 688-1047
*Contact:* Rita J. Kaplan, Secy.
*FAX:* (212) 688-6907; E-mail: skaplanzoo@aol.com

Incorporated in 1984 in NY.
**Donor(s):** Stanley H. Kaplan, Rita J. Kaplan.
**Grantmaker type:** Independent foundation
**Financial data** (yr. ended 12/31/99): Assets, $25,715,239 (M); gifts received, $1,500,000; expenditures, $2,417,147; qualifying distributions, $2,046,917; giving activities include $1,902,342 for 396 grants (high: $330,000; low: $10; average: $100–$5,000).
**Purpose and activities:** Support for cultural programs, including music, arts, theater, performing arts, and museums; libraries; medical research and education, including mental illness, AIDS and cancer research; social and family services, including programs for the homeless, children, and women; Jewish giving; and organizations promoting human rights.
**Fields of interest:** Visual arts; museums; performing arts; dance; theater; music; humanities; arts/cultural programs; education, association; education, research; education, fund raising; elementary/secondary education; early childhood education; child development, education; elementary school/education; higher education; medical school/education; theological school/education; libraries/library science; education; mental health/crisis services; cancer; AIDS; biomedicine; medical research; cancer research; AIDS research; gun control; domestic violence prevention; recreation; youth development, services; human services; children & youth, services; child development, services; family services; international affairs, goodwill promotion; human rights (international); race/intergroup relations; Roman Catholic federated giving programs; Jewish federated giving programs; leadership development; Jewish agencies & temples; religion; disabled; aging; women; gays/lesbians; economically disadvantaged; homeless; general charitable giving.
**International interests:** Israel.
**Types of support:** General/operating support; continuing support; annual campaigns; capital campaigns; building/renovation; equipment; endowments; program development; professorships; seed money; fellowships; internship funds; research; in-kind gifts.
**Limitations:** Applications not accepted. Giving primarily in Boston, MA, and New York, NY; giving also in Israel. No grants to individuals.
**Application information:** Contributes only to pre-selected organizations.

**Officers and Directors:*** Stanley H. Kaplan,* Pres.; Nancy Kaplan Belsky, V.P.; Susan Beth Kaplan, V.P.; Rita J. Kaplan,* Secy.; Nancy W. Greenblatt, Exec. Dir.
**Number of staff:** 1 full-time professional; 1 part-time support.
**EIN:** 133221298

## 456
## The J. M. Kaplan Fund, Inc. ▼
261 Madison Ave., 19th Fl.
New York, NY  10016  (212) 767-0630
*Contact:* William P. Falahee, Cont.
*FAX:* (212) 767-0639; Application address for publication program: Futhermore, P.O. Box 667, Hudson, NY 12534; tel.: (518) 828-8900

Incorporated in 1948 in NY as Faigel Leah Foundation, Inc.; The J.M. Kaplan Fund, Inc., a DE corporation, merged with it in 1975 and was renamed The J.M. Kaplan Fund, Inc.
**Donor(s):** Members of the J.M. Kaplan family.
**Grantmaker type:** Independent foundation
**Financial data** (yr. ended 12/31/98): Assets, $134,342,052 (M); gifts received, $9,427,211; expenditures, $11,152,896; qualifying distributions, $7,968,506; giving activities include $7,236,580 for 259 grants (high: $1,827,910; low: $1,500; average: $5,000–$150,000).
**Purpose and activities:** Giving primarily in five areas: City Life (the arts, reading and knowledge acquisition, urban greening, and human services programs); Environment and Sustainable Business (partnerships between environmental groups and business); Exploration and New Technologies (the application of new technologies in archeology, geology, and geography); Human Rights; and Research and Public Policy. The fund offers program-related investments to encourage ventures of particular interest. The fund also has a trustee-initiated grants program that considers grant requests invited by the trustees.
**Fields of interest:** History & archaeology; arts/cultural programs; libraries/library science; natural resource conservation & protection; environment; human services; community development; public policy, research.
**Types of support:** General/operating support; continuing support; program development; publication; seed money; research; technical assistance; program-related investments/loans.
**Limitations:** Giving primarily in NY, with emphasis on New York City. No grants to individuals, including scholarships and fellowships, or for construction or building programs, endowment funds, operating budgets of educational or medical institutions, film or video, or sponsorship of books, dances, plays, or other works of art.
**Publications:** Annual report (including application guidelines).
**Application information:** Proposals received by FAX not considered. Application form required.
  *Initial approach:* 2- to 3-page letter or pre-application questionnaire
  *Copies of proposal:* 1
  *Deadline(s):* None; requests received after Oct. 1 will be carried over to next year
  *Board meeting date(s):* May, Aug. and Nov.
  *Final notification:* Formal letter

**Officers and Trustees:*** Peter W. Davidson,* Chair. and Treas.; Betsy Davidson,* Co-Chair.; Richard D. Kaplan,* Co-Chair.; William P. Falahee, Cont.; Conn Nugent, Exec. Dir.; G. Bradford Davidson, J. Matthew Davidson, Joan K. Davidson, Caio Fonseca, Elizabeth K. Fonseca, Isabel Fonseca, Quina Fonseca, Mary E. Kaplan.
**Number of staff:** 3 full-time professional; 1 full-time support.
**EIN:** 136090286
**Recent grants for library/information services:**
**456-1** Brooklyn Public Library, Brooklyn, NY, $150,000. For New Leadership Branch Project to create new management teams at branch level, broaden audiences and encourage active participation of local residents for Stone Avenue, Brownsville and Brower neighborhood libraries. 1998.
**456-2** Chancellors Literacy Campaign, NYC, NY, $40,000. For Fill-a-Bookshelf Program that creates mini-libraries in third grade public school classrooms throughout the city. 1998.
**456-3** New York Public Library, NYC, NY, $100,000. To expand Preschool Family Literacy Program to additional sites in the South Bronx: West Farms, High Bridge and Morrisania. 1998.
**456-4** New York Public Library, NYC, NY, $12,000. For book, Building New York City, by Rebecca Read Shana, published by W. W. Norton and Co. 1998.
**456-5** Poets House, NYC, NY, $10,000. For general support. 1998.
**456-6** Publicolor, NYC, NY, $36,000. For painting of Chancellor's school libraries by community of volunteer painters. 1998.
**456-7** Queens Library Foundation, Jamaica, NY, $110,000. To expand Dream Branches Pilot Project, effort to make underutilized branches dynamic centers of their local communities, to additional branches in Astoria and South Ozone Park. 1998.

## 457
## Ezra Jack Keats Foundation, Inc.
1005 E. 4th St.
Brooklyn, NY  11230
*Contact:* Deborah Pope, Exec. Dir.
*Application address for mini-grants:* 450 14th St., Brooklyn, NY 11215

Established in 1970.
**Grantmaker type:** Independent foundation
**Financial data** (yr. ended 12/31/99): Assets, $3,107,021 (M); expenditures, $123,753; qualifying distributions, $95,327; giving activities include $67,575 for 123 grants (high: $5,000; low: $25).
**Purpose and activities:** Giving for arts and culture, libraries and reading.
**Fields of interest:** Arts/cultural programs; libraries/library science; reading.
**Types of support:** Program development.
**Limitations:** Giving on a national basis. No grants to individuals.
**Application information:** Send SASE for application form. Application form required.
  *Deadline(s):* Sept. 15
  *Final notification:* Dec.

**Officers and Directors:** Martin Pope,* Pres.;
Lillie Pope,* V.P.; Reynold Ruffins, Treas.;
Deborah Pope, Exec. Dir.
**Number of staff:** 1 part-time support.
**EIN:** 237072750

## 458
## Stephen and Tabitha King Foundation, Inc. ▼
101 Park Ave.
New York, NY 10178 (212) 661-8200
*Contact:* Arthur B. Greene, Secy.

Established in 1986 in ME.
**Donor(s):** Stephen E. King.
**Grantmaker type:** Independent foundation
**Financial data** (yr. ended 12/31/98): Assets,
$5,609,881 (M); gifts received, $3,792,509;
expenditures, $3,584,047; qualifying
distributions, $3,571,234; giving activities
include $3,546,428 for 186 grants (high:
$1,000,000; low: $100; average:
$1,000–$50,000).
**Purpose and activities:** Giving primarily for the
arts, education (including libraries), and human
services.
**Fields of interest:** Orchestra (symphony);
arts/cultural programs; higher education;
libraries (public); education; health associations;
human services; federated giving programs.
**Limitations:** Giving primarily in ME.
**Application information:**
  *Initial approach:* Proposal
  *Deadline(s):* None
  *Final notification:* 2 months
**Officers:** Stephen E. King, Pres.; Tabitha King,
V.P.; Arthur B. Greene, Secy.
**EIN:** 133364647
**Recent grants for library/information services:**
**458-1** Carver Memorial Library, Searsport, ME,
  $10,000. 1998.
**458-2** Curtis Memorial Library, Brunswick, ME,
  $15,000. For capital campaign. 1998.
**458-3** Freeland Holmes Library, Oxford, ME,
  $15,000. 1998.
**458-4** Gardiner Public Library, Gardiner, ME,
  $60,000. 1998.
**458-5** Norway Memorial Library, Norway, ME,
  $25,000. 1998.
**458-6** Old Town Library, Old Town, ME,
  $30,000. For Girls Talk Program. 1998.
**458-7** Phillips Public Library, Phillips, ME,
  $30,000. 1998.
**458-8** Rockland Public Library Endowment
  Association, Rockland, ME, $50,000. 1998.
**458-9** Skidompha Library, Damariscotta, ME,
  $25,000. 1998.

## 459
## Kissinger Family Foundation, Inc.
c/o Walter B. Kissinger
200 Broadhollow Rd.
Melville, NY 11747

Established in 1997 in NY.
**Donor(s):** The Kissinger Family.
**Grantmaker type:** Independent foundation
**Financial data** (yr. ended 11/30/98): Assets,
$3,626,611 (M); gifts received, $11,998;
expenditures, $282,035; qualifying distributions,
$149,536; giving activities include $102,560 for
42 grants (high: $12,000; low: $50).

**Purpose and activities:** Giving primarily to
education, the arts, and human services.
**Fields of interest:** Arts/cultural programs;
libraries/library science; education; human
services; Jewish agencies & temples.
**Limitations:** Applications not accepted. No
grants to individuals.
**Application information:** Contributes only to
pre-selected organizations.
**Trustees:** Eugenie Kissinger, John Kissinger,
Thomas Kissinger, Walter B. Kissinger, William
Kissinger, Dana Kissinger-Matray.
**EIN:** 113397778

## 460
## Saul & Marion Kleinkramer Foundation
111 Cherry Valley Ave., Ste. 802
Garden City, NY 11530
*Contact:* Saul Kleinkramer, Pres.

Established in 1997 in NY.
**Donor(s):** Saul Kleinkramer.
**Grantmaker type:** Independent foundation
**Financial data** (yr. ended 12/31/99): Assets,
$1,300,765 (M); gifts received, $100,104;
expenditures, $71,999; qualifying distributions,
$56,433; giving activities include $61,250 for 6
grants (high: $35,000; low: $250).
**Purpose and activities:** Giving for the arts,
education, and Jewish organizations.
**Fields of interest:** Theater; libraries (public);
foundations (community); Jewish agencies &
temples.
**Officers:** Saul Kleinkramer, Pres.; Marion
Kleinkramer, Secy.
**Trustee:** Sandra L. Bruschi.
**EIN:** 113336273

## 461
## The Esther A. & Joseph Klingenstein Fund, Inc. ▼
787 7th Ave., 6th Fl.
New York, NY 10019-6016 (212) 492-6181
*Contact:* John Klingenstein, Pres.
*FAX:* (212) 492-7007

Incorporated in 1945 in NY.
**Donor(s):** Esther A. Klingenstein,‡ Joseph
Klingenstein.‡
**Grantmaker type:** Independent foundation
**Financial data** (yr. ended 09/30/99): Assets,
$140,576,947 (M); expenditures, $8,302,726;
qualifying distributions, $7,409,840; giving
activities include $5,754,060 for 91 grants (high:
$578,595; low: $1,000) and $1,210,000 for 30
grants to individuals (high: $45,000; low:
$40,000).
**Purpose and activities:** Primary interests in
neuroscientific research bearing on epilepsy and
in independent school education. Some support
also for the use of animals in biomedical
research and church and state separation.
**Fields of interest:** Elementary/secondary
education; epilepsy research; neuroscience
research; civil liberties, first amendment; public
policy, research.
**Types of support:** General/operating support;
continuing support; program development;
conferences/seminars; publication; seed money;
fellowships; research.

**Limitations:** No grants to individuals (except for
Neuroscience Fellowship Prog.), or for building
or endowment funds.
**Publications:** Informational brochure.
**Application information:** Application forms are
required for the Klingenstein Fellowship Awards,
and are available from department heads or
from the foundation.
  *Initial approach:* Letter or proposal
  *Copies of proposal:* 1
  *Deadline(s):* None
  *Board meeting date(s):* Generally 4 or 5 times
    a year
**Officers and Directors:** John Klingenstein,*
Pres. and Treas.; Frederick A. Klingenstein,* 1st
V.P. and Secy.; Patricia D. Klingenstein, Sharon
L. Klingenstein.
**Number of staff:** 2 full-time professional; 2
part-time professional; 1 full-time support.
**EIN:** 136028788
**Recent grants for library/information services:**
**461-1** Council for Basic Education, DC,
  $50,000. For program support. 1999.
**461-2** New York Public Library, NYC, NY,
  $500,000. For family programming. 1999.
**461-3** New York Public Library, NYC, NY,
  $24,585. For family programming. 1999.
**461-4** New York Public Library, NYC, NY,
  $23,350. For family programming. 1999.
**461-5** Sexuality Information and Education
  Council of the U.S. (SIECUS), NYC, NY,
  $25,000. For work on prevention of teenage
  pregnancy. 1999.

## 462
## The H. Frederick Krimendahl II Foundation
c/o Goldman Sachs & Co., Tax Dept.
85 Broad St., 30th Fl.
New York, NY 10004-2106

Established in 1968 in NY.
**Donor(s):** H. Frederick Krimendahl II.
**Grantmaker type:** Independent foundation
**Financial data** (yr. ended 05/31/99): Assets,
$8,126,179 (M); expenditures, $397,840;
qualifying distributions, $388,464; giving
activities include $393,320 for 102 grants (high:
$140,000; low: $100).
**Purpose and activities:** Giving primarily for
education and the arts, including substantial
support for The Library of Congress.
**Fields of interest:** Music; arts/cultural programs;
libraries/library science; education; hospitals
(general); health associations; children & youth,
services.
**Limitations:** Applications not accepted. Giving
primarily in New York, NY. No grants to
individuals.
**Application information:** Contributes only to
pre-selected organizations.
**Trustees:** Elizabeth K. Krimendahl, H. Frederick
Krimendahl II, Nancy C. Krimendahl, James S.
Marcus, Emilia A. Saint-Amand.
**EIN:** 237000391

## 463
### Kvistad Foundation
167 DuBois Rd.
Shokan, NY   12481
*Contact:* Diane Kvistad, Pres.
*E-mail:* fund@chimes.com

Established in 1988.
**Donor(s):** Garry Kvistad, Diane Herrick Kvistad, Woodstock Percussion, Inc.
**Grantmaker type:** Operating foundation
**Financial data** (yr. ended 12/31/99): Assets, $559,040 (M); gifts received, $90,000; expenditures, $90,339; qualifying distributions, $90,539; giving activities include $83,260 for grants.
**Purpose and activities:** Support primarily to organizations which provide food and shelter for the poor, including the elderly and children, and to arts organizations and libraries.
**Fields of interest:** Arts/cultural programs; libraries/library science; education; food services; human services; children & youth, services; aging, centers & services; aging; economically disadvantaged.
**Limitations:** Giving primarily in Ulster County, NY. No grants to individuals.
**Application information:** Application form not required.
  *Deadline(s):* Nov. 1
**Officers:** Diane Herrick Kvistad, Pres.; Garry Kvistad, Secy.
**EIN:** 141702791

## 464
### Lake Placid Education Foundation
157 Saranac Ave.
Lake Placid, NY   12946   (518) 523-4433
*Contact:* John Lansing, Exec. Dir.
*Application address:* Crestview Plz., Lake Placid, NY 12946; FAX: (518) 523-4434; E-mail: 76103.1673@compuserve.com

Established in 1922 in NY.
**Donor(s):** Melvil Dewey.‡
**Grantmaker type:** Independent foundation
**Financial data** (yr. ended 06/30/00): Assets, $10,229,580 (M); expenditures, $405,879; qualifying distributions, $366,117; giving activities include $341,705 for 34 grants (high: $70,000; low: $500; average: $500–$40,000).
**Purpose and activities:** Giving for public and private schools, the arts, and libraries.
**Fields of interest:** Arts/cultural programs; elementary/secondary education; higher education; libraries/library science; education.
**Types of support:** General/operating support; continuing support; equipment; program development; conferences/seminars; seed money; scholarship funds; program-related investments/loans; scholarships—to individuals; matching/challenge support.
**Limitations:** Giving primarily in the northern Adirondack region of NY.
**Publications:** Informational brochure (including application guidelines).
**Application information:** Application form not required.
  *Copies of proposal:* 1
  *Deadline(s):* Nov. 1
  *Board meeting date(s):* Jan., May, and Aug.
  *Final notification:* Feb. 1

**Officers and Directors:*** Frederick C. Calder,* Pres.; Meredith Prime, V.P.; George Hart,* Secy.; Peter F. Roland, Treas.
**Number of staff:** 1 part-time professional; 1 part-time support.
**EIN:** 510243919

## 465
### Larsen Fund
575 Madison Ave., Ste. 1006
New York, NY   10022
*Contact:* Patricia S. Palmer, Grants Admin.
*Application address:* 2537 Post Rd., Ste. 224, Southport, CT 06490

Incorporated in 1941 in NY.
**Donor(s):** Roy E. Larsen.‡
**Grantmaker type:** Independent foundation
**Financial data** (yr. ended 12/31/99): Assets, $15,503,127 (M); expenditures, $954,771; qualifying distributions, $725,437; giving activities include $725,437 for 73 grants (high: $200,500; low: $500).
**Purpose and activities:** Support for education, including medical and secondary schools, educational research, computer sciences, and social sciences; human services, including youth, family services, and family planning; hospitals and population studies; law, justice and urban affairs; intercultural relations; conservation, ecology, and wildlife preservation; and the arts.
**Fields of interest:** Museums; theater; education, research; secondary school/education; higher education; medical school/education; libraries/library science; natural resource conservation & protection; environment; wildlife preservation & protection; hospitals (general); family planning; crime/law enforcement; children & youth, services; family services; race/intergroup relations; community development; computer science; social sciences; population studies; public affairs.
**Types of support:** Annual campaigns; capital campaigns; land acquisition; program development; professorships; curriculum development; fellowships; internship funds; scholarship funds; research; consulting services.
**Limitations:** Giving primarily in CT, MA, the Minneapolis, MN, area, and the New York, NY, area. No grants to individuals.
**Publications:** Annual report (including application guidelines).
**Application information:** Application form not required.
  *Initial approach:* Letter
  *Copies of proposal:* 1
  *Deadline(s):* Submit proposal at least 60 days prior to meeting dates
  *Board meeting date(s):* Beginning of June and Dec.
**Officers and Directors:*** Robert R. Larsen,* Pres. and Treas.; Christopher Larsen,* V.P.; Ann Larsen Simonson,* V.P.; Jonathan Z. Larsen,* Secy.
**Number of staff:** 2 part-time support.
**EIN:** 136104430

## 466
### Mary Woodard Lasker Charitable Trust
110 E. 42nd St., Ste. 1300
New York, NY   10017   (212) 286-0222
*Contact:* Dr. Neen Hunt, Exec. Dir.
*FAX:* (212) 286-0924; E-mail: nhunt@laskerfoundation.org

Established in 1994 in NY.
**Donor(s):** Mary W. Lasker.‡
**Grantmaker type:** Independent foundation
**Financial data** (yr. ended 12/31/97): Assets, $22,000,000 (M); gifts received, $37,000; expenditures, $1,600,000; qualifying distributions, $700,000; giving activities include $700,000 for grants.
**Fields of interest:** Higher education; libraries/library science; health associations; medical research.
**Limitations:** Giving primarily in NY.
**Application information:**
  *Initial approach:* Letter or Proposal
  *Deadline(s):* None
  *Board meeting date(s):* Quarterly
**Officers:** Neen Hunt, Exec. Dir.
**Trustees:** Christopher Brody, James W. Fordyce, James E. Hughes.
**Number of staff:** 1 full-time professional; 2 full-time support.
**EIN:** 137049274

## 467
### The Alice Lawrence Foundation, Inc.
c/o Graubard Mollen et al.
600 3rd Ave.
New York, NY   10016-1903

Incorporated in 1985 in NY.
**Donor(s):** Alice Lawrence.
**Grantmaker type:** Independent foundation
**Financial data** (yr. ended 12/31/99): Assets, $2,848,883 (M); gifts received, $403,000; expenditures, $332,000; qualifying distributions, $327,800; giving activities include $327,800 for 10 grants (high: $200,000; low: $100).
**Purpose and activities:** Giving primarily for health, education, the arts, and human services.
**Fields of interest:** Museums (art); orchestra (symphony); libraries/library science; education, alumni groups; hospitals (general); health associations; housing/shelter, homeless; homeless, human services.
**Limitations:** Applications not accepted. Giving primarily in NY. No grants to individuals.
**Application information:** Contributes only to pre-selected organizations.
**Officers and Directors:*** Alice Lawrence,* Pres.; C. Daniel Chill,* Secy.; E. Reich.
**EIN:** 133317659

## 468
### The Low Foundation, Inc.
c/o Grant Thornton, LLP
60 Broad St.
New York, NY   10004

Established in 1952.
**Donor(s):** Barbara L. Karatz.
**Grantmaker type:** Independent foundation
**Financial data** (yr. ended 08/31/99): Assets, $1,660,594 (M); expenditures, $127,985; qualifying distributions, $109,878; giving

activities include $107,753 for 47 grants (high: $40,000; low: $40).
**Purpose and activities:** Giving for art and cultural programs, education, and health services.
**Fields of interest:** Arts/cultural programs; libraries/library science; hospitals (general); health associations; human services.
**Limitations:** Applications not accepted. Giving primarily in NY. No grants to individuals.
**Application information:** Contributes only to pre-selected organizations.
**Officers and Directors:*** William W. Karatz,* Pres.; Joshua L. Gutfreund, V.P.; Nicholas Gutfreund, V.P.; Owen O. Gutfreund, V.P.; Lawrence Buttenwieser,* Treas.
**EIN:** 136062712

### 469
### Mandeville Foundation, Inc.
c/o Hubert T. Mandeville
230 Park Ave.
New York, NY 10169 (212) 697-4785
*Contact:* Hubert T. Mandeville, Pres.

Incorporated in 1963 in CT.
**Donor(s):** Ernest W. Mandeville.
**Grantmaker type:** Independent foundation
**Financial data** (yr. ended 12/31/99): Assets, $1,335,425 (M); expenditures, $336,078; qualifying distributions, $177,152; giving activities include $64,199 for 10 grants (high: $30,000; low: $13).
**Purpose and activities:** Giving for education and youth services.
**Fields of interest:** Secondary school/education; higher education; libraries/library science; education; hospitals (general); health associations; youth development, citizenship; children & youth, services.
**Limitations:** Giving primarily in CT and NY.
**Application information:** Application form not required.
*Deadline(s):* None
*Final notification:* 90 days
**Officers and Directors:*** Hubert T. Mandeville,* Pres. and Treas.; P. Kempton Mandeville,* V.P.; Maurice C. Greenbaum,* Secy.; Meredith H. Hollis, Matthew T. Mandeville.
**Number of staff:** 2
**EIN:** 066043343

### 470
### The Masinter Family Foundation
1 Colonial Rd.
White Plains, NY 10605

Established in 1997 in NY.
**Donor(s):** Edgar M. Masinter.
**Grantmaker type:** Independent foundation
**Financial data** (yr. ended 12/31/99): Assets, $417,821 (M); gifts received, $264,656; expenditures, $166,694; qualifying distributions, $161,243; giving activities include $162,320 for 13 grants (high: $79,320; low: $500).
**Purpose and activities:** Giving primarily for education.
**Fields of interest:** Higher education; libraries/library science.
**Types of support:** General/operating support.

**Limitations:** Applications not accepted. Giving primarily in New York, NY. No grants to individuals.
**Application information:** Contributes only to pre-selected organizations.
**Trustees:** Catherine M. Hildenbrand, Edgar M. Masinter, Margery F. Masinter, Robert A. Masinter.
**EIN:** 137133021

### 471
### The McGraw-Hill Companies, Inc. Corporate Giving Program
(Formerly McGraw-Hill, Inc. Corporate Giving Program)
1221 Ave. of the Americas
New York, NY 10020-1095 (212) 512-6480
*Contact:* Susan A. Wallman, Mgr., Corp. Contribs. and Community Rels., or Eileen Gabriele, Dir., Corp. Contribs. and Community Rels.
*FAX:* (212) 512-3611; *E-mail:* swallman@mcgraw-hill.com; *URL:* http://www.mcgraw-hill.com/community/community.html

**Grantmaker type:** Corporate giving program
**Purpose and activities:** The Corporate Contributions and Community Relations Program will give priority consideration to organizations and projects that promote and support excellence in education and learning, focus on initiatives that advance knowledge, work, and home skills, and contribute to the education of youth in the communities and markets where The McGraw-Hill Companies operate. Attention is also given to programs that utilize unique applications of new and developing technologies, extend their reach globally, can be evaluated and can serve as models elsewhere, and are staffed and administered by people with demonstrated competence and experience in their fields. The program will also encourage, recognize, and reward the involvement and contributions that company employees make to organizations in their communities which they value.
**Fields of interest:** Visual arts; museums; performing arts; dance; theater; arts/cultural programs; adult education—literacy & basic skills; libraries/library science; reading; education; health care; human services.
**Types of support:** General/operating support; continuing support; donated products; in-kind gifts.
**Limitations:** Giving primarily in areas of company operations. No support for sectarian or religious organizations, political activities or organizations established to influence legislation, organizations included in United Way drives, or institutions and agencies clearly outside the primary geographic concerns and interests of The McGraw-Hill Companies. No grants to individuals, or for courtesy advertising, pledge support for walk-a-thons and similiar activities, publication of books, magazines, films, or videos, or endowment funds; no loans of any kind.
**Application information:** If the request is considered eligible under The McGraw-Hill Companies' funding guidelines, a meeting may be arranged with Corporate Contributions and Community Relations staff. On-site visits may

also be made. The Corporate Contributions and Community Relations Program does not directly administer programs it supports. Recipients are asked, however, to submit periodic progress reports. Grants are not renewed automatically. Requests for support must be resubmitted each year.
*Initial approach:* Proposal letter
*Board meeting date(s):* Quarterly
**Number of staff:** 2 full-time professional; 2 full-time support.

### 472
### John L. McHugh Foundation, Inc.
60 E. 42nd St., Rm. 428
New York, NY 10165-0006 (212) 490-0190
*Contact:* Stanley B. Rich, Secy.-Treas.

Established in 1958.
**Donor(s):** John L. McHugh.‡
**Grantmaker type:** Independent foundation
**Financial data** (yr. ended 09/30/99): Assets, $1,221,591 (M); expenditures, $103,869; qualifying distributions, $64,800; giving activities include $64,800 for 44 grants (high: $4,000; low: $100).
**Purpose and activities:** Giving to human services.
**Fields of interest:** Arts/cultural programs; libraries (public); education; health care; cancer; medical research; cancer research; human services.
**Types of support:** General/operating support; program development; scholarship funds; research; exchange programs.
**Limitations:** Giving primarily in NY.
**Application information:**
*Deadline(s):* None
**Officers and Trustees:*** Trumbull Barton,* Pres.; Chas. Hollerith,* V.P.; Sally R. Harwood,* V.P.; Stanley B. Rich,* Secy.-Treas. and Mgr.
**EIN:** 136141528

### 473
### Meade Foundation, Inc.
425 E. Lake Rd.
Hammondsport, NY 14840
*Contact:* J.F. Meade, Jr., Tr.

Established in 1989 in NY.
**Donor(s):** J.F. Meade, Jr.
**Grantmaker type:** Independent foundation
**Financial data** (yr. ended 12/31/98): Assets, $1,368,945 (M); gifts received, $142,000; expenditures, $57,073; qualifying distributions, $56,578; giving activities include $56,548 for 24 grants (high: $37,000; low: $100).
**Purpose and activities:** Giving for art and cultural organizations and institutes and for health care.
**Fields of interest:** Museums; arts/cultural programs; libraries/library science; human services; public affairs; government agencies; Protestant agencies & churches.
**Limitations:** Giving primarily in Hammondsport, NY. No grants to individuals.
**Application information:** Application form not required.
*Deadline(s):* None
**Trustees:** Helen B. Meade, J.F. Meade, Jr., J.F. Meade III.
**EIN:** 161339424

## 474
### The Andrew W. Mellon Foundation ▼
140 E. 62nd St.
New York, NY 10021 (212) 838-8400
*Contact:* Michele S. Warman, Secy. and Genl. Counsel
*URL:* http://www.mellon.org

Trust established in 1940 in DE as Avalon Foundation; incorporated in 1954 in NY; merged with Old Dominion Foundation and renamed the Andrew W. Mellon Foundation in 1969.

**Donor(s):** Ailsa Mellon Bruce,‡ Paul Mellon.‡

**Grantmaker type:** Independent foundation

**Financial data** (yr. ended 12/31/99): Assets, $4,615,683,000 (M); expenditures, $195,673,133; qualifying distributions, $161,501,133; giving activities include $161,501,133 for grants (high: $3,000,000; low: $2,000; average: $100,000–$500,000).

**Purpose and activities:** Grants on a selective basis for higher education; cultural affairs, including the humanities, museums, art conservation, and performing arts; population; conservation and the environment; and public affairs. Graduate fellowship program in the humanities administered by the Woodrow Wilson National Fellowship Foundation, which makes all awards.

**Fields of interest:** Museums; performing arts; humanities; arts/cultural programs; higher education; natural resource conservation & protection; environment; population studies; public policy, research; public affairs.

**Types of support:** Continuing support; endowments; program development; fellowships; research; matching/challenge support.

**Limitations:** No support for primarily local organizations. No grants to individuals (including scholarships and fellowships); no loans.

**Publications:** Annual report.

**Application information:** Application form not required.
*Initial approach:* Descriptive letter or proposal
*Copies of proposal:* 1
*Deadline(s):* None
*Board meeting date(s):* Mar., June, Sept., and Dec.
*Final notification:* After board meetings

**Officers and Trustees:*** Hanna Holborn Gray,* Chair.; William G. Bowen,* Pres.; Harriet Zuckerman, Sr. V.P.; Mary Patterson McPherson, V.P.; T. Dennis Sullivan, V.P., Finance; Michele S. Warman, Secy. and Genl. Counsel; Eileen M. Scott, Treas.; Charles E. Exley, Jr., Walter E. Massey, Timothy Mellon, W. Taylor Reveley III, Charles Andrew Ryskamp, Anne M. Tatlock.

**Number of staff:** 19 full-time professional; 25 full-time support; 14 part-time support.

**EIN:** 131879954

**Recent grants for library/information services:**

**474-1** Agricultural University of Godollo, Godollo, Hungary, $34,000. For Phase II of Vision 2000 as part of European Educational Projects (EEP) Initiative. 1999.

**474-2** American Antiquarian Society, Worcester, MA, $500,000. For project, Strengthening Care and Access to Research Collections. 1999.

**474-3** American Council of Learned Societies, NYC, NY, $400,000. For fellowships at Library of Congress. 1999.

**474-4** American Museum of Natural History, NYC, NY, $2,000,000. To create Integrated Digital Library. 1999.

**474-5** American Music Center, NYC, NY, $250,000. For electronic media projects. 1999.

**474-6** American Philosophical Society, Philadelphia, PA, $452,000. For project, Strengthening Care and Access to Research Collections. 1999.

**474-7** Art Institute of Chicago, Chicago, IL, $26,500. For museum archives. 1999.

**474-8** Associated Colleges of the South, Atlanta, GA, $600,000. To enhance information fluency and training on ACS campuses using library directors and information technology specialists to increase campus awareness of information fluency issue in all dimensions while offering specific programs in which students, faculty, library staff, information technology staff and others can learn to make effective use of information resources. 1999.

**474-9** Brooklyn Institute of Arts and Sciences, Brooklyn, NY, $33,000. For work in Museum Archives. 1999.

**474-10** Brown University, John Carter Brown Library, Providence, RI, $211,000. For translations of works from Latin America. 1999.

**474-11** Bryn Mawr College, Bryn Mawr, PA, $450,000. For Tri-College Library Collaboration with Haverford, Swarthmore College and Five Colleges. 1999.

**474-12** California Institute of Technology, Pasadena, CA, $90,000. For dissertation seminars in collaboration with Henry E. Huntington Library and Art Gallery. 1999.

**474-13** Carleton College, Laurence McKinley Gould Library, Northfield, MN, $200,000. For experimental program of information literacy that will be completely integrated into curriculum of the college. 1999.

**474-14** Council on Library and Information Resources, DC, $2,600,000. For general support. 1999.

**474-15** Council on Library and Information Resources, DC, $250,000. To enable librarians and technology staff from liberal arts colleges to attend Frye Leadership Institute at Emory University to explore implications of changes in information technology. 1999.

**474-16** Council on Library and Information Resources, DC, $100,000. For Academic Image Exchange Initiative, part of Digital Library Federation work to explore ways of using digital libraries to enhance quality of art history teaching and research in nation's colleges and universities. 1999.

**474-17** Council on Library and Information Resources, DC, $12,000. To train staff in Latin and Central America in digitization and preservation techniques. 1999.

**474-18** Dillard University, New Orleans, LA, $300,000. For Archives and Special Collections. 1999.

**474-19** Eastern Cape Higher Education Association Trust, Port Elizabeth, South Africa, $44,500. For South East Academic Libraries System. 1999.

**474-20** Eastern Seaboard Association of Tertiary Institutions Trust, Dalbridge, South Africa, $816,000. For ESAL Library Consortium. 1999.

**474-21** Eleutherian Mills-Hagley Foundation, Wilmington, DE, $490,000. For project, Strengthening Care and Access to Research Collections. 1999.

**474-22** Five Colleges, Amherst, MA, $1,100,000. To create Five College Depository for selected journals and books now in collections of the libraries and to develop web-based database of finding aids to improve access to their archives and special collections; library Depository will be housed in two-story bunker that once served as headquarters of former U.S. Air Force Strategic Command. 1999.

**474-23** Five Colleges of Ohio, Granville, OH, $475,000. For Library Projects. 1999.

**474-24** Folger Shakespeare Library, DC, $500,000. For project, Strengthening Care and Access to Research Collections. 1999.

**474-25** Foundation Center, NYC, NY, $30,000. For general support. 1999.

**474-26** Foundation of Tertiary Institutions in the Northern Metropolis, Johannesburg, South Africa, $678,000. For Phase III of GAELIC (Gauteng and Environs Library Consortium), mission of GAELIC is to fully use and develop information resources of region for purpose of promoting education, research and lifelong learning amongst its clients, as contribution to development in South Africa with vision to create virtual library by linking together autonomous libraries via networks. 1999.

**474-27** Grantmakers in the Arts, Seattle, WA, $15,000. For Research, Publications and Information Services Program for the Performing Arts. 1999.

**474-28** Hampshire College, Amherst, MA, $25,000. For Liberal Arts College Library. 1999.

**474-29** Huntington Library, Art Collections and Botanical Gardens, San Marino, CA, $530,000. For project, Strengthening Care and Access to Research Collections. 1999.

**474-30** Huntington Library, Art Collections and Botanical Gardens, San Marino, CA, $40,000. For dissertation seminars in collaboration with California Institute of Technology. 1999.

**474-31** Huntington Library, Art Collections and Botanical Gardens, San Marino, CA, $10,000. For dissertation seminars in collaboration with California Institute of Technology. 1999.

**474-32** Journal Storage Project (JSTOR), NYC, NY, $1,750,000. For Phase II of Arts and Humanities Initiatives. 1999.

**474-33** Library Company of Philadelphia, Philadelphia, PA, $300,000. For project, Strengthening Care and Access to Research Collections. 1999.

**474-34** Library Information Network Consortium (LINC), Riga, Latvia, $33,000. To create LINC Unified Data Base for use throughout the Former Soviet Union as part of European Educational Projects (EEP). 1999.

**474-35** Library Information Network Consortium (LINC), Riga, Latvia, $25,000. For computer improvements throughout the

Former Soviet Union as part of European Educational Projects (EEP). 1999.

**474-36** Medici Archive Project, NYC, NY, $458,000. For technology support. 1999.

**474-37** Medici Archive Project, NYC, NY, $50,000. For technology support. 1999.

**474-38** Minnesota Private College Research Foundation, Saint Paul, MN, $335,000. For Electronic Library Resources Project. 1999.

**474-39** Modern Language Association of America, NYC, NY, $2,000,000. For Journal Storage Project (JSTOR) Modern Language and Literature Journals. 1999.

**474-40** Modern Language Association of America, NYC, NY, $1,500,000. For Modern Language Association (MLA) International Bibliography. 1999.

**474-41** Mount Holyoke College, South Hadley, MA, $27,000. For materials for Czech and Slovak Library Information Network (CASLIN) Conference held in Kolin in the Czech Republic, as part of European Educational Projects (EEP). 1999.

**474-42** Museum of Fine Arts, Boston, MA, $29,200. For work in museum archives. 1999.

**474-43** Museum of Modern Art, NYC, NY, $160,000. For work in museum and library archives. 1999.

**474-44** Museum of Modern Art, NYC, NY, $18,800. For work in museum archives. 1999.

**474-45** Mystic Seaport Museum, Mystic, CT, $385,000. For 19th Century American Merchant Marine Digital Library Project. 1999.

**474-46** New York Academy of Medicine, NYC, NY, $435,000. For access to Library Collection. 1999.

**474-47** New York Public Library, NYC, NY, $3,000,000. For Fellowships at Center for Scholars and Writers. 1999.

**474-48** Newberry Library, Chicago, IL, $500,000. For project, Strengthening Care and Access to Research Collections. 1999.

**474-49** Northeast Document Conservation Center, Andover, MA, $45,000. For scanning workshop. 1999.

**474-50** Oxford University, Refugee Studies Centre, Oxford, England, $200,000. For Library Project. 1999.

**474-51** Pierpont Morgan Library, NYC, NY, $500,000. For project, Strengthening Care and Access to Research Collections. 1999.

**474-52** Princeton University, Princeton, NJ, $264,000. For Library Technology Initiative. 1999.

**474-53** Reed College, Portland, OR, $200,000. For Libraries Initiative. 1999.

**474-54** Royal Society, London, England, $50,000. To participate in Journal Storage (JSTOR) Projects. 1999.

**474-55** South African Bibliographic and Information Network (SABINET), Centurion, South Africa, $650,000. For Phase 2 of SABINET National Union Catalogue. 1999.

**474-56** Tulane University, New Orleans, LA, $45,000. For operating support for libraries. 1999.

**474-57** University of California, Los Angeles, CA, $25,500. For Eastern European Library Automation Program. 1999.

**474-58** University of California, Riverside, CA, $400,000. To publish English Short Title Catalogue. 1999.

**474-59** University of Florida, Gainesville, FL, $12,100. To digitize Caribbean newspapers as part of IAS-Library Resources and Networks Initiative. 1999.

**474-60** University of Pennsylvania, Philadelphia, PA, $218,000. For Digital Books Project in partnership with Oxford University Press. 1999.

**474-61** University of Virginia, Charlottesville, VA, $500,000. For Part II of Early American Fiction Initiative. 1999.

**474-62** Vassar College, Poughkeepsie, NY, $200,000. For Libraries Initiative. 1999.

**474-63** Virginia Historical Society, Richmond, VA, $500,000. For project, Strengthening Care and Access to Research Collections. 1999.

**474-64** Western Cape Tertiary Institutions Trust, Cape Town, South Africa, $25,000. To automate libraries in Cape Library Consortium (CALICO). 1999.

**474-65** Yale University, New Haven, CT, $33,000. For study of JSTOR applications. 1999.

## 475
## The Memton Fund, Inc.
515 Madison Ave., Ste. 3702
New York, NY 10022
*Contact:* Lillian I. Daniels, Exec. Dir.

Incorporated in 1936 in NY.
**Donor(s):** Albert G. Milbank,‡ Charles M. Cauldwell.‡
**Grantmaker type:** Independent foundation
**Financial data** (yr. ended 12/31/99): Assets, $11,911,323 (M); expenditures, $489,997; qualifying distributions, $489,997; giving activities include $392,400 for 133 grants (high: $25,000; low: $500; average: $1,000–$5,000).
**Purpose and activities:** Giving primarily for education.
**Fields of interest:** Media/communications; museums; performing arts; historic preservation/historical societies; arts/cultural programs; adult education—literacy & basic skills; libraries/library science; education; natural resource conservation & protection; environment; animal welfare; animals/wildlife; health care; AIDS; youth development, citizenship; human services; children & youth, services; family services; public affairs, citizen participation.
**Types of support:** General/operating support; continuing support; annual campaigns; capital campaigns; building/renovation; endowments; program development; curriculum development; internship funds; scholarship funds.
**Limitations:** Applications not accepted. Giving limited to the U.S. and U.S. Pacific Islands. No grants to individuals.
**Application information:** Contributes only to pre-selected organizations.
*Board meeting date(s):* Spring and fall
**Officers and Directors:*** Elenita M. Drumwright,* Pres.; Samuel L. Milbank, V.P.; Lillian I. Daniels,* Secy.-Treas.; Robert V. Edgar, Olivia Farrar-Wellman, Alexandra Giordano,

Ellen White Levy, Michelle R. Milbank, Thomas Milbank.
**Number of staff:** 1 full-time professional; 1 part-time professional.
**EIN:** 136096608

## 476
## Merrill Lynch & Co., Inc. Corporate Giving Program
World Financial Ctr., S. Tower
New York, NY 10080-6106 (212) 236-4319
*Contact:* Eddy Bayardelle, Dir., Philanthropic Progs.; or Linda Federici, Dir., Special Events

**Grantmaker type:** Corporate giving program
**Financial data** (yr. ended 12/31/99): Total giving, $17,789,008; giving activities include $13,776,119 for grants and $4,012,889 for 11,931 employee matching gifts.
**Purpose and activities:** As a complement to its foundation, Merrill Lynch also makes charitable contributions to nonprofit organizations directly. Support is given primarily in areas of company operations.
**Fields of interest:** Museums; dance; theater; music; historic preservation/historical societies; arts/cultural programs; higher education; business school/education; libraries/library science; education; natural resource conservation & protection; energy; hospitals (general); health care; substance abuse, services; health organizations; housing/shelter; youth, services; family services; human services; business & industry; community development; public affairs; minorities; women; economically disadvantaged.
**Types of support:** General/operating support; continuing support; capital campaigns; building/renovation; endowments; employee volunteer services; sponsorships; employee matching gifts; employee-related scholarships; donated equipment; in-kind gifts; matching/challenge support.
**Limitations:** Giving primarily in areas of company operations, particularly the greater New York, NY, area, including NJ. No support for fraternal, social, or athletic organizations or political organizations. No grants to individuals (except for employee-related scholarships) or political candidates, or for general operating support of government agencies or debt reduction.
**Publications:** Grants list, corporate giving report (including application guidelines).
**Application information:** Proposals should be no longer than 3 pages in length. The Philanthropic Programs Department handles giving. The company has a staff that only handles contributions. Application form not required.
*Initial approach:* Proposal to nearest company facility
*Copies of proposal:* 1
*Deadline(s):* None
*Final notification:* 1 month
**Administrators:** Eddy Bayardelle, Dir., Philanthropic Progs.; Paul W. Critchlow, Pres., Merrill Lynch & Co. Fdn., Inc.
**Number of staff:** 5 full-time professional; 6 full-time support; 1 part-time support.

## 477
### Louise Hauss Miller Foundation
c/o Winthrop, Stimson, Putnam & Roberts
1 Battery Park Pl., Ste. 32
New York, NY 10004-1490
*Contact:* H. Williamson Ghriskey, Secy.-Treas.

Established in 1982.
**Grantmaker type:** Independent foundation
**Financial data** (yr. ended 01/31/99): Assets,
$1,262,996 (M); expenditures, $111,851;
qualifying distributions, $93,728; giving
activities include $76,000 for 9 grants (high:
$34,000; low: $1,000).
**Purpose and activities:** Giving for art and
culture, education, and human services.
**Fields of interest:** Elementary school/education;
higher education; libraries/library science; youth
development; scouting agencies (general);
human services; children & youth, services.
**Limitations:** Applications not accepted. No
grants to individuals.
**Application information:** Contributes only to
pre-selected organizations.
**Officers:** Allen Carlow Phillips, Pres.; Susan
Phillips Decker, V.P.; H. Williamson Ghriskey,
Secy.-Treas.
**Trustee:** Bonnie Barnes.
**EIN:** 133109190

## 478
### Paul and Irma Milstein Foundation
1271 Ave. of the Americas, Ste. 4200
New York, NY 10020

Established in 1995.
**Donor(s):** Paul Milstein, Irma Milstein.
**Grantmaker type:** Independent foundation
**Financial data** (yr. ended 12/31/99): Assets,
$4,850,431 (M); gifts received, $917,630;
expenditures, $6,005,106; qualifying
distributions, $5,994,017; giving activities
include $5,995,380 for 23 grants (high:
$3,000,000; low: $250).
**Purpose and activities:** Giving to a public
library and for education, the arts and Jewish
causes.
**Fields of interest:** Museums; secondary
school/education; higher education; theological
school/education; libraries (public); cancer;
Jewish federated giving programs; Jewish
agencies & temples.
**Limitations:** Applications not accepted. Giving
primarily in New York, NY. No grants to
individuals.
**Application information:** Contributes only to
pre-selected organizations.
**Officer:** Paul Milstein, Pres.
**Directors:** Roslyn M. Meyer, Edward Milstein,
Howard Milstein, Irma Milstein, Barbara M.
Zalaznick.
**EIN:** 133771891

## 479
### J. P. Morgan Charitable Trust ▼
60 Wall St., 36th Fl.
New York, NY 10260-0060 (212) 648-9673
*Contact:* Hildy Simmons, Managing Dir.
*FAX:* (212) 648-5082; URL: http://
www.jpmorgan.com/communityinvolvement

Trust established in 1961 in NY.

**Donor(s):** J.P. Morgan & Co. Incorporated,
Morgan Guaranty Trust Co. of New York.
**Grantmaker type:** Company-sponsored
foundation
**Financial data** (yr. ended 12/31/99): Assets,
$5,737,191 (M); gifts received, $1,008,516;
expenditures, $12,939,100; qualifying
distributions, $12,874,508; giving activities
include $7,920,582 for 413 grants (high:
$375,000; low: $1,000; average:
$5,000–$50,000) and $5,009,380 for employee
matching gifts.
**Purpose and activities:** Emphasis is on helping
to find solutions to social problems and needs
through support of competent agencies in fields
of health, social services, culture, education, the
environment, and international affairs. Special
attention to job training, youth programs,
international relief, housing, economic
development, and advocacy and citizen
involvement programs in New York City.
Matches employee gifts to educational
programs, cultural institutions, hospitals and
health care agencies, human services and local
development organizations, and environmental
and international organizations.
**Fields of interest:** Performing arts; arts/cultural
programs; elementary school/education; higher
education; libraries/library science; education;
environment; hospitals (general); health care;
health associations; AIDS; medical research;
housing/shelter, development; human services;
children & youth, services; aging, centers &
services; minorities/immigrants, centers &
services; international relief; international affairs;
economic development; urban/community
development; community development;
minorities.
**Types of support:** General/operating support;
continuing support; annual campaigns; capital
campaigns; building/renovation; equipment;
endowments; program development; seed
money; technical assistance; employee
matching gifts; matching/challenge support.
**Limitations:** Giving limited to New York, NY,
except for certain higher education programs
and in the area of international affairs. No
support for organizations working with chemical
dependency, specific disabilities or diseases
(except AIDS), or churches for non-secular
purposes. No grants to individuals, or for
scholarly research, scholarships, fellowships, or
conferences; no loans.
**Publications:** Corporate giving report (including
application guidelines), annual report.
**Application information:** Accepts New York
Common Application Form. Application form
required.
  *Initial approach:* Letter
  *Copies of proposal:* 1
  *Deadline(s):* Sept. 1
  *Board meeting date(s):* Every 9 weeks
  *Final notification:* 3 months
**Advisory Committee:** Michael E. Patterson,
Nicolas S. Rohatyn, Hildy J. Simmons.
**Trustee:** Morgan Guaranty Trust Co. of New
York.
**Number of staff:** 1 full-time professional; 2
full-time support.
**EIN:** 136037931

## 480
### Morse Family Foundation, Inc.
(Formerly Enid & Lester S. Morse, Jr. Foundation,
Inc.)
c/o Lester Morse Co.
60 E. 42nd St., Ste. 2446
New York, NY 10165-0015

Established in 1967 in NY.
**Donor(s):** Lester S. Morse, Jr.
**Grantmaker type:** Independent foundation
**Financial data** (yr. ended 03/31/99): Assets,
$4,584,594 (M); gifts received, $76,421;
expenditures, $600,768; qualifying distributions,
$574,167; giving activities include $577,964 for
201 grants (high: $50,000; low: $10).
**Purpose and activities:** Giving primarily for
education and the arts, including music and the
performing arts.
**Fields of interest:** Museums; performing arts;
dance; music; arts/cultural programs; higher
education; libraries/library science; education;
health care; human services; Jewish federated
giving programs.
**Limitations:** Applications not accepted. Giving
primarily in New York, NY. No grants to
individuals.
**Application information:** Contributes only to
pre-selected organizations.
  *Board meeting date(s):* Apr.
**Officers:** Lester S. Morse, Jr., Pres.; Enid W.
Morse, V.P.; Douglas A. Morse, Treas.
**EIN:** 136220174

## 481
### Northern Chautauqua Community Foundation, Inc.
212 Lake Shore Dr. W.
Dunkirk, NY 14048 (716) 366-4892
*Contact:* Diane Hannum, Exec. Dir.
*FAX:* (716) 366-4279; E-mail: nccf@netsync.net;
URL: http://fdncenter.org/grantmaker/nccf

Incorporated in 1986 in NY.
**Grantmaker type:** Community foundation
**Financial data** (yr. ended 12/31/99): Assets,
$7,300,000 (M); gifts received, $770,184;
expenditures, $555,000; giving activities
include $358,769 for 28 grants (high: $10,000;
low: $500; average: $25–$8,000) and $79,754
for 130 grants to individuals (high: $2,500; low:
$25; average: $70–$2,000).
**Purpose and activities:** Primary areas of interest
include education, libraries, family services,
community funds, cultural programs, and other
general charitable activities.
**Fields of interest:** Arts/cultural programs; higher
education; adult education—literacy & basic
skills; libraries/library science; reading;
education; environment; hospitals (general);
substance abuse, services; recreation; family
services; hospices; aging, centers & services;
community development; voluntarism
promotion; federated giving programs; aging;
general charitable giving.
**Types of support:** Building/renovation;
equipment; endowments; program
development; seed money; scholarship funds;
scholarships—to individuals;
matching/challenge support.
**Limitations:** Giving limited to northern
Chautauqua County, NY. No support for
religious organizations. No grants to individuals

(except for designated scholarship funds), or for capital campaigns, general operating budgets, publication of books, conferences, or annual fundraising campaigns.

**Publications:** Annual report (including application guidelines), application guidelines, newsletter.

**Application information:** Applications are considered in the spring and fall. Application form required.

  *Initial approach:* Letter or telephone
  *Copies of proposal:* 1
  *Deadline(s):* 15 days prior to grants committee meetings
  *Board meeting date(s):* Quarterly
  *Final notification:* 10 days following board meeting

**Officers and Directors:*** R. Bard Schaack,* Pres.; James H. Mintun, Jr.,* V.P.; Susan Marsh,* Treas.; Rosemary Banach, Michael Brunecz, Andrew W. Dorn, Donald Eno, Jean Foley, Richard Ketcham, James Koch, Kurt Maytum, Robert Miller, Jr., Jeffrey G. Passafaro, John Potter, Gerald Rocque, J. Carter Rowland, Ph.D., Darla Wasko, H.K. Williams IV, Terry Wolfenden.

**Number of staff:** 1 full-time professional; 1 part-time professional; 1 part-time support.

**EIN:** 161271663

---

### 482
### Northern New York Community Foundation, Inc.

(Formerly Watertown Foundation, Inc.)
120 Washington St.
Watertown, NY  13601  (315) 782-7110
*Contact:* Alex C. Velto, Exec. Dir.
*FAX:* (315) 782-0047; E-mail: nnycf@northnet.org

Incorporated in 1929 in NY.
**Grantmaker type:** Community foundation
**Financial data** (yr. ended 12/31/99): Assets, $23,217,420 (M); gifts received, $1,151,259; expenditures, $1,507,479; giving activities include $1,302,146 for grants.
**Purpose and activities:** To promote charitable, educational, cultural, recreational, and health programs through grants to community organizations and agencies, and through a student scholarship program in Jefferson and Lewis counties, NY.
**Fields of interest:** Historic preservation/historical societies; arts/cultural programs; education, fund raising; child development, education; adult/continuing education; libraries/library science; education; environment; hospitals (general); nursing care; health care; substance abuse, services; health associations; AIDS; food services; housing/shelter, development; recreation; human services; children & youth, services; child development, services; family services; hospices; aging, centers & services; homeless, human services; community development; federated giving programs; government/public administration; disabled; aging; economically disadvantaged; homeless; general charitable giving.
**Types of support:** Annual campaigns; capital campaigns; building/renovation; equipment; land acquisition; program development; conferences/seminars; publication; seed money; scholarship funds; technical assistance;

scholarships—to individuals; matching/challenge support.
**Limitations:** Giving limited to organizations and individuals in Jefferson and Lewis counties, NY. No grants for endowment funds or deficit financing.
**Publications:** Annual report, newsletter.
**Application information:** Application form not required.
  *Initial approach:* Letter
  *Copies of proposal:* 1
  *Deadline(s):* Feb. 1, May 1, Aug. 1, and Nov. 1
  *Board meeting date(s):* Mar., June, Sept., and Dec.
  *Final notification:* 1 to 2 months
**Officers and Directors:*** John B. Johnson, Jr.,* Pres.; Janet J. George, V.P.; Jane N. Lormore,* Secy.-Treas.; Alex C. Velto, Exec. Dir.; Donald C. Alexander, Douglas Brodie, Joe Clary, James R. Kanik, Donna D. Macsuga, Tony Morgia, James L. O'Donnell, Mark S. Purcell, Jan K. Turcotte, Anderson Wise, Grace A. Wright.
**Number of staff:** 1 full-time professional; 1 full-time support; 1 part-time support.
**EIN:** 156020989

---

### 483
### A. Lindsay and Olive B. O'Connor Foundation ▼

P.O. Box D
Hobart, NY  13788  (607) 538-9248
*Contact:* Donald F. Bishop II, Exec. Dir.
*FAX:* (607) 538-9136

Trust established in 1965 in NY.
**Donor(s):** Olive B. O'Connor.‡
**Grantmaker type:** Independent foundation
**Financial data** (yr. ended 12/31/99): Assets, $74,707,970 (M); expenditures, $3,117,014; qualifying distributions, $2,728,256; giving activities include $2,515,845 for 233 grants (high: $149,981; low: $315; average: $1,000–$75,000).
**Purpose and activities:** Emphasis on quality of life, including hospitals, libraries, community centers, higher education, nursing and other vocational education, child development and youth agencies, religious organizations, museums, and historic restoration; support also for civic affairs and town, village, and environmental conservation and improvement.
**Fields of interest:** Architecture; museums; performing arts; history & archaeology; historic preservation/historical societies; arts/cultural programs; early childhood education; child development, education; vocational education; higher education; business school/education; libraries/library science; natural resource conservation & protection; environment; animal welfare; wildlife preservation & protection; hospitals (general); nursing care; substance abuse, services; alcoholism; delinquency prevention/services; employment; agriculture; housing/shelter, development; human services; children & youth, services; child development, services; women, centers & services; rural development; community development; federated giving programs; religious federated giving programs; biological sciences; economics; government/public administration; Christian agencies & churches; Protestant agencies & churches; religion; women; economically disadvantaged.

**Types of support:** Continuing support; annual campaigns; capital campaigns; building/renovation; equipment; land acquisition; endowments; emergency funds; program development; conferences/seminars; publication; seed money; scholarship funds; research; technical assistance; program-related investments/loans; matching/challenge support.
**Limitations:** Giving primarily in Delaware County, NY, and 7 contiguous rural counties in upstate NY. No grants to individuals, or for operating budgets or deficit financing.
**Publications:** Program policy statement, multi-year report.
**Application information:** Application form required.
  *Initial approach:* Letter or telephone
  *Copies of proposal:* 1
  *Deadline(s):* Apr. 1 and Sept. 1; 1st of each month for grants under $5,000
  *Board meeting date(s):* May or June and Sept. or Oct.; committee meets monthly to consider grants under $5,000
  *Final notification:* 7 to 10 days after semiannual meeting
**Officers:** Donald F. Bishop II, Pres. and Exec. Dir.; Pamela Hill, Secy.-Treas.
**Advisory Committee:** Robert L. Bishop II, Chair.; Charlotte Bishop Hill, Vice-Chair.; William J. Murphy, Eugene E. Peckham.
**Trustee:** BSB Bank & Trust.
**Number of staff:** 2 full-time professional.
**EIN:** 166063485

---

### 484
### The Ohrstrom Foundation, Inc. ▼

c/o Curtis Mallet
101 Park Ave., 35th Fl.
New York, NY  10178-0061

Incorporated in 1953 in DE.
**Donor(s):** Members of the Ohrstrom family.
**Grantmaker type:** Independent foundation
**Financial data** (yr. ended 05/31/99): Assets, $74,101,299 (M); expenditures, $3,113,438; qualifying distributions, $3,028,878; giving activities include $2,907,145 for 198 grants (high: $935,183; low: $425; average: $1,000–$50,000).
**Purpose and activities:** Emphasis on elementary, secondary, and higher education; support also for civic affairs, conservation, hospitals and medical research, and museums.
**Fields of interest:** Museums; education, fund raising; elementary/secondary education; elementary school/education; secondary school/education; higher education; libraries/library science; natural resource conservation & protection; environment; hospitals (general); alcoholism; medical research; government/public administration; religion; general charitable giving.
**Types of support:** General/operating support; continuing support; annual campaigns; building/renovation; equipment; land acquisition; endowments; emergency funds; program development; seed money; matching/challenge support.
**Limitations:** Applications not accepted. Giving primarily in NY and VA. No grants to individuals, or for deficit financing, scholarships, fellowships, research, special projects, publications, or conferences; no loans.

**Application information:** Contributes only to pre-selected organizations.
**Officers and Directors:*** George L. Ohrstrom, Jr.,* Pres.; George F. Ohrstrom,* Exec. V.P.; Magalen O. Bryant,* V.P.; Peter A. Kalat,* Secy.; Dorothy Barry, Treas.; Kristiane C. Graham, George L. Ohrstrom II, Winifred E.A. Ohrstrom, Mark J. Ohrstrom.
**Number of staff:** 1 part-time support.
**EIN:** 546039966
**Recent grants for library/information services:**
**484-1** National Sporting Library, Middleburg, VA, $37,000. For unrestricted support. 1999.
**484-2** Redwood Library and Athenaeum, Newport, RI, $15,000. For unrestricted support. 1999.

## 485
### The David G. Ormsby Charitable Foundation
c/o Cravath Swaine & Moore
825 8th Ave.
New York, NY 10019-7475

**Donor(s):** David G. Ormsby.
**Grantmaker type:** Independent foundation
**Financial data** (yr. ended 12/31/98): Assets, $20,085 (M); expenditures, $68,251; qualifying distributions, $68,131; giving activities include $68,016 for 16 grants (high: $35,000; low: $25).
**Purpose and activities:** Giving primarily for education.
**Fields of interest:** College; law school/education; libraries (public); cemetery company.
**Types of support:** General/operating support.
**Limitations:** Applications not accepted. Giving on a national basis. No grants to individuals.
**Application information:** Contributes only to pre-selected organizations.
**Trustee:** David G. Ormsby.
**EIN:** 133382151

## 486
### Jan and Betka Papanek Foundation
500 5th Ave., Ste. 4810
New York, NY 10110 (212) 382-3357
*Contact:* Jiri Brotan, Tr.

Established in 1992.
**Donor(s):** Betka Papanek.
**Grantmaker type:** Independent foundation
**Financial data** (yr. ended 12/31/99): Assets, $1,128,718 (M); gifts received, $500; expenditures, $772,932; qualifying distributions, $753,479; giving activities include $713,203 for 8 grants (high: $290,157; low: $24,575).
**Fields of interest:** Higher education; libraries/library science.
**International interests:** Czech Republic; Slovakia.
**Limitations:** Giving in New York, NY, the Czech Republic, and Slovakia. No grants to individuals.
**Application information:**
*Initial approach:* Letter
*Deadline(s):* None
**Trustees:** Jiri Brotan, Anne E. Lesak Scott.
**EIN:** 133694358

## 487
### Park Foundation, Inc. ▼
P.O. Box 550
Ithaca, NY 14851 (607) 272-9124
*Contact:* Joanne V. Florino, Exec. Dir.
*FAX:* (607) 272-6057

Established in 1966.
**Donor(s):** RHP, Inc., Roy H. Park.‡
**Grantmaker type:** Independent foundation
**Financial data** (yr. ended 12/31/99): Assets, $650,276,904 (M); gifts received, $2,852,613; expenditures, $27,876,683; qualifying distributions, $23,252,526; giving activities include $22,369,904 for 362 grants (high: $1,004,940; low: $1,000; average: $5,000–$500,000).
**Purpose and activities:** Giving primarily for public television, higher education, the environment, and animal welfare.
**Fields of interest:** Television; higher education; education; environment; animal welfare; general charitable giving.
**Types of support:** General/operating support; program development; professorships; seed money; fellowships; scholarship funds; research; matching/challenge support.
**Limitations:** Giving limited to the East Coast (primarily in central NY) and the southeastern U.S. No grants to individuals.
**Publications:** Informational brochure (including application guidelines).
**Application information:** Application form required.
*Initial approach:* Letter
*Copies of proposal:* 1
*Deadline(s):* None
*Board meeting date(s):* Mar., June, Aug., Oct., and Dec.
**Officers and Board Members:** Dorothy D. Park,* Pres.; Roy H. Park, Jr., 1st V.P.; Adelaide P. Gomer,* 2nd V.P. and Secy.; Elizabeth Fowler,* Treas.; Joanne V. Florino, Exec. Dir.; Jerome Libin, Richard Robb.
**Junior Advisors:** Alicia P. Gomer, Roy H. Park III.
**Number of staff:** 3 full-time professional; 4 full-time support.
**EIN:** 166071043
**Recent grants for library/information services:**
**487-1** Child Care, NYC, NY, $57,500. For Phase I of Implementation Project. 1998.
**487-2** Earth Action Network, Norwalk, CT, $30,000. For three-part series on water resources and conservation. 1998.
**487-3** Tompkins County Economic Opportunity Corporation, Ithaca, NY, $30,000. For Family Resources Department. 1998.
**487-4** Tompkins County Public Library Foundation, Ithaca, NY, $2,500,000. To purchase Woolworth Building for new public library space. 1998.
**487-5** Ulysses Philomathic Library, Trumansburg, NY, $10,000. To develop Young Adult section of new library. 1998.

## 488
### The Park Foundation
500 5th Ave., No. 1710
New York, NY 10110-0002

Incorporated in 1949 in DC.
**Donor(s):** Joseph P. Kennedy, Jr. Foundation.
**Grantmaker type:** Independent foundation

**Financial data** (yr. ended 12/31/98): Assets, $112,299 (M); gifts received, $310,000; expenditures, $287,697; qualifying distributions, $287,166; giving activities include $287,184 for 50 grants (high: $80,000; low: $1,000).
**Fields of interest:** Theater; arts/cultural programs; libraries/library science; children & youth, services; human rights (international); federated giving programs; disabled.
**Types of support:** General/operating support; annual campaigns; research.
**Limitations:** Applications not accepted. Giving primarily in Washington, DC, MA, and NY. No grants to individuals; no loans or program-related investments.
**Application information:** Contributes only to pre-selected organizations.
**Officers and Trustee:*** Jean K. Smith,* V.P.; James S. Benvenuto, Treas.
**EIN:** 136163065

## 489
### Peck Stacpoole Foundation
17 W. 94th St., 1st Fl.
New York, NY 10025
*Contact:* Robert W. Ashton, Secy.
*FAX:* (212) 932-0316

Established in 1997 in NY.
**Donor(s):** S. Allyn Peck.‡
**Grantmaker type:** Independent foundation
**Financial data** (yr. ended 06/30/99): Assets, $4,247,211 (M); gifts received, $913,569; expenditures, $544,208; qualifying distributions, $499,918; giving activities include $500,000 for 2 grants of $250,000 each.
**Purpose and activities:** Giving primarily for libraries, museums and historic sites.
**Fields of interest:** Museums; historic preservation/historical societies; genealogy; arts/cultural programs; libraries/library science.
**Types of support:** General/operating support.
**Limitations:** Applications not accepted.
**Application information:** Unsolicited requests for funds not accepted.
**Officers:** Frederic W. Schaen, Pres.; Robert W. Ashton, Secy.-Treas.
**Trustee:** Lawrence L. Reger.
**EIN:** 133966373

## 490
### The Carl and Lily Pforzheimer Foundation, Inc. ▼
650 Madison Ave., 23rd Fl.
New York, NY 10022 (212) 223-6500
*Contact:* Carl H. Pforzheimer III, Pres.

Incorporated in 1942 in NY.
**Donor(s):** members of the Pforzheimer family.
**Grantmaker type:** Independent foundation
**Financial data** (yr. ended 12/31/99): Assets, $56,365,728 (M); expenditures, $6,918,560; qualifying distributions, $6,503,829; giving activities include $6,285,500 for 59 grants (high: $1,040,000; low: $5,000; average: $10,000–$50,000) and $243,592 for 1 foundation-administered program.
**Purpose and activities:** Maintains publishing and research activities in connection with the Carl H. Pforzheimer Library collection at the New York Public Library in the general field of American and English literature; giving primarily

for higher and secondary education; support also for cultural programs, public administration, a national municipal organization, and health care.

**Fields of interest:** Performing arts; theater; language & linguistics; literature; arts/cultural programs; secondary school/education; higher education; adult education—literacy & basic skills; libraries/library science; reading; education; hospitals (general); nursing care; health care; health associations; youth development, citizenship; government/public administration; public affairs, citizen participation.

**Types of support:** Endowments; program development; professorships; publication; seed money; fellowships; internship funds; scholarship funds; matching/challenge support.

**Limitations:** No grants to individuals, or for building funds; no loans.

**Application information:** Application form not required.

> *Initial approach:* Letter or proposal
> *Copies of proposal:* 1
> *Deadline(s):* None
> *Board meeting date(s):* Apr., June, Oct., and Dec.
> *Final notification:* Immediately following board meeting

**Officers and Directors:*** Carl H. Pforzheimer III,* Pres. and Treas.; Nancy P. Aronson,* V.P.; Martin F. Richman, Secy.; Anthony L. Ferranti, Compt.; Edgar D. Aronson, George L.K. Frelinghuysen, Carl A. Pforzheimer, Carol K. Pforzheimer, Elizabeth S. Pforzheimer, Alison A. Sherman, Thomas Sobol.

**Number of staff:** 3 full-time professional; 2 full-time support.

**EIN:** 135624374

**Recent grants for library/information services:**

**490-1** New York Public Library, NYC, NY, $5,047,600. 1998.

**490-2** Pierpont Morgan Library, NYC, NY, $100,000. 1998.

**490-3** Rosenbach Museum and Library, Philadelphia, PA, $10,000. 1998.

**490-4** White Plains Library Foundation, White Plains, NY, $25,000. 1998.

## 491
## Allen F. Pierce Foundation

33 Gates Cir., Apt. A
Buffalo, NY  14209
*Contact:* Jean M. Elfvin, Pres.

**Grantmaker type:** Independent foundation
**Financial data** (yr. ended 12/31/98): Assets, $1,278 (M); gifts received, $8,389; expenditures, $124,590; qualifying distributions, $123,017; giving activities include $123,700 for 16 grants (high: $46,000; low: $1,000).
**Purpose and activities:** Giving for the arts, animal welfare, hospitals, and human services.
**Fields of interest:** Arts/cultural programs; libraries/library science; animals/wildlife; hospitals (general); human services; Christian agencies & churches.
**Limitations:** Giving limited to Bradford County, PA. No grants to individuals.
**Application information:** Application form not required.

> *Deadline(s):* None

**Officer and Directors:*** Jean Margaret Elfvin,* Pres.; Ann D. DiLauro, Carole DiLauro, Hon. John T. Elfvin, Janet A. Knapp.
**Agent:** First Union National Bank.
**Number of staff:** None.
**EIN:** 232044356

## 492
## Pine Level Foundation, Inc.

c/o Ernst & Young
787 7th Ave.
New York, NY  10019
*Contact:* Iola Haverstick, Pres.

Incorporated in 1968 in CT as a successor to the Stetson Foundation, a trust established in 1936 in CT.
**Donor(s):** Iola Wise Stetson.
**Grantmaker type:** Independent foundation
**Financial data** (yr. ended 12/31/99): Assets, $2,092,863 (M); expenditures, $263,779; qualifying distributions, $244,116; giving activities include $241,661 for 64 grants (high: $55,116; low: $500).
**Fields of interest:** Arts, multipurpose centers/programs; secondary school/education; higher education; libraries/library science; education; hospitals (general); human services.
**Limitations:** Giving primarily in the Northeast. No grants to individuals.
**Application information:** Application form not required.

> *Initial approach:* Letter
> *Deadline(s):* None

**Officers and Directors:*** Iola Haverstick,* Pres.; Elizabeth Kratovil,* V.P.; S. Alexander Haverstick,* Secy.
**EIN:** 237008912

## 493
## Pinky Foundation

c/o Ernst & Young LLP
787 7th Ave.
New York, NY  10019-6018
*Contact:* Arthur Gordon

Established in 1997 in NY.
**Donor(s):** Cathy B. Graham.
**Grantmaker type:** Independent foundation
**Financial data** (yr. ended 12/31/98): Assets, $1,259,790 (M); expenditures, $549,882; qualifying distributions, $509,463; giving activities include $508,265 for 19 grants (high: $175,000; low: $1,000).
**Purpose and activities:** Giving primarily for the arts and health and human services.
**Fields of interest:** Theater; arts/cultural programs; higher education; libraries/library science; education; health associations; human services; community development.
**Limitations:** Giving primarily in NY.
**Application information:**

> *Initial approach:* Letter
> *Deadline(s):* None

**Trustees:** Cathy B. Graham, Stephen M. Graham.
**EIN:** 137107821

## 494
## Stephen J. Potter Memorial Foundation, Inc.

47 Sunnyside East
Queensbury, NY  12804
*Contact:* John Austin, Jr., Secy.-Treas.

Established in 1955 in NY.
**Donor(s):** Stephen J. Potter.‡
**Grantmaker type:** Independent foundation
**Financial data** (yr. ended 09/30/99): Assets, $873,498 (M); expenditures, $77,553; qualifying distributions, $72,811; giving activities include $22,750 for 11 grants (high: $4,000; low: $500) and $46,500 for 46 grants to individuals (high: $1,500; low: $500).
**Purpose and activities:** Scholarships to graduating seniors of Ticonderoga High School, NY; also supports historical organizations in Ticonderoga and Fort Edward, NY, and the immediate area.
**Fields of interest:** History & archaeology; historic preservation/historical societies; libraries/library science; education.
**Types of support:** General/operating support; scholarships—to individuals.
**Limitations:** Giving primarily in Ticonderoga, NY.
**Application information:** Application form not required.

> *Initial approach:* Letter
> *Deadline(s):* None
> *Board meeting date(s):* Late Nov.

**Officers and Directors:*** Jane M. Lape,* Pres.; John McDonald,* V.P.; John Austin, Jr.,* Secy.-Treas.; Gerald Abbott, William B. Wetherbee.
**Number of staff:** None.
**EIN:** 146016858

## 495
## The Reader's Digest Association, Inc. Corporate Giving Program

Reader's Digest Rd.
Pleasantville, NY  10570  (914) 241-5370
*Contact:* J. Edward Hall, V.P., Corp. Contribs.; or Carole M. Howard (sponsorships and special events)

**Grantmaker type:** Corporate giving program
**Purpose and activities:** As a complement to its foundation, Reader's Digest also makes charitable contributions to nonprofit organizations directly. Support is given primarily in areas of company operations.
**Fields of interest:** Literature; child development, education; libraries/library science; reading.
**Types of support:** General/operating support; sponsorships; in-kind gifts.
**Limitations:** Giving primarily in areas of company operations. No support for religious organizations or veterans', political, or fraternal organizations. No grants for advertisements, public television, film or media projects, capital or building campaigns, sporting events, or religious endeavors; no loaned talent.
**Publications:** Informational brochure.
**Application information:** Application form not required.

> *Initial approach:* Proposal to headquarters
> *Copies of proposal:* 1
> *Deadline(s):* None
> *Final notification:* Following review

Administrators: J. Edward Hall, V.P., Corp. Contribs.; Claudia Edwards-Watts, Assoc. Dir., Corp. Contribs.
Number of staff: 2 part-time professional; 2 part-time support.

## 496
### Reader's Digest Foundation ▼
Reader's Digest Rd.
Pleasantville, NY 10570-7000 (914) 244-5370
Contact: Claudia L. Edwards, Exec. Dir.
FAX: (914) 238-7642; URL: http://www.readersdigest.com/corporate/rd_foundation.html

Incorporated in 1938 in NY.
Donor(s): The Reader's Digest Association, Inc.
Grantmaker type: Company-sponsored foundation
Financial data (yr. ended 06/30/99): Assets, $28,743,233 (M); expenditures, $4,415,782; qualifying distributions, $4,207,783; giving activities include $1,781,825 for 62 grants (high: $612,931; low: $300), $144,700 for 57 grants to individuals and $1,860,166 for employee matching gifts.
Purpose and activities: The foundation believes that people can make a difference in society, and that education is the key to individuals realizing their full potential. To achieve this mission, the foundation invests in programs and partnerships that: 1) encourage employees and retirees of the Reader's Digest Association, Inc. to contribute to their communities through volunteerism and individual philanthropy; 2) offer local grants in education, literacy and library services, primarily for young people in kindergarten through grade 12; and 3) help Reader's Digest employees send their children to college and provide assistance to other college students pursuing careers in publishing and direct mail marketing. The programs initiated will be concentrated primarily in communities where employees live and work and where there are greater needs.
Fields of interest: Journalism & publishing; elementary/secondary education; libraries/library science; reading; human services.
Types of support: Employee matching gifts; employee-related scholarships.
Limitations: Giving primarily in Westchester County, NY. No support for religious organizations or endeavors, veterans' or fraternal organizations, private foundations, cultural organizations, environmental groups, local chapters of national organizations, medical research or health-related activities. No grants to individuals (except for employee-related scholarships), or for capital, building or endowment funds, operating budgets, annual campaigns, seed money, emergency funds, deficit financing, special projects, charitable dinners or fundraising events, television, film, or video productions, publications, workshops, conferences, or seminars; no loans.
Publications: Annual report (including application guidelines).
Application information: If request falls within the foundation's grant guidelines, a proposal will be required. Application form not required.
Initial approach: Letter
Copies of proposal: 1

Deadline(s): Apr. 1, Aug. 1, and Dec. 1
Board meeting date(s): June, Nov., and Feb.
Final notification: The foundation replies to all inquiries within 2 weeks of receipt; 60 days
Officers and Directors:* Thomas O. Ryder,* Chair.; Mary L. Terry, Secy.; William H. Magill, Treas.; Claudia L. Edwards, Exec. Dir.; M. John Bohane, Michael A. Brizel, Elizabeth G. Chambers, Thomas D. Gardner, Gary S. Rich, George S. Scimone, Christopher P. Willcox.
Number of staff: 3
EIN: 136120380
Recent grants for library/information services:
496-1 Mid-Hudson Library, Poughkeepsie, NY, $22,000. 1998.
496-2 Norwalk Public Library, Norwalk, CT, $16,500. 1998.
496-3 Westchester Library System, Elmsford, NY, $432,069. 1998.

## 497
### The Reed Foundation, Inc.
444 Madison Ave., Ste. 2901
New York, NY 10022 (212) 223-1330
FAX: (212) 754-0078; E-mail: jsa@reedfoundation.org

Incorporated in 1949 in NY.
Donor(s): Samuel Rubin.‡
Grantmaker type: Independent foundation
Financial data (yr. ended 12/31/98): Assets, $12,190,513 (M); expenditures, $1,398,409; qualifying distributions, $1,150,765; giving activities include $1,150,765 for 36 grants (high: $330,295; low: $2,500; average: $2,500–$25,000).
Purpose and activities: The foundation's focus is on the support of programs in the arts, including dance and music, related libraries, social services, and both domestic and international civil rights. The arts and literature of the Caribbean Basin, through programs at a university and a research institute, are of major interest at present.
Fields of interest: Visual arts; performing arts; dance; theater; music; arts/cultural programs; higher education; libraries/library science; education; crime/law enforcement; human services; children & youth, services; minorities/immigrants, centers & services; human rights (international); civil rights; minorities; economically disadvantaged.
International interests: Caribbean.
Types of support: General/operating support; continuing support; endowments; program development; fellowships; scholarship funds; research; exchange programs; matching/challenge support.
Limitations: Giving primarily in the metropolitan New York, NY, area. No grants to individuals.
Publications: Program policy statement.
Application information: Applications generally considered only from organizations that have been pre-selected or those with which the foundation has a funding history. Application form not required.
Initial approach: Letter
Copies of proposal: 1
Deadline(s): None
Board meeting date(s): Varies

Final notification: Immediately following board meetings
Officer and Directors:* Reed Rubin,* Pres.; Jane Gregory Rubin.
Number of staff: 1 part-time professional; 1 part-time support.
EIN: 131990017

## 498
### Robbins Foundation, Inc.
515 Madison Ave.
New York, NY 10022

Established in 1945.
Grantmaker type: Independent foundation
Financial data (yr. ended 02/28/98): Assets, $2,467,059 (M); expenditures, $154,281; qualifying distributions, $110,203; giving activities include $110,203 for 28 grants (high: $22,000; low: $100).
Purpose and activities: Giving primarily for education.
Fields of interest: Elementary/secondary education; higher education; libraries/library science.
Limitations: Applications not accepted. Giving primarily in NY. No grants to individuals.
Application information: Contributes only to pre-selected organizations.
Officers: Allan J. Robbins, Pres.; Anita Robbins Gordon-Wright, V.P.
Trustee: Stanley B. Rich.
EIN: 136116442

## 499
### Billy Rose Foundation, Inc.
805 3rd Ave., 23rd Fl.
New York, NY 10022 (212) 407-7745
Contact: Terri C. Mangino, Exec. Dir.

Incorporated in 1958 in NY.
Donor(s): Billy Rose.‡
Grantmaker type: Independent foundation
Financial data (yr. ended 12/31/98): Assets, $15,844,974 (M); expenditures, $1,213,152; qualifying distributions, $1,050,870; giving activities include $1,022,000 for 89 grants (high: $325,000; low: $2,000; average: $5,000–$25,000).
Purpose and activities: Support for museums, particularly a museum in Israel, and the performing and fine arts; some giving also for higher education.
Fields of interest: Arts, research; visual arts; museums; performing arts; theater, playwriting; orchestra (symphony); arts/cultural programs; higher education; libraries (public).
Types of support: Program development; research.
Limitations: Giving primarily in New York, NY. No grants to individuals.
Application information: Application form not required.
Initial approach: Letter
Deadline(s): None
Board meeting date(s): Usually in June
Final notification: Varies
Officers and Directors:* Arthur Cantor,* Chair.; James R. Cherry,* Pres. and Treas.; James R. Cherry, Jr., V.P.; John Wohlstetter, V.P.; Edward T. Walsh, Jr., Secy.
Number of staff: 1 full-time professional.

EIN: 136165466

## 500
### Frederick P. & Sandra P. Rose Foundation ▼
200 Madison Ave., 5th Fl.
New York, NY 10016

Established in 1982 in DE.
**Donor(s):** Frederick P. Rose,‡ Samuel and David Rose Charitable Foundation.
**Grantmaker type:** Independent foundation
**Financial data** (yr. ended 11/30/98): Assets, $41,883,552 (M); gifts received, $4,634,159; expenditures, $8,799,479; qualifying distributions, $6,899,243; giving activities include $6,955,182 for 313 grants (high: $500,000; low: $50; average: $500–$25,000).
**Purpose and activities:** Giving primarily for performing arts and other cultural organizations; support also for higher education.
**Fields of interest:** Performing arts; arts/cultural programs; higher education.
**Limitations:** Applications not accepted. Giving primarily in New York, NY. No grants to individuals.
**Application information:** Contributes only to pre-selected organizations.
**Officers and Directors:*** Sandra P. Rose,* V.P.; Jonathan F.P. Rose,* Secy.-Treas.; Adam R. Rose, Deborah Rose.
**EIN:** 133136740
**Recent grants for library/information services:**
**500-1** Irvington Library, Irvington, NY, $10,000. 1998.
**500-2** New York Public Library, NYC, NY, $3,000,000. 1998.
**500-3** New York Public Library, NYC, NY, $25,000. For Library Lions. 1998.
**500-4** New York Public Library, NYC, NY, $21,587. 1998.
**500-5** New York Public Library, NYC, NY, $19,000. 1998.
**500-6** New York Public Library, NYC, NY, $10,000. 1998.

## 501
### Helena Rubinstein Foundation, Inc.
477 Madison Ave., 7th Fl.
New York, NY 10022-5802 (212) 750-7310
*Contact:* Diane Moss, Pres. and C.E.O.

Incorporated in 1953 in NY.
**Donor(s):** Helena Rubinstein Gourielli.‡
**Grantmaker type:** Independent foundation
**Financial data** (yr. ended 05/31/99): Assets, $39,513,686 (M); expenditures, $3,084,720; qualifying distributions, $2,552,954; giving activities include $2,062,742 for 126 grants (high: $150,000; low: $500; average: $5,000–$25,000).
**Purpose and activities:** Focus on projects that benefit women and children. Funding primarily for higher and other education, community services, health, the arts and arts in education.
**Fields of interest:** Arts education; arts/cultural programs; vocational education; higher education; education; health care; human services; children & youth, services; women; economically disadvantaged.
**Types of support:** General/operating support; continuing support; endowments; program

development; seed money; fellowships; internship funds; scholarship funds.
**Limitations:** Giving primarily in New York, NY. No grants to individuals, or for emergency funds or film or video projects; no loans.
**Publications:** Biennial report (including application guidelines), application guidelines, grants list.
**Application information:** Accepts NYRAG Common Grant Application Form. Application form not required.
*Initial approach:* Letter
*Copies of proposal:* 1
*Deadline(s):* None
*Board meeting date(s):* May and Nov.
*Final notification:* 1 to 3 months
**Officers and Directors:*** Gertrude G. Michelson,* Chair.; Diane Moss,* Pres. and C.E.O.; Robert Moss,* V.P.; Louis E. Slesin,* Secy.-Treas.; Laurie Shapley, Exec. Dir.; Robin F. Grossman, Suzanne Slesin, Deborah A. Zoullas.
**Number of staff:** 4 full-time professional; 1 full-time support; 1 part-time support.
**EIN:** 136102666
**Recent grants for library/information services:**
**501-1** Child Care, NYC, NY, $15,000. For continued general support of child care referral, research, training and advocacy initiatives. 2000.
**501-2** National Womens Health Network, DC, $10,000. For Women's Health Advocacy Internship project. 2000.
**501-3** New York Public Library, NYC, NY, $500,000. For continued support for renovation of 115th Street Branch Library in Harlem as part of Adopt-A-Branch Program. 2000.

## 502
### The Scherman Foundation, Inc. ▼
16 E. 52nd St., Ste. 601
New York, NY 10022-5306 (212) 832-3086
*Contact:* Sandra Silverman, Pres. and Exec. Dir.
*FAX:* (212) 838-0154

Incorporated in 1941 in NY.
**Donor(s):** Members of the Scherman family.
**Grantmaker type:** Independent foundation
**Financial data** (yr. ended 12/31/99): Assets, $119,515,809 (M); expenditures, $7,275,834; qualifying distributions, $6,863,969; giving activities include $6,416,680 for 179 grants (high: $300,000; low: $200; average: $10,000–$100,000).
**Purpose and activities:** Grants largely for environment, disarmament and peace, reproductive rights and services, human rights and liberties, the arts and social welfare. In the social welfare field, grants are made to organizations concerned with social justice, housing, public affairs, and community self-help.
**Fields of interest:** Performing arts; theater; music; arts/cultural programs; libraries/library science; natural resource conservation & protection; environment; family planning; gun control; legal services; housing/shelter, development; human services; peace; arms control; human rights (international); civil rights, minorities; reproductive rights; civil rights; community development; economically disadvantaged; homeless.
**Types of support:** General/operating support; continuing support; program development;

technical assistance; matching/challenge support.
**Limitations:** Giving primarily in New York, NY for arts and social welfare. No support for colleges, universities, or other higher educational institutions. No grants to individuals, or for building or endowment funds, scholarships, fellowships, conferences or symposia, specific media or arts production, or medical, science or engineering research.
**Publications:** Annual report (including application guidelines).
**Application information:** Application form not required.
*Initial approach:* Letter
*Copies of proposal:* 1
*Deadline(s):* None
*Board meeting date(s):* Quarterly
*Final notification:* 6 to 8 weeks
**Officers and Directors:*** Karen R. Sollins, Chair.; Axel G. Rosin,* Chair, Emeritus; Sandra Silverman, Pres. and Exec. Dir.; Katharine S. Rosin,* Secy.; Mitchell C. Pratt, Treas. and Prog. Off.; Susanna Bergtold, Hillary Brown, Gordon N. Litwin, Archibald R. Murray, John J. O'Neil, Anthony M. Schulte, Marcia Thompson.
**Number of staff:** 2 full-time professional; 1 full-time support; 1 part-time support.
**EIN:** 136098464
**Recent grants for library/information services:**
**502-1** Educators for Social Responsibility, NYC, NY, $20,000. For Abolition Education and Action Project. 1999.
**502-2** Sexuality Information and Education Council of the U.S. (SIECUS), NYC, NY, $30,000. For general support. 1999.

## 503
### The Schloss Family Foundation, Inc.
c/o Walter J. Schloss
350 Park Ave., 9th Fl.
New York, NY 10022-6022

Established in 1997 in NY.
**Donor(s):** Walter J. Schloss.
**Grantmaker type:** Independent foundation
**Financial data** (yr. ended 12/31/99): Assets, $2,226,448 (M); expenditures, $101,900; qualifying distributions, $85,200; giving activities include $85,200 for 13 grants (high: $20,000; low: $1,000).
**Purpose and activities:** Giving for art and cultural programs, and for education.
**Fields of interest:** Museums; museums (art); libraries/library science; libraries (public); environment; animals/wildlife.
**Limitations:** Applications not accepted. Giving limited to Washington, DC, and NY. No grants to individuals.
**Application information:** Contributes only to pre-selected organizations.
**Officers:** Walter J. Schloss, Pres. and Treas.; Edwin W. Schloss, V.P.; Stephanie Cassel Scott, Secy.
**EIN:** 133935646

## 504
### The Thomas P. & Cynthia D. Sculco Foundation
132 E. 95th St.
New York, NY 10128
*Contact:* Thomas P. Sculco, M.D., Pres.

Established in 1997.
**Donor(s):** Thomas P. Sculco, M.D., Cynthia D. Sculco.
**Grantmaker type:** Independent foundation
**Financial data** (yr. ended 02/28/98): Assets, $1,152,654 (M); gifts received, $780,942; expenditures, $79,500; qualifying distributions, $79,500; giving activities include $79,500 for 8 grants (high: $55,000; low: $1,000).
**Purpose and activities:** Giving primarily for education.
**Fields of interest:** Theater; higher education; libraries (public).
**Application information:** Application form not required.
*Initial approach:* Letter
*Deadline(s):* None
**Officers:** Thomas P. Sculco, M.D., Pres.; Cynthia D. Sculco, Secy.
**EIN:** 133952927

## 505
### The Herbert J. Seligmann Charitable Trust
c/o Windels Marx, et al.
156 W. 56th St.
New York, NY 10019
*Contact:* John Kriz

Established in 1997 in NY.
**Donor(s):** Lise R. Seligmann.
**Grantmaker type:** Independent foundation
**Financial data** (yr. ended 12/31/97): Assets, $1,008,550 (M); gifts received, $967,626; expenditures, $85,302; qualifying distributions, $79,453; giving activities include $75,000 for 3 grants of $25,000 each.
**Purpose and activities:** Giving to higher education.
**Fields of interest:** University; libraries/library science.
**Limitations:** Giving primarily in NY.
**Application information:**
*Initial approach:* Proposal
*Deadline(s):* None
**Trustees:** Lise R. Seligmann, W. David Wister, Robert Nathaniel Zicht.
**EIN:** 137114871

## 506
### Ralph C. Sheldon Foundation, Inc.
P.O. Box 417
Jamestown, NY 14702-0417 (716) 664-9890
*Contact:* Miles L. Lasser, Exec. Dir.
*Application address:* 7 E. 3rd St., Jamestown, NY 14701; FAX: (716) 483-6116

Incorporated in 1948 in NY.
**Donor(s):** Julia S. Livengood,‡ Isabell M. Sheldon.‡
**Grantmaker type:** Independent foundation
**Financial data** (yr. ended 05/31/99): Assets, $10,431,982 (M); gifts received, $1,086,144; expenditures, $1,173,598; qualifying distributions, $1,124,883; giving activities

include $1,102,117 for 69 grants (high: $170,000; low: $100).
**Purpose and activities:** Support for youth development organizations, community improvement, cultural organizations, hospitals, social service organizations, and education.
**Fields of interest:** Visual arts; performing arts; theater; arts/cultural programs; libraries/library science; education; environment; hospitals (general); human services; youth, services; community development.
**Types of support:** General/operating support; annual campaigns; capital campaigns; building/renovation; equipment; emergency funds.
**Limitations:** Giving limited to southern Chautauqua County, NY. No support for religious organizations. No grants to individuals.
**Publications:** Application guidelines.
**Application information:** Contact foundation for deadlines. Application form required.
*Copies of proposal:* 6
*Deadline(s):* None
*Board meeting date(s):* Varies, approx. 5 times a year
*Final notification:* Immediately after determination
**Officers and Directors:*** Jane E. Sheldon,* Pres.; Mark Hampton,* V.P.; Barclay O. Wellman,* V.P.; Miles L. Lasser,* Secy. and Exec. Dir.; Peter B. Sullivan,* Treas.
**Number of staff:** 1 part-time professional; 1 part-time support.
**EIN:** 166030502

## 507
### The Arnold Simon Family Foundation, Inc.
c/o Schneider, Schecter and Yoss, PC
1979 Marcus Ave., Ste. 232
New Hyde Park, NY 11042-1002

Established in 1996 in NJ.
**Donor(s):** Arnold Simon.
**Grantmaker type:** Operating foundation
**Financial data** (yr. ended 12/31/99): Assets, $5,156,604 (M); gifts received, $581,100; expenditures, $1,675,757; qualifying distributions, $1,553,901; giving activities include $1,557,368 for 29 grants (high: $500,000; low: $80).
**Purpose and activities:** Giving primarily for health care; support also for the arts and education and for a presidential library.
**Fields of interest:** Libraries/library science; education; hospitals (general); health associations.
**Limitations:** Applications not accepted. No grants to individuals.
**Application information:** Contributes only to pre-selected organizations.
**Trustees:** Howard Schneider, Arnold Simon, Debra Simon.
**EIN:** 223480373

## 508
### The Robert and Sara Smith Foundation, Inc.
291 Genesee St.
Utica, NY 13501

Established in 1993 in NY.
**Grantmaker type:** Independent foundation

**Financial data** (yr. ended 12/31/98): Assets, $491,262 (M); expenditures, $60,257; qualifying distributions, $59,408; giving activities include $59,500 for 12 grants (high: $20,000; low: $500).
**Purpose and activities:** Giving primarily for education and youth programs.
**Fields of interest:** Libraries (public); education; youth development, association.
**Limitations:** Applications not accepted. No grants to individuals.
**Application information:** Contributes only to pre-selected organizations.
**Officers:** Michael Silverman, Pres.; Charles Silverman, V.P.; Lois Silverman, Secy.-Treas.
**EIN:** 161448678

## 509
### The John Ben Snow Foundation, Inc.
50 Presidential Plz., Ste. 106
Syracuse, NY 13202
*Contact:* Rollan D. Melton, Pres., or Jonathan L. Snow, Treas.

Incorporated in 1948 in NY.
**Donor(s):** John Ben Snow.‡
**Grantmaker type:** Independent foundation
**Financial data** (yr. ended 12/31/99): Assets, $6,863,557 (M); expenditures, $471,776; qualifying distributions, $373,377; giving activities include $336,800 for 27 grants (high: $40,000; low: $300; average: $10,000–$15,000).
**Purpose and activities:** The mission of the foundation is to make grants within specific focus areas to enhance the quality of life in central and northern NY state. The focus areas are: Arts and Culture, Community, Education, and Journalism.
**Fields of interest:** Journalism & publishing; historic preservation/historical societies; higher education; libraries/library science; education; environment; children & youth, services; community development; minorities; disabled.
**Types of support:** Building/renovation; equipment; program development; publication; seed money; fellowships; scholarship funds; matching/challenge support.
**Limitations:** Giving limited to central NY, with emphasis on Onondaga and Oswego counties. No support for religious organizations or for-profit groups. No grants to individuals, or for operating budgets, endowment funds, or contingency financing.
**Publications:** Annual report (including application guidelines), financial statement.
**Application information:** All inquiries by mail. Application form required.
*Initial approach:* Letter of inquiry
*Copies of proposal:* 1
*Deadline(s):* Apr. 1
*Board meeting date(s):* June
*Final notification:* July 1
**Officers and Directors:*** Rollan D. Melton,* Pres.; David H. Snow,* V.P. and Secy.; Jonathan L. Snow,* V.P. and Treas.; Valerie A. Macfie, Allen R. Malcolm, Bruce Malcolm, Emelie Melton-Williams.
**Number of staff:** 1 part-time support.
**EIN:** 136112704

## 510
### John Ben Snow Memorial Trust
50 Presidential Plz., Ste. 106
Syracuse, NY 13202
*Contact:* Jonathan L. Snow, Tr.

Trust established in 1975 in NY.
**Donor(s):** John Ben Snow.‡
**Grantmaker type:** Independent foundation
**Financial data** (yr. ended 12/31/99): Assets,
$29,932,152 (M); expenditures, $1,396,295;
qualifying distributions, $1,105,934; giving
activities include $1,007,300 for grants
(average: $15,000–$25,000).
**Purpose and activities:** Support primarily for
higher education, scholarship funds, and
minority students; the humanities and cultural
institutions, especially libraries, the performing
arts, theater, and historical preservation;
environmental groups; media and
communications; and community development.
Support also for the handicapped, and science
and technology.
**Fields of interest:** Performing arts; theater;
arts/cultural programs; higher education;
libraries/library science; environment; health
associations; community development; disabled.
**Types of support:** Building/renovation;
equipment; program development; publication;
seed money; fellowships; scholarship funds;
matching/challenge support.
**Limitations:** Giving primarily in MD, NV, and
central NY. No support for unspecified projects,
religious organizations, or for-profit groups. No
grants to individuals, or for operating budgets,
endowment funds, or contingency financing; no
loans.
**Publications:** Annual report (including
application guidelines).
**Application information:** Application form
required.
*Initial approach:* Letter of inquiry
*Copies of proposal:* 1
*Deadline(s):* Submit proposal preferably from
July through Jan.; deadline Apr. 1
*Board meeting date(s):* June
*Final notification:* July 1
**Trustees:** Allen R. Malcolm, Rollan D. Melton,
Jonathan L. Snow, The Bank of New York.
**Number of staff:** None.
**EIN:** 136633814

## 511
### Solow Foundation
9 W. 57th St., Ste. 4500
New York, NY 10019-2601
*Contact:* Rosalie S. Wolff, V.P.

Established in 1978 in DE.
**Donor(s):** Sheldon H. Solow.
**Grantmaker type:** Independent foundation
**Financial data** (yr. ended 10/31/99): Assets,
$9,592,912 (M); expenditures, $747,622;
qualifying distributions, $211,456; giving
activities include $210,500 for 16 grants (high:
$100,000; low: $1,000).
**Fields of interest:** Visual arts; architecture;
museums; history & archaeology; arts/cultural
programs; higher education; libraries/library
science; education; Jewish agencies & temples.
**Types of support:** General/operating support;
continuing support; professorships; fellowships.

**Limitations:** Giving primarily in New York, NY.
No grants to individuals.
**Application information:** Application form not
required.
*Initial approach:* Letter
*Copies of proposal:* 1
*Deadline(s):* None
**Officers:** Sheldon H. Solow, Pres.; Rosalie S.
Wolff, V.P.; Leonard Lazarus, Secy.; Steven M.
Cherniak, Treas.
**EIN:** 132950685

## 512
### The Soros Foundation-Hungary, Inc.
400 W. 59th St.
New York, NY 10019 (212) 548-0630
*Contact:* Steve Gutmann
*FAX:* (212) 548-4679

Established in 1983 in NY.
**Donor(s):** George Soros, George Soros
Charitable Lead Trust, Tivadar Charitable Lead
Trust.
**Grantmaker type:** Independent foundation
**Financial data** (yr. ended 12/31/99): Assets,
$181,503,220 (M); expenditures, $55,124,428;
qualifying distributions, $48,533,465; giving
activities include $50,000,000 for 1 grant.
**Purpose and activities:** Supports Hungarian
organizations and projects, including the fields
of language, culture, and education; also awards
grants and scholarships to individuals for higher
education and medical research.
**Fields of interest:** Elementary school/education;
law school/education; medical
school/education; adult education—literacy &
basic skills; libraries/library science; reading;
education; health care; health associations;
youth development, services; youth, services;
international affairs, goodwill promotion;
race/intergroup relations; civil rights; community
development; public policy, research;
government/public administration; leadership
development.
**International interests:** Hungary.
**Types of support:** Program development;
conferences/seminars; fellowships; internship
funds; research; grants to individuals;
scholarships—to individuals; exchange
programs.
**Limitations:** Giving primarily in Hungary.
**Publications:** Annual report, newsletter,
informational brochure (including application
guidelines).
**Application information:** Application form
required for scholarship programs only.
*Copies of proposal:* 1
*Deadline(s):* None
*Board meeting date(s):* Usually within 1 month
**Officers and Directors:*** George Soros,*
Co-Chair.; Susan Weber Soros,* Co-Chair.;
Aryeh Neier,* Pres.; Gary Gladstein, Secy.-Treas.
**Number of staff:** 4 full-time professional; 2
full-time support.
**EIN:** 133210361

## 513
### Bella Spewack Article 5 Trust
c/o The Bank of New York, Tax Dept.
1 Wall St., 28th Fl.
New York, NY 10286
*Application address:* c/o Robin Khan, The Bank
of New York, 1290 Ave. of the Americas, New
York, NY 10286

Established in 1991 in NY.
**Donor(s):** Bella Spewack.‡
**Grantmaker type:** Independent foundation
**Financial data** (yr. ended 06/30/98): Assets,
$1,617,699 (M); expenditures, $82,154;
qualifying distributions, $71,436; giving
activities include $65,000 for 12 grants (high:
$54,000; low: $500).
**Purpose and activities:** Giving primarily for
Jewish organizations.
**Fields of interest:** Theater; libraries/library
science; human services; Jewish federated giving
programs; Jewish agencies & temples; disabled;
homeless.
**Limitations:** Giving primarily in New York, NY.
**Application information:**
*Initial approach:* Letter
*Deadline(s):* None
**Trustees:** Arthur Elias, Lois Elias, The Bank of
New York.
**EIN:** 133669246

## 514
### Springate Corporation
25 Central Park W., Ste. 1B
New York, NY 10023-7253

Established about 1959 in NY.
**Donor(s):** Leonard Bernstein,‡ Amberson
Enterprises, Inc.
**Grantmaker type:** Independent foundation
**Financial data** (yr. ended 12/31/98): Assets,
$29,081 (M); gifts received, $75,000;
expenditures, $326,718; qualifying distributions,
$319,117; giving activities include $253,368 for
1 grant.
**Purpose and activities:** Support primarily for arts
and cultural activities, including theater, the
performing arts, music, museums, and libraries;
hospitals and AIDS and cancer research;
education, especially vocational and higher
education; Jewish welfare and Israel; community
funds; youth; the environment; race relations,
minorities, and immigrants; public policy and
public affairs; civil and human rights;
organizations promoting freedom and peace;
and other charitable giving.
**Fields of interest:** Museums; performing arts;
theater; music; arts/cultural programs;
vocational education; higher education;
libraries/library science; education;
environment; hospitals (general); cancer; cancer
research; human services; youth, services;
minorities/immigrants, centers & services;
peace; human rights (international);
race/intergroup relations; civil rights; federated
giving programs; Jewish federated giving
programs; public policy, research; public affairs;
minorities; immigrants/refugees.
**International interests:** Israel.
**Types of support:** General/operating support;
continuing support; endowments; scholarship
funds.

**Limitations:** Applications not accepted. Giving primarily in New York, NY. No grants to individuals.
**Application information:** Contributes only to pre-selected organizations.
**Officers and Directors:*** Nina Bernstein,* Pres.; Harry J. Kraut,* V.P.; Paul H. Epstein,* Secy.; Jaime Bernstein Thomas,* Treas.; Alexander Bernstein, Schuyler G. Chapin, Lukas Foss, Robert Lantz, Michael Tilson Thomas.
**Number of staff:** 1 part-time professional.
**EIN:** 136091607

## 515
### The Harold & Mimi Steinberg Charitable Trust ▼

c/o Schulte Roth & Zabel
900 3rd Ave.
New York, NY 10022

Established in 1986 in NY.
**Donor(s):** Harold Steinberg.‡
**Grantmaker type:** Independent foundation
**Financial data** (yr. ended 12/31/99): Assets, $24,104,667 (M); expenditures, $3,182,333; qualifying distributions, $2,843,398; giving activities include $2,790,295 for 118 grants (high: $200,000; low: $129; average: $1,000–$25,000).
**Purpose and activities:** Giving primarily for arts and cultural organizations, higher education, and the environment.
**Fields of interest:** Visual arts; performing arts; theater; higher education; libraries/library science; hospitals (general); human services; Jewish federated giving programs.
**Limitations:** Applications not accepted. Giving primarily in New York, NY. No grants to individuals.
**Application information:** Contributes only to pre-selected organizations. Unsolicited requests for funds not considered.
**Trustees:** Charles Benenson, Carole A. Krumland, James D. Steinberg, Michael A. Steinberg, Seth Weingarten, William D. Zabel.
**EIN:** 133383348

## 516
### The Miriam & Harold Steinberg Foundation, Inc.

c/o Steinberg Asset Mgmt. Co., Inc.
12 E. 49th St., Ste. 1202
New York, NY 10017-1028

Established in 1960 in NY.
**Grantmaker type:** Independent foundation
**Financial data** (yr. ended 06/30/00): Assets, $1,644,783 (M); expenditures, $79,105; qualifying distributions, $59,570; giving activities include $56,750 for 45 grants (high: $10,000; low: $150).
**Fields of interest:** Arts/cultural programs; libraries/library science; education; human services.
**Limitations:** Applications not accepted. Giving primarily in the San Francisco Bay Area, CA, and New York, NY. No grants to individuals.
**Application information:** Contributes only to pre-selected organizations.

**Officers:** Michael A. Steinberg, Pres.; Carol A. Krumland, V.P. and Secy.; James D. Steinberg, V.P. and Treas.
**EIN:** 136126000

## 517
### The Stevens Kingsley Foundation, Inc.

c/o Sullivan & Cromwell
125 Broad St.
New York, NY 10004-2498
*Contact:* George B. Waters, Dir.
*Application address:* 1205 N. Madison St., Rome, NY 13440-2725

Established in 1960 in NY.
**Grantmaker type:** Independent foundation
**Financial data** (yr. ended 12/31/98): Assets, $3,185,404 (M); expenditures, $115,033; qualifying distributions, $107,979; giving activities include $104,500 for 17 grants (high: $30,000; low: $400).
**Purpose and activities:** Giving primarily for community development, art and culture, and education.
**Fields of interest:** Historic preservation/historical societies; arts/cultural programs; libraries (public); education; YM/YWCAs & YM/YWHAs; community development; general charitable giving.
**Types of support:** Building/renovation; equipment; seed money.
**Limitations:** Giving limited to the Rome, NY, area. No grants to individuals, or for operating expenses.
**Application information:** Application form not required.
*Initial approach:* Letter
*Copies of proposal:* 1
*Deadline(s):* None
*Board meeting date(s):* Fall
**Officers and Directors:*** Donald R. Osborn,* Pres.; Henry Christensen III,* Secy.-Treas.; Mark F. Hinman, William Curtis Pierce, George B. Waters.
**Number of staff:** None.
**EIN:** 136150722

## 518
### Bradford Field and Lee Bottome Story Foundation

c/o Walter Conston, et al.
90 Park Ave.
New York, NY 10016

Established in 1988 in NY; foundation also files a copy of tax return in NJ.
**Donor(s):** Lee Bottome Story.‡
**Grantmaker type:** Independent foundation
**Financial data** (yr. ended 12/31/98): Assets, $306,088 (M); expenditures, $64,473; qualifying distributions, $60,192; giving activities include $60,500 for 6 grants (high: $15,000; low: $2,500).
**Fields of interest:** Libraries (public).
**Types of support:** General/operating support.
**Limitations:** Applications not accepted. Giving primarily in MA. No grants to individuals.
**Application information:** Contributes only to pre-selected organizations.
**Trustees:** Martha H. Dwyer, William B. Fisher.
**EIN:** 133487720

## 519
### The Philip A. and Lynn Straus Foundation, Inc.

1037 Constable Dr. S.
Mamaroneck, NY 10543

Incorporated about 1957 in NY.
**Donor(s):** Philip A. Straus.
**Grantmaker type:** Independent foundation
**Financial data** (yr. ended 03/31/99): Assets, $34,230,514 (M); gifts received, $6,000; expenditures, $1,777,097; qualifying distributions, $1,450,050; giving activities include $1,449,235 for 85 grants (high: $250,000; low: $50).
**Purpose and activities:** Giving primarily for education from birth to age 21, the arts, libraries, civil rights and human services.
**Fields of interest:** Museums; arts/cultural programs; libraries/library science; education; human services; civil rights.
**Limitations:** Applications not accepted. Giving primarily in NY. No grants to individuals.
**Application information:** Contributes only to pre-selected organizations.
**Officers:** Philip A. Straus, Pres.; Lynn G. Straus, V.P. and Treas.
**Number of staff:** None.
**EIN:** 136161223

## 520
### Strong Foundation of New York

30 E. 71st St.
New York, NY 10021-4956 (212) 249-1253
*Contact:* Roger L. Strong, Pres.

Established in 1961 in NY.
**Donor(s):** Marguerite Strong,‡ Roger L. Strong, Jeffrey Strong, Lee Strong, Roger Strong, Jr., Thomas Strong.
**Grantmaker type:** Independent foundation
**Financial data** (yr. ended 03/31/99): Assets, $4,436,988 (M); gifts received, $401,938; expenditures, $248,391; qualifying distributions, $190,010; giving activities include $186,195 for 112 grants (high: $40,000; low: $100).
**Purpose and activities:** Giving primarily for education and the arts, and to Jewish agencies.
**Fields of interest:** Arts/cultural programs; education, fund raising; higher education; libraries/library science; natural resource conservation & protection; Jewish agencies & temples; general charitable giving.
**Types of support:** General/operating support; annual campaigns; capital campaigns; matching/challenge support.
**Limitations:** Applications not accepted. Giving primarily in New York, NY. No grants to individuals.
**Publications:** Annual report.
**Application information:** Contributes only to pre-selected organizations.
*Board meeting date(s):* Quarterly
**Officers:** Roger L. Strong, Pres.; Roger L. Strong, Jr., V.P.; Lee Strong, Secy.
**Directors:** Jeffrey Strong, Thomas Strong.
**Number of staff:** None.
**EIN:** 136093147

## 521
**The Stuart Foundation, Inc.**
599 Lexington Ave.
New York, NY 10022 (212) 750-0055

Incorporated in 1951 in NY.
**Donor(s):** Members of the Stuart family.
**Grantmaker type:** Independent foundation
**Financial data** (yr. ended 12/31/97): Assets,
$3,519,616 (M); expenditures, $197,653;
qualifying distributions, $158,186; giving
activities include $153,960 for 42 grants (high:
$46,000; low: $50; average: $1,000–$60,000).
**Purpose and activities:** Giving primarily for
education, including educational research and
associations, building funds, organizations
providing assistance to minority students, early
childhood, elementary, secondary, higher and
medical education; support also for the arts,
including museums, theaters, and the fine and
performing arts, libraries, cancer research and
hospitals, and family services, including child
welfare and development.
**Fields of interest:** Visual arts; museums;
performing arts; theater; arts/cultural programs;
education, association; education, research;
education, fund raising; early childhood
education; child development, education;
elementary school/education; secondary
school/education; higher education; medical
school/education; libraries/library science;
education; natural resource conservation &
protection; environment; hospitals (general);
mental health/crisis services; cancer; cancer
research; children & youth, services; child
development, services; family services;
homeless, human services; federated giving
programs; homeless.
**Types of support:** General/operating support;
annual campaigns; capital campaigns;
building/renovation; equipment; endowments;
program development; fellowships; scholarship
funds; research.
**Limitations:** Applications not accepted. Giving
primarily in NY and New England, with
emphasis on CT, MA, and RI. No grants to
individuals.
**Application information:** Contributes only to
pre-selected organizations.
*Board meeting date(s):* Annually
**Officers and Directors:*** Alan L. Stuart,* Chair.;
John E. Stuart, Pres.; James M. Stuart, Jr., V.P.;
Jacqueline B. Stuart, Secy.; Edward Polito, Treas.;
Carolyn A. Stuart.
**Number of staff:** 1 full-time professional.
**EIN:** 136066191

## 522
**Time Warner Inc. Corporate Giving
   Program**
75 Rockerfeller Plz.
New York, NY 10019 (212) 484-8000
*Contact:* Kay M. Nishiyama, Mgr., Corp.
Contribs.

**Grantmaker type:** Corporate giving program
**Purpose and activities:** Social involvement and
concern are an integral part of Time Warner's
day-to-day operations. The company is a
national leader on work and family issues,
including innovative child care centers in
Burbank, CA, and New York, NY. The company
has also taken a leadership role in youth

employment and has responded with money,
effort, and imagination to the needs of people in
crisis. Time Warner gives to nonprofit
organizations for which employees provide
voluntary services. One-third of support is for
educational institutions. Giving also for literacy,
the arts and culture, and civic and welfare
issues. Employee support is through United
Student Aid Funds, three-for-one matching
grants (to education and art and culture),
scholarships for children of employees, and free
admission to art institutions and discount
performing arts tickets. The company also
provides in-kind donations of company services
and employee expertise. Emphasis is on
geographic relevance and benefit to company
business, staff, and shareholders.
**Fields of interest:** Museums; performing arts;
theater; humanities; arts/cultural programs;
elementary school/education; higher education;
medical school/education; adult/continuing
education; adult education—literacy & basic
skills; libraries/library science; reading;
education; employment; safety/disasters; human
services; children, day care; youth, services;
family services; minorities/immigrants, centers &
services; urban/community development;
voluntarism promotion; federated giving
programs; government/public administration;
minorities; economically disadvantaged.
**Types of support:** General/operating support;
emergency funds; program development;
research; consulting services; employee
volunteer services; employee matching gifts;
employee-related scholarships; in-kind gifts.
**Limitations:** Giving primarily in the New York,
NY, area. No support for sectarian, religious, or
political organizations, United Way recipients,
or medical or health-related organizations. No
grants to individuals (except for
employee-related scholarships), or for
memorials, publishing or filmmaking trips or
tours, endowment funds, or capital fund drives
(including building funds).
**Application information:** Separate,
locally-oriented giving programs are maintained
by some Time Warner subsidiary companies; the
parent company will not make grants on their
behalf. Telephone requests are not honored.
Application form not required.
*Initial approach:* 1- to 2-page letter
*Deadline(s):* None
*Final notification:* Meeting to be arranged if
   funding is possible; all requests are
   acknowledged.

## 523
**Tioga County Senior Citizens Foundation**
c/o Chemung Canal Trust Co.
P.O. Box 1522
Elmira, NY 14902
*Contact:* Dean Fowler
*Application address:* c/o Dean Fowler, 348 Front
St., Oswego, NY 13827, tel.: (607) 687-3083

Established in 1951.
**Grantmaker type:** Independent foundation
**Financial data** (yr. ended 09/30/99): Assets,
$1,513,366 (M); expenditures, $101,551;
qualifying distributions, $87,646; giving
activities include $86,900 for grants.
**Purpose and activities:** Support only to senior
citizen related programs in Tioga County, NY.

**Fields of interest:** Performing arts;
libraries/library science; human services; aging.
**Limitations:** Giving limited to Tioga County, NY.
**Application information:** Request application
form. Application form required.
*Deadline(s):* June 1
**Officers:** J. Dickson Edson, Pres.; Gary
Williams,* V.P.; Regina Williams,* Secy.; Richard
Waltman, Treas.
**EIN:** 150543615

## 524
**Tisch Foundation, Inc.** ▼
655 Madison Ave., 8th Fl.
New York, NY 10021-8087 (212) 521-2930
*Contact:* Mark J. Krinsky, V.P.

Incorporated in 1957 in FL.
**Donor(s):** Hotel Americana, Tisch Hotels, Inc.,
members of the Tisch family, and closely held
corporations.
**Grantmaker type:** Independent foundation
**Financial data** (yr. ended 12/31/98): Assets,
$132,383,122 (M); expenditures, $11,705,257;
qualifying distributions, $11,229,534; giving
activities include $11,297,946 for 145 grants
(high: $2,000,000; low: $100; average:
$1,000–$50,000).
**Purpose and activities:** Emphasis on higher
education, including institutions in Israel, and
research-related programs; support also for
Jewish organizations and welfare funds,
museums, and secondary education.
**Fields of interest:** Museums; secondary
school/education; higher education; AIDS;
medical research; human services; Jewish
federated giving programs; Jewish agencies &
temples.
**International interests:** Israel.
**Types of support:** Continuing support;
building/renovation; equipment; research.
**Limitations:** Applications not accepted. Giving
primarily in NY. No grants to individuals, or for
endowment funds, scholarships, fellowships, or
matching gifts; no loans.
**Application information:** Contributes only to
pre-selected organizations.
*Board meeting date(s):* Mar., June, Sept., Dec.,
   and as required
**Officers and Directors:*** Preston R. Tisch,*
Pres.; Laurence A. Tisch,* Sr. V.P.; Mark J.
Krinsky, V.P.; Thomas M. Steinberg, V.P.; Laurie
Tisch Sussman, V.P.; Andrew H. Tisch, V.P.;
Daniel R. Tisch, V.P.; James S. Tisch, V.P.;
Jonathan M. Tisch, V.P.; Steven E. Tisch, V.P.;
Thomas J. Tisch, V.P.; Barry L. Bloom,
Secy.-Treas.; Joan H. Tisch, Wilma S. Tisch.
**Number of staff:** None.
**EIN:** 591002844
**Recent grants for library/information services:**
**524-1** Center for Jewish History, NYC, NY,
   $55,000. For continued support. 1998.
**524-2** Rye Free Reading Room, Rye, NY,
   $25,000. For continued support. 1998.
**524-3** Survivors of the Shoah Visual History
   Foundation, Los Angeles, CA, $250,000. For
   continued support. 1998.
**524-4** Tufts University, Tisch Library, Medford,
   MA, $1,000,000. For continued support.
   1998.

## 525
### Mildred Faulkner Truman Foundation
c/o The Chase Manhattan Bank, N.A.
P.O. Box 1412
Rochester, NY 14603
*Contact:* Irene C. Graven, Exec. Dir.
*Application address:* 195 Front St., P.O. Box 89,
Owego, NY 13827, tel.: (607) 687-1350;
Additional tel.: (607) 785-2355

Established in 1985 in NY.
**Donor(s):** Mildred Faulkner Truman.‡
**Grantmaker type:** Independent foundation
**Financial data** (yr. ended 08/31/99): Assets,
$9,147,887 (M); expenditures, $514,817;
qualifying distributions, $468,887; giving
activities include $400,768 for 34 grants (high:
$100,000; low: $900; average: $500–$50,000).
**Purpose and activities:** Giving primarily for
community improvement.
**Fields of interest:** Arts/cultural programs;
libraries/library science; education;
environment; children & youth, services;
community development; Christian agencies &
churches.
**Types of support:** Capital campaigns;
building/renovation; equipment; emergency
funds; program development; seed money;
scholarship funds; scholarships—to individuals;
matching/challenge support.
**Limitations:** Giving primarily in Tioga County,
NY, with emphasis on the Owego area.
**Publications:** Annual report (including
application guidelines).
**Application information:** Application form
required.
   *Initial approach:* Proposal
   *Copies of proposal:* 11
   *Deadline(s):* 3 weeks before board meeting
   *Board meeting date(s):* Quarterly
   *Final notification:* 1 week after board meeting
**Officer:** Irene C. Graven, Exec. Dir.
**Corporate Trustee:** The Chase Manhattan Bank,
N.A.
**Number of staff:** 1 part-time professional.
**EIN:** 166271201

## 526
### Michael Tuch Foundation, Inc.
122 E. 42nd St., Ste. 1003
New York, NY 10168 (212) 986-9082
*Contact:* Martha Tuck Rozett, Pres.

Incorporated in 1946 in NY.
**Donor(s):** Michael Tuch.‡
**Grantmaker type:** Independent foundation
**Financial data** (yr. ended 12/31/99): Assets,
$9,687,157 (M); gifts received, $53,645;
expenditures, $528,590; qualifying distributions,
$460,941; giving activities include $407,050 for
119 grants (high: $12,000; low: $250).
**Purpose and activities:** Giving primarily for the
arts, including museums, and for educational
institutions and programs.
**Fields of interest:** Museums; performing arts;
theater; music; arts/cultural programs;
elementary school/education; higher education;
libraries/library science; education; food
services; human services; children & youth,
services; Jewish federated giving programs;
Jewish agencies & temples; economically
disadvantaged.

**Types of support:** Program development;
fellowships; internship funds; scholarship funds.
**Limitations:** Giving primarily in New York, NY.
No support for religion or health. No grants to
individuals, or for study or new general support.
**Application information:** Application form not
required.
   *Initial approach:* Proposal
   *Copies of proposal:* 1
   *Deadline(s):* None
   *Board meeting date(s):* May
**Officers and Trustees:*** Martha Tuck Rozett,*
Pres. and Exec. Dir.; Jonathan S. Tuck, V.P. and
Secy.-Treas.; Daniel H. Tuck.
**Number of staff:** 2 part-time professional; 2
part-time support.
**EIN:** 136002848

## 527
### The Mark Twain Foundation
c/o The Chase Manhattan Bank, N.A.
1 Chase Manhattan Plz., 5th Fl.
New York, NY 10081
*Contact:* John Boncada, Sr. Trust Off.
*Application address:* c/o The Chase Manhattan
Bank, N.A., 1211 Ave. of the Americas, New
York, NY 10036-8890

Established in 1978.
**Grantmaker type:** Independent foundation
**Financial data** (yr. ended 10/31/98): Assets,
$1,610,488 (M); expenditures, $94,409;
qualifying distributions, $57,753; giving
activities include $55,000 for grants.
**Purpose and activities:** Contributes only to Mark
Twain revivals, retrospectives, and associated
activities.
**Fields of interest:** Performing arts; history &
archaeology; college; libraries/library science.
**Types of support:** General/operating support.
**Application information:** Application form not
required.
   *Copies of proposal:* 2
   *Deadline(s):* None
**Trustees:** Richard A. Watson, The Chase
Manhattan Bank, N.A.
**EIN:** 133058782

## 528
### U.S. Trust Corporation Foundation
(Formerly United States Trust Company of New
York Foundation)
c/o U.S. Trust Co. of New York
114 W. 47th St.
New York, NY 10036 (212) 852-1400
*Contact:* Carol A. Strickland, Contrib. Comm.
Chair., U.S. Trust Co. of New York
*FAX:* (212) 852-1314; E-mail:
foundation@ustrust.com

Trust established in 1955 in NY.
**Donor(s):** U.S. Trust Co. of New York.
**Grantmaker type:** Company-sponsored
foundation
**Financial data** (yr. ended 12/31/99): Assets, $0
(M); expenditures, $499,263; qualifying
distributions, $499,263; giving activities include
$325,000 for 27 grants (high: $50,000; low:
$5,000; average: $5,000–$10,000) and
$174,263 for 352 employee matching gifts.
**Purpose and activities:** Primary areas of interest
include the arts, community development,

employment programs, and housing. Support for
the performing arts and other cultural programs,
and civic and urban affairs and development
organizations, including programs for the
disadvantaged that assist in building or
maintaining an improved quality of life.
Preference given to innovative, broad-based,
privately supported, and efficient organizations
in which company employees are active.
**Fields of interest:** Performing arts; dance;
theater; music; arts/cultural programs;
libraries/library science; employment;
housing/shelter, development; human services;
homeless, human services; urban/community
development; community development;
minorities; economically disadvantaged;
homeless.
**Types of support:** General/operating support;
continuing support; annual campaigns; capital
campaigns; building/renovation; program
development; employee matching gifts.
**Limitations:** Giving primarily in New York and
Nassau County, NY. No support for religious or
political organizations or member agencies of
the United Way. No grants to individuals, or for
emergency funds, deficit financing,
scholarships, or fellowships; no loans.
**Publications:** Annual report (including
application guidelines).
**Application information:** Cultural and arts
proposals reviewed in the spring; civic and
community proposals reviewed in the fall;
accepts NYRAG Common Application Form.
Application form not required.
   *Initial approach:* Letter or proposal
   *Copies of proposal:* 1
   *Deadline(s):* Apr. 1 and Sept. 1
   *Board meeting date(s):* May and Oct.
   *Final notification:* 2 to 6 months, depending
    on date proposal submitted
**Corporate Contributions Committee:** Carol A.
Strickland, Chair.
**Number of staff:** 1 part-time professional; 1
part-time support.
**EIN:** 136072081

## 529
### The Ungar Foundation
325 Sky Farm Rd.
Copake, NY 12516
*Contact:* Mrs. Aine Ungar, Tr.
*Application address:* P.O. Box 753, Copake, NY
12516

**Grantmaker type:** Independent foundation
**Financial data** (yr. ended 11/30/99): Assets,
$2,772,441 (M); expenditures, $418,400;
qualifying distributions, $383,324; giving
activities include $345,500 for 15 grants (high:
$60,000; low: $500).
**Purpose and activities:** Giving to education,
Native American organizations, human services
and Jewish agencies.
**Fields of interest:** Visual arts; museums;
performing arts; dance; theater; music; historic
preservation/historical societies; arts/cultural
programs; education, fund raising; early
childhood education; libraries/library science;
natural resource conservation & protection;
environment; animal welfare; wildlife
preservation & protection; hospitals (general);
health associations; marine science; engineering
& technology; science; Native Americans.

International interests: Israel.
**Types of support:** Continuing support; annual campaigns; building/renovation; program development; professorships; internship funds; scholarship funds; research.
**Limitations:** Giving primarily in New York, NY. No grants to individuals.
**Application information:**
*Initial approach:* Letter
*Deadline(s):* None
**Trustee:** Mrs. Aine Ungar.
**Number of staff:** 1 part-time support.
**EIN:** 136937282

**530**
**Lillian Vernon Foundation**
c/o Nathan Berkman & Co.
29 Broadway, Ste. 2900
New York, NY 10006-3296

Established in 1995 in CT.
**Donor(s):** Lillian Vernon.
**Grantmaker type:** Independent foundation
**Financial data** (yr. ended 06/30/99): Assets, $6,615,258 (M); expenditures, $937,999; qualifying distributions, $915,474; giving activities include $916,776 for grants (high: $470,250).
**Purpose and activities:** Giving primarily for the arts, including museums and the performing arts; also giving for education.
**Fields of interest:** Museums; performing arts; higher education; libraries/library science; human services.
**Limitations:** Applications not accepted. Giving primarily in NY. No grants to individuals.
**Application information:** Contributes only to pre-selected organizations.
**Trustee:** Lillian Vernon.
**EIN:** 223390451

**531**
**The G. Unger Vetlesen Foundation ▼**
c/o Fulton, Rowe, Hart & Coon
1 Rockefeller Plz., Ste. 301
New York, NY 10020-2002 (212) 586-0700
*Contact:* George Rowe, Jr., Pres.
*URL:* http://www.monellvetlesen.org

Incorporated in 1955 in NY.
**Donor(s):** George Unger Vetlesen.‡
**Grantmaker type:** Independent foundation
**Financial data** (yr. ended 12/31/98): Assets, $94,844,955 (M); expenditures, $3,254,314; qualifying distributions, $3,101,353; giving activities include $3,022,500 for 20 grants (high: $650,000; low: $5,000; average: $10,000–$100,000).
**Purpose and activities:** Established a biennial international science award for discoveries in the earth sciences; grants for biological, geophysical, and environmental research, including scholarships, and cultural organizations, including those emphasizing Norwegian-American relations and maritime interests. Support also for public policy research and libraries.
**Fields of interest:** Arts/cultural programs; libraries/library science; environment; marine science; physical/earth sciences; engineering & technology; biological sciences; science; public policy, research.

**Types of support:** General/operating support; continuing support; annual campaigns; capital campaigns; building/renovation; equipment; endowments; program development; professorships; scholarship funds; research.
**Limitations:** No grants to individuals.
**Publications:** Annual report, application guidelines.
**Application information:** Application form not required.
*Initial approach:* Letter
*Copies of proposal:* 1
*Deadline(s):* None
*Board meeting date(s):* June and Dec.
**Officers and Directors:*** George Rowe, Jr.,* Pres.; Laura Naus, Secy.; J.T.C. Hart, Treas.; Eugene P. Grisanti, Ambrose K. Monell, Henry G. Walter, Jr.
**Number of staff:** None.
**EIN:** 131982695

**532**
**Viburnum Foundation, Inc.**
c/o Molly Turner
160 Prospect Park, W., No. 4
Brooklyn, NY 11215
*Contact:* Molly L. Turner, Exec. Dir.
*E-mail:* Mollyt@mindspring.com

Established in 1989 in NY.
**Grantmaker type:** Independent foundation
**Financial data** (yr. ended 09/30/99): Assets, $6,680,152 (M); gifts received, $5,000; expenditures, $462,333; qualifying distributions, $405,566; giving activities include $382,900 for 51 grants (high: $97,900; low: $2,000).
**Purpose and activities:** Support for public libraries, and library advocacy and services, literary arts.
**Fields of interest:** Literature; adult education—literacy & basic skills; libraries/library science; reading.
**Types of support:** Continuing support; program development; conferences/seminars; publication; seed money.
**Limitations:** Applications not accepted. Giving on a national basis. No grants to individuals.
**Publications:** Occasional report.
**Application information:**
*Board meeting date(s):* Annually in late spring or summer
**Officer and Director:*** Molly L. Turner,* Exec. Dir.
**Number of staff:** 1 part-time professional.
**EIN:** 223019875

**533**
**Wallace-Readers Digest Funds ▼**
2 Park Ave., 23rd Fl.
New York, NY 10016 (212) 251-9700
*Contact:* Mary Lee Fitzgerald, Sr. Prog. Off., Education; Michael Moore, Sr. Prog. Off., Arts; Lydia Barrett Dir., Communities
*E-mail:* wrdf@wallacefunds.org; *URL:* http://www.wallacefunds.org

Lila Wallace-Reader's Digest Fund and DeWitt Wallace-Reader's Digest Fund Inc., incorporated in NY in 1956 and 1965 respectively.
**Donor(s):** DeWitt Wallace,‡ Lila Acheson Wallace.‡
**Grantmaker type:** Independent foundation

**Financial data** (yr. ended 12/31/99): Assets, $1,465,753,149; expenditures, $86,317,491; qualifying distributions, $72,860,231; giving activities include $71,985,231 for 335 grants (high: $1,759,972; low: $1,000; average: $15,000–$1,000,000) and $875,000 for 25 grants to individuals of $35,000 each.
**Purpose and activities:** The fund focuses on developing effective educational leaders to improve student learning; providing informal learning opportunities for children and families in communities; and increasing participation in the arts.
**Fields of interest:** Arts/cultural programs; education; community development.
**Types of support:** Program development.
**Limitations:** Giving on a national basis. No support for religious, fraternal, or veterans' organizations; government and public policy organizations, or private foundations. No grants for annual campaigns, endowments, capital purpose, or scholarly research.
**Application information:** Application form not required.
*Initial approach:* Letter of inquiry
*Copies of proposal:* 1
*Board meeting date(s):* 4 times per year
*Final notification:* 12 weeks
**Officers and Directors:*** George V. Grune,* Chair.; M. Christine DeVita,* Pres.; Laraine S. Rothenberg, Walter V. Shipley, C.J. Silas.
**Recent grants for library/information services:**
**533-1** Brooklyn Public Library Foundation, Brooklyn, NY, $400,000. For Public Libraries as Partners in Youth Development initiative. 1999.
**533-2** Education Resources Institute, Boston, MA, $901,000. For national expansion of community-based model for providing information to low-inome youth about how to prepare for and pursue a college education. 1999.
**533-3** Enoch Pratt Free Library, Baltimore, MD, $400,000. For Public Libraries as Partners in Youth Development initiative. 1999.
**533-4** Fort Bend County Library Systems, Richmond, TX, $400,000. For Public Libraries as Partners in Youth Devlopment Initiative. 1999.
**533-5** Foundation Center, NYC, NY, $25,000. For general support. 1999.
**533-6** Foundation Center, NYC, NY, $25,000. For general support. 1999.
**533-7** Free Library of Philadelphia, Philadelphia, PA, $400,000. For Public Libraries as Partners in Youth Development initiative. 1999.
**533-8** Greensboro Public Library, Friends of, Greensboro, NC, $275,000. To improve adult literacy instruction, including support services. 1999.
**533-9** Jacksonville Public Library Foundation, Jacksonville, FL, $225,000. To improve adult literacy instruction, including support services. 1999.
**533-10** King County Library System, Seattle, WA, $400,000. For Public Libraries as Partners in Youth Development initiative. 1999.
**533-11** Leon County Library, Friends of the, Tallahassee, FL, $225,000. To improve adult litearcy instruction, including support services. 1999.

**533-12** Lexington Public Library, Lexington, KY, $225,000. To improve adult literacy instruction, including support services. 1999.

**533-13** National Institute for Literacy, DC, $72,500. For consortium to improve services for adult learners and advance the field of adult learning and literacy. 1999.

**533-14** New Orleans Public Library, New Orleans, LA, $215,000. To improve adult literacy instruction, including support services. 1999.

**533-15** New York Public Library, NYC, NY, $270,000. To improve adult literacy instruction, including support services. 1999.

**533-16** Oakland Public Library, Oakland, CA, $400,000. For Public Libraries as Partners in Youth Development initiative. 1999.

**533-17** Oakland Public Library, Friends of the, Oakland, CA, $270,000. To improve adult literacy instruction, including support services. 1999.

**533-18** Plymouth Public Library, Plymouth, MA, $175,000. To improve adult literacy instruction, including support services. 1999.

**533-19** Public Library of Charlotte and Mecklenburg County, Charlotte, NC, $400,000. For Public Libraries as Partners in Youth Development initiative. 1999.

**533-20** Queens Library Foundation, Jamaica, NY, $315,000. To improve adult literacy instruction, including support services. 1999.

**533-21** Redwood City Public Library, Redwood City, CA, $270,000. To improve adult literacy instruction, including support services. 1999.

**533-22** Robinson Public Library District, Robinson, IL, $200,000. To improve adult literacy instruction, including support services. 1999.

**533-23** San Jose Public Library Foundation, San Jose, CA, $225,000. To improve adult literacy instruction, including support services. 1999.

**533-24** Santa Clara County Library, San Jose, CA, $225,000. To improve adult literacy instruction, including support services. 1999.

**533-25** Springfield City Library, Springfield, MA, $225,000. To improve adult literacy instruction, including support services. 1999.

**533-26** Tucson-Pima Public Library, Tucson, AZ, $400,000. For Public Libraries as Partners in Youth Development initiative. 1999.

**533-27** Urban Libraries Council, Evanston, IL, $749,000. To coordinate and serve as spokespersons for Public Libraries as Partners in Youth Development initiative. 1999.

**533-28** Washoe County Public Library System, Reno, NV, $371,000. For Public Libraries as Partners in Youth Development initiative. 1999.

**533-29** Waukegan Public Library, Waukegan, IL, $180,000. To improve adult literacy instruction, including support services. 1999.

### 534
**Miriam G. and Ira D. Wallach Foundation ▼**
3 Manhattanville Rd.
Purchase, NY 10577-2110

Incorporated in 1956 in NY.
**Grantmaker type:** Independent foundation
**Financial data** (yr. ended 10/31/99): Assets, $16,037,726 (M); gifts received, $66,938; expenditures, $1,580,955; qualifying

distributions, $1,415,441; giving activities include $1,360,947 for 95 grants (high: $500,000; low: $100; average: $1,000–$25,000).
**Purpose and activities:** Support primarily for higher education, and international relations, including peace; support also for social services, Jewish organizations, and cultural programs.
**Fields of interest:** Museums; performing arts; historical activities; higher education; libraries/library science; hospitals (general); AIDS; medical research; human services; peace; international affairs; community development; neighborhood development; Jewish federated giving programs; Jewish agencies & temples.
**Limitations:** Applications not accepted. Giving primarily in NY. No grants to individuals.
**Application information:** Contributes only to pre-selected organizations.
**Officers and Directors:\*** Ira D. Wallach,\* Chair.; Miriam G. Wallach,\* Vice-Chair.; Kenneth L. Wallach,\* Pres.; Edgar Wachenheim III,\* V.P.; Peter C. Siegfried, Secy.; Reginald Reinhardt, Treas.; Kate W. Cassidy, Martin W. Cassidy, Sue W. Wachenheim, Mary K. Wallach, Susan S. Wallach.
**EIN:** 136101702

### 535
**The Rosalind P. Walter Foundation**
509 Madison Ave., Ste. 1216
New York, NY 10022

Established in 1951 as the Walter Foundation.
**Donor(s):** Henry G. Walter, Jr.‡
**Grantmaker type:** Independent foundation
**Financial data** (yr. ended 12/31/99): Assets, $3,036,039 (M); expenditures, $588,154; qualifying distributions, $581,328; giving activities include $580,008 for 47 grants (high: $300,000; low: $35).
**Purpose and activities:** Giving for art and cultural programs, boys and girls clubs, and higher education.
**Fields of interest:** Arts/cultural programs; education; libraries (public); wildlife, sanctuaries; athletics/sports, racquet sports; boys & girls clubs; human services.
**Limitations:** Applications not accepted. Giving primarily in NY. No grants to individuals.
**Application information:** Contributes only to pre-selected organizations.
**Trustee:** Rosalind P. Walter.
**EIN:** 136177284

### 536
**Riley J. and Lillian N. Warren and Beatrice W. Blanding Foundation**
6 Ford Ave.
Oneonta, NY 13820 (607) 432-6720
*Contact:* Henry L. Hulbert, Mgr.

Trust established in 1972 in NY.
**Donor(s):** Beatrice W. Blanding.
**Grantmaker type:** Independent foundation
**Financial data** (yr. ended 12/31/99): Assets, $23,296,172 (M); gifts received, $147,428; expenditures, $1,088,890; qualifying distributions, $1,055,533; giving activities include $972,049 for 30 grants (high: $220,000; low: $1,500).

**Purpose and activities:** Giving primarily to a library foundation and a hospital foundation, as well as for education and youth services.
**Fields of interest:** Elementary/secondary education; higher education; libraries/library science; libraries (public); hospitals (general); boys clubs; children & youth, services; religion.
**Limitations:** Giving primarily in the Oneonta, NY, area.
**Application information:**
*Initial approach:* Letter
*Deadline(s):* Nov. 1
**Officer and Trustees:\*** Henry L. Hulbert,\* Mgr.; Robert A. Harlem, Maureen P. Hulbert.
**EIN:** 237203341

### 537
**The David Wasserman Foundation, Inc.**
Adirondack Ctr., 4722 State Hwy. 30
Amsterdam, NY 12010 (518) 843-2800
*Contact:* Norbert J. Sherbunt, Pres.

Incorporated in 1953 in NY.
**Donor(s):** David Wasserman.‡
**Grantmaker type:** Independent foundation
**Financial data** (yr. ended 02/28/99): Assets, $1,795,014 (M); expenditures, $134,882; qualifying distributions, $94,127; giving activities include $70,100 for 9 grants (high: $31,000; low: $100).
**Purpose and activities:** Grants for scientific, educational, and charitable purposes, including a scholarship fund.
**Fields of interest:** Education, fund raising; libraries/library science; education; hospitals (general); recreation; hospices; community development; general charitable giving.
**Types of support:** Capital campaigns; building/renovation; equipment; emergency funds; program development.
**Limitations:** Giving limited to Montgomery County, NY. No grants for operating budgets.
**Application information:** Application form not required.
*Copies of proposal:* 1
*Deadline(s):* None
*Board meeting date(s):* Varies
**Officers and Directors:\*** Norbert J. Sherbunt,\* Pres. and Treas.; Judith M. Sherbunt,\* V.P. and Secy.
**Number of staff:** 1 part-time professional.
**EIN:** 237183522

### 538
**Isak and Rose Weinman Foundation, Inc.**
c/o BDO Seidman, LLP
330 Madison Ave.
New York, NY 10017-5001

Established in 1956.
**Donor(s):** Lilliana Teruzzi.‡
**Grantmaker type:** Independent foundation
**Financial data** (yr. ended 12/31/99): Assets, $18,689,796 (M); expenditures, $1,019,102; qualifying distributions, $897,924; giving activities include $870,000 for 48 grants (high: $100,000; low: $2,500).
**Purpose and activities:** Giving primarily for the arts.
**Fields of interest:** Performing arts, education; circus arts; arts education; museums; choreography; university; libraries (public);

natural resource conservation & protection; hospitals (general); medical care, outpatient care; family planning; health care, blood supply; nursing home/convalescent facility; geriatrics research; children, services; federated giving programs; Jewish agencies & temples.
**Limitations:** Applications not accepted. Giving primarily in NY, with emphasis on New York City. No grants to individuals.
**Application information:** Contributes only to pre-selected organizations.
**Officers and Directors:*** W. Loeber Landau,* Chair. and Secy.; Alexander E. Slater,* Pres. and Treas.; Donna Landau Hardsman, Barbara Landau, Frederick P. Terry, Blair Landau Trippe.
**EIN:** 136110132

### 539
### The Margaret L. Wendt Foundation ▼
40 Fountain Plz., Ste. 277
Buffalo, NY 14202-2220 (716) 855-2146
*Contact:* Robert J. Kresse, Secy.-Treas.

Trust established in 1956 in NY.
**Donor(s):** Margaret L. Wendt.‡
**Grantmaker type:** Independent foundation
**Financial data** (yr. ended 01/31/99): Assets, $118,487,222 (M); expenditures, $5,319,907; qualifying distributions, $3,793,629; giving activities include $3,457,705 for 123 grants (high: $400,000; low: $197; average: $5,000–$50,000) and $116,069 for 3 program-related investments.
**Purpose and activities:** Emphasis on education, the arts, and social services; support also for churches and religious organizations, health associations, public interest organizations, and youth agencies.
**Fields of interest:** Visual arts; museums; performing arts; theater; history & archaeology; historic preservation/historical societies; arts/cultural programs; education, fund raising; early childhood education; higher education; libraries/library science; education; natural resource conservation & protection; hospitals (general); substance abuse, services; mental health/crisis services; health associations; cancer; AIDS; alcoholism; biomedicine; medical research; cancer research; AIDS research; legal services; crime/law enforcement; human services; children & youth, services; hospices; aging, centers & services; minorities/immigrants, centers & services; human rights (international); community development; federated giving programs; political science; government/public administration; public affairs; religion; minorities; disabled; aging; economically disadvantaged.
**Types of support:** Program-related investments/loans.
**Limitations:** Giving primarily in Buffalo and western NY. No grants to individuals, or for scholarships.
**Publications:** Application guidelines.
**Application information:** Application form not required.
*Initial approach:* Letter or application form
*Copies of proposal:* 4
*Deadline(s):* 1 month prior to board meeting
*Board meeting date(s):* Quarterly; no fixed dates
*Final notification:* Usually 4 to 6 months

**Officer and Trustees:*** Robert J. Kresse,* Secy.-Treas.; Janet L. Day, Thomas D. Lunt.
**Number of staff:** 1 part-time support.
**EIN:** 166030037

### 540
### The Western New York Foundation
Main Seneca Bldg., Ste. 1402
237 Main St.
Buffalo, NY 14203 (716) 847-6440
*Contact:* Welles V. Moot, Jr., Pres.

Incorporated in 1951 in NY as the Wildroot Foundation; present name adopted in 1958.
**Donor(s):** Welles V. Moot.‡
**Grantmaker type:** Independent foundation
**Financial data** (yr. ended 07/31/99): Assets, $13,674,597 (M); expenditures, $513,081; qualifying distributions, $438,669; giving activities include $359,979 for 32 grants (high: $50,000; low: $50; average: $50–$70,000).
**Purpose and activities:** Grants to nonprofit institutions, with emphasis on capital needs, seed funds for new projects, or expanding services. Support primarily for the fine and performing arts, youth agencies, the natural sciences, and social service agencies; some support also for health services and libraries and other educational institutions.
**Fields of interest:** Visual arts; museums; performing arts; dance; theater; music; arts/cultural programs; child development, education; secondary school/education; libraries (public); medical care, rehabilitation; substance abuse, services; mental health/crisis services; alcoholism; legal services; crime/law enforcement; housing/shelter, development; human services; children & youth, services; family services; hospices; aging, centers & services; women, centers & services; civil liberties, advocacy; community development; minorities; disabled; aging.
**Types of support:** Capital campaigns; building/renovation; equipment; land acquisition; emergency funds; program development; conferences/seminars; publication; seed money; technical assistance; program-related investments/loans; matching/challenge support.
**Limitations:** Giving limited to the 8th Judicial District of NY (Erie, Niagara, Genesee, Wyoming, Allegany, Cattaraugus, and Chautauqua counties). No support for hospitals or religious organizations. No grants to individuals, or for scholarships, fellowships, or generally for operating budgets or deficit financing.
**Publications:** Annual report (including application guidelines), informational brochure.
**Application information:** Application form required.
*Initial approach:* Letter or telephone to request application
*Copies of proposal:* 3
*Deadline(s):* None
*Board meeting date(s):* 3 or 4 times a year
*Final notification:* 8 to 12 weeks

**Officers and Trustees:*** Welles V. Moot, Jr.,* Pres.; Cecily M. Johnson,* V.P.; John R. Moot,* Secy.; Richard E. Moot,* Treas.; Brenda McDuffie, Trudy A. Mollenberg, Andrew R. Moot, John N. Walsh III.

**Number of staff:** 1 full-time professional; 1 part-time support.
**EIN:** 160845962

### 541
### White Flowers Foundation
c/o Goldman Sachs & Co., Tax Dept.
85 Broad St.
New York, NY 10004
*Contact:* Mary H. White, Tr.
*Mailing address:* 4 E. 70th St., No. 9A, New York, NY 10021

Established in 1989 in NY.
**Donor(s):** J. Christopher Flowers.
**Grantmaker type:** Independent foundation
**Financial data** (yr. ended 05/31/98): Assets, $1,100,973 (M); gifts received, $973,558; expenditures, $740,809; qualifying distributions, $731,686; giving activities include $736,604 for grants.
**Purpose and activities:** Giving primarily for higher education and churches.
**Fields of interest:** Museums (art); higher education; libraries (public); education; federated giving programs; Christian agencies & churches.
**Types of support:** General/operating support; continuing support; annual campaigns; capital campaigns; endowments; emergency funds; research.
**Limitations:** Applications not accepted. Giving primarily in New York, NY. No grants to individuals.
**Application information:** Contributes only to pre-selected organizations.
**Trustees:** J. Christopher Flowers, Mary H. White.
**EIN:** 133532030

### 542
### The Whittemore Foundation
c/o Frederick B. Whittemore, Morgan Stanley and Co.
1221 Ave. of the Americas, 30th Fl.
New York, NY 10020

Established in 1988 in NY.
**Donor(s):** Frederick B. Whittemore.
**Grantmaker type:** Independent foundation
**Financial data** (yr. ended 12/31/98): Assets, $4,718,043 (M); gifts received, $1,147; expenditures, $1,683,143; qualifying distributions, $1,621,016; giving activities include $1,621,016 for 62 grants (high: $1,000,000; low: $100; average: $1,000–$10,000).
**Purpose and activities:** Giving for libraries, youth centers and Protestant churches.
**Fields of interest:** Higher education; libraries/library science; recreation, community facilities; youth development, centers & clubs; Protestant agencies & churches.
**Limitations:** Applications not accepted. Giving primarily in NH. No grants to individuals.
**Application information:** Contributes only to pre-selected organizations.
**Officers and Trustees:*** Frederick B. Whittemore,* Pres. and Treas.; Edward B. Whittemore,* V.P.; Lawrence F. Whittemore,* V.P.
**EIN:** 133527578

## 543
## Wild Wings Foundation
c/o AMCO
667 Madison Ave., 20th Fl.
New York, NY 10021 (212) 973-8219

Established in 1981.
**Donor(s):** Rockefeller Charitable Trust, Anna M. Rockefeller Charitable Trust.
**Grantmaker type:** Independent foundation
**Financial data** (yr. ended 12/31/99): Assets, $9,393,601 (M); gifts received, $375,000; expenditures, $547,599; qualifying distributions, $431,726; giving activities include $275,000 for 2 grants (high: $150,000; low: $125,000).
**Purpose and activities:** Giving primarily for education and the environment and conservation.
**Fields of interest:** Museums (art); ballet; higher education; libraries/library science; education; natural resource conservation & protection; environment; human services.
**Limitations:** Applications not accepted. Giving primarily in NY. No grants to individuals or for scholarly research.
**Publications:** Annual report, financial statement.
**Application information:** Unsolicited requests for funds not accepted.
**Trustees:** Christopher Elliman, David D. Elliman, David M. McAlpin.
**Number of staff:** 1 part-time support.
**EIN:** 133096074

## 544
## John Wiley & Sons, Inc. Corporate Giving Program
605 3rd Ave.
New York, NY 10158 (212) 850-6000
*Contact:* Deborah E. Wiley, Sr. V.P., Corp. Comm.

**Grantmaker type:** Corporate giving program
**Financial data** (yr. ended 04/30/99): Total giving, $685,133; giving activities include $216,522 for 66 grants (high: $25,000; low: $100; average: $100–$25,000), $260,965 for 500 employee matching gifts and $207,646 for in-kind gifts.
**Purpose and activities:** John Wiley makes charitable contributions to nonprofit organizations involved with arts and culture, adult education, business, science, public affairs, and to libraries. Support is given primarily in areas of company operations.
**Fields of interest:** Museums; performing arts; theater; music; arts/cultural programs; adult education—literacy & basic skills; libraries/library science; business & industry; chemistry; physics; engineering & technology; biological sciences; science; public affairs.
**Types of support:** General/operating support; annual campaigns; capital campaigns; endowments; emergency funds; conferences/seminars; publication; curriculum development; fellowships; scholarship funds; employee volunteer services; use of facilities; employee matching gifts; donated products; in-kind gifts; matching/challenge support.
**Limitations:** Giving primarily in areas of company operations, particularly in the greater New York, NY, metropolitan area.
**Publications:** Program policy statement.
**Application information:** The Corporate Communications Department handles giving. Application form not required.

*Initial approach:* Proposal to headquarters
*Copies of proposal:* 1
*Deadline(s):* None
*Final notification:* Following review

## 545
## The H. W. Wilson Foundation, Inc.
950 University Ave.
Bronx, NY 10452
*Contact:* William V. Joyce, Pres.
*Tel.:* (718) 588-8400, ext. 2205

Incorporated in 1952 in NY.
**Donor(s):** H.W. Wilson,‡ Mrs. H.W. Wilson,‡ The H.W. Wilson Co., Inc.
**Grantmaker type:** Independent foundation
**Financial data** (yr. ended 11/30/99): Assets, $16,566,705 (M); expenditures, $751,495; qualifying distributions, $555,900; giving activities include $555,900 for 53 grants (high: $50,000; low: $1,000).
**Purpose and activities:** Grants largely to accredited library schools for scholarships; support also for cultural programs, including historical societies, and library associations.
**Fields of interest:** Higher education; libraries/library science.
**Types of support:** Scholarship funds; research.
**Limitations:** No grants for building or endowment funds or operating budgets.
**Application information:** Application form not required.

*Initial approach:* Proposal
*Copies of proposal:* 1
*Deadline(s):* None
*Board meeting date(s):* Jan., Mar., May, Aug., and Oct.
*Final notification:* 3 months
**Officers and Directors:*** William V. Joyce,* Pres. and Treas.; James M. Matarazzo,* V.P.; William E. Stanton,* Secy.
**EIN:** 237418062

## 546
## Ann Eden Woodward Foundation
c/o J. Lapatin, Esq.
989 Ave. of the Americas
New York, NY 10016

Established in 1963 in NY.
**Donor(s):** Ann Eden Woodward.‡
**Grantmaker type:** Independent foundation
**Financial data** (yr. ended 05/31/98): Assets, $609,330 (M); gifts received, $375,000; expenditures, $348,948; qualifying distributions, $344,424; giving activities include $340,000 for grants.
**Purpose and activities:** Giving for the arts, including museums, and for hospitals, environmental and wildlife preservation, and public libraries.
**Fields of interest:** Museums; arts/cultural programs; libraries/library science; natural resource conservation & protection; wildlife preservation & protection; hospitals (general).
**Limitations:** Applications not accepted. Giving primarily in New York, NY. No grants to individuals.
**Application information:** Grants awarded at discretion of managers.
**Officers:** J.A. Lapatin, Mgr.; J.A. Wood, Mgr.
**EIN:** 136126021

## 547
## The Worby Charitable Foundation
11 Martine Ave., Ste. PH
White Plains, NY 10606
*Contact:* David E. Worby, Tr.

Established in 1993 in NY.
**Donor(s):** Davi E. Worby.
**Grantmaker type:** Independent foundation
**Financial data** (yr. ended 12/31/98): Assets, $237,539 (M); gifts received, $94,000; expenditures, $79,719; qualifying distributions, $79,719; giving activities include $66,886 for grants (high: $25,000).
**Purpose and activities:** Giving for education, the arts, libraries, and Jewish organizations.
**Fields of interest:** Arts/cultural programs; higher education; libraries/library science; Jewish federated giving programs; Jewish agencies & temples.
**Application information:** Application form not required.

*Initial approach:* Letter
*Deadline(s):* None
**Trustee:** David E. Worby.
**EIN:** 137031450

## 548
## Yaron Foundation, Inc.
201 E. 37th St., Lobby Ste.
New York, NY 10016-3142
*Contact:* Norman Horowitz, Exec. Dir.

Established in 1984.
**Donor(s):** Isaac Steven Herschkopf, Debrah Lee Charatan, Robert Durst, Martin L. Markowitz, Leon Miller, Charles Ramat, Jay Susman.
**Grantmaker type:** Independent foundation
**Financial data** (yr. ended 12/31/98): Assets, $650,936 (M); gifts received, $108,097; expenditures, $138,314; qualifying distributions, $133,581; giving activities include $133,763 for 58 grants (high: $15,500; low: $10).
**Purpose and activities:** Giving to Jewish agencies, cultural institutes, public services and youth services.
**Fields of interest:** Film/video; museums; theater; music; arts/cultural programs; education, research; education, fund raising; higher education; medical school/education; adult/continuing education; adult education—literacy & basic skills; libraries/library science; reading; education; natural resource conservation & protection; environment; wildlife preservation & protection; hospitals (general); health care; health associations; biomedicine; medical research; human services; youth, services; hospices; aging, centers & services; women, centers & services; minorities/immigrants, centers & services; peace; human rights (international); Jewish federated giving programs; psychology, behavioral science; Jewish agencies & temples; minorities; disabled; aging; women.
**International interests:** Israel.
**Types of support:** Annual campaigns; building/renovation; equipment; emergency funds; curriculum development; research.
**Limitations:** Giving primarily in New York, NY.
**Application information:** Academic qualifications required for individual applicants; proposal required for research grants. Application form not required.

*Copies of proposal:* 1
*Deadline(s):* None
*Board meeting date(s):* Monthly
*Final notification:* 2 months
**Officers:** Isaac Steven Herschkopf, Pres.; and six additional officers.
**Number of staff:** 1 full-time professional; 1 part-time support.
**EIN:** 133209791

### 549
### The Christine and Jaime Yordan Foundation
c/o Goldman Sachs & Co., Tax Dept.
85 Broad St.
New York, NY 10004

Established in 1993 in CT.
**Donor(s):** Jaime E. Yordan.
**Grantmaker type:** Independent foundation
**Financial data** (yr. ended 07/31/99): Assets, $361,097 (M); gifts received, $184,048; expenditures, $148,807; qualifying distributions, $144,750; giving activities include $144,750 for 19 grants (high: $25,000; low: $250).
**Purpose and activities:** Giving primarily for education and religion.
**Fields of interest:** Libraries/library science; education; children & youth, services; Christian agencies & churches.
**Limitations:** Applications not accepted. Giving primarily in CT. No grants to individuals.
**Application information:** Contributes only to pre-selected organizations.
**Trustees:** Kevin W. Kennedy, Michael R. Lynch, Jaime E. Yordan.
**EIN:** 133755228

# NORTH CAROLINA

### 550
### E. H. Barnard Charitable Trust
c/o Central Carolina Bank & Trust Co.
P.O. Box 931
Durham, NC 27702

Established in 1988 in NC.
**Donor(s):** E.H. Barnard.‡
**Grantmaker type:** Independent foundation
**Financial data** (yr. ended 05/31/98): Assets, $5,431,877 (M); expenditures, $229,270; qualifying distributions, $195,699; giving activities include $200,000 for 3 grants (high: $100,000; low: $8,000).
**Purpose and activities:** Giving primarily for education, sports programs, and federated giving programs.
**Fields of interest:** Libraries (public); athletics/sports, amateur leagues; federated giving programs.
**Limitations:** Applications not accepted. Giving primarily in Yadkin County, NC. No grants to individuals.
**Application information:** Contributes only to pre-selected organizations.
**Trustee:** Central Carolina Bank & Trust Co.
**EIN:** 566299574

### 551
### Irwin Belk Educational Foundation
6100 Fairview Rd., Ste. 640
Charlotte, NC 28210-3277 (704) 553-8296
*Contact:* Carl G. Belk

Established in 1992.
**Donor(s):** Carl G. Belk, Irwin Belk.
**Grantmaker type:** Independent foundation
**Financial data** (yr. ended 12/31/98): Assets, $720,018 (M); expenditures, $342,693; qualifying distributions, $339,783; giving activities include $340,000 for 6 grants (high: $100,000; low: $10,000).
**Purpose and activities:** Giving primarily for arts and culture, libraries, and to religious organizations.
**Fields of interest:** Museums (science & technology); arts/cultural programs; libraries (public); Protestant agencies & churches.
**Types of support:** General/operating support.
**Limitations:** Giving primarily in NC. No grants to individuals.
**Application information:**
*Initial approach:* Letter
*Deadline(s):* None
**Trustee:** William I. Belk.
**EIN:** 561783301

### 552
### Chapin Foundation of Myrtle Beach, South Carolina
c/o Bank of America
1 NationsBank Plz., T09-1
Charlotte, NC 28255
*Contact:* Harold D. Clardy, Chair.
*Application address:* P.O. Box 2568, Myrtle Beach, SC 29577

Trust established in 1943 in SC.
**Donor(s):** S.B. Chapin.
**Grantmaker type:** Independent foundation
**Financial data** (yr. ended 07/31/99): Assets, $18,634,514 (L); expenditures, $896,210; qualifying distributions, $857,054; giving activities include $864,122 for 35 grants (high: $200,600; low: $5,000; average: $1,500–$70,000).
**Purpose and activities:** Support for all religious organizations in Myrtle Beach, SC, that qualify; support also for public libraries and YM-YWCAs within the city limits.
**Fields of interest:** Libraries/library science; YM/YWCAs & YM/YWHAs; Christian agencies & churches.
**Limitations:** Giving limited to the Myrtle Beach, SC, area. No grants to individuals.
**Application information:** Application form required.
*Initial approach:* Letter or proposal
*Copies of proposal:* 1
*Deadline(s):* None
*Board meeting date(s):* Twice a year
**Officers and Directors:*** Harold D. Clardy,* Chair.; Claude M. Epps,* Vice-Chair.; Claire Chapin Epps, Secy.; Lawton Benton, Ruth T. Gore, Harold Hartshorne, Jr.
**Trustee:** Bank of America.
**EIN:** 566039453

### 553
### The Coffey Foundation, Inc.
P.O. Box 1170
Lenoir, NC 28645
*Contact:* Mrs. Hope Huffstetler
*Application address:* 406 Norwood St., S.W., Lenoir, NC 28645

Established about 1979 in NC.
**Donor(s):** Harold F. Coffey Trust.
**Grantmaker type:** Independent foundation
**Financial data** (yr. ended 11/30/99): Assets, $11,584,586 (M); expenditures, $483,314; qualifying distributions, $375,216; giving activities include $165,800 for 38 grants (high: $30,000; low: $50) and $196,346 for 79 grants to individuals of $2,500 each.
**Purpose and activities:** Giving for higher education, youth, and social services; support also for student loans and individual scholarships.
**Fields of interest:** Arts councils; higher education; university; libraries (public); housing/shelter, development; human services; youth, services; hospices; aging, centers & services; federated giving programs.
**Types of support:** General/operating support; scholarships—to individuals; student loans—to individuals.
**Limitations:** Giving primarily in Caldwell County, NC; scholarships limited to residents of Caldwell County.
**Application information:** Application forms for student grants available at high schools in Caldwell County. Application form required.
*Deadline(s):* Apr. 15
**Trustees:** Gary W. Bradford, Charles E. Dobbin, Leslie D. Hines, Jr., Betty Lou Miller, Wayne J. Miller, Jr.
**EIN:** 566047501

### 554
### Cumberland Community Foundation, Inc.
P.O. Box 2171
Fayetteville, NC 28302-2171 (910) 483-4449
*Contact:* Monika Simmons, Prog. and Comm. Mgr.
*FAX:* (910) 483-2905; *E-mail:* ccfnd@infi.net, or ccf3@infi.net

Established in 1980 in NC.
**Donor(s):** Lucile Hutaff.‡
**Grantmaker type:** Community foundation
**Financial data** (yr. ended 06/30/99): Assets, $14,400,000 (M); gifts received, $3,600,000; expenditures, $1,277,000; giving activities include $1,070,000 for 221 grants (high: $50,000; low: $500; average: $500–$50,000).
**Purpose and activities:** Support primarily for innovative and collaborative projects.
**Fields of interest:** Museums; performing arts; dance; humanities; history & archaeology; language & linguistics; literature; arts/cultural programs; early childhood education; child development, education; secondary school/education; vocational education; higher education; adult/continuing education; libraries/library science; education; natural resource conservation & protection; environment; wildlife preservation & protection; family planning; medical care, rehabilitation; health care; substance abuse, services; mental health/crisis services; AIDS; delinquency

prevention/services; crime/law enforcement; employment; nutrition; housing/shelter, development; recreation; youth development, services; human services; children & youth, services; child development, services; family services; hospices; women, centers & services; minorities/immigrants, centers & services; homeless, human services; international affairs, goodwill promotion; human rights (international); race/intergroup relations; civil rights; urban/community development; rural development; community development; voluntarism promotion; population studies; military/veterans' organizations; leadership development; minorities; Native Americans; disabled; women; economically disadvantaged; homeless.

**Types of support:** General/operating support; endowments; program development; conferences/seminars; publication; seed money; scholarship funds; technical assistance; scholarships—to individuals; in-kind gifts; matching/challenge support.

**Limitations:** Giving limited to southeastern NC.

**Publications:** Annual report, informational brochure, application guidelines, occasional report, financial statement, grants list, newsletter, program policy statement.

**Application information:** Competitive grants are awarded in the county of the donor. Application form required.

> *Initial approach:* Letter
> *Copies of proposal:* 1
> *Deadline(s):* Spring and fall; telephone for dates
> *Board meeting date(s):* 2nd Thur. of every other month
> *Final notification:* 1st weeks in Apr. and Dec.

**Officers and Directors:*** John T. Henley, Jr.,* Pres.; Ramon L. Yarborough,* V.P.; J. Gary Ciccone,* Secy.; Robert W. Drake,* Treas.; Mildred Braxton, Mary Lynn M. Bryan, Alfred E. Cleveland, Margaret H. Dickson, Ellie Fleishman, Leslie A. Griffin, Joseph H. Hollinshed, Henry G. Hutaff, J. Wes Jones, Robert O. McCoy, Jr., Walter C. Moorman, Ruby S. Murchison, Donald Porter, Robert G. Ray, Sammy Short, Iris M. Thornton, Dot Wyatt.

**Number of staff:** 2 full-time professional; 1 part-time professional; 1 full-time support.
**EIN:** 581406831

## 555
## Harry L. Dalton Foundation, Inc.
736 Wachovia Ctr.
Charlotte, NC   28285   (704) 332-5380
*Contact:* R. Alfred Brand III, V.P.
*FAX:* (704) 378-5320

Established about 1979 in NC.
**Grantmaker type:** Independent foundation
**Financial data** (yr. ended 07/31/99): Assets, $5,201,544 (M); expenditures, $180,976; qualifying distributions, $170,000; giving activities include $170,000 for 34 grants (high: $56,500; low: $500).

**Purpose and activities:** Giving primarily for education, including higher education and libraries; support also for cultural programs, youth, family planning, drug abuse programs, mental health, and historic preservation.

**Fields of interest:** Visual arts; museums; performing arts; historic preservation/historical

societies; arts/cultural programs; education, fund raising; higher education; libraries/library science; education; family planning; substance abuse, services; mental health/crisis services; alcoholism; children & youth, services; community development; federated giving programs; government/public administration.

**Types of support:** Capital campaigns; building/renovation; endowments.

**Limitations:** Giving primarily in Mecklenburg County, NC.

**Publications:** Annual report.

**Application information:** Application form not required.

> *Initial approach:* Letter
> *Deadline(s):* None
> *Board meeting date(s):* Quarterly

**Officers and Directors:*** Elizabeth D. Brand,* Pres.; R. Alfred Brand III, V.P. and Treas.; Deeda M. Coffey,* Secy.

**Number of staff:** 1 part-time support.
**EIN:** 566061267

## 556
## The Duke Endowment ▼
100 N. Tryon St., Ste. 3500
Charlotte, NC   28202-4012   (704) 376-0291
*Contact:* Elizabeth H. Locke, Ph.D., Pres.
*FAX:* (704) 376-9336 (Charlotte); Rural Church Div. address: 3329 Chapel Hill Blvd., P.O. Box 51307, Durham, NC 27717-1307, tel.: (919) 489-3359; E-mail: droberson@tde.org; URL: http://www.dukeendowment.org

Trust established in 1924 in NJ.
**Donor(s):** James Buchanan Duke.‡
**Grantmaker type:** Independent foundation
**Financial data** (yr. ended 12/31/99): Assets, $2,335,495,956 (M); expenditures, $91,442,272; qualifying distributions, $82,000,000; giving activities include $80,230,455 for 1,045 grants (high: $9,191,500; low: $500; average: $500–$9,191,500).

**Purpose and activities:** Grants to nonprofit health care and child care institutions in NC and SC; rural United Methodist churches and its pastors in NC; and Duke, Furman, and Johnson C. Smith Universities, and Davidson College.

**Fields of interest:** Higher education; hospitals (general); health care; children & youth, services; Protestant agencies & churches.

**Types of support:** General/operating support; continuing support; capital campaigns; building/renovation; equipment; endowments; emergency funds; program development; conferences/seminars; professorships; publication; seed money; curriculum development; fellowships; internship funds; scholarship funds; research; technical assistance; consulting services; matching/challenge support.

**Limitations:** Giving limited to NC and SC. No grants to individuals (except for internship program), or for deficit financing; no loans.

**Publications:** Annual report (including application guidelines), informational brochure (including application guidelines), grants list, occasional report, informational brochure.

**Application information:** Application form not required.

> *Initial approach:* Letter
> *Copies of proposal:* 1

> *Deadline(s):* None
> *Board meeting date(s):* 10 months of the year
> *Final notification:* 2 to 6 months

**Officers and Trustees:*** Mary D.B.T. Semans,* Chair.; Hugh M. Chapman,* Vice-Chair.; Louis C. Stephens, Jr.,* Vice-Chair.; Elizabeth H. Locke, Ph.D., Pres. and Dir., Education Div.; Eugene W. Cochrane, Jr., V.P. and Dir., Health Care Div.; Terri W. Honeycutt, Secy.; Janice C. Walker, C.F.O. and Treas.; Stephanie S. Lynch, C.I.O.; William G. Anlyan, M.D., Erskine B. Bowles, John Hope Franklin, Ph.D., Constance F. Gray, Richard H. Jenrette, Mary D.T. Jones, Thomas S. Kenan III, Juanita M. Kreps, Ph.D., John G. Medlin, Jr., Russell M. Robinson II, Minor M. Shaw, L. Neil Williams, Jr.

**Number of staff:** 17 full-time professional; 16 full-time support.
**EIN:** 560529965
**Recent grants for library/information services:**
**556-1** Cannon Memorial Hospital, Pickens, SC, $190,632. To develop Partners Healthwise Initiative, community health information program. 1999.
**556-2** Davidson College, Davidson, NC, $220,703. For library acquisitions, publications and operating support. 1999.
**556-3** Duke University, Durham, NC, $9,191,500. For library. 1999.
**556-4** Duke University Medical Center, Durham, NC, $1,000,000. For information technology equipment. 1999.
**556-5** Foundation Center, NYC, NY, $20,000. For annual support. 1999.
**556-6** Furman University, Greenville, SC, $585,000. For library. 1999.
**556-7** Haywood Regional Medical Center, Clyde, NC, $145,400. To develop community-based health information system. 1999.
**556-8** Johnson C. Smith University, Charlotte, NC, $225,000. To renovate James B. Duke Library. 1999.
**556-9** Johnson C. Smith University, Charlotte, NC, $194,550. For library administration. 1999.
**556-10** WESTCARE Health System, Sylva, NC, $134,902. To establish community-based computer information and referral system. 1999.

## 557
## Thomas Austin Finch Foundation
c/o Wachovia Bank of North Carolina
P.O. Box 3099
Winston-Salem, NC   27150-7131
*Contact:* Linda G. Tilley, V.P.

Trust established in 1944 in NC.
**Donor(s):** Ernestine L. Finch Mobley,‡ Thomas Austin Finch, Jr.‡
**Grantmaker type:** Independent foundation
**Financial data** (yr. ended 12/31/99): Assets, $14,117,130 (M); expenditures, $546,067; qualifying distributions, $474,674; giving activities include $468,093 for 21 grants (high: $240,000; low: $100).

**Fields of interest:** Elementary/secondary education; secondary school/education; libraries/library science; hospitals (general); federated giving programs; government/public administration; Protestant agencies & churches; religion.

**Types of support:** General/operating support; continuing support; annual campaigns; building/renovation; equipment; program development; scholarship funds.
**Limitations:** Giving limited to Thomasville, NC. No grants to individuals, or for emergency funds, deficit financing, endowment funds, or fellowships; no loans.
**Publications:** Informational brochure (including application guidelines).
**Application information:** Application form required.
  *Initial approach:* Letter
  *Copies of proposal:* 1
  *Deadline(s):* None
  *Board meeting date(s):* Mar. and Nov.
  *Final notification:* 2 weeks
**Foundation Committee:** David Finch, Chair.; Kermit Cloninger, John L. Finch, Sumner Finch, Meredith Slane Person.
**Trustee:** Wachovia Bank of North Carolina.
**Number of staff:** None.
**EIN:** 566037907

## 558
### The First Union Foundation ▼
c/o First Union Corp.
301 S. College St.
Charlotte, NC   28288-0143   (704) 374-4689
*Contact:* Judy Allison, Dir.
*FAX:* (704) 374-2484; Local bank addresses: (CT, NJ, NY): Fran Durst, 370 Scotch Rd., Trenton, NJ 08628, Tel.: (609) 530-7357; FL: Debbie Clark, P.O. Box 4425, Jacksonville, FL 32231, Tel.: (904) 361-3147; GA: Gwen Adams, 999 Peachtree St., N.E., Atlanta, GA 30309, Tel.: (404) 827-7566; PA & DE: Bronal Harris, P.O. Box 7618, Philadelphia, PA 19101, Tel.: (215) 973-4181; TN: Chris McComish, 150 N. 4th Ave., 23rd Fl., Nashville, TN 37219, Tel.: (615) 251-0746; DC, MD, & VA: Carol Jarratt, 7 N. 8th St., Richmond, VA 23219, Tel.: (804) 771-7847, and First Union Securities, Inc.: Robin Schilling, 10750 Wheat 1st Dr., Glen Allen, VA 23060, Tel.: (804) 965-2415

Established in 1987 in NC.
**Donor(s):** First Union Corp.
**Grantmaker type:** Company-sponsored foundation
**Financial data** (yr. ended 12/31/98): Assets, $29,028,405 (M); gifts received, $33,878,583; expenditures, $19,486,282; qualifying distributions, $19,482,113; giving activities include $19,154,856 for 2,464 grants (high: $500,000; low: $50; average: $250–$20,000) and $294,708 for employee matching gifts.
**Purpose and activities:** Support for higher education and special programs for public elementary and secondary schools; arts funds or councils; community improvement; and family and social services, minorities, and the handicapped. Special consideration for children and youth and the disadvantaged to help them become productive and self-sufficient. Types of support include capital grants, made only when there is a community-wide fundraising campaign that includes the entire business community. Grants are made for one year only unless a multi-year pledge is made.
**Fields of interest:** Arts councils; visual arts; museums; performing arts; dance; music; education; fund raising; elementary/secondary

education; early childhood education; child development, education; elementary school/education; secondary school/education; higher education; business school/education; adult/continuing education; adult education—literacy & basic skills; libraries/library science; reading; education; natural resource conservation & protection; environment; hospitals (general); medical care, rehabilitation; health care; substance abuse, services; mental health/crisis services; health associations; heart & circulatory diseases; alcoholism; heart & circulatory research; youth development, citizenship; human services; children & youth, services; child development, services; family services; hospices; aging, centers & services; minorities/immigrants, centers & services; homeless, human services; urban/community development; community development; voluntarism promotion; federated giving programs; government/public administration; public affairs, citizen participation; minorities; disabled; aging; economically disadvantaged; homeless.
**Types of support:** General/operating support; annual campaigns; capital campaigns; building/renovation; endowments; program development; seed money; scholarship funds; employee matching gifts.
**Limitations:** Giving limited to CT, Washington, DC, DE, FL, GA, MD, NC, NJ, NY, PA, SC, TN, and VA. No support for political, religious, veterans', or fraternal organizations, retirement homes, precollege level private schools except through employee matching gifts, or organizations supported through the United Way, except for approved capital campaigns, international organizations, or intermediary organizations or agents. No grants to individuals, or for travel or conferences, or capital projects.
**Publications:** Annual report, informational brochure (including application guidelines).
**Application information:** Application form not required.
  *Initial approach:* Proposal to the nearest First Union National Bank
  *Copies of proposal:* 1
  *Deadline(s):* None
  *Board meeting date(s):* Feb. 5, May 7, Aug. 27, and Nov. 5
**Directors:** Judy Allison, Robert Atwood, Malcolm E. Everett, Jane Henderson, Don Johnson, Don McMullen, Ken Thompson, Mark Treanor.
**Trustee:** First Union National Bank.
**Number of staff:** None.
**EIN:** 566288589
**Recent grants for library/information services:**
558-1 Cheyney University of Pennsylvania, Cheyney, PA, $50,000. For construction and renovation of Leslie Pinckney Hill Library and Biddle Hall. 1998.
558-2 Community College of Philadelphia, Philadelphia, PA, $100,000. For capital campaign to improve library. 1998.
558-3 Free Library of Philadelphia, Philadelphia, PA, $50,000. 1998.
558-4 Free Library of Philadelphia, Philadelphia, PA, $32,000. 1998.
558-5 Free Library of Philadelphia Foundation, Philadelphia, PA, $200,000. For Changing Lives campaign to provide community

libraries with computers and internet access. 1998.
558-6 Free Library of Philadelphia Foundation, Philadelphia, PA, $25,000. For Changing Lives campaign to provide community libraries with computers and internet access. 1998.
558-7 National Housing Institute, Orange, NJ, $15,000. 1998.

## 559
### Gambrill Foundation
c/o Wachovia Bank of North Carolina, N.A.
P.O. Box 3099
Winston-Salem, NC   27150-7153
*Contact:* Jerry Lane, Tr. Off., Wachovia Bank of North Carolina, N.A.
*Application address:* c/o Wachovia Bank of North Carolina, N.A., 1401 Main St., Ste. 501, Columbia, SC 29226-9365, tel.: (803) 765-3671

Established in 1967.
**Donor(s):** Anne J. Gambrill.‡
**Grantmaker type:** Independent foundation
**Financial data** (yr. ended 12/31/99): Assets, $5,655,308 (M); expenditures, $279,151; qualifying distributions, $235,660; giving activities include $241,553 for 23 grants (high: $50,000; low: $1,000).
**Fields of interest:** Music; higher education; libraries/library science; food services; human services; Christian agencies & churches.
**Limitations:** Giving limited to Anderson, SC.
**Application information:**
  *Initial approach:* 2-page typewritten letter
  *Copies of proposal:* 6
  *Deadline(s):* Mar. 1 and Sept. 1
**Trustees:** Lila F. Albergotti, Harry W. Findley, Robert M. Rainey, William L. Watkins, F. McKinnon Wilkinson, Wachovia Bank of North Carolina, N.A.
**EIN:** 576029520

## 560
### The Leonard G. Herring Family Foundation, Inc.
310 Coffey St.
North Wilkesboro, NC   28659
*Contact:* Leonard G. Herring, Pres.

Established in 1994.
**Donor(s):** Leonard G. Herring.
**Grantmaker type:** Independent foundation
**Financial data** (yr. ended 12/31/98): Assets, $4,062,382 (M); gifts received, $514,062; expenditures, $71,856; qualifying distributions, $67,178; giving activities include $67,408 for 24 grants (high: $12,500; low: $100).
**Purpose and activities:** Giving for arts and culture, education, and public service organizations.
**Fields of interest:** University; libraries/library science; zoos/zoological societies; American Red Cross.
**Limitations:** Applications not accepted. No grants to individuals.
**Application information:** Contributes only to pre-selected organizations.
**Officers:** Leonard G. Herring, Pres.; Rozelia S. Herring, V.P.; Sandra Herring Gaddy, Secy.; Albert Lee Herring, Treas.
**EIN:** 561881015

## 561
## Rostan Family Foundation

P.O. Box 970
Valdese, NC  28690-0970

Established in 1995 in NC.
**Donor(s):** John P. Rostan, Jr.,‡ Naomi B. Rostan.
**Grantmaker type:** Independent foundation
**Financial data** (yr. ended 12/31/99): Assets, $8,278,472 (M); expenditures, $244,763; qualifying distributions, $224,363; giving activities include $227,500 for 15 grants (high: $33,000; low: $5,000).
**Purpose and activities:** Giving primarily for education and for human services.
**Fields of interest:** University; libraries (public); Boy Scouts; Girl Scouts; Salvation Army; hospices; Christian agencies & churches.
**Limitations:** Applications not accepted. Giving limited to NC. No grants to individuals.
**Application information:** Contributes only to pre-selected organizations.
**Officers and Trustees:*** Mrs. John P. Rostan, Jr.,* C.E.O. and Pres.; John P. Rostan III,* V.P. and Secy.; James H. Rostan,* V.P. and Treas.
**EIN:** 561901626

## 562
## Triangle Community Foundation

100 Park Offices, Ste. 209
P.O. Box 12834
Research Triangle Park, NC  27709
(919) 549-9840
*Contact:* Polly Guthrie, Prog. Dir.
*FAX:* (919) 990-9066; E-mail: info@trianglecf.org; URL: http://www.trianglecf.org

Incorporated in 1983 in NC.
**Grantmaker type:** Community foundation
**Financial data** (yr. ended 06/30/99): Assets, $74,563,651 (M); gifts received, $14,822,360; expenditures, $6,925,941; giving activities include $6,061,202 for 1,744 grants and $16 for in-kind gifts.
**Fields of interest:** Visual arts; museums; performing arts; dance; theater; music; humanities; historic preservation/historical societies; arts/cultural programs; early childhood education; child development, education; elementary school/education; vocational education; higher education; adult/continuing education; adult education—literacy & basic skills; libraries/library science; reading; education; natural resource conservation & protection; energy; environment; animal welfare; wildlife preservation & protection; family planning; medical care, rehabilitation; health care; substance abuse, services; mental health/crisis services; health associations; AIDS; alcoholism; delinquency prevention/services; legal services; crime/law enforcement; food services; housing/shelter, development; recreation; youth development, services; human services; children & youth, services; child development, services; family services; hospices; aging, centers & services; women, centers & services; minorities/immigrants, centers & services; homeless, human services; peace; race/intergroup relations; urban/community development; rural development; community development; voluntarism promotion; government/public

administration; leadership development; public affairs; minorities; Native Americans; disabled; aging; women; gays/lesbians; economically disadvantaged; homeless; general charitable giving.
**Types of support:** Continuing support; emergency funds; program development; seed money; scholarship funds; technical assistance; program-related investments/loans; employee-related scholarships; scholarships—to individuals.
**Limitations:** Giving limited to Durham, Orange, Chatham and Wake counties, NC. No grants for annual campaigns or operating budgets.
**Publications:** Annual report (including application guidelines), newsletter, application guidelines, financial statement, grants list.
**Application information:** Application form required.
*Initial approach:* Letter, telephone or e-mail (jan@trianglecf.org) for application
*Copies of proposal:* 6
*Deadline(s):* Feb. 1 and Aug. 1
*Board meeting date(s):* Feb., May, Aug., and Nov.
*Final notification:* June 15 and Dec. 1
**Officers and Directors:*** Stephen D. Corman, Pres.; Sara Brooks Creagh,* V.P.; Thomas F. Keller, Secy.; Shannon E. St. John, Exec. Dir.; and 14 additional directors.
**Number of staff:** 9
**EIN:** 561380796

## 563
## The Wachovia Foundation, Inc. ▼

c/o Wachovia Bank of North Carolina, N.A.
P.O. Box 3099
Winston-Salem, NC  27150-7131
*Contact:* Ed Loflin, Asst. Treas.
*Application addresses:* for NC, contact local bank office; for SC: Charlton E. Law, 1426 Main St., Columbia, SC 29226; for GA: Ben Boswell, P.O. Box 4148, MC-1102, Atlanta, GA 30302; for VA: Kenneth L. Flemins, 1021 E. Cary St., Richmond, VA 23219; and for FL: Teresa Weaver, 100 N. Tampa St., Ste. 4100, Tampa, FL 33609

Incorporated in 1982 in NC.
**Donor(s):** Wachovia Corp.
**Grantmaker type:** Company-sponsored foundation
**Financial data** (yr. ended 12/31/99): Assets, $18,015,472 (M); expenditures, $10,478,512; qualifying distributions, $10,192,014; giving activities include $10,171,030 for 902 grants (high: $150,000; low: $199; average: $800–$100,000).
**Purpose and activities:** Grants made primarily for general purposes and capital campaigns.
**Fields of interest:** Media/communications; museums; performing arts; humanities; historic preservation/historical societies; arts/cultural programs; higher education; business school/education; libraries/library science; education; natural resource conservation & protection; environment; hospitals (general); health care; substance abuse, services; health associations; crime/law enforcement; housing/shelter, development; recreation; human services; children & youth, services; hospices; community development; economics; disabled; economically disadvantaged.

**Types of support:** General/operating support; annual campaigns; capital campaigns; building/renovation; equipment; endowments; emergency funds; program development; conferences/seminars; professorships; seed money; curriculum development; fellowships; scholarship funds; matching/challenge support.
**Limitations:** Giving primarily in FL, GA, NC, SC, and VA. No grants to individuals.
**Application information:** Applications available at local Wachovia branch office. Application form required.
*Copies of proposal:* 1
*Deadline(s):* None
**Directors:** L.M. Baker, Jr., Chair.; Joyce T. Adger, James C. Cherry, Jean E. Davis, Stanhope A. Kelly, G. Joseph Prendergast, Will B. Spence, D. Gary Thompson.
**Number of staff:** None.
**EIN:** 581485946
**Recent grants for library/information services:**
**563-1** Burke County Public Library, Morganton, NC, $20,000. For capital campaign and building fund. 1998.
**563-2** Greensboro Public Library, Friends of, Greensboro, NC, $12,500. For continued support. 1998.
**563-3** Moravian Music Foundation, Winston-Salem, NC, $50,000. Toward construction of new Archival Research Center. 1998.
**563-4** New Hanover County Public Library, Friends of the, Wilmington, NC, $10,000. Toward renovations at new facility in Northeast area. 1998.
**563-5** South Carolina Archives and History Foundation, Columbia, SC, $50,000. For capital campaign. 1998.
**563-6** Spartanburg County Public Library, Landrum Branch, Friends of the, Landrum, SC, $10,000. For capital campaign. 1998.
**563-7** Work-Family Resource Center, Winston-Salem, NC, $15,000. For child and elder care resource and referral. 1998.

## 564
## Mary and Elliott Wood Foundation

(Formerly Elliott S. Wood Foundation)
c/o Wachovia Bank of North Carolina, N.A.
P.O. Box 3099
Winston-Salem, NC  27150-7153
*Contact:* Elliott S. Wood, Committee Member
*Application address:* P.O. Box 2448, High Point, NC 27261, tel.: (336) 885-5051

**Donor(s):** Elliott S. Wood, Mary W. Wood.
**Grantmaker type:** Independent foundation
**Financial data** (yr. ended 12/31/98): Assets, $2,444,212 (M); expenditures, $98,220; qualifying distributions, $71,584; giving activities include $43,000 for 39 grants (high: $5,000; low: $50).
**Purpose and activities:** Giving primarily for scholarships.
**Fields of interest:** Libraries (public); students, sororities/fraternities.
**Limitations:** Giving primarily in NC. No grants to individuals.
**Application information:**
*Initial approach:* Letter
*Deadline(s):* None
**Trustee:** Wachovia Bank of North Carolina, N.A.

**Foundation Committee:** Elliott S. Wood, Mary W. Wood, William Pennuel Wood.
**EIN:** 566055686

# OHIO

## 565
## The Burgett Family/Kokosing Foundation
c/o William B. Burgett
17531 Waterford Rd., P.O. Box 226
Fredericktown, OH  43019  (419) 522-7508
*Contact:* Shirley Burgett, Pres.
*Application address:* 2922 Lost Run Rd., Fredericktown, OH 43019

Established in 1992 in OH.
**Donor(s):** William Burgett, Shirley Burgett.
**Grantmaker type:** Independent foundation
**Financial data** (yr. ended 12/31/98): Assets, $72,708 (M); gifts received, $68,727; expenditures, $75,827; qualifying distributions, $75,743; giving activities include $75,750 for 9 grants (high: $34,000; low: $50).
**Fields of interest:** Libraries/library science; community development; federated giving programs; Christian agencies & churches; disabled.
**Limitations:** Giving limited to OH. No grants to individuals.
**Application information:**
*Initial approach:* Letter
**Officers and Trustees:*** Shirley Burgett,* Pres.; William Barth Burgett,* V.P.; William Brian Burgett, V.P.; Marsha Rinehart,* Secy.; Valerie Matusik,* Treas.; Janenne Burgett, William B. Burgett.
**EIN:** 311367299

## 566
## Charles H. Dater Foundation, Inc.
302 Gwynne Bldg.
602 Main St.
Cincinnati, OH  45202  (513) 241-1234
*Contact:* Bruce A. Krone, Secy.
*E-mail:* BruceA.Krone@Dater.org

Established in 1985 in OH.
**Grantmaker type:** Independent foundation
**Financial data** (yr. ended 08/31/99): Assets, $58,494,367 (M); expenditures, $3,636,787; qualifying distributions, $2,737,638; giving activities include $2,472,500 for 114 grants (high: $250,000; low: $1,000; average: $5,000–$100,000).
**Purpose and activities:** Support primarily for social and family services, with emphasis on services for children and the disadvantaged; support also for hospitals, education, including libraries, and museums and other fine arts groups.
**Fields of interest:** Historic preservation/historical societies; arts/cultural programs; child development, education; higher education; libraries/library science; education; hospitals (general); medical care, rehabilitation; delinquency prevention/services; recreation; human services; children & youth, services; child development, services; family services;

Christian agencies & churches; disabled; economically disadvantaged.
**Types of support:** General/operating support; continuing support; annual campaigns; building/renovation; equipment; program development; seed money; scholarship funds; consulting services; program-related investments/loans.
**Limitations:** Giving primarily in the greater Cincinnati, OH, area.
**Application information:** Application form required.
*Initial approach:* Letter requesting application form
*Copies of proposal:* 4
*Deadline(s):* None
*Board meeting date(s):* Monthly
*Final notification:* Within 2 months
**Officers and Trustees:*** Stanley J. Frank, Jr.,* V.P.; Dorothy G. Krone,* V.P.; David L. Olberding,* V.P.; John D. Silvati,* V.P.; Bruce A. Krone,* Secy.
**EIN:** 311150951

## 567
## Laura B. Frick Trust
c/o Wayne County National Bank
P.O. Box 757
Wooster, OH  44691  (330) 264-7111
*Contact:* Arianna Liggett, Trust Off., Wayne County National Bank
*E-mail:* aliggett@wcnb.com

Established in 1959 in OH.
**Grantmaker type:** Independent foundation
**Financial data** (yr. ended 12/31/99): Assets, $4,261,062 (M); expenditures, $180,274; qualifying distributions, $160,474; giving activities include $150,539 for 27 grants (high: $25,550; low: $240).
**Purpose and activities:** Giving primarily for libraries, hospitals, and elementary and secondary education, including religious schools; some support also for social services and health.
**Fields of interest:** Elementary/secondary education; elementary school/education; secondary school/education; libraries/library science; hospitals (general); health care; health associations; human services; Christian agencies & churches; religion.
**Types of support:** General/operating support.
**Limitations:** Giving limited to Wayne or Holmes counties, OH. No grants to individuals.
**Application information:** Application form required.
*Initial approach:* Letter
*Copies of proposal:* 1
*Deadline(s):* Apr. 1 and Oct. 1
*Board meeting date(s):* May and Nov.
*Final notification:* May and Nov.
**Trustee:** Wayne County National Bank.
**EIN:** 346513247

## 568
## The Sidney Frohman Foundation
c/o Muehlhauser & Moore
P.O. Box 790
Sandusky, OH  44871-0790

Trust established in 1952 in OH.
**Donor(s):** Sidney Frohman,‡ Blanche P. Frohman.‡

**Grantmaker type:** Independent foundation
**Financial data** (yr. ended 12/31/99): Assets, $11,966,648 (M); expenditures, $621,495; qualifying distributions, $589,109; giving activities include $583,494 for 59 grants (high: $77,000; low: $475).
**Purpose and activities:** Funding for education, a library association, arts, human services and federated giving programs.
**Fields of interest:** Arts/cultural programs; libraries/library science; education; health organizations; human services; federated giving programs.
**Types of support:** General/operating support; capital campaigns; equipment.
**Limitations:** Applications not accepted. Giving primarily in OH, with emphasis on Erie County. No grants to individuals.
**Application information:** Contributes only to pre-selected organizations.
**Trustees:** Daniel C. Frohman, George T. Henderson, Donald G. Koch.
**EIN:** 346517809

## 569
## The Gale Foundation
c/o Thomas F. Allen; Blossom Business Office, Inc.
20325 Center Ridge Rd., Ste. 629
Rocky River, OH  44116  (440) 331-8220

Established in 1995 in OH.
**Donor(s):** Elizabeth B. Blossom, The William Bingham Foundation.
**Grantmaker type:** Independent foundation
**Financial data** (yr. ended 12/31/99): Assets, $9,123,582 (M); expenditures, $549,863; qualifying distributions, $502,334; giving activities include $497,820 for 14 grants (high: $200,000; low: $4,000).
**Fields of interest:** Libraries (school); animal welfare; hospitals (general); boys clubs.
**Types of support:** General/operating support; land acquisition; program-related investments/loans.
**Limitations:** Applications not accepted. Giving on a national basis.
**Application information:** Contributes only to pre-selected organizations.
**Officers and Trustees:*** Benjamin Gale,* Pres.; Deborah B. Gale,* V.P.; Thomas F. Allen, Secy.-Treas.; Charles L. Freer, Deborah G. Freer, Mary B. Gale, Thomas V. Gale.
**EIN:** 341812999

## 570
## The GAR Foundation ▼
50 S. Main St.
P.O. Box 1500
Akron, OH  44309  (330) 643-0201
*Contact:* Robert W. Briggs, Exec. Dir.
*E-mail:* RBriggs@BDBlaw.com

Trust established in 1967 in OH.
**Donor(s):** Ruth C. Roush,‡ Galen Roush.‡
**Grantmaker type:** Independent foundation
**Financial data** (yr. ended 12/31/99): Assets, $190,215,740 (M); expenditures, $5,226,511; qualifying distributions, $3,957,996; giving activities include $3,090,663 for 70 grants (high: $300,000; low: $2,000; average: $10,000–$50,000).

**Purpose and activities:** Grants for education, the arts, and civic and social service agencies, including youth activities.

**Fields of interest:** Arts/cultural programs; secondary school/education; higher education; domestic violence prevention; human services; youth, services; economics; minorities; disabled; aging; economically disadvantaged; homeless.

**Types of support:** General/operating support; continuing support; annual campaigns; capital campaigns; building/renovation; equipment; land acquisition; endowments; debt reduction; program development; seed money; curriculum development; scholarship funds; matching/challenge support.

**Limitations:** Giving primarily in the Akron-Summit County area and secondarily in Cuyahoga, Stark, Medina, Portage and Wayne counties, OH. No support for private non-operating foundations, health care institutions, or national organizations. No grants to individuals, or for medical research, capital funding for churches or synagogues, fundraising campaigns or general operating expenses of the donee not directly related to its exempt purpose, or computers for schools.

**Publications:** Application guidelines.

**Application information:** Application form required.

  *Initial approach:* Request application form
  *Copies of proposal:* 1
  *Deadline(s):* Feb. 1, May 1, Aug. 1, and Nov. 1
  *Board meeting date(s):* Feb., May, Aug., and Nov.
  *Final notification:* 2 to 3 weeks after meeting

**Officer and Trustees:*** Robert W. Briggs,* Exec. Dir.; National City Bank.

**Distribution Committee:** Richard A. Chenoweth, Joseph Clapp, John L. Tormey, S.R. Werner, Douglas A. Wilson.

**Number of staff:** 2 full-time professional; 6 part-time professional; 2 full-time support; 1 part-time support.

**EIN:** 346577710

**Recent grants for library/information services:**

**570-1** Info Line, Akron, OH, $43,125. For start-up support for Community Computer Intiative project. 1998.

**570-2** Western Reserve Academy, Hudson, OH, $250,000. For construction of John D. Ong Library. 1998.

**570-3** Western Reserve Academy, Hudson, OH, $250,000. For educational materials for John D. Ong Library. 1998.

## 571
## Haman Family Foundation
c/o The Huntington National Bank
P.O. Box 1558, HC1012
Columbus, OH   43216
*Contact:* Lawrence Markworth, V.P., The Huntington National Bank
*Application address:* 232 W. 3rd St., Dover, OH 44622

Established in 1997 in OH.
**Donor(s):** Robert L. Haman,‡ Freda I. Haman.‡
**Grantmaker type:** Independent foundation
**Financial data** (yr. ended 03/31/00): Assets, $1,262,914 (M); expenditures, $65,770; qualifying distributions, $56,550; giving activities include $54,666 for 11 grants (high: $12,767; low: $1,485).

**Fields of interest:** Museums; theater; arts/cultural programs; education, management/technical aid; libraries/library science; education; YM/YWCAs & YM/YWHAs.

**Types of support:** Capital campaigns; building/renovation; equipment; matching/challenge support.

**Limitations:** Giving primarily in Tuscarawas County, OH. No grants for capital improvement projects.

**Application information:** Application form required.

  *Copies of proposal:* 4
  *Board meeting date(s):* Feb. and Aug.

**Trustee:** The Huntington National Bank.
**EIN:** 316565640

## 572
## Hildreth Foundation, Inc.
41 S. High St.
Columbus, OH   43215-3406
*Contact:* Mark Merkle, V.P.

Established in 1949.
**Donor(s):** Helen R. Davies.
**Grantmaker type:** Independent foundation
**Financial data** (yr. ended 12/31/99): Assets, $1,442,853 (M); expenditures, $85,973; qualifying distributions, $65,082; giving activities include $67,000 for 36 grants (high: $18,000; low: $100).

**Purpose and activities:** Giving for museums, education, health, and the environment.

**Fields of interest:** Museums; libraries (public); education; natural resource conservation & protection; medical care, rehabilitation; cancer.

**Types of support:** General/operating support.

**Limitations:** Giving primarily in Columbus, OH. No grants to individuals.

**Officers:** Louis H. Sanford, Pres.; Louis Hildreth II, V.P. and Secy.; Mark Merkle, V.P. and Treas.
**EIN:** 316026444

## 573
## Edwin P. Kell Charitable Trust
c/o Key Trust Co. of Ohio, N.A.
P.O. Box 10099
Toledo, OH   43699-0099

Established in 1998 in OH.
**Donor(s):** Edwin P. Kell Trust.
**Grantmaker type:** Independent foundation
**Financial data** (yr. ended 12/31/99): Assets, $1,416,232 (M); gifts received, $199; expenditures, $79,762; qualifying distributions, $79,203; giving activities include $57,111 for 4 grants (high: $30,840; low: $8,757).

**Fields of interest:** Education, volunteer services; libraries (public); Salvation Army.

**Limitations:** Applications not accepted. Giving primarily in OH. No grants to individuals.

**Application information:** Contributes only to pre-selected organizations.

**Trustee:** Key Trust Co. of Ohio, N.A.
**EIN:** 341882259

## 574
## Austin E. Knowlton Foundation, Inc.
1800 Star Bank Ctr.
425 Walnut St.
Cincinnati, OH   45202-3957
*Contact:* Charles D. Lindberg, Tr.

Established in 1982.
**Donor(s):** Austin E. Knowlton.
**Grantmaker type:** Independent foundation
**Financial data** (yr. ended 12/31/99): Assets, $4,431,320 (M); expenditures, $86,360; qualifying distributions, $86,210; giving activities include $77,775 for 14 grants (high: $50,000; low: $275).

**Purpose and activities:** Giving primarily for education.

**Fields of interest:** Higher education; libraries/library science.

**Limitations:** Giving primarily in OH. No grants to individuals.

**Application information:** Application form not required.

  *Copies of proposal:* 1
  *Deadline(s):* None
  *Board meeting date(s):* As needed

**Trustees:** Robert Fite, Austin E. Knowlton, Charles D. Lindberg.
**Number of staff:** None.
**EIN:** 311044475

## 575
## Kulas Foundation ▼
50 Public Sq., Ste. 924
Cleveland, OH   44113-2203   (216) 623-4770
*FAX:* (216) 623-4773; URL: http://fdncenter.org/grantmaker/kulas

Incorporated in 1937 in OH.
**Donor(s):** Fynette H. Kulas,‡ E.J. Kulas.‡
**Grantmaker type:** Independent foundation
**Financial data** (yr. ended 12/31/99): Assets, $43,872,471 (M); gifts received, $354,085; expenditures, $2,314,754; qualifying distributions, $2,046,771; giving activities include $1,907,284 for 74 grants (high: $150,000; low: $245; average: $2,000–$50,000).

**Purpose and activities:** Grants largely to music institutions and for higher education; some support also for local performing arts and social services.

**Fields of interest:** Museums; performing arts; music; arts/cultural programs; education, association; education, fund raising; higher education; libraries/library science; education; human services.

**Types of support:** General/operating support; continuing support; annual campaigns; capital campaigns; building/renovation; equipment; land acquisition; program development; conferences/seminars; professorships; research; consulting services; program-related investments/loans; matching/challenge support.

**Limitations:** Giving limited to Cuyahoga County, OH, and its contiguous counties. No grants to individuals, or for endowment funds.

**Publications:** Application guidelines, informational brochure (including application guidelines).

**Application information:** Special policy on Music Therapy - telephone for information. Application form required.

*Initial approach:* Letter or telephone
*Copies of proposal:* 5
*Deadline(s):* Submit proposal preferably 6 weeks before a meeting; no set deadline
*Board meeting date(s):* 4 times per year
*Final notification:* Within 2 weeks after board meeting
**Officers and Trustees:*** Patrick F. McCartan,* V.P.; Richard W. Pogue,* V.P.; Allan J. Zambie, Secy.; Nancy McCann.
**Number of staff:** None.
**EIN:** 340770687

## 576
### Fred Lazarus, Jr. Foundation
2800 Cincinnati Commerce Ctr.
600 Vine St., 28th Fl.
Cincinnati, OH 45202-2409
*Contact:* Stuart A. Schloss, Jr., Tr.

**Grantmaker type:** Independent foundation
**Financial data** (yr. ended 12/31/99): Assets, $857,858 (M); expenditures, $53,315; qualifying distributions, $50,000; giving activities include $50,000 for 4 grants (high: $25,000; low: $5,000).
**Purpose and activities:** Giving primarily for education.
**Fields of interest:** Higher education; libraries/library science; education.
**Limitations:** Giving primarily in MA and MD. No grants to individuals.
**Application information:** Application form not required.
   *Initial approach:* Letter
   *Deadline(s):* None
**Trustees:** Carol Lazarus, Fred Lazarus IV, John R. Lazarus, Stuart A. Schloss, Jr.
**EIN:** 316021207

## 577
### F. T. and Anna C. Manley Memorial Fund
c/o Key Trust Co.
800 Superior Ave.
Cleveland, OH 44114

Established in 1987 in NY.
**Grantmaker type:** Independent foundation
**Financial data** (yr. ended 12/31/99): Assets, $4,361,102 (M); expenditures, $139,729; qualifying distributions, $110,251; giving activities include $110,000 for grants.
**Fields of interest:** Elementary/secondary education; higher education; libraries/library science; hospitals (general); medical care, rehabilitation; human services; children & youth, services.
**Limitations:** Applications not accepted. Giving limited to organizations in Allegheny and Cattaraugus counties, NY. No grants to individuals.
**Application information:** Contributes only to pre-selected organizations.
**Trustee:** Key Trust Co.
**EIN:** 136905221

## 578
### Middletown Community Foundation
36 Donham Plz., Ste. 110
Middletown, OH 45042  (513) 424-7369
*Contact:* Kay Wright, Exec. Dir.
*FAX:* (513) 424-7555; E-mail: mcf@mailexcite.com; URL: http://www.mcfoundation.org

Incorporated in 1976 in OH.
**Grantmaker type:** Community foundation
**Financial data** (yr. ended 12/31/99): Assets, $17,482,860 (M); gifts received, $1,115,321; expenditures, $1,120,647; giving activities include $1,024,187 for 197 grants (high: $50,000; low: $100; average: $100–$50,000) and $71,460 for 307 grants to individuals.
**Purpose and activities:** The mission of the foundation is to: 1) serve as a leader, catalyst and resource for philanthropy; 2) to serve as a permanent and growing endowment for the community's changing needs and opportunities; 3) to strive for excellence through strategic grantmaking in the areas of the arts, education, health, social services, recreation and community development; 4) to provide a flexible and cost-effective way for donors to improve their community.
**Fields of interest:** Performing arts; arts/cultural programs; elementary/secondary education; early childhood education; elementary school/education; higher education; libraries/library science; education; health care; youth development, services; youth development, citizenship; human services; youth, services; family services; community development; public affairs, citizen participation; leadership development; aging.
**Types of support:** Capital campaigns; building/renovation; equipment; endowments; emergency funds; program development; seed money; scholarship funds; scholarships—to individuals; matching/challenge support.
**Limitations:** Giving limited to the greater Middletown, OH, area. No support for religious organizations other than religious schools. No grants to individuals (except for scholarships); few grants given for ongoing support.
**Publications:** Annual report, newsletter, application guidelines, informational brochure (including application guidelines), financial statement.
**Application information:** Application form not required.
   *Initial approach:* Proposal
   *Copies of proposal:* 1
   *Deadline(s):* Mar. 1, June 1, Sept. 1, and Dec. 1
   *Board meeting date(s):* Quarterly
   *Final notification:* Apr. 30, July 30, Oct. 30, and Dec. 30
**Officers and Trustees:*** John Peterson,* Pres.; Joseph Lyons,* V.P.; Vicki Frazer, Secy.; John Venturella, Treas.; Kay Wright, Exec. Dir.; John Burley, Sue Butcher, Sanford Casper, Joe Cristo, David Daugherty, Michael Dickenson, Michael Governanti, Gregg Grimes, David Haft, Loretta Harrison, Carolyn Henderson, Seth Johnston, Ronald Olson, Jack O'Neil, Sandra Ongkiko, Elmon Prier, Michael J. Sanders, Gary Shupe, Gene Snow, Molly Williams, Thomas Wortley.
**Number of staff:** 1 full-time professional; 1 full-time support.
**EIN:** 310898380

## 579
### John P. Murphy Foundation ▼
50 Public Sq., Ste. 924
Cleveland, OH 44113-2203  (216) 623-4770
*FAX:* (216) 623-4773; URL: http://fdncenter.org/grantmaker/jpmurphy

Incorporated in 1960 in OH.
**Donor(s):** John P. Murphy.‡
**Grantmaker type:** Independent foundation
**Financial data** (yr. ended 12/31/99): Assets, $68,459,481 (M); expenditures, $4,330,745; qualifying distributions, $3,795,980; giving activities include $3,620,915 for 119 grants (high: $1,000,000; low: $400; average: $1,000–$100,000).
**Purpose and activities:** Giving primarily for higher education, civic affairs, the performing arts, community development and health; support also for social services and youth.
**Fields of interest:** Visual arts; museums; performing arts; dance; theater; history & archaeology; historic preservation/historical societies; arts/cultural programs; vocational education; higher education; medical school/education; nursing school/education; adult/continuing education; libraries/library science; education; hospitals (general); medical care, rehabilitation; nursing care; health care; health associations; alcoholism; medical research; gun control; crime/law enforcement; youth development, services; human services; children & youth, services; women, centers & services; urban/community development; community development; federated giving programs; economics; public policy, research; government/public administration; leadership development; public affairs; disabled; women.
**Types of support:** General/operating support; continuing support; annual campaigns; capital campaigns; building/renovation; equipment; program development; publication; curriculum development; research; consulting services; program-related investments/loans; exchange programs; matching/challenge support.
**Limitations:** Giving primarily in the greater Cleveland, OH, area. No grants to individuals, or for endowment funds; no loans (except for program-related investments).
**Publications:** Informational brochure, application guidelines.
**Application information:** Application form required.
   *Initial approach:* Letter or telephone
   *Copies of proposal:* 8
   *Deadline(s):* 4 weeks before meeting
   *Board meeting date(s):* 4 times a year
   *Final notification:* Within 2 weeks of meeting
**Officers and Trustees:*** Nancy W. McCann,* 1st V.P.; Allan J. Zambie,* V.P. and Secy.; Robert R. Broadbent,* V.P.; R. Bruce Campbell,* V.P.; Marie S. Strawbridge,* V.P.
**Number of staff:** 1 full-time professional; 2 full-time support.
**EIN:** 346528308

## 580
## Muskingum County Community Foundation

534 Putnam Ave.
Zanesville, OH  43701  (740) 453-5734
*Contact:* Dr. David Mitzel, Exec. Dir.
*Mailing address:* P.O. Box 3042, Zanesville, OH
43702-3042; FAX: (740) 453-5734; E-mail:
giving@mccf.org; URL: http://www.mccf.org

Established in 1985 in OH.
**Grantmaker type:** Community foundation
**Financial data** (yr. ended 12/31/99): Assets,
$12,500,000 (M); gifts received, $2,600,000;
expenditures, $1,000,000; giving activities
include $414,000 for grants.
**Purpose and activities:** The foundation seeks to
support worthwhile organizations and programs
that enhance the quality of life in Muskingum
County, OH.
**Fields of interest:** Performing arts; music;
arts/cultural programs; elementary/secondary
education; libraries/library science; education;
animal welfare; wildlife preservation &
protection; hospitals (general); health care;
recreation; youth development, services;
children & youth, services; hospices;
community development; leadership
development; aging.
**Types of support:** Capital campaigns;
building/renovation; land acquisition;
endowments; program development;
conferences/seminars; publication; seed money;
fellowships; scholarships—to individuals;
matching/challenge support.
**Limitations:** Giving limited to Muskingum
County, OH.
**Publications:** Annual report (including
application guidelines), newsletter,
informational brochure, grants list.
**Application information:** Application form
required.
*Copies of proposal:* 10
*Deadline(s):* Mar. 1 and Nov. 1
*Board meeting date(s):* Bimonthly on 4th Wed.
*Final notification:* Mar. 31 and Nov. 30
**Officers and Trustee:\*** Douglas Mock, Pres.;
James McDonald, V.P.; Sondra Kopf, Secy.;
Frank Dosch,\* Treas.
**Number of staff:** 1 full-time professional; 1
full-time support; 1 part-time support.
**EIN:** 311147022

## 581
## Mary K. Peabody Foundation

c/o National City Bank of Indiana
P.O. Box 94651
Cleveland, OH  44101-4651

Established in 1991 in IN.
**Grantmaker type:** Independent foundation
**Financial data** (yr. ended 07/31/99): Assets,
$8,015,712 (M); gifts received, $246,672;
expenditures, $943,645; qualifying distributions,
$907,761; giving activities include $863,908 for
8 grants (high: $738,314; low: $831).
**Purpose and activities:** Giving to community
foundations in East Jordan, Michigan and North
Manchester, Indiana, and a library in Boyne
Falls, Michigan.
**Fields of interest:** Libraries (public); foundations
(community).

**Types of support:** Building/renovation;
equipment.
**Limitations:** Applications not accepted. Giving
primarily in Boyne Falls and East Jordan, MI;
some giving in North Manchester, IN. No grants
to individuals.
**Application information:** Contributes only to
pre-selected organizations.
**Trustees:** Frances H. Fisher, National City Bank
of Indiana.
**EIN:** 356546371

## 582
## Helmer Rabild Charitable Trust

c/o National City Bank of Pennsylvania
P. O. Box 94651
Cleveland, OH  44101-4651
*Contact:* Lynette A. Pedensky, Trust Off.,
National City Bank of Pennsylvania
*Application address:* c/o National City Bank of
Pennsylvania, 127 W. Spring St., Titusville, PA
16354, tel.: (814) 827-5972

**Grantmaker type:** Independent foundation
**Financial data** (yr. ended 12/31/98): Assets,
$1,076,151 (M); expenditures, $53,391;
qualifying distributions, $46,388; giving
activities include $45,005 for 7 grants (high:
$10,000; low: $505).
**Fields of interest:** Libraries/library science;
human services; federated giving programs.
**Limitations:** Giving primarily in the Titusville,
PA, area. No grants to individuals.
**Application information:**
*Initial approach:* Letter
*Deadline(s):* None
**Trustee:** National City Bank of Pennsylvania.
**EIN:** 256013302

## 583
## Reeves Foundation

232-4 W. 3rd St.
P.O. Box 441
Dover, OH  44622-0441  (330) 364-4660
*Contact:* Don A. Ulrich, Exec. Dir.

Trust established in 1966 in OH.
**Donor(s):** Margaret J. Reeves,‡ Helen F.
Reeves,‡ Samuel J. Reeves.‡
**Grantmaker type:** Independent foundation
**Financial data** (yr. ended 12/31/99): Assets,
$25,691,874 (M); expenditures, $1,362,293;
qualifying distributions, $1,232,566; giving
activities include $1,201,826 for 45 grants
(high: $155,000; low: $1,363; average:
$10,000–$25,000).
**Purpose and activities:** Emphasis on health
agencies, including hospitals; grants also for
youth agencies, education, and public
administration. Priority given to capital
improvement projects.
**Fields of interest:** Education; hospitals (general);
health care; health associations; children &
youth, services; government/public
administration.
**Types of support:** Continuing support;
building/renovation; equipment; program
development; matching/challenge support.
**Limitations:** Giving primarily in OH, with
emphasis on the Dover area. No grants to
individuals, or for annual campaigns, seed
money, emergency funds, deficit financing, land

acquisition, endowment funds, fellowships,
special projects, publications, or conferences;
no loans.
**Application information:** Application form not
required.
*Initial approach:* Proposal
*Copies of proposal:* 2
*Deadline(s):* 14 days prior to those months
when board meets
*Board meeting date(s):* Bimonthly starting in
Feb.
*Final notification:* 1 month
**Officers and Trustees:\*** W.E. Lieser,\* Pres.;
Thomas J. Patton,\* V.P.; Jeffrey Wagner,\*
Secy.-Treas.; Don A. Ulrich, Exec. Dir.; Ronald
L. Pissocra, Peter F. Wagner.
**Number of staff:** 1 part-time professional; 1
part-time support.
**EIN:** 346575477
**Recent grants for library/information services:**
**583-1** Bolivar, Village of, Bolivar, OH, $50,000.
For new library project. 1998.
**583-2** Newcomerstown Public Library,
Newcomerstown, OH, $200,000. For new
library building. 1998.

## 584
## Richland County Foundation

(Formerly The Richland County Foundation of
Mansfield, Ohio)
24 W. 3rd St., Ste. 100
Mansfield, OH  44902-1209  (419) 525-3020
*Contact:* Pamela H. Siegenthaler, Pres.
*FAX:* (419) 525-1590; E-mail:
info@rcfoundation.org; URL: http://
www.rcfoundation.org

Incorporated in 1945 in OH.
**Grantmaker type:** Community foundation
**Financial data** (yr. ended 12/31/99): Assets,
$58,849,280 (M); gifts received, $4,466,682;
expenditures, $2,441,300; giving activities
include $1,989,298 for 449 grants (high:
$200,000; low: $150).
**Purpose and activities:** To improve the quality of
life in Richland County through organized
philanthropy; to provide leadership and act as a
catalyst in identifying and addressing evolving
community needs, and to distribute grants for
charitable purposes in the areas of health,
economic development, basic human needs,
education, cultural activities, environment, and
community services. Also provides grants,
through other local nonprofits, to aged and
incurably ill Richland County residents.
**Fields of interest:** Historic
preservation/historical societies; arts/cultural
programs; early childhood education; child
development, education; elementary
school/education; secondary school/education;
vocational education; higher education;
adult/continuing education; adult
education—literacy & basic skills;
libraries/library science; reading; education;
hospitals (general); health care; substance
abuse, services; mental health/crisis services;
health associations; human services; children &
youth, services; child development, services;
aging, centers & services; women, centers &
services; race/intergroup relations; community
development; government/public
administration; minorities; disabled; aging;

women; economically disadvantaged; general charitable giving.
**Types of support:** General/operating support; capital campaigns; building/renovation; equipment; endowments; emergency funds; program development; publication; seed money; technical assistance; program-related investments/loans.
**Limitations:** Giving primarily in Richland County, OH. No support for sectarian religious purposes. No grants for annual campaigns, fellowships, highly technical or specialized research, maintenance funds, or travel.
**Publications:** Annual report (including application guidelines), application guidelines, newsletter, informational brochure.
**Application information:** Scholarship applications available after Jan. 1. Application form required.
*Initial approach:* Telephone or appointment
*Copies of proposal:* 1
*Deadline(s):* 1st Fri. of Jan., Mar., May, July, Sept., and Nov.
*Board meeting date(s):* 2nd Mon. of Feb., Apr., June, Aug., Oct., and Dec. Annual Meeting in May
*Final notification:* At least 8 weeks
**Officers and Trustees:*** Edith B. Humphrey,* Chair.; Pamela H. Siegenthaler, Pres. and C.E.O.; Deborah M. Schenk, Secy.; Bill Goldman, Treas.; Ivy Amos, Col. Daniel G. Arnold, Richard S. Cummins, Suzanne C. Davis, Katherine N. Fernyak, Lawrence L. Gibson, M.D., William J. Hartnett, J. Jeffrey Heck, Robert L. Konstam, Robert L. Lee, Sarah S. Lichtenstein, E. William McCarrick, Laurie McKeon, Burton Preston, Rev. Clifford Schutjer, Linda H. Smith, Rev. Wray C. Smith, D.D., John W. Welsh, J. George Williams.
**Trustee Banks:** Bank One, Mansfield, N.A., Key Trust Co. of Ohio, N.A., National City Bank, Columbus, Richland Bank, Mansfield.
**Number of staff:** 3 full-time professional; 1 full-time support.
**EIN:** 340872883

---

**585**
**The Scott & Fetzer Foundation**
c/o The Scott Fetzer Co.
28800 Clemens Rd.
Westlake, OH 44145 (440) 892-3000
*Contact:* Edie DeSantis

Established in 1967 in OH.
**Donor(s):** The Scott Fetzer Co.
**Grantmaker type:** Company-sponsored foundation
**Financial data** (yr. ended 12/31/98): Assets, $451,974 (M); gifts received, $313,202; expenditures, $249,912; qualifying distributions, $249,675; giving activities include $249,675 for 87 grants (high: $55,000; low: $25).
**Purpose and activities:** Giving for the arts, education, federated giving programs, and community service organizations.
**Fields of interest:** Museums; arts/cultural programs; elementary/secondary education; higher education; libraries/library science; hospitals (general); human services; federated giving programs.
**Limitations:** Applications not accepted. Giving primarily in OH. No grants to individuals.
**Publications:** Program policy statement.

**Application information:** Contributes only to pre-selected organizations.
**Officers:** Ralph E. Schey, Chair.; Kenneth J. Semelsberger, Pres.; Timothy S. Guster, V.P. and Secy.; William W.T. Stephans, V.P. and Treas.
**EIN:** 346596076

---

**586**
**Dorothy T. & Myron Seifert Charitable Trust**
c/o National City Bank, Columbus
P.O. Box 94651
Cleveland, OH 44101-4651

Established in 1996 in OH.
**Grantmaker type:** Independent foundation
**Financial data** (yr. ended 12/31/98): Assets, $7,098,310 (M); gifts received, $5,448; expenditures, $278,322; qualifying distributions, $253,868; giving activities include $235,338 for 23 grants (high: $19,611; low: $7,354).
**Fields of interest:** Museums; historic preservation/historical societies; libraries/library science; lung diseases; Protestant agencies & churches; religion.
**Limitations:** Applications not accepted. Giving limited to OH. No grants to individuals.
**Application information:** Contributes only to pre-selected organizations.
**Trustee:** National City Bank, Columbus.
**EIN:** 316535424

---

**587**
**The Slemp Foundation**
c/o Firstar Bank
P.O. Box 1118
Cincinnati, OH 45201
*Contact:* Patricia L. Durbin
*Application address:* P.O. Box 5208, ML. 7155 Cincinnati, OH 45201-5208

Trust established in 1943 in VA.
**Donor(s):** C. Bascom Slemp.‡
**Grantmaker type:** Independent foundation
**Financial data** (yr. ended 06/30/99): Assets, $23,926,018 (M); gifts received, $300; expenditures, $1,035,490; qualifying distributions, $922,902; giving activities include $543,617 for 37 grants (high: $100,000; low: $100) and $307,000 for 159 grants to individuals (high: $2,000; low: $1,000).
**Purpose and activities:** Giving for the maintenance of three named institutions, charitable and educational purposes, and for the improvement of health of residents of Lee and Wise counties, VA, or their descendants, wherever located, including a state department of conservation and recreation, undergraduate scholarships, public education, and volunteer fire departments and rescue squads.
**Fields of interest:** Arts/cultural programs; elementary/secondary education; libraries/library science; natural resource conservation & protection; recreation, community facilities; government/public administration.
**Types of support:** Building/renovation; equipment; endowments; emergency funds; seed money; curriculum development; scholarship funds; scholarships—to individuals.
**Limitations:** Giving primarily in Lee and Wise counties, VA.

**Application information:** Application forms provided for scholarship applicants.
*Initial approach:* Letter
*Copies of proposal:* 1
*Deadline(s):* Sept. 15 for scholarships
*Board meeting date(s):* Apr., July, and Nov.
**Trustees:** Mary Virginia Edmonds, John A. Reid, Melissa Smith Sircy, James Smith, Nancey E. Smith.
**Agent:** Firstar Bank.
**EIN:** 316025080

---

**588**
**The Kelvin and Eleanor Smith Foundation ▼**
26380 Curtiss Wright Pkwy., Ste. 105
Cleveland, OH 44143 (216) 289-5789
*Contact:* Carol W. Zett, Grants Mgr.
*FAX:* (216) 289-5948

Incorporated in 1955 in OH.
**Donor(s):** Kelvin Smith.‡
**Grantmaker type:** Independent foundation
**Financial data** (yr. ended 10/31/99): Assets, $142,007,830 (M); gifts received, $36,917,437; expenditures, $6,939,417; qualifying distributions, $6,501,153; giving activities include $6,452,384 for 48 grants (high: $2,195,000; low: $2,250; average: $3,000–$200,000).
**Purpose and activities:** The foundation's principal interests are in the fields of nonsectarian education, the performing and visual arts, and the environment.
**Fields of interest:** Arts/cultural programs; education; environment; health care; human services.
**Types of support:** General/operating support; continuing support; annual campaigns; capital campaigns; building/renovation.
**Limitations:** Giving primarily in the greater Cleveland, OH, area. No grants to individuals, or for endowment funds, scholarships, fellowships, or matching gifts; no loans.
**Publications:** Application guidelines.
**Application information:** Application form not required.
*Initial approach:* Letter
*Copies of proposal:* 1
*Deadline(s):* None
*Board meeting date(s):* No set time
*Final notification:* By mail
**Officers and Trustees:*** Lucia S. Nash,* Co-Chair.; Cara S. Stirn,* Co-Chair.; Ellen S. Mavec,* Pres.; Andrew L. Fabens III, Secy.; William B. LaPlace,* Treas.; Carol Zett, Grants Mgr.; Charles P. Bolton, Michael D. Eppig, M.D., William J. O'Neill, Jr.
**Number of staff:** 1 full-time professional.
**EIN:** 346555349
**Recent grants for library/information services:**
**588-1** Case Western Reserve University, Kelvin Smith Library, Cleveland, OH, $1,500,000. For capital campaign. 1998.

---

**589**

**The Harry Stensen Memorial Trust Fund**
c/o Key Trust Co. of Ohio, N.A.
P.O. Box 10099
Toledo, OH  43699-0099  (419) 259-8391
*Contact:* Imogene S. Ripps, Admin., Key Trust
Co. of Ohio, N.A.

Established in 1986 in OH.
**Grantmaker type:** Independent foundation
**Financial data** (yr. ended 05/31/99): Assets,
$3,400,856 (M); expenditures, $100,863;
qualifying distributions, $89,831; giving
activities include $85,000 for 9 grants (high:
$25,000; low: $5,000).
**Purpose and activities:** Giving primarily for
community development.
**Fields of interest:** Arts/cultural programs;
libraries (public); education; crime/law
enforcement; housing/shelter; aging; human
services; community development; federated
giving programs.
**Types of support:** General/operating support;
building/renovation; equipment.
**Limitations:** Giving limited to the Port Clinton,
OH, area. No grants to individuals.
**Application information:** Information available
upon request.
　*Deadline(s):* Nov. 1
　*Board meeting date(s):* May
　*Final notification:* May 31
**Trustee:** Key Trust Co. of Ohio, N.A.
**Number of staff:** None.
**EIN:** 346619471

**590**

**J. William & Mary Helen Straker
　Charitable Foundation**
925 Military Rd.
Zanesville, OH  43701
*Contact:* Susan Straker Henderson, Pres.

Established in 1994.
**Donor(s):** J. Wm. Straker, Mary H. Straker.
**Grantmaker type:** Independent foundation
**Financial data** (yr. ended 12/31/99): Assets,
$3,366,692 (M); expenditures, $153,342;
qualifying distributions, $492,782; giving
activities include $55,952 for 15 grants
(average: $1,000–$90,000).
**Fields of interest:** Arts/cultural programs;
libraries/library science; education; youth
development, services; human services.
**Types of support:** Capital campaigns;
building/renovation; land acquisition; program
development.
**Limitations:** Giving primarily in Muskingum
County, OH.
**Application information:** Application form
required.
　*Initial approach:* Letter
　*Copies of proposal:* 6
　*Deadline(s):* May 15
　*Board meeting date(s):* June
　*Final notification:* July 15
**Officers and Board Members:*** Susan Straker
Henderson,* Pres. and Treas.; John W. Straker,
Jr.,* Secy.; Anne Straker Plosser, J.W. Straker,
Jane Straker, M.H. Straker.
**Number of staff:** 1 part-time professional.
**EIN:** 311396841

**591**

**Timken Foundation of Canton ▼**
236 3rd St., S.W.
Canton, OH  44702
*Contact:* Don D. Dickes, Secy.-Treas.

Incorporated in 1934 in OH.
**Donor(s):** members of the Timken family.
**Grantmaker type:** Independent foundation
**Financial data** (yr. ended 09/30/99): Assets,
$152,914,132 (M); expenditures, $11,627,387;
qualifying distributions, $11,415,298; giving
activities include $11,370,433 for 113 grants
(high: $1,994,850; low: $2,323; average:
$10,000–$500,000).
**Purpose and activities:** To promote broad civic
betterment by capital fund grants; support
largely for colleges, schools, hospitals, cultural
centers, conservation and recreation, and other
charitable institutions.
**Fields of interest:** Historic
preservation/historical societies; arts/cultural
programs; early childhood education; child
development, education; elementary
school/education; secondary school/education;
higher education; adult education—literacy &
basic skills; libraries/library science; reading;
education; hospitals (general); health care;
health associations; abuse prevention;
recreation; youth development, services; child
development, services; community
development; computer science; leadership
development; economically disadvantaged.
**International interests:** Canada; France; Italy;
United Kingdom; Poland; Romania; South
Africa; Brazil; Australia.
**Types of support:** Capital campaigns;
building/renovation; equipment; land
acquisition; endowments; program
development; seed money; curriculum
development; research; matching/challenge
support.
**Limitations:** Applications not accepted. Giving
primarily in local areas of Timken Co. domestic
operations in Ashland, Bucyrus, Canton,
Columbus, Eaton, New Philadelphia, Wauseon,
and Wooster, OH; Ashboro, Columbus, and
Lincolnton, NC; Concord, Keene, and Lebanon,
NH; Latrobe, PA; Gaffney, SC; and Altavista, VA.
Giving also in local areas in Australia, Brazil,
Canada, France, Great Britain, Italy, Poland,
Romania, and South Africa where Timken Co.
has manufacturing facilities. No grants to
individuals, or for operating budgets.
**Application information:**
　*Board meeting date(s):* As required
**Officers and Trustees:*** Ward J. Timken,* Pres.;
W.R. Timken, Jr.,* V.P.; Don D. Dickes,*
Secy.-Treas.
**Number of staff:** 2 part-time professional; 1
part-time support.
**EIN:** 346520254
**Recent grants for library/information services:**
**591-1** Cherokee County Public Library, Gaffney,
　SC, $212,172. For library expansion. Grant
　made in form of stock. 1998.
**591-2** Lincoln County Public Library,
　Lincolnton, NC, $10,000. For Galaxy project.
　1998.
**591-3** READ Educational Trust, Braamfontein,
　South Africa, $59,983. For Library and
　Language development program. 1998.

**592**

**Tipp City Foundation**
c/o Star Bank, N.A.
910 W. Main St.
Troy, OH  45373
*Contact:* Thomas Kleptz, Trust Off., Star Bank,
N.A.
*Application address:* 730 Hathaway Terr., Tipp
City, OH 45371

Established in 1943 in OH.
**Grantmaker type:** Independent foundation
**Financial data** (yr. ended 12/31/97): Assets,
$1,843,667 (M); expenditures, $81,021;
qualifying distributions, $70,869; giving
activities include $70,369 for 27 grants (high:
$9,450; low: $250) and $500 for 1 grant to an
individual.
**Purpose and activities:** Support for local
schools, including library, art, and computer
programs; and community services, including
civic groups, aid for the handicapped, the
hungry, and recreation.
**Fields of interest:** Libraries/library science;
education; human services; federated giving
programs; disabled; aging.
**Limitations:** Giving limited to Miami County,
with emphasis on Tipp City, OH.
**Application information:** Application form not
required.
　*Initial approach:* Letter
　*Deadline(s):* None
　*Board meeting date(s):* Quarterly
**Trustee:** Star Bank, N.A.
**Number of staff:** None.
**EIN:** 316018697

**593**

**Tod Foundation**
c/o Mahoning National Bank of Youngstown,
Trust Dept.
23 Federal Plz., P.O. Box 479
Youngstown, OH  44501-0479  (330) 742-7000
*Contact:* Fred Tod, Jr., Pres.

**Donor(s):** Fred Tod, Jr., David Tod.
**Grantmaker type:** Independent foundation
**Financial data** (yr. ended 12/31/98): Assets,
$310,250 (M); gifts received, $373;
expenditures, $80,059; qualifying distributions,
$78,638; giving activities include $78,450 for
24 grants (high: $25,000; low: $100).
**Fields of interest:** Libraries (public); hospitals
(general); general charitable giving.
**Limitations:** Giving primarily in FL and OH.
**Application information:**
　*Initial approach:* Letter
　*Deadline(s):* None
**Officers:** Fred Tod, Jr., Pres.; David Tod, V.P.
**Director:** James E. Mitchell.
**Trustee:** Mahoning National Bank of
Youngstown.
**EIN:** 346557813

## 594
## The Troy Foundation

c/o Star Bank, N.A.
910 W. Main St.
Troy, OH 45373 (937) 335-8513
*Contact:* Melissa A. Kleptz, Exec. Dir.
*FAX:* (937) 332-8305; E-mail:
mkleptz@thetroyfoundation.org

Established in 1924 in OH by bank resolution
and declaration of trust.
**Donor(s):** Nannie Kendall,‡ A.G. Stouder,‡ J.M.
Spencer.‡
**Grantmaker type:** Community foundation
**Financial data** (yr. ended 12/31/99): Assets,
$31,952,476 (M); expenditures, $3,474,514;
giving activities include $3,111,111 for grants.
**Purpose and activities:** To assist, encourage, and
promote the well-being of mankind.
**Fields of interest:** Museums; historic
preservation/historical societies; arts/cultural
programs; education, fund raising;
elementary/secondary education; child
development, education; elementary
school/education; vocational education;
business school/education; libraries/library
science; education; natural resource
conservation & protection; environment;
hospitals (general); health care; substance abuse,
services; biomedicine; recreation; human
services; children & youth, services; child
development, services; hospices; community
development.
**Types of support:** Annual campaigns; capital
campaigns; building/renovation; equipment;
emergency funds; program development; seed
money; curriculum development; scholarship
funds; matching/challenge support.
**Limitations:** Giving limited to the Troy City, OH,
School District. No support for religious
organizations. No grants to individuals, or for
endowment funds, operating budgets,
continuing support, deficit financing, land
acquisition, research, demonstration projects,
publications, conferences, or fellowships; no
loans.
**Publications:** Annual report, informational
brochure (including application guidelines),
application guidelines, informational brochure.
**Application information:** Application form
required.
   *Initial approach:* Proposal
   *Copies of proposal:* 6
   *Deadline(s):* 15th of the month preceeding
      board meeting
   *Board meeting date(s):* 3rd Friday of Mar.,
      June, Sept., and Dec.
   *Final notification:* 1 to 2 months
**Trustees:** Michael E. Pfeffenberger, R. Daniel
Sadlier, Ronald B. Scott.
**Distribution Committee:** Doris Blackmore,
Chair.; R. Murray Dalton, Vice-Chair.; Steve
Baker, Beth Earhart, Cindy Meeker.
**Number of staff:** 1 full-time professional.
**EIN:** 316018703

## 595
## The Van Wert County Foundation

138 E. Main St.
Van Wert, OH 45891 (419) 238-1743
*Contact:* Larry L. Wendel, Exec. Secy.
*FAX:* (419) 238-3374; E-mail: vwcf@bright.net

Incorporated in 1925 in OH.
**Donor(s):** Charles F. Wassenberg,‡ Gaylord
Saltzgaber,‡ John D. Ault,‡ Kernan Wright,‡
Richard L. Klein,‡ Hazel Gleason,‡ Constance
Eirich.‡
**Grantmaker type:** Independent foundation
**Financial data** (yr. ended 12/31/99): Assets,
$17,912,618 (M); gifts received, $247,929;
expenditures, $1,043,990; qualifying
distributions, $1,020,227; giving activities
include $576,875 for grants and $303,093 for
108 grants to individuals (high: $2,650; low:
$300).
**Purpose and activities:** Emphasis on
scholarships in art, music, agriculture, and
home economics; support also for elementary,
secondary and higher education, youth
agencies, an art center, recreational facilities,
and programs dealing with alcoholism and drug
abuse.
**Fields of interest:** Music; historic
preservation/historical societies; arts/cultural
programs; elementary school/education;
secondary school/education; higher education;
libraries/library science; substance abuse,
services; alcoholism; agriculture; recreation;
human services; children & youth, services.
**Types of support:** General/operating support;
building/renovation; equipment; research;
scholarships—to individuals.
**Limitations:** Giving limited to Van Wert and
Paulding counties, OH. No grants to individuals
(except for designated scholarship funds), or for
endowment funds or matching gifts.
**Publications:** Application guidelines,
informational brochure.
**Application information:** The foundation has
discontinued its loans to individuals program.
Previous commitments will be honored.
Application form required.
   *Initial approach:* Letter
   *Copies of proposal:* 1
   *Deadline(s):* Submit proposal in May or Nov.;
      deadlines May 15 and Nov. 15; June 1 for
      scholarships
   *Board meeting date(s):* Semiannually
   *Final notification:* 1 week
**Officers and Trustees:*** Bruce C. Kennedy,*
Pres.; Robert C. Young,* V.P.; F.W. Purmort III,*
Secy.; Larry L. Wendel, Exec. Secy.; D.L.
Brumback III, Michael T. Cross, William S.
Derry, Kenneth Koch, Watson Ley, Paul W.
Purmort, Jr., C. Allan Runser, Donald C. Sutton,
Roger K. Thompson, Hon. Sumner J. Walters,
Michael R. Zedaker.
**Number of staff:** 1 full-time professional; 1
full-time support; 1 part-time support.
**EIN:** 340907558

## 596
## The Wagnalls Memorial

P.O. Box 217
Lithopolis, OH 43136 (614) 833-4767
*Contact:* Jerry W. Neff, Exec. Dir.
*E-mail:* jneff@clc.lib.oh.us

Incorporated in 1924 in OH.
**Donor(s):** Mabel Wagnalls-Jones.‡
**Grantmaker type:** Independent foundation
**Financial data** (yr. ended 08/31/98): Assets,
$20,196,675 (M); gifts received, $13,121;
expenditures, $1,699,050; qualifying
distributions, $1,314,084; giving activities
include $13,240 for grants, $190,944 for grants
to individuals (high: $3,000) and $1,236,579 for
1 foundation-administered program.
**Purpose and activities:** Primary areas of interest
include education, including scholarships and
fellowships, cultural programs, youth, and
libraries; support also for community
development, citizenship and civic affairs.
**Fields of interest:** Arts/cultural programs;
libraries/library science; education; youth
development, citizenship; children & youth,
services; community development;
government/public administration; public affairs,
citizen participation.
**Types of support:** Fellowships; scholarship
funds; scholarships—to individuals;
matching/challenge support.
**Limitations:** Giving limited to the Bloom
Township and Fairfield County, OH, areas.
**Publications:** Annual report, newsletter,
application guidelines, financial statement.
**Application information:** Application forms
required for scholarships.
   *Initial approach:* Letter or telephone
   *Deadline(s):* June 15
   *Board meeting date(s):* 1st Monday of each
      month
**Officers and Trustees:*** Edwin A. Wisner, J.D.,*
Chair.; Jerry A. Solt,* Vice-Chair.; Jerry W. Neff,
Exec. Dir.; Wm. Haynes, Robert O. Jepsen, Scott
Phillips, John R. Watkins, David Wynkoop.
**Number of staff:** 4 full-time professional; 2
part-time professional; 10 full-time support; 22
part-time support.
**EIN:** 314379589

## 597
## Charles Westheimer Family Fund

36 E. 4th St., Ste. 905
Cincinnati, OH 45202-3810
*Contact:* Charles Westheimer, Pres., or May O.
Westheimer, V.P.
*FAX:* (513) 421-9343

Established in 1980 in OH.
**Donor(s):** Charles Westheimer, Irwin F.
Westheimer,‡ May O. Westheimer.
**Grantmaker type:** Independent foundation
**Financial data** (yr. ended 12/31/98): Assets,
$531,605 (M); expenditures, $103,099;
qualifying distributions, $101,309; giving
activities include $101,028 for 161 grants (high:
$20,200; low: $10).
**Purpose and activities:** Giving for the arts,
education, and human services.
**Fields of interest:** Visual arts; museums;
performing arts; music; history & archaeology;
language & linguistics; literature; historic
preservation/historical societies; arts/cultural
programs; early childhood education; secondary
school/education; higher education; adult
education—literacy & basic skills;
libraries/library science; reading; education;
environment; family planning; delinquency
prevention/services; youth development,
citizenship; hospices; homeless, human
services; peace; arms control; foreign policy;
race/intergroup relations; civil rights;
urban/community development; community
development; anthropology & sociology;
government/public administration; public affairs,
citizen participation; minorities; homeless;
general charitable giving.

**Types of support:** Continuing support; annual campaigns; capital campaigns; building/renovation; emergency funds; program development; conferences/seminars; publication; seed money; scholarship funds; matching/challenge support.
**Limitations:** Giving primarily in Cincinnati, OH.
**Application information:** Application form not required.
> *Initial approach:* Letter
> *Deadline(s):* None
> *Board meeting date(s):* Varies
**Officers:** Charles Westheimer, Pres.; May O. Westheimer, V.P. and Treas.; John R. Westheimer, Secy.
**Number of staff:** None.
**EIN:** 311016766

# OKLAHOMA

## 598
## K. S. Adams Foundation
c/o WestStar Bank
P.O. Box 2248
Bartlesville, OK   74005-2248   (918) 337-3279
*Contact:* Jack I. Seidle

Established in 1953 in OK.
**Grantmaker type:** Independent foundation
**Financial data** (yr. ended 12/31/98): Assets, $1,760,503 (M); expenditures, $106,962; qualifying distributions, $91,500; giving activities include $91,500 for 46 grants (high: $5,000; low: $500).
**Purpose and activities:** Giving to religion, higher education, youth services, community foundations, medical foundations and research.
**Fields of interest:** Child development, education; higher education; libraries/library science; education; children & youth, services; child development, services.
**Types of support:** Continuing support; annual campaigns.
**Limitations:** Giving primarily in Bartlesville, OK. No grants to individuals.
**Application information:** Application form not required.
> *Initial approach:* Letter
> *Deadline(s):* None
**Trustees:** Dorothy Glynn Adams, WestStar Bank.
**Number of staff:** None.
**EIN:** 736091602

## 599
## American Fidelity Corporation Founders Fund, Inc.
2000 N. Classen Blvd.
Oklahoma City, OK   73106
*Contact:* Jo Ella Ramsey, Secy.
*Application address:* P.O. Box 25523, Oklahoma City, OK 73125

Established in 1984 in OK.
**Donor(s):** American Fidelity Assurance Co.
**Grantmaker type:** Company-sponsored foundation
**Financial data** (yr. ended 12/31/99): Assets, $4,783,703 (M); expenditures, $257,491;

qualifying distributions, $252,342; giving activities include $152,388 for grants (high: $10,000; low: $100; average: $500–$2,500) and $101,692 for employee matching gifts.
**Purpose and activities:** Support for education, including higher education and educational research, health associations and clinics, various arts councils, local cultural events and museums, community and civic affairs groups.
**Fields of interest:** Museums; arts/cultural programs; adult education—literacy & basic skills; libraries/library science; reading; education; environment; health care; health associations; medical research; federated giving programs; government/public administration.
**Types of support:** Annual campaigns; program development; research; employee matching gifts.
**Limitations:** Giving primarily in OK. No grants to individuals.
**Publications:** Application guidelines.
**Application information:** Application form required.
> *Initial approach:* Letter
> *Copies of proposal:* 1
> *Board meeting date(s):* Varies
**Officers and Directors:*** William M. Cameron,* Pres.; John W. Rex,* Exec V.P. and Treas.; Jo Ella Ramsey,* Secy.; Brett Barrowman, Jo Carol Cameron, Laura Cameron, William E. Durrett.
**EIN:** 731236059

## 600
## The Mervin Bovaird Foundation ▼
100 W. 5th St., Ste. 800
Tulsa, OK   74103-4291   (918) 583-1777
*Contact:* R. Casey Cooper, Pres.

Established in 1955.
**Donor(s):** Mabel W. Bovaird.‡
**Grantmaker type:** Independent foundation
**Financial data** (yr. ended 12/31/99): Assets, $47,656,838 (M); expenditures, $2,786,058; qualifying distributions, $2,565,590; giving activities include $2,346,123 for 96 grants (high: $125,000; low: $500; average: $25,000–$100,000).
**Purpose and activities:** Support for social services, health, and education; also funds a scholarship program for Tulsa County high school graduating seniors and graduates of Tulsa Community College at the University of Tulsa (not for graduate or professional study).
**Fields of interest:** Arts/cultural programs; education; environment; health care; health associations; human services; community development.
**Types of support:** General/operating support; continuing support; annual campaigns; capital campaigns; building/renovation; equipment; endowments; program development; conferences/seminars; curriculum development; scholarship funds; research; matching/challenge support.
**Limitations:** Giving limited to the Tulsa, OK, area. No grants to individuals; no loans.
**Publications:** Program policy statement.
**Application information:** Scholarship recipients are chosen by Tulsa public high schools and Tulsa Community College based on need and ability to attend Tulsa University. Application form not required.
> *Initial approach:* Brief letter
> *Copies of proposal:* 1

*Deadline(s):* May 1 (or date established by schools selecting a recipient for scholarships); Nov. 15 for grants
*Board meeting date(s):* Quarterly
*Final notification:* Dec. 15 through 20
**Officers and Trustees:*** R. Casey Cooper,* Pres.; David B. McKinney,* V.P. and Treas.; Wanda W. Brown, Secy.; Tilford H. Eskridge, Lance Stockwell, Thomas H. Trower.
**Number of staff:** 3 part-time professional.
**EIN:** 736102163
**Recent grants for library/information services:**
600-1 Tulsa Area Book Bank, Tulsa, OK, $15,000. 1998.
600-2 University of Tulsa, Tulsa, OK, $625,000. For Legal Center and Law Library. 1998.

## 601
## The Helmerich Foundation ▼
1579 E. 21st St.
Tulsa, OK   74114
*Contact:* W.H. Helmerich III, Tr.

Established in 1965 in OK.
**Donor(s):** W.H. Helmerich,‡ Walter H. Helmerich III.
**Grantmaker type:** Independent foundation
**Financial data** (yr. ended 09/30/99): Assets, $88,297,866 (M); expenditures, $4,187,512; qualifying distributions, $3,854,672; giving activities include $3,840,355 for 79 grants (high: $500,000; low: $2,500; average: $10,000–$50,000).
**Purpose and activities:** Limited to large capital needs in the Tulsa, OK, area for charitable, and educational purposes. Primary areas of interest include community development, higher education, health services, museums, and the performing arts.
**Fields of interest:** Museums; performing arts; arts/cultural programs; higher education; education; health care; youth, services; community development.
**Types of support:** Capital campaigns; building/renovation; equipment; land acquisition.
**Limitations:** Giving limited to the Tulsa, OK, area. No grants to individuals, or for general support, continuing support, annual campaigns, seed money, emergency funds, deficit financing, matching gifts, scholarships, fellowships, program support, operating budgets, research, demonstration projects, publications, or conferences; generally, no support for endowment funds; no loans.
**Publications:** Application guidelines, program policy statement.
**Application information:** Application form not required.
> *Initial approach:* Letter
> *Copies of proposal:* 1
> *Deadline(s):* None
> *Board meeting date(s):* As required
> *Final notification:* 6 weeks
**Trustee:** Walter H. Helmerich III.
**Number of staff:** 1 full-time support; 1 part-time support.
**EIN:** 736105607
**Recent grants for library/information services:**
601-1 Library of Congress, James Madison Council, DC, $10,000. For capital campaign. 1998.

**601-2** Piney Woods Country Life School, Piney Woods, MS, $10,000. For library renovations. 1998.
**601-3** Tulsa Library Trust, Tulsa, OK, $25,000. For rejuvenation project. 1998.
**601-4** University of Oklahoma Foundation, Norman, OK, $1,000,000. For library fund. 1998.

## 602
## Montfort Jones and Allie Brown Jones Foundation
P.O. Box 1234
Bristow, OK  74010

Trust established in 1960 in OK.
**Donor(s):** Allie B. Jones.‡
**Grantmaker type:** Independent foundation
**Financial data** (yr. ended 08/31/99): Assets, $4,445,239 (M); expenditures, $159,178; qualifying distributions, $132,807; giving activities include $107,640 for 6 grants (high: $50,000; low: $1,000).
**Purpose and activities:** Support primarily for higher education and a library; support also for community development.
**Fields of interest:** Higher education; libraries/library science; recreation; community development.
**Limitations:** Applications not accepted. Giving limited to organizations that specifically benefit Bristow, OK. No grants to individuals, or for scholarships (except funds at Southern Methodist University and University of Mississippi).
**Application information:** Contributes only to pre-selected organizations.
**Officers and Trustees:*** David H. Loeffler, Jr.,* Chair.; Hazel S. Earnhardt,* Secy.; Roger Collins, Velma J. Collins, Stan Earnhardt.
**EIN:** 730721557

## 603
## The Kerr Foundation, Inc.
12501 N. May Ave.
Oklahoma City, OK  73120  (405) 749-7991
*Contact:* Robert S. Kerr, Jr., Chair. and C.E.O.
*FAX:* (405) 749-2877; E-mail: kerr@ionet.net

Incorporated in 1963 in OK, and reincorporated in 1985.
**Donor(s):** Grayce B. Kerr Flynn.‡
**Grantmaker type:** Independent foundation
**Financial data** (yr. ended 12/31/98): Assets, $30,126,191 (M); expenditures, $2,248,063; qualifying distributions, $1,466,828; giving activities include $987,444 for grants.
**Purpose and activities:** Giving primarily for education, the fine arts and other cultural activities, and health. Generally all grants are challenge grants.
**Fields of interest:** Visual arts; museums; performing arts; arts/cultural programs; libraries/library science; education; health care; health associations; youth, services; government/public administration.
**Types of support:** Building/renovation; equipment; program development; professorships; curriculum development; fellowships; internship funds; research; program evaluation; in-kind gifts; matching/challenge support.

**Limitations:** Giving primarily in AR, CO, Washington, DC, KS, MO, NM, OK, and TX. No grants to individuals, or generally for continuing support.
**Publications:** Annual report.
**Application information:** Application form available on website. Application form required.
  *Initial approach:* Letter
  *Copies of proposal:* 3
  *Deadline(s):* None
  *Board meeting date(s):* Quarterly
**Officers and Trustees:*** Robert S. Kerr, Jr.,* Chair. and C.E.O.; Lou C. Kerr,* Pres. and Vice-Chair.; Steven S. Kerr, Secy.; Royce M. Hammons,* Treas.; Cody T. Kerr, Sharon L. Kerr, Ray Kline, Laura K. Ogle, Elmer B. Staats.
**Number of staff:** 4 full-time professional; 1 part-time professional; 1 full-time support.
**EIN:** 731256122

## 604
## Krueger Charitable Foundation
6929 E. 62nd Pl.
Tulsa, OK  74133

Established in 1994 in OK.
**Donor(s):** W.C. Krueger, Carol Krueger, Alma M. Krueger.
**Grantmaker type:** Independent foundation
**Financial data** (yr. ended 10/31/99): Assets, $2,463,516 (M); gifts received, $2,242,343; expenditures, $59,007; qualifying distributions, $56,745; giving activities include $57,300 for 5 grants (high: $18,000; low: $6,000).
**Purpose and activities:** Giving for the arts, youth services, and libraries.
**Fields of interest:** Arts/cultural programs; libraries/library science; children & youth, services.
**Limitations:** Applications not accepted. Giving primarily in CO and OK. No grants to individuals.
**Application information:** Contributes only to pre-selected organizations.
**Trustees:** Robert Bernthal, Angie Jackson, Carol K. Krueger, W.C. Krueger, Gary Edward Morris.
**EIN:** 731459816

## 605
## Irene M. and Julian J. Rothbaum Foundation
P.O. Box 21468
Tulsa, OK  74121-1468

Established in 1994 in OK.
**Donor(s):** Julian Rothbaum, Irene Rothbaum.
**Grantmaker type:** Independent foundation
**Financial data** (yr. ended 12/31/99): Assets, $608,448 (M); expenditures, $309,283; qualifying distributions, $304,134; giving activities include $305,750 for 55 grants (high: $140,900; low: $100).
**Purpose and activities:** Giving for education and Jewish federated giving programs.
**Fields of interest:** University; libraries (public); Jewish federated giving programs.
**Limitations:** Applications not accepted. No grants to individuals.
**Application information:** Contributes only to pre-selected organizations.
**Trustee:** Julian J. Rothbaum.
**EIN:** 731463214

## 606
## Nelle and Milt Thompson Foundation
P.O. Drawer 1770
Cushing, OK  74023-1770

Established in 1988 in OK.
**Donor(s):** Nelle J. Thompson.
**Grantmaker type:** Independent foundation
**Financial data** (yr. ended 12/31/99): Assets, $1,238,012 (M); expenditures, $59,714; qualifying distributions, $56,655; giving activities include $37,516 for 16 grants (high: $10,000; low: $150) and $6,250 for 6 grants to individuals of $1,250 each.
**Purpose and activities:** Giving for the arts, health and welfare , education, youth services, and Christian organizations.
**Fields of interest:** Arts/cultural programs; libraries/library science; housing/shelter, development; human services; children & youth, services; Christian agencies & churches; aging.
**Limitations:** Giving limited to Cushing, OK. No grants to individuals.
**Trustees:** Charles E. Phelps, Jr., Kelly Phelps, Margaret Phelps, Sherrie Plunkett.
**EIN:** 736242219

# OREGON

## 607
## The Carpenter Foundation
711 E. Main St., Ste. 10
Medford, OR  97504  (541) 772-5851
*Contact:* Dunbar Carpenter, Treas., or Jane Carpenter, Pres.
*Additional tel.:* (541) 772-5732; FAX: (541) 773-3970; E-mail: carpdn@internetcds.com

Incorporated in 1957 in OR.
**Donor(s):** Helen Bundy Carpenter,‡ Alfred S.V. Carpenter.‡
**Grantmaker type:** Independent foundation
**Financial data** (yr. ended 06/30/99): Assets, $19,548,514 (M); gifts received, $1,000; expenditures, $934,520; qualifying distributions, $889,910; giving activities include $792,828 for 68 grants (high: $40,000; low: $1,100).
**Purpose and activities:** Primary areas of interest include the arts, education, public interest, regional planning, and human services, including child welfare and youth.
**Fields of interest:** Visual arts; performing arts; theater; arts/cultural programs; early childhood education; child development, education; secondary school/education; higher education; adult/continuing education; adult education—literacy & basic skills; libraries/library science; reading; education; natural resource conservation & protection; environment; health care; substance abuse, services; mental health/crisis services; legal services; housing/shelter, development; human services; children & youth, services; child development, services; family services; rural development; community development; government/public administration; economically disadvantaged.

**Types of support:** General/operating support; continuing support; annual campaigns; capital campaigns; building/renovation; equipment; land acquisition; program development; conferences/seminars; publication; seed money; curriculum development; scholarship funds; technical assistance; consulting services; program evaluation; matching/challenge support.
**Limitations:** Giving limited to Jackson and Josephine counties, OR. No grants to individuals, or for deficit financing.
**Publications:** Annual report (including application guidelines), financial statement, grants list, informational brochure (including application guidelines).
**Application information:** Application form not required.
  *Initial approach:* Letter or telephone for guidelines
  *Copies of proposal:* 1
  *Deadline(s):* Submit proposal 6 weeks before board meeting
  *Board meeting date(s):* Usually in Mar., June, Sept., and Dec.
  *Final notification:* 1 to 2 weeks after board meeting
**Officers and Trustees:*** Jane H. Carpenter,* Pres.; Emily C. Mostue,* V.P.; Karen C. Allan,* Secy.; Dunbar Carpenter,* Treas.; Bill Moffat, Brian Mostue.
**Public Trustees:** Rev. David Close, Susan G. Cohen, Mary Ellen Fleeger, Virginia Post.
**Number of staff:** 1 part-time professional; 1 part-time support.
**EIN:** 930491360

---

### 608
### C. Giles Hunt Charitable Trust
c/o Wells Fargo Bank
P.O. Box 609
Eugene, OR  97440-0609
*Contact:* C.Q. Dukehart, V.P. and Trust Off., Wells Fargo Bank

Trust established in 1974 in OR.
**Donor(s):** C. Giles Hunt.‡
**Grantmaker type:** Independent foundation
**Financial data** (yr. ended 12/31/99): Assets, $6,253,455 (M); expenditures, $342,263; qualifying distributions, $286,248; giving activities include $274,054 for 48 grants (high: $30,418; low: $350).
**Purpose and activities:** Giving primarily for education, including for public libraries.
**Fields of interest:** Secondary school/education; libraries/library science; human services; children & youth, services; government/public administration.
**Types of support:** General/operating support; capital campaigns; building/renovation; equipment.
**Limitations:** Giving primarily in Douglas County, OR. No grants to individuals.
**Publications:** Application guidelines.
**Application information:** Application form required.
  *Initial approach:* Letter or proposal
  *Copies of proposal:* 7
  *Deadline(s):* Submit proposal in Jan. or Feb.; deadline Feb. 28
  *Board meeting date(s):* Mar. and Apr.
**Trustee:** Wells Fargo Bank.
**EIN:** 237428278

---

### 609
### Libri Foundation
P.O. Box 10246
Eugene, OR  97440-2246  (541) 747-9655
*Contact:* Barbara J. McKillip, Pres. and Treas.
*FAX:* (541) 747-4348; E-mail:
librifdn@teleport.com; URL: http://
www.teleport.com/~librifdn

Established in 1989.
**Grantmaker type:** Public charity
**Financial data** (yr. ended 09/30/98): Assets, $249,085; gifts received, $200,712; expenditures, $186,564.
**Purpose and activities:** The foundation seeks to help rural libraries acquire quality children's books they could not otherwise afford to buy.
**Fields of interest:** Adult education—literacy & basic skills; libraries (public).
**Types of support:** Matching/challenge support.
**Publications:** Annual report, application guidelines.
**Application information:** Applications are accepted from school libraries only if they serve as a public library. Application form required.
  *Initial approach:* Letter, telephone, FAX, or e-mail for application packet
  *Copies of proposal:* 1
**Officers and Directors:*** Barbara J. McKillip,* Pres. and Treas.; G.L. McKillip,* V.P.; Rodney A. Slade,* Secy.; Lowell A. Barto.
**Number of staff:** 1 full-time professional.
**EIN:** 930995572

---

### 610
### Second Dorothy F. Martin Charitable Foundation
c/o U.S. Bank, N.A.
P.O. Box 3168
Portland, OR  97208
*Application address:* c/o U.S. Bank, N.A., P.O. Box 3058, Salt Lake City, UT 84110-3058, tel.: (801) 534-6085

Established in 1985 in UT.
**Grantmaker type:** Independent foundation
**Financial data** (yr. ended 11/30/99): Assets, $984,383 (M); expenditures, $59,278; qualifying distributions, $47,602; giving activities include $45,300 for 9 grants (high: $22,500; low: $100).
**Purpose and activities:** Giving primarily for religion and human services.
**Fields of interest:** Human services, information services; civil rights, women; Roman Catholic agencies & churches.
**Limitations:** Giving primarily in Salt Lake City, UT. No grants to individuals.
**Application information:**
  *Initial approach:* Letter
  *Deadline(s):* None
**Trustee:** U.S. Bank, N.A.
**EIN:** 876197628

---

### 611
### McGraw Family Foundation, Inc.
707 S.W. Washington St., No. 934
Portland, OR  97205
*Contact:* Nancie S. McGraw, Pres.

Established in 1986 in OR.

**Donor(s):** Donald H. McGraw, Nancie S. McGraw.
**Grantmaker type:** Independent foundation
**Financial data** (yr. ended 09/30/99): Assets, $1,802,580 (M); expenditures, $114,193; qualifying distributions, $87,518; giving activities include $88,500 for grants (high: $30,000; low: $1,000).
**Purpose and activities:** Primarily giving to educational, cultural and social service organizations in OR.
**Fields of interest:** Libraries/library science; animal welfare; hospitals (specialty); children, services.
**Limitations:** Giving limited to Portland, OR. No grants to individuals.
**Application information:**
  *Initial approach:* Letter
  *Deadline(s):* None
**Officers:** Nancie S. McGraw, Pres. and Treas.; Mary M. Richenstein, V.P. and Secy.
**EIN:** 930934831

---

### 612
### PGE Corporate Giving Program
1 World Trade Ctr.
121 S.W. Salmon St.
Portland, OR  97204  (503) 464-7618
*Contact:* Kathy Carlson, Mgr., Community Resources

**Grantmaker type:** Corporate giving program
**Purpose and activities:** PGE's involvement in programs like the Stop Oregon Litter and Vandalism annual clean-up efforts, and affordable energy efficient housing projects like City Life, make a direct and tangible difference to the company's customers and neighbors.
**Fields of interest:** Arts, cultural/ethnic awareness; visual arts; museums; performing arts; theater; humanities; arts/cultural programs; early childhood education; elementary school/education; higher education; adult education—literacy & basic skills; libraries/library science; reading; education; energy; environment; wildlife preservation & protection; health care; substance abuse, services; legal services; crime/law enforcement; housing/shelter; youth development, services; youth development, citizenship; human services; children & youth, services; children, services; youth, services; family services; aging, centers & services; women, centers & services; minorities/immigrants, centers & services; homeless, human services; community development; economics; government/public administration; public affairs, citizen participation; leadership development; public affairs; minorities; aging; women; economically disadvantaged; homeless.
**Types of support:** General/operating support; capital campaigns; building/renovation; program development; scholarship funds; research; employee volunteer services; use of facilities; donated equipment; in-kind gifts; matching/challenge support.
**Limitations:** Giving primarily in company areas in OR. No grants to individuals.
**Publications:** Corporate report, annual report, application guidelines.
**Application information:** Application form not required.

*Initial approach:* Letter and proposal to headquarters
*Copies of proposal:* 1
*Deadline(s):* Sept.
*Board meeting date(s):* Quarterly
*Final notification:* 6 weeks
**Administrators:** Kathy Carlson, Mgr., Community Resources; Christine Crossland, Community Resources Specialist.
**Number of staff:** 2 full-time professional; 1 full-time support.

---

### 613
### Paul R. and Anna Lee White Family Charitable Foundation
c/o U.S. Bank, N.A., Tax Svcs. Dept.
P.O. Box 3168
Portland, OR  97208-3168
*Contact:* J.T. Garcia
*FAX:* (503) 275-6746

Established in 1985 in CO.
**Grantmaker type:** Independent foundation
**Financial data** (yr. ended 12/31/99): Assets, $3,923,180 (M); expenditures, $198,359; qualifying distributions, $168,949; giving activities include $165,000 for 14 grants (high: $20,000; low: $3,000).
**Purpose and activities:** Giving primarily for education, health, and youth organizations.
**Fields of interest:** Higher education; libraries/library science; hospitals (general); health care; mental health, clinics; children & youth, services.
**Limitations:** Applications not accepted. Giving primarily in CO and Sheridan, WY. No grants to individuals.
**Application information:** Contributes only to pre-selected organizations; unsolicited requests for funds not accepted.
**Trustees:** Lela Green, Dorothy Oliveira, George J. Robinson, U.S. Bank, N.A.
**EIN:** 846191934

---

# PENNSYLVANIA

---

### 614
### Arthur F. and Alice E. Adams Charitable Foundation
c/o First Union National Bank
Broad and Walnut Sts.
Philadelphia, PA  19109
*Application address:* c/o First Union National Bank, Attn: Susan Best, 200 S. Biscayne Blvd., 14th Fl., Miami, FL 33131

Established in 1987 in FL.
**Donor(s):** Alice E. Adams.‡
**Grantmaker type:** Independent foundation
**Financial data** (yr. ended 09/30/98): Assets, $22,965,089 (M); expenditures, $1,108,468; qualifying distributions, $914,975; giving activities include $882,000 for grants.
**Fields of interest:** Performing arts; music; higher education; libraries/library science.
**Limitations:** Giving primarily in FL and TN. No grants to individuals.
**Application information:**

*Initial approach:* Letter
*Deadline(s):* None
*Board meeting date(s):* May and Nov.
**Trustees:** R. Grady Barrs, Henry C. Clark, William B. Warren, First Union National Bank of Florida.
**EIN:** 656003785

---

### 615
### The Albert Trust
c/o Asher & Co., Ltd.
1845 Walnut St., 13th Fl.
Philadelphia, PA  19103

Established in 1992 in PA.
**Donor(s):** Richard A. Greenawalt, Margaret A. Greenawalt.
**Grantmaker type:** Independent foundation
**Financial data** (yr. ended 12/31/99): Assets, $3,347,454 (M); expenditures, $185,625; qualifying distributions, $170,798; giving activities include $170,798 for 38 grants (high: $71,200; low: $40).
**Purpose and activities:** Giving primarily for schooling and educational purposes; support also for the arts.
**Fields of interest:** Museums (art); performing arts; elementary/secondary education; higher education; university; libraries (public); parks/playgrounds; neighborhood centers; community development, women's clubs.
**Limitations:** Applications not accepted. Giving primarily in Philadelphia, PA. No grants to individuals.
**Application information:** Contributes only to pre-selected organizations.
**Trustees:** Margaret A. Greenawalt, Richard A. Greenawalt.
**EIN:** 237709316

---

### 616
### The Arcadia Foundation ▼
105 E. Logan St.
Norristown, PA  19401-3058   (610) 275-8460
*Contact:* Marilyn Lee Steinbright, Pres.

Incorporated in 1964 in PA.
**Donor(s):** Edith C. Steinbright,‡ Marilyn Lee Steinbright.
**Grantmaker type:** Independent foundation
**Financial data** (yr. ended 09/30/99): Assets, $58,925,136 (M); gifts received, $22,958; expenditures, $5,309,042; qualifying distributions, $4,881,565; giving activities include $4,943,003 for 158 grants (high: $500,000; low: $500; average: $1,000–$25,000).
**Purpose and activities:** Emphasis on hospitals and hospital building funds, health agencies and services, nursing, hospices, early childhood, adult and higher education, libraries, child development and welfare agencies, youth organizations, and social service and general welfare agencies, including care of the handicapped, aged, and hungry; support also for family services, the environment and conservation, wildlife and animal welfare, religious organizations, historical preservation, and music organizations.
**Fields of interest:** Music; historic preservation/historical societies; early childhood education; child development, education;

higher education; adult/continuing education; libraries/library science; education; natural resource conservation & protection; environment; animal welfare; wildlife preservation & protection; hospitals (general); nursing care; health care; health associations; food services; human services; children & youth, services; child development, services; family services; hospices; aging, centers & services; Christian agencies & churches; Protestant agencies & churches; religion; disabled; aging; economically disadvantaged; general charitable giving.
**Types of support:** General/operating support; continuing support; annual campaigns; capital campaigns; building/renovation; equipment; endowments; program development; scholarship funds; research.
**Limitations:** Giving limited to eastern PA organizations whose addresses have zip codes of 18000 - 19000. Generally, low support for cultural programs. No grants to individuals, or for deficit financing, land acquisition, fellowships, demonstration projects, publications, or conferences; no loans.
**Publications:** Annual report, application guidelines.
**Application information:** Application form not required.
*Initial approach:* Letter or proposal (not exceeding 2 pages; otherwise entire proposal will be discarded)
*Copies of proposal:* 1
*Deadline(s):* Submit proposal only between Sept. 1 and Nov. 1; deadline Nov. 1 for the calendar year
*Board meeting date(s):* Dec.
*Final notification:* Up to 3 months after Nov. 1
**Officers and Directors:\*** Marilyn Lee Steinbright,\* Pres.; Tanya Hashorva,\* V.P.; David P. Sandler,\* Secy.; Harvey S.S. Miller,\* Treas.; Edward L. Jones, Jr., Kathleen Shellington.
**Number of staff:** None.
**EIN:** 236399772
**Recent grants for library/information services:**
**616-1** Free Library of Philadelphia, Philadelphia, PA, $25,000. 1999.
**616-2** Mennonite Resources Network, Souderton, PA, $12,000. 1999.
**616-3** Montgomery County Norristown Public Library, Norristown, PA, $25,000. 1999.
**616-4** Schwenkfelder Library, Pennsburg, PA, $25,000. 1999.

---

### 617
### Charles F. Bartolomei Trust B
c/o First Union National Bank
Broad & Walnut Sts., Ste. P1308
Philadelphia, PA  19109-1199

Established in 1997 in FL.
**Grantmaker type:** Independent foundation
**Financial data** (yr. ended 12/31/98): Assets, $3,356,070 (M); expenditures, $173,154; qualifying distributions, $140,266; giving activities include $141,854 for 5 grants (high: $56,742; low: $21,278).
**Purpose and activities:** Giving primarily to a hospital, as well as for education and human services.
**Fields of interest:** Libraries/library science; secondary school/education; education;

hospitals (general); Goodwill Industries; human services.
**Limitations:** Applications not accepted. Giving primarily in MA. No grants to individuals.
**Application information:** Contributes only to pre-selected organizations.
**Trustee:** First Union National Bank.
**EIN:** 596976099

## 618
## Benevolent Association of Pottsville
1632 Lightfoot Dr.
Auburn, PA 17922
*Contact:* Marian A. Yanaitis

**Grantmaker type:** Independent foundation
**Financial data** (yr. ended 12/31/99): Assets, $800,343 (M); gifts received, $4,563; expenditures, $59,974; qualifying distributions, $50,474; giving activities include $46,713 for 19 grants (high: $9,000; low: $333).
**Fields of interest:** Libraries/library science; human services; YM/YWCAs & YM/YWHAs.
**Limitations:** Giving limited to Schuylkill County, PA. No grants to individuals.
**Application information:** Application form required.
*Initial approach:* Write for application
*Deadline(s):* Aug. 1
**Officers:** William C. Schuettler, Pres.; Frances Weiss, V.P.; Robert Yanaitis, Treas.
**EIN:** 236279703

## 619
## William L. & Margaret L. Benz Foundation
c/o Mellon Bank, N.A.
3 Mellon Bank Ctr., Rm. 4000
Pittsburgh, PA 15259-0001 (412) 234-0023
*Contact:* Laurie A. Moritz, Asst. V.P., Mellon Bank, N.A.

Established in 1987 in PA.
**Donor(s):** Margaret L. Benz.‡
**Grantmaker type:** Independent foundation
**Financial data** (yr. ended 05/31/99): Assets, $4,619,864 (M); expenditures, $227,035; qualifying distributions, $195,231; giving activities include $13,000 for 1 grant and $162,800 for 283 grants to individuals (high: $1,500; low: $250).
**Purpose and activities:** Primarily awards scholarships to Blairsville, PA residents for higher education; support also for the Blairsville public library.
**Fields of interest:** Libraries/library science; scholarships/financial aid.
**Types of support:** General/operating support; scholarships—to individuals.
**Limitations:** Giving limited to residents of Blairsville, PA for scholarships.
**Application information:** Request application information from Blairsville, PA, High School. Requests for grants to organizations are not accepted. Application form required.
*Deadline(s):* Apr. 30
**Trustee:** Mellon Bank, N.A.
**EIN:** 256276186

## 620
## Brodart Co. Contributions Program
c/o Corp. Contribs.
500 Arch St.
Williamsport, PA 17705

**Grantmaker type:** Corporate giving program
**Purpose and activities:** Brodart makes charitable contributions to nonprofit organizations involved with education. Support is given on a national basis and in Canada.
**Fields of interest:** Libraries/library science; libraries (school); education.
**International interests:** Canada.
**Types of support:** General/operating support; employee volunteer services; sponsorships; in-kind gifts.
**Limitations:** Giving in the U.S. and Canada.
**Application information:** Application form not required.
*Initial approach:* Proposal to headquarters
*Copies of proposal:* 1
*Deadline(s):* None
*Final notification:* Following review

## 621
## The Buhl Foundation ▼
650 Smithfield St., Ste. 2300
Pittsburgh, PA 15222 (412) 566-2711
*Contact:* Dr. Doreen E. Boyce, Pres.

Established as a trust in 1927 in PA; reincorporated in 1992.
**Donor(s):** Henry Buhl, Jr.,‡ Henry C. Frick.‡
**Grantmaker type:** Independent foundation
**Financial data** (yr. ended 06/30/00): Assets, $95,984,414 (M); gifts received, $175; expenditures, $5,515,420; qualifying distributions, $5,371,919; giving activities include $5,019,403 for 113 grants (high: $1,500,000; low: $800; average: $1,000–$150,000) and $25,065 for 35 employee matching gifts.
**Purpose and activities:** Emphasis on developmental or innovative grants to regional institutions, with special interest in education at all levels and in regional concerns, particularly those related to problems of children and youth.
**Fields of interest:** Early childhood education; child development, education; elementary school/education; secondary school/education; higher education; adult/continuing education; libraries/library science; education; children & youth, services; child development, services; engineering & technology; science; minorities.
**Types of support:** Continuing support; program development; seed money; research; program-related investments/loans.
**Limitations:** Giving primarily in southwestern PA, with emphasis on the Pittsburgh area. No support for religious or political activities, or nationally funded organizations. No grants to individuals, or for building or endowment funds, operating budgets, scholarships, fellowships, equipment, land acquisition, annual campaigns, emergency funds, deficit financing, fundraising campaigns, renovation projects, publications, conferences or seminars (unless grant-related).
**Publications:** Annual report, informational brochure (including application guidelines).
**Application information:** Submit final proposal upon invitation only. Application form not required.

*Initial approach:* Letter of inquiry
*Copies of proposal:* 1
*Deadline(s):* None
*Board meeting date(s):* Bimonthly
*Final notification:* Approximately 3 months
**Officers and Directors:*** Francis B. Nimick, Jr.,* Chair.; William H. Rea,* Vice-Chair.; Jean A. Robinson,* Vice-Chair.; Albert C. Van Dusen,* Vice-Chair.; Doreen E. Boyce, Pres.; Marsha Zahumensky.
**Number of staff:** 2 full-time professional; 2 full-time support.
**EIN:** 250378910
**Recent grants for library/information services:**
**621-1** Allegheny County Library Association, Pittsburgh, PA, $10,000. For Future of Libraries Fund feasibility study. 1999.
**621-2** University of Pittsburgh, University Library System, Pittsburgh, PA, $37,670. For supplemental funding for oral history of Pittsburgh from 1960 to present for Archives of Industrial Society. 1999.

## 622
## Chester County Community Foundation
The Lincoln Bldg.
28 W. Market St.
West Chester, PA 19382 (610) 696-8211
*Contact:* Michael J. Rawl, Pres.
*FAX:* (610) 696-8213; URL: http://www.chescocf.org

Established in 1994 in PA.
**Grantmaker type:** Community foundation
**Financial data** (yr. ended 06/30/99): Assets, $5,800,000 (L); gifts received, $3,500,000; expenditures, $2,400,000; giving activities include $1,800,000 for grants and $10,000 for 1 loan.
**Purpose and activities:** To maintain and enhance the quality of life in Chester County, PA.
**Fields of interest:** Arts/cultural programs; libraries/library science; scholarships/financial aid; education; health care; community development, neighborhood development; women; youth development.
**Types of support:** General/operating support; building/renovation; endowments; program development; conferences/seminars; scholarship funds; consulting services.
**Limitations:** Giving primarily in Chester County, PA. No grants to individuals.
**Publications:** Annual report, financial statement, newsletter, informational brochure, application guidelines.
**Application information:** Ninety percent of funding is donor-directed or institutional. Limited funding is available in current issue areas. Interested parties are invited to submit a letter of inquiry by Mar. 1.
*Initial approach:* Letter
*Deadline(s):* May 1
*Board meeting date(s):* Feb., May., Sept., and Nov.
**Officers and Directors:*** Henry A. Jordan, M.D.,* Chair.; Michael J. Rawl,* Pres.; John A. Featherman III,* Secy.; and 14 additional directors.
**Number of staff:** 3 full-time professional; 2 part-time professional; 1 full-time support.
**EIN:** 232773822

**623**
**The Doris Crane Charitable Trust**
c/o Mellon Bank, N.A.
P.O. Box 7236 Aim No. 193-0224
Philadelphia, PA 19101-7236

Established in 1992 in PA.
**Grantmaker type:** Independent foundation
**Financial data** (yr. ended 07/31/99): Assets,
$1,370,231 (M); expenditures, $83,409;
qualifying distributions, $64,170; giving
activities include $58,506 for 2 grants (high:
$29,578; low: $28,926).
**Purpose and activities:** Giving for education and
to a library.
**Fields of interest:** Libraries (public); animal
welfare; animal population control.
**Limitations:** Applications not accepted. Giving
primarily in PA. No grants to individuals.
**Application information:** Contributes only to
pre-selected organizations.
**Trustee:** Mellon Bank, N.A.
**EIN:** 256391613

**624**
**E. R. Crawford Estate Trust Fund "A"**
P.O. Box 487
Mc Keesport, PA 15134-0487 (412) 672-6670
*Contact:* Francis E. Neish, Jr., Tr.

Trust established in 1936 in PA.
**Donor(s):** E.R. Crawford.‡
**Grantmaker type:** Independent foundation
**Financial data** (yr. ended 12/31/99): Assets,
$7,501,227 (M); expenditures, $426,495;
qualifying distributions, $405,904; giving
activities include $366,750 for 87 grants (high:
$45,000; low: $500) and $5,475 for 8 grants to
individuals (high: $2,250; low: $83).
**Purpose and activities:** Giving for religious,
educational, charitable, and public purposes,
with emphasis on Allegheny County, PA and the
employees or former employees of the
McKeesport Tin Plate Company.
**Fields of interest:** Arts/cultural programs;
libraries/library science; hospitals (general);
Salvation Army; YM/YWCAs & YM/YWHAs;
religion.
**Types of support:** General/operating support;
scholarship funds; grants to individuals.
**Limitations:** Giving primarily in PA, with
emphasis on Allegheny County.
**Application information:** Application form
required for individuals.
    *Initial approach:* Proposal
    *Deadline(s):* None
**Trustees:** William O. Hunter, Francis E. Neish,
Jr., George F. Young, Jr.
**Number of staff:** 4
**EIN:** 256031554

**625**
**The 1994 Charles B. Degenstein**
    **Foundation**
c/o Mellon Bank, N.A.
P.O. Box 7236, AIM 193-0224
Philadelphia, PA 19101-7236
*Contact:* Appelbaum & Appelbaum
*Application address:* 43 S. 5th St., Sunbury, PA
17801-2896

Established in 1996 in PA.

**Grantmaker type:** Independent foundation
**Financial data** (yr. ended 06/30/99): Assets,
$105,906,118 (M); gifts received, $88,673,079;
expenditures, $1,381,865; qualifying
distributions, $1,136,050; giving activities
include $1,028,198 for 32 grants (high:
$175,000; low: $1,000) and $30,000 for 2
employee matching gifts.
**Purpose and activities:** Giving primarily for
libraries and YMCA's, as well as for the arts,
health, playgrounds, human services, and
federated giving programs.
**Fields of interest:** Arts/cultural programs;
libraries (public); education; health care;
disasters, fire prevention/control;
parks/playgrounds; human services; YM/YWCAs
& YM/YWHAs; children, services; federated
giving programs.
**Types of support:** Matching/challenge support.
**Limitations:** Giving within a 75-mile radius of
Sunbury, PA.
**Application information:** Application form
required.
    *Deadline(s):* None
**Trustees:** Sidney Appelbaum, Mellon Bank, N.A.
**EIN:** 237792979

**626**
**Ralph M. and Ella M. Eccles Foundation**
c/o National City Bank of Pennsylvania
20 Stanwix St.
Pittsburgh, PA 15222 (814) 678-3546
*Contact:* Emily Eisenman

Trust established in 1972 in PA.
**Grantmaker type:** Independent foundation
**Financial data** (yr. ended 12/31/98): Assets,
$4,438,706 (M); expenditures, $229,652;
qualifying distributions, $200,953; giving
activities include $184,234 for 4 grants (high:
$142,842; low: $505).
**Purpose and activities:** Support primarily for a
hospital, library and other community programs
and projects in Clarion county, PA.
**Fields of interest:** Libraries/library science;
hospitals (general); community development.
**Types of support:** General/operating support;
continuing support; annual campaigns;
building/renovation; equipment; land
acquisition; debt reduction; emergency funds;
seed money.
**Limitations:** Giving limited to Clarion County,
PA. No grants for endowment funds, special
projects, research, publications, conferences,
fellowships, or matching gifts; no loans.
**Publications:** Application guidelines.
**Application information:** Application form
required.
    *Initial approach:* Letter
    *Copies of proposal:* 3
    *Deadline(s):* None
    *Board meeting date(s):* May and Dec.
    *Final notification:* 2 months
**Trustee:** National City Bank of Pennsylvania.
**Number of staff:** 1 full-time professional; 1
part-time support.
**EIN:** 237261807

**627**
**Eichleay Foundation**
6585 Penn Ave.
Pittsburgh, PA 15206-4491

Established about 1956.
**Grantmaker type:** Independent foundation
**Financial data** (yr. ended 12/31/98): Assets,
$1,845,534 (M); expenditures, $88,623;
qualifying distributions, $85,399; giving
activities include $87,000 for 17 grants (high:
$30,000; low: $500).
**Fields of interest:** Arts/cultural programs; higher
education; libraries/library science; education.
**Limitations:** Applications not accepted. Giving
primarily in Pittsburgh, PA. No grants to
individuals.
**Application information:** Contributes only to
pre-selected organizations.
**Trustees:** George F. Eichleay, John W. Eichleay, Jr.
**EIN:** 256065754

**628**
**Lewis Elkins Fund**
c/o First Union National Bank
P.O. Box 7558, PA 1308
Philadelphia, PA 19101-7558
*Contact:* Paul Keperling

Established in 1903.
**Grantmaker type:** Independent foundation
**Financial data** (yr. ended 12/31/98): Assets,
$24,801,234 (M); expenditures, $1,136,648;
qualifying distributions, $1,071,489; giving
activities include $1,055,869 for 5 grants (high:
$211,174; low: $211,173).
**Purpose and activities:** Giving primarily for
children's services and a hospital.
**Fields of interest:** Libraries (special); hospitals
(general); children & youth, services;
residential/custodial care; foundations
(non-grantmaking, non-operating).
**Limitations:** Applications not accepted. Giving
limited to Philadelphia, PA. No grants to
individuals.
**Application information:** Contributes only to
pre-selected organizations.
**Trustee:** First Union National Bank.
**EIN:** 236214962

**629**
**Evans Foundation**
225 N. Olive St.
P.O. Box 258
Media, PA 19063 (610) 566-5800
*Contact:* Megan E. Zavawski, Secy.-Treas.

Established in 1983 in NY.
**Donor(s):** Anita Seits.
**Grantmaker type:** Independent foundation
**Financial data** (yr. ended 01/31/99): Assets,
$2,124,938 (M); expenditures, $375,402;
qualifying distributions, $114,660; giving
activities include $96,060 for 24 grants (high:
$25,000; low: $500).
**Purpose and activities:** Giving for the arts and
education.
**Fields of interest:** Arts, multipurpose
centers/programs; museums (science &
technology); elementary/secondary education;
higher education; libraries/library science;
education.

**Limitations:** Giving primarily in Delaware County, PA. No grants to individuals.
**Application information:**
*Initial approach:* Letter
*Deadline(s):* May
*Board meeting date(s):* June
**Officers:** Anita Seits, Pres.; Kevin D. Seits, V.P.; Megan E. Zavawski, Secy.-Treas.
**EIN:** 133178754

---

### 630
### The Fredricksen Foundation
4718 Old Gettysburg Rd., Ste. 209
Mechanicsburg, PA 17055-4380
(717) 731-9405
*Contact:* Miles J. Gibbons, Jr., Exec. Dir.

Established in 1987 in PA.
**Donor(s):** L.B. Smith Medical Foundation, Inc., C.J. Fredricksen.‡
**Grantmaker type:** Independent foundation
**Financial data** (yr. ended 12/31/99): Assets, $1,456,372 (M); expenditures, $461,118; qualifying distributions, $455,847; giving activities include $454,250 for 9 grants (high: $400,000; low: $1,000; average: $5,000–$20,000).
**Purpose and activities:** Giving primarily for libraries and health care.
**Fields of interest:** Libraries (school); health care.
**Types of support:** General/operating support; capital campaigns; building/renovation; program development; seed money.
**Limitations:** Giving limited to the Harrisburg, PA, and the Marco Island and Naples, FL, areas. No grants to individuals.
**Application information:** Application form not required.
*Initial approach:* Letter
*Copies of proposal:* 1
*Deadline(s):* None
*Board meeting date(s):* As needed
**Officer and Trustees:\*** Miles J. Gibbons, Jr.,\* Exec. Dir.; Cleve L. Fredricksen, Mary Jane Fredricksen.
**Number of staff:** None.
**EIN:** 222852610

---

### 631
### The Hamer Foundation
2470 Fox Hill Rd.
State College, PA 16803 (814) 355-8004
*Contact:* Donald W. Hamer, Tr.

Established in 1989 in PA.
**Donor(s):** Donald W. Hamer.
**Grantmaker type:** Independent foundation
**Financial data** (yr. ended 12/31/99): Assets, $4,584,475 (L); gifts received, $892,250; expenditures, $331,367; qualifying distributions, $323,500; giving activities include $323,500 for grants (average: $1,000–$40,000).
**Purpose and activities:** Giving primarily for conservation programs.
**Fields of interest:** Visual arts; museums; performing arts; higher education; libraries/library science; natural resource conservation & protection; animal welfare; human services; Christian agencies & churches; religion.

**Types of support:** General/operating support; annual campaigns; capital campaigns; building/renovation.
**Limitations:** Giving primarily in Centre County, PA. No grants to individuals.
**Application information:** Application form not required.
*Initial approach:* Proposal
*Copies of proposal:* 1
*Deadline(s):* None
*Board meeting date(s):* As needed
**Trustees:** Donald W. Hamer, Diane M. Kerly, Edward Matosziuk.
**Number of staff:** None.
**EIN:** 251610780

---

### 632
### The HBE Foundation
350 Pond View
Devon, PA 19333-1732 (610) 688-0143
*Contact:* Bruce M. Brown, Tr.

Established in 1988.
**Donor(s):** Bruce Maitland Brown.
**Grantmaker type:** Independent foundation
**Financial data** (yr. ended 06/30/00): Assets, $1,450,650 (M); gifts received, $274; expenditures, $70,856; qualifying distributions, $64,730; giving activities include $62,745 for 14 grants (high: $25,000; low: $100).
**Purpose and activities:** Giving for the arts, culture, education, and human services.
**Fields of interest:** Journalism & publishing; genealogy; arts/cultural programs; elementary school/education; secondary school/education; higher education; libraries/library science; education; botanical/landscape services; environment, beautification programs; human services; philanthropy/voluntarism; science; religion; general charitable giving.
**International interests:** Bermuda; Ireland; Scotland; Soviet Union (Former); Central America.
**Types of support:** General/operating support; capital campaigns; building/renovation; emergency funds; program development; publication; seed money; scholarship funds; research; in-kind gifts.
**Limitations:** Giving primarily in southeastern PA. No grants to individuals, charities making "payments in lieu of taxes," debt reduction or "emergencies".
**Publications:** Multi-year report (including application guidelines).
**Application information:** Unsolicited proposals not acknowledged unless trustee is interested. Application form not required.
*Initial approach:* Telephone or letter
*Copies of proposal:* 1
*Deadline(s):* None
*Board meeting date(s):* After site visit
**Trustee:** Bruce Maitland Brown.
**Number of staff:** None.
**EIN:** 236910944

---

### 633
### Drue Heinz Trust ▼
(Formerly H. J. & Drue Heinz Trust)
606 Oliver Bldg.
535 Smithfield St.
Pittsburgh, PA 15222 (412) 281-5737
*Contact:* Julia V. Shea, Fdn. Mgr.

Established in 1954 in PA.
**Grantmaker type:** Independent foundation
**Financial data** (yr. ended 12/31/99): Assets, $35,540,496 (M); expenditures, $2,674,041; qualifying distributions, $2,596,743; giving activities include $2,524,355 for 82 grants (high: $615,000; low: $250; average: $1,000–$100,000).
**Purpose and activities:** Emphasis on higher education, medical research, conservation, recreation, fine arts, and prevention of cruelty to children and animals.
**Fields of interest:** Visual arts; architecture; museums; performing arts; arts/cultural programs; higher education; libraries/library science; natural resource conservation & protection; animal welfare; hospitals (general); medical research; recreation; children & youth, services.
**Types of support:** General/operating support; program development.
**Limitations:** Giving primarily in Washington, DC, NY, and PA.
**Application information:**
*Initial approach:* Letter or telephone for application guidelines
*Board meeting date(s):* Nov.
**Trustees:** James F. Dolan, Drue Heinz, William D. Rea, Mellon Bank, N.A.
**Number of staff:** 1 full-time professional; 1 part-time professional; 1 full-time support.
**EIN:** 256018930

---

### 634
### Horsehead Community Development Fund, Inc.
P.O. Box 351
Palmerton, PA 18071-0351 (610) 826-4377
*Contact:* Charles H. Campton, Exec. Consultant
*Additional tel.:* (610) 826-4377

Established in 1989 in PA.
**Donor(s):** Horsehead Resource Development Co., Inc.
**Grantmaker type:** Company-sponsored foundation
**Financial data** (yr. ended 12/31/99): Assets, $142,790 (M); gifts received, $139,815; expenditures, $145,208; qualifying distributions, $145,102; giving activities include $136,875 for 40 grants (high: $25,000; low: $500).
**Purpose and activities:** Giving primarily to a hospital and library associations; support also for community development and sports activities for youth.
**Fields of interest:** Performing arts; libraries/library science; natural resource conservation & protection; environment; hospitals (general); recreation; children & youth, services; community development; federated giving programs; disabled; aging.
**Types of support:** Capital campaigns; building/renovation; equipment; emergency funds; program development.

**Limitations:** Giving limited to the Palmerton, PA, area. No grants to individuals, or for start-up funds.
**Publications:** Annual report (including application guidelines), informational brochure (including application guidelines), grants list, occasional report, program policy statement, financial statement.
**Application information:** Grants must be used in same year awarded. Application form required.
  *Initial approach:* Letter or telephone
  *Copies of proposal:* 1
  *Deadline(s):* Apr. 1, July 1, Sept. 1, and Dec. 1
  *Board meeting date(s):* Jan., Apr., July, and Oct.
  *Final notification:* After board meeting
**Officers and Directors:*** William Bechdolt,* Chair.; Fred L. Masenheimer,* Vice-Chair; Richard Hager,* Secy.; Willard Doll,* Treas.; Charles H. Campton, Exec. Consultant; Joseph Bechtel, Mary Elizabeth Cyr, Michael R. Harleman.
**Number of staff:** 1 part-time professional.
**EIN:** 232588172

---

**635**
**Hughes Foundation, Inc.**
P.O. Box 149
Stroudsburg, PA  18360-0149   (717) 393-1226
*Contact:* R. Clinton Hughes, Jr., Pres.

Established in 1959 in PA.
**Donor(s):** Russell C. Hughes Trust.
**Grantmaker type:** Independent foundation
**Financial data** (yr. ended 04/30/00): Assets, $2,112,244 (M); expenditures, $230,000; qualifying distributions, $140,300; giving activities include $140,300 for 8 grants (high: $60,000; low: $300).
**Purpose and activities:** Grants primarily for education and youth organizations; support also for a community association, a public library, and a hospital.
**Fields of interest:** Libraries/library science; education; hospitals (general); children & youth, services; community development.
**Types of support:** General/operating support; annual campaigns; capital campaigns; building/renovation; program development; scholarship funds.
**Limitations:** Giving only in the Stroudsburg and Monroe County, PA, area. No grants to individuals.
**Application information:** Application form not required.
  *Initial approach:* Letter
  *Copies of proposal:* 1
  *Deadline(s):* Mar. 31
  *Board meeting date(s):* Oct. and Apr.
**Officers and Directors:*** R. Clinton Hughes, Jr.,* Pres.; R. Dale Hughes,* V.P.; Kevin Hughes,* Secy.; Terri Cramer,* Treas.; Bernard Billick, Bryan E. Hughes, Raymond Price III.
**EIN:** 236298104

---

**636**
**Margaret G. Jacobs Charitable Trust**
c/o Brown Brothers Harriman Trust Co.
1531 Walnut St.
Philadelphia, PA  19102-8910
*Contact:* William R. Levy, Tr.

Established in 1992 in PA.
**Donor(s):** Margaret G. Jacobs.‡
**Grantmaker type:** Independent foundation
**Financial data** (yr. ended 06/30/99): Assets, $3,082,379 (M); expenditures, $110,829; qualifying distributions, $108,711; giving activities include $104,000 for 35 grants (high: $15,000; low: $500; average: $1,000–$10,000).
**Purpose and activities:** Giving primarily for human services, American Red Cross, Boys Scouts, elementary education, and health associations.
**Fields of interest:** Elementary/secondary education; libraries/library science; hospitals (specialty); health associations; Boy Scouts; human services; American Red Cross.
**Types of support:** Equipment; emergency funds; matching/challenge support.
**Limitations:** Giving limited to PA.
**Application information:** Application form not required.
  *Initial approach:* Letter
  *Copies of proposal:* 1
  *Deadline(s):* None
  *Board meeting date(s):* Rolling
**Trustees:** Philip Brown, William R. Levy.
**Number of staff:** 1 part-time support.
**EIN:** 232743317

---

**637**
**Jerome Foundation**
c/o PNC Bank, N.A., MS: P3-POLV-27-1
One Oliver Plaza, 210 Sixth Ave.
Pittsburgh, PA  15222-2602
*Application address:* Benny J. Jerome, 800 Fourth Ave., New Kensington, PA 15068

**Donor(s):** Benny J. Jerome.
**Grantmaker type:** Independent foundation
**Financial data** (yr. ended 12/31/98): Assets, $1,251,640 (M); expenditures, $55,262; qualifying distributions, $51,049; giving activities include $50,750 for 27 grants (high: $10,000; low: $50).
**Fields of interest:** Libraries/library science; human services; Protestant agencies & churches.
**Limitations:** Giving primarily in PA. No grants to individuals.
**Application information:** Application form not required.
  *Deadline(s):* None
**Trustee:** PNC Bank, N.A.
**EIN:** 256066649

---

**638**
**The Roy F. Johns, Jr. Family Foundation**
200 Marshall Dr.
Coraopolis, PA  15108   (412) 264-8383
*Contact:* Roy F. Johns, Jr., Dir.

Established in 1993.
**Donor(s):** Roy F. Johns, Jr.
**Grantmaker type:** Independent foundation
**Financial data** (yr. ended 12/31/99): Assets, $2,464,834 (M); expenditures, $123,704; qualifying distributions, $53,912; giving activities include $53,020 for 11 grants (high: $10,000; low: $120).
**Purpose and activities:** Giving primarily to arts, culture and education.
**Fields of interest:** Orchestra (symphony); college; libraries (school).

**Limitations:** Giving primarily in western PA. No grants to individuals.
**Application information:** Application form not required.
  *Initial approach:* Letter
  *Copies of proposal:* 1
  *Deadline(s):* None
  *Board meeting date(s):* Oct.
  *Final notification:* Dec.
**Officer and Directors:*** Roy F. Johns, Jr.,* Mgr.; Barbara Johns.
**Number of staff:** 1 part-time support.
**EIN:** 256426447

---

**639**
**H. D. Jones Charitable Trust**
c/o National City Bank of Pennsylvania
20 Stanwix St., Loc. 25-155
Pittsburgh, PA  15222

Established in 1989 in PA.
**Grantmaker type:** Independent foundation
**Financial data** (yr. ended 12/31/98): Assets, $1,384,264 (M); expenditures, $99,819; qualifying distributions, $88,456; giving activities include $85,576 for 7 grants (high: $29,024; low: $3,312).
**Fields of interest:** Higher education; libraries/library science; human services; federated giving programs.
**Limitations:** Applications not accepted. Giving limited to PA. No grants to individuals.
**Application information:** Contributes only to pre-selected organizations.
**Trustee:** National City Bank of Pennsylvania.
**EIN:** 256119452

---

**640**
**Hess & Helyn Kline Foundation**
c/o Wolf, Block, Schorr & Solis-Cohen
1650 Arch St., 22nd Fl.
Philadelphia, PA  19103

Established around 1954.
**Donor(s):** Hess Kline.‡
**Grantmaker type:** Independent foundation
**Financial data** (yr. ended 12/31/99): Assets, $1,645,772 (M); expenditures, $106,844; qualifying distributions, $102,028; giving activities include $101,500 for 39 grants (high: $10,000; low: $50).
**Fields of interest:** Museums (art); libraries (public); hospitals (general).
**Limitations:** Giving primarily in MA. No grants to individuals.
**Application information:** Application form not required.
  *Deadline(s):* None
**Trustees:** Barbara Ann Eldridge, Denise Jo Levy, Jennifer Mentzer.
**EIN:** 236243380

---

**641**
**Laughlin Memorial, Inc.**
202 Orchard Ln., Edgeworth
Sewickley, PA  15143   (412) 741-8889
*Contact:* Frederick C. Emerick, Jr., Secy.-Treas.

Established about 1927 in PA.
**Donor(s):** Mary M. Laughlin.‡

**Grantmaker type:** Independent foundation
**Financial data** (yr. ended 12/31/00): Assets, $3,001,884 (M); gifts received, $14,513; expenditures, $112,838; qualifying distributions, $112,838; giving activities include $71,500 for 15 grants (high: $20,000; low: $500).
**Purpose and activities:** Giving support for libraries, health, and human services.
**Fields of interest:** Libraries/library science; medical care, rehabilitation; human services; children & youth, services.
**Types of support:** General/operating support.
**Limitations:** Giving limited to the Ambridge, PA, area. No grants to individuals.
**Application information:** Application form required.
*Initial approach:* Letter
*Copies of proposal:* 1
*Deadline(s):* Nov. 30
*Board meeting date(s):* Dec.
**Officers and Trustees:*** Alexander M. Laughlin,* Pres.; Frederick C. Emerick, Jr.,* Secy.-Treas.; Carl M. Kerchner, David W. Laughlin, John E. Matter, James F. Schell, William J. Simpson, James P. Wetzel, Jr.
**Number of staff:** 1 part-time professional.
**EIN:** 251072140

## 642
## Jerry Lee Foundation

c/o WBEB FM Radio, Inc.
10 Presidential Blvd.
Bala Cynwyd, PA  19004  (610) 667-8400
*Contact:* Gloria Dreon, Admin.
*E-mail:* jerryl@101-FM.com

Established in 1996 in PA.
**Donor(s):** David Kurtz, Gerald Lee.
**Grantmaker type:** Independent foundation
**Financial data** (yr. ended 12/31/99): Assets, $275,932 (M); gifts received, $227,000; expenditures, $224,953; qualifying distributions, $224,850; giving activities include $204,075 for 10 grants (high: $130,000; low: $3,075).
**Purpose and activities:** Giving limited for educational purposes.
**Fields of interest:** Higher education; libraries/library science; education.
**Types of support:** Conferences/seminars; fellowships; matching/challenge support.
**Limitations:** Applications not accepted. No grants to individuals.
**Application information:** Contributes only to pre-selected organizations.
**Directors:** David Kurtz, Gerald Lee.
**EIN:** 232867684

## 643
## Martha and Spencer Love Foundation

c/o First Union National Bank
Broad and Walnut Sts.
Philadelphia, PA  19109-1199

Trust established in 1947 in NC.
**Donor(s):** J. Spencer Love,‡ Martha E. Love Ayers.
**Grantmaker type:** Independent foundation
**Financial data** (yr. ended 12/31/98): Assets, $2,522,296 (M); expenditures, $100,149; qualifying distributions, $80,887; giving activities include $80,876 for 3 grants (high: $50,000; low: $10,000).

**Purpose and activities:** Funding primarily for higher education.
**Fields of interest:** Arts, formal/general education; law school/education; libraries (public).
**Limitations:** Applications not accepted. Giving primarily in NC. No grants to individuals.
**Application information:** Contributes only to pre-selected organizations.
*Board meeting date(s):* As required
**Directors:** Charles E. Love, Cornelia Spencer Love, Julian Love, Lela Porter Love, Martin E. Love.
**Trustee:** First Union National Bank.
**EIN:** 566040789

## 644
## Samuel P. Mandell Foundation

1735 Market St., Ste. 3410
Philadelphia, PA  19103-7501  (215) 979-3410
*Contact:* Seymour Mandell, Tr.

Trust established in 1955 in PA.
**Donor(s):** Samuel P. Mandell,‡ Ida S. Mandell.‡
**Grantmaker type:** Independent foundation
**Financial data** (yr. ended 12/31/99): Assets, $20,354,344 (M); expenditures, $1,407,266; qualifying distributions, $1,298,784; giving activities include $1,233,779 for grants.
**Purpose and activities:** Emphasis on religious funds, hospitals, medical research, health associations and services, higher and other education, the fine arts and other cultural programs, community affairs, and the environment.
**Fields of interest:** Media/communications; visual arts; museums; performing arts; arts/cultural programs; higher education; libraries/library science; education; environment; hospitals (general); health care; health associations; cancer; medical research; cancer research; crime/law enforcement; human services; Jewish federated giving programs; religious federated giving programs; government/public administration; Roman Catholic agencies & churches; minorities; disabled; general charitable giving.
**Types of support:** General/operating support; continuing support; annual campaigns; capital campaigns; building/renovation; program development; professorships; research.
**Limitations:** Giving primarily in PA. No support for private operating foundations. No grants to individuals.
**Application information:** Application form not required.
*Initial approach:* Letter
*Copies of proposal:* 1
*Deadline(s):* None
*Board meeting date(s):* Quarterly
**Trustees:** Harold Cramer, Gerald Mandell, M.D., Judith Mandell, Morton Mandell, M.D., Ronald Mandell, Seymour Mandell.
**Number of staff:** 2 part-time support.
**EIN:** 236274709

## 645
## Helen McBee Irrevocable Trust

c/o First Union National Bank
Broad and Walnut Sts., PA 1308
Philadelphia, PA  19109-1199

Established in 1995.
**Donor(s):** Helen McBee.
**Grantmaker type:** Independent foundation
**Financial data** (yr. ended 12/31/99): Assets, $3,242,866 (M); expenditures, $129,903; qualifying distributions, $99,476; giving activities include $99,388 for 7 grants (high: $29,818; low: $4,970).
**Purpose and activities:** Giving for art and cultural programs, education, and for medical and public services.
**Fields of interest:** Historic preservation/historical societies; university; libraries (public); scholarships/financial aid; medicine/medical care, community health systems; community development, neighborhood development; Christian agencies & churches; cemeteries/burial services.
**Limitations:** Applications not accepted. Giving primarily in Bakersville, NC. No grants to individuals.
**Application information:** Contributes only to pre-selected organizations.
**Trustee:** First Union National Bank.
**EIN:** 566453865

## 646
## Anne McCormick Trust

c/o Dauphin Deposit Bank & Trust Co.
3607 Derry St.
Harrisburg, PA  17111
*Contact:* Larry A. Hartman, Trust Off., Dauphin Deposit Bank & Trust Co.
*Application address:* c/o Allfirst Bank, P.O.Box 2961, Harrisburg, PA 17105

Trust established in PA.
**Donor(s):** Anne McCormick.‡
**Grantmaker type:** Independent foundation
**Financial data** (yr. ended 12/31/99): Assets, $9,096,978 (M); expenditures, $718,086; qualifying distributions, $662,591; giving activities include $662,700 for 32 grants (high: $100,000; low: $2,000).
**Fields of interest:** Arts/cultural programs; higher education; libraries (public); eye diseases; boys & girls clubs; youth development, scouting agencies (general); human services; children & youth, services; federated giving programs; Protestant agencies & churches.
**Limitations:** Giving limited to Dauphin, Cumberland, Perry, and Franklin counties, PA. No grants to individuals.
**Application information:**
*Initial approach:* Proposal
*Deadline(s):* None
**Trustee:** Allfirst Bank.
**EIN:** 236471389

## 647
## McCune Foundation ▼

750 6 PPG Pl.
Pittsburgh, PA  15222  (412) 644-8779
*Contact:* Henry S. Beukema, Exec. Dir.
*FAX:* (412) 644-8059; URL: http://www.mccune.org

Established in 1979 in PA.
**Donor(s):** Charles L. McCune.‡
**Grantmaker type:** Independent foundation
**Financial data** (yr. ended 09/30/00): Assets, $618,651,395 (M); expenditures, $30,640,588;

qualifying distributions, $29,478,528; giving activities include $28,391,003 for 143 grants (high: $2,500,000; low: $1,053; average: $50,000–$500,000) and $350,000 for 1 program-related investment.

**Purpose and activities:** Following the donor's granting interests, the foundation emphasizes two major program areas: independent higher education and human services. The foundation also recognizes the importance of civic, cultural, and community-based organizations that are working to remedy the effects of economic dislocation, while addressing future issues. The foundation is particularly interested in collaborative approaches among groups addressing strategic regional issues and bringing innovative approaches to traditional challenges.

**Fields of interest:** Museums; performing arts; historic preservation/historical societies; arts/cultural programs; higher education; adult education—literacy & basic skills; libraries/library science; health care; medical research; employment; housing/shelter, development; youth development, services; human services; economic development; urban/community development.

**Types of support:** Capital campaigns; building/renovation; equipment; program development; seed money; technical assistance; program-related investments/loans.

**Limitations:** Giving primarily in southwestern PA, with emphasis on the Pittsburgh area. No grants to individuals, or for general operating purposes.

**Publications:** Annual report (including application guidelines), application guidelines.

**Application information:** Applicants are encouraged to wait at least 3 years after receiving a grant before reapplying. Application form required.

*Initial approach:* 2- to 3-page letter of inquiry
*Copies of proposal:* 1
*Deadline(s):* None
*Board meeting date(s):* Mar., June, Sept., and Dec.
*Final notification:* Minimum 90 days

**Officers:** Henry S. Beukema, Exec. Dir.; Martha J. Perry, Assoc. Exec. Dir.

**Distribution Committee:** James M. Edwards, Chair.; Richard D. Edwards, Chair. Emeritus; Michael M. Edwards, John R. McCune VI.

**Trustee:** National City Bank of Pennsylvania.

**Number of staff:** 4 full-time professional; 2 full-time support.

**EIN:** 256210269

**Recent grants for library/information services:**

**647-1** Lebanese American University, NYC, NY, $300,000. Toward construction of Gibran Khalil Gibran Library at Byblos. 1999.

**647-2** Sewickley Public Library, Sewickley, PA, $250,000. Toward building expansion and renovation. 1999.

**647-3** University of Pittsburgh, Center for American Music, Pittsburgh, PA, $500,000. For endowment. 1999.

---

**648**
**Glenn and Ruth Mengle Foundation**
c/o First Commonwealth Trust Co.
P.O. Box 1046
DuBois, PA 15801
*Contact:* D. Edward Chaplin, V.P., First Commonwealth Trust Co.

Trust established in 1956 in PA.
**Donor(s):** Glenn A. Mengle,‡ Ruth E. Mengle Blake.‡
**Grantmaker type:** Independent foundation
**Financial data** (yr. ended 12/31/99): Assets, $13,910,299 (M); expenditures, $819,147; qualifying distributions, $819,147; giving activities include $623,289 for 53 grants (high: $67,500; low: $50).
**Purpose and activities:** Giving primarily to public television, education, hospitals, food services, the Boy Scouts of America, children's and social services, the YMCA, federated giving programs, and Roman Catholic organizations and schools.
**Fields of interest:** Television; secondary school/education; libraries/library science; education; hospitals (general); food services; Boy Scouts; human services; YM/YWCAs & YM/YWHAs; children, services; federated giving programs; Roman Catholic agencies & churches.
**Types of support:** General/operating support; capital campaigns.
**Limitations:** Giving limited to the Brockway, DuBois, and Erie, PA, areas. No grants to individuals.
**Application information:**
*Initial approach:* Letter
*Copies of proposal:* 1
*Deadline(s):* Sept. 1
**Trustees:** DeVere L. Sheesley, First Commonwealth Trust Co.
**EIN:** 256067616

---

**649**
**P. M. Moore Foundation**
1531 2nd St.
P.O. Box 416
Beaver, PA 15009-0416 (724) 774-4997
*Contact:* Dana L. Duff, Treas.

Incorporated in 1958 in PA.
**Donor(s):** Paul M. Moore.‡
**Grantmaker type:** Independent foundation
**Financial data** (yr. ended 12/31/99): Assets, $6,003,378 (M); expenditures, $254,158; qualifying distributions, $249,000; giving activities include $249,000 for 30 grants (high: $25,000; low: $1,000).
**Purpose and activities:** Giving primarily to youth scouting agencies, YMCA's, libraries, and for social services, arts and culture, higher education, federated giving programs, and religion, particularly Presbyterian churches.
**Fields of interest:** Arts/cultural programs; higher education; libraries/library science; health associations; Boy Scouts; Girl Scouts; human services; YM/YWCAs & YM/YWHAs; federated giving programs; Protestant agencies & churches; religion.
**Limitations:** Giving primarily in Beaver County, PA. No grants to individuals.
**Application information:** Application form not required.
*Deadline(s):* None

**Officers:** Ruth Ann Duff, Secy.; Dana L. Duff, Treas.
**Directors:** David M. Duff, Paul W. Duff.
**EIN:** 256066268

---

**650**
**Neisler Foundation**
c/o First Union National Bank
Broad and Walnut Sts.
Philadelphia, PA 19109-1199

Established in 1952 in NC.
**Grantmaker type:** Independent foundation
**Financial data** (yr. ended 12/31/99): Assets, $2,292,138 (M); expenditures, $147,375; qualifying distributions, $111,464; giving activities include $114,215 for 90 grants (high: $10,000; low: $100).
**Purpose and activities:** Giving for health and human services, cultural programs and historical preservation, Christian churches, and education.
**Fields of interest:** History & archaeology; libraries/library science; education; human services; voluntarism promotion; federated giving programs; government/public administration; Protestant agencies & churches.
**Limitations:** Applications not accepted. Giving primarily in the South. No grants to individuals.
**Application information:** Contributes only to pre-selected organizations.
**Trustee:** First Union National Bank.
**EIN:** 566042484

---

**651**
**The Paul H. O'Neill Charitable Foundation**
3 Von Lent Pl.
Pittsburgh, PA 15232-1444

Established in 1991 in PA.
**Grantmaker type:** Independent foundation
**Financial data** (yr. ended 12/31/99): Assets, $1,966,478 (M); gifts received, $634,809; expenditures, $570,932; qualifying distributions, $568,507; giving activities include $570,511 for 27 grants (high: $250,000; low: $200).
**Purpose and activities:** Giving for federated giving programs, health, children's services, the arts, education, and cultural programs.
**Fields of interest:** Historic preservation/historical societies; libraries (special); education; children & youth, services; federated giving programs; public policy, research; public affairs.
**Limitations:** Giving primarily in southwestern PA. No support for specialized health or medical programs, or for sectarian or religious organizations. No grants to individuals; or for general operating support or for professorships.
**Publications:** Application guidelines.
**Application information:**
*Initial approach:* Letter of inquiry
*Deadline(s):* None
*Board meeting date(s):* June and Dec.
**Officer:** Paul H. O'Neill, Chair.
**Director:** Nancy J. O'Neill.
**EIN:** 256378671

## 652

### Horace B. Packer Foundation

P.O. Box 732
Wellsboro, PA  16901   (570) 724-1800
*Contact:* Carl Carson, Pres.

Incorporated in 1951 in PA.
**Donor(s):** Horace B. Packer.‡
**Grantmaker type:** Independent foundation
**Financial data** (yr. ended 12/31/99): Assets,
$5,551,558 (M); expenditures, $316,028;
qualifying distributions, $270,588; giving
activities include $266,416 for 34 grants (high:
$75,000; low: $650).
**Purpose and activities:** To furnish services to
benefit the youth of Tioga County; grants to
educational institutions for scholarships to
students residing in the county.
**Fields of interest:** Libraries/library science;
education; children & youth, services.
**Types of support:** Scholarship funds;
scholarships—to individuals.
**Limitations:** Giving limited to Tioga County, PA.
**Application information:** Application form
required.
  *Initial approach:* Letter
  *Copies of proposal:* 1
  *Deadline(s):* None
  *Board meeting date(s):* May and Oct.
**Officers:** Carl E. Carson, Pres.; Edward H.
Owlett, V.P.; Robert M. Kemp, Secy.; David K.
Esquire, Treas.
**Directors:** R. James Dunham, Rev. Gregory P.
Hinton, Rhonda Litchfield, Debra Schneider.
**Trustees:** Harold Hershberger, Keystone
Financial.
**Number of staff:** 1 part-time support.
**EIN:** 236390932

## 653

### W. I. Patterson Charitable Fund

407 Oliver Bldg.
Pittsburgh, PA  15222   (412) 281-5580
*Contact:* Robert B. Shust, Tr.

Trust established in 1955 in PA.
**Donor(s):** W.I. Patterson.‡
**Grantmaker type:** Independent foundation
**Financial data** (yr. ended 07/31/00): Assets,
$4,989,028 (M); expenditures, $293,056;
qualifying distributions, $259,675; giving
activities include $259,675 for 69 grants (high:
$51,935; low: $1,000; average: $1,000–$7,000).
**Purpose and activities:** Support for higher and
other education, a library, health associations
and hospitals, and welfare funds.
**Fields of interest:** Higher education; libraries
(public); education; hospitals (general); health
associations; human services.
**Types of support:** General/operating support;
continuing support; annual campaigns; capital
campaigns; building/renovation; equipment;
land acquisition; debt reduction; emergency
funds; publication; seed money; research.
**Limitations:** Giving primarily in Allegheny
County, PA. No grants to individuals, or for
endowment funds, scholarships, fellowships, or
matching gifts; no loans.
**Application information:** Application form not
required.
  *Initial approach:* Proposal
  *Copies of proposal:* 1

*Deadline(s):* Submit proposal preferably in
  May or June; deadline June 30
*Board meeting date(s):* At least 6 times a year,
  including Feb., May, July, Sept., and Nov.
**Trustees:** Martin L. Moore, Jr., Robert B. Shust,
Robert B. Wolf.
**Number of staff:** None.
**EIN:** 256028639

## 654

### Sylvia Perkin Perpetual Charitable Trust

c/o James Kressler, First Union National Bank
702 Hamilton Mall
Allentown, PA  18101
*Contact:* Arnold C. Rapoport, Tr.
*Application address:* c/o Arnold C. Rapaport,
P.O. Box 443, Allentown, PA 18105-0443

Established in 1986 in PA.
**Donor(s):** Sylvia Perkin.‡
**Grantmaker type:** Independent foundation
**Financial data** (yr. ended 04/30/99): Assets,
$9,337,469 (M); expenditures, $398,631;
qualifying distributions, $359,431; giving
activities include $350,000 for 38 grants (high:
$50,000; low: $1,000).
**Purpose and activities:** Giving primarily for
Jewish agencies and federated giving programs,
education, human services, and arts and culture.
**Fields of interest:** Arts/cultural programs; higher
education; libraries (public); human services;
Jewish federated giving programs; Jewish
agencies & temples.
**Types of support:** General/operating support;
scholarship funds.
**Limitations:** Giving primarily in Allentown, PA.
**Application information:** Application form not
required.
  *Deadline(s):* None
**Trustees:** James D. Christie, Arnold C. Rapoport,
First Union National Bank.
**EIN:** 236792999

## 655

### S. Wilson & Grace M. Pollock Foundation

c/o Allfirst Bank, Tax Dept.
3607 Derry St., MC 900-02-06
Harrisburg, PA  17111
*Contact:* Heath Allen, Esq.
*Application address:* P.O. Box 11963,
Harrisburg, PA 17108-1963

Established in 1997 in PA.
**Donor(s):** Grace Pollock, S. Wilson Pollock.
**Grantmaker type:** Independent foundation
**Financial data** (yr. ended 04/30/99): Assets,
$90,149,947 (M); expenditures, $603,685;
qualifying distributions, $324,095; giving
activities include $329,000 for 14 grants (high:
$88,000; low: $3,000).
**Purpose and activities:** Funding primarily for
arts and culture, education, and human services.
**Fields of interest:** Libraries (public); education;
animals/wildlife, single organization support;
hospitals (general); cancer; heart & circulatory
diseases; lung diseases; human services;
Protestant agencies & churches.
**Limitations:** No grants to individuals.
**Application information:**
  *Deadline(s):* None
**Director:** Heath Allen.
**Trustee:** Allfirst Bank.

**EIN:** 237889770

## 656

### PPL Corporation Contributions Program

(Formerly PP&L Resources, Inc. Corporate
Giving Program)
2 N. 9th St., A9-4
Allentown, PA  18101   (610) 774-5222
*Contact:* Annette B. Derkacs

**Grantmaker type:** Corporate giving program
**Purpose and activities:** PPL makes charitable
contributions to nonprofit organizations
involved with arts and culture, K-12 education,
youth development, and to libraries and
hospitals. Support is given primarily in areas of
company operations.
**Fields of interest:** Arts/cultural programs;
elementary/secondary education;
libraries/library science; medical care, in-patient
care; youth development.
**Types of support:** General/operating support;
scholarship funds; employee volunteer services;
sponsorships; employee matching gifts;
scholarships—to individuals.
**Limitations:** Giving primarily in areas of
company operations.
**Application information:** The Delivery Services
and Economic Development Department
handles giving. Application form not required.
  *Initial approach:* Proposal to nearest company
    facility
  *Copies of proposal:* 1
  *Final notification:* Following review
**Number of staff:** None.

## 657

### J. Bowman Proper Charitable Trust

c/o National City Bank of Pennsylvania
127 W. Spring St.
Titusville, PA  16354
*Application address:* c/o Stephen J. Kosak, P.O.
Box 374, Oil City, PA 16301, tel.: (814)
677-5085

Established in 1991 in PA.
**Donor(s):** J. Bowman Proper.‡
**Grantmaker type:** Independent foundation
**Financial data** (yr. ended 09/30/99): Assets,
$2,658,123 (M); expenditures, $71,213;
qualifying distributions, $56,818; giving
activities include $43,803 for 9 grants (high:
$8,437; low: $600).
**Purpose and activities:** Giving for youth
programs, Christian organizations, and
education.
**Fields of interest:** Libraries/library science;
education; children & youth, services; Christian
agencies & churches.
**Types of support:** Scholarship funds.
**Limitations:** Giving for scholarships limited to
West Forest County, PA; giving for organizations
limited to the Tionesta, PA, area.
**Application information:**
  *Initial approach:* Letter for grants; formal
    application for scholarships
  *Deadline(s):* Apr. 30 for scholarships; none for
    grants
**Trustee:** National City Bank of Pennsylvania.
**EIN:** 251670828

## 658
### Edith L. Reynolds Trust
c/o Mellon Bank, N.A.
P.O. Box 7236
Philadelphia, PA 19101-7236

Established in 1965 in PA.
**Grantmaker type:** Independent foundation
**Financial data** (yr. ended 12/31/99): Assets, $538,096 (M); expenditures, $58,718; qualifying distributions, $52,376; giving activities include $51,744 for 17 grants (high: $7,500; low: $500).
**Purpose and activities:** Giving for the arts, education, the environment, hospitals, and family services.
**Fields of interest:** Performing arts; history & archaeology; historic preservation/historical societies; libraries (public); environment; hospitals (general); family services; federated giving programs.
**Types of support:** General/operating support.
**Limitations:** Applications not accepted. Giving primarily in Wilkes-Barre, PA. No grants to individuals.
**Application information:** Generally contributes to pre-selected organizations.
**Selection Committee:** Dorrence R. Belin, Edward Darling, Mrs. Harry B. Schooley, Jr.
**Trustee:** Mellon Bank, N.A.
**EIN:** 236409220

## 659
### The Ross Family Foundation
5 Overlook Rd.
Clarks Green, PA 18411 (717) 587-1365
*Contact:* Adrian E. Ross, Pres.

Established in 1954 in PA.
**Donor(s):** Adrian E. Ross, Daniel R. Ross, James A. Ross,‡ James A. Ross.
**Grantmaker type:** Independent foundation
**Financial data** (yr. ended 12/31/99): Assets, $3,499,219 (M); gifts received, $39,475; expenditures, $149,974; qualifying distributions, $140,030; giving activities include $135,505 for 87 grants (high: $29,500; low: $50).
**Fields of interest:** Museums; music; higher education; libraries/library science; education; natural resource conservation & protection; children & youth, services; Christian agencies & churches.
**Types of support:** Annual campaigns; capital campaigns; endowments.
**Limitations:** Giving primarily in the Scranton, PA, area.
**Application information:**
 *Initial approach:* Letter
 *Deadline(s):* None
**Officers and Trustees:*** Adrian E. Ross,* Pres.; James A. Ross,* V.P.; Daniel R. Ross,* Secy.-Treas.
**Number of staff:** None.
**EIN:** 246017499

## 660
### S & T Bancorp Charitable Foundation
c/o S & T Bank, Trust Dept.
P.O. Box 220
Indiana, PA 15701
*Contact:* James C. Miller, Pres.
*Application address:* P.O. Box 190, Indiana, PA 15701, tel: (724) 465-1443

Established in 1993 in PA.
**Donor(s):** S & T Bancorp, Inc., S & T Bank.
**Grantmaker type:** Company-sponsored foundation
**Financial data** (yr. ended 12/31/99): Assets, $813,246 (M); gifts received, $64,800; expenditures, $305,805; qualifying distributions, $299,327; giving activities include $261,800 for 93 grants (high: $25,000; low: $500).
**Purpose and activities:** Giving primarily for health and human services, support also for education.
**Fields of interest:** Performing arts; historic preservation/historical societies; arts, services; higher education; university; libraries (public); cancer; Big Brothers/Big Sisters; Boy Scouts; Girl Scouts; YM/YWCAs & YM/YWHAs; foundations (community).
**Types of support:** General/operating support; capital campaigns; building/renovation.
**Limitations:** Giving limited to areas of company operations in PA. No grants to individuals.
**Application information:**
 *Initial approach:* Letter
 *Deadline(s):* None
**Officers:** James C. Miller, Pres.; Edward C. Hauck, V.P.; H. William Klumpp, Treas.
**Trustee:** S & T Bank.
**EIN:** 251716950

## 661
### Schuylkill Area Community Foundation
(Formerly Ashland Trusts)
101 N. Centre St., 2nd Fl., Ste. A
Pottsville, PA 17901 (570) 624-1580
*Contact:* Harry Strouse, Secy.
*FAX:* (570) 624-1581

Established in 1967 in PA.
**Grantmaker type:** Community foundation
**Financial data** (yr. ended 04/30/98): Assets, $3,372,888 (M); gifts received, $216,289; expenditures, $244,995; giving activities include $143,831 for grants and $79,479 for grants to individuals.
**Purpose and activities:** Scholarships principally for residents of the borough of Ashland and graduates of North Schuylkill, Cardinal Brennan, and Tri-Veller high schools. Support also for libraries and projects benefiting the general public, including improving public parks, sponsoring a recreation program for youth, and supporting volunteer fire companies. Also support of numerous human service organizations.
**Fields of interest:** Libraries/library science; education; recreation; human services; children & youth, services; community development; government/public administration.
**Types of support:** General/operating support; scholarships—to individuals.
**Limitations:** Applications not accepted. Giving primarily in the Schuylkill County, PA, area; some programs extend to neighboring counties.

**Application information:** Scholarships paid to educational institutions for named individuals.
 *Board meeting date(s):* Feb., June, Sept., and Nov.
**Officer and Board Member:*** Harry Strouse,* Secy.
**Number of staff:** None.
**EIN:** 236422789

## 662
### The Scranton Area Foundation, Inc.
Bank Towers, Ste. 608
321 Spruce St.
Scranton, PA 18503-1409 (570) 347-6203
*Contact:* Jeanne A. Bovard, Exec. Dir.
*FAX:* (717) 347-7587

Established in 1954 in PA by resolution and declaration of trust; reorganized in 1998.
**Grantmaker type:** Community foundation
**Financial data** (yr. ended 12/31/99): Assets, $19,834,064 (M); gifts received, $394,996; expenditures, $728,569; giving activities include $414,884 for 78 grants (high: $75,000; low: $200; average: $200–$75,000).
**Purpose and activities:** Encourages and helps to build community endowment through grants for new projects and services to address unmet needs; provides a variety of donor services.
**Fields of interest:** Historic preservation/historical societies; arts/cultural programs; child development, education; vocational education; higher education; libraries/library science; education; natural resource conservation & protection; health care; mental health/crisis services; health associations; youth development, services; human services; children & youth, services; child development, services; human rights (international); community development; voluntarism promotion; leadership development; public affairs; religion.
**Types of support:** Continuing support; endowments; program development; conferences/seminars; publication; seed money; scholarship funds; research; consulting services; matching/challenge support.
**Limitations:** Giving limited to the Scranton and Lackawanna County, PA, area. No grants for building funds, annual campaigns, deficit financing, or emergency funds; generally no support for operating budgets; no loans.
**Publications:** Annual report, informational brochure (including application guidelines), occasional report, newsletter, grants list, application guidelines.
**Application information:** Application form required.
 *Initial approach:* Letter or telephone
 *Copies of proposal:* 1
 *Deadline(s):* None
 *Board meeting date(s):* Jan., Apr., July, Oct. and Dec.
 *Final notification:* Jan., Apr., July, Oct. and Dec.
**Officer:** Jeanne A. Bovard, Exec. Dir.
**Governors:** Richard C. Marquardt, Sr., Chair.; Dorrance R. Belin, Vice-Chair.; James F. Bell III, Richard S. Bishop, Harmar D. Brereton, M.D., Austin J. Burke, Mary Ellen Coleman, Eugene F. Cosgrove, Sr. Jean Coughlin, I.H.M., Carlene Gallo, Kathleen Graff, Kelly Kane, Robert N. Lettieri, Thomas R. Nealon, Carlon E. Preate,

James W. Reid, Leitha Reinheimer, Gerald W. Seibert.
**Investment Managers:** PNC Bank, N.A., Penn Security.
**Number of staff:** 1 full-time professional; 3 full-time support.
**EIN:** 232890364

## 663
## Arlene H. Smith Charitable Foundation
c/o MacDonald, Illig, Jones & Britton
100 State St., Ste. 700
Erie, PA 16507-1459
*Contact:* Timothy M. Hunter, Treas.
*Application address:* c/o McInnes Steel Co., 441 E. Main St., Corry, PA 16407-0901

Established in 1982 in PA.
**Donor(s):** Arlene H. Smith.‡
**Grantmaker type:** Independent foundation
**Financial data** (yr. ended 12/31/99): Assets, $5,061,306 (M); expenditures, $288,046; qualifying distributions, $251,498; giving activities include $255,971 for 15 grants (high: $100,000; low: $2,500).
**Purpose and activities:** Giving primarily for arts, education, and children's and human services.
**Fields of interest:** Education, association; higher education; libraries (public); hospitals (general); recreation; human services; economically disadvantaged.
**Limitations:** Giving limited to the Corry, PA, area. No grants to individuals.
**Application information:** Application form required.
  *Copies of proposal:* 2
  *Deadline(s):* None
**Officers and Directors:*** Stephen J. Mahoney,* Pres.; Frank K. Smith,* V.P.; James D. Cullen,* Secy.; Timothy M. Hunter, Treas.; John E. Britton.
**EIN:** 251515142

## 664
## Marguerite Carl Smith Foundation
c/o First Union National Bank
P.O. Box 7558 FC 1-3-9-20
Philadelphia, PA 19101-7558

Established in 1989 in PA.
**Donor(s):** Marguerite Carl Smith.
**Grantmaker type:** Independent foundation
**Financial data** (yr. ended 05/31/99): Assets, $3,077,673 (M); expenditures, $114,569; qualifying distributions, $95,996; giving activities include $14,400 for 4 grants (high: $6,400; low: $1,000) and $74,478 for 30 grants to individuals (high: $2,500; low: $1,978).
**Purpose and activities:** Giving primarily in the form of scholarships.
**Fields of interest:** Higher education; libraries/library science; human services; Christian agencies & churches.
**Types of support:** Scholarships—to individuals.
**Limitations:** Giving primarily in Jersey Shore, PA.
**Application information:**
  *Initial approach:* Letter
  *Deadline(s):* None
**Trustees:** Ralph Kuhns, Mrs. Ralph Kuhns, Shirley Loud, Lee Smith, Mary Tuefel.
**EIN:** 232564406

## 665
## Ethel Sergeant Clark Smith Memorial Fund
c/o First Union National Bank
123 S. Broad St., PA 1279
Philadelphia, PA 19109   (215) 985-3920
*Contact:* Camie Morrison, V.P., First Union National Bank
*FAX:* (215) 985-3922

Trust established in 1977 in PA.
**Donor(s):** Ethel Sergeant Clark Smith.‡
**Grantmaker type:** Independent foundation
**Financial data** (yr. ended 05/31/98): Assets, $18,345,180 (M); expenditures, $971,753; qualifying distributions, $857,613; giving activities include $717,330 for grants (average: $5,000–$25,000).
**Purpose and activities:** Giving for health associations and hospitals, education, including early childhood and secondary schools, child welfare and development, social service organizations, libraries, fine and performing arts groups and culture, museums and historical buildings, recreation, music and drama facilities, and programs for women, the handicapped and exceptional persons, and community reinvestment.
**Fields of interest:** Visual arts; museums; performing arts; theater; music; historic preservation/historical societies; arts/cultural programs; early childhood education; child development, education; secondary school/education; higher education; libraries/library science; education; hospitals (general); medical care, rehabilitation; substance abuse, services; health associations; recreation; human services; children & youth, services; child development, services; women, centers & services; community development; disabled; women.
**Types of support:** General/operating support; capital campaigns; building/renovation; equipment; land acquisition; emergency funds; program development; seed money; research; exchange programs; matching/challenge support.
**Limitations:** Giving limited to Delaware County, PA, or organizations benefiting county residents. No support for single-disease organizations, salaries, or consultants. No grants to individuals, or for deficit financing, scholarships, or fellowships; no gifts longer than three years consecutively; no loans.
**Publications:** Application guidelines, financial statement, informational brochure (including application guidelines), program policy statement.
**Application information:** Personal visits prior to proposal submission discouraged; accepts Delaware Valley Grantmakers Common Grant Application and Common Report Form. Application form required.
  *Initial approach:* Letter
  *Copies of proposal:* 1
  *Deadline(s):* Mar. 1 and Sept. 1
  *Board meeting date(s):* May and Nov.
  *Final notification:* 1 month after trustee meets with advisory committee
**Trustee:** First Union National Bank.
**Number of staff:** None.
**EIN:** 236648857

## 666
## Smiy Family Foundation Trust
626 Iroquois St.
Irwin, PA 15642   (724) 238-3341
*Contact:* Paul Smiy, Tr.
*Application address:* c/o Patrick K. Wallace, PNC Bank, 204 E. Main St., Ligoner, Pa 15658, tel.: (412) 238-3340

Established in 1996 in PA.
**Grantmaker type:** Independent foundation
**Financial data** (yr. ended 06/30/99): Assets, $2,466,050 (M); expenditures, $169,534; qualifying distributions, $129,074; giving activities include $115,000 for 40 grants (high: $15,000; low: $500) and $15,000 for 3 grants to individuals of $5,000 each.
**Purpose and activities:** Giving to provide assistance to the elderly and to other individuals who are in financial need and cannot afford their own medical care and equipment or need help paying for basic supplies and services.
**Fields of interest:** Music, ensembles & groups; libraries (public); education; medicine/medical care, research; Roman Catholic agencies & churches.
**Limitations:** Giving primarily in PA.
**Application information:**
  *Initial approach:* Letter
  *Deadline(s):* None
**Trustee:** Paul Smiy.
**EIN:** 232905105

## 667
## Snee-Reinhardt Charitable Foundation
2101 1 Mellon Bank Ctr.
500 Grant St.
Pittsburgh, PA 15219   (412) 471-2944
*Contact:* Joan E. Szymanski, Fdn. Mgr.

Established in 1987 in PA.
**Donor(s):** Katherine E. Snee.
**Grantmaker type:** Independent foundation
**Financial data** (yr. ended 12/31/97): Assets, $7,919,467 (M); expenditures, $457,246; qualifying distributions, $403,705; giving activities include $362,958 for grants (average: $500–$25,000).
**Fields of interest:** Arts/cultural programs; libraries/library science; education; environment; health care; substance abuse, services; health associations; cancer; children & youth, services; aging, centers & services; community development; aging.
**Types of support:** Building/renovation; equipment; program development.
**Limitations:** Giving primarily in northern MD, PA (especially the southwestern region) and northeast WV. No support for sectarian or religious organizations or organizations that promote abortion or euthanasia. No grants to individuals, or for capital improvement, endowment funds, or general operating expenses.
**Publications:** Application guidelines, informational brochure (including application guidelines), grants list, annual report.
**Application information:** Application form required.
  *Initial approach:* Telephone for guidelines
  *Copies of proposal:* 1
  *Deadline(s):* Varies
  *Board meeting date(s):* May, Sept., and Nov.

*Final notification:* 2 weeks after board meeting
**Directors:** Paul A. Heasley, Chair.; Virginia M. Davis, Christina R. Heasley, Karen L. Heasley, Timothy N. Heasley, James W. Ummer, Richard T. Vail.
**Trustee:** PNC Bank, N.A.
**Number of staff:** 2 full-time support.
**EIN:** 256292908

## 668
### Harrison & Margaret Snyder Charitable Trust
c/o Mid-State Bank & Trust Co., Trust Dept.
P.O. Box 2007
Altoona, PA 16603-2007
*Contact:* Marie Boyle, Asst. V.P. and Trust Off.

Established in 1994 in PA.
**Donor(s):** Margaret Snyder,‡ Harrison Snyder.‡
**Grantmaker type:** Independent foundation
**Financial data** (yr. ended 12/31/98): Assets, $1,609,011 (M); expenditures, $97,362; qualifying distributions, $72,646; giving activities include $72,646 for 25 grants (high: $7,500; low: $1,000).
**Purpose and activities:** Giving primarily for education and human services.
**Fields of interest:** Libraries/library science; human services.
**Limitations:** Giving limited to Blair County, PA.
**Application information:**
  *Initial approach:* Proposal
  *Copies of proposal:* 1
  *Deadline(s):* Nov. 1
  *Board meeting date(s):* Dec.
**Trustees:** William R. Collins, Daniel Ratchford, Mid-State Bank & Trust Co.
**EIN:** 256436588

## 669
### Stackpole-Hall Foundation
44 S. Saint Marys St.
St. Marys, PA 15857 (814) 834-1845
*Contact:* William C. Conrad, Exec. Secy.
*FAX:* (814) 834-1869; E-mail: s-hf@ncentral.com

Trust established in 1951 in PA.
**Donor(s):** Lyle G. Hall, Sr.,‡ J. Hall Stackpole,‡ Harrison C. Stackpole, Lyle G. Hall, Jr., Adelaide Stackpole.
**Grantmaker type:** Independent foundation
**Financial data** (yr. ended 12/31/98): Assets, $27,330,693 (M); expenditures, $1,418,775; qualifying distributions, $1,095,827; giving activities include $1,095,827 for 86 grants (high: $97,223; low: $200).
**Purpose and activities:** Support for higher and secondary education, and literacy and vocational projects; Christian agencies and churches; social services, including youth and child welfare agencies; the arts and cultural programs; health services, including mental health and drug abuse issues; and community development, including civic affairs and leadership development, conservation concerns, rural development, and voluntarism.
**Fields of interest:** Visual arts; performing arts; arts/cultural programs; education, fund raising; secondary school/education; vocational education; adult/continuing education; higher education; adult education—literacy & basic skills; libraries/library science; reading;

education; natural resource conservation & protection; hospitals (general); nursing care; health care; substance abuse, services; mental health/crisis services; alcoholism; recreation; youth development, services; human services; children & youth, services; hospices; rural development; community development; voluntarism promotion; government/public administration; leadership development; Christian agencies & churches; disabled.
**Types of support:** Annual campaigns; capital campaigns; building/renovation; equipment; program development; seed money; matching/challenge support.
**Limitations:** Giving primarily in Elk County, PA. No grants to individuals, or for scholarships or fellowships; generally, no grants for operating budgets or endowment funds; no loans.
**Publications:** Annual report (including application guidelines), newsletter, informational brochure.
**Application information:** Application form not required.
  *Initial approach:* Letter
  *Copies of proposal:* 1
  *Deadline(s):* None
  *Board meeting date(s):* Quarterly
**Trustees:** Lyle G. Hall, Jr., Chair.; Douglas R. Dobson, Vice-Chair.; Helen Hall Drew, Megan Hall, J.M. Hamlin Johnson, Alexander Sheble-Hall, R. Dauer Stackpole, Sara-Jane Stackpole, T. Scott Stackpole.
**Board Members:** Heather Conrad, Jeff Drew, Laurey Nixon, Charlotte Perkins, Alex Stackpole.
**Number of staff:** 1 full-time professional; 2 part-time support.
**EIN:** 256006650

## 670
### Alexander Stewart, M.D. Foundation
c/o Mellon Bank, N.A.
P.O. Box 7236 AIM 193-0224
Philadelphia, PA 19101-7236 (215) 553-2557
*Contact:* Pat Kling, Trust Off., Mellon Bank, N.A.

Established in 1981 in PA.
**Grantmaker type:** Independent foundation
**Financial data** (yr. ended 06/30/99): Assets, $8,599,365 (M); expenditures, $353,499; qualifying distributions, $300,250; giving activities include $281,560 for 43 grants (high: $20,000; low: $1,000).
**Purpose and activities:** Giving primarily for human services and mental health. Support also for historical societies and libraries.
**Fields of interest:** Historic preservation/historical societies; libraries/library science; natural resource conservation & protection; mental health/crisis services; youth development, scouting agencies (general); human services; Salvation Army; YM/YWCAs & YM/YWHAs.
**Types of support:** General/operating support.
**Limitations:** Giving limited to Shippensburg, PA, and vicinity, including Cumberland, Franklin, Fulton, and Perry counties. No grants to individuals.
**Application information:**
  *Initial approach:* Proposal
  *Deadline(s):* Apr. 1
**Trustee:** Mellon Bank, N.A.
**EIN:** 236732616

## 671
### Teleflex Foundation
630 W. Germantown Pike, Ste. 461
Plymouth Meeting, PA 19462 (610) 834-6364
*Contact:* Thelma A. Fretz, V.P.

Established in 1980 in PA.
**Donor(s):** Teleflex Incorporated.
**Grantmaker type:** Company-sponsored foundation
**Financial data** (yr. ended 12/31/99): Assets, $2,510 (M); gifts received, $250,000; expenditures, $253,311; qualifying distributions, $255,311; giving activities include $234,750 for grants (high: $25,000; low: $2,000; average: $1,000–$5,000).
**Purpose and activities:** Support for higher, elementary, and vocational education and literacy programs; hospitals and health, medical research, rehabilitation programs for alcohol and drug abuse, science, and technology; community funds and social services, including women and child welfare, family planning, and the handicapped; public affairs and policies; culture, especially fine and performing arts; environmental issues; and urban and civic affairs.
**Fields of interest:** Visual arts; museums; performing arts; dance; theater; music; historic preservation/historical societies; arts/cultural programs; elementary school/education; vocational education; higher education; business school/education; engineering school/education; adult education—literacy & basic skills; libraries/library science; reading; education; natural resource conservation & protection; environment; wildlife preservation & protection; hospitals (general); family planning; medical care, rehabilitation; health care; substance abuse, services; mental health/crisis services; health associations; cancer; alcoholism; crime/law enforcement; human services; children & youth, services; family services; hospices; aging, centers & services; women, centers & services; minorities/immigrants, centers & services; human rights (international); urban/community development; community development; federated giving programs; engineering & technology; engineering; science; public policy, research; government/public administration; public affairs; minorities; disabled; aging; women; economically disadvantaged.
**Types of support:** Program development; seed money; curriculum development; technical assistance; employee matching gifts.
**Limitations:** No grants to individuals.
**Publications:** Application guidelines.
**Application information:** Application form required.
  *Initial approach:* Preliminary phone call recommended; proposal
  *Copies of proposal:* 1
  *Deadline(s):* Sept. 30 and Mar. 24
  *Board meeting date(s):* Fall and spring
**Officers:** Lennox K. Black, Pres.; Thelma A. Fretz, V.P.; John H. Remer, Treas.
**Directors:** Christopher Black, Thomas Byrne, M.C. Chisholm, Janine Dusossoit, Diane Fukuda, William Haussmann, Stephen Holland, Anita Piacentino, Palmer Retzlaff.
**Number of staff:** 1 part-time professional.
**EIN:** 232104782

**672**

## Trumbower Hospital Foundation

124 Belvidere St.
Nazareth, PA 18064-2105
*Application address:* P.O. Box 57, Nazareth, PA
18064, tel.: (610) 759-1420

Established in 1977.
**Grantmaker type:** Operating foundation
**Financial data** (yr. ended 10/31/99): Assets,
$1,533,146 (M); expenditures, $81,930;
qualifying distributions, $71,916; giving
activities include $64,505 for 18 grants (high:
$12,495; low: $760).
**Purpose and activities:** Support only for health
services and education benefiting the residents
of the Nazareth, PA, area.
**Fields of interest:** Libraries/library science;
hospitals (general); YM/YWCAs & YM/YWHAs;
federated giving programs.
**Limitations:** Giving primarily in the Nazareth,
PA, area. No grants to individuals.
**Application information:**
*Initial approach:* Letter
*Copies of proposal:* 7
*Deadline(s):* Feb. 1
*Final notification:* June 30
**Officers:** Richard W. Kraemer, Pres.; Helen
Ziegler, Secy.; Rosemarie Potope, Treas.
**EIN:** 237377310

**673**

## Unisys Corporate Giving Program

P.O. Box 500 M.S. A2-13
Blue Bell, PA 19424-0001 (215) 986-2867
*Contact:* David Curry, V.P., Corp. Public Affairs

**Grantmaker type:** Corporate giving program
**Purpose and activities:** As a good corporate
citizen, Unisys is working to advance social
progress in the communities where they do
business across the globe. The company focuses
its philanthropic resources on promoting literacy
and excellence in science, math, and
technology. Unisys supports the United Way
and other selected community causes. Key
activities include a multi-year sponsorship of the
Philadelphia Liberty Medal.
**Fields of interest:** Museums (science &
technology); libraries/library science;
arts/cultural programs; education; human
services; voluntarism promotion; federated
giving programs; engineering & technology;
computer science; science.
**Types of support:** Donated products.
**Limitations:** No support for religious, fraternal,
or labor organizations or United Way recipients.
No grants to individuals.
**Publications:** Corporate report.

**674**

## USX Foundation, Inc. ▼

600 Grant St., Rm. 685
Pittsburgh, PA 15219-4776 (412) 433-5237
*Contact:* James L. Hamilton III, Genl. Mgr.
*FAX:* (412) 433-6847; URL: http://
www.usx.aa.psiweb.com/USXFAR99.pdf

Incorporated in 1953 in DE.
**Donor(s):** USX Corp., and certain subsidiaries.
**Grantmaker type:** Company-sponsored
foundation

**Financial data** (yr. ended 11/30/99): Assets,
$7,401,244 (M); gifts received, $3,513,840;
expenditures, $6,470,699; qualifying
distributions, $6,373,725; giving activities
include $5,117,626 for 498 grants (high:
$200,000; low: $50; average: $1,000–$25,000)
and $1,075,850 for 1,798 employee matching
gifts.
**Purpose and activities:** Giving for capital and
operating grants primarily for higher education,
including matching gifts and support of
educational associations; health and human
services, including the United Way; arts and
culture; and scientific affairs.
**Fields of interest:** Museums; performing arts;
historic preservation/historical societies;
arts/cultural programs; education, association;
higher education; business school/education;
law school/education; engineering
school/education; libraries (public); natural
resource conservation & protection; energy;
environment; health care; substance abuse,
services; mental health/crisis services;
delinquency prevention/services;
safety/disasters; human services; children &
youth, services; federated giving programs;
engineering & technology; computer science;
engineering; science; economics; public policy,
research; public affairs; minorities; Native
Americans; disabled; economically
disadvantaged.
**Types of support:** General/operating support;
capital campaigns; building/renovation;
equipment; scholarship funds; employee
matching gifts; employee-related scholarships.
**Limitations:** Giving primarily in areas of
company operations in the U.S., including AK,
AL, CO, IL, IN, LA, MI, MN, OH, OK, western
PA, and TX. No support for religious
organizations for religious purposes, economic
development projects, or preschool to grade 12
education, hospitals or nursing homes. No
grants to individuals (except for
employee-related scholarships), or for
conferences, seminars, symposia, travel,
exhibits, special or fundraising events,
fellowships, publication of papers, books or
magazines, production of films, videotapes, or
other audio-visual materials, or operating
support of United Way agencies; no loans.
**Publications:** Annual report (including
application guidelines), application guidelines.
**Application information:** Grantmakers of
Western PA. Common Grant Application
Format. Application form not required.
*Copies of proposal:* 1
*Deadline(s):* Jan. 15 for public, cultural, and
scientific affairs; Apr. 15 for education; July.
15 for health and human services
*Board meeting date(s):* Apr., July, and Oct.
*Final notification:* Following board meetings
**Officers and Trustees:*** Thomas J. Usher,*
Chair.; Marilyn A. Harris,* Pres.; Edward F.
Guna, V.P. and Treas.; Larry G. Schultz, V.P. and
Compt.; Gary A. Glynn, V.P., Investments; Dan
D. Sandman,* Secy. and Genl. Counsel; Robert
M. Hernandez,* C.F.O.; James L. Hamilton III,
Genl. Mgr.; Randall Wynkoop, Tax Counsel;
Jerry Howard, John T. Mills, Paul J. Wilhelm.
**Number of staff:** 1 full-time professional; 1
part-time professional; 2 full-time support.
**EIN:** 136093185
**Recent grants for library/information services:**

**674-1** Braddock Carnegie Library and
Community Center, Braddock, PA, $20,000.
For capital support. 1998.

**675**

## Peggy & Ellis Wachs Family Foundation

612 Zollinger Way
Merion Station, PA 19066

Established in 1985 in PA.
**Donor(s):** Ellis G. Wachs
**Grantmaker type:** Independent foundation
**Financial data** (yr. ended 12/31/99): Assets,
$2,326,082 (M); expenditures, $93,414;
qualifying distributions, $90,252; giving
activities include $88,484 for 53 grants (high:
$25,300; low: $15).
**Purpose and activities:** Giving primarily for
education, Jewish agencies and temples and a
public library.
**Fields of interest:** Higher education; libraries
(public); medical research; federated giving
programs; Jewish agencies & temples.
**Types of support:** Annual campaigns.
**Limitations:** Applications not accepted. Giving
primarily in Philadelphia, PA. No grants to
individuals.
**Application information:** Contributes only to
pre-selected organizations.
**Trustees:** Ellis G. Wachs, Peggy B. Wachs.
**EIN:** 236802696

**676**

## Walden Trust

c/o Henry P. Hoffstot, Jr., et al.
P.O. Box 2009
Pittsburgh, PA 15230

**Grantmaker type:** Independent foundation
**Financial data** (yr. ended 12/31/98): Assets,
$1,187,268 (M); expenditures, $51,268;
qualifying distributions, $48,216; giving
activities include $46,500 for 22 grants (high:
$7,500; low: $500).
**Fields of interest:** Historical activities;
libraries/library science.
**Limitations:** Applications not accepted. Giving
on a national basis. No grants to individuals.
**Application information:** Contributes only to
pre-selected organizations.
**Trustees:** Thayer H. Drew, Robert R. Garvey, Jr.,
Henry P. Hoffstot, Jr., Henry P. Hoffstot III, Lora
H. Jenkins, Lorna K. Tahtinen, Arthur P. Ziegler,
Jr.
**EIN:** 256027635

**677**

## Whalley Charitable Trust

1210 Graham Ave.
Windber, PA 15963 (814) 467-4000
*Contact:* David Klementik, Tr.

Trust established in 1961 in PA.
**Donor(s):** John J. Whalley, John Whalley, Jr.,
Mary Whalley.
**Grantmaker type:** Independent foundation
**Financial data** (yr. ended 12/31/99): Assets,
$6,023,956 (M); expenditures, $685,339;
qualifying distributions, $643,807; giving

activities include $635,012 for 44 grants (high: $300,000; low: $100).

**Purpose and activities:** Giving primarily for education and health care.

**Fields of interest:** Education; libraries (public); hospitals (general); disasters, fire prevention/control; recreation; human services; community development; Protestant agencies & churches.

**Limitations:** Giving primarily in PA, with emphasis on Windber and Johnstown.

**Application information:** Application form not required.

   *Initial approach:* Letter
   *Deadline(s):* None
**Trustees:** David Klementik, G. Lesko.
**EIN:** 237128436

## 678
**Wolf-Kuhn Foundation**
129 Summit Dr.
Hollidaysburg, PA 16648 (814) 696-2721
*Contact:* Gerald P. Wolf, Chair.
*FAX:* (814) 696-7510

Established in 1957.

**Donor(s):** George A. Wolf,‡ Herbert T. Wolf, Sr.,‡ Margery Wolf-Kuhn.‡

**Grantmaker type:** Independent foundation

**Financial data** (yr. ended 09/30/98): Assets, $1,343,615 (M); expenditures, $78,122; qualifying distributions, $73,350; giving activities include $73,350 for 18 grants (high: $12,500; low: $100).

**Purpose and activities:** Giving for arts and culture, and education.

**Fields of interest:** Museums; performing arts; higher education; libraries/library science; Christian agencies & churches.

**Types of support:** General/operating support; continuing support; annual campaigns; seed money; curriculum development; scholarship funds.

**Limitations:** Giving primarily in central PA. No grants to individuals.

**Publications:** Occasional report.

**Application information:** Application form required.

   *Initial approach:* Letter
   *Copies of proposal:* 1
   *Board meeting date(s):* Mar., June, Sept., and Dec.
**Officer and Trustees:*** Gerald P. Wolf,* Chair.; Anne S. Borland, Michael Master, Marie Riley, Steven Sloan, Herbert T. Wolf II.
**Number of staff:** 1 part-time professional.
**EIN:** 256064237

# PUERTO RICO

## 679
**The Luis A. Ferre Foundation, Inc.**
P.O. Box 9066590
San Juan, PR 00906-6590 (787) 641-8070
*Contact:* Orlando Vazquez, Treas.

Incorporated in 1966 in PR.
**Donor(s):** Luis A. Ferre.

**Grantmaker type:** Public charity

**Financial data** (yr. ended 12/31/99): Gifts received, $2,619,229; expenditures, $3,755,016.

**Purpose and activities:** The foundation operates, maintains, and conserves the art at the Ponce Museum of Art.

**Fields of interest:** Museums; libraries/library science.

**Limitations:** Applications not accepted. Giving primarily in PR.

**Publications:** Financial statement.

**Application information:** Contributes only to pre-selected organizations; unsolicited requests for funds not considered or acknowledged.

   *Board meeting date(s):* Jan. and July
**Officers:** Luis A. Ferre, Pres.; Antonio Luis Ferre, V.P.; Rosario J. Ferre, V.P.; Etienne Totti, Secy.; Orlando Vazquez, Treas.; Carmen T. Ruiz de Fischler, Exec. Dir.
**EIN:** 660235625

# RHODE ISLAND

## 680
**Ashaway Charitable Trust**
c/o The Washington Trust Co.
23 Broad St.
Westerly, RI 02891
*Contact:* Pamela Crandall, Mgr.
*Application address:* c/o Ashaway Line & Twine Mfg. Co., Ashaway, RI 02804

Established in 1950 in RI.

**Grantmaker type:** Operating foundation

**Financial data** (yr. ended 12/31/98): Assets, $1,228,493 (M); expenditures, $69,851; qualifying distributions, $55,740; giving activities include $54,467 for 52 grants (high: $7,000; low: $100).

**Fields of interest:** Libraries/library science; health associations; community development; Protestant agencies & churches; general charitable giving.

**Limitations:** Giving primarily in CT and RI.

**Application information:**
   *Initial approach:* Letter
   *Deadline(s):* None
**Officer:** Pamela Crandall, Mgr.
**Trustee:** The Washington Trust Co.
**EIN:** 056003255

## 681
**The Champlin Foundations ▼**
300 Centerville Rd, Ste. 300S
Warwick, RI 02886-0203 (401) 736-0370
*Contact:* David A. King, Exec. Dir.
*FAX:* (401) 736-7248; E-mail: champlinfdns@worldnet.att.net; URL: http://fdncenter.org/grantmaker/champlin

Trusts established in 1932, 1947, and 1975 in DE.

**Donor(s):** George S. Champlin,‡ Florence C. Hamilton,‡ Hope C. Neaves.‡

**Grantmaker type:** Independent foundation

**Financial data** (yr. ended 12/31/99): Assets, $502,288,387 (M); expenditures, $25,263,631; qualifying distributions, $22,884,344; giving

activities include $22,798,134 for 310 grants (high: $2,000,000; low: $500; average: $15,000–$70,000).

**Purpose and activities:** Giving primarily for conservation; higher, secondary, and other education, including libraries; health and hospitals; cultural activities, including historic preservation; scientific activities; and social and family services, including programs for youth and the elderly.

**Fields of interest:** Historic preservation/historical societies; arts/cultural programs; secondary school/education; higher education; libraries/library science; education; natural resource conservation & protection; environment; animal welfare; hospitals (general); family planning; health care; health associations; human services; youth, services; engineering & technology; science.

**Types of support:** Capital campaigns; building/renovation; equipment; land acquisition.

**Limitations:** Giving primarily in RI. No support for religious schools, books, films, videos, or plays. No grants to individuals, or for general support, program or operating budgets, matching gifts, special projects, research, publications, conferences, or continuing support; no loans.

**Publications:** Program policy statement, application guidelines, annual report, grants list.

**Application information:** No grants are awarded on a continuing basis, but applicants may qualify annually. Application form not required.

   *Initial approach:* 1-page letter
   *Copies of proposal:* 1
   *Deadline(s):* Submit public school requests by May 31 if invited; submit all other requests between Mar. 1 and June 30; deadline June 30
   *Board meeting date(s):* Nov.
   *Final notification:* After Nov. meeting
**Distribution Committee:** David A. King, Exec. Dir.; John Gorham, Louis R. Hampton, Earl W. Harrington, Jr., Robert W. Kenyon, Norma B. LaFreniere, Keith H. Lang, John W. Linnell.
**Trustee:** PNC Bank, N.A.
**Number of staff:** 3 full-time professional; 1 part-time professional; 1 full-time support; 1 part-time support.

**Recent grants for library/information services:**

**681-1** Barrington Public Library, Barrington, RI, $62,850. For PCs, switch, tape check, edge repair system, DVD collection, music CD's, special needs equipment, large print books, window film and carpeting. 1999.

**681-2** Brownell Library, Little Compton, RI, $10,850. For switches, computers, software and printers to complement CLAN equipment. 1999.

**681-3** Burrillville High School, Burrillville, RI, $25,000. For computer and other equipment for library, math, science, humanities and journalism programs. 1999.

**681-4** Central Falls Free Public Library, Central Falls, RI, $136,215. For computer equipment, renovations and interior decorations. 1999.

**681-5** Cooperating Libraries Automated Network (CLAN), Providence, RI, $44,954. To convert non-MARC records in CLAN database, and for computer and other equipment. 1999.

**681-6** Coventry Public Library, Coventry, RI, $45,059. For computer and other equipment and collection development. 1999.

**681-7** Cranston Public Library, Cranston, RI, $126,795. For computer and other equipment, encyclopedias and digital photo conversion. 1999.

**681-8** Cumberland Public Library, Cumberland, RI, $29,390. For computer and other equipment. 1999.

**681-9** Davisville Free Library Association, North Kingstown, RI, $70,275. For book acquisitions, CLAN installation, computer and other equipment, book and artifact restoration and renovations. 1999.

**681-10** East Greenwich Free Library, East Greenwich, RI, $36,450. For CLAN equipment upgrades and other computer equipment. 1999.

**681-11** Greene Public Library, Greene, RI, $100,000. To build addition to existing library building. 1999.

**681-12** Greenville Public Library, Greenville, RI, $53,400. For computer equipment, video and photography equipment and reference collection development. 1999.

**681-13** Harmony Library, Harmony, RI, $20,800. For updated CLAN equipment, insulation in Community Room, adult and juvenile nonfiction and storage shelving. 1999.

**681-14** Hope Library Association, Hope, RI, $38,300. For computer equipment, copy machine, water fountains and young adult materials. 1999.

**681-15** Island Free Library, Block Island, RI, $250,000. For construction, equipment and collection expansion. 1999.

**681-16** Jamestown Philomenian Library, Jamestown, RI, $30,000. For reader-printer, network upgrades, lighting and stairs. 1999.

**681-17** Joseph H. Gaudet Middle School, Middletown, RI, $25,000. For computers, printers and software for computer labs and library. 1999.

**681-18** Lincoln Public Library, Lincoln, RI, $40,121. For computer and other equipment. 1999.

**681-19** Memorial and Library Association of Westerly, Westerly, RI, $114,655. To upgrade elevator, for computers and LAN, for document management system and for Images of RI project. 1999.

**681-20** Narragansett Public Library, Narragansett, RI, $42,800. To upgrade computers, to replace terminals and for equipment. 1999.

**681-21** Newport Public Library, Newport, RI, $320,000. For computer systems upgrade, software and building project. 1999.

**681-22** North Kingstown Free Library, North Kingstown, RI, $28,544. For library materials, computer and other equipment and Images of RI project. 1999.

**681-23** North Scituate Public Library, North Scituate, RI, $32,700. For collection development, print conservation, computer and other equipment and renovations. 1999.

**681-24** North Smithfield Public Library, Slatersville, RI, $40,529. For collection development, computer and other equipment and Images of RI project. 1999.

**681-25** Portsmouth Free Public Library, Portsmouth, RI, $24,750. To replace flooring and for computer and other equipment. 1999.

**681-26** Providence Public Library, Providence, RI, $1,873,000. For books and other collection development, computer and other equipment and capital campaign. 1999.

**681-27** Providence Public Library, Providence, RI, $325,000. To implement high-speed digital connections at every LAN site. 1999.

**681-28** Redwood Library and Athenaeum, Newport, RI, $50,000. To install new HVAC. 1999.

**681-29** Rhode Island College, Providence, RI, $115,300. For technology learning center at Adams Library, video microscopy, electronic biological imaging and CD ROM preparation lab. 1999.

**681-30** South Kingstown Public Library, Peace Dale, RI, $60,760. For repairs to Kingston Free Library exterior, computer and other equipment and Images of RI project. 1999.

**681-31** Tiverton Library Services, Tiverton, RI, $34,300. For computer equipment, circulation desk and collection development. 1999.

**681-32** Tollgate High School, Warwick, RI, $25,000. To extend internet access to library and all classrooms. 1999.

**681-33** Union Public Library, Tiverton, RI, $55,432. For CLAN and other computer equipment. 1999.

**681-34** Warwick Public Library, Warwick, RI, $400,000. Toward construction of library addition. 1999.

**681-35** West Warwick Public Library System, West Warwick, RI, $98,040. Toward computer equipment, books, furnishings and equipment, emergency repairs and conversion of Quiet Study room into lab. 1999.

**681-36** Willett Free Library, Saunderstown, RI, $28,380. For hardware and software for CLAN membership and other equipment. 1999.

## 682
### The Cranston Foundation
1381 Cranston St.
Cranston, RI 02920-6789 (401) 943-4800
*Contact:* The Trustees

Trust established in 1960 in RI.
**Donor(s):** Cranston Print Works Co.
**Grantmaker type:** Company-sponsored foundation
**Financial data** (yr. ended 06/30/00): Assets, $3,646 (M); gifts received, $164,872; expenditures, $188,057; qualifying distributions, $187,103; giving activities include $50,000 for 20 grants (high: $10,000; low: $250), $100,837 for 35 grants to individuals (high: $4,000; low: $1,000) and $28,266 for 114 employee matching gifts.
**Purpose and activities:** Grants largely for higher education, including a scholarship program for children of Cranston Print Works Co. employees. Support also for community funds, hospitals, cultural programs, the environment, and textile institutions and organizations.
**Fields of interest:** Arts/cultural programs; higher education; libraries/library science; education; environment; hospitals (general); health care;

human services; community development; federated giving programs.
**Types of support:** General/operating support; employee matching gifts; employee-related scholarships.
**Limitations:** Giving primarily in MA, NY, and RI.
**Application information:** Application form required for scholarships.
  *Initial approach:* Proposal
  *Copies of proposal:* 1
  *Deadline(s):* Aug. 31 for grants; Feb. 15 for scholarships
  *Board meeting date(s):* Semiannually
  *Final notification:* Sept. 30
**Trustees:** Brian Adriance, A. Baker, G. Carlson, B. Grandison, J. Menzies, Frederic L. Rockefeller, George W. Shuster, S. Wollseiffen.
**Number of staff:** 1 full-time professional.
**EIN:** 056015348

## 683
### Dorot Foundation ▼
439 Benefit St.
Providence, RI 02903 (401) 351-8866
*Contact:* Ernest S. Frerichs, Exec. Dir.
*E-mail:* info@dorot.org; URL: http://www.dorot.org

Incorporated in 1958 in NY as Joy and Samuel Ungerleider Foundation.
**Donor(s):** Joy G. Ungerleider-Mayerson,‡ D.S. and R.H. Gottesman Foundation.
**Grantmaker type:** Independent foundation
**Financial data** (yr. ended 03/31/99): Assets, $37,252,803 (M); gifts received, $2,683,030; expenditures, $4,272,102; qualifying distributions, $3,610,886; giving activities include $2,244,000 for 36 grants (high: $800,000; low: $50; average: $2,500–$25,000) and $516,520 for grants to individuals.
**Purpose and activities:** Grants primarily for higher education and educational organizations including fellowships to individuals studying in Israel; support also for Jewish organizations.
**Fields of interest:** Museums; education, association; higher education; medical school/education; libraries (public); environment, administration/regulation; human services; Jewish agencies & temples.
**International interests:** Israel.
**Types of support:** General/operating support; endowments; program development; professorships; fellowships.
**Limitations:** Applications not accepted. Giving primarily in the U.S.; some giving also in Israel.
**Application information:** Contributes only to pre-selected organizations. Does not accept unsolicited requests for funds.
**Officers and Directors:\*** Jeane U. Springer,\* Pres.; Steven Ungerleider,\* V.P.; Steven Baum, Secy. and Treas.; Ernest S. Frerichs, Exec. Dir.
**Number of staff:** 2 full-time professional; 4 part-time professional; 1 full-time support.
**EIN:** 136116927
**Recent grants for library/information services:**
**683-1** Jewish Womens Archives, Brookline, MA, $100,000. 1999.
**683-2** New York Public Library, NYC, NY, $800,000. 1999.

## 684
## The Hassenfeld Foundation ▼
1011 Newport Ave.
Pawtucket, RI 02861

Established in 1944 in RI.
**Donor(s):** Hasbro, Inc., Stephen Hassenfeld Charitable Lead Trust, and members of the Hassenfeld family.
**Grantmaker type:** Independent foundation
**Financial data** (yr. ended 12/31/99): Assets, $23,279,920 (M); gifts received, $2,218,041; expenditures, $3,787,976; qualifying distributions, $3,781,669; giving activities include $3,780,583 for 68 grants (high: $387,500; low: $1,000; average: $1,000–$300,000).
**Purpose and activities:** Giving primarily for higher education, Jewish federated giving programs, and arts and cultural organizations.
**Fields of interest:** Arts/cultural programs; higher education; Jewish federated giving programs.
**Limitations:** Applications not accepted. No grants to individuals.
**Application information:** Contributes only to pre-selected organizations.
**Officers and Director:*** Sylvia K. Hassenfeld,* Pres.; Alan G. Hassenfeld, V.P. and Treas.; Ellen Block, Secy.
**EIN:** 056015373
**Recent grants for library/information services:**
**684-1** American Jewish Historical Society, NYC, NY, $10,000. 1998.
**684-2** Survivors of the Shoah Visual History Foundation, Los Angeles, CA, $247,195. For grant made in form of stock. 1998.

## 685
## Mildred & Charles Page Fund
c/o Fleet Private Clients Group
P.O. Box 6767
Providence, RI 02940 (401) 435-7256

Established in 1998.
**Grantmaker type:** Independent foundation
**Financial data** (yr. ended 12/31/99): Assets, $1,858,973 (M); expenditures, $74,911; qualifying distributions, $67,695; giving activities include $56,101 for 9 grants (high: $11,221; low: $5,610).
**Purpose and activities:** Giving primarily to education, health care, human services, and religious organizations.
**Fields of interest:** Libraries (public); hospitals (general); medical care, rehabilitation; family services; human services, special populations; Protestant agencies & churches.
**Limitations:** Applications not accepted. No grants to individuals.
**Application information:** Contributes only to pre-selected organizations.
**Trustee:** Fleet Bank.
**EIN:** 046479105

## 686
## The Rhode Island Foundation ▼
1 Union Sta.
Providence, RI 02903 (401) 274-4564
*Contact:* Ronald D. Thorpe, V.P., Prog.
*FAX:* (401) 331-8085; URL: http://www.rifoundation.org

Incorporated in 1916 in RI (includes The Rhode Island Community Foundation in 1984).
**Grantmaker type:** Community foundation
**Financial data** (yr. ended 12/31/99): Assets, $388,290,979 (M); gifts received, $6,644,419; expenditures, $19,278,547; giving activities include $15,583,369 for grants.
**Purpose and activities:** To promote educational and charitable activities that tend to improve the living conditions and well-being of the inhabitants of RI; grants for capital and operating purposes principally to agencies working in the fields of education, health care, the arts and cultural affairs, youth, the aged, social services, urban affairs, historic preservation, and the environment. Some restricted grants for scholarships and medical research.
**Fields of interest:** Performing arts; historic preservation/historical societies; arts/cultural programs; libraries/library science; education; natural resource conservation & protection; environment; animal welfare; hospitals (general); health care; health associations; AIDS; alcoholism; AIDS research; legal services; food services; human services; children & youth, services; family services; aging, centers & services; minorities/immigrants, centers & services; homeless, human services; community development; voluntarism promotion; government/public administration; public affairs; minorities; aging; immigrants/refugees; economically disadvantaged; homeless.
**Types of support:** General/operating support; capital campaigns; building/renovation; equipment; land acquisition; emergency funds; program development; conferences/seminars; publication; seed money; fellowships; scholarship funds; technical assistance; consulting services; scholarships—to individuals; matching/challenge support.
**Limitations:** Giving limited to RI. No support for religious organizations for sectarian purposes (except as specified by donors). No grants to individuals (except from donor-advised and designated funds), or for endowment funds, research, hospital equipment, capital needs of health organizations, annual campaigns, deficit financing, or educational institutions for general operating expenses; no loans.
**Publications:** Annual report (including application guidelines), program policy statement, application guidelines, newsletter, informational brochure, occasional report.
**Application information:** Organizations are invited to submit a full application after letter of intent is received. For scholarship information from the designated and donor-advised funds contact the foundation. Application form not required.
*Initial approach:* 3- to 4-page letter of intent
*Copies of proposal:* 5
*Deadline(s):* Varies
*Board meeting date(s):* 3 times per year
*Final notification:* One week after board meeting
**Officers:** Ronald V. Gallo, Pres. and C.E.O.; Carol Golden, V.P., Devel.; Ronald D. Thorpe, Jr., V.P., Prog.; Jennifer Reid, Cont.
**Board of Directors:** Norman Estes McCulloch, Jr., Chair.; Pablo Rodriguez, Vice-Chair.; Elizabeth Z. Chace, Ann F. Conner, George Graboys, Margaret Goddard Leeson, Florence K. Murray, Walter R. Stone, John W. Wall.

**Trustees:** Citizens National Bank, Fleet Bank, N.A., BankBoston, N.A., Van Liew Trust Co., Washington Trust Bank.
**Number of staff:** 16 full-time professional; 2 part-time professional; 11 full-time support.
**EIN:** 050208270

## 687
## Elva S. Smith Trust
c/o Citizens Bank New Hampshire
870 Westminster St.
Providence, RI 02903 (603) 229-3574
*Application address:* c/o Martha Washington, Office of the Dean, Univ. of Pittsburgh, School of Library & Information Science, 509 SLIS Bldg., Pittsburgh, PA 15260, tel.: (412) 624-5230

Established in 1965 in NH.
**Donor(s):** Elva S. Smith.‡
**Grantmaker type:** Independent foundation
**Financial data** (yr. ended 12/31/98): Assets, $2,535,685 (M); expenditures, $63,766; qualifying distributions, $57,165; giving activities include $38,952 for 1 grant and $12,648 for 1 grant to an individual.
**Purpose and activities:** Primarily supports the scholarship program at the School of Library and Information Management at the University of Pittsburgh, PA.
**Fields of interest:** Libraries/library science.
**Types of support:** General/operating support; scholarships—to individuals.
**Limitations:** Giving limited to Pittsburgh, PA, and VT.
**Application information:**
*Initial approach:* Letter or telephone
*Deadline(s):* None
**Trustee:** Citizens Bank New Hampshire.
**EIN:** 026014169

## 688
## Washington Trust Charitable Foundation
c/o The Washington Trust Co.
23 Broad St.
Westerly, RI 02891
*Contact:* John C. Warren

Established in 1994 in RI.
**Donor(s):** The Washington Trust Co.
**Grantmaker type:** Company-sponsored foundation
**Financial data** (yr. ended 12/31/99): Assets, $1,127,580 (M); gifts received, $11,474; expenditures, $303,949; qualifying distributions, $294,333; giving activities include $294,333 for 63 grants (high: $37,000; low: $250).
**Fields of interest:** Libraries/library science; education; hospitals (general); housing/shelter; YM/YWCAs & YM/YWHAs.
**Types of support:** General/operating support; capital campaigns; building/renovation.
**Limitations:** Giving primarily in New England, with emphasis on CT and RI.
**Application information:**
*Initial approach:* Letter
*Deadline(s):* Oct. 1
**Trustee:** The Washington Trust Co.
**EIN:** 050477294

# SOUTH CAROLINA

## 689
### The Bailey Foundation
P.O. Box 494
Clinton, SC 29325 (864) 938-2632
*Contact:* Thomas E. Sebrell, IV, Admin.
*FAX:* (864) 938-2669

Trust established in 1951 in SC.
**Donor(s):** M.S. Bailey & Son, Bankers, Clinton Investment Co.
**Grantmaker type:** Independent foundation
**Financial data** (yr. ended 08/31/99): Assets, $5,752,283 (M); gifts received, $66,250; expenditures, $324,977; qualifying distributions, $291,217; giving activities include $254,000 for 34 grants (high: $100,000; low: $2,000) and $36,900 for 23 employee matching gifts.
**Purpose and activities:** Support primarily for higher education, including a scholarship program for graduating seniors of Laurens County public high schools accepted at a degree-granting four-year college or university; support also for churches, community services, libraries, museums, and social services including child welfare and development and the elderly located in or serving Laurens County, SC.
**Fields of interest:** Higher education; libraries/library science; education; human services; children & youth, services; child development, services; aging, centers & services; community development; religion; aging.
**Types of support:** Capital campaigns; building/renovation; endowments; employee matching gifts; scholarships—to individuals; matching/challenge support.
**Limitations:** Giving limited to Laurens County, SC. No grants to individuals (except scholarships for students attending local high schools), or for operating expenses.
**Publications:** Annual report, informational brochure (including application guidelines).
**Application information:** Applications for students available from guidance counselors at Clinton High School and Laurens High School. Application form not required.
*Initial approach:* For grants, write administrator
*Copies of proposal:* 1
*Deadline(s):* For scholarships, Apr. 15 of applicant's senior year in high school
*Board meeting date(s):* Periodically
*Final notification:* May 15
**Trustee:** Carolina First Bank.
**Advisory Committee:** George H. Cornelson, Chair.; Emily F. Bailey, C. Bailey Dixon, Toccoa W. Switzer, Robert M. Vance, James Von Hollen.
**Grants Advisory Committee:** Joseph O. Nixon, Chair.; Sonia Cheek, Wanda B. Isaac, Sam Moore, Susan Polson, Donny Ross, Donny Wilder.
**Number of staff:** None.
**EIN:** 576018387

## 690
### Robert S. Campbell Foundation
101 N. Main St.
Greenville, SC 29601

Established in 1995 in SC.
**Grantmaker type:** Independent foundation
**Financial data** (yr. ended 12/31/98): Assets, $15,570,325 (M); gifts received, $400,856; expenditures, $691,782; qualifying distributions, $521,990; giving activities include $475,000 for 8 grants (high: $200,000; low: $5,000).
**Purpose and activities:** Funding primarily for a public library and higher education. Funding also for youth services.
**Fields of interest:** Higher education; libraries (public); children & youth, services.
**Limitations:** Giving primarily in SC, some funding also in NC. No grants to individuals.
**Application information:** Application form not required.
*Deadline(s):* None
**Trustee:** William W. Brown.
**EIN:** 571031564

## 691
### Colonial Life and Accident Insurance Company Contributions Program
1200 Colonial Life Blvd.
Columbia, SC 29202 (803) 798-7000
*Contact:* Edwina Carns, Public and Comm. Rels.

**Grantmaker type:** Corporate giving program
**Purpose and activities:** Primary support for education, especially K-12. Giving also for economic development.
**Fields of interest:** Visual arts; performing arts; humanities; historic preservation/historical societies; arts/cultural programs; education, association; education, research; education, fund raising; early childhood education; elementary school/education; business school/education; adult/continuing education; libraries/library science; natural resource conservation & protection; environment; animal welfare; hospitals (general); family planning; nursing care; health care; substance abuse, services; mental health/crisis services; cancer; heart & circulatory diseases; AIDS; alcoholism; health organizations; cancer research; heart & circulatory research; AIDS research; crime/law enforcement; food services; housing/shelter, development; youth development, citizenship; human services; children & youth, services; family services; aging, centers & services; human rights (international); civil rights; government/public administration; public affairs, citizen participation; minorities; disabled; aging; economically disadvantaged.
**Types of support:** General/operating support; continuing support; annual campaigns; capital campaigns; building/renovation; land acquisition; endowments; emergency funds; conferences/seminars; fellowships; internship funds; scholarship funds; employee volunteer services; loaned talent; use of facilities; employee matching gifts.
**Limitations:** Giving primarily in the Columbia, OH, area and some parts of SC. No support for for-profit organizations. No grants to individuals.
**Application information:** The Vice-Chairman's office handles giving. Application form required.
*Initial approach:* Send letter to headquarters

*Deadline(s):* None
*Final notification:* 4 weeks
**Number of staff:** 1 full-time professional; 1 full-time support.

## 692
### Hamrick Mills Foundation, Inc.
P.O. Box 48
Gaffney, SC 29342-0048
*Contact:* Wylie L. Hamrick, Pres.

Established in 1952.
**Donor(s):** Hamrick Mills Inc.
**Grantmaker type:** Company-sponsored foundation
**Financial data** (yr. ended 12/31/99): Assets, $2,135,946 (M); expenditures, $112,591; qualifying distributions, $89,845; giving activities include $89,710 for 25 grants (high: $13,403; low: $275).
**Purpose and activities:** Giving for higher education, art and cultural programs, and for children and human services.
**Fields of interest:** Elementary school/education; higher education; libraries/library science; cancer; cancer research; children & youth, services.
**Types of support:** General/operating support.
**Limitations:** Giving primarily in Cherokee County, SC. No grants to individuals.
**Application information:**
*Initial approach:* Letter
*Deadline(s):* None
**Officers and Directors:*** Wylie L. Hamrick,* Pres.; C.F. Hamrick II,* Secy.-Treas.; J.M. Hamrick, L.W. Hamrick, W.C. Hamrick, R.C. Thomson.
**EIN:** 576024261

## 693
### Herman N. Hipp First Foundation
P.O. Box 546
Greenville, SC 29602

Established in 1958.
**Grantmaker type:** Independent foundation
**Financial data** (yr. ended 12/31/99): Assets, $1,018,935 (M); expenditures, $616,407; qualifying distributions, $608,936; giving activities include $609,375 for 8 grants (high: $300,375; low: $2,000).
**Purpose and activities:** Giving for youth services, higher education, federated giving programs and for a theater.
**Fields of interest:** Libraries/library science.
**Limitations:** Applications not accepted. Giving primarily in Greenville, SC. No grants to individuals.
**Application information:** Contributes only to pre-selected organizations.
**Trustee:** H. Neel Hipp.
**EIN:** 576017334

# SOUTH DAKOTA

## 694
**Welk Family Foundation**
c/o Dacotah Bank
P.O. Box 1210
Aberdeen, SD  57402   (605) 225-5611

Established in 1988 in SD.
**Grantmaker type:** Independent foundation
**Financial data** (yr. ended 12/31/99): Assets,
$3,887,801 (M); expenditures, $158,207;
qualifying distributions, $134,851; giving
activities include $136,721 for 10 grants (high:
$35,000; low: $721).
**Fields of interest:** Libraries/library science;
education; hospitals (general); Christian
agencies & churches.
**Types of support:** Scholarship funds.
**Limitations:** Giving limited to Roberts County,
SD. No grants to individuals.
**Application information:** Application form
required.
   *Deadline(s):* None
**Trustee:** Dacotah Bank.
**Advisory Committee:** Kaye Cahill, Lavonne
Grimsrud, Harlan Hammer, Guy Mackner,
Laurel Pistorius.
**EIN:** 363579562

# TENNESSEE

## 695
**Harrison Family Foundation, Inc.**
901 Tallan Bldg.
Chattanooga, TN  37402
*Contact:* Dorothy B. Jones, Secy.-Treas.

Established in 1994 in TN.
**Grantmaker type:** Independent foundation
**Financial data** (yr. ended 12/31/99): Assets,
$6,997,031 (M); expenditures, $1,271,874;
qualifying distributions, $1,270,833; giving
activities include $1,271,829 for 25 grants (high:
$1,043,523; low: $10).
**Purpose and activities:** Giving primarily for the
arts, education, and for health associations.
**Fields of interest:** Museums; ballet; arts/cultural
programs; secondary school/education; higher
education; libraries/library science; education;
environment; medical care, rehabilitation; heart
& circulatory diseases; arthritis; epilepsy;
diabetes; Boy Scouts; YM/YWCAs &
YM/YWHAs; religion.
**Limitations:** Giving primarily in TN.
**Application information:** Application form not
required.
   *Deadline(s):* None
**Officers:** J. Frank Harrison, Jr., Chair.; J. Frank
Harrison III, Pres.; Dorothy B. Jones, Secy.-Treas.
**EIN:** 621569138

## 696
**Plough Foundation ▼**
6410 Poplar Ave., Ste. 710
Memphis, TN  38119   (901) 761-9180
*Contact:* Noris R. Haynes, Jr., Exec. Dir.
*FAX:* (901) 761-6186; E-mail:
Haynes@plough.org

Trust established in 1972 in TN.
**Donor(s):** Abe Plough.‡
**Grantmaker type:** Independent foundation
**Financial data** (yr. ended 12/31/99): Assets,
$212,746,356 (M); gifts received, $626,447;
expenditures, $12,210,590; qualifying
distributions, $10,490,649; giving activities
include $9,799,879 for 67 grants (high:
$2,000,000; low: $1,000; average:
$5,000–$500,000).
**Purpose and activities:** Grants to community
projects, including a community fund, early
childhood and elementary education, substance
abuse prevention-early intervention, social
service agencies, housing and homelessness,
civic affairs groups, and the arts.
**Fields of interest:** Arts/cultural programs; early
childhood education; elementary
school/education; health care; crime/violence
prevention; housing/shelter, temporary shelter;
housing/shelter, homeless; human services;
youth, services; family services; homeless,
human services; economic development;
homeless.
**Types of support:** Capital campaigns;
building/renovation; equipment; land
acquisition; endowments; program
development; professorships; seed money;
curriculum development; program evaluation;
matching/challenge support.
**Limitations:** Giving primarily in Shelby County,
TN, with an emphasis on Memphis. No grants to
individuals, and generally no grants for annual
operating funds; no loans.
**Publications:** Informational brochure (including
application guidelines), application guidelines.
**Application information:** Application form
required.
   *Initial approach:* Letter describing project, no
   more than 3 pages; full application by
   invitation only
   *Copies of proposal:* 1
   *Deadline(s):* 10th of month prior to board
   meeting for full application
   *Board meeting date(s):* Feb., May, Aug., and
   Nov.
   *Final notification:* Generally within 2 weeks
**Officer and Trustees:*** Noris R. Haynes, Jr.,*
Exec. Dir.; Patricia R. Burnham, Eugene J.
Callahan, DD Eisenberg, Diane R. Goldstein,
Larry Papasan, Jocelyn P. Rudner, James
Springfield, Steve Wishnia, National Bank of
Commerce.
**Number of staff:** 4 full-time professional; 2
full-time support.
**EIN:** 237175983
**Recent grants for library/information services:**
**696-1** Foundation for the Memphis Shelby
County Public Library, Memphis, TN,
$1,000,000. For building fund. 1998.
**696-2** Grant Information Center, Memphis, TN,
$30,000. For general operating support. 1998.

## 697
**Justin & Valerie Blair Potter Foundation**
1 NationsBank Plz.
Nashville, TN  37239-1697   (615) 749-3164
*Contact:* Otis Goodin, Tr. Off.

Established in 1953.
**Grantmaker type:** Independent foundation
**Financial data** (yr. ended 12/31/99): Assets,
$29,394,806 (M); expenditures, $1,614,267;
qualifying distributions, $1,484,218; giving
activities include $1,435,000 for 22 grants (high:
$200,000; low: $20,000).
**Fields of interest:** Archives; medical care,
rehabilitation; athletics/sports, equestrianism;
boys & girls clubs; civil liberties, right to life;
Roman Catholic agencies & churches.
**Limitations:** Giving primarily in Nashville, TN.
**Application information:**
   *Initial approach:* Letter
   *Deadline(s):* None
**Trustees:** Albert I. Menefee, Jr., Valerie Menefee,
Bank of America.
**EIN:** 626306577

# TEXAS

## 698
**Harry Bass Foundation**
4809 Cole Ave., Ste. 252
Dallas, TX  75205   (214) 599-0300
*Contact:* David Calhoun, V.P., Grants
*FAX:* (214) 599-0405; E-mail:
dcalhoun@airmail.net

Established in 1983 in TX.
**Donor(s):** Harry W. Bass, Jr.‡
**Grantmaker type:** Independent foundation
**Financial data** (yr. ended 12/31/99): Assets,
$9,551,118 (M); expenditures, $188,048;
qualifying distributions, $145,573; giving
activities include $106,500 for grants (average:
$100–$3,000).
**Purpose and activities:** Support for numismatic
organizations nationwide; primary areas of
interest include education, museums, and health
associations in the Dallas, TX, area.
**Fields of interest:** Museums; libraries/library
science; education; hospitals (general); health
associations; government/public administration;
religion; general charitable giving.
**Types of support:** General/operating support;
continuing support; annual campaigns;
equipment; scholarship funds; research;
employee matching gifts.
**Limitations:** Applications not accepted. Giving
primarily in the Dallas, TX, area. No grants to
individuals.
**Application information:** Contributes only to
pre-selected organizations.
   *Board meeting date(s):* Quarterly
**Officers and Trustees:*** Doris L. Bass,* Pres.;
David Calhoun,* V.P., Grants; Michael Calhoun,
V.P.; J. Michael Wylie.
**Number of staff:** None.
**EIN:** 751876307

## 699
## Bertha Foundation
P.O. Box 1110
Graham, TX 76450 (940) 549-1400
*Contact:* Douglas A. Stroud, V.P.

Established in 1967 in TX.
**Donor(s):** E. Bruce Street, M. Boyd Street.
**Grantmaker type:** Independent foundation
**Financial data** (yr. ended 12/31/99): Assets,
$10,226,191 (M); gifts received, $8,855;
expenditures, $509,034; qualifying distributions,
$445,784; giving activities include $432,192 for
26 grants (high: $100,000; low: $108).
**Fields of interest:** Libraries/library science;
education; hospitals (general); recreation;
human services; government/public
administration.
**Types of support:** General/operating support;
building/renovation; scholarship funds.
**Limitations:** Giving limited to Young County and
Graham, TX. No grants to individuals.
**Application information:**
 *Initial approach:* Letter
 *Deadline(s):* None
**Officers and Directors:*** Alice Ann Street,*
Pres.; Douglas A. Stroud,* V.P.; J.R.
Montgomery,* Secy.; Sandra Street Estess, E.
Bruce Street, M.B. Street, Jr., Melissa Street York.
**EIN:** 756050023

## 700
## Bowden-Massey Foundation
P.O. Box 90436
San Antonio, TX 78209
*Contact:* Charles L. Bowden, Pres.

Established in 1992 in TX.
**Donor(s):** Charles L. Bowden, Virginia M.
Bowden.
**Grantmaker type:** Independent foundation
**Financial data** (yr. ended 12/31/99): Assets,
$3,212,354 (M); gifts received, $147,360;
expenditures, $106,602; qualifying distributions,
$106,284; giving activities include $106,000 for
9 grants (high: $82,000; low: $200).
**Purpose and activities:** Support primarily for
psychiatric research, education, and libraries.
**Fields of interest:** Arts/cultural programs;
libraries/library science; education; mental
health, treatment; religion.
**Types of support:** Fellowships; research.
**Limitations:** Giving primarily in TX.
**Publications:** Annual report.
**Application information:** Application form not
required.
 *Initial approach:* Proposal
 *Copies of proposal:* 1
 *Deadline(s):* None
 *Board meeting date(s):* Nov.
**Officers and Directors:*** Charles L. Bowden,*
Pres. and Treas.; Virginia M. Bowden,* V.P. and
Secy.; Ellen M. Bowden, Sharon B. Davis.
**EIN:** 742637829

## 701
## Margaret C. B. & S. Spencer N. Brown
 Foundation, Inc.
P.O. Box 8739
Waco, TX 76714

Established in 1983.

**Donor(s):** Margaret Boyce Brown, S. Spencer
Brown, National Diversified.
**Grantmaker type:** Independent foundation
**Financial data** (yr. ended 12/31/99): Assets,
$1,828,982 (M); gifts received, $481,263;
expenditures, $122,259; qualifying distributions,
$120,487; giving activities include $105,155 for
40 grants (high: $34,407; low: $35).
**Purpose and activities:** Giving for higher
education, Christian churches and institutes,
and for a hospital.
**Fields of interest:** Museums; college; libraries
(public); Protestant agencies & churches.
**Limitations:** Applications not accepted. Giving
primarily in TX. No grants to individuals; or for
fellowships.
**Application information:** Contributes only to
pre-selected organizations.
**Officers:** S. Spencer Brown, Sr., Pres.; S. Spencer
Brown, Jr., V.P.; Margaret Boyce Brown, Secy.
**Trustees:** Maria Stanton Brown, Stanton Boyce
Brown, Margaret Brown Lewis, ExTraCo Banks.
**EIN:** 746046197

## 702
## Flora Cameron Foundation
4600 Broadway, Ste. 106
San Antonio, TX 78209 (210) 824-8301
*Contact:* Flora C. Atherton, Pres.

Established in 1952 in TX.
**Grantmaker type:** Independent foundation
**Financial data** (yr. ended 08/31/98): Assets,
$1,834,977 (M); gifts received, $233,000;
expenditures, $211,624; qualifying distributions,
$196,507; giving activities include $194,000 for
16 grants (high: $25,000; low: $500).
**Purpose and activities:** Giving primarily for the
arts, education, Protestant agencies, and
community services.
**Fields of interest:** Arts/cultural programs; higher
education; libraries/library science; reading.
**Types of support:** General/operating support.
**Limitations:** Giving primarily in the San
Antonio, TX, area. No grants to individuals.
**Application information:**
 *Initial approach:* Proposal
 *Deadline(s):* None
**Officers:** Flora C. Atherton, Pres. and Treas.;
John H. Crichton, V.P.; Gloria Labatt, Secy.
**Trustee:** Gilbert M. Denman.
**EIN:** 746038681

## 703
## Coastal Bend Community Foundation
The Six Hundred Bldg.
600 Leopard St., Ste. 1716
Corpus Christi, TX 78473 (361) 882-9745
*Contact:* Jim Moloney, Exec. Dir.
*FAX:* (361) 882-2865; E-mail:
jmoloney@cbcfoundation.org; URL: http://
www.cbcfoundation.org

Established in 1980 in TX.
**Grantmaker type:** Community foundation
**Financial data** (yr. ended 12/31/99): Assets,
$27,428,425 (L); gifts received, $3,079,687;
expenditures, $3,124,305; giving activities
include $2,697,371 for 261 grants and $84,350
for 85 grants to individuals.
**Purpose and activities:** Giving primarily for
social services, including alcohol and drug

abuse programs, youth and child welfare, the
disadvantaged, the homeless and hungry, and
welfare; hospitals; voluntarism; community
development; animal welfare; higher and other
education, including scholarship funds, literacy,
and libraries; and arts and culture, including
museums and history.
**Fields of interest:** Museums; history &
archaeology; arts/cultural programs; higher
education; adult education—literacy & basic
skills; libraries/library science; reading;
education; animal welfare; hospitals (general);
substance abuse, services; alcoholism; food
services; human services; children & youth,
services; homeless, human services; community
development; voluntarism promotion;
economically disadvantaged; homeless; general
charitable giving.
**Types of support:** General/operating support;
equipment; program development; seed money;
fellowships; scholarship funds.
**Limitations:** Giving limited to Aransas, Bee, Jim
Wells, Kleberg, Nueces, Refugio, and San
Patricio counties, TX.
**Publications:** Grants list, informational
brochure, application guidelines, annual report.
**Application information:** Cover form required.
Application form required.
 *Initial approach:* Letter requesting guidelines
 *Copies of proposal:* 1
 *Deadline(s):* Sept. 1
 *Board meeting date(s):* Feb., May, Aug., and
  Nov.
 *Final notification:* Nov.
**Officers and Directors:*** T.D. Sells, Jr.,* Pres.;
Ginger D. Fagen,* V.P.; Pat M. Eisenhauer,*
Secy.-Treas.; Jim Moloney,* Exec. Dir.; Harry Lee
Adams, Jr., Deb Bauer, Susie Bracht Black,
Roberto Bosquez, M.D., Austin Brown, John
Chapman, Lawrence Cornelius, Patricia Cypher,
Joe DeLeon, Jr., Lucien Flournoy, Joe Fulton,
John H. Garner, Paul R. Haas, Ed Harte, Jace C.
Hoffman, Mark H. Hulings, Harris A. Kaffe,
Glenda Kane, Lou Adele May, Leon McNinch,
Patty P. Mueller, Gorman Ritchie, Robert Rooke,
Chela Storm, Alfred C. Thomas, Norman P.
Wilcox, Nan Wilson.
**Number of staff:** 1 full-time professional; 1
full-time support.
**EIN:** 742190039

## 704
## Coastal Bend Foundation, Inc.
140 W. Cleveland Blvd.
Aransas Pass, TX 78336-2766
*Contact:* Tom Andrews, Exec. Dir.

Established in 1988 in TX.
**Grantmaker type:** Independent foundation
**Financial data** (yr. ended 12/31/98): Assets,
$2,028,473 (M); expenditures, $95,035;
qualifying distributions, $87,337; giving
activities include $41,075 for 10 grants (high:
$25,000; low: $75) and $25,000 for 1 grant to
an individual.
**Purpose and activities:** Giving to museums and
libraries.
**Fields of interest:** Museums; libraries/library
science.
**Types of support:** Scholarships—to individuals.
**Limitations:** Giving limited to within 15 miles of
Aransas Pass, TX. No grants to individuals
(except for designated scholarship funds).

**Application information:** Application form required.

*Deadline(s):* None

**Directors:** Tom Andrews, Exec. Dir.; Charles Benbow, Jan Pate, Wendell Roberts.

**EIN:** 742129257

---

**705**

## The Constantin Foundation

4809 Cole Ave., LB 127
Dallas, TX  75205-3578   (214) 522-9300
*Contact:* Betty S. Hillin, Exec. Dir.

Trust established in 1947 in TX.

**Donor(s):** E. Constantin, Jr.,‡ Mrs. E. Constantin, Jr.‡

**Grantmaker type:** Independent foundation

**Financial data** (yr. ended 12/31/98): Assets, $45,767,362 (M); expenditures, $2,250,461; qualifying distributions, $1,665,433; giving activities include $1,626,717 for 25 grants (high: $600,000; low: $1,000; average: $10,000–$65,000).

**Purpose and activities:** Emphasis on higher and other education; some support for cultural programs, social service and youth agencies, and hospitals and health, including alcohol and drug abuse programs.

**Fields of interest:** Media/communications; museums; music; humanities; arts/cultural programs; secondary school/education; vocational education; higher education; adult/continuing education; libraries/library science; education; hospitals (general); medical care, rehabilitation; health care; substance abuse, services; health associations; delinquency prevention/services; housing/shelter, development; human services; children & youth, services; disabled; economically disadvantaged.

**Types of support:** Continuing support; capital campaigns; building/renovation; equipment; land acquisition; program development; matching/challenge support.

**Limitations:** Giving limited to Dallas County, TX. No support for state schools, theater groups, churches, or state supported institutions. No grants to individuals, or for research, special events, fund raisers, or second party request; no loans.

**Publications:** Application guidelines.

**Application information:** Application form not required.

*Initial approach:* Letter (up to 3 pages)

*Copies of proposal:* 1

*Deadline(s):* Sept. 30 for letters of inquiry; grants reviewed at quarterly meetings; grant meeting in Dec.

*Board meeting date(s):* Feb., May, Aug., Nov., and Dec.

*Final notification:* Jan.

**Officer:** Betty S. Hillin, Exec. Dir.

**Trustees:** Henry C. Beck, Jr., Gene H. Bishop, Walter L. Fleming, Jr., Paul A. Lockhart, Jr., Joseph Boyd Neuhoff, Joel T. Williams, Jr.

**Number of staff:** 1 full-time professional.

**EIN:** 756011289

---

**706**

## Joe and Louise Cook Foundation

505 Cherokee Dr.
Temple, TX  76504
*Contact:* Barbara Wendland, Pres.

Established in 1989 in TX.

**Donor(s):** Joe B. Cook,‡ Louise P. Cook.‡

**Grantmaker type:** Independent foundation

**Financial data** (yr. ended 12/31/99): Assets, $12,347,191 (M); expenditures, $583,679; qualifying distributions, $478,276; giving activities include $478,276 for 26 grants (high: $103,150; low: $500; average: $500–$103,150).

**Purpose and activities:** Giving primarily to Methodist churches, education, and human services.

**Fields of interest:** Arts/cultural programs; theological school/education; libraries/library science; education; Christian agencies & churches.

**Types of support:** General/operating support; continuing support; annual campaigns; capital campaigns; building/renovation; endowments; program development; professorships; scholarship funds; matching/challenge support.

**Limitations:** Applications not accepted. Giving primarily in TX. No grants to individuals.

**Application information:** Contributes only to pre-selected organizations. Unsolicited applications not accepted.

**Officers and Directors:*** Barbara Wendland,* Pres.; C. Wendland,* V.P.; E. Wendland,* Treas.

**Number of staff:** None.

**EIN:** 742541278

---

**707**

## The Diamond M Foundation, Inc.

909 25th St.
Snyder, TX  79549
*Contact:* John Mark McLaughlin, Pres.
*Application address:* 2201 Sherwood Way, San Angelo, TX 76901

Trust established in 1950; incorporated in 1957 in TX.

**Donor(s):** C.T. McLaughlin.‡

**Grantmaker type:** Operating foundation

**Financial data** (yr. ended 12/31/98): Assets, $1,073,762 (M); expenditures, $89,580; qualifying distributions, $87,788; giving activities include $71,651 for 2 grants (high: $44,190; low: $27,461).

**Purpose and activities:** A private operating foundation; primary activity is to operate a museum; limited giving for charitable activities, including community funds, community services, and higher education.

**Fields of interest:** Arts/cultural programs; libraries/library science; education.

**Limitations:** Giving limited to TX.

**Officers:** John Mark McLaughlin, Pres.; Jean McLaughlin Kahle, Secy.

**Directors:** Evelyn McLaughlin Davies, Barbara Riddle Fendley, Max Von Roeder.

**Number of staff:** 1 full-time professional; 1 full-time support; 1 part-time support.

**EIN:** 756015426

---

**708**

## Clifton C. and Henryetta C. Doak Charitable Trust

c/o Norwest Bank Texas, N.A.
P.O. Drawer 913
Bryan, TX  77805   (409) 776-3267
*Contact:* Kenneth Loke

Established in 1993 in TX.

**Donor(s):** Henryetta C. Doak.‡

**Grantmaker type:** Independent foundation

**Financial data** (yr. ended 12/31/99): Assets, $4,707,429 (M); expenditures, $177,309; qualifying distributions, $142,800; giving activities include $142,800 for 15 grants (high: $20,000; low: $300).

**Fields of interest:** Museums; arts/cultural programs; libraries/library science; medical care, rehabilitation; youth development, centers & clubs; human services.

**Limitations:** Giving limited to the Brazos County, TX area. No grants to individuals.

**Application information:** Application form required.

*Deadline(s):* Mar. 15

**Trustee:** Norwest Bank Texas, N.A.

**EIN:** 746402510

---

**709**

## Dougherty Foundation

P.O. Box 640
Beeville, TX  78104-0640   (512) 358-3560
*Contact:* Daren R. Wilder, Secy.-Treas.

Established in 1940 in TX.

**Donor(s):** Genevieve T. Dougherty,‡ James R. Dougherty.‡

**Grantmaker type:** Independent foundation

**Financial data** (yr. ended 07/31/99): Assets, $2,186,597 (M); expenditures, $119,127; qualifying distributions, $113,993; giving activities include $114,675 for 24 grants (high: $14,000; low: $1,000).

**Purpose and activities:** Giving primarily for education and for health and human services.

**Fields of interest:** Higher education; libraries/library science; hospitals (general); human services; Christian agencies & churches; general charitable giving.

**Types of support:** General/operating support; continuing support; annual campaigns; capital campaigns; building/renovation; equipment; endowments; program development; conferences/seminars; scholarship funds; research.

**Limitations:** Giving primarily in southern TX. No grants to individuals.

**Application information:** Application form not required.

*Initial approach:* Letter

*Copies of proposal:* 1

*Deadline(s):* None

*Board meeting date(s):* Varies

**Officer:** Daren R. Wilder, Secy.-Treas.

**Trustees:** Mrs. Alvin Grimsinger, Mrs. John Allen King, Ben F. Vaughan III.

**Number of staff:** None.

**EIN:** 746039859

---

## 710
### The R. W. Fair Foundation
P.O. Box 689
Tyler, TX 75710 (903) 592-3811
*Contact:* Wilton H. Fair, Pres.

Trust established in 1936; incorporated in 1959 in TX.
**Donor(s):** R.W. Fair,‡ Mattie Allen Fair.‡
**Grantmaker type:** Independent foundation
**Financial data** (yr. ended 12/31/98): Assets, $14,676,660 (M); expenditures, $1,453,347; qualifying distributions, $899,881; giving activities include $899,121 for 89 grants (high: $170,000; low: $100; average: $1,000–$10,000).
**Purpose and activities:** Grants largely for Protestant church support and church-related programs, and for secondary and higher education. Some support for hospitals, youth and social service agencies, libraries, and cultural activities.
**Fields of interest:** Arts/cultural programs; education, fund raising; secondary school/education; higher education; libraries/library science; education; hospitals (general); cancer; heart & circulatory diseases; cancer research; heart & circulatory research; human services; youth, services; Protestant agencies & churches.
**Types of support:** Building/renovation; equipment; endowments; program development; seed money; research; matching/challenge support.
**Limitations:** Giving primarily in the Southwest, with emphasis on TX. No grants to individuals, or for operating budgets.
**Publications:** Application guidelines.
**Application information:** Application form required.
> *Initial approach:* Letter
> *Copies of proposal:* 1
> *Deadline(s):* Mar. 1, June 1, Sept. 1, and Dec. 1
> *Board meeting date(s):* Mar., June, Sept., and Dec.
> *Final notification:* 3 months
**Officers and Directors:*** Wilton H. Fair,* Pres.; James W. Fair,* Sr. V.P.; Sam Bright,* V.P.; Wilma Stenhouse,* Secy.-Treas.; Herbert Buie, B.G. Hartley, Will A. Knight, B.B. Palmore.
**Number of staff:** 2 part-time professional.
**EIN:** 756015270

## 711
### I. D. & Marguerite Fairchild Foundation
P.O. Box 150143
Lufkin, TX 75915-0143 (936) 634-2771
*Contact:* C. James Haley, Jr., Pres.

Established in 1977 in TX.
**Donor(s):** Marguerite Fairchild.‡
**Grantmaker type:** Independent foundation
**Financial data** (yr. ended 06/30/99): Assets, $4,466,243 (M); expenditures, $249,126; qualifying distributions, $230,781; giving activities include $220,000 for 9 grants (high: $110,000; low: $2,000).
**Purpose and activities:** Giving primarily for a college and museums. Giving also for libraries, a zoo, and education.
**Fields of interest:** Museums; arts/cultural programs; higher education; libraries (public);

education; zoos/zoological societies; community development.
**Types of support:** Endowments; program development; scholarship funds.
**Limitations:** Giving primarily in Angelina County, TX. No grants to individuals.
**Application information:** Application form not required.
> *Initial approach:* Letter
> *Copies of proposal:* 9
> *Deadline(s):* None
> *Board meeting date(s):* June
> *Final notification:* June 30
**Officers:** C. James Haley, Jr., Pres.; Hilda Mitchell, V.P.; Mary Duncan, Secy.
**Number of staff:** None.
**EIN:** 751572514

## 712
### Ray C. Fish Foundation
2001 Kirby Dr., Ste. 1005
Houston, TX 77019 (713) 522-0741
*Contact:* Paula Hooton, Secy.

Incorporated in 1957 in TX.
**Donor(s):** Raymond Clinton Fish,‡ Mirtha G. Fish.‡
**Grantmaker type:** Independent foundation
**Financial data** (yr. ended 06/30/99): Assets, $31,459,766 (M); gifts received, $68,676; expenditures, $1,591,814; qualifying distributions, $1,146,176; giving activities include $1,044,800 for 137 grants (high: $75,000; low: $500).
**Purpose and activities:** Giving for a presidential library, health, education, the arts, and children and youth services.
**Fields of interest:** Performing arts; arts/cultural programs; higher education; libraries (special); education; hospitals (general); medical research; human services; children & youth, services.
**Types of support:** General/operating support; continuing support; annual campaigns; capital campaigns; building/renovation; endowments; program development; professorships; seed money; scholarship funds; research; matching/challenge support.
**Limitations:** Giving primarily in TX, with emphasis on Houston. No grants to individuals.
**Publications:** Financial statement, informational brochure (including application guidelines), application guidelines.
**Application information:** Application form not required.
> *Copies of proposal:* 1
> *Board meeting date(s):* Quarterly
> *Final notification:* By mail
**Officers and Trustees:*** Barbara F. Daniel,* Pres.; Robert J. Cruikshank,* V.P.; James L. Daniel, Jr.,* V.P.; Paula Hooton,* Secy.; Christopher J. Daniel,* Treas.; Catherine Daniel.
**Number of staff:** 1 full-time professional.
**EIN:** 746043047

## 713
### Garvey Texas Foundation, Inc.
P.O. Box 9600
Fort Worth, TX 76147-2600
*Contact:* Shirley F. Garvey, Pres.

Incorporated in 1962 in TX.

**Donor(s):** James S. Garvey, Shirley F. Garvey, Garvey Foundation.
**Grantmaker type:** Independent foundation
**Financial data** (yr. ended 12/31/99): Assets, $9,957,199 (M); expenditures, $571,079; qualifying distributions, $473,569; giving activities include $479,043 for 89 grants (high: $130,000; low: $18).
**Fields of interest:** Orchestra (symphony); arts/cultural programs; elementary/secondary education; higher education; libraries/library science; health care; human services; children & youth, services; Christian agencies & churches.
**Types of support:** Capital campaigns; program-related investments/loans.
**Limitations:** Giving primarily in CO, KS, NE, OK and TX. No grants to individuals.
**Application information:** Application form required.
> *Initial approach:* Letter
> *Copies of proposal:* 1
> *Deadline(s):* None
**Officers:** Shirley F. Garvey, Pres.; James S. Garvey, V.P.; Richard F. Garvey, Secy.; Bedford L. Burgher, Treas.
**EIN:** 756031547

## 714
### The Gorges Foundation
(Formerly Patty Gorges Foundation)
P.O. Box 3547
Harlingen, TX 78551-3547
*Contact:* Matt Gorges, Pres.

Established in 1993 in TX.
**Donor(s):** Matt F. Gorges, Patricia C. Gorges.
**Grantmaker type:** Independent foundation
**Financial data** (yr. ended 12/31/98): Assets, $1,701,500 (M); expenditures, $230,190; qualifying distributions, $220,669; giving activities include $220,669 for grants (average: $2,500–$10,000).
**Purpose and activities:** Giving primarily for projects related to higher education, the Roman Catholic Church, or community improvement in Cameron County, TX.
**Fields of interest:** Higher education; libraries (public); Christian agencies & churches; Roman Catholic agencies & churches.
**Types of support:** Annual campaigns; capital campaigns; endowments; emergency funds; matching/challenge support.
**Limitations:** Giving primarily in Cameron County, TX. No grants to individuals.
**Application information:** Application form not required.
> *Initial approach:* Detailed letter
> *Deadline(s):* None
> *Board meeting date(s):* May 15
**Officers and Trustees:*** Matt F. Gorges,* Pres.; Patty Gorges,* Secy.-Treas.; Daniel Hightower.
**EIN:** 742690463

## 715
### Gray-Pampa Foundation, Inc.
412 Combs-Worley Bldg.
Pampa, TX 79065
*Contact:* Wesley Green, Chair.
*Application address:* 401 Combs-Worley Bldg., Pampa, TX 79065, tel.: (806) 669-3191

Established in 1954.

**Grantmaker type:** Independent foundation
**Financial data** (yr. ended 12/31/99): Assets, $1,930,457 (M); gifts received, $3,390; expenditures, $46,347; qualifying distributions, $44,032; giving activities include $42,782 for 16 grants (high: $17,282; low: $500).
**Purpose and activities:** Emphasis on library endeavors and support for the underprivileged.
**Fields of interest:** Libraries/library science; human services; federated giving programs.
**Types of support:** General/operating support; equipment.
**Limitations:** Giving limited to the Panhandle of TX, with emphasis on Gray and Pampa counties.
**Application information:**
   *Initial approach:* Proposal
   *Deadline(s):* July 1 and Dec. 1
**Officer and Trustees:*** Wesley Green,* Chair.; Kenneth W. Fields, Aubrey Steele, Bill W. Waters, Floyd Watson.
**EIN:** 756021715

### 716
### Hall-Voyer Foundation
(Formerly David Graham Hall Foundation)
502 N. Sixth St.
P.O. Box 47
Honey Grove, TX  75446
*Contact:* Mary A. Thurman, Exec. V.P.
*E-mail:* mat@1starnet.com; URL: http://www2.1starnet.com/hallv

Established around 1940 in TX.
**Donor(s):** David Graham Hall.‡
**Grantmaker type:** Operating foundation
**Financial data** (yr. ended 12/31/99): Assets, $4,383,258 (M); gifts received, $23,844; expenditures, $220,993; qualifying distributions, $188,787; giving activities include $130,000 for 3 grants (high: $10,000; low: $1,000) and $80,755 for foundation-administered programs.
**Fields of interest:** Libraries/library science; children & youth, services; rural development.
**Types of support:** General/operating support; program development.
**Limitations:** Applications not accepted. Giving limited to TX. No grants to individuals.
**Publications:** Informational brochure.
**Application information:** Contributes only to pre-selected organizations. Unsolicited requests for funds not considered.
   *Board meeting date(s):* Jan. and July
**Officers and Directors:*** Evelyn F. Wise,* Pres. and Treas.; Mary A. Thurman,* Exec. V.P.; Cheryl Beavers, Beverly Felts, Abraham Goldfarb, Ben Holland, Frank I. Millar.
**Number of staff:** 1 full-time professional; 2 part-time professional; 4 part-time support.
**EIN:** 750868394

### 717
### The Robert and Marie Hansen Family Foundation
3300 S. Gessner Rd.
Houston, TX  77063  (713) 735-3274
*Contact:* John P. Hansen, Dir.

Established in 1994 in TX.
**Donor(s):** Robert A. Hansen, Marie T. Hansen.
**Grantmaker type:** Independent foundation
**Financial data** (yr. ended 12/31/99): Assets, $2,215,934 (M); expenditures, $160,624;

qualifying distributions, $137,325; giving activities include $137,325 for 62 grants (high: $25,000; low: $25).
**Purpose and activities:** Giving primarily for education, health and human services, and religious organizations.
**Fields of interest:** Secondary school/education; libraries/library science; education; health associations; human services; Roman Catholic agencies & churches.
**Limitations:** No grants to individuals.
**Application information:** Application form not required.
   *Deadline(s):* None
**Directors:** Karen A. Clifton, Paul T. Clifton, John P. Hansen, Marie T. Hansen, Mark W. Hansen, Robert A. Hansen.
**EIN:** 760442783

### 718
### Wilton & Effie Mae Hebert Foundation
P.O. Box 908
Port Neches, TX  77651  (409) 727-2345
*Contact:* Pauline Womack, Dir.
*Application address:* 802 West Dr., Port Neches, TX 77651

Established in 1992 in TX.
**Donor(s):** Wilton P. Hebert,‡ Effie Mae Hebert.‡
**Grantmaker type:** Independent foundation
**Financial data** (yr. ended 12/31/99): Assets, $15,603,664 (M); expenditures, $869,349; qualifying distributions, $757,331; giving activities include $739,265 for 29 grants (high: $175,000; low: $1,055).
**Fields of interest:** Literature; arts/cultural programs; libraries/library science; education; hospitals (general); human services; aging, centers & services; science; religion; aging.
**Types of support:** General/operating support; building/renovation.
**Limitations:** Giving primarily in TX. No grants to individuals.
**Application information:** Application form required.
   *Copies of proposal:* 6
   *Deadline(s):* None
   *Board meeting date(s):* Mar., June, Sept., and Dec.
**Directors:** Earl Black, James Black, Jimmy Foster, Joe Hebert, Ed Hughes, Joe Vernon, Pauline Womack.
**Number of staff:** 1 full-time professional; 1 part-time professional.
**EIN:** 760065521

### 719
### Esther L. Heit Foundation
815 Montreal
Longview, TX  75601

Established in 1991 in TX.
**Donor(s):** Esther L. Smith.
**Grantmaker type:** Operating foundation
**Financial data** (yr. ended 12/31/99): Assets, $1,322,452 (M); expenditures, $115,064; qualifying distributions, $92,916; giving activities include $88,855 for 14 grants (high: $26,250; low: $100).
**Purpose and activities:** Giving for higher education, with an emphasis on scholarships.

**Fields of interest:** Higher education; libraries/library science; scholarships/financial aid; human services.
**Types of support:** Scholarship funds; scholarships—to individuals.
**Limitations:** Applications not accepted. Giving primarily in TX.
**Application information:** Contributes only to pre-selected organizations.
**Officers:** John G. Heit, Pres.; John A. Heit, V.P.; Carol G. Heit, Secy.-Treas.
**Directors:** James M. Heit, Carol A. Hicks, James P. Hicks, Mary Lou Lubbers.
**EIN:** 752392220

### 720
### The Thomas O. Hicks Family Foundation
200 Crescent Ct., Ste. 1600
Dallas, TX  75201

Established in 1994 in TX.
**Donor(s):** Thomas O. Hicks.
**Grantmaker type:** Independent foundation
**Financial data** (yr. ended 11/30/99): Assets, $11,789,158 (M); expenditures, $745,761; qualifying distributions, $726,672; giving activities include $727,700 for 10 grants (high: $441,667; low: $5,000).
**Purpose and activities:** Support primarily for higher education and a public library; some support also for the arts.
**Fields of interest:** Arts/cultural programs; higher education; libraries (public).
**Limitations:** Applications not accepted. Giving primarily in TX. No grants to individuals.
**Application information:** Contributes only to pre-selected organizations.
**Officers:** Thomas O. Hicks, Pres.; Cinda C. Hicks, V.P.
**Director:** Rebecca A. McConnell.
**EIN:** 752570214

### 721
### Albert & Bessie Mae Kronkosky Charitable Foundation
112 E. Pecan, Ste. 830
San Antonio, TX  78205  (210) 475-9000
*Contact:* Palmer Moe, Exec. Dir.
*Additional tel.:* (888) 309-9001; FAX: (210) 354-2204; E-mail: kronfndn@kronkosky.org; URL: http://www.kronkosky.org

Established in 1991 in TX.
**Donor(s):** Albert Kronkosky,‡ Bessie Mae Kronkosky.
**Grantmaker type:** Independent foundation
**Financial data** (yr. ended 12/31/99): Assets, $395,012,313 (M); gifts received, $155,000; expenditures, $17,359,597; qualifying distributions, $16,002,044; giving activities include $14,478,724 for 234 grants (high: $1,700,000; low: $192).
**Purpose and activities:** Support for the arts, museums, libraries, animal welfare, wildlife, medical research, child abuse prevention, parks, youth development, disabled, and aging.
**Fields of interest:** Arts, multipurpose centers/programs; museums; libraries (public); animal welfare; wildlife, sanctuaries; zoos/zoological societies; medical research; child abuse prevention; parks/playgrounds;

youth development, centers & clubs; disabled; aging.
**Types of support:** General/operating support; continuing support; capital campaigns; building/renovation; equipment; endowments; program development; research; consulting services; matching/challenge support.
**Limitations:** Giving limited to Bandera, Bexar, Comal, and Kendall counties, TX.
**Publications:** Application guidelines.
**Application information:** Application form required.
*Initial approach:* Letter of Inquiry
*Copies of proposal:* 1
*Deadline(s):* None
*Board meeting date(s):* 6 times annually
*Final notification:* Within 2 weeks of Dist. Comm. meeting
**Trustee:** Bank of America.
**Number of staff:** 6 full-time professional; 4 part-time support.
**EIN:** 746385152

## 722
## The Lende Foundation
701 N. St. Mary's St., Ste. 24
San Antonio, TX 78205

Established in 1978.
**Donor(s):** H.W. Lende, Jr., R.R. Lende, Elizabeth Lende.
**Grantmaker type:** Independent foundation
**Financial data** (yr. ended 11/30/99): Assets, $1,628,573 (M); gifts received, $900; expenditures, $88,984; qualifying distributions, $82,213; giving activities include $78,961 for 11 grants (high: $43,000; low: $1,000).
**Purpose and activities:** Giving to arts and culture, and education.
**Fields of interest:** Media/communications; libraries/library science; environment, research; environment, plant conservation; medicine/medical care, single organization support; hospitals (general); children & youth, services; human services, special populations; Christian agencies & churches.
**Limitations:** Applications not accepted. Giving primarily in San Antonio, TX. No grants to individuals.
**Application information:** Contributes only to pre-selected organizations.
**Officers:** H.W. Lende, Jr., Pres. and Treas.; R.R. Lende, V.P.
**EIN:** 741985933

## 723
## The Eugene McDermott Foundation ▼
3808 Euclid Ave.
Dallas, TX 75205
*Contact:* Mrs. Mary McDermott Cook, Pres.

Incorporated in 1972 in TX; absorbed The McDermott Foundation in 1977.
**Donor(s):** Eugene McDermott,‡ Mrs. Eugene McDermott.
**Grantmaker type:** Independent foundation
**Financial data** (yr. ended 08/31/99): Assets, $110,836,016 (M); expenditures, $4,829,680; qualifying distributions, $4,300,179; giving activities include $4,229,890 for 118 grants (high: $1,000,000; low: $500; average: $1,000–$25,000).

**Purpose and activities:** Support primarily for cultural programs, higher and secondary education, health, and general community interests.
**Fields of interest:** Museums; historic preservation/historical societies; arts/cultural programs; early childhood education; elementary school/education; secondary school/education; higher education; education; hospitals (general); health care; health associations; medical research; children & youth, services; human rights (international); community development; federated giving programs; government/public administration; minorities.
**Types of support:** General/operating support; continuing support; annual campaigns; capital campaigns; building/renovation; equipment; land acquisition; endowments; program development; professorships; seed money; curriculum development; scholarship funds; research; matching/challenge support.
**Limitations:** Giving primarily in Dallas, TX. No grants to individuals.
**Application information:** No printed material available. Application form not required.
*Initial approach:* Letter
*Copies of proposal:* 1
*Deadline(s):* None
*Board meeting date(s):* Quarterly
*Final notification:* Prior to Aug. 31
**Officers and Trustees:*** Mary McDermott Cook,* Pres.; Charles E. Cullum,* V.P.; Vincent Prothro,* Secy.-Treas.; Mrs. Eugene McDermott, C.J. Thomsen.
**Agent:** Bank of America.
**Number of staff:** 2 part-time professional.
**EIN:** 237237919
**Recent grants for library/information services:**
723-1 Dallas Public Library, Friends of the, Dallas, TX, $500,000. To renovate eighth floor of central Library. 1999.

## 724
## John P. McGovern Foundation ▼
2211 Norfolk St., Ste. 900
Houston, TX 77098-4044 (713) 661-4808
*Contact:* John P. McGovern, M.D., Pres.
*FAX:* (713) 661-3031

Established in 1961 in TX.
**Donor(s):** John P. McGovern, M.D.
**Grantmaker type:** Independent foundation
**Financial data** (yr. ended 08/31/99): Assets, $180,094,718 (M); gifts received, $4,410,914; expenditures, $9,194,031; qualifying distributions, $8,537,920; giving activities include $8,350,000 for 82 grants (high: $5,788,900; low: $100).
**Purpose and activities:** To carry on the charitable interests of the donor to support the activities of established nonprofit organizations, which are of importance to human welfare with special focus on children and family health education and promotion, treatment and disease prevention.
**Fields of interest:** Education; health care; children & youth, services; family services; community development, neighborhood development.
**Types of support:** General/operating support; continuing support; building/renovation; endowments; emergency funds;

conferences/seminars; professorships; publication; curriculum development; scholarship funds; research; matching/challenge support.
**Limitations:** Applications not accepted. Giving primarily in TX, with emphasis on Houston; giving also in the Southwest. No grants to individuals.
**Application information:** Contributes only to pre-selected organizations.
*Board meeting date(s):* Usually on or before Aug. 31
**Officers and Director:** John P. McGovern, M.D., Pres.; Kathrine G. McGovern, V.P. and Treas.; Gay Collette, Secy.; Orville L. Story.
**Number of staff:** 1 part-time professional; 6 part-time support.
**EIN:** 746053075
**Recent grants for library/information services:**
724-1 Houston Academy of Medicine, Texas Medical Center Library, Houston, TX, $30,000. For John P. McGovern History of Medicine Collection. 1999.
724-2 Ronald Reagan Presidential Foundation, Simi Valley, CA, $250,000. 1999.

## 725
## Meadows Foundation, Inc. ▼
Wilson Historic Block
3003 Swiss Ave.
Dallas, TX 75204-6090 (214) 826-9431
*Contact:* Bruce H. Esterline, V.P., Admin.
*URL:* http://www.mfi.org

Incorporated in 1948 in TX.
**Donor(s):** Algur Hurtle Meadows,‡ Virginia Meadows.‡
**Grantmaker type:** Independent foundation
**Financial data** (yr. ended 12/31/99): Assets, $901,119,098 (M); expenditures, $48,843,524; qualifying distributions, $38,667,333; giving activities include $24,897,355 for 230 grants (average: $25,000–$250,000), $43,361 for employee matching gifts, $759,045 for foundation-administered programs, $5,743,680 for program-related investments and $1,184,000 for 26 in-kind gifts.
**Purpose and activities:** Support for the arts, social services, community and rural development, health, education, and civic and cultural programs. Operates a historic preservation investment-related program using a cluster of Victorian homes as offices for nonprofit agencies.
**Fields of interest:** Media/communications; architecture; museums; humanities; history & archaeology; historic preservation/historical societies; arts/cultural programs; education, public education; early childhood education; child development, education; medical school/education; adult/continuing education; adult education—literacy & basic skills; libraries/library science; reading; education; natural resource conservation & protection; environment; wildlife preservation & protection; dental care; medical care, rehabilitation; nursing care; health care; substance abuse, services; mental health/crisis services; AIDS; alcoholism; AIDS research; crime/law enforcement; employment; agriculture; nutrition; housing/shelter, development; safety/disasters; recreation; youth development, services; human services; children & youth, services; child

development, services; family services; hospices; aging, centers & services; homeless, human services; race/intergroup relations; urban/community development; rural development; community development; voluntarism promotion; government/public administration; transportation; leadership development; public affairs; Christian agencies & churches; aging; economically disadvantaged; homeless.

**Types of support:** General/operating support; continuing support; capital campaigns; building/renovation; equipment; land acquisition; endowments; debt reduction; emergency funds; program development; seed money; curriculum development; research; technical assistance; consulting services; program evaluation; program-related investments/loans; employee matching gifts; matching/challenge support.

**Limitations:** Giving limited to TX. No grants to individuals; generally, no grants for annual campaigns, fundraising events, professional conferences and symposia, travel expenses for groups to perform or compete outside of TX, or construction of churches and seminaries.

**Publications:** Annual report (including application guidelines), application guidelines.

**Application information:** Application form not required.

> *Initial approach:* Proposal
> *Copies of proposal:* 1
> *Deadline(s):* None
> *Board meeting date(s):* Grants review committee meets monthly; full board meets 2 or 3 times a year
> *Final notification:* 3 to 4 months

**Officers and Directors:*** Robert A. Meadows,* Chair. and V.P.; Linda P. Evans,* Pres. and C.E.O.; Martha L. Benson, V.P., Treas. and C.F.O.; Larry Meadows Broadfoot, V.P.; Michael E. Patrick, V.P. and C.I.O.; Bruce H. Esterline, V.P., Grants Admin.; Robert E. Weiss, V.P., Admin.; Emily J. Jones, Corp. Secy.; Evelyn Meadows Acton, Dir. Emeritus; John W. Broadfoot, J.W. Bullion, True Miller Campbell, Daniel H. Chapman, Judy B. Culbertson, Deborah Rouse Gill, John A. Hammack, Sally R. Lancaster, Dir. Emeritus; P. Mike McCullough, Curtis W. Meadows, Jr., Dir. Emeritus; Mark A. Meadows, Michael L. Meadows, Sally C. Miller, Dir. Emeritus; G. Tomas Rhodus, Evy Kay Ritzen, Eloise Meadows Rouse, Dir. Emeritus; Stephen Wheeler Wilson, Dorothy C. Wilson, Dir. Emeritus.

**Number of staff:** 23 full-time professional; 1 part-time professional; 21 full-time support; 2 part-time support.

**EIN:** 756015322

**Recent grants for library/information services:**

**725-1** Blanco Library, Blanco, TX, $50,000. Toward renovating and expanding facility to house library. 1999.

**725-2** Clute Public Library Association, Clute, TX, $75,000. Toward construction. 1999.

**725-3** Comfort Public Library, Comfort, TX, $50,000. Toward expansion and renovation. 1999.

**725-4** Floyd County Library, Friends of the, Floydada, TX, $50,000. Toward constructing Library. 1999.

**725-5** Jourdanton Library and Community Center Foundation, Jourdanton, TX, $75,250. Toward construction. 1999.

**725-6** Lockhart, City of, Lockhart, TX, $100,000. Toward restoring and expanding Dr. Eugene Clark Library. 1999.

**725-7** National Council for Science and the Environment, DC, $24,600. Toward developing online resource of Texas environmental information. 1999.

**725-8** Shiner Public Library, Friends of the, Shiner, TX, $57,500. Toward constructing Library and cultural center. 1999.

**725-9** Spur, City of, Spur, TX, $40,000. Toward purchasing and renovating building to house new public library. 1999.

## 726
## Meredith Foundation

P.O. Box 117
Mineola, TX 75773

Trust established in 1958 in TX.
**Donor(s):** Harry W. Meredith.‡
**Grantmaker type:** Independent foundation
**Financial data** (yr. ended 12/31/99): Assets, $16,504,249 (M); expenditures, $797,580; qualifying distributions, $702,637; giving activities include $706,991 for 10 grants (high: $168,893; low: $2,000).
**Purpose and activities:** Giving primarily for civic projects; support also for educational and cultural projects and a library.
**Fields of interest:** Arts/cultural programs; libraries/library science; education; children & youth, services; civic centers; government/public administration.
**Types of support:** General/operating support; equipment; scholarship funds.
**Limitations:** Applications not accepted. Giving limited to the Mineola, TX, area. No grants to individuals.
**Publications:** Program policy statement.
**Application information:** Contributes only to pre-selected organizations.

> *Board meeting date(s):* Monthly

**Officers:** James Dear,* Chair.; Coulter Templeton,* Vice-Chair.; Ray Williams,* Secy.-Treas.
**Trustees:** W.T. Harrison, J. Carl Norris.
**EIN:** 756024469

## 727
## Navarro Community Foundation

P.O. Box 1035
Corsicana, TX 75151 (903) 874-4301
*Contact:* W. Bruce Robinson, Exec. Secy.-Treas.

Established in 1938 in TX.
**Donor(s):** Frank N. Drane.‡
**Grantmaker type:** Independent foundation
**Financial data** (yr. ended 12/31/99): Assets, $21,825,089 (M); expenditures, $1,053,225; qualifying distributions, $955,915; giving activities include $968,365 for 41 grants (high: $400,000; low: $1,200).
**Purpose and activities:** Support largely for public schools, higher education, community development, and a community fund; grants also for Protestant church support, child welfare, youth agencies, a hospital, a library, and cultural programs.
**Fields of interest:** Elementary/secondary education; higher education; libraries/library science; hospitals (general); children & youth,

services; community development; federated giving programs; Protestant agencies & churches.
**Types of support:** General/operating support; annual campaigns; capital campaigns; building/renovation; seed money; scholarship funds; matching/challenge support.
**Limitations:** Giving limited to Navarro County, TX. No grants to individuals, or for research, conferences, endowment funds, publications, or special projects; no loans.
**Application information:** Application form not required.

> *Initial approach:* Proposal
> *Copies of proposal:* 2
> *Deadline(s):* Jan. 1, Apr. 1, July 1, and Oct. 1
> *Board meeting date(s):* Jan., Apr., July, and Oct.

**Officers and Trustees:*** William Clarkson III,* Chair.; W. Bruce Robinson,* Exec. Secy.-Treas.; O.L. Albritton, Jr., C.L. Brown III, C. David Campbell, M.D., Lynn Cooper, Embry Ferguson, Gioia Keeney, Billie Love McFerran, Halsey M. Settle III, M.D., John B. Stroud.
**Trustee Banks:** Bank One, Texas, N.A., Corsicana National Bank, Bank of America.
**Number of staff:** 1 full-time professional; 1 part-time professional.
**EIN:** 750800663

## 728
## John and Florence Newman Foundation

112 E. Pecan, Ste. 1725
San Antonio, TX 78205 (210) 226-0371

Established in 1988 in TX.
**Donor(s):** Florence B. Newman.
**Grantmaker type:** Independent foundation
**Financial data** (yr. ended 12/31/98): Assets, $11,759,817 (M); expenditures, $686,146; qualifying distributions, $526,369; giving activities include $471,905 for 38 grants (high: $165,000; low: $14).
**Purpose and activities:** Giving primarily for the arts and education.
**Fields of interest:** Media/communications; museums; arts/cultural programs; libraries/library science; education; animal welfare; community development; Christian agencies & churches.
**Types of support:** General/operating support; equipment; scholarship funds.
**Limitations:** Applications not accepted. Giving primarily in San Antonio, TX. No grants to individuals.
**Application information:** Contributes only to pre-selected organizations.
**Directors:** Catherine Houston, Ann J. Newman, John E. Newman, Jr.
**EIN:** 742525348

## 729
## The Kathryn O'Connor Foundation

1 O'Connor Plz., Ste. 1100
Victoria, TX 77901 (512) 578-6271
*Contact:* D.H. Braman, Jr., Pres.

Incorporated in 1951 in TX.
**Donor(s):** Kathryn S. O'Connor,‡ Tom O'Connor, Jr.,‡ Dennis O'Connor, Mary O'Connor Braman.‡
**Grantmaker type:** Independent foundation
**Financial data** (yr. ended 12/31/99): Assets, $6,393,143 (M); expenditures, $427,002;

qualifying distributions, $376,138; giving activities include $376,138 for 19 grants (high: $135,000; low: $1,000; average: $10,000–$50,000).

**Purpose and activities:** Support for institutions for the advancement of religion, education, and the relief of poverty; grants also for hospitals. The foundation also operates and maintains a church.

**Fields of interest:** Elementary/secondary education; secondary school/education; higher education; libraries/library science; hospitals (general); cancer; cancer research; hospices; Christian agencies & churches; Roman Catholic agencies & churches; religion.

**Types of support:** General/operating support; continuing support; annual campaigns; building/renovation.

**Limitations:** Giving limited to southern TX, with emphasis on Victoria and Refugio counties and surrounding area. No grants to individuals, or for matching gifts; no loans.

**Publications:** Annual report.

**Application information:** Application form not required.

   *Initial approach:* Letter
   *Deadline(s):* None
   *Board meeting date(s):* As required

**Officers:** D.H. Braman, Jr.,* Pres.; Venable B. Proctor, Secy.; Robert L. Coffey, Treas.

**Number of staff:** None.

**EIN:** 746039415

---

### 730
### David D. & Nona S. Payne Foundation, Inc.

Hughes Bldg., Ste. 436
Pampa, TX 79065 (806) 665-7281
*Contact:* Adelaide S. Colwell, Secy.
*Application address:* 2000 Charles St., Pampa, TX 79065, tel.: (806) 665-3488

Established in 1980 in TX.

**Donor(s):** Nona S. Payne.‡

**Grantmaker type:** Independent foundation

**Financial data** (yr. ended 06/30/99): Assets, $2,180,572 (M); expenditures, $129,088; qualifying distributions, $114,380; giving activities include $115,700 for grants (average: $5,000–$10,000).

**Purpose and activities:** Primary areas of interest include the fine arts, education, social services, the elderly, and youth.

**Fields of interest:** Visual arts; museums; performing arts; adult education—literacy & basic skills; libraries/library science; reading; education; mental health/crisis services; human services; youth, services; hospices; aging, centers & services; government/public administration; Christian agencies & churches; aging.

**Types of support:** General/operating support; building/renovation; equipment; emergency funds; matching/challenge support.

**Limitations:** Giving primarily in the TX Panhandle area. No grants to individuals.

**Application information:** Application form required.

   *Initial approach:* Letter or telephone
   *Copies of proposal:* 3
   *Deadline(s):* Sept. 23 and Mar. 23; grant awards are made semiannually in Apr. and Oct.

   *Board meeting date(s):* 1st Tuesday of each calendar quarter
   *Final notification:* 2 weeks

**Officers and Trustees:*** Vanessa G. Buzzard,* Pres.; Rebecca L. Holmes,* V.P. and Treas.; Adelaide S. Colwell,* Secy.

**EIN:** 751736339

---

### 731
### The Pineywoods Foundation

P.O. Box 1647
Lufkin, TX 75902 (936) 634-7444
*Contact:* Bob Bowman, Secy.
*Application address:* 515 S. 1st St., Lufkin, TX 75901; FAX: (409) 634-7750

Established in 1984 in TX.

**Donor(s):** The Southland Foundation.

**Grantmaker type:** Independent foundation

**Financial data** (yr. ended 12/31/98): Assets, $3,352,000 (M); expenditures, $128,547; qualifying distributions, $124,740; giving activities include $115,816 for 21 grants (high: $20,000; low: $1,000; average: $1,000–$20,000).

**Fields of interest:** Museums; history & archaeology; historic preservation/historical societies; libraries/library science; education; health care; human services; children & youth, services; rural development; community development; government/public administration.

**Types of support:** General/operating support; building/renovation; equipment; program development; publication; seed money; research; matching/challenge support.

**Limitations:** Giving limited to Angelina, Cherokee, Houston, Jasper, Nacogdoches, Panola, Polk, Sabine, San Augustine, San Jacinto, Shelby, Trinity, and Tyler counties, TX. No support for governmental agencies, state colleges, universities, or churches and other religious organizations. No grants to individuals, or for salaries or annual operating budgets.

**Publications:** Informational brochure, application guidelines.

**Application information:** Application form required.

   *Initial approach:* Proposal
   *Copies of proposal:* 8
   *Deadline(s):* None
   *Board meeting date(s):* Quarterly, at will
   *Final notification:* Following board meetings

**Officers and Trustees:*** John F. Anderson,* Chair.; Bob Bowman,* Secy.; George Henderson,* Treas.

**Number of staff:** 1 part-time professional.

**EIN:** 751922533

---

### 732
### Pollock Foundation

2626 Howell St., Ste. 895
Dallas, TX 75204 (214) 871-7155
*Contact:* Robert G. Pollock

Established in 1955 in TX.

**Donor(s):** Lawrence S. Pollock, Sr.,‡ Lawrence S. Pollock, Jr.‡

**Grantmaker type:** Independent foundation

**Financial data** (yr. ended 12/31/99): Assets, $13,010,197 (M); gifts received, $3,344,933; expenditures, $564,150; qualifying distributions,

$530,543; giving activities include $529,700 for 16 grants (high: $150,000; low: $500).

**Fields of interest:** Arts/cultural programs; public health school/education; dental school/education; libraries/library science; nursing care; youth development, centers & clubs; human services; Jewish agencies & temples.

**Limitations:** Giving primarily in Dallas, TX.

**Application information:** Application form required.

   *Deadline(s):* None

**Trustees:** Lawrence S. Pollock III, Richard Pollock, Robert G. Pollock, Shirley Pollock.

**EIN:** 756011985

---

### 733
### Ed Rachal Foundation

210 S. Carancahua, Ste. 303
Corpus Christi, TX 78401-3040
(361) 881-9040
*Contact:* Paul D. Atheide, C.E.O. and Secy.
*FAX:* (361) 881-9885; E-mail: edrachel@edrachel.org; URL: http://www.edrachel.org

Established in 1965 in TX.

**Grantmaker type:** Independent foundation

**Financial data** (yr. ended 08/31/98): Assets, $20,864,691 (M); expenditures, $1,869,607; qualifying distributions, $1,019,259; giving activities include $206,641 for 48 grants (high: $25,000; low: $500) and $692,437 for foundation-administered programs.

**Purpose and activities:** Giving primarily to a university.

**Fields of interest:** Higher education; libraries/library science; health associations; human services; Christian agencies & churches.

**Types of support:** General/operating support; building/renovation.

**Limitations:** Giving limited to TX.

**Application information:** Application form required.

   *Initial approach:* Request for application
   *Deadline(s):* None
   *Board meeting date(s):* Nov., Feb., May, and Aug.

**Officers and Directors:*** John D. White,* Chair.; Robert L. Walker,* Vice-Chair.; Paul D. Altheide,* C.E.O. and Secy.; Richard Schendel,* Treas.

**Director:** John White.

**Number of staff:** 3 full-time professional; 5 full-time support; 1 part-time support.

**EIN:** 741116595

---

### 734
### Rockwell Fund, Inc. ▼

1330 Post Oak Blvd., Ste. 1825
Houston, TX 77056 (713) 629-9022
*Contact:* R. Terry Bell, Pres.
*FAX:* (713) 629-7702; URL: http://www.rockfund.org

Trust established in 1931; incorporated in 1949 in TX; merged with Rockwell Brothers Endowment, Inc. in 1981.

**Donor(s):** Members of the James M. Rockwell family.

**Grantmaker type:** Independent foundation

**Financial data** (yr. ended 12/31/99): Assets, $132,653,552 (M); expenditures, $5,896,150; qualifying distributions, $5,070,984; giving activities include $4,772,360 for 142 grants (high: $100,000; low: $500; average: $10,000–$20,000).
**Purpose and activities:** Giving primarily for charitable, religious, educational, medical, arts and humanities, and civic purposes.
**Fields of interest:** Visual arts; museums; performing arts; theater; music; humanities; historic preservation/historical societies; arts/cultural programs; early childhood education; child development, education; elementary school/education; secondary school/education; higher education; adult/continuing education; adult education—literacy & basic skills; libraries/library science; reading; education; natural resource conservation & protection; environment; animal welfare; hospitals (general); family planning; medical care, rehabilitation; nursing care; health care; health associations; cancer; AIDS; biomedicine; delinquency prevention/services; crime/law enforcement; food services; human services; children & youth, services; child development, services; homeless, human services; Protestant federated giving programs; government/public administration; Christian agencies & churches; Protestant agencies & churches; minorities; disabled; aging; homeless; general charitable giving.
**Types of support:** General/operating support; continuing support; annual campaigns; capital campaigns; building/renovation; equipment; land acquisition; endowments; program development; professorships; publication; seed money; curriculum development; fellowships; scholarship funds; matching/challenge support.
**Limitations:** Giving primarily in TX, with emphasis on Houston. No grants to individuals or for medical or scientific research projects, underwriting benefits, dinners, galas, and fundraising special events, or mass appeal solicitations; no loans; grants primarily awarded on a year-to-year basis only.
**Publications:** Annual report, application guidelines.
**Application information:** Applicants should not submit more than 1 proposal per year. Application form required.
  *Initial approach:* Letter requesting application and guidelines
  *Copies of proposal:* 1
  *Deadline(s):* Feb. 1, May 1, Aug. 1, and Nov. 1
  *Board meeting date(s):* Quarterly
  *Final notification:* After each quarterly meeting
**Officers and Trustees:*** R. Terry Bell,* Pres.; Helen N. Sterling,* V.P.; Mary Jo Loyd,* Secy.; Bennie Green,* Treas.; Lucian L. Morrison.
**Number of staff:** 3 full-time professional; 3 part-time professional; 1 full-time support.
**EIN:** 746040258
**Recent grants for library/information services:**
**734-1** Children at Risk, Houston, TX, $10,000. To update children's services database. 1998.
**734-2** Clute Public Library Association, Clute, TX, $10,000. For construction of new library building. 1998.
**734-3** Houston Academy of Medicine, Houston, TX, $20,000. To create HealthNET at medical library. 1998.

**734-4** Nederland, City of, Nederland, TX, $10,000. For public library furnishings and equipment. 1998.

---

**735**
**Shell Oil Company Foundation ▼**
(Formerly Shell Companies Foundation, Inc.)
910 Louisiana, Ste. 4137
P.O. Box 2099
Houston, TX  77252  (713) 241-3616
*Contact:* J.N. Doherty, Pres.
*FAX:* (713) 241-3329; URL: http://www.countonshell.com/community/community_found.html

Incorporated in 1953 in NY.
**Donor(s):** Shell Oil Co., and other participating companies.
**Grantmaker type:** Company-sponsored foundation
**Financial data** (yr. ended 12/31/99): Assets, $60,752,688 (M); gifts received, $987,900; expenditures, $37,349,620; qualifying distributions, $20,356,550; giving activities include $19,958,211 for 686 grants (high: $2,464,000; low: $500; average: $1,000–$100,000) and $2,584,240 for employee matching gifts.
**Purpose and activities:** Preferred areas of giving are education and community funds. About 48 percent of the budget is channeled through a number of planned programs that provide student aid, faculty development, basic research grants, and departmental grants to some 725 colleges and universities (three-quarters of these schools participate in Shell Matching Gifts Program only), and to a few national educational organizations. Main interests in education are math, engineering, science, and business. Approximately 24 percent of the budget is directed to United Way organizations in cities or towns where Shell employees reside. The remaining funds are paid to a limited number of national organizations concerned with a broad range of needs and, to a greater extent, to local organizations in communities where significant numbers of Shell employees reside.
**Fields of interest:** Visual arts; museums; performing arts; dance; theater; music; arts/cultural programs; education, association; elementary school/education; secondary school/education; higher education; business school/education; law school/education; engineering school/education; libraries/library science; education; natural resource conservation & protection; energy; environment; wildlife preservation & protection; hospitals (general); health care; substance abuse, services; health associations; cancer; medical research; cancer research; youth development; citizenship; human services; children & youth, services; hospices; minorities/immigrants, centers & services; business & industry; federated giving programs; chemistry; mathematics; engineering & technology; computer science; engineering; science; economics; public policy, research; government/public administration; public affairs; citizen participation; minorities; disabled; economically disadvantaged; general charitable giving.

**Types of support:** General/operating support; continuing support; annual campaigns; capital campaigns; program development; professorships; publication; curriculum development; fellowships; scholarship funds; research; consulting services; employee matching gifts; matching/challenge support.
**Limitations:** Giving primarily in areas of company operations. No support for special requests of colleges, universities, and college fundraising associations, or hospital operating expenses. No grants to individuals, or for endowment funds, capital campaigns of national organizations, or development funds; no loans.
**Publications:** Corporate giving report (including application guidelines).
**Application information:** Scholarship programs administered through National Merit Scholarship Corp. Application form not required.
  *Initial approach:* Letter
  *Copies of proposal:* 1
  *Deadline(s):* Submit proposal Jan. through Aug.; deadline Aug. 31
  *Board meeting date(s):* Mar. and Dec.
  *Final notification:* 1 month
**Officers and Directors:*** J.N. Doherty,* Pres.; N.J. Caruso,* V.P.; B.W. Levan,* V.P.; B.L. McHam, Secy.; R.W. Leftwich, Treas.; G.E. Banister, S.M. Borches, P.D. Ching, C.E. Dunagan, J.L. Golden, S.A. Lackey, S.C. Stryker.
**Number of staff:** 5 full-time professional; 2 full-time support.
**EIN:** 136066583
**Recent grants for library/information services:**
**735-1** Charter School Resource Center of Texas, San Antonio, TX, $10,000. 1998.
**735-2** George Bush Presidential Library Center, College Station, TX, $50,000. 1998.
**735-3** Houston Education Resource Network (HERN), Houston, TX, $10,000. 1998.
**735-4** Houston Public Library, Houston, TX, $10,000. 1998.
**735-5** Houston Public Library, Houston, TX, $10,000. 1998.
**735-6** Library of Congress, DC, $100,000. 1998.
**735-7** People with AIDS Coalition (PWAC) Houston, Houston, TX, $10,000. 1998.

---

**736**
**J. E. Smothers, Sr. Memorial Foundation**
P.O. Box 17423
San Antonio, TX  78217  (210) 829-1783
*Contact:* Mary Ann Smothers Bruni, Tr.

Established in 1990 in TX.
**Grantmaker type:** Independent foundation
**Financial data** (yr. ended 09/30/99): Assets, $2,770,093 (M); expenditures, $93,449; qualifying distributions, $87,680; giving activities include $89,400 for 13 grants (high: $50,000; low: $1,500).
**Purpose and activities:** Giving for higher education, arts and sciences, and religion.
**Fields of interest:** Arts/cultural programs; libraries/library science.
**Types of support:** General/operating support; building/renovation; program development.
**Limitations:** Giving primarily in TX. No grants to individuals.
**Application information:**
  *Initial approach:* Letter
  *Deadline(s):* None

**Trustees:** Mary Ann Smothers Bruni, J.E. Smothers, Jr.
**EIN:** 742608200

## 737
### Sterling-Turner Foundation
(Formerly Turner Charitable Foundation)
811 Rusk, Ste. 205
Houston, TX 77002-2811 (713) 237-1117
*Contact:* Eyvonne Moser, Exec. Dir.
*FAX:* (713) 223-4638

Incorporated in 1960 in TX.
**Donor(s):** Isla Carroll Turner,‡ P.E. Turner.‡
**Grantmaker type:** Independent foundation
**Financial data** (yr. ended 12/31/99): Assets, $55,771,569 (M); expenditures, $2,577,639; qualifying distributions, $2,392,207; giving activities include $2,415,689 for 125 grants (high: $172,667; low: $800; average: $5,000–$25,000).
**Purpose and activities:** Giving for higher and secondary education, social services, youth, the elderly, fine and performing arts groups and other cultural programs, Catholic, Jewish, and Protestant church support and religious programs, hospitals, health services, AIDS research, hospices, programs for women and children, minorities, the homeless, the handicapped, urban and community development, civic and urban affairs, libraries, and conservation programs.
**Fields of interest:** Visual arts; museums; performing arts; theater; historic preservation/historical societies; arts/cultural programs; education, association; education, research; education, fund raising; elementary/secondary education; child development, education; secondary school/education; higher education; adult education—literacy & basic skills; libraries/library science; reading; natural resource conservation & protection; animal welfare; hospitals (general); medical care, rehabilitation; health care; substance abuse, services; mental health/crisis services; cancer; heart & circulatory diseases; AIDS; cancer research; heart & circulatory research; AIDS research; domestic violence prevention; food services; recreation; children & youth, services; child development, services; family services; hospices; minorities/immigrants, centers & services; homeless, human services; civil rights, minorities; civil rights, disabled; civil rights, women; civil rights, aging; civil rights, gays/lesbians; community development, business promotion; community development; federated giving programs; government/public administration; Protestant agencies & churches; Roman Catholic agencies & churches; Jewish agencies & temples; religion; minorities; African Americans; Latinos; aging; women; people with AIDS (PWAs); homeless.
**Types of support:** General/operating support; continuing support; annual campaigns; capital campaigns; building/renovation; equipment; land acquisition; endowments; debt reduction; emergency funds; program development; conferences/seminars; professorships; publication; seed money; curriculum development; fellowships; scholarship funds; research; matching/challenge support.

**Limitations:** Giving limited to TX. No grants to individuals.
**Publications:** Application guidelines.
**Application information:** Contact foundation for guidelines. Application form required.
  *Initial approach:* Written request
  *Copies of proposal:* 1
  *Deadline(s):* Mar. 1
  *Board meeting date(s):* Apr.
  *Final notification:* Positive responses only
**Officers and Trustees:*** T.R. Reckling III,* Pres.; Bert F. Winston, Jr.,* V.P.; Christiana R. McConn,* Secy.; Isla C. Reckling,* Treas.; Eyvonne Moser, Exec. Dir.; Thomas E. Berry, Blake W. Caldwell, Carroll R. Goodman, Chaille W. Hawkins, James S. Reckling, John B. Reckling, Stephen M. Reckling, T.R. "Cliffe" Reckling IV, Thomas K. Reckling, L. David Winston.
**Number of staff:** 2 full-time professional.
**EIN:** 741460482

## 738
### Roy and Christine Sturgis Charitable and Educational Trust ▼
c/o Bank of America
P.O. Box 830241
Dallas, TX 75283-0241 (214) 209-1965
*Contact:* Daniel J. Kelly, V.P., Bank of America

Established in 1981 in AR.
**Donor(s):** Christine Sturgis.‡
**Grantmaker type:** Independent foundation
**Financial data** (yr. ended 09/30/98): Assets, $56,911,802 (M); expenditures, $3,797,422; qualifying distributions, $3,023,053; giving activities include $3,004,000 for 61 grants (high: $500,000; low: $6,000; average: $10,000–$20,000).
**Purpose and activities:** Support primarily for religious, charitable, scientific, literary, and educational organizations.
**Fields of interest:** Arts/cultural programs; education, fund raising; libraries/library science; education; hospitals (general); health care; health associations; medical research; food services; human services; homeless, human services; engineering & technology; science; economically disadvantaged; homeless.
**Types of support:** General/operating support; capital campaigns; building/renovation; equipment; endowments; program development; scholarship funds; research; matching/challenge support.
**Limitations:** Giving primarily in AR and the Dallas, TX, area. No grants to individuals or for seminars; no loans.
**Publications:** Application guidelines, program policy statement.
**Application information:** No personal interviews granted. Application form required.
  *Initial approach:* Letter
  *Copies of proposal:* 2
  *Deadline(s):* Dec. 31
  *Board meeting date(s):* Apr.
  *Final notification:* May
**Trustee Bank:** Bank of America.
**Number of staff:** 1 part-time professional; 1 part-time support.
**EIN:** 756331832
**Recent grants for library/information services:**

**738-1** Arkansas Sheriffs Boys and Girls Ranches, Batesville, AR, $75,000. For Tutorial Center and Library. 1998.
**738-2** Dallas Public Library, Friends of the, Dallas, TX, $15,000. For Mobile Learning Center. 1998.

## 739
### Swalm Foundation ▼
11511 Katy Fwy., Ste. 430
Houston, TX 77079 (281) 497-5280
*Contact:* Mimi Minkoff, Secy. and Grant Admin.
*FAX:* (281) 497-7340; URL: http://www.swalm.org

Established in 1980 in TX.
**Donor(s):** Dave C. Swalm, Texas Olefins Co.
**Grantmaker type:** Independent foundation
**Financial data** (yr. ended 11/30/99): Assets, $100,273,247 (M); gifts received, $2,880,000; expenditures, $5,134,275; qualifying distributions, $4,472,671; giving activities include $4,200,522 for 104 grants (high: $210,000; low: $3,450).
**Purpose and activities:** Giving primarily for human service organizations, education, and health.
**Fields of interest:** Education, research; education, fund raising; early childhood education; child development, education; elementary school/education; higher education; engineering school/education; adult/continuing education; adult education—literacy & basic skills; libraries/library science; reading; education; medical care, rehabilitation; health care; substance abuse, services; mental health/crisis services; skin disorders; AIDS; alcoholism; skin disorders research; AIDS research; food services; nutrition; housing/shelter, development; human services; children & youth, services; child development, services; family services; hospices; aging, centers & services; women, centers & services; homeless, human services; engineering; Christian agencies & churches; minorities; disabled; aging; women; economically disadvantaged; homeless; general charitable giving.
**Types of support:** General/operating support; building/renovation; endowments; emergency funds; scholarship funds; matching/challenge support.
**Limitations:** Giving primarily in TX. No support for programs with no local community support, religious social service programs, summer camps, retreats, field trips unless a large component is for the disadvantaged and for their theraputic, cultural or educational use, medical research, experimental programs in public education including charter schools. No grants to individuals or fellowships, buildings or operations of individual churches, synagogues, or mosques, capital campaigns and operations of institutes of higher education and medical facilities, galas or other social fundraisers, large national or international organization's giving campaign, organization whose geographic locations preclude or inhibit foundation staff monitoring or oversight.
**Publications:** Informational brochure (including application guidelines).
**Application information:** Application form required.

*Initial approach:* Letter or telephone requesting application form
*Copies of proposal:* 1
*Deadline(s):* 90 days prior to board meetings for consideration in current quarter
*Board meeting date(s):* Mar., June, Sept., and Jan.
**Officers and Directors:*** Beth C. Swalm,* Chair.; Billy C. Ward,* Pres. and C.E.O.; Dave C. Swalm,* V.P.; Mimi Minkoff,* Secy. and Grant Admin.; Mark C. Mendelovitz,* Treas.
**Number of staff:** 1 part-time professional; 1 part-time support.
**EIN:** 742073420
**Recent grants for library/information services:**
**739-1** Cedar Creek Library, Seven Points, TX, $35,000. To purchase furniture for new facility. 1998.

## 740
### Tocker Foundation
3814 Medical Pkwy.
Austin, TX 78756-4002 (512) 452-1044
*Contact:* Darryl Tocker, Exec. Dir.
*FAX:* (512) 452-7690; E-mail: Grants@Tocker.org; URL: http://www.tocker.org

Established in 1964 in TX.
**Donor(s):** Phillip Tocker,‡ Mrs. Phillip Tocker.‡
**Grantmaker type:** Independent foundation
**Financial data** (yr. ended 11/30/99): Assets, $39,731,832 (M); gifts received, $1,000; expenditures, $1,565,318; qualifying distributions, $1,672,574; giving activities include $1,220,945 for 121 grants (high: $100,000; low: $100; average: $7,000–$400,000).
**Purpose and activities:** Giving primarily to public libraries.
**Fields of interest:** Libraries/library science; education.
**Limitations:** Giving primarily in TX. No grants to individuals.
**Publications:** Informational brochure (including application guidelines).
**Application information:** Application form required.
*Initial approach:* Letter
*Copies of proposal:* 1
*Deadline(s):* Jan. 15 and June 1
**Officer:** Darryl Tocker, Exec. Dir.
**Directors:** Mel Kunze, Barbara Tocker, Robert Tocker.
**Number of staff:** 1 full-time professional.
**EIN:** 756037871

## 741
### The Trull Foundation
404 4th St.
Palacios, TX 77465 (361) 972-5241
*Contact:* E. Gail Purvis, Exec. Dir.
*FAX:* (361) 972-1109; E-mail: info@trullfoundation.org; URL: http://www.trullfoundation.org

Trust established in 1967 in TX.
**Donor(s):** R.B. Trull, Florence M. Trull,‡ Gladys T. Brooking, Jean T. Herlin, Laura Shiflett.
**Grantmaker type:** Independent foundation
**Financial data** (yr. ended 12/31/98): Assets, $26,181,492 (M); expenditures, $1,253,625; qualifying distributions, $1,068,472; giving

activities include $1,007,106 for 242 grants (high: $80,000; low: $290).
**Purpose and activities:** Primary areas of interest include youth, minorities, and education. Giving also for child welfare, the disadvantaged, Protestant church support and welfare programs, denominational giving, higher, elementary, and secondary education with emphasis on religious schools, theological education, and literacy programs, child development, and youth agencies; some support for community development, assistance for immigrants, international relief activities, organizations promoting peace, ecology and the environment, (particularly the TX coast environment), population studies, AIDS research, museums, and the performing arts.
**Fields of interest:** Museums; performing arts; history & archaeology; elementary/secondary education; child development, education; elementary school/education; secondary school/education; higher education; theological school/education; adult education—literacy & basic skills; libraries/library science; reading; education; natural resource conservation & protection; environment; substance abuse, services; food services; human services; children & youth, services; child development, services; family services; minorities/immigrants, centers & services; homeless, human services; international relief; peace; community development; Protestant federated giving programs; population studies; Protestant agencies & churches; religion; minorities; Latinos; immigrants/refugees; economically disadvantaged; homeless.
**Types of support:** General/operating support; continuing support; annual campaigns; equipment; program development; conferences/seminars; publication; seed money; curriculum development; internship funds; scholarship funds; technical assistance; consulting services.
**Limitations:** Giving primarily in southern TX, with emphasis on the Palacios, TX, area. No grants to individuals directly, and rarely for building or endowment funds; no loans.
**Publications:** Biennial report (including application guidelines), application guidelines.
**Application information:** Proposals submitted by FAX not considered. Application form required.
*Initial approach:* Letter, telephone or visit website
*Copies of proposal:* 4
*Deadline(s):* None
*Board meeting date(s):* Usually 3 to 5 times a year; contributions committee meets monthly and as required
*Final notification:* 6 weeks
**Officers and Trustees:*** Colleen Claybourn,* Chair.; Rose C. Lancaster,* Vice-Chair.; J. Fred Huitt,* Secy.-Treas.; E. Gail Purvis, Exec. Dir.; Cara P. Herlin, Jean T. Herlin, Sarah H. Olfers, R.B. Trull, R. Scott Trull.
**Number of staff:** 1 full-time professional; 1 full-time support; 1 part-time support.
**EIN:** 237423943

## 742
### Adolf & Kaethe Wechsler Memorial Foundation
c/o Bank of America, Trust Dept.
P.O. Box 831041
Dallas, TX 75283-1041 (214) 580-2411

Established in 1993.
**Grantmaker type:** Independent foundation
**Financial data** (yr. ended 12/31/99): Assets, $1,345,727 (M); expenditures, $84,239; qualifying distributions, $74,909; giving activities include $70,000 for 18 grants (high: $17,500; low: $1,000).
**Purpose and activities:** Giving to education, arts and culture and religion.
**Fields of interest:** Media/communications; performing arts; libraries/library science; human services; Protestant agencies & churches.
**Limitations:** Applications not accepted. Giving primarily in Galveston, TX. No grants to individuals.
**Application information:** Contributes only to pre-selected organizations.
**Trustees:** Barker, Lain, Bank of America.
**EIN:** 760442309

# UTAH

## 743
### The Don-Kay-Clay Cash Foundation
377 E. Canyon Oak Way
Salt Lake City, UT 84103

Established in 1997 in UT.
**Donor(s):** Roy D. Cash, Sondra K. Cash.
**Grantmaker type:** Independent foundation
**Financial data** (yr. ended 12/31/99): Assets, $1,244,467 (M); gifts received, $15,000; expenditures, $61,403; qualifying distributions, $60,897; giving activities include $59,475 for 21 grants (high: $25,000; low: $25).
**Purpose and activities:** Giving for education and human services.
**Fields of interest:** University; libraries (public); American Red Cross.
**Limitations:** Applications not accepted. Giving primarily in UT. No grants to individuals.
**Application information:** Contributes only to pre-selected organizations.
**Officers:** Roy Don Cash, Pres.; Clay Collin Cash, V.P.; Sondra Kay Cash, Secy.-Treas.
**EIN:** 841381970

## 744
### First Security Foundation
79 S. Main St., Rm. 201
Salt Lake City, UT 84111-1921

Established in 1952 in UT.
**Donor(s):** First Security Corp.
**Grantmaker type:** Company-sponsored foundation
**Financial data** (yr. ended 12/31/99): Assets, $4,169,289 (M); expenditures, $165,802; qualifying distributions, $150,615; giving activities include $149,675 for 47 grants (high: $12,000; low: $300).

**Purpose and activities:** Giving for scholarships and libraries at selected universities and colleges in UT, ID, NM, NV, OR and WY.
**Fields of interest:** Higher education; libraries (school).
**Types of support:** General/operating support; scholarship funds.
**Limitations:** Applications not accepted. Giving limited to ID, NM, NV, OR, UT, and WY. No grants to individuals.
**Application information:** Contributes only to pre-selected organizations.
**Officers and Trustees:\*** Spencer F. Eccles,\* Pres.; Amelia Critchfield, Secy.; Verna Lee Johnston, Treas.; Morgan J. Evans, First Security Bank, N.A.
**EIN:** 876118149

## 745
### The Jon and Karen Huntsman Foundation ▼
c/o Huntsman, Inc.
500 Huntsman Way
Salt Lake City, UT   84108-1235

Established in 1988 in UT.
**Donor(s):** Jon M. Huntsman.
**Grantmaker type:** Independent foundation
**Financial data** (yr. ended 12/31/98): Assets, $78,883,469 (M); expenditures, $4,362,536; qualifying distributions, $3,697,297; giving activities include $3,838,750 for 41 grants (high: $1,000,000; low: $1,000; average: $1,000–$100,000).
**Purpose and activities:** Giving primarily for music, education, health care, science, and Christian agencies and churches.
**Fields of interest:** Music; education; health care; science; Christian agencies & churches.
**Limitations:** Applications not accepted. Giving on a national basis. No grants to individuals.
**Application information:** Contributes only to pre-selected organizations.
**Officers and Trustees:\*** Jon M. Huntsman,\* Pres.; J. Kimo Esplin, V.P. and Treas.; Christena Durham, V.P.; David H. Huntsman,\* V.P.; James H. Hunstman, V.P.; Jon M. Hunstman, Jr.,\* V.P.; Karen H. Huntsman,\* V.P.; Paul C. Huntsman,\* V.P.; Jennifer Parkin, V.P.; Elizabeth A. Whitsett, V.P.; Robert B. Lence,\* Secy.; Richard P. Durham, Kathleen H. Huffman, Peter R. Huntsman.
**EIN:** 742521914
**Recent grants for library/information services:**
**745-1** Brigham Young University, J. Reuben Clark Law School, Provo, UT, $1,000,000. For Howard W. Hunter Law Library. 1998.
**745-2** Southern Utah University, Library Foundation, Cedar City, UT, $100,000. 1998.

## 746
### John A. & Telitha E. Lindquist Foundation
3408 Washington Blvd.
Ogden, UT   84401-4108
*Contact:* Robert E. Lindquist, Dir.

Established in 1994 in UT.
**Donor(s):** John A. Lindquist, Telitha E. Lindquist.
**Grantmaker type:** Independent foundation
**Financial data** (yr. ended 12/31/98): Assets, $2,322,062 (M); expenditures, $102,208; qualifying distributions, $97,852; giving

activities include $97,600 for 26 grants (high: $53,000; low: $100).
**Purpose and activities:** Giving primarily to educational and charitable entities in northern Utah.
**Fields of interest:** Performing arts; arts/cultural programs; higher education; libraries (public); education; cancer research; human services.
**Limitations:** Giving limited to northern UT.
**Application information:**
*Initial approach:* Proposal
*Deadline(s):* None
**Officers:** Kathryn Lindquist, Pres.; Peter N. Lindquist, Secy.; Steven E. Lindquist, C.F.O.
**Directors:** Laurie L. Babilis, Telitha L. Greiner, John E. Lindquist, Robert E. Lindquist.
**EIN:** 870530598

## 747
### Junior E. & Blanche B. Rich Foundation
c/o First Security Bank of Utah, N.A.
P.O. Box 30007
Salt Lake City, UT   84130
*Contact:* Sharon Rich Lewis, Chair.
*Application address:* 2826 Pierce Ave., Ogden, UT 84409

Established in 1975 in UT.
**Grantmaker type:** Independent foundation
**Financial data** (yr. ended 12/31/99): Assets, $6,731,067 (M); expenditures, $224,149; qualifying distributions, $212,253; giving activities include $196,592 for 55 grants (high: $10,250; low: $100).
**Purpose and activities:** Giving primarily for the arts, education, and health organizations.
**Fields of interest:** Visual arts; performing arts; history & archaeology; language & linguistics; literature; arts/cultural programs; elementary school/education; secondary school/education; higher education; libraries/library science; education; hospitals (general); medical research; human services; children & youth, services; hospices; homeless, human services; Christian agencies & churches; religion; homeless.
**Types of support:** General/operating support; continuing support; capital campaigns; building/renovation; scholarship funds.
**Limitations:** Giving primarily in Weber County, UT.
**Application information:** Application form not required.
*Initial approach:* Letter
*Copies of proposal:* 1
*Deadline(s):* Preferably by Sept. 30; no set deadline
*Board meeting date(s):* Nov.
**Directors:** Sharon Rich Lewis, Chair.; Lynne R. Lichfield, Carolyn R. Nebeker, Edward B. Rich.
**Trustee:** First Security Bank of Utah, N.A.
**EIN:** 876173654

# VERMONT

## 748
### Terry F. Allen Family Charitable Trust
256 Fuller Mountain Rd.
Ferrisburg, VT   05456

Established in 1997.
**Donor(s):** Terry F. Allen.
**Grantmaker type:** Independent foundation
**Financial data** (yr. ended 12/31/99): Assets, $2,110,642 (M); expenditures, $273,994; qualifying distributions, $211,447; giving activities include $215,675 for 126 grants (high: $15,000; low: $75).
**Purpose and activities:** Giving primarily for education and youth development.
**Fields of interest:** Orchestra (symphony); elementary/secondary education; higher education; libraries/library science; food banks; youth development, centers & clubs.
**Limitations:** Applications not accepted. Giving primarily in VT. No grants to individuals.
**Application information:** Contributes only to pre-selected organizations.
**Director:** Terry F. Allen.
**EIN:** 046837908

## 749
### Lamson-Howell Foundation, Inc.
R.D. 2, Box 48
Randolph, VT   05060
*Contact:* Hannah Jeffery, Pres.

Established about 1972.
**Donor(s):** Samuel L. Howell.‡
**Grantmaker type:** Independent foundation
**Financial data** (yr. ended 09/30/99): Assets, $12,618 (M); gifts received, $96,360; expenditures, $101,934; qualifying distributions, $100,158; giving activities include $100,580 for 32 grants (high: $20,000; low: $380).
**Purpose and activities:** Primary areas of interest are education, libraries, recreation, music, and cultural programs. Grants made only to tax exempt organizations in Randolph, VT, and contiguous towns.
**Fields of interest:** Music; historic preservation/historical societies; arts/cultural programs; higher education; libraries/library science; education; recreation; community development.
**Types of support:** Capital campaigns; building/renovation; program development; seed money; scholarship funds.
**Limitations:** Giving limited to Randolph, VT, and contiguous towns. No grants to individuals.
**Application information:** Application form not required.
*Initial approach:* Letter
*Copies of proposal:* 4
*Deadline(s):* None
*Board meeting date(s):* Feb., June, and Sept.
*Final notification:* Positive replies only
**Officers and Trustees:\*** Hannah Jeffery,\* Pres.; Robert J. Lamson,\* Secy.; Sheldon Dimick,\* Treas.; Karl Miller.
**Number of staff:** None.
**EIN:** 036010574

## 750
## Mortimer R. Proctor Trust

c/o Chittenden Trust Co.
P.O. Box 729
Rutland, VT 05702-0729
*Contact:* Jeanne Gilbert

Established around 1978.
**Grantmaker type:** Independent foundation
**Financial data** (yr. ended 12/31/99): Assets, $4,551,535 (M); expenditures, $272,919; qualifying distributions, $253,922; giving activities include $253,922 for 18 grants (high: $48,000; low: $250; average: $2,000–$15,000).
**Fields of interest:** Theater; arts/cultural programs; elementary school/education; higher education; libraries/library science; education; community development; federated giving programs; government/public administration; Protestant agencies & churches; Roman Catholic agencies & churches; religion; general charitable giving.
**Types of support:** General/operating support; continuing support; capital campaigns; building/renovation; equipment; emergency funds; program development; curriculum development; technical assistance.
**Limitations:** Giving limited to Proctor, VT. No grants to individuals.
**Application information:** Application form required.
*Initial approach:* Letter
*Copies of proposal:* 2
*Deadline(s):* Jan. 15 and June 15
*Board meeting date(s):* Jan. 15 and June 15
*Final notification:* 6 weeks after application deadline
**Trustee:** Chittenden Trust Co.
**Number of staff:** None.
**EIN:** 036020099

## 751
## Vermont Community Foundation

P.O. Box 30
3 Court St.
Middlebury, VT 05753 (802) 388-3355
*Contact:* Judy Dunning
*FAX:* (802) 388-3398; E-mail: vcf@vermontcf.org; URL: http://www.vermontcf.org

Established in 1986 in VT.
**Grantmaker type:** Community foundation
**Financial data** (yr. ended 12/31/98): Assets, $49,815,311 (L); expenditures, $8,599,816; giving activities include $5,500,000 for grants.
**Purpose and activities:** Support for the arts and humanities, education, the environment, health, historic preservation, public affairs and community development, and social services. The foundation is interested in projects which increase citizens' commitment to community needs, increase efficiency of nonprofit agencies, eliminate duplication of services, develop self-reliance, and emphasize prevention as well as treatment.
**Fields of interest:** Historic preservation/historical societies; arts/cultural programs; early childhood education; child development, education; elementary school/education; secondary school/education; higher education; adult/continuing education; libraries/library science; natural resource conservation & protection; environment; animal welfare; family planning; substance abuse, services; mental health/crisis services; AIDS; alcoholism; health organizations; human services; children & youth, services; youth, services; child development, services; family services; minorities/immigrants, centers & services; homeless, human services; civil rights; community development; public affairs; disabled; aging; economically disadvantaged.
**Types of support:** Program development; seed money; scholarship funds; technical assistance; consulting services; program-related investments/loans.
**Limitations:** Giving limited to VT. No support for religious purposes. No grants to individuals, or for annual campaigns, building funds, continuing support, debt reduction, equipment and materials, general endowments, or operating budgets.
**Publications:** Annual report, multi-year report, application guidelines, financial statement, grants list, informational brochure (including application guidelines), program policy statement, occasional report.
**Application information:** Proposal summary form required. Application form not required.
*Initial approach:* Proposal
*Copies of proposal:* 3
*Deadline(s):* Apr. 1 and Oct. 1
*Board meeting date(s):* 8 times annually
*Final notification:* 2 months
**Officers and Directors:*** Stephen C. Terry,* Chair.; David G. Rahr, Pres.; Faith Brown, V.P. Finance and Operations; Charlotte Stetson, V.P.; Paul A. Bruhn, Charles R. Cummings, John T. Ewing, Cornelius D. Hogan, George E. Little, Jr., John H. Marshall, Emily R. Morrow, Caroline Morse, Carolyn C. Roberts, Sr. Janice E. Ryan, John F. Taylor, Alec Webb, Richard C. White.
**Number of staff:** 2 full-time professional; 1 part-time professional; 3 part-time support.
**EIN:** 222712160

## 752
## The WELD Foundation

c/o J. David Shenk
P.O. Box 1092
Manchester, VT 05254

Established in 1992.
**Donor(s):** Willis W. Shenk, Elsie S. Shenk.
**Grantmaker type:** Independent foundation
**Financial data** (yr. ended 12/31/99): Assets, $2,145,681 (M); gifts received, $15,610; expenditures, $71,696; qualifying distributions, $61,289; giving activities include $61,750 for 43 grants (high: $15,500; low: $250).
**Purpose and activities:** Giving to general charitable giving.
**Fields of interest:** Museums (art); libraries (public).
**Limitations:** Applications not accepted. Giving primarily in Lancaster County, PA. No grants to individuals.
**Application information:** Contributes only to pre-selected organizations.
**Officers:** Willis W. Shenk, Chair.; J. David Shenk, Pres.; Elsie S. Shenk, V.P. and Secy.; Mary Louise Shenk, Treas.
**EIN:** 232680871

# VIRGINIA

## 753
## Camp Foundation

P.O. Box 813
Franklin, VA 23851 (757) 562-3439
*Contact:* Bobby B. Worrell, Exec. Dir.

Incorporated in 1942 in VA.
**Donor(s):** James L. Camp,‡ P.D. Camp,‡ and their families.
**Grantmaker type:** Independent foundation
**Financial data** (yr. ended 12/31/99): Assets, $19,272,388 (M); expenditures, $1,183,863; qualifying distributions, $1,106,700; giving activities include $1,022,313 for grants (average: $1,000–$20,000).
**Purpose and activities:** To provide or aid in providing, in or near the town of Franklin, VA, parks, playgrounds, recreational facilities, libraries, hospitals, clinics, homes for the aged or needy, refuge for delinquent, dependent or neglected children, training schools, or other like institutions or activities. Grants also to select organizations statewide, with emphasis on youth agencies, safety programs, hospitals, mental illness, and nursing programs, higher and secondary education, including scholarships filed through high school principals, recreation, the environment, historic preservation, and cultural programs.
**Fields of interest:** Historic preservation/historical societies; arts/cultural programs; secondary school/education; higher education; libraries/library science; education; environment; hospitals (general); nursing care; health care; mental health/crisis services; safety/disasters; recreation; children & youth, services; aging, centers & services; government/public administration; aging.
**Types of support:** Annual campaigns; building/renovation; equipment; land acquisition; emergency funds; seed money; scholarship funds; research; scholarships—to individuals; matching/challenge support.
**Limitations:** Giving primarily in the city of Franklin, and Southampton and Isle of Wight counties, VA.
**Publications:** Application guidelines.
**Application information:** 4-year scholarships awarded to graduating high school seniors who are residents of the City of Franklin or the counties of Southampton and Isle of Wight. Application form not required.
*Initial approach:* Proposal
*Copies of proposal:* 7
*Deadline(s):* Submit proposal between June and Aug.; deadline Sept. 1. Scholarship application deadlines: Feb. 26 for filing with high school principals
*Board meeting date(s):* May and Nov.
*Final notification:* 3 months
**Officers and Directors:*** Robert C. Ray,* Chair.; Sol W. Rawls, Jr.,* Pres.; Westbrook Parker,* V.P.; John M. Camp, Jr.,* Treas.; Bobby B. Worrell,* Exec. Dir.; John M. Camp III, W.M. Camp, Jr., Clifford A. Cutchins III, William W. Cutchins, Randy B. Drake, John R. Marks, Paul Camp Marks, J. Edward Moyler, Jr., John D. Munford, L.H. Puckett, Jr., S. Waite Rawls, Jr., J.E. Ray III, Richard E. Ray, Toy D. Savage, Jr.

**Number of staff:** 2 full-time professional; 1 part-time support.
**EIN:** 546052488

## 754

### Quincy Cole Trust

c/o Bank of America
P.O. Box 26606
Richmond, VA 23261 (804) 788-2143
*Contact:* Rita Smith
*Application address:* c/o Bank of America, P.O. Box 26903, Richmond, VA 23261

Established in 1969 in VA.
**Donor(s):** Quincy Cole.‡
**Grantmaker type:** Independent foundation
**Financial data** (yr. ended 06/30/98): Assets, $12,674,072 (M); gifts received, $32,563; expenditures, $596,726; qualifying distributions, $552,854; giving activities include $559,595 for grants.
**Purpose and activities:** Giving primarily for the arts and cultural organization, including museums and historical societies.
**Fields of interest:** Museums; historic preservation/historical societies; arts/cultural programs; libraries/library science; horticulture & garden clubs.
**Limitations:** Giving limited to the metropolitan Richmond, VA, area.
**Application information:**
*Initial approach:* Letter
*Deadline(s):* Apr. 20
*Board meeting date(s):* June
**Trustee:** Bank of America.
**EIN:** 546086247

## 755

### Freedom Forum, Inc. ▼

1101 Wilson Blvd., 22nd Fl.
Arlington, VA 22209 (703) 528-0800
*Contact:* Charles L. Overby, Chair., or Gene Policinski, Special Asst. to Pres.
*FAX:* (703) 284-3770; E-mail: news@freedomforum.org; URL: http://www.freedomforum.org

Incorporated in 1991 in VA.
**Grantmaker type:** Operating foundation
**Financial data** (yr. ended 12/31/98): Assets, $1,053,745,893 (M); expenditures, $76,683,784; qualifying distributions, $66,970,660; giving activities include $25,749,717 for grants, $745,155 for employee matching gifts and $28,887,071 for 4 foundation-administered programs.
**Purpose and activities:** The foundation, an operating program foundation making only a limited number of grants, is dedicated primarily to conducting and supporting national, international, and community programs that foster the First Amendment freedom of press, speech, assembly, petition, and religion and the free exercise thereof by all peoples. The foundation also operates the Freedom Forum Media Studies Center in New York City, the Freedom Forum First Amendment Center at Vanderbilt University, and the Paul Miller Washington Reporting Fellowships in Washington, DC.
**Fields of interest:** Media/communications; film/video; television; journalism & publishing;

museums; arts/cultural programs; education, public policy; elementary/secondary education; higher education; libraries/library science; education; health care; human services; civil rights, minorities; civil liberties, first amendment; African Americans.
**Types of support:** General/operating support; continuing support; annual campaigns; capital campaigns; building/renovation; equipment; program development; conferences/seminars; professorships; publication; seed money; curriculum development; fellowships; scholarship funds; research; program-related investments/loans; employee matching gifts; grants to individuals; scholarships—to individuals; exchange programs.
**Limitations:** Giving on a national and international basis.
**Officers and Trustees:\*** Charles L. Overby,* Chair. and C.E.O.; Peter S. Prichard,* Pres.; Robert H. Giles, Sr. V.P. and Exec. Dir., The Freedom Forum; Felix F. Gutierrez, Sr. V.P. and Exec. Dir., Pacific Coast Center; Kenneth A. Paulson, Sr. V.P. and Exec. Dir., First Amendment Center; Joe Urschel, Sr. V.P. and Exec. Dir., Newseum; Christine Wells, Sr. V.P., International; Mary Kay Blake, V.P., Partnerships and Initiatives; Harvey S. Cotter, V.P., and Treas.; Maurice Fliess, V.P., Publications; Pamela Y. Galloway-Tabb, V.P., Genl. Svcs.; Jack Hurley, V.P., Broadcasting; Max Page, V.P., and Deputy Dir., Newseum; Adam Clayton Powell III, V.P., Technology and Progs.; Tracy A. Quinn, V.P., Newseum; Nate Ruffin, V.P., Human Resources; Roderick Sandeen, V.P., Admin.; Beth Tuttle, V.P., Marketing and Communications; Robert G. McCullough, Secy.; Martin F. Birmingham, Bernard B. Brody, Genl. Harry W. Brooks, Jr., John E. Heselden, Madelyn P. Jennings, Malcolm R. Kirschenbaum, Bette Bao Lord, Brian Mulroney, Allen H. Neuharth, Jan Neuharth, Will Norton, Jr., John C. Quinn, Carl Rowan, Josefina Salas-Porras, John Seigenthaler, Paul Simon.
**EIN:** 541604427

## 756

### Greater Lynchburg Community Trust

c/o Central Fidelity National Bank Bldg., 19th Fl.
P.O. Box 714
Lynchburg, VA 24505 (804) 845-6500
*Contact:* Stuart J. Turille, Exec. Dir.
*FAX:* (804) 845-6530; E-mail: glct@inmind.com; URL: http://www.lynchburgtrust.org

Established as a community trust in 1972 in VA.
**Grantmaker type:** Community foundation
**Financial data** (yr. ended 09/30/99): Assets, $11,893,932 (M); gifts received, $2,748,761; expenditures, $426,817; giving activities include $261,194 for 75 grants (low: $107; average: $117–$10,000) and $3,000 for 3 grants to individuals of $1,000 each.
**Purpose and activities:** Giving primarily for education and human services.
**Fields of interest:** Arts/cultural programs; libraries/library science; education; food services; human services; children & youth, services; family services; aging, centers & services; women, centers & services; homeless, human services; community development; social sciences; disabled; aging; women;

economically disadvantaged; homeless; general charitable giving.
**Types of support:** Capital campaigns; building/renovation; equipment; emergency funds; program development; seed money; scholarship funds; technical assistance; employee-related scholarships; scholarships—to individuals; matching/challenge support.
**Limitations:** Giving limited to Lynchburg and Bedford City, and Amherst, Bedford, and Campbell counties, VA. No support for religious organizations for sectarian or religious purposes. No grants to individuals (except for designated scholarship funds), or for continuing support, annual campaigns, deficit financing, employee matching gifts, or non-grant support; no loans or multiple-year grants.
**Publications:** Application guidelines, program policy statement, annual report, informational brochure, newsletter.
**Application information:** Application form not required.
*Initial approach:* Letter (no more than 2 pages) or telephone
*Copies of proposal:* 10
*Deadline(s):* Apr. 15 and Oct. 15
*Board meeting date(s):* June, Sept., Dec., Feb., and Apr.
*Final notification:* June and Dec.
**Officers and Directors:\*** Samuel P. Cardwell,* Chair.; John P. Eckert,* Chair., Distribs. Comm.; Yuille Holt III,* Chair., Investment Comm.; Terry Hall Jamerson,* Vice-Chair.; Shanda K. Rowe, Secy.; William F. Quillian, Jr., Advisor; Elliot S. Schewel, Advisor; G. Edward Calvert, Robert H. Gillian, Rev. D. Jack Hamilton, Joyce Houck, Joseph C. Knakal, Jr., Amy Ray, Irma Seiferth, Benny R. Shrader, Daniel B. Sweeney, John A. Watts, Jr., T. Ashby Watts III.
**Trustee Banks:** BB & T, SunTrust Bank, One Valley Bank, N.A., Wachovia Bank, N.A., Bank of America.
**Number of staff:** 1 full-time professional; 1 part-time professional.
**EIN:** 546112680

## 757

### The Norfolk Foundation

1 Commercial Pl., Ste 1410
Norfolk, VA 23510-2113 (757) 622-7951
*Contact:* Angelica D. Light, Exec. Dir.
*FAX:* (757) 622-1751; E-mail: info@norfolkfoundation.org; URL: http://www.norfolkfoundation.org

Established in 1950 in VA by resolution and declaration of trust.
**Grantmaker type:** Community foundation
**Financial data** (yr. ended 12/31/99): Assets, $120,621,018 (M); gifts received, $10,606,828; expenditures, $4,415,080; giving activities include $3,963,441 for 115 grants (high: $463,398; low: $500; average: $5,000–$100,000).
**Purpose and activities:** Support for local hospitals; higher, medical, and other educational institutions; family and child welfare agencies; a community fund; programs for drug abuse, the aged, the homeless, and the handicapped; and cultural and civic programs.
**Fields of interest:** Museums; historic preservation/historical societies; arts/cultural programs; child development, education; higher

education; medical school/education; adult/continuing education; adult education—literacy & basic skills; libraries/library science; reading; education; natural resource conservation & protection; environment; animal welfare; hospitals (general); family planning; medical care, rehabilitation; health care; substance abuse, services; mental health/crisis services; health associations; AIDS; medical research; AIDS research; youth development, services; human services; children & youth, services; child development, services; family services; aging, centers & services; homeless, human services; community development; voluntarism promotion; government/public administration; leadership development; disabled; aging; economically disadvantaged; homeless.

**Types of support:** Capital campaigns; building/renovation; equipment; land acquisition; seed money; scholarships—to individuals.

**Limitations:** Giving limited to Norfolk, VA, and a 50-mile area from its boundaries. No support for national or international organizations, or religious organizations for religious purposes, hospitals and similar health care facilities, or projects normally the responsibility of the government. No grants to individuals (except for donor-designated scholarships), or for operating budgets, annual campaigns, research, endowment funds, or deficit financing; no loans.

**Publications:** Annual report (including application guidelines), application guidelines, informational brochure, newsletter, financial statement, grants list.

**Application information:** Application form required for scholarships only; applications available Dec. 1.

   *Initial approach:* Letter or telephone
   *Copies of proposal:* 1
   *Deadline(s):* Mar. 1 for scholarships; none for other grants
   *Board meeting date(s):* 4 times a year
   *Final notification:* 3 to 4 months
**Officers:** Martha B. Ambler, Cont.; Angelica D. Light, Exec. Dir.
**Distribution Committee:** Joshua P. Darden, Jr., Chair.; Toy D. Savage, Jr., Vice-Chair.; Jean C. Bruce, John H. Foster, H.P. McNeal, Kurt M. Rosenbach, John O. Wynne.
**Number of staff:** 3 full-time professional; 2 part-time professional; 1 full-time support.
**EIN:** 540722169
**Recent grants for library/information services:**
**757-1** Norfolk Public Library, Friends of the, Norfolk, VA, $33,372. For public computer labs. 1999.

### 758
### Patricia and Douglas Perry Foundation
4600 Ocean Front Ave.
Virginia Beach, VA   23451-2521

Established in 1993 in VA.
**Donor(s):** J. Douglas Perry, Patricia W. Perry.
**Grantmaker type:** Independent foundation
**Financial data** (yr. ended 12/31/99): Assets, $7,670,229 (M); expenditures, $336,671; qualifying distributions, $335,704; giving activities include $335,704 for 16 grants (high: $165,400; low: $25).

**Purpose and activities:** Giving primarily for the arts and education.
**Fields of interest:** Arts/cultural programs; university; libraries/library science; Salvation Army; Protestant agencies & churches.
**Types of support:** Scholarships—to individuals.
**Limitations:** Giving limited to residents of Virginia Beach and Norfolk, VA.
**Application information:** Application form required.
   *Initial approach:* Letter
   *Deadline(s):* Feb. 15
**Officers:** Patricia W. Perry, Pres.; Brandon D. Perry, V.P.; J. Douglas Perry, Treas.
**Director:** J. Christopher Perry.
**EIN:** 541691140

### 759
### Portsmouth Community Trust
P.O. Box 1394
Portsmouth, VA   23705   (757) 397-5424
*Contact:* Nancy G. Wren, Exec. Dir.

Established in 1965 in VA.
**Grantmaker type:** Community foundation
**Financial data** (yr. ended 12/31/99): Assets, $3,084,675 (M); gifts received, $203,404; expenditures, $214,853; giving activities include $169,857 for 66 grants (high: $6,100; low: $100; average: $100–$20,000).

**Purpose and activities:** Primary areas of interest include community development, community funds, hospital building funds, and general charitable giving. Support also for museums, music, and other arts groups, libraries, public and civic affairs, recreational programs, medical, and education, including higher, secondary, adult education, and programs for minorities.
**Fields of interest:** Museums; music; arts/cultural programs; secondary school/education; higher education; medical school/education; adult/continuing education; libraries/library science; education; hospitals (general); health care; recreation; human services; community development; federated giving programs; marine science; government/public administration; public affairs; minorities.
**Types of support:** General/operating support; continuing support; annual campaigns; capital campaigns; equipment; scholarship funds.
**Limitations:** Giving limited to within a 50 mile radius of Portsmouth, VA. No support for any agency which has received a discretionary grant from the Portsmouth Community Trust within the preceding year. No grants to individuals, or for operating support, religious purposes, deficit financing, government agencies.
**Publications:** Annual report, application guidelines, financial statement, grants list, informational brochure.
**Application information:** Application form required.
   *Initial approach:* Letter requesting application form
   *Copies of proposal:* 2
   *Deadline(s):* Feb. 1, May 1, Aug. 1, and Nov. 1
   *Board meeting date(s):* 1st Wednesday in Mar., June, Sept., and Dec.
**Officers:** Andrew H. Hook, Chair.; Nancy G. Wren, Exec. Dir.
**Number of staff:** 1 part-time professional.
**EIN:** 546062589

### 760
### Emma May Ridgeway Charitable Trust
c/o Farmers & Merchants Trust Co.
P.O. Box 2800
Winchester, VA   22604

Established in 1983.
**Grantmaker type:** Independent foundation
**Financial data** (yr. ended 07/31/99): Assets, $1,687,088 (M); expenditures, $108,299; qualifying distributions, $96,344; giving activities include $94,247 for 29 grants (high: $11,781; low: $250).

**Purpose and activities:** Giving primarily for personal services in the surrounding areas.
**Fields of interest:** Libraries/library science; education; health associations; housing/shelter; youth development; human services; federated giving programs; Protestant agencies & churches.
**Limitations:** Giving primarily in the Winchester, VA, area.
**Application information:** Application form not required.
   *Deadline(s):* May 31
**Trustee:** Farmers & Merchants Trust Co.
**EIN:** 546202908

### 761
### Rouse-Bottom Foundation
115 Harbor Dr.
Hampton, VA   23661-3301
*Contact:* Viola K. Wood, Admin. Asst.

Established in 1989 in VA.
**Donor(s):** Dorothy Bottom.‡
**Grantmaker type:** Independent foundation
**Financial data** (yr. ended 12/31/99): Assets, $4,020,202 (M); expenditures, $193,368; qualifying distributions, $166,170; giving activities include $168,000 for grants (average: $500–$2,500).

**Fields of interest:** Museums; historic preservation/historical societies; arts/cultural programs; higher education; libraries/library science; environment.
**Limitations:** Giving primarily in VA, with emphasis on the Tidewater and Lower Peninsula areas. No support for health, social services, or youth or civic programs. No grants to individuals.
**Application information:** Giving strictly limited to the foundation's fields of interest; funds are committed mainly to core group of grantees. Application form not required.
   *Initial approach:* Letter
   *Copies of proposal:* 6
   *Deadline(s):* Aug. 15
   *Board meeting date(s):* Quarterly
   *Final notification:* Following board meeting
**Officers and Directors:\*** Raymond B. Bottom, Jr.,\* Pres.; Dorothy Rouse-Bottom,\* Secy.-Treas.; Lewis T. Booker, M. Whitney Gilkey, Jesse R. Forst, Lester Migdal.
**Number of staff:** None.
**EIN:** 541521527

### 762
### St. Andrew's Association
6123 St. Andrew's Ln.
Richmond, VA   23226

Charter granted in 1900 by Act of General Assembly of VA; incorporated in 1912.
**Grantmaker type:** Independent foundation
**Financial data** (yr. ended 10/31/99): Assets, $9,080,544 (M); expenditures, $580,132; qualifying distributions, $429,070; giving activities include $430,567 for 2 grants (high: $423,567; low: $7,000).
**Purpose and activities:** Giving primarily for a school. Some giving also for a library.
**Fields of interest:** Libraries/library science; education.
**Types of support:** General/operating support.
**Limitations:** Applications not accepted. Giving limited to Richmond, VA. No grants to individuals.
**Application information:** Contributes only to pre-selected organizations.
**Officers and Directors:\*** Randolph F. Totten,\* Pres.; J. F. Williams III, V.P.; McDonald Wellford, Jr., Secy.; John D. Blackwell, Treas.; Harry W. Baldwin, Jr., Harry Baldwin III, and five additional directors.
**EIN:** 546039947

### 763
### Tara Foundation, Inc.
P.O. Box 1850
Middleburg, VA 20118 (540) 687-8884
*Contact:* Mary Painter

**Donor(s):** Magalen O. Bryant.
**Grantmaker type:** Independent foundation
**Financial data** (yr. ended 12/31/99): Assets, $6,751,870 (M); gifts received, $726,551; expenditures, $155,758; qualifying distributions, $153,698; giving activities include $152,094 for grants.
**Fields of interest:** Arts/cultural programs; libraries/library science; education; natural resource conservation & protection; human services; government/public administration; religion.
**Limitations:** Giving on a national basis. No grants to individuals.
**Application information:**
    *Deadline(s):* None
**Officers and Directors:\*** Magalen C. Webert,\* Pres.; John C.O. Bryant,\* V.P.; John Gordon,\* Secy.-Treas.; Magalen O. Bryant, Michael R. Crane, W. Carey Crane III, Kristiane W. Graham.
**Number of staff:** 1 shared staff
**EIN:** 541596203

# WASHINGTON

### 764
### Anderson Foundation
P.O. Box 24304
Seattle, WA 98124
*Contact:* Barbara A. Lawrence, Secy.-Treas.

Established in 1952.
**Donor(s):** Charles M. Anderson, Dorothy I. Anderson, William Anderson, Barbara A. Lawrence.
**Grantmaker type:** Independent foundation

**Financial data** (yr. ended 06/30/99): Assets, $19,508,667 (M); gifts received, $2,739,089; expenditures, $1,006,778; qualifying distributions, $886,774; giving activities include $895,000 for 34 grants (high: $125,000; low: $1,000).
**Purpose and activities:** Giving primarily for education, health care, and to Protestant churches.
**Fields of interest:** Museums; higher education; libraries (public); education; hospitals (general); health associations; medical research; human services; children & youth, services; Protestant agencies & churches.
**Types of support:** Building/renovation; equipment; professorships; scholarship funds; research.
**Limitations:** Applications not accepted. Giving primarily in WA, with emphasis on Seattle. No grants to individuals, or for endowment funds or matching gifts; no loans.
**Application information:** Unsolicited requests for funds not accepted.
    *Board meeting date(s):* Annually
**Officers:** Charles M. Anderson, Pres.; Helen Anderson, V.P.; Barbara A. Lawrence, Secy.-Treas.
**Trustee:** William Anderson.
**Number of staff:** 2 part-time support.
**EIN:** 916031724

### 765
### Norman Archibald Charitable Foundation
c/o Wells Fargo Bank, MAC 6540-141
P.O. Box 21927, 14th Fl.
Seattle, WA 98111 (206) 343-8367
*Contact:* Stuart H. Prestrud, Secy. of Board of Managers
*Additional tel.:* (206) 343-2217

Established in 1976 in WA.
**Donor(s):** Norman Archibald.‡
**Grantmaker type:** Independent foundation
**Financial data** (yr. ended 09/30/99): Assets, $11,125,219 (M); expenditures, $646,980; qualifying distributions, $559,887; giving activities include $543,500 for 97 grants (high: $50,000; low: $1,200).
**Purpose and activities:** Support youth and child development programs; support also for medical research, higher education and libraries, museums and the performing arts, social services for the aged and the handicapped, housing programs, and animal welfare and conservation.
**Fields of interest:** Museums; performing arts; theater; music; history & archaeology; arts/cultural programs; child development, education; higher education; libraries/library science; education; natural resource conservation & protection; environment; animal welfare; hospitals (general); health care; health associations; AIDS; medical research; AIDS research; housing/shelter, development; youth development, services; human services; children & youth, services; child development, services; hospices; aging, centers & services; federated giving programs; engineering & technology; science; leadership development; Native Americans; disabled; aging.
**Types of support:** General/operating support; building/renovation; equipment; land

acquisition; program development; seed money; research.
**Limitations:** Giving primarily in the Puget Sound region of WA. No support for government entities, private foundations, or religious organizations for religious purposes. No grants to individuals, or for ongoing operational support, deficit financing, endowment funds, or scholarships; no loans.
**Publications:** Annual report, application guidelines (including application guidelines).
**Application information:** Application form not required.
    *Initial approach:* Letter
    *Copies of proposal:* 3
    *Deadline(s):* None
**Advisory Board:** Robert L. Gerth, J. Shan Mullin, Stuart H. Prestrud.
**Trustee:** Wells Fargo Bank.
**Number of staff:** None.
**EIN:** 911098014

### 766
### Leonard X. Bosack & Bette M. Kruger Foundation
8422 154th Ave., N.E.
Redmond, WA 98052-3800
*Contact:* Exec. Dir.

Established in 1990 in CA.
**Donor(s):** Leonard X. Bosack,‡ Sandra K. Lerner, Leonard Bosack.
**Grantmaker type:** Independent foundation
**Financial data** (yr. ended 01/31/98): Assets, $34,032,459 (M); gifts received, $132,217; expenditures, $2,843,265; qualifying distributions, $3,392,901; giving activities include $853,463 for 17 grants (high: $209,728; low: $145).
**Purpose and activities:** Funding specifically in support of scientific education and the promotion of animal welfare, with special emphasis on the treatment of zoo and laboratory animals, and the day-to-day operation needs of animal welfare agencies; funding also for a library.
**Fields of interest:** Higher education; libraries/library science; animal welfare; engineering & technology; science.
**International interests:** United Kingdom.
**Types of support:** Program development.
**Limitations:** Applications not accepted. No grants to individuals, or for operating budgets.
**Publications:** Informational brochure.
**Application information:** Contributes only to pre-selected organizations.
**Officers and Directors:\*** Sandra K. Lerner,\* Chair. and Pres.; Leonard Bosack,\* V.P. and Secy.
**Number of staff:** 1 full-time professional; 5 full-time support.
**EIN:** 943128478

### 767
### The Foster Foundation ▼
1201 3rd Ave., Ste. 2101
Seattle, WA 98101
*Contact:* Jill Goodsell, Admin.

Established in 1984 in WA.
**Donor(s):** Evelyn W. Foster.
**Grantmaker type:** Independent foundation

**Financial data** (yr. ended 12/31/98): Assets, $39,368,378 (M); expenditures, $2,088,693; qualifying distributions, $2,014,114; giving activities include $2,000,000 for 72 grants (high: $330,000; low: $5,000; average: $5,000–$40,000).

**Purpose and activities:** Giving primarily for education, including a university and community literacy programs, the performing arts, including opera and the symphony, and social services, with emphasis on at-risk youth and food and shelter programs for the homeless.

**Fields of interest:** Performing arts; higher education; education; health care; health associations; human services; children & youth, services.

**Types of support:** Building/renovation; equipment; program development; seed money; scholarship funds; research; matching/challenge support.

**Limitations:** Giving primarily in the Pacific Northwest. No grants to individuals, or for fundraising, endowment funds, or unrestricted operating funds; no loans.

**Application information:**
*Initial approach:* Letter
*Deadline(s):* None
*Final notification:* 3 months
**Officers and Trustees:*** Michael G. Foster, Jr.,* Dir.; Jill Goodsell,* Admin.; Evelyn W. Foster, Michael G. Foster, Sr., Thomas B. Foster.
**EIN:** 911265474
**Recent grants for library/information services:**
**767-1** Seattle Public Library Foundation, Seattle, WA, $290,000. 1998.

---

**768**
**Microsoft Corporation Community Affairs**
1 Microsoft Way
Redmond, WA 98052-6399 (425) 936-8185
*Contact:* Bruce Brooks, Dir., Community Affairs
*Application addresses for software donations outside WA:* CompuMentor, 487 3rd St., San Francisco, CA 94107, tel.: (415) 512-7784, Gifts In Kind International, 333 N. Fairfax St., Ste. 100, Alexandria, VA 22314, tel.: (703) 836-2121; E-mail: giving@microsoft.com; URL: http://www.microsoft.com/giving

**Grantmaker type:** Corporate giving program
**Financial data** (yr. ended 06/30/99): Total giving, $104,659,000; giving activities include $13,034,000 for grants, $12,612,000 for employee matching gifts and $79,013,000 for in-kind gifts.

**Purpose and activities:** Microsoft makes charitable contributions to nonprofit organizations involved with arts and culture, education, the environment, human services, science, public affairs, and senior citizens. Support is given on an international basis.

**Fields of interest:** Arts/cultural programs; higher education; college (community/junior); libraries (public); education; environment; human services; science; public affairs; aging.

**Types of support:** General/operating support; annual campaigns; capital campaigns; fellowships; scholarship funds; employee volunteer services; employee matching gifts; scholarships—to individuals; donated products; in-kind gifts; matching/challenge support.

**Limitations:** Giving on an international basis, particularly in the Puget Sound, WA, area. No

support for political, labor, religious, or fraternal organizations, amateur or professional sports groups or teams, hospitals or medical clinics, or U.S.-based organizations active in areas abroad. No grants to individuals (except for scholarships), or for sports events, conferences or symposia, sponsorships, exhibitions or performances, or fundraising.

**Publications:** Application guidelines, corporate giving report.

**Application information:** Unsolicited proposals for general operating support from organizations located outside the Puget Sound, WA, area are not accepted. Unsolicited proposals for software donations from organizations located outside the U.S. are not accepted. An application form is required for software donations. The Law and Corporate Affairs Department handles giving. The company has a staff that only handles contributions. A contributions committee reviews all requests.
*Initial approach:* Proposal to headquarters; contact headquarters for software donation application form
*Deadline(s):* Apr. 30 for Nonprofit Technology Leadership Grants
*Final notification:* Following review
**Administrators:** Bruce Brooks, Dir., Community Affairs; Joanna Demirian, Sr. Prog. Mgr.; Emily Hine, Prog. Mgr.; Chris Jones, Sr. Prog. Mgr.; Sarah Meyer, Sr. Prog. Mgr.; Jane Meseck Yeager, Prog. Mgr.
**Number of staff:** 6 full-time professional; 7 full-time support.

---

**769**
**The Norcliffe Foundation ▼**
(Formerly The Norcliffe Fund)
First Interstate Ctr.
999 3rd Ave., Ste. 1006
Seattle, WA 98104 (206) 682-4820
*Contact:* Dana Pigott, Pres.

Incorporated in 1952 in WA.
**Donor(s):** Theiline M. McCone.‡
**Grantmaker type:** Independent foundation
**Financial data** (yr. ended 11/30/99): Assets, $66,056,205 (M); gifts received, $1,949,553; expenditures, $5,622,757; qualifying distributions, $5,463,418; giving activities include $5,389,052 for 130 grants (high: $1,025,700; low: $13; average: $1,000–$25,000).

**Purpose and activities:** Emphasis on the arts and cultural activities, Roman Catholic church support and religious associations, hospitals, early childhood, higher and secondary education, and historic preservation; support also for medical research and health associations, hospices, the environment and conservation, and social services, including programs for the disabled, the homeless, child welfare, youth agencies, wildlife organizations, and the aged.

**Fields of interest:** Visual arts; architecture; performing arts; theater; music; historic preservation/historical societies; arts/cultural programs; education, association; education, fund raising; elementary/secondary education; vocational education; higher education; adult education—literacy & basic skills; libraries/library science; reading; education; natural resource conservation & protection;

environment; wildlife preservation & protection; hospitals (general); dental care; health care; substance abuse, services; mental health/crisis services; health associations; cancer; AIDS; alcoholism; biomedicine; medical research; cancer research; AIDS research; legal services; employment; food services; nutrition; housing/shelter, development; recreation; human services; children & youth, services; child development, services; family services; hospices; human services, special populations; community development; voluntarism promotion; federated giving programs; mathematics; computer science; government/public administration; Christian agencies & churches; minorities; Native Americans; disabled; aging; women; economically disadvantaged; homeless.

**Types of support:** General/operating support; capital campaigns.

**Limitations:** Giving in the Puget Sound region of WA, with emphasis on Seattle. No grants to individuals, or for deficit financing, matching gifts, or scholarships; no loans.

**Publications:** Program policy statement, application guidelines.

**Application information:** Application form not required.
*Initial approach:* Letter
*Copies of proposal:* 1
*Deadline(s):* None
*Board meeting date(s):* As required
*Final notification:* 3 to 6 months
**Officers and Trustees:*** Dana Pigott,* Pres.; Arline Hefferline, Secy. and Fdn. Mgr.; Theiline P. Scheumann,* Treas.; Mary Ellen Hughes, Charles M. Pigott, Dana Pigott, James C. Pigott, Lee W. Rolfe, Ann Pigott Wyckoff.
**Number of staff:** 1 full-time professional.
**EIN:** 916029352

---

**770**
**The Orrico Foundation**
c/o Dan Kettman
20565 N.E. 33rd Ct.
Redmond, WA 98053

Established in 1993 in WA.
**Grantmaker type:** Independent foundation
**Financial data** (yr. ended 12/31/98): Assets, $1,313,460 (M); expenditures, $62,839; qualifying distributions, $59,032; giving activities include $60,000 for 2 grants (high: $50,000; low: $10,000).

**Fields of interest:** Libraries (public); hospitals (general).

**Limitations:** Applications not accepted. Giving primarily in Seattle, WA. No grants to individuals.

**Application information:** Contributes only to pre-selected organizations.

**Officers and Directors:*** Brent A. Orrico,* Pres.; Mark V. Orrico,* V.P.; Paul E. Orrico,* Secy.; Daniel Kettman,* Treas.; Diane M. Kettman, Dean H. Orrico, F. Kevin Orrico, Phyllis Orrico.
**EIN:** 911597380

## 771
## Potlatch Foundation II
c/o Potlatch Corp.
601 W. Riverside Ave., Ste. 1100
Spokane, WA 99201 (509) 835-1515
*Contact:* Hubert D. Travaille, Pres.
*E-mail:* hdtravai@potlatchcorp.com

Established in 1985 in CA.
**Donor(s):** Potlatch Corp.
**Grantmaker type:** Company-sponsored
foundation
**Financial data** (yr. ended 12/31/98): Assets,
$594,244 (M); gifts received, $1,206,950;
expenditures, $1,104,913; qualifying
distributions, $1,104,422; giving activities
include $1,039,600 for 204 grants (high:
$192,500; low: $200; average: $300–$200,000)
and $64,691 for 155 employee matching gifts.
**Purpose and activities:** Giving primarily for arts,
elementary/secondary education, higher
education, libraries, natural resources
conservation and protection, health care,
human services, community development, and
public policy.
**Fields of interest:** Arts/cultural programs;
elementary/secondary education; higher
education; libraries/library science; natural
resource conservation & protection; health care;
human services; community development;
public policy, research.
**Types of support:** General/operating support;
continuing support; capital campaigns;
building/renovation; program development;
professorships; curriculum development;
fellowships; research; employee matching gifts;
scholarships—to individuals.
**Limitations:** Giving primarily in southeastern
AR, northern ID, and northern MN.
**Application information:** Submit Contribution
Authorization form. Application form not
required.
*Initial approach:* Letter
*Deadline(s):* None
**Officers and Trustees:*** Hubert D. Travaille,*
Pres.; L. Pendleton Siegel,* V.P.; Betty R.
Fleshman, Secy.; Gerald L. Zuehlke, Treas.;
Ralph M. Davisson, Barbara M. Failing, George
F. Jewett, Jr., Charles R. Pottenger, Sandra T.
Powell, John M. Richards, Thomas R. Smrekar.
**Number of staff:** None.
**EIN:** 942948030

## 772
## The Greater Tacoma Community
## Foundation
P.O. Box 1995
Tacoma, WA 98401-1995 (253) 383-5622
*Contact:* Lynn Rumball, Prog. Off.
*FAX:* (253) 272-8099; *E-mail:* lynn@gtcf.org;
URL: http://www.gtcf.org

Incorporated in 1977 in WA.
**Grantmaker type:** Community foundation
**Financial data** (yr. ended 06/30/99): Assets,
$55,495,234 (M); gifts received, $8,545,929;
expenditures, $3,201,464; giving activities
include $1,816,859 for 500 grants (low: $100;
average: $50–$7,500).
**Fields of interest:** Museums; performing arts;
theater; historic preservation/historical societies;
arts/cultural programs; child development,
education; higher education; adult/continuing

education; libraries/library science; education;
natural resource conservation & protection;
environment; hospitals (general); health care;
substance abuse, services; mental health/crisis
services; health associations; AIDS; AIDS
research; food services; housing/shelter,
development; recreation; youth development,
services; human services; children & youth,
services; child development, services; family
services; hospices; aging, centers & services;
homeless, human services; community
development; voluntarism promotion;
government/public administration; leadership
development; disabled; aging; economically
disadvantaged; homeless.
**Types of support:** General/operating support;
continuing support; capital campaigns;
building/renovation; equipment; emergency
funds; program development; seed money;
technical assistance; consulting services;
program-related investments/loans;
matching/challenge support.
**Limitations:** Giving limited to Pierce County,
WA. No support for religious or political
activities. No grants for annual campaigns,
scholarships, fellowships, seminars, meetings or
travel, or publications, unless specified by donor.
**Publications:** Annual report, informational
brochure (including application guidelines),
newsletter, application guidelines.
**Application information:** Application form
available on website. Application form required.
*Initial approach:* Letter of intent due 1 month
prior to deadlines
*Copies of proposal:* 2
*Deadline(s):* Mar. 15, July 15, and Nov. 15
*Board meeting date(s):* 5 times yearly
*Final notification:* Within 3 months
**Officers and Directors:*** Michael A. Tucci,*
Chair.; Steven Hill,* Vice-Chair.; Gregory M.
Tanbara,* Secy.; Donald R. Williams,* Treas.;
Elizabeth Brenner, Piper Cheney, Ray E. Corpuz,
Jr., James P. Dawson, Dick DeVine, Andrea S.
Gernon, Bill Gill, Sally B. Leighton, Jose Palmas,
Valarie Zeeck.
**Number of staff:** 3 full-time professional; 1
full-time support.
**EIN:** 911007459

## 773
## Greater Wenatchee Community
## Foundation
7 N. Wenatchee Ave., Ste. 201
P.O. Box 3332
Wenatchee, WA 98807-3332 (509) 663-7716
*Contact:* G. Raymond Taylor, Pres. and C.E.O.
*FAX:* (509) 664-9569; *E-mail:*
manager@gwcfncw.org

Incorporated in 1986 in WA.
**Grantmaker type:** Community foundation
**Financial data** (yr. ended 06/30/99): Assets,
$10,844,800 (M); gifts received, $806,284;
expenditures, $573,066; giving activities
include $336,024 for grants and $45,076 for 84
grants to individuals (high: $6,000; low: $200;
average: $250–$1,000).
**Purpose and activities:** Primary areas of interest
include the arts, education, the environment,
and the disadvantaged, with emphasis on child
welfare and the elderly.
**Fields of interest:** Media/communications;
visual arts; museums; performing arts; theater;

music; humanities; history & archaeology;
historic preservation/historical societies;
arts/cultural programs; early childhood
education; child development, education;
elementary school/education; higher education;
adult/continuing education; adult
education—literacy & basic skills;
libraries/library science; reading; education;
natural resource conservation & protection;
environment; animal welfare; wildlife
preservation & protection; hospitals (general);
family planning; medical care, rehabilitation;
health care; substance abuse, services; mental
health/crisis services; AIDS; alcoholism; food
services; housing/shelter, development;
safety/disasters; recreation; human services;
children & youth, services; child development,
services; family services; hospices; aging,
centers & services; women, centers & services;
minorities/immigrants, centers & services;
homeless, human services; community
development; voluntarism promotion;
minorities; disabled; aging; women;
economically disadvantaged; homeless.
**Types of support:** Capital campaigns;
building/renovation; equipment; land
acquisition; program development; seed money;
technical assistance; scholarships—to
individuals; matching/challenge support.
**Limitations:** Giving limited to north central WA,
especially Chelan, Douglas, Grant, and
Okanogan counties. No support for religious
sectarian purposes. No grants to individuals
(except for designated scholarships), or for
continuing support, annual campaigns, general
operating budgets, or conferences.
**Publications:** Annual report, application
guidelines, informational brochure, occasional
report, grants list.
**Application information:** Contact foundation for
application guidelines or use the PNGF
Common Form. Application form not required.
*Initial approach:* Telephone or letter
*Copies of proposal:* 4
*Deadline(s):* Varies; telephone to verify
*Board meeting date(s):* Quarterly
*Final notification:* 2 months
**Officers and Trustees:*** John R. Applegate,
M.D.,* Chair.; Leon McKinney,* Vice-Chair.; G.
Raymond Taylor,* Pres. and C.E.O.; Jane
Hensel,* Secy.-Treas.; Lloyd L. Berry, Roger
Bumps, Benjamin Flores, Dale M. Foreman,
Gerald E. Gibbons, M.D., Douglas B. Harper,
Dennis S. Johnson, Terrence M. McCawley, John
C. "Joe" Merritt, John J. "Jack" Snyder, Jr., Terry
Sorom, Bing Uylangco, Mary Ann Warren,
Robert L. White.
**Number of staff:** 1 full-time professional; 1
full-time support; 1 part-time support.
**EIN:** 911349486

# WEST VIRGINIA

## 774
**Hollowell Foundation, Inc.**
(Formerly Hollowell-Ford Foundation, Inc.)
103 E. Washington St.
Lewisburg, WV 24901-1326 (304) 645-5414
*Contact:* Thomas G. Potterfield, Pres.

Established in 1975 in WV.
**Donor(s):** Margaret F. Hollowell,‡ Otto Hollowell Unitrust.
**Grantmaker type:** Independent foundation
**Financial data** (yr. ended 06/30/98): Assets, $4,841,581 (M); expenditures, $290,265; qualifying distributions, $224,800; giving activities include $224,800 for 24 grants (high: $50,000; low: $500).
**Purpose and activities:** Giving primarily for public libraries and community improvement.
**Fields of interest:** Arts, multipurpose centers/programs; higher education; libraries (public); community development.
**Types of support:** General/operating support; building/renovation; matching/challenge support.
**Limitations:** Giving limited to Greenbrier County, WV. No grants to individuals.
**Application information:** Application form required.
*Deadline(s):* Apr. 1
*Board meeting date(s):* Jan., Apr., June, and Sept.
**Officers:** Thomas G. Potterfield, Pres.; Thomas G. McMillan, V.P.; Jesse O. Guills, Jr., Treas.
**Director:** Marshall Musser.
**Number of staff:** 1 part-time professional.
**EIN:** 510183517

## 775
**The Greater Kanawha Valley Foundation**
Huntington Sq., Ste. 1600
900 Lee St., E.
Charleston, WV 25301 (304) 346-3620
*Contact:* Rebecca C. Cain
*FAX:* (304) 346-3640; E-mail: tgkvf@tgkvf.com; URL: http://www.tgkvf.com

Established in 1962 in WV.
**Grantmaker type:** Community foundation
**Financial data** (yr. ended 12/31/99): Assets, $95,168,297 (M); gifts received, $518,027; expenditures, $3,997,942; giving activities include $2,670,543 for grants (average: $200–$18,000) and $577,930 for grants to individuals (average: $375–$8,000).
**Purpose and activities:** Primary areas of interest include higher and other education, youth, recreation, the arts, and the social sciences. Support also for child welfare and family services, women, housing, the medical sciences, including research on AIDS, heart disease, and cancer, ecology and the environment, and community development programs.
**Fields of interest:** Film/video; visual arts; museums; performing arts; dance; humanities; historic preservation/historical societies; arts/cultural programs; education, association; education, research; early childhood education;
elementary school/education; higher education; libraries/library science; education; natural resource conservation & protection; environment; dental care; nursing care; health care; substance abuse, services; health associations; cancer; eye diseases; heart & circulatory diseases; AIDS; biomedicine; medical research; cancer research; eye research; heart & circulatory research; AIDS research; housing/shelter, development; recreation; human services; children & youth, services; family services; hospices; women, centers & services; homeless, human services; community development; social sciences; disabled; women; homeless.
**Types of support:** General/operating support; continuing support; annual campaigns; capital campaigns; building/renovation; equipment; program development; conferences/seminars; publication; seed money; scholarship funds; research; technical assistance; employee-related scholarships; scholarships—to individuals; matching/challenge support.
**Limitations:** Giving limited to the greater Kanawha Valley, WV, area, except scholarships which are limited to residents of WV. No grants to individuals (except for designated scholarship funds), or for deficit financing or general endowments; no loans.
**Publications:** Annual report (including application guidelines), informational brochure, application guidelines, financial statement.
**Application information:** Application form required.
*Initial approach:* Letter, telephone, FAX, or E-mail
*Copies of proposal:* 1
*Deadline(s):* Varies; contact foundation for information; Feb. 14 for scholarships
*Board meeting date(s):* Quarterly, usually in Apr., June, Sept., and Dec.
*Final notification:* Immediately after board action
**Officers and Trustees:*** Sandra Murphy,* Chair.; Stephan R. Crislip, Vice-Chair.; Lesley A. Russo, Secy.; Charles L. Capito, Jr., T. Randolph Cox, Daniel S. Foster, M.D., Rebecca B. Goldman, Judith N. McJunkin, Mary Anne Michael, Harry Moone, Barbara Rose.
**Advisory Committee:** Paul Arbogast, G. Thomas Battle, Frederick H. Belden, Jr., Elsie P. Carter, Elizabeth E. Chilton, William M. Davis, Deborah A. Faber, Brooks F. McCabe, Jr., Charles R. McElwee, Thomas N. McJunkin, Harry Moore, William E. Mullett, Ph.D., Warren Point, M.D., Virginia Rugeley, Mark H. Schaul, Dolly Sherwood, K. Richard C. Sinclair, Olivia R. Singleton, Louis B. Southworth, Charles B. Stacy, L. Newton Thomas, Jr., Adeline J. Voorhees, Thomas C. Wetzel.
**Trustee Banks:** Bank One, West Virginia, N.A., City National Bank of Charleston, Huntington National Bank West Virginia, One Valley Bank, N.A., United National Bank, WesBanco Bank.
**Number of staff:** 6 full-time professional; 1 part-time professional.
**EIN:** 556024430

## 776
**Elizabeth Sarah Kraft Memorial Trust**
c/o WesBanco Bank Wheeling
1 Bank Plz.
Wheeling, WV 26003 (304) 234-9400

Established in 1993 in WV.
**Donor(s):** Elizabeth Sarah Kraft.‡
**Grantmaker type:** Independent foundation
**Financial data** (yr. ended 12/31/98): Assets, $1,756,686 (M); expenditures, $64,636; qualifying distributions, $59,383; giving activities include $56,728 for 6 grants (high: $17,018; low: $2,836).
**Purpose and activities:** Giving primarily for education and youth programs.
**Fields of interest:** Education, single organization support; libraries (public); medical care, rehabilitation; children & youth, services; Protestant agencies & churches.
**Limitations:** Applications not accepted. Giving limited to WV. No grants to individuals.
**Application information:** Contributes only to pre-selected organizations.
**Trustee:** WesBanco Bank Wheeling.
**EIN:** 556118512

## 777
**Parkersburg Area Community Foundation**
501 Avery St.
P.O. Box 1762
Parkersburg, WV 26102-1762 (304) 428-4438
*Contact:* Judy Sjostedt, Exec. Dir.
*FAX:* (304) 428-1200; E-mail: PACF@wirefire.com; URL: http://home.wirefire.com/pacf

Established in 1963 in WV.
**Donor(s):** Albert Wolfe,‡ Members of the Wolfe family,‡ The Keystone Foundation.‡
**Grantmaker type:** Community foundation
**Financial data** (yr. ended 06/30/99): Assets, $8,093,218 (M); gifts received, $419,749; expenditures, $468,940; giving activities include $233,442 for 148 grants (high: $25,000; low: $10; average: $1,000–$4,000) and $108,525 for 109 grants to individuals (high: $2,500; low: $20; average: $100–$1,000).
**Purpose and activities:** Support for programs leading toward the improvement or fulfillment of charitable, educational, cultural, health, and welfare activities, including direct human services and scholarships to individuals.
**Fields of interest:** Museums; historic preservation/historical societies; arts/cultural programs; child development, education; higher education; adult education—literacy & basic skills; libraries/library science; reading; education; health care; animal welfare; mental health/crisis services; health associations; human services; children & youth, services; child development, services; family services; community development; disabled.
**Types of support:** Capital campaigns; building/renovation; equipment; emergency funds; program development; seed money; scholarship funds; scholarships—to individuals; matching/challenge support.
**Limitations:** Giving limited to Calhoun, Doddridge, Gilma, Wirt, Wood, Jackson, Pleasants, Ritchie, and Reane counties, WV. No grants for travel, meetings, seminars, conferences, student exchange programs,

annual campaigns, endowment funds, operating budgets, debt reduction, or maintenance needs.
**Publications:** Annual report, informational brochure, newsletter, application guidelines.
**Application information:** Application form required.
*Initial approach:* Letter, E-mail, or telephone for guidelines
*Copies of proposal:* 10
*Deadline(s):* Mar. 1 and Sept. 15 for local grants; Apr. 1 for the Ruth Hornbrook Memorial Fund
*Board meeting date(s):* 3rd Friday in Jan., Mar., May, Sept., and Nov.
*Final notification:* May/Nov.; will consider emergency grants at other times
**Officers and Governors:\*** Thomas Weyer,\* Chair.; Barbara N. Fish, Vice-Chair.; Judy Sjostedt,\* Exec. Dir.; and 15 additional members.
**Trustee Banks:** One Valley Bank, N.A., The Peoples Bank, United National Bank, WesBanco Bank Parkersburg, WesBanco Bank Wheeling.
**Number of staff:** 2 full-time professional.
**EIN:** 556027764

# WISCONSIN

## 778
### Alliant Energy Foundation, Inc.
(Formerly Wisconsin Power and Light Foundation, Inc.)
P.O. Box 192
Madison, WI  53701-0192  (608) 252-5545
*Contact:* Jo Ann Healy, Admin.
*E-mail:* joannhealy@alliant-energy.com; URL: http://www.alliantenergy.com/ourinvolvement/charity.php3

Established in 1984 in WI.
**Donor(s):** Wisconsin Power and Light Co., Alliant Energy Corp.
**Grantmaker type:** Company-sponsored foundation
**Financial data** (yr. ended 12/31/98): Assets, $11,109,155 (M); gifts received, $3,499; expenditures, $952,168; qualifying distributions, $819,402; giving activities include $625,878 for 475 grants (high: $97,744; low: $10; average: $250–$1,000), $88,500 for 39 grants to individuals (high: $3,000; low: $1,500) and $47,118 for 177 employee matching gifts.
**Fields of interest:** Visual arts; museums; performing arts; dance; theater; music; arts/cultural programs; education, association; higher education; business school/education; adult education—literacy & basic skills; libraries/library science; reading; education; hospitals (general); health associations; youth development, citizenship; human services; children & youth, services; family services; hospices; community development; government/public administration; public affairs, citizen participation; minorities.
**Types of support:** General/operating support; continuing support; annual campaigns; capital campaigns; building/renovation; equipment; emergency funds; seed money; fellowships; scholarship funds; employee matching gifts; employee-related scholarships.

**Limitations:** Giving limited to areas of company operations in central and southcentral WI. No support for religious, fraternal, or social clubs, organized sports teams, or political organizations. No grants for ads in programs, door prizes, raffles, dinner tables, travel funds, scholarships, endowments, fundraising, or tours.
**Publications:** Annual report (including application guidelines), informational brochure (including application guidelines).
**Application information:** Application form required.
*Initial approach:* Proposal
*Copies of proposal:* 1
*Deadline(s):* Sept. 1
*Board meeting date(s):* Quarterly
*Final notification:* Jan.
**Officers and Directors:\*** Pamela Wegner,\* Pres.; Robert Rusch, Secy.-Treas.; Joanne Acomb, Erroll B. Davis, Jr., William Holewinski, Thaddeus A. Miller, Jules A. Nicolet, Jan Scott, Linda Taplin-Canto.
**Number of staff:** 1 full-time professional.
**EIN:** 391444065

## 779
### Annmarie Foundation, Inc.
c/o Phillips Plastic Customer Ctr.
1201 Hanley Rd.
Hudson, WI  54016
*Contact:* Kandare Becker

Established in 1973 in WI.
**Donor(s):** Phillips Plastics Corp.
**Grantmaker type:** Independent foundation
**Financial data** (yr. ended 04/30/99): Assets, $3,993,680 (M); gifts received, $500,250; expenditures, $384,778; qualifying distributions, $353,428; giving activities include $324,350 for 212 grants (high: $5,250; low: $100) and $29,078 for 29 grants to individuals (high: $2,078; low: $500).
**Purpose and activities:** Awards scholarships to students pursuing education in the profession of a plastic-related field, and residing in areas where Phillips Plastics operates; support also for youth development, recreation, pre-school through higher education, community services, and culture.
**Fields of interest:** Arts/cultural programs; libraries (public); education; health associations; Big Brothers/Big Sisters; youth development; scouting agencies (general); youth, services; federated giving programs; Christian agencies & churches; Protestant agencies & churches; Roman Catholic agencies & churches.
**Types of support:** General/operating support; scholarships—to individuals.
**Limitations:** Giving limited to the Phillips, WI, area.
**Application information:** Application form required.
*Initial approach:* Letter
*Deadline(s):* None
**Members:** Jim Anderson, Doug Berends, Brad Chapman, Tom Gehrke, Sally Griese, Marilyn McCarty, Karl Murch, Kay Stevens.
**EIN:** 237301323

## 780
### Associated Banc-Corp Foundation
(Formerly First Financial Foundation, Inc.)
1200 Hansen Rd.
Green Bay, WI  54304
*Contact:* Jon Drayna
*E-mail:* jon.drayna@associatedbank.com

Established in 1977 in WI.
**Donor(s):** First Financial Bank, Associated Banc-Corp.
**Grantmaker type:** Company-sponsored foundation
**Financial data** (yr. ended 12/31/99): Assets, $903,220 (M); expenditures, $48,106; qualifying distributions, $47,501; giving activities include $47,440 for grants.
**Fields of interest:** Performing arts; higher education; business school/education; libraries/library science; hospitals (general); health care; health associations; medical research; housing/shelter, development; community development; federated giving programs; economics; government/public administration.
**Types of support:** Annual campaigns; capital campaigns; building/renovation; program development.
**Limitations:** Giving limited to areas of business in IL and WI. No support for labor organizations, veterans organizations, or religious or church-affiliated organizations. No grants to individuals.
**Application information:** Not actively making grants in 2000. Application form required.
*Initial approach:* Letter
*Copies of proposal:* 1
*Deadline(s):* Sept. 1
*Board meeting date(s):* Oct.
*Final notification:* Dec.
**Officers and Directors:\*** Ralph R. Staven,\* Chair. and Pres.; Robert M. Salinger, Secy.; David W. Drought, Treas.; Robert S. Gaiswinkler, James O. Heinecke, Ignatius H. Robers.
**Number of staff:** 1 part-time professional.
**EIN:** 391277461

## 781
### Pat and Jay Baker Foundation, Inc.
6350 W. Lake Dr.
Whitefish Bay, WI  53217

Established in 1993.
**Grantmaker type:** Independent foundation
**Financial data** (yr. ended 12/31/99): Assets, $8,321,703 (M); gifts received, $1,530; expenditures, $4,481,737; qualifying distributions, $4,437,813; giving activities include $4,482,100 for 16 grants (high: $1,000,000; low: $100).
**Fields of interest:** Museums (art); performing arts; university; libraries (public); federated giving programs; Protestant agencies & churches.
**Limitations:** Applications not accepted. Giving primarily in Milwaukee, WI. No grants to individuals.
**Application information:** Contributes only to pre-selected organizations.
**Officers and Directors:\*** Jay H. Baker,\* Pres. and Treas.; Pat Good Baker,\* V.P. and Secy.; Peter M. Sommerhauser.
**EIN:** 391776268

## 782
### Theodore W. Batterman Family Foundation, Inc.
c/o Theodore W. Batterman
1450 Janesville Ave.
Fort Atkinson, WI 53538

Established in 1990 in WI.
**Donor(s):** Theodore W. Batterman, Spacesaver Corp.
**Grantmaker type:** Independent foundation
**Financial data** (yr. ended 12/31/98): Assets, $40,782,102 (M); gifts received, $1,748,148; expenditures, $1,676,008; qualifying distributions, $1,545,999; giving activities include $1,513,826 for 52 grants (high: $150,000; low: $2,500).
**Purpose and activities:** Giving primarily for education and human services.
**Fields of interest:** Libraries (public); education; human services; children & youth, services; Protestant agencies & churches.
**Limitations:** Applications not accepted. Giving limited to WI. No grants to individuals.
**Application information:** Contributes only to pre-selected organizations.
**Officers and Directors:\*** Theodore W. Batterman,\* Pres. and Treas.; Marilyn H. Batterman,\* V.P. and Secy.; Christopher T. Batterman, Eric D. Batterman, Linda C. Batterman Johnson, Andrew R. Lauritzen, Laura G. Batterman Wilkins.
**EIN:** 391688812

## 783
### Bidwell Foundation
P.O. Box 873
Portage, WI 53901
*Contact:* Donald Witt, Tr.

Established in 1980.
**Grantmaker type:** Independent foundation
**Financial data** (yr. ended 01/31/98): Assets, $1,634,625 (M); expenditures, $179,678; qualifying distributions, $98,500; giving activities include $98,500 for 7 grants (high: $50,000; low: $500).
**Purpose and activities:** Giving primarily to animal welfare associations and Christian churches.
**Fields of interest:** Libraries/library science; scholarships/financial aid.
**Types of support:** General/operating support.
**Limitations:** Giving primarily in Columbia County, WI.
**Application information:** Application form not required.
*Deadline(s):* None
**Trustees:** Robert D. Miller, Richard Rehm, Donald Witt.
**EIN:** 391340893

## 784
### Black River Falls Area Foundation
c/o Jackson County Bank
8 Main St.
Black River Falls, WI 54615 (715) 284-5341
*Contact:* Gilbert L. Homstad, Chair.
*Application address:* P.O. Box 99, Black River Falls, WI 54615

Established in 1985 in WI.

**Grantmaker type:** Community foundation
**Financial data** (yr. ended 12/31/99): Assets, $1,170,000 (M); expenditures, $584,000; giving activities include $557,000 for 15 grants (high: $500,000; low: $500) and $17,000 for 15 grants to individuals.
**Fields of interest:** Libraries/library science; education; recreation; community development; federated giving programs; disabled.
**Types of support:** Capital campaigns; building/renovation; program development; seed money; scholarship funds.
**Limitations:** Giving limited to Jackson County, WI, with emphasis on the city of Black River Falls. No grants to individuals (except for local scholarships).
**Publications:** Application guidelines, informational brochure, multi-year report.
**Application information:** Applications accepted between Apr. 1 and May 15. Application form required.
*Initial approach:* Letter
*Deadline(s):* May 15
*Board meeting date(s):* Annually
**Officers and Trustees:\*** Gilbert L. Homstad,\* Chair.; David Hoffman, Vice-Chair.; A.T. Lahmeyer, Secy.; John Lund,\* Treas.; Todd Anderson, Ruth Buswell, Mike Dougherty, John Hogden, Mary O'Brien, Jerry Kitowski.
**Number of staff:** None.
**EIN:** 391563654

## 785
### A. Keith Brewer Trust
c/o Marshall & Ilsley Trust Co.
P.O. Box 2980
Milwaukee, WI 53201

**Grantmaker type:** Independent foundation
**Financial data** (yr. ended 12/31/98): Assets, $1,069,281 (M); expenditures, $76,121; qualifying distributions, $64,225; giving activities include $63,175 for 1 grant.
**Purpose and activities:** Support for an affiliated private science library and research in the physical sciences.
**Fields of interest:** Libraries/library science; physical/earth sciences.
**Types of support:** General/operating support.
**Limitations:** Applications not accepted. Giving limited to WI. No grants to individuals.
**Application information:** Contributes only to pre-selected organizations.
**Trustee:** Marshall & Ilsley Trust Co.
**EIN:** 396432314

## 786
### Community Foundation for the Fox Valley Region, Inc.
P.O. Box 563
118 S. State St., F-2
Appleton, WI 54912 (920) 830-1290
*Contact:* Larry L. Kath, Exec. Dir., Lori Miller, Dir., Finance, or Lynn VanLankvelt, Financial Admin.
*FAX:* (920) 830-1293; E-mail: cffvr@cffoxvalley.org; URL: http://www.cffoxvalley.org

Organized in 1986 in WI.
**Grantmaker type:** Community foundation

**Financial data** (yr. ended 06/30/99): Assets, $59,776,847 (M); gifts received, $7,844,386; expenditures, $5,152,763; giving activities include $4,287,373 for grants (average: $24–$100,000).
**Purpose and activities:** The foundation exists to enhance the quality of life for all citizens of the Fox Valley region by using funds entrusted to the foundation's stewardship to address community problems and opportunities.
**Fields of interest:** Arts/cultural programs; libraries/library science; education; pharmacology; health care; substance abuse, services; health associations; AIDS; alcoholism; AIDS research; human services; children & youth, services; homeless, human services; community development; government/public administration; transportation; women; homeless.
**Types of support:** Emergency funds; program development; seed money.
**Limitations:** Giving limited to the Fox Valley, WI, area. No support for sectarian or religious purposes or medical projects. No grants for operating expenses (except from donor-advised funds), annual fund drives, deficit financing, endowment funds, capital projects, travel expenses, or specific research.
**Publications:** Annual report, informational brochure (including application guidelines), newsletter.
**Application information:** Application form required.
*Initial approach:* Letter or telephone
*Copies of proposal:* 4
*Deadline(s):* Jan. 10, Apr. 10, July 10, and Sept. 30
*Board meeting date(s):* Feb., May, Aug., and Nov.
*Final notification:* Feb., May, Aug., and Nov.
**Officers and Directors:\*** Jim Hayes,\* Chair.; Larry L. Kath,\* Pres.; Jane Gorton,\* V.P.; Richard Auchter,\* Treas.; and 43 additional directors.
**Number of staff:** 7 full-time professional; 4 full-time support.
**EIN:** 391548450

## 787
### Green Bay Packers Foundation
1265 Lombardi Ave.
Green Bay, WI 54304-3928 (920) 496-5700
*Contact:* Phillip Pionek, Secy.
*URL:* http://www.packers.com/community/foundation.html

Established in 1986 in WI.
**Donor(s):** Green Bay Packers, Inc.
**Grantmaker type:** Company-sponsored foundation
**Financial data** (yr. ended 03/31/00): Assets, $2,859,663 (M); gifts received, $101,108; expenditures, $154,987; qualifying distributions, $131,830; giving activities include $134,571 for 62 grants (high: $5,000; low: $500; average: $500–$5,000).
**Purpose and activities:** Giving primarily for library services, botanical gardens, and youth services.
**Fields of interest:** Libraries/library science; botanical gardens; substance abuse, services; children & youth, services; family services, domestic violence.

**Limitations:** Applications not accepted. Giving primarily in WI. No grants to individuals.
**Publications:** Annual report, financial statement.
**Application information:** Contributes only to pre-selected organizations.
*Board meeting date(s):* Aug. and Dec.
**Officer and Trustees:*** John "Jack" Meng,* Chair.; Donald F. Harden, Michael Reese, Leo Scherer, Fred Trowbridge, Jr., Associated Bank, N.A.
**EIN:** 391577137

### 788
### H. J. Hagge Foundation, Inc.
500 3rd St., Ste. 506
Wausau, WI 54403-4896 (715) 845-1818
*Contact:* Carol M. Krieg, Asst. Secy.-Treas.

Established in 1956 in WI.
**Donor(s):** H.J. Hagge,‡ Helen S. Hagge.‡
**Grantmaker type:** Independent foundation
**Financial data** (yr. ended 12/31/99): Assets, $2,058,177 (M); expenditures, $118,474; qualifying distributions, $112,366; giving activities include $108,107 for 72 grants (high: $22,573; low: $100; average: $500–$1,000).
**Purpose and activities:** Giving for education, civic projects, community and human services.
**Fields of interest:** Arts/cultural programs; education, association; libraries/library science; wildlife preservation & protection; health associations; cancer; cancer research; human services; Protestant agencies & churches; religion; minorities.
**Types of support:** General/operating support; continuing support; annual campaigns; capital campaigns; emergency funds.
**Limitations:** Giving primarily in WI. No grants to individuals.
**Application information:** Application form not required.
*Initial approach:* Letter
*Copies of proposal:* 1
*Deadline(s):* None
*Board meeting date(s):* Jan. and July
**Officers and Directors:*** Robert S. Hagge, Jr.,* Pres. and Treas.; Kristin Single Hagge,* V.P.; Leigh Hagge Tuckey,* Secy.; A. Woodson Hagge, Daniel L. Hagge, Jr.
**Number of staff:** None.
**EIN:** 396037112

### 789
### Jones Family Foundation
P.O. Box 1167
481 E. Division St., Ste. 800
Fond du Lac, WI 54936-1167

Established in 1989 in WI.
**Donor(s):** Donald Jones, Terri Jones.
**Grantmaker type:** Independent foundation
**Financial data** (yr. ended 12/31/99): Assets, $2,756,412 (M); expenditures, $784,168; qualifying distributions, $755,009; giving activities include $740,871 for 19 grants (high: $350,000; low: $100).
**Purpose and activities:** Giving primarily for education, health, and human services. Support also for the Library of Congress.
**Fields of interest:** Libraries (special); education; health care; human services.
**Types of support:** General/operating support.

**Limitations:** Applications not accepted. Giving primarily in Fond du Lac, WI. No grants to individuals.
**Application information:** Contributes only to pre-selected organizations.
**Trustees:** Donald Jones, Terri Jones.
**EIN:** 396501525

### 790
### The George Kress Foundation, Inc.
P.O. Box 19006
Green Bay, WI 54307-9006
*Contact:* John F. Kress, Secy.
*Application address:* c/o Green Bay Packaging Co., 1700 N. Webster Ave., Green Bay, WI 54301

Incorporated in 1953 in WI.
**Donor(s):** Green Bay Packaging, Inc.
**Grantmaker type:** Independent foundation
**Financial data** (yr. ended 12/31/99): Assets, $8,364,651 (M); gifts received, $2,400,000; expenditures, $1,740,107; qualifying distributions, $1,704,657; giving activities include $1,700,891 for 238 grants (high: $500,000; low: $50).
**Purpose and activities:** Giving primarily to federated giving programs, libraries, Christian agencies and churches, and higher education; funding also for arts and culture, historical preservation, hospitals, health associations, recreation, particularly local sporting events, children and youth services, social and family services, community development, and the United Way.
**Fields of interest:** Historic preservation/historical societies; arts/cultural programs; higher education; libraries (public); education; hospitals (general); health associations; recreation; boys & girls clubs; human services; YM/YWCAs & YM/YWHAs; children & youth, services; family services; community development; federated giving programs; Christian agencies & churches.
**Types of support:** Continuing support; annual campaigns; capital campaigns; building/renovation; program development; professorships; scholarship funds; research.
**Limitations:** Giving primarily in Green Bay and Madison, WI.
**Application information:** Application form not required.
*Initial approach:* Letter
*Copies of proposal:* 1
*Deadline(s):* None
**Officers:** George F. Kress, Pres.; James F. Kress, V.P.; John Kress, Secy.
**Number of staff:** 1 full-time professional; 1 part-time support.
**EIN:** 396050768

### 791
### Viola E. Lundeberg Trust
c/o R.V. Alexander
P.O. Box 46
River Falls, WI 54022-0046

Established in 1995 in WI.
**Grantmaker type:** Independent foundation
**Financial data** (yr. ended 12/31/99): Assets, $752,998 (M); expenditures, $61,766; qualifying distributions, $45,000; giving

activities include $45,000 for 6 grants (high: $15,000; low: $5,000).
**Fields of interest:** Higher education; libraries/library science; education.
**Limitations:** Applications not accepted. Giving limited to MN and WI. No grants to individuals.
**Application information:** Contributes only to pre-selected organizations.
**Trustees:** R.V. Alexander, Roland Hammer.
**EIN:** 396503917

### 792
### Earl & Eugenia Quirk Foundation, Inc.
314 W. Main St., Ste. 11
Watertown, WI 53094-7630 (920) 261-0223
*Contact:* Claude C. Held II

Established in 1962 in WI.
**Donor(s):** Catherine J. Quirk,‡ Eugenia B. Quirk.‡
**Grantmaker type:** Independent foundation
**Financial data** (yr. ended 04/30/99): Assets, $4,202,172 (M); expenditures, $276,253; qualifying distributions, $244,407; giving activities include $232,100 for 19 grants (high: $150,000; low: $600).
**Fields of interest:** Arts/cultural programs; libraries/library science; hospitals (general); community development; general charitable giving.
**Limitations:** Applications not accepted. Giving limited to WI. No grants to individuals.
**Application information:** Contributes only to pre-selected organizations.
**Officers and Directors:*** Lillian Q. Conley,* Pres.; Ellen P. Conley,* V.P.; Wendy Q. Schuett,* Secy.; Darby R. Quirk,* Treas.; James E. Conley, M.D., James B. Quirk.
**Number of staff:** None.
**EIN:** 396059626

### 793
### Dr. R. G. & Sarah Raymond Foundation
c/o National Exchange Bank and Trust
130 S. Main St.
Fond du Lac, WI 54935-4210
*Contact:* Robert V. Edgarton, Secy.
*Application address:* P.O. Box 1003, Fond du Lac, WI 54931, tel.: (920) 922-0470

Established in 1957.
**Grantmaker type:** Independent foundation
**Financial data** (yr. ended 12/31/98): Assets, $1,519,013 (M); expenditures, $92,333; qualifying distributions, $77,576; giving activities include $76,500 for 35 grants (high: $7,000; low: $300).
**Fields of interest:** Libraries/library science; education; health care; recreation; human services; Christian agencies & churches; religion.
**Types of support:** General/operating support.
**Limitations:** Giving primarily in Fond du Lac and Dodge counties, WI.
**Application information:**
*Initial approach:* Letter
*Deadline(s):* None
**Officers and Directors:*** Leland Friedrich,* Pres.; Michael W. Bachhuber, V.P.; Robert V. Edgarton,* Secy.; Peter Stone,* Treas.
**EIN:** 396051142

## 794
### Schoenleber Foundation, Inc.
111 E. Wisconsin Ave., Ste. 1800
Milwaukee, WI  53202-4802   (414) 276-3400
*Contact:* Peter C. Haensel, Pres.

Established in 1965 in WI.
**Donor(s):** Marie Schoenleber,‡ Louise
Schoenleber,‡ Gretchen Schoenleber.‡
**Grantmaker type:** Independent foundation
**Financial data** (yr. ended 12/31/99): Assets,
$7,024,166 (M); expenditures, $498,368;
qualifying distributions, $396,142; giving
activities include $400,100 for 19 grants (high:
$100,000; low: $5,000).
**Purpose and activities:** Giving primarily to a
public library foundation, as well as for arts and
culture, education, and human services,
particularly to a center for people who are blind
and/or deaf, and federated giving programs.
**Fields of interest:** Arts/cultural programs;
libraries (public); education; human services;
federated giving programs; disabled.
**Types of support:** General/operating support;
endowments; scholarship funds.
**Limitations:** Giving primarily in WI, with
emphasis on Milwaukee. No support for
religious purposes, or for primary or secondary
education. No grants to individuals.
**Publications:** Informational brochure (including
application guidelines).
**Application information:** Application form
required.
  *Initial approach:* Letter
  *Copies of proposal:* 1
  *Deadline(s):* Aug. 30
**Officers and Directors:** Peter C. Haensel,*
Pres.; Frank W. Bastian,* Secy.; Walter Schorrak.
**Number of staff:** 1 full-time professional; 1
part-time support.
**EIN:** 391049364

## 795
### Frank C. Shattuck Charitable Trust
c/o Bank One Trust Co., N.A.
P.O. Box 1308
Milwaukee, WI  53201-1308
*Application address:* c/o Bank One Trust Co.,
N.A., P.O. Box 789, Neenah, WI 54956

Established in 1950.
**Grantmaker type:** Independent foundation
**Financial data** (yr. ended 06/30/98): Assets,
$2,399,315 (M); expenditures, $133,333;
qualifying distributions, $105,454; giving
activities include $100,000 for 5 grants (high:
$30,000; low: $5,000).
**Purpose and activities:** Support for youth
services, a public library, and a Presbyterian
church.
**Fields of interest:** Libraries/library science;
children & youth, services; Protestant agencies
& churches.

**Limitations:** Giving primarily in WI. No grants to
individuals.
**Application information:**
  *Initial approach:* Letter
  *Deadline(s):* None
**Trustee:** Bank One Trust Co., N.A.
**EIN:** 396048813

## 796
### Jane & Arthur Stangel Fund, Inc.
1047 W. Crescent Dr.
Manitowoc, WI  54220
*Contact:* Richard R. Jodarski, Pres.
*Application address:* P.O. Box 2303,
Manitowoc, WI 54221-2303, tel.: (920)
682-5290

Established in 1968.
**Grantmaker type:** Independent foundation
**Financial data** (yr. ended 12/31/98): Assets,
$1,579,115 (M); expenditures, $83,688;
qualifying distributions, $77,779; giving
activities include $70,600 for 26 grants (high:
$10,000; low: $400).
**Purpose and activities:** Giving to secondary and
higher education, art and cultural institutes, and
to human service organizations.
**Fields of interest:** Arts/cultural programs;
elementary/secondary education; higher
education; libraries (public); hospitals (general);
human services.
**Limitations:** Giving primarily in Manitowoc
County, WI. No grants to individuals.
**Application information:**
  *Initial approach:* Proposal
  *Deadline(s):* None
**Officers:** Richard R. Jodarski, Pres.; Nicholas B.
Jagemann, V.P.; Kaye E. Johnson, Secy.-Treas.
**EIN:** 396120403

## 797
### Harriet Steel Charitable Trust
c/o Bank One Trust Co., N.A.
P.O. Box 1308
Milwaukee, WI  53201

Established in 1997 in WI.
**Donor(s):** Harriet Steel.‡
**Grantmaker type:** Independent foundation
**Financial data** (yr. ended 12/31/99): Assets,
$561,901 (M); expenditures, $62,022;
qualifying distributions, $58,330; giving
activities include $56,947 for 7 grants (high:
$10,951; low: $2,190).
**Purpose and activities:** Giving for women's
services, food and human services, and for
religion.
**Fields of interest:** Libraries/library science; food
services; women, centers & services; Christian
agencies & churches.
**Limitations:** Applications not accepted. Giving
primarily in WI. No grants to individuals.

**Application information:** Contributes only to
pre-selected organizations.
**Trustee:** Bank One Trust Co., N.A.
**EIN:** 396496152

## 798
### C. Kevin Walker Foundation
P.O. Box 30
New Lisbon, WI  53950

Established in 1996 in WI.
**Grantmaker type:** Independent foundation
**Financial data** (yr. ended 12/31/99): Assets,
$489,887 (M); expenditures, $72,196;
qualifying distributions, $70,888; giving
activities include $71,500 for 2 grants (high:
$66,500; low: $5,000).
**Purpose and activities:** Giving for libraries.
**Fields of interest:** Libraries (public).
**Limitations:** Applications not accepted. No
grants to individuals.
**Application information:** Contributes only to
pre-selected organizations.
**Trustees:** Donald Boudreau, Wes R. Christensen,
Kevin C. Walker.
**EIN:** 391869238

## 799
### Lester G. Wood Foundation, Inc.
3290 Vista Rd.
Green Bay, WI  54301-2632   (920) 336-1222
*Contact:* Patricia W. Baer, Pres.

Established in 1955.
**Donor(s):** Members of the Baer and Lea families.
**Grantmaker type:** Independent foundation
**Financial data** (yr. ended 12/31/99): Assets,
$3,243,160 (M); gifts received, $535,097;
expenditures, $213,624; qualifying distributions,
$204,418; giving activities include $206,000 for
24 grants (high: $30,000; low: $1,000).
**Purpose and activities:** Giving primarily to a
community foundation, a library, a community
church, and a museum; funding also for
education and social services.
**Fields of interest:** Museums; nursing
school/education; libraries/library science;
education; cancer; human services; Salvation
Army; YM/YWCAs & YM/YWHAs; children,
services; foundations (community); religion.
**Types of support:** General/operating support;
scholarship funds; research.
**Limitations:** Giving primarily in WI, with
emphasis on Green Bay. No grants to
individuals.
**Application information:** Application form not
required.
  *Deadline(s):* None
**Officers and Directors:** Patricia W. Baer,*
Pres.; Charles S. Baer,* V.P.; Frederick E. Baer,*
Secy.-Treas.; Frederick W. Baer, Richard R. Baer.
**Number of staff:** None.
**EIN:** 396055567

# INDEX TO DONORS, OFFICERS, TRUSTEES

NATIONAL GUIDE TO FUNDING FOR LIBRARIES AND INFORMATION SERVICES

# GEOGRAPHIC INDEX

Grantmakers in boldface type make grants on a national, regional, or international basis; the others generally limit giving to the city or state in which they are located. For local funders with a history of giving in another state, consult the "see also" references at the end of each state section.

*Montville:* **International 375**
*New Brunswick:* Robb 381
*Paramus:* Armour 367
*Park Ridge:* Gilmartin 373
*Princeton:* **Johnson 376**
*Rumson:* Cowles 371
*Secaucus:* Stern 383
*Summit:* Fredrickson 372
*Warren:* Schwartz 382
*Weehawken:* PaineWebber 379
*Wyckoff:* Heidtke 374

*see also* 114, 256, 397, 476, 544

## NEW MEXICO

*Santa Fe:* McCune 385

*see also* 292, 603, 744

## NEW YORK

*Albany:* **Hunter 452**
*Amsterdam:* Children's 408, CTW 414, Wasserman 537
*Auburn:* Columbian 410, Emerson 426
*Bronx:* **Wilson 545**
*Brooklyn:* **Keats 457, Viburnum 532**
*Buffalo:* Elster 425, Pierce 491, Wendt 539, Western 540
*Copake:* Ungar 529
*Dunkirk:* Northern 481
*Elmira:* Tioga 523
*Garden City:* **Brooks 400,** Kleinkramer 460
*Glen Head:* Barker 396
*Hammondsport:* Meade 473
*Hobart:* O'Connor 483
*Hudson:* Hudson 448
*Ithaca:* Park 487
*Jamestown:* Chautauqua 407, Gebbie 431, Sheldon 506
*Lake Placid:* Lake Placid 464
*Long Island City:* Darrah 416
*Mamaroneck:* Straus 519
*Melville:* Kissinger 459
*Millbrook:* Dyson 423
*New Hyde Park:* Simon 507
*New York:* Abrons 386, Acorn 387, Adler 388, Alexander 390, Ash 391, **AT&T 392,** B & L 393, **Baker 394, Balanchine 395,** Birkelund 397, Blue 398, Brine 399, Calf 402, Carbetz 403, **Carnegie 404,** Chase 406, **China 409,** Constans 412, Covey 413, Cullman 415, deCoizart 417, Delacorte 418, **Delmas 419, Deutsche 420,** Dimon 421, Duberg 422, Eckert 424, **Engelhard 427, Engineering 428,** Fife 429, Forchheimer 430, Gellert 432, GGM 433, Gilder 434, Goldman 435, Goldsmith 436, Goldsmith 437, Gramercy 439, Greenhill 440, Gregory 441, Hebrew 442, Heckscher 443, Heilbrunn 444, **Heineman 445,** Huguenot 449, Hultquist 451, Kaplan 455, Kaplan 456, King 458, **Klingenstein 461,** Krimendahl 462, Larsen 465, Lasker 466, Lawrence 467, Low 468, Mandeville 469, McGraw 471, McHugh 472, **Mellon 474, Memton 475,** Merrill 476, **Miller 477,** Milstein 478, Morgan 479, Morse 480, Ohrstrom 484, **Ormsby 485, Papanek 486,** Park 488, Peck 489, **Pforzheimer 490, Pine 492,** Pinky 493, Reed 497, Robbins 498, Rose 499, Rose 500, Rubinstein 501, Scherman 502, Schloss 503, Sculco 504, Seligmann 505, Solow 511, **Soros 512,** Spewack 513, Springate 514, Steinberg 515, Steinberg 516, Stevens 517, Story 518, Strong 520, Stuart 521, Time 522, Tisch 524, Tuch 526, **Twain 527,** U.S. 528, Vernon 530, **Vetlesen 531, Wallace 533,** Walter 535, Weinman 538, White 541, Whittemore 542, Wild 543, Wiley 544, Woodward 546, Yaron 548, **Yordan 549**
*Oneida:* Chapman 405
*Oneonta:* Hulbert 450, Warren 536
*Pleasantville:* Reader's 495, Reader's 496
*Purchase:* Gottesman 438, International 453, Wallach 534
*Queensbury:* Potter 494

*Rochester:* Agrilink 389, Johnson 454, Truman 525
*Rome:* Hinman 446
*Rye:* Burke 401
*Shokan:* Kvistad 463
*Syracuse:* Snow 509, Snow 510
*Troy:* Howard 447
*Utica:* Community 411, Smith 508
*Watertown:* Northern 482
*White Plains:* Masinter 470, Worby 547

*see also* 62, 79, 94, 95, 99, 108, 115, 128, 255, 256, 257, 298, 354, 367, 368, 371, 374, 377, 379, 380, 383, 577, 633, 682, 760

## NORTH CAROLINA

*Charlotte:* Belk 551, Chapin 552, Dalton 555, Duke 556, **First 558**
*Durham:* Barnard 550
*Fayetteville:* Cumberland 554
*Lenoir:* Coffey 553
*North Wilkesboro:* **Herring 560**
*Research Triangle Park:* Triangle 562
*Valdese:* Rostan 561
*Winston-Salem:* Finch 557, Gambrill 559, Wachovia 563, Wood 564

*see also* 135, 487, 643, 645, 690

## NORTH DAKOTA

*see* 334

## OHIO

*Akron:* GAR 570
*Canton:* **Timken 591**
*Cincinnati:* Dater 566, Knowlton 574, Lazarus 576, Slemp 587, Westheimer 597
*Cleveland:* Kulas 575, Manley 577, Murphy 579, Peabody 581, Rabild 582, Seifert 586, Smith 588
*Columbus:* Haman 571, Hildreth 572
*Dover:* Reeves 583
*Fredericktown:* Burgett 565
*Lithopolis:* Wagnalls 596
*Mansfield:* Richland 584
*Middletown:* Middletown 578
*Rocky River:* **Gale 569**
*Sandusky:* Frohman 568
*Toledo:* Kell 573, Stensen 589
*Troy:* Tipp City 592, Troy 594
*Van Wert:* Van Wert 595
*Westlake:* Scott 585
*Wooster:* Frick 567
*Youngstown:* Tod 593
*Zanesville:* Muskingum 580, Straker 590

*see also* 50, 320, 691

## OKLAHOMA

*Bartlesville:* Adams 598
*Bristow:* Jones 602
*Cushing:* Thompson 606
*Oklahoma City:* American 599, Kerr 603
*Tulsa:* Bovaird 600, Helmerich 601, Krueger 604, Rothbaum 605

*see also* 112, 713

## OREGON

*Eugene:* Hunt 608, Libri 609
*Medford:* Carpenter 607
*Portland:* Martin 610, McGraw 611, PGE 612, White 613

*see also* 51, 171, 744, 767

## PENNSYLVANIA

*Allentown:* Perkin 654, PPL 656
*Altoona:* Snyder 668
*Auburn:* Benevolent 618
*Bala Cynwyd:* **Lee 642**
*Beaver:* Moore 649
*Blue Bell:* Unisys 673
*Clarks Green:* Ross 659
*Coraopolis:* Johns 638
*Devon:* HBE 632
*DuBois:* Mengle 648
*Erie:* Smith 663
*Harrisburg:* McCormick 646, Pollock 655
*Hollidaysburg:* Wolf 678
*Indiana:* S & T 660
*Irwin:* Smiy 666
*Mc Keesport:* Crawford 624
*Mechanicsburg:* Fredricksen 630
*Media:* Evans 629
*Merion Station:* Wachs 675
*Nazareth:* Trumbower 672
*Norristown:* Arcadia 616
*Palmerton:* Horsehead 634
*Philadelphia:* Adams 614, Albert 615, Bartolomei 617, Crane 623, Degenstein 625, Elkins 628, Jacobs 636, Kline 640, Love 643, Mandell 644, McBee 645, **Neisler 650,** Reynolds 658, Smith 664, Smith 665, Stewart 670
*Pittsburgh:* Benz 619, Buhl 621, Eccles 626, Eichleay 627, Heinz 633, Jerome 637, Jones 639, McCune 647, O'Neill 651, Patterson 653, Snee 667, **USX 674, Walden 676**
*Plymouth Meeting:* **Teleflex 671**
*Pottsville:* Schuylkill 661
*Scranton:* Scranton 662
*Sewickley:* Laughlin 641
*St. Marys:* Stackpole 669
*State College:* Hamer 631
*Stroudsburg:* Hughes 635
*Titusville:* Proper 657
*Wellsboro:* Packer 652
*West Chester:* Chester 622
*Williamsport:* **Brodart 620**
*Windber:* Whalley 677

*see also* 50, 99, 114, 115, 138, 377, 491, 582, 687, 752

## PUERTO RICO

*San Juan:* Ferre 679

## RHODE ISLAND

*Cranston:* Cranston 682
*Pawtucket:* **Hassenfeld 684**
*Providence:* **Dorot 683,** Page 685, Rhode Island 686, Smith 687
*Warwick:* Champlin 681
*Westerly:* Ashaway 680, Washington 688

*see also* 108, 384, 521

## SOUTH CAROLINA

*Clinton:* Bailey 689
*Columbia:* Colonial 691
*Gaffney:* Hamrick 692
*Greenville:* Campbell 690, Hipp 693

*see also* 172, 552, 556, 559, 563

## SOUTH DAKOTA

*Aberdeen:* Welk 694

*see also* 234

## TENNESSEE

*Chattanooga:* Harrison 695

# TYPES OF SUPPORT INDEX

Grantmakers in boldface type make grants on a national, regional, or international basis; the others generally limit giving to the city or state in which they are located.

**Annual campaigns:** any organized effort by a nonprofit to secure gifts on an annual basis; also called annual appeals.

**Building/renovation:** money raised for construction, renovation, remodeling, or rehabilitation of buildings; may be part of an organization's capital campaign.

**Capital campaigns:** a campaign, usually extending over a period of years, to raise substantial funds for enduring purposes, such as building or endowment funds.

**Cause-related marketing:** linking gifts to charity with marketing promotions. This may involve donating products which will then be auctioned or given away in a drawing with the proceeds benefiting a charity. The advertising campaign for the product will be combined with the promotion for the charity. In other cases it will be advertised that when a customer buys the product a certain amount of the proceeds will be donated to charity. Often gifts made to charities stemming from cause-related marketing are not called charitable donations and may be assigned as expenses to the department in charge of the program. Public affairs and marketing are the departments usually involved.

**Conferences/seminars:** a grant to cover the expenses of holding a conference or seminar.

**Consulting services:** professional staff support provided by the foundation to a nonprofit to consult on a project of mutual interest or to evaluate services (not a cash grant).

**Continuing support:** a grant that is renewed on a regular basis.

**Curriculum development:** grants to schools, colleges, universities, and educational support organizations to develop general or discipline-specific curricula.

**Debt reduction:** also known as deficit financing. A grant to reduce the recipient organization's indebtedness; frequently refers to mortgage payments.

**Donated equipment:** surplus furniture, office machines, paper, appliances, laboratory apparatus, or other items that may be given to charities, schools, or hospitals.

**Donated land:** land or developed property. Institutions of higher education often receive gifts of real estate; land has also been given to community groups for housing development or for parks or recreational facilities.

**Donated products:** companies giving away what they make or produce. Product donations can include periodic clothing donations to a shelter for the homeless or regular donations of pharmaceuticals to a health clinic resulting in a reliable supply.

**Emergency funds:** a one-time grant to cover immediate short-term funding needs on an emergency basis.

**Employee matching gifts:** a contribution to a charitable organization by a corporate employee which is matched by a similar contribution from the employer. Many corporations support employee matching gift programs in higher education to stimulate their employees to give to the college or university of their choice. In addition, many foundations support matching gift programs for their officers and directors.

**Employee volunteer services:** an ongoing coordinated effort through which the company promotes involvement with nonprofits on the part of employees. The involvement may be during work time or after hours. (Employees may also volunteer on their own initiative; however, that is not described as corporate volunteerism). Many companies honor their employees with awards for outstanding volunteer efforts. In making cash donations, many favor the organizations with which their employees have worked as volunteers. Employee volunteerism runs the gamut from school tutoring programs to sales on work premises of employee-made crafts or baked goods to benefit nonprofits. Management of the programs can range from fully-staffed offices of corporate volunteerism to a part-time coordinating responsibility on the part of one employee.

**Employee-related scholarships:** a scholarship program funded by a company-sponsored foundation usually for children of employees; programs are frequently administered by the National Merit Scholarship Corporation which is responsible for selection of scholars.

**Endowments:** a bequest or gift intended to be kept permanently and invested to provide income for continued support of an organization.

**Equipment:** a grant to purchase equipment, furnishings, or other materials.

**Exchange programs:** usually refers to funds for educational exchange programs for foreign students.

**Fellowships:** usually indicates funds awarded to educational institutions to support fellowship programs. A few foundations award fellowships directly to individuals.

**General/operating support:** a grant made to further the general purpose or work of an organization, rather than for a specific purpose or project; also called unrestricted grants.

**Grants to individuals:** awards made directly by the foundation to individuals rather than to nonprofit organizations; includes aid to the needy. (See also "Fellowships," "Scholarships—to individuals," and "Student loans—to individuals.")

**In-kind gifts:** a contribution of equipment, supplies, or other property as distinct from a monetary grant. Some organizations may also donate space or staff time as an in-kind contribution.

**Internship funds:** usually indicates funds awarded to an institution or organization to support an internship program rather than a grant to an individual.

**Land acquisition:** a grant to purchase real estate property.

**Lectureships:** see "Curriculum development."

**Loaned talent:** an aspect of employee volunteerism. It differs from the usual definition of such in that it usually involves loaned professionals and executive staff who are helping a nonprofit in an area involving their particular skills. Loaned talents can assist a nonprofit in strategic planning, dispute resolution or negotiation services, office administration, real estate technical assistance, personnel policies, lobbying, consulting, fundraising, and legal and tax advice.

**Loans:** see "Program-related investments/loans" and "Student loans—to individuals.")

**Matching/challenge support:** a grant which is made to match funds provided by another donor. (See also "Employee matching gifts.")

**Operating budgets:** see "General/operating support."

**Professorships:** a grant to an educational institution to endow a professorship or chair.

**Program development:** grants to support specific projects or programs as opposed to general purpose grants.

**Program evaluation:** grants to evaluate a specific project or program; includes awards both to agencies to pay for evaluation costs and to research institutes and other program evaluators.

**Program-related investments/loans:** a loan is any temporary award of funds that must be repaid. A program-related investment is a loan or other investment (as distinguished from a grant) made by a foundation to another organization for a project related to the foundation's stated charitable purpose and interests.

**Public relations services:** may include printing and duplicating, audio-visual and graphic arts services, helping to plan special events such as festivals, piggyback advertising (advertisements that mention a company while also promoting a nonprofit), and public service advertising.

**Publication:** a grant to fund reports or other publications issued by a nonprofit resulting from research or projects of interest to the foundation.

**Renovation projects:** see "Building/renovation."

**Research:** usually indicates funds awarded to institutions to cover costs of investigations and clinical trials. Research grants for individuals are usually referred to as fellowships.

**Scholarship funds:** a grant to an educational institution or organization to support a scholarship program, mainly for students at the undergraduate level. (See also "Employee-related scholarships.")

**Scholarships—to individuals:** assistance awarded directly to individuals in the form of educational grants or scholarships. (See also "Employee-related scholarships.")

**Seed money:** a grant or contribution used to start a new project or organization. Seed grants may cover salaries and other operating expenses of a new project. Also known as "start-up funds."

**Special projects:** see "Program development."

**Sponsorships:** endorsements of charities by corporations; or corporate contributions to all or part of a charitable event.

**Student aid:** see "Fellowships," "Scholarships—to individuals," and "Student loans—to individuals."

**Student loans—to individuals:** assistance awarded directly to individuals in the form of educational loans.

**Technical assistance:** operational or management assistance given to nonprofit organizations; may include fundraising assistance, budgeting and financial planning, program planning, legal advice, marketing, and other aids to management. Assistance may be offered directly by a foundation staff member or in the form of a grant to pay for the services of an outside consultant.

**Use of facilities:** this may include rent free office space for temporary periods, dining and meeting facilities, telecommunications services, mailing services, transportation services, or computer services.

---

## Curriculum development

## Debt reduction

## Donated equipment

## Donated products

## Emergency funds

## Employee matching gifts

## Employee volunteer services

## Employee-related scholarships

## Endowments

McDermott 723, McGovern 724, Meadows 725, Rockwell 734, Sterling 737, Sturgis 738, Swalm 739
*Wisconsin:* Schoenleber 794

## Equipment

*Alabama:* Crampton 1, Smith 6
*Alaska:* Alaska 9
*Arizona:* **Southwestern 13**
*California:* Ahmanson 16, Auburn 18, Copley 33, Glendale 45, Jewett 55, Lytel 58, Sonora 71, Stewart 73, Weingart 77
*Colorado:* El Pomar 80, Gates 82, Joslin 83, Kitzmiller 85
*Connecticut:* Auerbach 89, Bodenwein 90, Community 93, New Britain 98, Palmer 100, Rayonier 101, Woodward 108
*Delaware:* Crystal 109, Marmot 111
*Georgia:* Callaway 141, Newland 147
*Illinois:* CharitaBulls 165, Chicago 167, Dillon 170, Heath 178, Puckett 188, Scholl 191, Timm 196
*Indiana:* Community 201, Decatur 202, Dekko 203, Indianapolis 206, Thompson 212
*Iowa:* Armstrong 216, Carver 219, Community 220, McElroy 227
*Kansas:* Murdock 237
*Kentucky:* Community 239, Nettelroth 242
*Louisiana:* Booth 246, Huie 247
*Maryland:* **Knapp 259,** Marpat 260, **Westport 264**
*Massachusetts:* Bayrd 268, Community 271, Daniels 277, Ham 279, Hathaway 280, High 281, Kelley 284, Thompson 298
*Michigan:* Community 305, Delano 306, Dow 308, Fremont 310, Library 313, Stubnitz 324, Vicksburg 326, Wickes 328, Wickson 329
*Minnesota:* Bremer 334, Otter 338
*Missouri:* Green 343, Oppenstein 348, Shaw 354
*Montana:* Montana 356
*Nebraska:* Perkins 359, **Union 360**
*Nevada:* **Wiegand 364**
*New Jersey:* Cowles 371, Fredrickson 372, **International 375,** Schwartz 382, Stern 383
*New Mexico:* McCune 385
*New York:* Agrilink 389, Alexander 390, Barker 396, **Brooks 400,** Chase 406, Chautauqua 407, Columbian 410, Community 411, Dyson 423, Emerson 426, Gebbie 431, Heckscher 443, Howard 447, Kaplan 455, Lake Placid 464, Morgan 479, Northern 481, Northern 482, O'Connor 483, Ohrstrom 484, Sheldon 506, Snow 509, Snow 510, Stevens 517, Stuart 521, Tisch 524, Truman 525, **Vetlesen 531,** Wasserman 537, Western 540, Yaron 548
*North Carolina:* Duke 556, Finch 557, Wachovia 563
*Ohio:* Dater 566, Frohman 568, GAR 570, Haman 571, Kulas 575, Middletown 578, Murphy 579, Peabody 581, Reeves 583, Richland 584, Slemp 587, Stensen 589, **Timken 591,** Troy 594, Van Wert 595
*Oklahoma:* Bovaird 600, Helmerich 601, Kerr 603
*Oregon:* Carpenter 607, Hunt 608
*Pennsylvania:* Arcadia 616, Eccles 626, Horsehead 634, Jacobs 636, McCune 647, Patterson 653, Smith 665, Snee 667, Stackpole 669, **USX 674**
*Rhode Island:* Champlin 681, Rhode Island 686
*Tennessee:* Plough 696
*Texas:* Bass 698, Coastal 703, Constantin 705, Dougherty 709, Fair 710, Gray 715, Kronkosky 721, McDermott 723, Meadows 725, Meredith 726, Newman 728, Payne 730, Pineywoods 731, Rockwell 734, Sterling 737, Sturgis 738, Trull 741
*Vermont:* Proctor 750
*Virginia:* Camp 753, **Freedom 755,** Lynchburg 756, Norfolk 757, Portsmouth 759
*Washington:* Anderson 764, Archibald 765, Foster 767, Tacoma 772, Wenatchee 773
*West Virginia:* Kanawha 775, Parkersburg 777
*Wisconsin:* Alliant 778

## Exchange programs

*Iowa:* Community 220

New York: Alexander 390, McHugh 472, Reed 497, **Soros 512**
*Ohio:* Murphy 579
*Pennsylvania:* Smith 665
*Virginia:* **Freedom 755**

## Fellowships

*Alabama:* Moody 4
*Arizona:* **Southwestern 13**
*California:* **Getty 43**
*Colorado:* Gates 82
*Connecticut:* **Tenneco 105**
*Illinois:* American 158, Bank 159, First 174, Scholl 191
*Iowa:* McElroy 227
*Maine:* Smith 254
*Massachusetts:* Community 271, Kennedy 285
*New York:* Agrilink 389, **China 409,** Community 411, Dyson 423, **Heineman 445,** International 453, Kaplan 455, **Klingenstein 461,** Larsen 465, **Mellon 474,** Park 487, **Pforzheimer 490,** Reed 497, Rubinstein 501, Snow 509, Snow 510, Solow 511, **Soros 512,** Stuart 521, Tuch 526, Wiley 544
*North Carolina:* Duke 556, Wachovia 563
*Ohio:* Muskingum 580, Wagnalls 596
*Oklahoma:* Kerr 603
*Pennsylvania:* **Lee 642**
*Rhode Island:* **Dorot 683,** Rhode Island 686
*South Carolina:* Colonial 691
*Texas:* Bowden 700, Coastal 703, Rockwell 734, Shell 735, Sterling 737
*Virginia:* **Freedom 755**
*Washington:* **Microsoft 768,** Potlatch 771
*Wisconsin:* Alliant 778

## General/operating support

*Alabama:* Crampton 1, First 2, Moody 4, Smith 6, **Vulcan 8**
*Alaska:* Alaska 9
*California:* AIDS 17, Berkman 25, Cheeryble 31, Coleman 32, Essick 38, Hanover 47, Hewlett 49, Hexcel 50, Irvine 54, Jewett 55, Leavey 56, Lytel 58, Silberstein 69, Sonora 71, Stewart 73
*Colorado:* El Pomar 80, Flug 81, Joslin 83, Weckbaugh 87
*Connecticut:* Auerbach 89, Champion 92, Community 93, Mills 97, New Britain 98, Rayonier 101, Weller 107
*Florida:* Eaton 127, Schultz 134
*Georgia:* Callaway 141, Johnston 144, Newland 147, Williams 150
*Idaho:* Simplot 155
*Illinois:* **Allen 157,** American 158, Bank 159, Caestecker 163, Centralia 164, Chicago 166, Chicago 167, Comer 168, Dillon 170, Donnelley 171, Donnelley 172, Hume 180, OMRON 186, Tesuque 195, Timm 196
*Indiana:* Auburn 199, Community 201, Dekko 203, Indianapolis 206, Journal 208, Marshall 209, Thompson 212
*Iowa:* Armstrong 216, Barr 217, Green 223, MidAmerican 230
*Kansas:* Garvey 236
*Kentucky:* Community 239, LG&E 241, Nettelroth 242
*Louisiana:* Huie 247
*Maine:* Aldermere 248
*Maryland:* Marpat 260, **Westport 264**
*Massachusetts:* American 266, Burnham 270, Concord's 272, Daniels 277, Eaton 278, Hathaway 280, Kelley 284, Knowlton 287, Memorial 289, Newburyport 290, Stearns 296, Wheatland 300, White 301
*Michigan:* Berrien 303, Camp 304, Delano 306, DeVos 307, Dow 308, Fremont 310, Library 313, Vicksburg 326, Wickson 329
*Minnesota:* Andersen 331, Ankeny 332, Boss 333, Bremer 334, Federated 335, General 337
*Missouri:* Dula 342, Hall 344, Oppenstein 348, Pierson 350, Pitzman 351, Richardson 352, Russell 353, Shaw 354
*Montana:* Montana 356

*Nebraska:* Perkins 359, **Union 360**
*New Jersey:* **Burns 370,** Cowles 371, Fredrickson 372, Martini 378, Schwartz 382, Stern 383
*New Mexico:* McCune 385
*New York:* Agrilink 389, Alexander 390, **AT&T 392, Baker 394,** Barker 396, Calf 402, Chapman 405, Chase 406, Chautauqua 407, Columbian 410, Community 411, Constans 412, **Delmas 419, Deutsche 420,** Duberg 422, Dyson 423, **Engelhard 427,** Fife 429, Gebbie 431, Goldsmith 437, Hebrew 442, **Heineman 445,** Hinman 446, Hultquist 451, International 453, Kaplan 455, Kaplan 456, **Klingenstein 461,** Lake Placid 464, Masinter 470, McGraw 471, McHugh 472, **Memton 475,** Merrill 476, Morgan 479, Ohrstrom 484, **Ormsby 485,** Park 487, Park 488, Peck 489, Potter 494, Reader's 495, Reed 497, Rubinstein 501, Scherman 502, Sheldon 506, Solow 511, Springate 514, Story 518, Strong 520, Stuart 521, Time 522, **Twain 527,** U.S. 528, **Vetlesen 531,** White 541, Wiley 544
*North Carolina:* Belk 551, Coffey 553, Cumberland 554, Duke 556, Finch 557, **First 558,** Wachovia 563
*Ohio:* Dater 566, Frick 567, Frohman 568, **Gale 569,** GAR 570, Hildreth 572, Kulas 575, Murphy 579, Richland 584, Smith 588, Stensen 589, Van Wert 595
*Oklahoma:* Bovaird 600
*Oregon:* Carpenter 607, Hunt 608, PGE 612
*Pennsylvania:* Arcadia 616, Benz 619, **Brodart 620,** Chester 622, Crawford 624, Eccles 626, Fredricksen 630, Hamer 631, HBE 632, Heinz 633, Hughes 635, Laughlin 641, Mandell 644, Mengle 648, Patterson 653, Perkin 654, PPL 656, Reynolds 658, S & T 660, Schuylkill 661, Smith 665, Stewart 670, **USX 674,** Wolf 678
*Rhode Island:* Cranston 682, **Dorot 683,** Rhode Island 686, Smith 687, Washington 688
*South Carolina:* Colonial 691, Hamrick 692
*Texas:* Bass 698, Bertha 699, Cameron 702, Coastal 703, Cook 706, Dougherty 709, Fish 712, Gray 715, Hall 716, Hebert 718, Kronkosky 721, McDermott 723, McGovern 724, Meadows 725, Meredith 726, Navarro 727, Newman 728, O'Connor 729, Payne 730, Pineywoods 731, Rachal 733, Rockwell 734, Shell 735, Smothers 736, Sterling 737, Sturgis 738, Swalm 739, Trull 741
*Utah:* First 744, Rich 747
*Vermont:* Proctor 750
*Virginia:* **Freedom 755,** Portsmouth 759, St. Andrew's 762
*Washington:* Archibald 765, **Microsoft 768,** Norcliffe 769, Potlatch 771, Tacoma 772
*West Virginia:* Hollowell 774, Kanawha 775
*Wisconsin:* Alliant 778, Annmarie 779, Bidwell 783, Brewer 785, Hagge 788, Jones 789, Raymond 793, Schoenleber 794, Wood 799

## Grants to individuals

*Alabama:* Moody 4
*Alaska:* Alaska 9
*California:* **Getty 43**
*Florida:* **Eagles 126**
*Illinois:* American 158
*Indiana:* Community 201
*Massachusetts:* Kennedy 285, Knowlton 287, Newburyport 290
*Minnesota:* Federated 335
*New York:* Children's 408, **Delmas 419, Soros 512**
*Pennsylvania:* Crawford 624
*Virginia:* **Freedom 755**

## In-kind gifts

*Alabama:* **Vulcan 8**
*California:* Stewart 73
*Connecticut:* Rayonier 101, **Tenneco 105**
*Georgia:* Callaway 141
*Idaho:* Simplot 155
*Illinois:* American 158, Bank 159, Dillon 170, OMRON 186
*Indiana:* Community 201

*Massachusetts:* Community 271, Ham 279, Hathaway 280, Kelley 284, White 301
*Michigan:* Berrien 303, Community 305, DeVos 307, Dow 308, Fremont 310, Hillsdale 311, Stubnitz 324, Vicksburg 326, Wickes 328, Wilkinson 330
*Minnesota:* Andersen 331, Bremer 334
*Missouri:* Green 343, Hall 344, Oppenstein 348, Shaw 354
*New Hampshire:* Sidore 366
*New Jersey:* Cowles 371, **International 375,** Stern 383
*New Mexico:* McCune 385
*New York:* **Carnegie 404,** Chautauqua 407, Community 411, Dyson 423, Gebbie 431, Heckscher 443, **Heineman 445,** Howard 447, International 453, Kaplan 455, Kaplan 456, **Klingenstein 461,** Lake Placid 464, Morgan 479, Northern 481, Northern 482, O'Connor 483, Ohrstrom 484, Park 487, **Pforzheimer 490,** Rubinstein 501, Snow 509, Snow 510, Stevens 517, Truman 525, **Viburnum 532,** Western 540
*North Carolina:* Cumberland 554, Duke 556, **First 558,** Triangle 562, Wachovia 563
*Ohio:* Dater 566, GAR 570, Middletown 578, Muskingum 580, Richland 584, Slemp 587, **Timken 591,** Troy 594, Westheimer 597
*Oregon:* Carpenter 607
*Pennsylvania:* Buhl 621, Eccles 626, Fredricksen 630, HBE 632, McCune 647, Patterson 653, Scranton 662, Smith 665, Stackpole 669, **Teleflex 671,** Wolf 678
*Rhode Island:* Rhode Island 686
*Tennessee:* Plough 696

*Texas:* Coastal 703, Fair 710, Fish 712, McDermott 723, Meadows 725, Navarro 727, Pineywoods 731, Rockwell 734, Sterling 737, Trull 741
*Vermont:* Lamson 749, Vermont 751
*Virginia:* Camp 753, **Freedom 755,** Lynchburg 756, Norfolk 757
*Washington:* Archibald 765, Foster 767, Tacoma 772, Wenatchee 773
*West Virginia:* Kanawha 775, Parkersburg 777
*Wisconsin:* Alliant 778, Black River Falls 784, Community 786

## Sponsorships

*Connecticut:* **Tenneco 105**
*Minnesota:* Otter 338
*New York:* Merrill 476, Reader's 495
*Pennsylvania:* **Brodart 620,** PPL 656

## Student loans—to individuals

*California:* Glendale 45
*Illinois:* Centralia 164
*North Carolina:* Coffey 553

## Technical assistance

*Alaska:* Alaska 9
*California:* Glendale 45, Irvine 54, Jewett 55, Sonora 71
*Connecticut:* New Britain 98
*District of Columbia:* Benton 116

*Illinois:* Chicago 167
*Indiana:* Community 201, Decatur 202, Dekko 203, Indianapolis 206
*Kentucky:* Community 239
*Massachusetts:* Community 271, Kelley 284, White 301
*Michigan:* Fremont 310, Library 313
*Minnesota:* Andersen 331, Bremer 334
*Missouri:* Hall 344
*New Mexico:* McCune 385
*New York:* Abrons 386, **AT&T 392, China 409,** Community 411, **Deutsche 420,** Dyson 423, **Heineman 445,** Kaplan 456, Morgan 479, Northern 482, O'Connor 483, Scherman 502, Western 540
*North Carolina:* Cumberland 554, Duke 556, Triangle 562
*Ohio:* Richland 584
*Oregon:* Carpenter 607
*Pennsylvania:* McCune 647, **Teleflex 671**
*Rhode Island:* Rhode Island 686
*Texas:* Meadows 725, Trull 741
*Vermont:* Proctor 750, Vermont 751
*Virginia:* Lynchburg 756
*Washington:* Tacoma 772, Wenatchee 773
*West Virginia:* Kanawha 775

## Use of facilities

*Connecticut:* **Tenneco 105**
*Minnesota:* Otter 338
*New York:* Wiley 544
*Oregon:* PGE 612
*South Carolina:* Colonial 691

# INDEX TO GRANTMAKERS BY SUBJECT

Terms used in this index are listed below and generally conform to the Foundation Center's Grants Classification System. In the index itself, foundations and corporate giving programs are arranged under each term by state location, abbreviated name, and sequence number. Organizations in boldface type make grants on a national, regional, or international basis. The others generally limit their giving to the state or city in which they are located. For a subject index to the individual grants in this volume, see the Index to Grants by Subject.

---

## Archives

*Massachusetts:* Kennedy 285
*New York:* **Balanchine 395**
*Tennessee:* Potter 697

## Arts, information services

*California:* Banky 23

## Education, information services

*District of Columbia:* Special 120
*Illinois:* **Moen 184**

## Human services, information services

*Oregon:* Martin 610

## Libraries (academic/research)

*California:* Frankel 41, Hewlett 49
*Florida:* Lattman 132
*Illinois:* American 158
*Massachusetts:* Langrock 288

## Libraries (medical)

*California:* **Delzell 35**
*Hawaii:* Mamiya 151
*Illinois:* Marion 183

## Libraries (public)

*Alabama:* Crampton 1, Moody 4, Sanders 5
*California:* Braddock 26, Folger 39, Foothill 40, Glendale 45, Heller 48, Hurt 52, Jewett 55, Sajak 65, Schott 66, Smittcamp 70, Stone 74, White 78
*Colorado:* Weckbaugh 87
*Connecticut:* Alden 88, Auerbach 89, Fromson 96, Roberts 102, Roosa 103
*Delaware:* Robson 112, Zock 114
*District of Columbia:* Haft 117
*Florida:* BCR 123, Doyle 125, Funkhouser 129
*Georgia:* Georgia 143, Price 148, **Singletary 149**
*Illinois:* American 158, Caestecker 163, Centralia 164, CharitaBulls 165, H.B.B. 176, Lumpkin 182, Myers 185, Puckett 188, Rauch 189, Sycamore 194

*Indiana:* Decatur 202, Marshall 209, Thompson 212, Van Arnam 214
*Iowa:* AmerUs 215, Heath 224, Melick 228
*Kansas:* Bramlage 235
*Kentucky:* LG&E 241, Nettelroth 242, Richardt 245
*Maine:* Aldermere 248, Brook 249, Heald 250
*Maryland:* Gorlitz 257, Thomas 263, **Westport 264**
*Massachusetts:* Austin 267, Connell 273, Cottle 274, Memorial 289, Tillotson 299
*Michigan:* Delano 306, Frazier 309, Library 313, **Meritor 314, Sagan 321,** St. Clair 323, Thayer 325
*Minnesota:* Bremer 334, Garmar 336
*Missouri:* Boylan 340
*Montana:* Boe 355
*Nebraska:* Nelson 358
*New Jersey:* Armour 367, **Burns 370,** Stern 383
*New York:* Adler 388, Birkelund 397, Blue 398, Burke 401, CTW 414, Gellert 432, GGM 433, Goldman 435, Greenhill 440, Hebrew 442, Heilbrunn 444, Johnson 454, King 458, Kleinkramer 460, McHugh 472, Milstein 478, **Ormsby 485,** Rose 499, Schloss 503, Sculco 504, Smith 508, Stevens 517, Story 518, Walter 535, Warren 536, Weinman 538, Western 540, White 541
*North Carolina:* Barnard 550, Belk 551, Coffey 553, Rostan 561, Wood 564
*Ohio:* Hildreth 572, Kell 573, Peabody 581, Stensen 589, Tod 593
*Oklahoma:* Rothbaum 605
*Oregon:* Libri 609
*Pennsylvania:* Albert 615, Crane 623, Degenstein 625, Kline 640, Love 643, McBee 645, McCormick 646, Patterson 653, Perkin 654, Pollock 655, Reynolds 658, S & T 660, Smith 663, Smiy 666, **USX 674,** Wachs 675, Whalley 677
*Rhode Island:* **Dorot 683,** Page 685
*South Carolina:* Campbell 690
*Texas:* Brown 701, Fairchild 711, Gorges 714, Hicks 720, Kronkosky 721
*Utah:* Cash 743, Lindquist 746
*Vermont:* WELD 752
*Washington:* Anderson 764, **Microsoft 768,** Orrico 770
*West Virginia:* Hollowell 774, Kraft 776
*Wisconsin:* Annmarie 779, Baker 781, Batterman 782, Kress 790, Schoenleber 794, Stangel 796, Walker 798

## Libraries (school)

*California:* Coleman 32

*Florida:* Flaherty 128, Skinner 135
*Georgia:* Johnston 144
*Illinois:* American 158, **Brooker 162,** Glossberg 175
*Michigan:* Pierce 318
*New York:* Calf 402, Covey 413
*Ohio:* **Gale 569**
*Pennsylvania:* **Brodart 620,** Fredricksen 630, Johns 638
*Utah:* First 744

## Libraries (special)

*California:* **Central 30, Muth 61**
*District of Columbia:* Silverstein 119, Special 120
*Georgia:* **Singletary 149**
*Illinois:* Deering 169
*Maryland:* Minkoff 262
*Massachusetts:* Kessler 286
*New Jersey:* Heidtke 374
*Pennsylvania:* Elkins 628, O'Neill 651
*Texas:* Fish 712
*Wisconsin:* Jones 789

## Libraries/library science

*Alabama:* First 2, Linn 3, Smith 6, Talton 7, **Vulcan 8**
*Alaska:* Doyon 10
*Arizona:* Chapman 12, **Southwestern 13**
*Arkansas:* Dishongh 14, Ottenheimer 15
*California:* Ahmanson 16, Bacon 19, Baker 20, Baker 21, Bandai 22, Bartman 24, Berkman 25, Braun 27, Brewster 28, C.M.J. 29, Cheeryble 31, Copley 33, Cotton 34, Edelman 36, Endurance 37, Essick 38, Geschke 42, Givens 44, Green 46, Hanover 47, Hexcel 50, Huntington 51, Irell 53, Long 57, Lytel 58, **McLaughlin 59,** Novak 62, Parker 63, Pelosi 64, Shannon 67, Silberstein 68, Simpson 69, Sonora 71, Steiner 72, Stewart 73, Straus 75, Taper 76, Winnick 79
*Colorado:* El Pomar 80, Flug 81, Gates 82, Joslin 83, Kinder 84, Kitzmiller 85, Pioneer 86
*Connecticut:* Bodenwein 90, Burton 91, Champion 92, Community 93, Donchian 95, Mills 97, New Britain 98, 1919 99, Palmer 100, Rayonier 101, Sayles 104, **Tenneco 105,** Thomaston 106, Weller 107, Woodward 108
*Delaware:* Crystal 109, Marmot 111, **Ross 113**
*District of Columbia:* Baruch 115, Benton 116, **National 118,** Telecommuncations 121, Wilkes 122

## Medicine/medical care, information services

## Philanthropy/voluntarism, information services

## Public affairs, information services

## Recreation, information services

## Science, information services

# INDEX TO GRANTS BY SUBJECT

For each subject term, grants are listed first by grantmaker entry number, then by grant number within the grantmaker entry. For a general subject index to the purposes and activities of the grantmakers in this volume, see the Index to Grantmakers by Subject.

# GRANTMAKER NAME INDEX